Woodrow Wilson

Boy President

Illustrated by Mel Bolden

Woodrow Wilson

Boy President

By Helen Albee Monsell

the NEW *Bobbs-Merrill* COMPANY, INC.

® AN ASSOCIATE OF HOWARD W. SAMS & CO., INC.

Publishers • INDIANAPOLIS • NEW YORK

To Eudora Elizabeth Thomas,
my favorite librarian

Illustrations

Contents

CHILDHOOD OF FAMOUS AMERICANS ®

★ ★ ★

Books by Helen Albee Monsell

DOLLY MADISON: QUAKER GIRL
HENRY CLAY: YOUNG KENTUCKY ORATOR
JOHN MARSHALL: BOY OF YOUNG AMERICA
ROBERT E. LEE: BOY OF OLD VIRGINIA
SUSAN ANTHONY: GIRL WHO DARED
TOM JACKSON: YOUNG STONEWALL
TOM JEFFERSON: BOY OF COLONIAL DAYS

Woodrow Wilson

Boy President

That Means War!

IT WAS a crisp cool morning in the fall of 1860. The sun was shining down on the little city of Augusta, Georgia. A stiff breeze was blowing. It caught the leaves from the big tree by the gate and tossed them around the yard. Tommy Wilson's puppy was chasing them. When Tommy looked down from the upstairs window, he could hardly wait to get outdoors himself.

He ran to the head of the steps, slid down the banister and raced through the hall. Then he stopped. There was a smell of hot molasses cookies in the air. Maybe he'd better go by the kitchen on his way out.

Mother was rolling out the cooky dough on the table by the window. Old Mitty, the cook, was putting a fresh batch in the oven. The pan she had just taken out was on the back of the stove.

Tommy didn't even have to ask. Mother smiled at him and nodded her head. "They're hot," she said. "Don't burn your fingers."

Mitty ran a knife under three of the biggest cookies and lifted them from the pan. "Here."

They were so hot that he had to keep tossing them from one hand to the other.

"Don't play too hard," said Mother as he started toward the door. "You mustn't wear yourself out."

The puppy came racing to meet him. "Yap!" she said in a tone which plainly meant, "Cooky, please!"

"Wait a minute," said Tommy. "Let's see if they are cool enough to eat."

He bit into one of the cookies. It was only pleasantly warm now.

"Here! Ask for it."

The puppy sat up on her hind legs. "Yap!" she said again.

Tommy tossed her a big piece of cooky. Then they raced together down the walk. Father and a friend were just coming in the gate. Tommy nearly bumped into them.

"Hold on there," said Father. "Look where you're going." But he wasn't cross. He was only laughing. Father was never cross with Tommy. Now he spoke to his friend as if Tommy were a man instead of a four-year-old boy.

"This is my son, Thomas Woodrow Wilson."

The man looked at Tommy. "That is a right big name for such a scrap of a boy."

"It is indeed," said Father. "So we call him Tommy."

DOES THERE HAVE TO BE WAR?

Tommy didn't like to have anyone think he was "a scrap of a boy." He didn't like to have Mother tell him, "Don't play too hard." He wanted to show everyone that he was really big and strong. He looked up at the gate. It was very tall.

"I am going to climb it," he decided. "That ought to show them."

But Father and his friend had gone on into the house. There was only the puppy to watch him. Maybe that was just as well. He had to try quite a few times before he reached the top of the gate. He didn't have much breath left. "I reckon I'll sit on one of the gateposts and rest for a while," he told himself.

More people than usual were going by. They looked worried and excited. Tommy wondered if there could be a fire uptown. He started to climb down from his post so that he could run and see.

Just then two men passed close by.

"Lincoln has been elected," one was saying. He sounded angry.

"Yes," said the other. "Lincoln has been elected. That means war."

They both looked so worried that Tommy felt worried, too. What did it all mean?

When Tommy was bothered about anything, he always went straight to Father. Father would stop to explain things, no matter how busy he was. Tommy hurried up the walk now. He ran up the steps, across the porch and into the big hall. The door to Father's study was open. He and his friend were sitting in front of the fireplace. They were busy talking. They sounded worried, too.

"Father," Tommy began, even before he reached the door, "who is Lincoln? Why is there going to be a war?"

He hoped Father would laugh his big, jolly laugh and say, "Stuff and nonsense. Who has been filling your head with such foolishness?" Then everything would be all right again.

But Father didn't laugh. He looked as worried and upset as the two men had been.

"Mr. Lincoln," he said, "is going to be the next President of the United States. He has been elected by men who want to make the Southern states give up their slaves. A good many men in the South think slavery is wrong, too. But they want to take care of the question in their own way. They aren't going to let anybody *make* them do anything."

Tommy nodded. He knew that feeling very well, himself.

"The Southern states have said they would withdraw from the United States if Mr. Lincoln was elected. They believe they have a perfect right to do so. The Northern states say they haven't. They will fight to keep them in."

"Look here," said Father's friend. "What is the use of trying to explain things to the boy? He's too young to understand."

"Maybe so," said Father. "But then again, maybe he'll remember it later, even if he doesn't understand now."

Tommy bit into his last cooky. "Does there *have* to be a war?" he asked.

"I am afraid so," the friend answered before

Father could speak, "although it does seem as if there ought to be some other way out."

"There is," said Father. "Men who aren't selfish and who try to understand one another don't fight. But the world has never been willing to try that way."

"No," the other man said sadly, "and it never will."

"I am not so sure. Someday a leader may arise——"

"What is a leader?" asked Tommy.

"A man who can show the people what to do and make them want to do it."

"Just like the game the big boys play—Follow the Leader?"

"Exactly, Tommy. Now run outdoors and play. We will be busy for a while."

Tommy turned away thoughtfully. He was still thinking about what his father had said about war. As he opened the door he saw Joe

Lamar from next door coming up the walk. Tommy forgot all the questions that had been tumbling about in his mind.

"Can you come out, Tommy?" asked Joe. "Phil has to stay in the house. He went out of the yard when he wasn't supposed to. Now I don't have anyone to play with."

The two boys ran to the back yard and began to roll and tumble in some leaves that had been raked into a pile. The puppy wanted to join in the fun. She ran from one boy to the other, yapping excitedly.

After a while Tommy's sister Annie, who was two years older, came to find him.

"Oh, there you are, Tommy!" she said. "Goodness, you're dirty. It's time to come in and get ready for dinner."

Tommy ran ahead of Annie into the house. As he looked into the study, he saw Father and his friend still talking seriously.

20

Tommy started upstairs. Father's friend had been right. He didn't understand everything Father had tried to explain. But Father had been right, too. Even if he didn't understand entirely, some of the things Father had said stayed tucked away in his mind. "Someday a leader may arise——"

Company's Coming!

THE MEN in the street had been right. War was declared between the North and the South. At first it didn't seem to be the terrible thing Tommy had been afraid of. Sometimes he forgot about it. So many other interesting things were happening!

Almost a year had gone by when he came downstairs one summer morning to find the kitchen full of odors. He could smell chicken frying, pies bubbling, cakes baking.

"We're going to have company," his sister Annie told him.

"As if I couldn't guess it!" said Tommy.

Father was a minister. He was always having company. Usually Tommy was glad to see people come. Today, though, he wasn't the least bit glad.

"We'll have extra good things for dinner," Annie reminded him. "Just smell."

"But not everything about having company is good. Will they stay all night?"

Annie nodded. "Just look at that long row of piecrusts. Ever so many people must be coming. Or else they are going to stay for a long time."

"But if they are here tonight, Father won't be able to read to us."

"I reckon not."

"And he left off last night at the most exciting place. The Indians have just captured Hawk-eye——"

"Tommy!" called Mother. "Will you run down to the garden and get me a few sprigs of mint?"

Tommy ran out to the kitchen garden behind

the brick wall. He was still thinking about the Indians and Hawkeye. "Maybe Marion will read to us," he told himself. Marion was his other sister. She was nearly twelve. "But she'll probably be busy helping Mother. There's always a lot to do when we have company."

Now he remembered another thing he didn't like about having company. Mother always wanted him to be dressed up. Sometimes she even made him put on his Sunday clothes!

HAWKEYE

As soon as he took Mother the mint, he slipped away next door.

"Let's play in your attic," he told the Lamar boys. "Maybe, if Mother doesn't see me, she'll forget about how I look."

The Lamar boys knew how he felt. Their father was a minister, too. "Even if it isn't Sun-

24

day, you can't play games very well if you have your Sunday clothes on," they agreed.

They went up to the attic to play. They watched through the window as the Wilsons' company began to arrive. One man came on horseback. Another came in a buggy. Two of them came from the steamcars. They all carried big carpetbags.

"That means they are going to stay all night." Tommy groaned. "I'll never find out how Hawkeye got away from those Indians!"

"Let's play Indians," Joe suggested. "You be a white man. Phil and I will be Indians. We'll hide behind Grandfather's trunk. Then we'll jump out and scalp you."

"No, you won't. Because I am Hawkeye. I've got my rifle——"

"We'll have war clubs——"

"Come on. Let's start."

"Ye-ow!" shouted Big Chief Joe. He grabbed

up a feather duster and began to dance a war dance around the attic.

Hawkeye Tommy knelt behind the trunk. He used an old broom for his rifle.

Bang!

Phil had been creeping up behind him. Now he jumped on Tommy with a yell that sounded like an Indian war whoop.

"Boys! Boys!" called Mrs. Lamar from the foot of the attic steps. "Won't you please play something quieter?"

That ended the big fight. The boys sat down on the old trunk.

"What *can* we play?" they grumbled. "There isn't anything that's fun that doesn't make a noise."

Tommy had an idea. "Let's play church. I don't believe your mother will mind the noise if we are singing hymns. And we can take turns preaching."

They were just beginning to enjoy themselves again when Marion came to the foot of the steps.

"Tommy! Mother says it's time for you to come home."

Phil Lamar looked out the little window at the sun. "It isn't nearly dinnertime yet," he objected.

"We children will probably have dinner by ourselves, anyway," said Tommy. "What Marion means is that it's time to get me dressed up. I surely hope she isn't going to make me put on my new shoes!"

When Mother Was Little

IT WAS a very neat and tidy Tommy who went into the parlor to meet Father's guests. Father put his arm around him. "This is my son," he told the men. "He was born on the twenty-eighth of December, 1856. We were living in Staunton, Virginia, then."

It was easy to see that Father was very proud of Tommy. Tommy was proud of Father, too. He was sure his father was the finest man there. He sat quietly for a while and listened, but sitting still was hard work. He wasn't sorry when dinnertime came.

The children had their dinner early. Then

they went outdoors to play. All afternoon they could see men coming and going at the Wilson house. Tommy was sure they had never had so much company in one day before.

Mother was still busy when suppertime came. She asked Marion to give the other children their bread and milk. "And then will you take them upstairs and keep an eye on them?"

Marion often kept an eye on the other children. She was Big Sister. Sometimes Tommy felt as if she were almost his second mother. She was almost as good as Mother, too, when it came to telling stories or answering his questions.

"Why are we having so much company at once?" he asked now.

"There's going to be a big meeting in Father's church. It begins tomorrow. Presbyterian ministers and elders are coming to it from all over the South."

"Will it last long?"

"Several days, I reckon."

"Through Sunday?" Tommy was worried. When a minister was a guest on Sunday, Father always asked him to preach the morning sermon. Suppose he asked all of the men here to preach!

"What is the meeting about, anyway?" he asked crossly.

"Well—we aren't in the United States any longer, you know," Marion told him. "Georgia is one of the Confederate States of America."

Tommy nodded. He was not quite five years old, but he knew that.

"And the Confederate States must have their own Presbyterian Church. Men have come from all the Southern states to get it started. They'll hold meetings in Father's church across the street."

"I wish they'd hold the meeting in some other church," Tommy said. "Then Father could go on reading to us about Hawkeye."

"No, he couldn't. He'd have to be at that other church, wherever it was."

Tommy knew she was right. He didn't even try to argue. Instead he started off on a new idea. "You go get the book and read it to us."

"I can't. It's in Father's study and some of the men are talking there."

"Then tell us a story. Tell about the time Mother was nearly drowned."

"Wait a minute," Annie said. "I want to hear it, too, but I want to get my doll first."

Marion sat down in a comfortable low chair. When Annie came back she sat on the rug, close by. Tommy lay down on the floor between them.

"Now we're ready."

A STORMY VOYAGE

"When Mother was a little girl," Marion began, "she lived over in England. Grandfather was a minister, just like Father. He had a big family. There were four brothers and sisters older than Mother. There were three younger than she was."

Four older brothers and sisters to take care of you and make you mind! Tommy was very fond of his older sisters, but he sympathized with little-girl Mother.

Marion sympathized with the big brothers and sisters. "It does seem as if the four of them could have kept an eye on little Jessie," she said, "but of course there were little James and Gene and Marion to look after, too. When I think how much time it takes to help Mother look after just you, I can understand how they felt with four youngsters on their hands.

"When Mother first remembers, they lived in a little house with a garden which went right back to a castle wall. She and Uncle James used to throw their ball against the wall. But when

Mother was eight years old, Grandfather decided to come to America. They sailed in a little packet ship, and they were on the ocean for over two months!"

"I'd like that," Tommy said.

"No, you wouldn't. Not when a storm was tossing the boat around as if it were a cat playing with a ball. And the winds were roaring and the waves were dashing——"

Tommy wriggled excitedly. This was the best part of the story. It always gave him shivers.

"Little-girl Mother didn't like it. The passengers were told to stay down in the cabin. She didn't like that, either. It was too hot and close and sticky. At last she managed to slip away.

"She climbed up to the deck. She wanted some fresh air, but the wind was so strong it almost took her breath away. It nearly blew her across the deck. She caught hold of a piece of rope.

"Just then a big wave came. She could see it,

like a big, green moving wall. She screamed, but the wind was too loud to let anyone hear her little voice. Then the wave struck.

"It buried the bow of the boat in the water. It swept Mother off her feet and washed her overboard. Her mouth was too full of water now to scream, but she held tight to the rope. It pulled her arms almost out of their sockets. It burned her hands, but she held on. She swung out far over the water. She could see it boiling and green below her. Then she swung back. She managed to catch at the railing. Then she crept back down to the cabin."

Tommy had been holding his breath. It was as good a story as an Indian story would be.

"So now Mother is afraid of the ocean," Marion finished. "And I don't blame her."

"I don't, either," Tommy agreed. "But I'd like to go on the water myself."

Mr. Moderator!

THE NEXT morning the Wilsons were up early. With four guests in the house there was work for everyone—Mother, Mitty, Annie, Marion, Tommy. Even the dog dashed around as if she were going on important errands.

Things grew quieter after the meeting started in the church. In fact, they grew too quiet. Tommy sat down on the porch steps, with the dog at his feet. The Lamar boys had gone somewhere to play. Everything was very still. He wondered what was happening in the church. Maybe Father was making a speech. Suddenly he made up his mind he would go see.

The meeting of course was for men, not boys. There was a big gallery, though, where the servants sat on Sunday mornings. Tommy knew where the stairs were. He could slip up to the gallery and sit on the floor behind the railing. The men downstairs couldn't see him, but he could see and hear everything.

He jumped up. He ran across the street and into the big church. Nobody was in the vestibule. He slipped up the dark stairs and into the gallery. He looked down.

One of Father's guests was standing by the pulpit. He wasn't preaching a sermon. He wasn't even talking. It was very plain, though, that he was in charge of everything.

Anyone in the church who wanted to speak would stand. "Mr. Moderator!" he would call.

39

"Dr. Palmer."

Then Dr. Palmer would speak.

Sometimes three or four men would jump to their feet at once. "Mr. Moderator!" they would all call.

Then "Mr. Moderator" would have to decide which one was first. "Dr. Hoge has the floor," he would say.

"I make a motion——"

It was very plain that Mr. Moderator kept things in order. Without him, everyone would be talking at once. Nobody would know what was happening. He had charge of the whole meeting.

"I'd like to be Mr. Moderator," Tommy decided.

Tomorrow he and the Lamar boys would play having a meeting instead of church. Only how did Mr. Moderator know what to do next? He would have to ask Father.

He was so interested watching that he didn't know how long he had been there. At last someone said, "Mr. Moderator, I move the morning meeting be adjourned."

Tommy wasn't sure what that meant. While he was trying to decide, everybody stood up. The meeting was over! It was dinnertime.

A GOOD ROMP

The meetings lasted nearly two weeks. Tommy slipped up the gallery steps nearly every day to watch and listen. But he was glad when they were over. There were ever so many questions he wanted to ask Father. Besides, he wanted his family to himself again.

Father took his last guest down to the steam-cars. As they were getting into the buggy, he looked at Tommy. "Do you want to come along?" he asked.

Of course Tommy wanted to go along. He climbed into the buggy. He sat quietly all the way to the station. It was very hard for him to sit quietly. He was rather proud of himself.

He liked the noise and bustle at the station. He wished he were going on the train. But maybe, after all, it was just as well he couldn't go. When the train had left they drove back home. Now Tommy had Father all to himself. He could ask all the questions he wanted to ask.

"Why did they call the man in front 'Mr. Moderator?'"

"He was the man in charge of the meeting. Sometimes he is called 'President' or 'Chairman.' We Presbyterians call him a moderator."

"How does he know what to do?"

"There are certain rules for him to go by. They are the same all over the country. They have a long name—parliamentary law."

Tommy liked long words. "Parliamentary

law." He said it over and over under his breath. He liked the way it rolled over his tongue. "Par-lia-men-tary law."

The mare knew she was headed home. There were oats waiting for her there. Tommy had so many questions to ask he wanted to go slowly, but the horse had other ideas. In almost no time she had them home again.

"Come into the study," Father said. "I'll show you the rules a moderator must follow."

In the study Father showed him a small black book. "These are our *Rules of Order*. When you can read, I'll give you a copy." He put the book back in his bookcase. "Now run along and get ready for supper."

Tommy felt cramped and stiff after his ride in the buggy. Besides, Father hadn't played with him for days. And there was plenty of time before supper.

"It's early yet," Tommy said.

"You need plenty of time. You're such a little slowpoke."

"Slowpoke, yourself!" teased Tommy. "You can't catch me!"

Father was tired of sitting still, too. He was ready for a romp. He made a dive for Tommy.

They ran through the big hall, across the porch, down the steps, and into the yard. Now they raced around the big snowball bush. Tommy tried dodging. Father could dodge, too.

Mother and the girls came to the window and stood there laughing. Finally Father chased Tommy into a corner of the yard. Tommy had one last idea. He began to climb the fence. Father caught him by the leg.

"I've got you now!" he crowed.

Both of them were breathless with running and laughing as they started back across the yard. *Rules of Order* were fun, Tommy decided, but this was more fun still.

The most fun of all, though, came that night. Supper was over. Mother sat in her low chair, knitting. The two girls sat on the sofa near by. Tommy turned a chair upside down near the candle table. Then he lay down on the floor.

He started to ask Mother to tell a story. But she would probably just get to the exciting point when Father would come in.

He jumped up and ran into the next room. When he came back he brought Mother's guitar. "Let's sing," he said.

Mother played the guitar softly. The children sang "The Minstrel Boy to the War Is Gone." With the second verse another voice joined in. Father had come from his study. He had a book in his hands. The song broke off in the middle of the verse.

"Now," cried Tommy, "we'll learn how Hawk-eye got away from the Indians!"

45

Father liked to sit on the floor almost as well as Tommy did. He sat down by the candle table. He leaned back against the upturned chair.

" 'When the Indians recognized their prisoner——' " he began.

Tommy wriggled happily. Mr. Cooper had certainly written a good book when he wrote *The Last of the Mohicans*.

Blackberries Are Ripe

"HEY, TOMMY!" called Joe Lamar. Tommy was up in the big oak tree. He hooked his arm over a limb and leaned down to call, "Come on up!"

"You come on down instead. Let's go blackberrying."

It was such a good idea Tommy wished he had thought of it himself. He climbed down to the lowest branch, swung by his arms and jumped.

"Wait until I get a pail," he said.

"Get a big one. Will Fleming says the berries are thick out his way."

Will was one of Tommy's friends who lived

out in the country. "I went out there last year," Tommy remembered, "when the berries were ripe."

He hurried to the kitchen. "I want a pail," he told Mitty.

Mother was busy by the kitchen table. "Don't make it too big a pail," she said. "You aren't strong enough to carry a heavy one, dear."

"But I am, Mother! I'm not a puny baby any more. I'm almost eight years old!"

"You're still thin and scrawny," said Mitty.

Tommy knew she was right, but he hated to be reminded that he wasn't strong. "I'm never exactly sick," he insisted. He wouldn't admit even to himself how tired he got doing the things the other boys did.

"Here is a pail that is middling big," said Mitty. "I hope you fill it. If this war doesn't hurry up and quit, there won't be anything for anybody to eat anywhere."

The war had been going on for three years now. Tommy could hardly remember when it had started. At first it had only been something which was happening far away. Now, every day, it was coming closer and closer. There were almost no young men left in town. They were all in the army. Father wasn't home very much. He was off preaching to the soldiers and helping take care of them.

"There's one good thing about the war," Tommy told Joe as they started for the gate. "All the schoolteachers are in the army. We'd be shut up in some schoolroom this very minute if they weren't."

"You're right," Joe agreed. "But the army needs more men still. Hey, wait a minute. There come some now."

Down the road came a small troop of men.

"They're off to join the army," said Joe.

The boys climbed up on the gateposts to watch them pass.

"They surely don't look like soldiers now."

Some were riding old horses. Some were on mules. Some were trudging through the dust on their own feet. Some of them were in their best clothes. Others were almost in rags. But they were all in a good humor. They joked with the boys as they passed by.

"Hey, bub," called one, "aren't you afraid you'll fall off that post?"

Tommy grinned. "Oh, go get your mule!" he called back. That was a new bit of slang he had just learned. He was rather proud of it.

The soldiers-to-be laughed. They trooped on down the road. Tommy and Joe laughed, too, but somehow, after the men had gone by, it didn't seem so funny.

"That man probably has a boy of his own back home," Tommy told Joe.

"I reckon nearly all of them do. If they didn't have families, they would have been in the army long ago."

"Their wives are going to have a hard time taking care of the children by themselves."

"And the boys are going to miss their fathers."

"I wish this war would end," said Tommy.

"So do I," Joe agreed.

"I wish we didn't have to have wars."

It was nearly four years since the day when Father had explained to Tommy about war. He couldn't remember it well enough to tell Joe. But he still felt as he did then, and, dimly, he remembered what Father had said. "Someday a leader may arise——"

Both boys sat still for two or three minutes. Then Tommy climbed down. "Well," he said, "we'd better be getting along if our folks are going to have blackberries for dinner."

IT IS NO FUN TO GO BLACKBERRYING

"You always *think* blackberrying is going to be fun," Tommy fussed some two or three hours later. "You take the biggest pail your mother will let you have. And then you find out all over again that it isn't fun at all.

"The sun gets too hot. The briers scratch you. Mosquitoes, gnats, and other kinds of bugs bite you. Besides, it takes just about sixteen million berries to fill a pail. And the more you pick, the heavier the pail is going to be when you carry it home."

Joe stood up and stretched. "And the best berries are so low you have to break your back picking them," he added. "Or else they are so high you almost stretch your arms out of their sockets reaching for them. And then the brier slaps you in the face when you let it go."

"And I'm thirsty, tired, hungry, and hot. And I have a stone bruise on my foot."

"Well, our pails are full, anyway. Let's go home."

They crossed the stubble field, back to the road. There the dust was soft to their bare feet. But the pails seemed to grow heavier and heavier as they trudged along.

"It's funny," said Tommy. "Right now, both of us feel as if we never want to go berrying again as long as we live. But our mothers will put something on our bites and scratches, and we'll have a good dinner. Then we'll lie down on the grass under the apple tree and maybe Marion will read to us for a while. We'll forget how miserable we are right now. We'll be ready to do it all over again."

"I won't," said Joe.

"By tomorrow morning you'll be ready to go again," said Tommy. "Just wait and see."

"LET'S DO IT AGAIN"

Mitty was glad to get the berries. She looked at the clock. "There's just time to make a berry pie for dinner."

Mother looked at Tommy's legs. They were all scratched and bitten. "Come on upstairs and wash them in cool water. Then I'll put some ointment on them."

When dinner was over, Tommy went out into the yard and lay down underneath the apple tree. A good breeze was blowing. He had never felt more comfortable. After a while Joe came over. He stretched out by Tommy. "We had blackberry pie for dinner," said Tommy.

"We had blackberry roll."

They lay sleepily quiet for a few minutes.

"My mother was mighty glad to get those berries," Tommy said.

"So was mine," said Joe.

"I'll bet you they are thicker behind the piney woods than in the bushes where we were."

"Um-hum. And remember that snake that crawled out from the bushes? Maybe we could catch him next time."

"If we went earlier in the day, we wouldn't get so hot," Tommy said.

"Shucks! I don't mind a little sun."

"I don't, either. It felt good on my back."

"Um-hum," Joe said. "You know, it's fun to go blackberrying."

Then both boys laughed. "What did I tell you?" crowed Tommy.

"Well, it is. You know it is, yourself."

"Of course I do. Let's go again tomorrow."

"I Wish I Had a Horse"

AFTER THE blackberry season was over, summer settled down to stay. In the fields outside the city, the cotton bolls grew fat. Then they burst into fluffy masses of white. Cotton pickers were busy from morning till night.

Tommy wasn't particularly interested in cotton. "I wish I had a horse." he told his sisters one warm Monday afternoon.

"I wish I had one, too," Annie said, "but there isn't a chance. Our soldiers need every horse that isn't being used on the farms."

"I know. But all the same it would be fun to go riding this afternoon."

"Would you rather do that than go walking with Father?" Marion asked.

"'Deed I wouldn't. I'd just like to do both. Say—that gives me an idea!"

Both girls laughed. Tommy was always having ideas.

"It must be a mighty good one if it fixes things so that you can go riding and walking at the same time," Marion teased.

Tommy jumped up from the porch step where he had been sitting. He started down the path around the house toward the kitchen. "If Father comes out, tell him I'll be right back."

"I know where you're going," Annie called after him. " You want some of the cookies Mother made this morning from the molasses Aunt Marion sent her. Bring me some too."

Cookies were a rare treat these days. As the war kept on, even molasses was hard to get. Aunt Marion lived on a plantation just outside the city. Her daughter Jessie was just about Tommy's age. Tommy often went out there to spend the day with them. Aunt Marion knew how fond he was of cookies. She had managed to save a little molasses for Mother to use.

When Tommy came back from the kitchen, his hands were full. He divided the cookies with the girls. Then, instead of eating his own, he put them in his pocket.

"Why don't you eat them?" Annie asked.

"He's saving them for his walk," Marion said.

But Tommy only said, "Has Father come out from his study yet?"

Annie shook her head.

"I wish he'd hurry up. If he doesn't it will be time to come home before we start."

"Nonsense. You have the whole afternoon ahead of you."

"But Monday is always the shortest day of the week. It is three times as short as Sunday."

"You feel that way because on Sunday you can't run about or play games."

"Maybe," Tommy agreed, "but that isn't the only reason."

"No?" Marion was teasing again. "Could it possibly be because Father is too busy on Sunday to pay his son any special attention?"

Tommy grinned. "I reckon so. Anyway, we always have an extra good time on Mondays. You ought to see the places we go to—mills, railroad yards, factories. If Joe and I tried to get into places like that by ourselves, we'd be chased away in a hurry. But when Father tells a man, 'I'd like to take my son through your mill,' he is as pleased as a peacock. He shows us everything."

"That's because Father is a minister. Everybody likes him."

"I should say they do! Folks who say they wouldn't like to be a minister's son don't know what they are talking about. Really, it is a great deal of fun."

Just then Father came out. "Are you ready, Tommy? It is time we were off."

Tommy jumped up in a hurry.

"Where shall we go?" asked his father as they started down the steps.

Tommy decided he'd not say anything about his special idea yet. He'd just head their walk in the right direction. "You've never shown me how a cotton gin works," he suggested.

"So I haven't. And that is something every Southern boy should know. We'll go out to Mr. Fielding's plantation. It will be a warm walk, but I hear he started ginning yesterday."

THE IDEA WORKS

Augusta was a small city. Soon Tommy and his father had left its houses behind them. In the fields on either side of the country road the cotton pickers were at work. They moved slowly down the rows, filling their big bags with the fluffy white cotton.

Tommy wasn't interested in the pickers. He wanted to get on to the cotton gin, but Father stopped to speak to everybody. It made Tommy as fidgety as a worm in hot ashes.

Finally they came to the gin shed at the far end of Mr. Fielding's plantation. There, on a shaft, was a great flat cogwheel. Two long poles, or sweeps, stretched out from the shaft. Horses were harnessed to these sweeps. They pulled them around and around. This turned the shaft. Other wheels fitted into the cogwheel. Belts connected them with the gin upstairs.

Now it was Father who pushed on ahead. He didn't notice that Tommy was pulling back. Father wanted to see the gin. Tommy wanted to see the horses. He climbed the narrow steps slowly. He looked back as long as he could see even the swish of the gray mare's tail.

"You must watch closely," said Father when they reached the gin room.

Tommy looked at the big box in front of him. Inside were two rollers. The first one was covered with saw teeth. When the gin man dumped a basket of cotton into the gin, it caught on those teeth and was carried through a grid. The grid was too narrow to let the seeds through. They were torn out and fell down a hole into the seed room below.

The second roller was covered with brushes. They brushed the seeded cotton from the saw teeth out into the lint room. Now the teeth were ready to bite into a new basketful of cotton.

"It's a wonderful machine," said the gin man. "When my father was a boy, cottonseed had to be picked out by hand. I've often heard him tell how he went over to the Widow Green's plantation just a short way from here, to watch the first cotton gin work.

"Mr. Eli Whitney was visiting her house and had invented it while he was there. It was a queer-looking contraption, Pa said. You had to turn it by hand. But even then it could do the work of a half-dozen men. Why, before we had the gin, it took a good worker a whole day to pick a shoeful of cottonseed! This machine can clean as much in an hour as he could have done in a week!"

"Wonderful!" Father agreed. "And just think what it has meant to our whole country! More cotton, more trade, more factories——"

He and the gin man talked on and on. They quite forgot Tommy. At last it occurred to Father that his son was unusually quiet. He turned around. Tommy had disappeared.

"Now where has the young rascal gone?"

"Probably he's down in the shed, helping whip the dust from the cotton. Youngsters always like to use switches. Or else he's out watching the big screw press the cotton into bales."

But Tommy's idea had nothing to do with switches or screws. He had slipped away as soon as Father and the gin man started talking.

When Father came downstairs, he didn't see his son at first. Instead, he almost bumped into the man who drove the gin horses. Right now, the man seemed to be taking a rest. His hands and mouth were full of molasses cookies. He looked as happy as a cow in a cornfield.

The gin hadn't stopped working. The horses were still going around and around, pulling the sweeps. Father looked. There on the gray mare's back sat Tommy. He had traded his cookies for a ride on a gin horse.

"SAY JUST WHAT YOU MEAN"

The best part of Monday afternoon walks came on the way home. Then Tommy could ask all the questions he wanted to. That didn't mean just two or three. His questions lasted more than halfway home. After that it was Father's turn. He wasn't satisfied with just two or three questions, either. He wanted to make sure his son understood everything he had seen.

Tommy enjoyed that, too, especially when he knew the answers. Today it was hard at first to pull his mind away from the horses. Still, there were a good many things he wanted to know. Where did Eli Whitney come from? What became of him? Did he ever invent anything else?

Father had to wait quite a while for his turn. At last Tommy's father said, "Now tell me exactly how a cotton gin works."

When Tommy's father said "exactly," he meant "exactly." Tommy knew better than to use such words as "kind of" or "something or other" or "sort of like." His answers must be clear-cut and plain.

Today he had a fine new word he'd been saving for a week. Father would be impressed. "The wheel at the top of the shaft was absolutely stupendous."

Instead of being impressed, Father laughed. "What do you mean by that?"

"Why," said Tommy, "I meant 'very big.'"

"Then why didn't you say 'very big'? Remember this. Always use the word that means exactly what you want to say. If that word is a big one, use it. But you will find that nearly always small words say what you mean better than big ones do."

"Yes, sir," said Tommy. "All the same," he added to himself, "I think stupendous is a fine word."

"Now start again."

Tommy started again, but he still felt peevish. He didn't like to be laughed at.

"What becomes of the cottonseed?" Father asked.

"It falls into the seed room. Mr. Fielding saves enough to plant next year and throws the rest away. That looks like a big waste to me."

"It is. Men are trying now to make cottonseed cake which can be fed to cattle. Some folks even say that cottonseed oil can be made for human beings to use."

Tommy wasn't sure he would like that.

"How is the cotton weighed?" asked Father. "How is it cleaned?" Then finally came the last question: "What made the machinery run?"

At that, Tommy forgot to feel cross. "I did," he said proudly, "because I drove the horses."

Anxious Days

IT WASN'T only that the war was taking such a long, long time to end. It wasn't only that food was hard to get. Now people were looking at one another with anxious faces. How much longer could the South hold out? Suppose the South should lose?

Tommy couldn't suppose any such thing, but the war was making the whole world turn upside down, it seemed to him.

Sunday was, as Tommy very well knew, a day of rest. Nobody was supposed to work. The catechism said that it must be spent "in public and private worship, except for such parts as were to be taken up in the works of necessity and mercy."

Father believed in the catechism. He saw to it that the Wilsons' Sundays were spent in just that way. He urged the people in his church to keep it that way, too.

But there came a Sunday morning that fall when Father prayed even longer than usual before he started across the street to the church. His face was set in strange new lines. The news all week had been bad, very bad.

Tommy crossed the street with Mother and the girls. The church seemed dark and dim after the glaring light outside. Everything was very still. It was hard to believe that a war was really going on.

There came the usual opening hymns and the long prayer. Then Father stepped forward to the pulpit. Tommy settled back for the sermon. It wasn't so hard to sit still as it used to be. He could understand nearly everything his father said now.

Suddenly he sat up straight in startled surprise. There was a quick rustle through the entire church. Everyone else seemed to be as surprised as Tommy was. Father was speaking, but he wasn't preaching a sermon.

His voice was clear and ringing. "There is a great battle raging today. Our men need ammunition. Immediately after this service you must go to the ammunition factory and help fill cartridges. You will now rise and receive the benediction."

Father was cutting the morning service short so that the people could go to work on Sunday! Tommy could hardly believe it. Then he remembered the catechism again. "Except for such parts as were to be taken up in the works of necessity." War was terrible. It could even upset Sunday!

Every day the news grew worse. Sherman's soldiers had reached Atlanta. They were starting their march to the sea. On that march they took everything their army would need. They set fire to everything they thought the Southern army could use.

Of course, other things caught on fire, too. When a blaze started, it spread over a whole farm. As the soldiers marched on, they left behind them home after home in burning ruins.

Augusta was only a small city, but there were big warehouses there. If the cotton in them could be sent to England, it could be sold for money to buy arms and supplies the Southern army needed. Would Sherman's army come to Augusta to burn the cotton warehouses? Nobody knew.

"But we'll find out mighty soon," Joe said to Tommy. "The Yankees are getting nearer."

The two boys had been on an errand for Mother. Now they were on their way home.

"Let's go down by the river," Tommy suggested. "It isn't much out of our way."

"Let's. I'll race you to the first warehouse."

Off they started, but when they reached the corner, Tommy stopped short.

"Look!" he cried. "What is happening?"

Men were dragging the heavy bales of cotton

from the warehouses. They were piling them in the street.

"It's the Yankees! They're here! They are going to burn the city!"

Joe shook his head. "They're not soldiers."

Tommy looked again. Joe was right. Most of them were too old for soldiers. And there was Dick Fulsom's brother, who had lost his arm at Manassas.

One of the old men had stopped to wipe his forehead with his sleeve. He gave the boys a tired grin. "Pushing cotton bales around is hard work," he said.

"Why are you doing it? We thought you were Yankees getting ready to burn the town."

"No, sirree, I'm not a Yankee. And nobody's getting ready to burn this town—yet. But there's no telling. Sherman's men may get here any time. We haven't much of anybody left to fight them. All our boys are in the army already."

He gave his shoulders a tired hitch and went back to his cotton bale. "So we thought we would get the cotton out in the road all ready for them. Maybe they would just put a match to it without burning the buildings.

"Then perhaps we could put out the blaze before the whole city caught fire. Maybe the idea will work. Maybe it won't. We don't know yet, but it's worth trying anyway."

A LONG NIGHT

That night as he lay in bed, Tommy could hear men marching past his home. They were going out of town, not into town. He jumped up and ran to the front of the house.

He peeped through the blinds into the moon-lit night. "What is it?" he whispered anxiously to Mother.

"We've had word that Northern soldiers are

close by. The few men left in town have gone out to meet them."

"Will there be a fight?"

"Let us pray not. But if there is, we must be ready. The wounded will be brought back. We'll use the church for a hospital. There will be hard work then for the women and children to do. Right now, there is nothing to do but wait."

All that night they waited. Sometimes Tommy dozed. Then he would wake with a start. Had the Yankees come? There was no sound of fighting. The girls joined their mother and Tommy. They sat there, waiting, watching.

At last the gray light of dawn crept through the blinds. It was morning. Nothing had happened.

Soon after sunrise the men of the town came trooping back. They looked sleepy and rumpled after a night in the open fields. There had been no fight. The enemy soldiers had taken another road. They wouldn't come to Augusta, after all.

THE END

The long war dragged on. Slowly the end grew near. First came the terrible news that

General Lee had surrendered. Then General Johnston surrendered. Soon after that an excited man stopped at the gate.

"The Yankees have captured President Davis," he called to Father. "Some folks say he was dressed in his wife's clothes, trying to get away. But they nabbed him!"

After that, rumors came thick and fast. "They are going to bring President Davis through Augusta."—— "They are taking him up north to prison."—— "The carriage will come down this street!"

Tommy hung over the gate excitedly.

"Come into the house, Tommy," called Mother sternly. When he came up the porch steps she added, "It is hard enough on the poor man to be a prisoner. There's no need to make it worse by having the road lined with folks staring at him as if he were a wild beast in a cage."

Tommy went upstairs. The front blinds were

drawn to keep out the hot sun. He peeped through them. Down the street came a carriage. He could see Jefferson Davis, President of the Confederacy, sitting in it. There were soldiers on each side of the carriage.

The President, himself, was a prisoner. Now Tommy knew that the war was over.

Why Read?

SAD DAYS followed. Many of the men of Augusta who had gone to war never came back. They were dead on the battlefield. Those who did return were tired and discouraged. Some of them were crippled.

The slaves who had been freed were not ready for freedom. They were like children. Men were sent down from the North to help them, but some of these men only tried to make themselves rich.

It was a hard time for the people of the South, but the days were not all black. Now that they knew the worst, they could face it. The war was over. Their boys were no longer being killed in battle. Life began to be filled once more with homey, everyday happenings.

The days were busy ones for Tommy. He was learning to read. "It is high time!" many of his mother's friends said. "The idea of a boy going on nine years old before he has even learned his letters! And a minister's son, too!"

They didn't understand. Tommy hadn't been able to learn to read as long as the war was going on. His eyesight was very poor. He needed glasses. To try to read without them would have strained his eyes still more. It might even have made him blind. But it was impossible to get glasses during the war.

"We'll just have to let his reading lessons go for a while," Father had decided. "There is plenty for him to learn without books. Besides, all of us can read to him."

Tommy liked to listen to other people read. He wasn't at all anxious to start reading for himself. But now the war was over. He had his glasses. They were a pesky nuisance! He couldn't play rough-and-tumble games for fear he would break them. The boys made fun of them. And worst of all, with glasses, he must learn to read.

Tommy liked to do things that none of the other boys could do. There was no fun in learning something they could already do better than he could.

"Will you hear Tommy's reading lesson for me this morning?" Mother asked Marion one warm summer day. "Your Grandfather Woodrow's train gets in at noon, and I shall be busy every minute getting ready for him."

The children knew how happy Mother would be to see Grandfather Woodrow again. He hadn't been able to come to Augusta during the war. Tommy could hardly remember him.

Marion was glad to help Mother, but it wasn't

easy to hear Tommy's lesson. He always wanted to argue about it.

"This primer is for babies," he told Marion. "What's the use of reading it? I know all the stories in it already."

Marion sighed. Tommy was *so* stubborn whenever he didn't want to do a thing. And he was right. The primer was babyish. Father had just finished reading one of Mr. Dickens' novels out loud to the family. Now he was reading Weems's *Life of Washington.* You couldn't expect a boy who enjoyed grown-up books like those to get any fun out of a primer.

"But you *have* to learn to read sometime," she told Tommy.

"I don't see why. I'd rather just listen to Father."

"He isn't always here."

"Then you or Mother or Annie can read to me."

"We won't be with you after you are grown."

"Then I'll learn to read after I'm grown. But right now I want to go play in the ditch by the church. The rain this morning filled it knee-deep."

"Mother wants you to read your lesson first."

"Oh, well, if I *have* to——"

With Marion's help he stumbled through the

lesson. Then he hurried to the ditch. The Lamar boys came over. Soon they were busy making boats out of leaves. They were sailing them when Grandfather Woodrow arrived. Tommy scampered up from the ditch in a hurry.

His grandfather was a small man, but he was almost as quick as Tommy himself. He had been born in Scotland and still spoke with a Scottish accent. It was hard at first to understand, but soon Tommy began to like it. Before Grandfather's visit was over he had begun to copy it, just a little.

"WILL YOU LEND ME YOUR GLASSES?"

Grandfather Woodrow came on Saturday. When Tommy awoke the next morning he had a feeling that it was going to be a good day. At first he couldn't think why. Then, all of a sudden, he remembered.

Grandfather was a minister. He would preach the morning sermon. Last night Tommy had watched him take his notes from his bag. The sermon wasn't going to be long.

After church they would all go to Aunt Marion Bone's plantation for dinner. Aunt Marion always had good dinners, but, with Grandfather visiting them, she would be sure to have something extra special. And, best of all, Sunday was a day of rest. There wouldn't be any reading lesson!

Tommy felt happy as he laced his shoes and slicked down his hair. This was going to be a good day!

There were a few bad minutes right at first. The minister's family sat only four pews from the front of the church. Everyone could see Tommy every minute of the service. They expected the minister's son to keep especially quiet. That wasn't what worried him. He had grown so used to that he didn't mind. But he did mind walking down the aisle with those glasses on.

Tommy knew he wasn't good-looking. He was too thin and wiry. His nose was long, his chin was sharp. "And when I put these glasses on," he groaned to Annie, "I must look like a big grasshopper."

But he wouldn't let the boys know he cared. He started down the aisle with his head held high. Will Fleming grinned at him as he passed. The boy in the pew ahead started to snicker. He managed to choke it back before his mother could notice, but Tommy heard him. His face grew red. He held his back straighter than ever.

"He'd be whispering names at me if he dared," Tommy thought to himself. "Huh! I can think of half a dozen good ones myself. 'Old Four-Eyes'—'Grandaddy Wilson'—'Tommy Frog-eye.'" He hoped he didn't look as miserable as he felt as he sat down by Mother.

After the first hymn he felt better. He liked to sing. The music made him forget about himself.

After the offering had been taken Grandfather Woodrow stepped forward. He put his notes on the reading desk. He felt in his pocket for his spectacles. A blank look came over his face. He felt in another pocket, then another. At last he turned to Father. They spoke for a moment in low tones. Then Father came forward.

"Dr. Woodrow has left his eyeglasses at home," he announced. "Will someone in the congregation lend him a pair?"

Every man in the church who was wearing glasses took them off. They brought them down the aisle. Tommy took off his glasses, too. He marched down the aisle with the men. None of the boys would snicker now. They would all envy him. He was sorry his pew was so far front. That made his march short.

Grandfather Woodrow tried on each pair of glasses without smiling. He chose the ones through which he could see best. With a polite "thank you" he motioned them all back to their pews. Then he began his sermon.

Tommy could hardly listen to a word he said. He was too interested in watching those glasses. They were too large. The day was warm. Grandfather's nose began to get moist with perspiration. The eyeglasses began to slide. Down they would come, all the way to the point of his nose.

Then, just when Tommy was sure they were going to fall off, up would go Grandfather's arm. He would push the glasses back in place without stopping a word in his sermon. For a moment they would stay still. Then they would start sliding again. Tommy grew so interested watching them, he was almost sorry when the sermon was over.

After church he stood by Grandfather. He heard him thank the owner of the spectacles when he gave them back. "I couldn't have read a word without them," he said. "And it is a very sad thing not to be able to read."

Marion looked at Tommy. Tommy grinned. "But Grandfather doesn't have to read just primer stuff," he whispered.

On Sunday Afternoon

AUNT MARION's dinner was just as good as Tommy had expected it to be. Fried chicken, rice and gravy, hot biscuits, baked tomatoes, with peach tarts to finish off—he ate and ate!

After dinner, though, came Sunday afternoon. None of the children ever enjoyed Sunday afternoons.

"We have to keep on our best clothes," Jessie fumed, "and sit around, with nothing to do."

"Even if we had on our everyday dresses," Annie reminded her, "we still couldn't *do* anything."

"That's right. I don't mind not climbing trees

or going into the woods, or wading in the creek on Sundays, but I do wish we could play games."

"We can play Bible games," said Tommy. "Let's try Guess Who."

The other children agreed. They sat down on the porch steps.

"I'm thinking of a boy in the Bible," Tommy began. "You can ask three questions. Then you must guess who it is."

"What did he do?" Annie asked.

"He tended his father's sheep."

"That's easy. We don't need three questions. It's David."

"That's right."

"Now it's my turn. I'm thinking of a man in the Bible. Ask your questions."

It was a good game, but after a while they couldn't think of any new names.

"Will it be a Sunday game if we use people in American history?" asked Jessie.

"I reckon that's all right," Tommy decided.

"Then I'm thinking of a boy in history. Ask your questions."

"Where did he live?"

"In Virginia."

"What did he do?"

"He cut down a tree."

"Oh! George Washington!"

"Father was reading to us last week in Dr. Weems's book about how Washington chopped down the cherry tree," said Tommy, "but some people say it is just a story and isn't really true. No one is sure that he really chopped it down."

"But Mother says," Annie told Jessie, "that it doesn't make any difference whether it is a true story or not. It *is* true that George Washington was the kind of boy who wouldn't let somebody else be blamed for what he did. He'd tell the truth and face whatever happened next."

"I don't see anything so extra special about

that," said Tommy. "Anybody can do that. Now the part of the book I liked best was when he was fighting with the Indians the time that General Braddock was killed. The bullets went whizzing through his coat——"

"Look," Jessie interrupted. "The next time

you come down on a weekday, let's play Wild Indians."

"Let's," agreed Tommy. "We'll make some bows and arrows——"

But just then Mother came out to the porch. "It's time to start home," she said.

"I'M READING"

Of course Monday couldn't be Tommy's day with Father while Grandfather was there. Neither could Tuesday or Wednesday. The *Life of Washington* lay unopened on the table. Tommy did wish they could go on with it.

"You read it to us," he begged Mother on Thursday.

Mother shook her head. "I want to be with your grandfather every minute I can."

"Then you go on with it, Marion."

"I'm busy." Marion laughed. "If you are so

tired of baby primers, why don't you read it to yourself?"

Tommy was startled. Reading was a lesson. It had never occurred to him that he could do it for fun.

He picked up the *Life of Washington*. Then he lay down on the floor near the table, where the lamplight would fall on the book. He opened it carefully. "When Washington saw that the Indians——" he read slowly.

He couldn't manage the big words, but there weren't very many of them. Why, he was really reading! At first he was as proud as a puppy with his first trick. Then he forgot all about himself. He was too interested in George Washington. Soon he was so deep in his book he didn't even hear the slow ticking of the big clock. He had no idea how time was passing.

At last Marion came back into the room. "Nine o'clock, Tommy," she said. "Mother says to tell you it's time to go to bed. You can read some more of that book tomorrow."

Tommy looked up in surprise. He shook his head. He might not always be stubborn about the same thing, but he could still be stubborn.

"I can't go to bed now," he said firmly. "I'm reading."

Wild Indians

NOT LONG after Grandfather's visit, Tommy's brother Joseph was born. Mother and the girls couldn't give all their attention to Tommy now. He wasn't sorry. It was good not to be the youngest child and the only boy in the family.

One morning his womenfolk were all busy with the new baby. Tommy decided he would go out to Aunt Marion's to spend the day. He and Jessie hadn't had that game of Wild Indians yet. He always liked to play with Jessie. She could run as fast as he could and climb just as high, even if she was a girl.

Now that the war was over, the Wilsons had

a horse again. Tommy had learned to drive. He would often take the reins when he and Mother started off together. He liked riding, though, even better than he did driving. The horse was big and black. She was so broad that when he sat on her back, his legs stuck out more than they did down. But he never fell off.

His puppy had grown to be a big dog now. She had puppies of her own. Tommy stopped to play with them a moment before he climbed up on the big horse. "It won't be long before you'll be running along with me when I ride off," he told them. "Then the rabbits along the way will have to watch out."

It wasn't a long ride to Jessie's home at Sand Hills. She saw him coming and ran to open the gate. She remembered their plan.

As soon as they put the horse in the stable, they hurried down to the thicket by the brook. They chose two long switches there for bows.

They found some reeds, too, to make into headless arrows. They sat on the back porch while they strung their bows with cord that Jessie had saved. This took quite a while, but at last it was finished. Tommy and Jessie stood up and tried out their bows and arrows.

Just beyond Sand Hills there was a strip of piney woods. Beyond the woods lived a large family of children.

"Sometimes they play Indian and chase me," said Jessie, "and sometimes I play Indian and chase them. It's a good game, no matter which side you play."

"Let's go down to the piney woods and hide," said Tommy. "Then if any of them come along, we'll give a war whoop and jump at them."

"We'll have to put on war paint first," said Jessie.

They ran down to the chicken yard. They got enough feathers to make their hair as wild as any

Indian's. Pokeberries were ripe. They stained their faces with rich purple pokeberry juice.

That meant hard scrubbing later. "It will be worth it, though," Tommy decided, "if I look as horrible as Jessie does. And I bet I do, only worse." He added another big dab of pokeberry juice.

Now the two Indians, in all their war paint, went down to the piney woods. They hardly had time to hide when through the woods came three children. Their mother had sent them to the store for some molasses.

"Sh," whispered Tommy. "Here come some unwary settlers. Is your bow ready? Now when I yell, shoot and then jump out at them."

The "settlers" came nearer. They were watching two squirrels chase each other. They didn't guess there were wild Indians close by.

"Ye-ow!" screamed Tommy. *Zing* went his arrow as it flew through the air.

Jessie screamed at almost the same moment. *Zing* went her arrow, too.

Of course, the arrows didn't hit anybody. The Indians hadn't meant for them to. If they did hit, they wouldn't do more than make a very little bruise. But the way they whizzed was as exciting as if they were really deadly weapons.

The settlers yelled. Then the Indians dashed on them. In another moment settlers and Indians were all screaming and chasing one another. It was hard to tell which were having the best time.

But the settlers' mother was waiting for her molasses. At last they had to go on.

TOO GOOD A SHOT

The Indians sat down on a log to catch their breath. "What shall we do next?" asked Tommy.

"Let's go to the house for some cookies."

That was a good idea. They went up to the house. A few minutes later they stood on the porch steps munching. Then Tommy had an idea.

"Let's play you are a squirrel and I am an Indian. I have a hungry squaw and three papooses back in my wigwam. I'll go behind the house and count to five hundred by fives while you hide. Then I'll come hunting for you."

Jessie darted to the front of the house while Tommy went back of the kitchen and started to count. She picked out a big maple with thick leaves that would hide her well. She climbed as easily as if she were a boy.

Soon Tommy came stalking through the woods. He looked up every tree. Finally he saw a flutter of blue. Jessie's dress was showing through the leaves. He drew his trusty bow and shot an arrow in the tree.

He didn't really aim at her. But just then Jessie

decided to climb to a higher branch. She was reaching up with one hand. The arrow hit her shoulder. It startled her. She lost her balance and tumbled down at Tommy's feet.

There she lay, white and still. Tommy was so frightened that for a second he couldn't move. He was sure she was dead.

"If I get my horse and dash home as fast as I can," he said to himself, "I'll be gone before anyone finds her. They will never know I did it."

But he couldn't just run away and leave her there. "I'll go call Aunt Marion," he decided. "Only I won't say I shot her. People will think one of the other children did it."

But while he raced toward the house he remembered the Sunday afternoon when they had talked about George Washington—how he wouldn't let someone else be blamed for what he did. "And I said," he remembered, "that I didn't see anything especially hard about telling the truth and facing what happened next. I know better now, but I'll have to do it."

"Aunt Marion," he called as he ran into the house. "Come quick! Jessie is dead! It wasn't an accident. I killed her!"

Aunt Marion and the servants came running. They picked up Jessie's limp little body. They carried her into the house and laid her on the sofa.

"Get some water," said Aunt Marion. "Go to my medicine chest. Bring me the tall bottle."

Just then Jessie's eyelids moved. She wasn't dead! Her eyes opened slowly. A minute later she was trying to sit up. "What happened?" she asked. Then she answered herself, slowly. "I— was falling—and I reckon—I bumped the breath out of me—when I hit the ground."

Sure enough, that was all that had happened. There were a few bruises, but not a bone was broken!

Tommy was so happy that he sang all the way home. Once or twice he gave a war whoop just to hear himself yell. But he didn't try to shoot a single arrow into the bushes along the roadside. No, sir! A boy who could hit a mark he wasn't even aiming at had to be careful!

Streetcars

THE CITY of Augusta was growing larger. Eleven-year-old Tommy could borrow Father's horse whenever he wanted to go farther than he could walk. But not everyone in town was so lucky. They needed streetcars.

All through the summer the boys had watched the workmen laying the tracks. The long metal rails glistened in the sun. Tommy could hardly wait to see the streetcars. At last, one evening, Father looked up from his paper.

"We'll have really up-to-date traveling in Augusta in a few days. I see that the streetcars have arrived. They are down at the carbarn now."

The next morning Tommy and Joe went down to see the streetcars. The carbarn was a huge building that looked like a shed.

"Look at that front wall," said Joe. "It is almost nothing but doors."

"It takes a big door," Tommy reminded him, "for a streetcar to go through."

"I know. Doesn't it look strange to see the tracks running right into a building like that?"

"I'm glad the mules are going to have such a fine stable," said Tommy. "They'll deserve it after they work hard all day. Just see those big cars they'll have to pull."

The streetcars were shining in their new paint. "They look like Noah's arks on wheels," said Joe. "Do you suppose just two mules can pull one of those big things—especially when it's full of people?"

"Sure! When they get on the tracks they run so easily I could almost pull one myself. And the driver puts on an extra mule at the foot of a steep hill."

The next day the streetcars were actually running. Tommy stood on the sidewalk and cheered when the first one went by. He wasn't satisfied, though, just to stand and watch. In less than a week he and Joe had saved enough money to take a ride themselves.

They climbed up the steps at the back of the car. Inside were two long benches facing each other. Tommy sat on one side and Joe on the other. For the first few blocks they sat stiff and straight, staring at each other. They were as solemn and dignified as two wooden Indians. Then they began to grin. Then they got together on one side to look out the window.

They were still in their own neighborhood, but the houses and stores seemed different when they were looked at sidewise through a street-car window. Then the neighborhood itself changed. The car took them past great warehouses filled with cotton. They went by the railroad shops. At last they came to the end of the line.

"How on earth are we going to turn around?" asked Joe.

"You wait and see," said Tommy. Father had explained it to him.

The car tracks ended on a low, round platform. The platform was sometimes called a turntable, because it could be turned around. The mules pulled the car onto the platform. Then they pulled the platform, with the car on it, around until the rails met again. Now the car was facing back toward town.

There were no other passengers as they started home. The boys stood in the front of the car and talked to the driver. He showed them how he worked the brakes when the car went downhill.

"Let us try it," begged Tommy.

"All right. Get ready. We're coming to a steep hill as soon as we turn this corner."

They turned the corner and started down the hill. The streetcar picked up speed on the smooth rails almost before the boys knew what was happening. Both of them grabbed at the brake. They got in each other's way. The car went faster and faster.

"Hey!" cried the driver. "Watch what you're doing!"

Tommy's hand closed on the handle. It wasn't a second too soon. Joe's hand was close by his. They pulled together. The brake squealed as the car slowed down.

"Whew!" said the driver. "In another minute we would have run into the mules and had them sitting in our laps. Now here is the end of the line, unless you boys want to take another round trip."

"Let's," said Tommy. "I'd like to try that hill again."

It was nearly dinnertime when they reached the home corner after the second trip. They put their fare in the little box in front and told the driver good-by as they climbed down the back steps.

That night the Wilson family sat out in their front yard under the trees. Far away they could see the lights of the streetcar bobbing slowly along. They looked like a string of colored lightning bugs.

"First of all, people walked," said Tommy. "Then they rode horseback. Then someone invented carriages for the horses to pull. Now there are tracks and streetcars. I wonder what someone will think up next?"

The Lightfoot Club

WILL FLEMING was coming to spend the day with Tommy. "I do hope he'll have a good time," said Mother. "You always have such fun at his house. It seems to me that there are many more things for boys to do out in the country, though, than there are here in town."

Tommy wasn't worried. "Will can always find plenty for us to do," he agreed. "But he can hardly ever get up a good ball game way out there. There aren't enough boys. Here we can start playing as soon as he comes."

"Maybe he won't be as anxious to play as you are," Marion suggested.

118

But he was. He was hardly in the yard before they were off again, with Tommy's bat and ball.

A short way down the street there was a vacant lot. Several boys were there already—Peter and Henry from down the street, the Lamar boys, Bob Smith, Dick Fulsom and others. They had already marked the bases.

"Hi, Tommy! Hello there, Will!" they called. "Hurry up. We're ready to choose sides."

Tommy and Will got on opposite sides. Tommy was first at bat. He missed the first ball. But he hit the next one. It rose high in the air. How Tommy ran! He touched first base and almost reached second. But Will was running, too. He made a beautiful catch. Tommy was out.

"Too bad," called Will.

It was Bob's turn next. He had hard luck, too. He struck out. Then Henry went to bat. He was tagged trying to reach second. Tommy's side had to go out into the field without having made a single run. The other side didn't do much better. One man reached first base, but he was left there. Soon it was Tommy's turn again. This time he made up his mind he would bat the ball clear into the next block.

The pitcher threw the ball. Then—*Crack!*

Even Tommy knew he couldn't have hit it that hard. Why, he hadn't hit it hard at all! The boys all looked up, startled. They had been too busy to notice the sky. Black thunderclouds were rolling up. A red flash of lightning zigzagged across the dark mass.

"We'd better run," said Bob.

"We can have one more inning," the others insisted.

The pitcher thought so, too. "Just time enough for me to put you out," he told Tommy.

He threw a hard, straight ball. Tommy struck. Then he ran—first base, second base, on to third. The ball went across the road and landed in the bushes by the sidewalk. Peter was still hunting for it when Tommy reached the home plate.

Then, just as Peter found the ball, the rain came down.

"Run!" they all shouted. "We'll get soaked."

No one even asked, "Where shall we run?"
They all knew. They made a beeline for Tommy's barn and climbed the ladder to the loft.

A CLUB IS BORN

The barn loft was big and roomy, with great
mounds of hay. Down below them the boys
could hear the horse moving in her stall. A hen
was nesting in the hay. She squawked angrily
at the boys, then scurried away. The rain
strummed on the roof over their heads. At first
it almost drowned their shouts as they rolled and
tumbled in the hay.

Finally, breathless, they lay down to cool off.
The rain quieted to a gentle steady beat.

"No more baseball today," said Joe.

"You know what I wish?" asked Will. "I wish
we could get up a regular team. I live a long way
out, but I could get in to play with the rest of

you. And we could play the boys from other parts of town."

Tommy had a sudden idea. "I tell you what! Let's start a club. We can have a name and a secret password and play baseball and make speeches and everything!"

"That's a good idea!"

"What will our name be?"

"The Rovers!"

"I don't like that!"

"The Wild Indians!"

"How about the Beavers?"

Everybody was talking at once. Nobody was listening to anyone else. One or two of the boys were ready to fight. They were making a great racket, but they were getting nowhere. Tommy remembered the meetings in Father's church. Those men had all been anxious to talk, but they managed better than this.

"Look here," he called to the boys. He jumped

up on a mound of hay. "Listen just a minute." At last he got their attention. "If we're going to have a club we must do it right. We'll have to have parliamentary law."

Tommy wasn't the only boy who liked big words. The others liked them, too. "What is parliamentary law?"

The rain had slowed down now to a drizzle. "I'll run up to the house," said Tommy, "and borrow Father's *Rules of Order*. That will explain it."

He ran through the drizzle up to the house and knocked on Father's study door. When he explained what he wanted, Father got his *Rules of Order* from the bookcase. Tommy put it inside his shirt to keep it dry. Then he ran back to the barn.

The more he read to the boys, the more excited they became. This would be fun. It would be as good as play-acting. "Come on. Let's elect a president right now."

"Let's elect Tommy, because he already knows most of the rules."

They brought a barrel up from down below to use as a table.

"Now," said the new president, "the first thing we must do is make a constitution."

"Mr. President!" called Will.

"Mr. Fleming has the floor," said Tommy gravely.

"I move our president write the constitution and bring it to the next meeting."

Everybody yelled "Aye" before Tommy could put the motion. He didn't have time to object.

But he didn't want to. Writing a constitution would be work, but he would like to try it.

"Is there further business to come before the meeting?" he asked.

"Mr. President!"

"Mr. Fulsom."

"I smell ham frying. That means it is close to dinnertime. I move we adjourn until the constitution's ready."

That motion was never seconded, voted on, or passed. Instead the boys began to jump and climb down from the loft. They were hungry, and they didn't want to miss their dinners.

126

Tommy worked hard on the constitution. At last it was ready. He wasn't sure about all of the spelling, but he couldn't show it even to Father because this was a secret society. Even if the words did look queer, the boys wouldn't know any more about them than he did.

When it was finished he called another meeting in the barn. One of the boys brought a rolled-up poster with him. "This is a secret society," he said, "so we ought to have something to scare folks away if they try to peep in on us. I brought this to tack up opposite the ladder."

He unrolled the poster. "I made a picture of an Indian," he said. "I think that ought to scare folks away."

All the boys laughed. The poster was a picture of a fierce-looking Indian with a many-colored feather headdress. The Indian held an upraised tomahawk in one hand.

"Where's the hammer?"

The meeting had to wait until the poster was tacked in place. Then Tommy read the constitution. The boys voted on it, article by article.

"Now for a name."

"I move," said one of the boys, "that we be named the Lightfoot Club. It sounds like an Indian name, but baseball players need light feet, too."

"Is there a second to the motion?"

"I second it," said Peter.

"Is there any discussion?"

There was, indeed. The president had a hard time to keep only one boy talking at a time. Many other names were suggested. Finally a vote was taken. The Lightfoot Club won.

Tommy looked through one of the little openings in the gable of the barn. The sun was shining and the wind was blowing.

"Now," said President Tommy, "one of the main objects of the Lightfoot Club is to play baseball. It is good baseball weather. Do I hear a motion that we adjourn to the ball field?"

President Tommy

It was several weeks later. The Wilsons were at dinner. From his seat between Mother and Marion, Tommy could look through the window which opened on the side yard. He had seen more than one boy go by on his way to the barn. As soon as their president could join them, there would be a meeting of the Lightfoot Club.

It seemed to Tommy that dinner would never end. Father had a guest. They talked and talked. Tommy grew more and more impatient.

Mother had seen the boys going by the window, too. Finally she said in a low tone, "You may be excused, Tommy, if you want to go."

130

Almost before she had finished speaking, Tommy was at the door.

Up in the loft the boys were all talking at once. They seemed to be very angry at somebody about something. As Tommy climbed the ladder, he could hear Peter's voice above the others.

"And she said she'd sick her dog on us if she ever caught us in her yard again."

"She always was the meanest old woman in town."

"Her old apples weren't fit to eat anyway. They were green as grass."

"What's happened?" Tommy asked Joe.

"Peter and Henry were coming past Mrs. Jones's place just now, and they saw some apples lying on the grass under her big tree. There wasn't any sense in leaving them there for the chickens to peck, so they climbed over the fence after them. Mrs. Jones caught them and gave them a good dressing down."

"We'll get even with her," said Henry. "We have a plan, but you boys will have to help us."

"Of course we'll help."

"Tonight after she has gone to bed we'll get her cow out of the cowshed. We'll fix her up fine, with ribbons on her horns and an apron around her neck. Then—you know how high Mrs. Jones's porch is?"

The boys nodded. "There must be a dozen steps," Bob said.

"We'll coax and push the cow up the steps and tie her rope to the front doorknob. Then we'll ring the bell, bang on the door and run. When Mrs. Jones comes down and opens the door, she'll pull the cow right inside the hall."

"Say, it's too bad it will be too dark to see her face from where we'll be hiding. But I'll bet she'll screech so loudly that she can be heard across the river!" said Peter. "And she'll have a time getting the cow down those steps again!"

"It will serve her right, the stingy old thing!" Henry said. "Making such a fuss over half a dozen wormy apples!"

"But they were her apples, after all," Tommy remarked.

"Yes—and it's going to be her cow, too!" said Peter.

The boys laughed. Tommy grinned. "I can't help feeling, though, that it is rather hard on poor old Bossy," he said.

That hadn't occurred to the boys before. "We wouldn't really hurt her," said Peter. But he didn't sound positive.

"My father says a man's house is his castle," Tommy went on. "And I reckon a woman's yard is, too."

"I never thought about it that way," Henry said, "but maybe you're right."

"Besides, if we're going to play tricks on anyone, we ought to choose somebody our own size.

133

A dozen boys against one little old lady—it really doesn't seem quite fair."

By this time most of the boys were beginning to feel that perhaps their trick wasn't such a good idea after all. Peter, however, was not yet quite ready to admit it.

"I'm not going to let Tommy Wilson tell me what to do and what not to do."

Henry laughed. "Tommy never does that. Somehow, though, he always manages to make us see things his way. Well, let's forget the cow and get along with the meeting."

"I'm ready," said Tommy. He banged on the barrel. "The meeting will please come to order."

A PINE CONE BATTLE

It was a short meeting. The weather was too fine for the boys to want to stay inside. Besides, President Tommy had a new game to suggest.

"After the rain this morning the field is too wet for baseball. Let's go down to the strip of piney woods back of Henry's house and have a pine cone battle. Half of us will be on one side of the path through the woods and half on the other."

The boys hurried down the street to the strip of piney woods. There Bob and Tommy were made the captains. Then they began to choose their sides. Tommy picked both Peter and Henry for his side.

"Now," said Joe, "we must decide on the rules of battle."

"If a man is hit by a cone, he's killed and has to drop out," Tommy suggested. "If he slips and falls he is a prisoner. The pine tags are so slippery we'll have plenty of prisoners. You keep yours back of those bushes, Bob, and we'll keep ours on the other side of the ditch.

"A prisoner can't fight until he escapes and

gets back on his own side of the path. If he's hit by a cone while he's escaping he's killed, but if he gets back safe he can fight again. The last man left alive wins the battle for his side."

"Come on, let's get ammunition," cried Bob.

The boys chased through the woods, gathering pine cones. Then Bob called, "Ready?"

"Wait a minute," said Tommy. "I'll have to take off my glasses."

"Now—one, two, three, *fire!*" cried Joe.

It was a wild battle. With whoops and yells they drove each other back and forth across the path. They ducked as the pine cones whizzed over their heads.

Without his glasses Tommy couldn't aim any too well. He was a good dodger and ducker, though. Nobody could hit him. One by one, as the boys were "killed," they dropped out. Then they stood back behind the bushes or the ditch and cheered their side on.

"There he goes, Bob!"

"Watch out, Tommy!"

At last only Tommy and Bob were left. Bob was hiding behind a tree. Tommy was crouched down behind a blackberry bush. Neither would show enough of himself for the other to aim at.

"They can stay like that all night," the other boys groaned. "We'll just have to call it a drawn battle."

But Tommy had another idea. He hung his cap on a stick. Then he stuck the stick in the ground so that the cap showed just a little above the bushes. He crept a few feet away.

Bob saw the cap. He thought it was on Tommy's head. He aimed and fired. His cone hit the cap and knocked it to the ground. "I've got him," he cried, jumping from behind the tree.

Then he saw the stick and knew he had been tricked. He jumped back, but it was too late. He had given Tommy a chance to aim and fire, too. Even without his glasses Tommy couldn't miss at such close range. His cone struck Bob squarely on the shoulder. The game was over.

"We've won!" cried Peter. "We've won!"

He had forgotten all about being angry with Tommy. As they trooped back up the street, they passed Mrs. Jones's yard. It was late afternoon. She was just driving her cow into the shed.

"There goes Mrs. Jones," said one of the boys. "And there goes her cow."

"Let her go," said Peter. "When Henry and I play tricks we'll pick someone our own size, not just a little old lady." He honestly believed it was his own idea!

Three Cheers for the Circus!

THE LIGHTFOOT CLUB had a good summer. The boys played teams from other parts of town. They held secret meetings, with the Indian poster on guard. But when the days grew shorter the boys began to grow gloomy. It was almost schooltime.

"If the war hadn't ended," Peter grumbled, "the teachers would still be in the army."

"They were in there too long," said Henry. "That's the trouble. They brought home all sorts of army ideas about discipline. Take Professor Derry, for instance. Look at the way he makes us toe the mark!"

Tommy felt anxious. His eyes were stronger now and his health was better. Now that he was nearly thirteen, it was time for him to begin Latin and Greek. He was to start in Professor Derry's school the next week.

"Don't worry," Joe told him. "You'll get along all right. Why, a bookworm like you will probably enjoy it!"

But he didn't. It was true that Tommy was a bookworm. When he became interested in a book, he wanted to keep on reading. Mother would only smile when she saw his lamp burning long after he was supposed to be asleep. "We mustn't be too hard on him," she would say. Mother was a bookworm herself, so she knew how Tommy felt about reading.

Professor Derry had very different ideas. He expected Tommy to keep on reading, too, but it mustn't be only in the books he liked. It must be in Latin and mathematics and Greek as well.

He never said, "We mustn't be too hard on the boy." He said, "We mustn't be too easy if we expect Tommy to learn his lessons."

"Oh, I know it is good for me," Tommy grumbled. "I have common sense. And Professor Derry is fair. To tell the truth, I believe I like him. But that doesn't mean I like the ruler he uses when I can't recite. And it doesn't mean that I like his cane, either."

"Things could be worse," Joe admitted. "We're lucky to be so near the cotton warehouses that we can play there during noon hour. And it's good so many of the Lightfoot boys are in the same school. That means we can keep up our baseball games."

THE CIRCUS PARADE

The winter wasn't bad, but when springtime came the boys grew restless. "Why can't you think up something new to do?" the Lightfoot Club asked its president.

One day a man came through town in a buggy. He had a big roll of posters at his feet and a bucket of paste. Before he drove on, he had posted notices all over the city. The circus was coming to town!

Not many circuses had been able to come south during the war. Few of the boys had ever seen one. They hadn't been so excited since the day the streetcars started running.

The day of the circus four of the boys were talking about it on their way to school.

"My cousin saw it in Macon. He says there's an elephant."

"Father says they have big torches so that they can have a show at night as well as in the day-time."

"I wish I could be a clown."

"I'd rather be a lion tamer."

"There's going to be a grand parade at ten o'clock."

"It won't do us any good. We'll be in school."

"Aw, I want to see the lions!"

"And the elephant!"

"And the ladies in spangled dresses!"

"And the clowns!"

Tommy knew perfectly well that he could go to the circus. If he hadn't saved up enough money for a ticket, his father would give him the rest. But right then the parade seemed more important than the circus itself. It came first. If he wasn't there, other people would see some of its wonders before he did. Besides, the boys had been wanting something new to do.

"Let's not go to school this morning," he said suddenly. "Let's go to the parade instead."

The boys were startled. Then some of them grinned. "Say—that's not a bad idea. But we'll catch it when we get back."

"What if we do? It will be worth it."

They hid their books behind some bushes. Then they started uptown. They couldn't go through the business section. Their fathers might see them. They couldn't go past the homes of any of the club members. Their mothers might be looking out the windows. It was a roundabout trip, but at last they reached the street down which the parade would come.

Quite a crowd was there already. The boys climbed onto a fence and perched there, like so many roosting chickens. Now that they had time to think they began to feel a bit worried. But it was too late to back out. The school bell had rung long ago.

At last they heard music. It was faint and far away. Then it grew nearer. They could see the band wagon. Men in bright uniforms were tooting and blowing and beating a big drum.

"Look! Yonder's the elephant!"

"Just look at those horses!" cried Tommy.

The parade passed slowly by—wild animal cages, trained dogs, clowns, everything. It was a good parade. There were ladies in fine sparkling dresses. The clowns turned handsprings. The wild animals roared. The boys enjoyed every minute of it.

Finally the last cage rumbled by. The women who had brought their little children to watch the parade turned away. "It's all over," they said.

It wasn't over for the boys. They jumped down from the fence. They rushed ahead until they caught up with the band. Then they marched along with it all the way to the circus grounds. There the parade broke up. Now it was really over. The boys looked at one another.

"Well," said Tommy at last, "I reckon it's time to go back and face the music."

The way back seemed very, very short. They didn't talk much. They were thinking about Professor Derry's cane.

Tommy put his hand in his pocket. "Hey!" he said. "I have a good-luck horse chestnut in my pocket. I traded my old knife to Peter for it the other day. Maybe if we rub it, it will give us luck." He took out the horse chestnut and passed it around. Each boy gave it a hard rub.

Just then they were going by the cotton warehouse. Tommy had another idea. He ran inside and came back with some big wads of waste cotton. "Here! We'll stick this cotton in our clothes where it will do the most good," he said. "It will soften the blows that we are sure to get from Professor Derry's cane."

The boys padded one another until they were so plump their seams were almost bursting. Then they went up the steps to Professor Derry's classroom.

Professor Derry looked at them. He looked at his big watch. "Take your seats," he said.

Tommy was tired. The day was warm. The cotton padding was warmer still. But he wasn't anxious to have school close. It seemed as if the time had never gone so quickly before.

At last Professor Derry closed his book. "The boys who played truant will remain. The rest of the class are dismissed." He reached for his cane.

It was some time later when the boys came down the school steps.

"Your lucky horse chestnut didn't do us a bit of good," they told Tommy.

"No," Tommy agreed. "The cotton didn't help much either." Then he grinned. "But it surely was a good parade."

A Subject for a Debate

AFTER the circus, life grew rather dull again. One fall day the boys had a club meeting. "Let's do something new," the boys insisted.

Tommy thought it over. "We might have a debate," he suggested. "All colleges have debate teams. If we practice now we'll have a better chance to get on one of the big teams when we go to college."

The Lightfoot boys liked the idea. "Maybe we can get up debates with some of the boys from other parts of town, the way we do baseball games," Phil suggested.

"We'll have to practice first," Peter said. "Let's

choose a subject and each of us get ready to debate it. Then we'll have a debate of our own and ask Dick Fulsom's brother to be the judge. He's been to college. He can choose the two best men, and we'll send them out against the other clubs."

Everyone liked that idea. There was a chorus of approval. Tommy rapped on the table sharply. "I think that's a good idea, too," he said. "But if we ask Dick's brother, we'll really have to work. We don't want him to think he's wasting his time."

After more discussion the boys agreed that Tommy was right. They really had to dig in. They set the time for the debate. It was to be next Friday in the Wilson barn.

Choosing a subject wasn't easy. Each boy had his own ideas. Suggestions came thick and fast. Tommy had to rap for order again and again during the discussion.

Peter wrote down all the subjects as they were suggested. Bob insisted that "Honesty is the best policy" would be good. Joe was equally sure that "Robert E. Lee is the greatest living American" was the best subject.

At first everyone agreed with Joe. Tommy smiled with relief when all the boys seemed satisfied. "Now who wants to be on the side to prove that General Lee is *not* the greatest American?" Tommy asked.

There was dead silence for a moment. Then murmurs of "Not I" and "I don't want to" came from all the boys.

Tommy took off his glasses. He polished them on the front of his shirt. Then he put them back on. He knew that General Lee was the hero of every boy in that room. Tommy couldn't imagine himself trying to prove that Robert E. Lee was *not* great. He rapped for order.

"We can't have a debate without two sides to a question," he said slowly. "I guess we all feel the same way about General Lee. Maybe we should choose another subject."

"Yes! Yes!" all the boys said.

Tommy said, "Let's choose a subject that really has two sides this time." Then the boys settled back to think. At last they agreed on an idea. The subject would be, "Resolved: That the pen is mightier than the sword."

The meeting broke up after that. Each boy was determined that Dick's brother would hear a good debate the next week. Tommy could hardly wait to tell his father about the club's plans.

Tommy found it harder than ever to study that week. He wanted to spend every minute getting ready for the debate. There were many things that the other boys in the club could do better than he did. Although he was stronger than he used to be, he was still worn out before they began to feel tired. Often, too, he couldn't play in the more exciting games for fear he'd break his glasses.

"But a fellow doesn't need to be strong to be a good debater," he told himself. "And my glasses won't be in the way, either. This is my chance and I'm going to make the most of it."

He sat down at his desk and started to work. When had the pen been mightier than the sword? That would be the first question.

Histories had always been Tommy's favorite books. He had more than one of them on his shelf. He went through them now to find times when whole countries had been influenced by the words some great men had written. "The Declaration of Independence," he told himself. "I'll start off with that."

After he had thought up his own arguments, he thought up the arguments the other side would be likely to make. He planned how to answer them. The more he worked, the more interested he became.

WHAT SHOULD HE DO?

When the afternoon for the debate came, the boys were ready. All of them were eager to represent the Lightfoot Club when it started to have debates with other clubs.

"But Tommy will win first place," said Peter while they waited for the judge to arrive. "Even when he hasn't studied up in advance, he always out-argues us. And you know how he can make us do things his way. He'll make the judge think his way, too."

"He'll win first place when we debate the other clubs, too," said Bob.

Just then Dick Fulsom's brother arrived. "Good afternoon, gentlemen," he said, as if they were college men, all of them.

He took his place where Tommy usually stood. Then he took some slips from his pocket. "I am sure you will want to carry on this debate just as the literary societies in my college would do it. So I prepared these slips of paper which I'll put in my hat. Each of you will draw one. It will tell you which side you are to take."

156

Each of the boys came forward and drew out a slip. When Tommy's turn came he put his hand in the hat. He opened the slip and read it.

"But this says I must argue that the sword is mightier than the pen," he exclaimed. "I can't take that side. I don't believe it."

"That doesn't make any difference," the boys told him. "We don't care which side you really believe in. Just give us a good debate."

Tommy shook his head. "I couldn't argue for something I thought was wrong."

"You'll have to, now you've drawn that slip," said the judge. "It must be that or nothing."

"Then it will have to be nothing."

"You sound like a spoiled child. 'If I can't have the side I want, I won't play.'"

"Maybe I do, but I can't help it. I can't argue for something I don't believe in. It would be dishonest."

Some of the boys called him stubborn. Some

said he was a poor sport. He was going back on his friends. They made him feel very uncomfortable, but they couldn't change his mind. He didn't debate.

"What can we do with a fellow like Tommy?" asked Peter disgustedly. "Nothing. Just nothing. But the strange thing about it is—no matter how angry I get with him, I still like him."

General Lee Comes to Town

TOMMY WAS sure that nothing would ever make Professor Derry give his school a holiday, but he was mistaken. Wonderful news came over the telegraph wire one morning. The whole city rocked with excitement. General Robert E. Lee, the great leader of the Confederate army, was on his way to Savannah. He would stop over in Augusta to spend the night!

Professor Derry was as excited as any of the boys. "To see Robert E. Lee—that will be something for you to tell your grandchildren! Tomorrow morning there will be no school until after his train leaves."

Tommy could hardly sleep that night. At half past nine he heard the engine whistle. General Lee's train was coming. It would be at the station by now. The committee would be there to meet him. The general would be tired. He had had a long illness. No one else could see him tonight. But tomorrow——!

Long before train time the next morning the sidewalks were lined with people. Men were crowding to see their old commander. Women and children wanted to greet their hero. The war was over. He was no longer a soldier. But he was still loved as no other man in the South had ever been loved.

Tommy could hardly wait for breakfast. As he left the house Joe joined him. They dashed down the street together. Suppose the general had left for the station earlier than had been expected! Suppose they had missed him!

They weren't too late. They had to wait and wait. The sun was hot. Mothers sat down on the curbs with their babies in their laps. Old soldiers leaned against the trees. Then word came from the hotel. General Lee was tired from his long trip. He wouldn't take the morning train. He was going to stay in Augusta all day.

The crowd cheered. Everyone started toward the hotel. Joe and Tommy found themselves being swept along by the crowd. Once Tommy almost lost his glasses. A woman beside him bumped them when she tried to raise her arm. Tommy caught them just before they fell off.

"You'd better put them in your pocket," Joe said. "You don't need to see where you're going. You have to go where the crowd pushes you anyway. Ouch! Someone bumped me."

Tommy thought that his glasses were as safe on his face as they would be in his pocket. He grinned as he put them back on.

Finally the boys were in front of the hotel. The yard in front of it was packed with people, and the hotel itself seemed to be full, too.

A young man with pencil and paper in his hand pushed his way out of the hotel doorway. He smiled at Tommy, who was crowded up against the building.

"Did you see him? Did he talk with you?" everyone asked the young man.

The man took out his handkerchief and mopped his forehead. "Yes, I saw him," he answered. "There's the biggest crowd in there that this hotel ever has had. But the general takes time to speak with each person. He looks old and sick, but he's still a great man."

A woman next to Tommy looked down at her little boy. With one hand he clung to his mother's skirts. In the other hand he clutched a big bunch of roses.

"Don't forget," the woman was saying to her son, "when we get into the general's room, tell him that your name is Robert E. Lee Simpson. Then give him the flowers. You can always remember that you saw the great general you were named for."

The crowd at the door moved forward a few steps. Tommy lost sight of the woman and boy, as they edged forward.

Just then two old soldiers came through the doorway. One of them was wiping his eyes. Tommy heard him say, "Imagine General Lee remembering that I was wounded at Gettysburg! What a memory he has!"

Tommy turned to look at Joe. Joe wasn't smiling now. The boys were only a few steps from the door, but Joe shook his head.

"We'll never get in, Tommy," he said. "You and I are the wrong age. We're too young to have been soldiers, but we're too old to have been named for him. We won't get in."

"We can try," said Tommy. The crowd inched forward. Tommy turned to say something to Joe, but several strangers were in the way. Tommy knew that there was no use trying to stay with Joe.

He wormed his way through the crowd. Finally he was in the hall. Then he slipped into the room. At last two soldiers who had been talking to the general turned away. Tommy slipped into their place. The next moment he was standing by General Lee.

The general saw him and smiled. Then a group of men pushed forward. They pushed Tommy to one side. He had seen the general, so he was ready to go home. He didn't even try to find Joe, but started home alone.

The first book Tommy ever read himself had been about General George Washington. Then and there Washington had become his first hero. Now he had a second one. He had seen Robert E. Lee—not from far away, but close up. He had seen the kindness in Lee's face and also the sadness.

A lump came into Tommy's throat. It was hard to put into words exactly what he felt, but Father had trained him to try. Why were Washington and Lee great men? He puzzled it out as he walked home under the hot sun. They were both brave soldiers, but that wasn't all. No, indeed!

"It sounds preachy," he said to himself, "but

it is true, all the same. Both of them were ready to give themselves in war and in peace to the building up of their country. That's it."

He gave a satisfied sigh because he had figured it out. Then he hurried up the porch steps. "I wonder what Mother is going to have for dinner today."

Good-by to the Lightfoot Club

"I'm going to have a busy time this fall," Tommy told his mother. "You should see the long lessons in Greek and Latin Professor Derry is giving us! Besides that, the Lightfoot Club still has two more games to play. And there are those new books Father bought last week. I'll have to squeeze them in somewhere."

The first of the two games came the next afternoon. The Lightfoot boys lost it in the ninth inning. Peter, at second, muffed the ball when the bases were full.

"But we still have one more game," Tommy told his team.

He was busy with his plans as he walked home. "Maybe, if we shifted Peter from——"

Annie was waiting for him in the hall. "Tommy!" she said. "The most exciting thing has happened! Father has been asked to teach in the theological school at Columbia. How would you like to live in South Carolina?"

Tommy's thoughts came back from the baseball field with a jolt. Leave Augusta! Leave Professor Derry! Leave the Lightfoot Club!

"Are we really going?" he asked.

"I don't know. Father hasn't decided yet."

Tommy listened anxiously that night when Father prayed for guidance. The next afternoon and the next and the next, he asked Mother as soon as he came in from school, "Have you and Father decided yet?"

"Yes," she told him at last. "Father has told the school at Columbia that he will come. We shall have to move in a few weeks."

A few weeks! Tommy gave a sigh of relief. He could still play in the last game of the season for the Lightfoot team.

THE LAST GAME

The sun shone clear the next Saturday morning. "We won't have any rain to stop us today," Tommy told the girls happily.

"We're coming to watch you," Annie said.

The Blues came from the other side of town. They were a strong team. Tommy watched them anxiously as they came on the field. Their captain's fingers looked battered and out of shape.

"A good many ball players have fingers like that," Tommy thought. "It would be a good thing if we could all wear gloves. It would save a lot of sprained fingers."

Sometimes Tommy played center field, but today he was at shortstop. "Come on, boys," he called as they ran out into the field. "Let's make this game a walkover."

But it wasn't a walkover at all. Both sides were retired with a blank for the first two innings. Then the Blues got a man on first base. The next player sent a daisy cutter to right field. It was a fine two-base hit. The first player came home. The next two men were out. The score was 1–0 in favor of the Blues.

When the Lightfoot boys went to bat, their luck changed, too. Joe made a fine hit over the center fielder's head and got to second base. Tommy hit an infield single which brought Joe to third. Henry came to bat. He struck at the ball twice but missed it. Then he sent a hot liner to third base. The third baseman muffed it, and the ball went far out into left field. Both Joe and Tommy came home. Tommy's team was ahead 2–1.

In the next inning the Blues made two runs.

The Lightfoot boys made another. The score was tied. After that, first one team, then the other would get ahead, but never by more than one run. When the last half of the eighth inning was over, the score was 7–6 in favor of the Lightfoot team.

"Let's keep it there!" called Tommy as they went out into the field for the last time.

The Blues' first man at bat went out. The next one reached first base. With a single the third player advanced him to second. Now their best hitter came to bat.

He didn't even try to swing at the first two balls. When the third came, he hit hard. The ball whizzed toward the shortstop. It was over his head. Tommy jumped as he reached for it. It was a fine catch, but the ball stung his hand so that he almost muffed it. He threw the ball to second. The Blue player was caught off base. A double play! The game was over!

The umpire called the final score. "Seven to six in favor of the Lightfoot team." How the club members cheered! They gave a special cheer, too, for Captain Wilson.

Tommy felt happy, but he was sad, too. He started home with his bat over his shoulder. His games with the Lightfoot Club were over.

Moving to Columbia

"I DON'T LIKE moving a bit," Tommy told his sisters. "It's as bad as spring housecleaning and getting ready for company rolled together."

"You haven't let it bother you too much," Annie answered. "All you did was to pack your books and your bat. Then you said, 'I'm ready.'"

"Well, I am."

Marion looked up from the trunk she was packing. She had been helping Mother ever since daybreak. "What about your clothes?" she asked.

Tommy looked sheepish. "I reckon I'll let you take care of them."

Marion laughed. "All right. You take care of Joseph. That will get both of you out from underfoot."

Tommy decided he would take Joseph for a ride on the streetcar. It would give him a chance to tell the driver good-by, too.

"I'm sorry you're leaving," the driver told him.

"I'm sorry, too," said Tommy.

But when they got back to the house nearly all the furniture was gone. The empty rooms looked so strange and unfriendly that he was glad when the time came to leave.

FIRST VIEW OF COLUMBIA

Aunt Marion and Jessie came down to the station to see them off. Father had gone on ahead. He met them at the station in Columbia. Soon they were driving to their new home. Tommy was busy trying to see both sides of the street.

For block after block there were no houses at all—only charred ruins with heaps of blackened bricks and half-burned walls. Green vines, weeds and even a few flowers were growing out of the cluttered cellars.

"What happened?" asked Tommy. "It looks as if the whole city was burned."

"Most of it was," said Father. "It happened right at the end of the war. Some people say the Yankees burned it. Some say our own men started it to keep the enemy back. But fire and war always go together. Columbia was destroyed."

"Oh!" Tommy thought back to the war days when he was a small boy in Augusta. "And I thought we were in the middle of the war there," he remembered. He looked again at the ruins they were passing. "The people of Columbia know what war really is."

Father nodded. "It is suffering," he said, "and starvation and cruelty."

"Pray God," said Mother, "that it may never happen again."

Tommy was nearly fifteen now. He was beginning to think for himself. "That prayer isn't quite right," he thought. He remembered the old proverb, "Heaven helps those who help themselves."

"I reckon that is it," he decided. They passed what had been a beautiful lawn. Now it was a mass of weeds choked with rubbish.

"Pray God," he murmured to himself, "that I may help keep war from ever happening again."

Princeton Days

TEEN-AGE Tommy had not yet won the struggle against poor health. He tried to start college at Davidson when he was seventeen, but the doctors sent him home. After another year he was stronger.

"You may try again," his father said. "There are many good schools. Maybe you would like to go to one of the northern colleges." So this time Tommy went to Princeton, in New Jersey.

There he soon became as busy as ever he had been when he was president of the Lightfoot Club. There were more debates and of course there was more baseball.

"I may not be strong enough yet to play on the team," he told himself, "but at least I can help clear the land for a diamond."

He learned a good deal, too, about a new game called football. He liked to plan plays for the team. Sometimes he would even referee a football game.

He started a new literary club. This meant a new constitution for him to write. He helped start a college newspaper, too.

Although Tommy was busy with extra activities, his schoolwork improved steadily. His health also was better than it ever had been.

As Tommy studied, he became more and more interested in history and government. He read everything he could on these subjects.

In his last year at Princeton, he was made editor of the college newspaper. It was his job to choose articles to print in this paper. Other students wrote about things that interested them. Then Tommy chose the best ones to print. Sometimes he printed one of his own articles on government.

It took a great deal of time and work to be a good editor. Tommy never forgot something that his father had taught him. "Be sure to say *exactly* what you mean," his father had told him. So when Tommy wrote for the college newspaper, he was careful to choose exactly the right words. He was proud of the paper.

As he worked and played, there was always a question in his mind. "After I leave college, what shall I do with my life?"

Then suddenly he found the answer. He had gone to the library to look up a quotation. A new magazine had just come in. He picked it up and began to read. It had come from England. It described the men who had been the heads of the English government. It told how they had made England what she was.

As Tommy read, his thoughts became clear. They weren't new thoughts exactly. For months they had been in the back of his mind.

Ever since he had written the constitution of the Lightfoot Club, he had liked to study the ways in which people could govern themselves. "What this magazine says is true," he told himself. "For good government there must be good leaders. And the United States needs them just as much as England does.

"I've been wondering what I'll do after I leave college. I'd like to become a good leader in the government."

The more he thought about it, the surer he became. "Of course it won't be easy. First I'll have to study. I must learn all the ways of good government. I must learn how to show these ways to other people. Maybe I'll write books or teach—or both. Maybe I'll become a senator or even a governor."

Half joking, half serious, he wrote the words down to see how they would look. Senator Tommy Wilson. Governor Tommy Wilson. "No, that isn't right. Tommy doesn't fit."

But he had another name—Woodrow. He tried again. Senator Woodrow Wilson. Governor Woodrow Wilson. That was better. He looked at the words with a grin.

Then Tommy became serious again. He turned back to the beginning of the article in the magazine. He read a few paragraphs. Then he thought about them. He read a few more paragraphs and thought about them.

When Tommy looked out the library window, he was surprised to see that it was getting dark. He had spent the whole afternoon reading and thinking about one article.

He hurried down the stairs and across the campus. Stars were coming out. A good fresh wind was blowing. Tommy felt as uplifted and free as the wind. His big question had been answered. He knew what he was going to do with his life.

Woodrow,
the Man

So Tommy Wilson, the boy, grew into Woodrow Wilson, the man. He studied good government. He wrote books about it. He taught it. He became President of Princeton University, then Governor of New Jersey. Finally, in 1913, he became President of the United States.

World War I broke out. President Wilson knew what war meant. He remembered the anxious days in Augusta. He remembered the black ruins of Columbia. He tried with all his heart and soul to keep it away from his country. At last he found that this was impossible.

"We must fight," he told his countrymen sorrowfully. "But if we go into this war heart and soul we shall win. And we can make it a war that will end all wars."

He began, even before the war was over, to plan a way to end wars. He explained his plan to Congress. He explained it to the people of the United States and to the whole world.

"There was a time," he said, "when every man fought his neighbor. Now neighbors have learned to live together in peace. Here in America our states have learned to live together in one country. Now the countries, too, must unite. We must have a League of Nations."

The war ended. The victorious allies made plans for a meeting where they would draw up a treaty of peace. Who should be sent to represent the United States?

"I shall go myself," said Woodrow Wilson.

No President had ever left the United States before while he was in office. Many people didn't like the idea. "A President's place is in his own country," they said.

"I *must* go," President Wilson insisted. "I must show the world how a League of Nations can keep the world at peace."

THE LEAGUE OF NATIONS

The people of Europe were tired of war, too. They gathered in crowds to cheer Wilson on. They loved him as, years before, the people of Augusta had loved General Lee.

Wherever he went—France, England, Italy— the same thing happened. Mothers brought their children to see the great man. Even the poorest home had his picture on the wall. Everywhere crowds cheered him. "He will make the world free!" the people cried.

But when the Peace Conference began, his popularity died. The world was not ready for the League as he planned it. To make it a success the nations of the world would have to be unselfish.

The politicians at the Peace Conference couldn't understand this. It seemed more sensible and patriotic for each one to grab as much land and money as he could for his own people.

President Wilson knew this was a sure way to bring on more wars. He knew, too, that many parts of the peace treaty were unwise. "After the League of Nations is started, though," he told himself, "it will straighten these things out."

He was still hopeful for the future when he returned to America. But there he found a new disappointment. Not even his own people were ready for the League.

"Why," they asked, "should the United States get mixed up again in the quarrels of Europe? Let Europe take care of herself. We'll take care of ourselves."

"But that is the way wars begin," Wilson insisted. "The United States cannot keep apart from the rest of the world—not in these days. There must be a place where all the nations can come and work out their problems together. We must have a League of Nations."

The people of the United States didn't agree with him.

"It is because they don't understand," he decided. "I must explain it all again. I'll make a trip across the country and hold meetings in every state."

He was an old man now and very tired. His doctor shook his head when he heard what the President wanted to do.

"You shouldn't try it," said the doctor.

"I must," said President Wilson.

He started on his long, hard trip. At first it looked as if his plan might work. As a boy, Tommy had usually been able to make people see

things his way. As President Wilson, he still had the same skill. But halfway through the trip his health gave way. Ill and helpless, he was carried back to Washington. His fight to have the United States join the League of Nations was lost. A few years later, in 1924, he died.

For a while it seemed that all for which he had worked died, too. The League of Nations, without America, was weak and powerless. At last his worst fears were realized. The world was caught up in another war.

But when World War II was over, Wilson's dream once more came into being. This time the organization was called the United Nations instead of the League of Nations, but its object was much the same. It was created to lead the world once more along the paths that Woodrow Wilson planned—toward freedom for all and a just and lasting peace.

More About This Book

WHEN WOODROW WILSON LIVED

1856 THOMAS WOODROW WILSON WAS BORN IN STAUNTON, VIRGINIA, DECEMBER 28.

There were thirty-one states in the Union.

Franklin D. Pierce was President.

The population of the country was about 28,140,000.

1856–1870 AFTER TWO YEARS IN STAUNTON, TOMMY LIVED IN AUGUSTA, GEORGIA.

Eleven states seceded from the Union and formed the Confederate States of America, 1860-1861.

The first transcontinental telegraph was completed, 1861.

The War between the States was fought, 1861-1865.

The Emancipation Proclamation was issued, 1863.

The first transcontinental railroad was completed, 1869.

1870– 1879	TOMMY COMPLETED HIGH SCHOOL AND GRADU- ATED FROM PRINCETON UNIVERSITY.

Alexander G. Bell invented the telephone, 1876.

Rutherford B. Hayes became President, 1877.

Thomas Edison invented the phonograph, 1878, and the electric light bulb, 1879.

1879– 1913	WILSON WAS A STUDENT, LAWYER, TEACHER, WRITER, AND GOVERNOR.

Clara Barton founded the American Red Cross, 1881.

The Spanish-American War was fought, 1898.

Wilbur and Orville Wright flew the first heavier-than-air aircraft, 1903.

Robert Peary discovered the North Pole, 1909.

1913– 1924	WILSON SERVED TWO TERMS AS PRESIDENT AND AFTERWARDS RETIRED.

The Panama Canal was completed and opened to world traffic, 1914.

The United States entered World War I, 1917.

World War I ended, 1918.

The League of Nations was formed, 1920.

1924 WILSON DIED FEBRUARY 3, IN WASHINGTON, D.C., AFTER THREE YEARS RETIREMENT.

There were forty-eight states in the Union.

Calvin Coolidge was President.

The population of the country was about 112,500,000.

DO YOU REMEMBER?

1. Why was Thomas Woodrow Wilson called Tommy when he was a boy?

2. What important news did Tommy overhear when he climbed one of the gateposts at his home?

3. Who was Tommy's father and how did he serve as a community leader?

4. How did Tommy and Joe Lamar happen to see men leaving to join the Confederate Army?

5. How did Tommy manage to get to take a horse-back ride even though horses were scarce?

6. What important events finally brought the War between the States to an end?

7. How did Tommy and his friends form the Light-foot Club, and who became president?

8. What happened when the boys stayed away from school to watch a circus parade?

9. Why did Tommy refuse to debate that the sword is mightier than the pen?

10. How did Tommy get to see Robert E. Lee when Lee came to Augusta?

11. What prayer did Tommy utter when the family first moved to Columbia?

12. What activities did Tommy carry on while he attended Princeton University?

13. What important positions did Woodrow Wilson hold during his lifetime?

14. What important organization did Wilson help to found after World War I?

IT'S FUN TO LOOK UP THESE THINGS

1. Where is Staunton, Virginia, the city where Wilson was born?

2. What other schools besides Princeton University did Wilson attend?

3. Where did Wilson practice law for a short period of time?

4. What was the famous Quad Plan which Wilson started at Princeton University?

5. When did fighting cease in World War I, and how is the date celebrated today?

6. What important Nobel Prize was awarded to Wilson following World War I?

7. What other countries besides the United States helped to found the League of Nations?

INTERESTING THINGS YOU CAN DO

1. Make a list of Presidents besides Wilson who were born in Virginia.

2. Prepare a report on the principal causes of World War I.

3. Find out what event caused the United States to enter World War I.

4. Make a list of popular songs which were sung during World War I.

5. Explain why the League of Nations lasted only a short period of time.

6. Collect pictures of Wilson as President for a display on the bulletin board.

OTHER BOOKS YOU MAY ENJOY READING

America Travels, Alice Dalgliesh. Macmillan.

George Washington: Boy Leader, Augusta Stevenson. Trade and School Editions, Bobbs-Merrill.

Heroes, Heroines and Holidays, Eleanor Thomas. Ginn.

Lee, the Gallant General, Jeanette Eaton. Morrow.

Pets at the White House, Carl Carmer. Dutton.

Rainbow Round the World, Elizabeth Yates. Bobbs-Merrill.

Story of the Presidents, Maud and Miska Petersham. Macmillan.

They Lived in the White House, Frances Cavanah. Macrae Smith.

INTERESTING WORDS IN THIS BOOK

adjourn (ă jûrn') : end a meeting

aisle (īl) : passageway, usually between rows of seats, as in a church or school

bale: large package of compressed raw material, bound tightly and often wrapped

banister (băn′ĭs tẽr) : railing at the side of an open stairway

beeline: direct or straight line

boll (bōl) : seed pod of cotton plant, which bursts open when cotton is ripe

brier (brī'ẽr) : bush with woody stems and branches covered with thorns

campus: grounds of a college or school

catechism (kăt'ẻ kĭz'm) : book or manual filled with questions and answers, used for providing religious instruction within a church

charred: burned black but not turned to ashes

congregation (kŏng'grẻ gā'shŭn) : group of people who belong to or attend a certain church

constitution (kŏn'stĭ tū'shŭn) : statement of purposes and rules or laws of an organization, a state, or a nation

debate: engages in an argument for or against a certain subject according to a set of rules

discipline (dis'ĭ plĭn) : enforcement of good behavior, often by rules

elder: person in certain churches who shares with other persons, including the minister, in deciding how the church should be run

fidgety: restless, impatient, nervous

gable: three-cornered top end of a building, with sides formed by sloping portions of a roof

gallery: upper floor of a building located over the back part of first floor, balcony

199

grid: grating or coarse screen used to sort out or hold back larger particles, while allowing smaller particles to fall through

moderator (mŏd′ẽr ā′tẽr) : person in charge of a meeting, chairman

parliamentary law (pär lĭ mĕn′tả rĭ) : rules of order, rules for carrying on a meeting

pine tags: needles from pine trees that have fallen to the ground and formed a thick covering

quotation (kwȯ tā′shŭn) : actual words or statement taken from the writings or sayings of another

snicker: short, smothered laugh

sprig: twig or small branch of a plant

steamcars: railroad cars

stubble: stumps of grainstalks, a few inches high, left in a field after the grain has been cut

surrender (sŭ rĕn′dẽr) : yield, give up

theological (thē′ȯ lŏj′ĭ kăl) : referring to religion, often applied to a special college or university where ministers are trained

truant (trōō′ănt) : child who stays away from school without permission

unwary: not suspecting, unguarded

vestibule (vĕs′tĭ būl) : entrance hall, room between outer door and inner part of a building

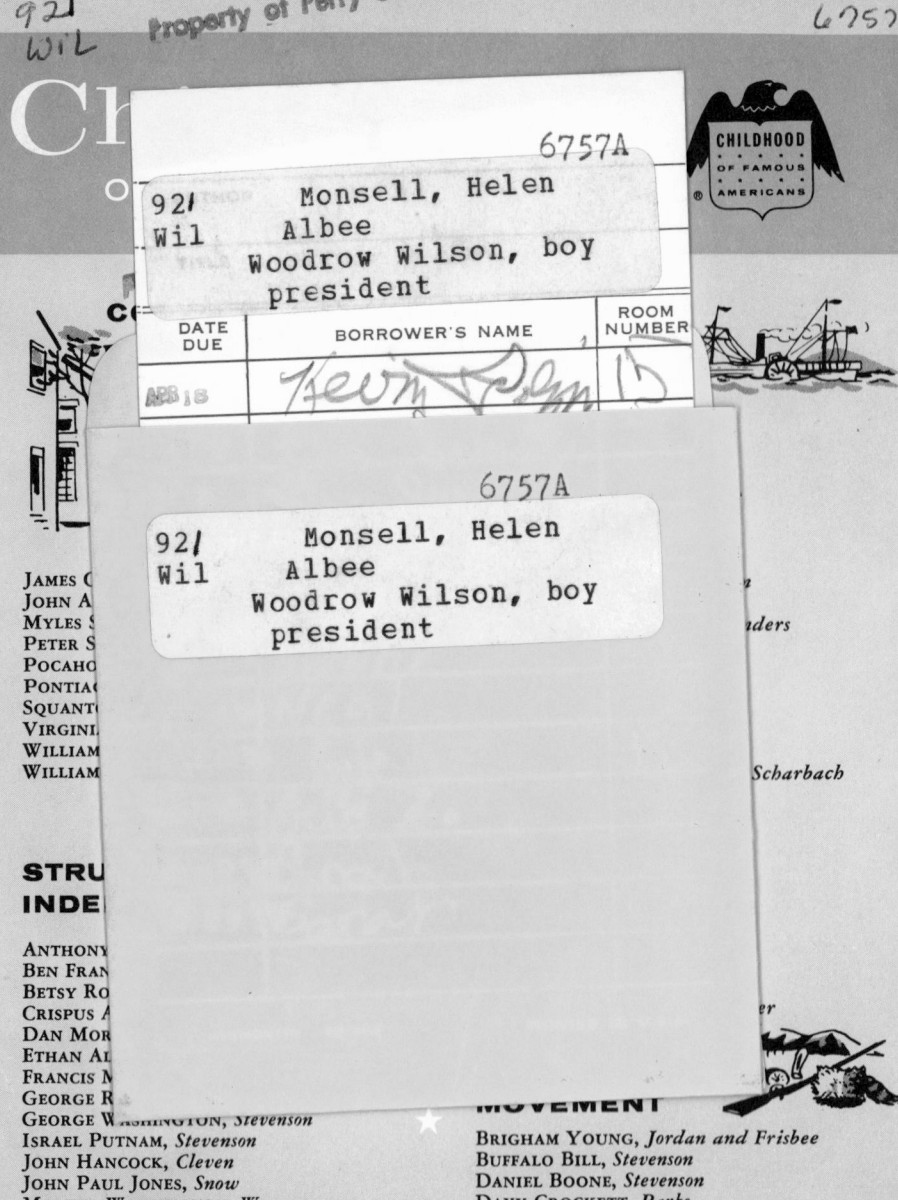

Ch
O

CHILDHOOD OF FAMOUS AMERICANS

6757A

921
Wil

Monsell, Helen
Albee
Woodrow Wilson, boy
president

DATE DUE	BORROWER'S NAME	ROOM NUMBER
APR 18	*Kevin*	D

6757A

921
Wil

Monsell, Helen
Albee
Woodrow Wilson, boy
president

Scharbach

JAMES
JOHN A
MYLES
PETER S
POCAHO
PONTIAC
SQUANTO
VIRGINI
WILLIAM
WILLIAM

STRU
INDE

ANTHONY
BEN FRAN
BETSY RO
CRISPUS A
DAN MOR
ETHAN AL
FRANCIS M
GEORGE R
GEORGE WASHINGTON, *Stevenson*
ISRAEL PUTNAM, *Stevenson*
JOHN HANCOCK, *Cleven*
JOHN PAUL JONES, *Snow*
MARTHA WASHINGTON, *Wagoner*
MOLLY PITCHER, *Stevenson*
NATHAN HALE, *Stevenson*
NATHANAEL GREENE, *Peckham*
PATRICK HENRY, *Barton*
PAUL REVERE, *Stevenson*
TOM JEFFERSON, *Monsell*

MOVEMENT

BRIGHAM YOUNG, *Jordan and Frisbee*
BUFFALO BILL, *Stevenson*
DANIEL BOONE, *Stevenson*
DAVY CROCKETT, *Parks*
GAIL BORDEN, *Paradis*
JED SMITH, *Burt*
JESSIE FREMONT, *Wagoner*
JIM BOWIE, *Winders*
JIM BRIDGER, *Winders*
KIT CARSON, *Stevenson*

CHICAGO

Where to Stay and Eat
for All Budgets

Must-See Sights
and Local Secrets

Ratings You Can Trust

Fodor's Travel Publications   New York, Toronto, London, Sydney, Auckland
www.fodors.com

rolyn Galgano

Heidi Moore, Jo Napolitano, Roberta Sotonoff

th, Mark Stroud, *cartographers*; Bob Blake, Rebecca
Bae, , *information graphics*

Design: Fabrizio La Rocca, *creative director*; Guido Caroti, Siobhan O'Hare, *art directors*; Tina Malaney, Chie Ushio, Ann McBride, Jessica Walsh, *designers*; Melanie Marin, *senior picture editor*

Cover Photo (Chicago Theater marquee): age fotostock/SuperStock, with permission from MSG, a division of Madison Square Garden, L.P. All rights reserved.

Production/Manufacturing: Amanda Bullock

COPYRIGHT

ISBN 978–1–4000–0700–4

ISSN 0743–9326

SPECIAL SALES

This book is available at special discounts for bulk purchases for sales promotions or premiums. Special editions, including personalized covers, excerpts of existing books, and corporate imprints, can be created in large quantities for special needs. For more information, write to Special Markets/Premium Sales, 1745 Broadway, MD 6-2, New York, New York 10019, or e-mail specialmarkets@randomhouse.com.

AN IMPORTANT TIP & AN INVITATION

Although all prices, opening times, and other details in this book are based on information supplied to us at press time, changes occur all the time in the travel world, and Fodor's cannot accept responsibility for facts that become outdated or for inadvertent errors or omissions. So **always confirm information when it matters**, especially if you're making a detour to visit a specific place. Your experiences—positive and negative— matter to us. If we have missed or misstated something, **please write to us.** We follow up on all suggestions. Contact the Chicago editor at editors@fodors.com or c/o Fodor's at 1745 Broadway, New York, NY 10019.

PRINTED IN THE UNITED STATES OF AMERICA

10 9 8 7 6 5 4 3 2 1

Be a Fodor's Correspondent

Your opinion matters. It matters to us. It matters to your fellow Fodor's travelers, too. And we'd like to hear it. In fact, we need to hear it.

When you share your experiences and opinions, you become an active member of the Fodor's community. That means we'll not only use your feedback to make our books better, but we'll publish your names and comments whenever possible. Throughout our guides, look for "Word of Mouth," excerpts of your unvarnished feedback.

Here's how you can help improve Fodor's for all of us.

Tell us when we're right. We rely on local writers to give you an insider's perspective. But our writers and staff editors—who are the best in the business—depend on you. Your positive feedback is a vote to renew our recommendations for the next edition.

Tell us when we're wrong. We're proud that we update most of our guides every year. But we're not perfect. Things change. Hotels cut services. Museums change hours. Charming cafés lose charm. If our writer didn't quite capture the essence of a place, tell us how you'd do it differently. If any of our descriptions are inaccurate or inadequate, we'll incorporate your changes in the next edition and will correct factual errors at fodors.com immediately.

Tell us what to include. You probably have had fantastic travel experiences that aren't yet in Fodor's. Why not share them with a community of like-minded travelers? Maybe you chanced upon a beach or bistro or B&B that you don't want to keep to yourself. Tell us why we should include it. And share your discoveries and experiences with everyone directly at fodors.com. Your input may lead us to add a new listing or highlight a place we cover with a "Highly Recommended" star or with our highest rating, "Fodor's Choice."

Give us your opinion instantly at our feedback center at www.fodors.com/feedback. You may also e-mail editors@fodors.com with the subject line "Chicago Editor." Or send your nominations, comments, and complaints by mail to Chicago Editor, Fodor's, 1745 Broadway, New York, NY 10019.

You and travelers like you are the heart of the Fodor's community. Make our community richer by sharing your experiences. Be a Fodor's correspondent.

Happy traveling!

Tim Jarrell, Publisher

CONTENTS

CHICAGO IN FOCUS

ABOUT THIS BOOK

Our Ratings

Sometimes you find terrific travel experiences and sometimes they just find you. But usually the burden is on you to select the right combination of experiences. That's where our ratings come in.

As travelers we've all discovered a place so wonderful that its worthiness is obvious. And sometimes that place is so experiential that superlatives don't do it justice: you just have to be there to know. These sights, properties, and experiences get our highest rating, **Fodor's Choice,** indicated by orange stars throughout this book.

Black stars highlight sights and properties we deem **Highly Recommended,** places that our writers, editors, and readers praise again and again for consistency and excellence.

By default, there's another category: any place we include in this book is by definition worth your time unless we say otherwise. And we will.

Disagree with any of our choices? Care to nominate a place or suggest that we rate one more highly? Visit our feedback center at www.fodors.com/feedback.

Budget Well

Hotel and restaurant price categories from ¢ to $$$$ are defined in the opening pages of each chapter. For attractions, we always give standard adult admission fees; reductions are usually available for children, students, and senior citizens. Want to pay with plastic? **AE, D, DC, MC, V** following restaurant and hotel listings indicate if American Express, Discover, Diners Club, MasterCard, and Visa are accepted.

Restaurants

Unless we state otherwise, restaurants are open for lunch and dinner daily. We mention dress only when there's a specific requirement and reservations only when they're essential or not accepted—it's always best to book ahead.

Hotels

Hotels have private bath, phone, TV, and air-conditioning and operate on the European Plan (aka EP, meaning without meals), unless we specify that they use the Continental Plan (CP, with a continental breakfast), Breakfast Plan (BP, with a full breakfast), or Modified American Plan (MAP, with breakfast and dinner) or are all-inclusive (including all meals and most activities). We always list facilities but not whether you'll be charged an extra fee to use them, so when pricing accommodations, find out what's included.

Many Listings

★	Fodor's Choice
★	Highly recommended
✉	Physical address
✛	Directions
⌑	Mailing address
☎	Telephone
🖷	Fax
⊕	On the Web
✎	E-mail
🎫	Admission fee
☉	Open/closed times
Ⓜ	Metro stations
▭	Credit cards

Hotels & Restaurants

🏨	Hotel
⇄	Number of rooms
⌂	Facilities
❍	Meal plans
✕	Restaurant
⌂	Reservations
⤬	Smoking
⌘	BYOB
✕🏨	Hotel with restaurant that warrants a visit

Outdoors

⚑	Golf
⛺	Camping

Other

☺	Family-friendly
⇨	See also
✉	Branch address
☞	Take note

Experience
Chicago

WORD OF MOUTH

"The architectural river cruise is great, but not for little kids, they'll be bored silly. If you want to take a boat, take a Duck Tour, or take the boat taxi that goes between museum campus and Navy Pier. For kids, the Shedd Aquarium and Field Museum are excellent. They'll love 'the Bean' in Millennium Park. How about a baseball game at Wrigley Field?"

—dmlove

CHICAGO PLANNER

The Second City?

New Yorkers will tell you theirs is the greatest city in the world. But Chicagoans beg to differ. Chicago's charm is indisputable—the impeccably clean streets; the friendly Midwestern vibe; the alluring mixture of lush parks, Lake Michigan, and sleek skyscrapers. It's what keeps the debate going (log onto the Fodors.com "Talk" forum and check out one of the "favorite city" debates!), and what keeps everyone coming back.

Word of Mouth

"We took the El up to Magnificent Mile area—it was a bit of an adventure because the red line was not running north, only south. But it just gave us more opportunities to walk! NYC is my favorite US city because it's so walking oriented, and Chicago has now won a place in my heart."

–Pisces

Highly, highly recommend the Segway tour . . . The route is incredibly scenic and riding the Segway is great fun.

–djkbooks

Getting Around

Chicago has an excellent network of buses as well as trains, which are collectively called the El (for "elevated," which many of them are). The combination should bring you within ¼ mile of any place you'd like to go. Those with city smarts will find it safe to take any train, any time. Others may want to take extra caution after 11 PM. Buses are almost always safe; there are several express buses running from downtown to destinations like the Museum of Science and Industry.

As of this writing, the fare for any bus or train is $1.75 and a transfer is 25¢ with a Transit Card; if you're paying cash, all rides are $2. Travelers may want to get a Visitor Pass at their hotel, airport CTA stations, or any visitor center. These passes allow unlimited rides for a small fee and are worth it as long as you take three trips a day.

For directions to specific places via public transportation, for public transportation maps, and for locations to buy Transit Cards, see ⊕ www.transitchicago.com.

Three free trolley lines (Navy Pier, Water Tower Park, Museum Campus) circulate downtown attractions. Originating at both Ogilvy and Union Metra stations, with a transfer point on State Street near Macy's, they run every 20 minutes from 10 AM to 6 PM daily. Most services begin on Memorial Day and run through Labor Day; the Navy Pier trolley, which travels between Navy Pier and State Street, operates year-round. More information is at ⊕ www.cityof chicago.org/transportation/trolleys.

If you drive downtown, park in one of the giant city-owned parking lots underneath Millennium Park or by the Museum Campus, which charge a flat fee. Private lots usually cost double.

A Few of Our Favorite Things

What do Fodor's editors do when they head to Chicago? Here are a few of our personal picks. We love walking along the Chicago River and watching the boats ply the water, then strolling down State Street to the old Carson Pirie Scott building, just to admire the iron scrollwork outside. We gallery-hop in River North, and duck into cute boutiques along Oak Street. We head to Hyde Park to gawk at the colorful, noisy monk parakeets. We never leave without indulging in deep-dish pizza. We won't tell you which baseball team we cheer for, but we do love going to the games. And at night? You can find us catching the blues at B.L.U.E.S., going to an outdoor concert (we've heard great ones at Grant Park), howling at Second City improvisers, or having drinks at the Signature Room at the John Hancock.

Visitor Centers

■ **Chicago Cultural Center** (⊠ 77 E. Randolph St., at Michigan Ave. ☎ 312/744–6630 ⊕ www.cityofchicago. org/tourism/culturalcenter ⊗ Mon.–Thurs. 8–7, Fri. 8–6, Sat. 9–6, Sun. 10–6).

■ **Chicago Water Works** (⊠ 163 E. Pearson St., at Michigan Ave. ☎ 877/244–2246 ⊕ www.877chicago.com or www.choosechicago.com ⊗ Daily 7:30–7).

■ **Millennium Park Welcome Center** (⊠ 201 E. Randolph St., in the Northwest Exelon Pavilion ☎ 312/742–1168 ⊕ www.millenniumpark.org ⊗ Apr. 1–Oct. 1, daily 9–7; Oct. 2– Mar. 31, daily 10–4).

■ **Chicago Greeters** (☎ 312/744–8000 ⊕ www.chicago greeter.com). This free service, offered by the Chicago Office of Tourism, pairs visitors with a city-smart volunteer guide for an informal two- to four-hour walking tour. Register two weeks in advance. Chicago Greeter tours step off from the Chicago Cultural Center.

When to Go

June, September, and October are mild and sunny. November through March the temperature ranges from crisp to bitter, April and May can fluctuate between cold/soggy and bright/warm, and July and August can either be perfect or serve up the deadly combo of high heat and high humidity. That said, the only thing certain about Chicago's weather, according to locals, is that it can change in an instant. If you head to Chicago in warmer months, you'll be able to catch some of the fantastic outdoor festivals; during the holiday season the city's decked out in lights.

Local Know-How

Most businesses in Chicago are open 10 to 6. Some shops stay open as late as 9. Restaurants can be closed on Monday and usually stop serving around 10 PM on weeknights, 11 PM on weekends. There are a few 24-hour diners, but they are rarer than you might expect. Bars close at 2 AM or 4 AM.

You can avoid the long lines at Chicago museums by buying tickets online at least a day in advance. The most popular architecture tour, led by the Chicago Architecture Foundation, always sells out—be sure to buy tickets in advance.

TOP CHICAGO ATTRACTIONS

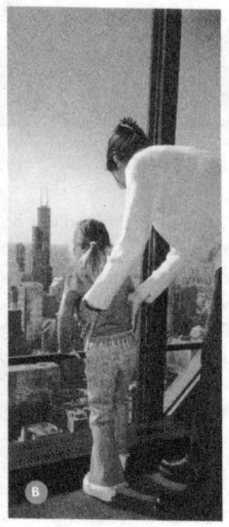

Sears Tower Skydeck

(A) Take the ear-popping ride to the 103rd-floor observatory, where, on a clear day you can see as far as Michigan, Wisconsin, and Indiana. At the top, interactive exhibits tell about Chicago's dreamers, schemers, architects, musicians, writers, and sports stars. Kids love Knee-High Chicago, a 4-foot-high exhibit that has cutouts of Chicago sports, history, and cultural icons at a child's eye-level. Security is very tight, so figure in a little extra time for your visit to the Skydeck.

John Hancock Center Observatory

(B) The third-tallest building in Chicago has the most impressive panoramic views of the lake and surrounding skyline—it's high enough to see the tops of neighboring buildings in vivid 3-D, but not so remote that you feel like you're looking out from a plane. Our tip? Skip the observatory and head to the bar that adjoins the Signature Room restaurant on the 95th floor—you'll spend your money on an exorbitantly priced cocktail instead of the entrance fee and enjoy the same view. Women can head to the 95th-floor ladies' room for the best view in the whole building.

Shopping on the Magnificent Mile

(C) Exclusive shops, department stores, and boutiques line the northern half of swanky Michigan Avenue. Even better, the concentration of prestigious stores in vertical malls means you can get a lot of shopping done in winter without venturing into the bluster outside.

The Blues Scene

(D) Explore jumping North Side clubs, like Kingston Mines, or South Side venues like the Checkerboard or Lee's Unleaded Blues (where greats like Muddy Waters and Buddy Guy first honed their talent) for the sound Chicago gave birth to—the scintillating electric blues. If you're here in June, don't miss the Chicago Blues Festival, which packs in fans every summer.

Navy Pier

(E) Yes, it's a little schlocky, but Navy Pier is fun, especially for families. Everyone can fan out to shop in the mall, play 18-hole minigolf in Pier Park in the summer, see a movie at the IMAX Theater, or explore the Chicago Children's Museum. Plus, there's a stained-glass museum, a funhouse maze with scenes of Chicago landmarks, and an old-fashioned swing ride. Meet up later at the Ferris wheel for a photo op or just settle on the pier with a drink and enjoy the view.

Art Institute of Chicago

(F) This Chicago cultural gem has the country's best collection of Impressionist and Postimpressionist art. It's also a great place to see all those paintings you've only seen on postcards, like *American Gothic* and *Nighthawks*.

Adler Planetarium & Astronomy Museum

(G) How can you not enjoy getting up close with the cosmos at the country's oldest planetarium? Older children and astronomy fanatics get geeked about the interactive science exhibits and the high-tech Sky Pavilion, while younger visitors set their sights on virtual-reality shows in the StarRider Theater.

Field Museum

(H) Say hello to Sue, the Field's beloved gigantic T. rex, before immersing yourself in this extraordinary museum's collection of anthropological and paleontological artifacts and animal dioramas. The dinosaurs are the thing here, but surprising collections like Tibetan Buddhist altars, mummies, and re-creations of famous gems may entice you to linger for hours.

Museum of Science & Industry

(I) Travel down an elevator shaft to a "working" coal mine, stroll the cobblestone streets of Chicago circa 1910, explore the caves of a human heart, or watch quietly as a baby chick pecks its way out of its shell at this endlessly interactive museum.

Shedd Aquarium

(J) We find the experience of watching entire universities—not just schools—of fantastically colored fish, as well as dolphins and whales, completely mesmerizing. Don't miss the Wild Reef exhibit, where stingrays slide quietly under the Plexiglas at your feet.

Frank Lloyd Wright Architecture

(K) Frank Lloyd Wright's Prairie School captured the flat, expansive Midwestern plains he saw around him. Oak Park, a Chicago suburb, has many fine examples, though one of the best is Robie House in Hyde Park, which is open for tours.

Millennium Park

Make a beeline for Frank Gehry's **Jay Pritzker Pavilion**, where an incredible sound system allows audiences to enjoy concert-hall sound in the great outdoors. The *Bean* is a luminous polished-steel sculpture that plays tricks with the reflection of Chicago's skyline. In warmer months, children of all ages can't resist a splash in the Crown Fountain, twin 50-foot towers that project close-up video images of Chicagoans "spitting" jets of water.

SOAKING IT ALL IN: RIVER & LAKE TOURS

Coursing through the heart of the Windy City is the majestic Chicago River, lined with some of the city's finest architecture and dotted with river walks and restaurants. Hop in a boat, kayak, canoe, or gondola and sail down for some of the prettiest views of the city. Some tours even head out to the lake for a skyscraper-studded panorama.

Best Tour Companies

The **ArchiCenter of the Chicago Architecture Foundation** (⊠ *224 S. Michigan Ave., Loop* ☎ *312/922–3432* ⊕ *www.archi tecture.org* ☉ *Daily 9–6:30*) conducts excellent, docent-led boat, walking, and bus tours of the Loop and beyond. Our favorite walking tours spotlight "Historic Skyscrapers" and "Modern Skyscrapers." The ArchiCenter also hosts exhibitions, lectures, and discussions.

Watch the panoply of Chicago's magnificent skyline slide by from the decks of *Chicago's First Lady, Chicago's Little Lady, and Chicago's Fair Lady,* the fleet of the **Chicago Architecture Foundation River Cruise.** Make reservations in advance for the popular 90-minute tours. **Ticketmaster** (☎ *312/902–1500* ⊕ *www.ticketmaster. com/illinois*) sells tickets by phone, online, and at the Hot Tix booth in the Chicago Water Works Visitor Center. Ticketmaster fees apply at these outlets. You can also purchase tickets at the *Chicago's First Lady* ticket window or at the Chicago Archi-Center (224 S. Michigan Ave.). ⊠ *Southeast corner of Michigan Ave. Bridge* ☎ *847/358–1330* ⊕ *www.cruisechicago. com* ☳ *$28 weekdays, $30 weekends and holidays* ☉ *May–Nov., daily.*

TOUR ALTERNATIVES

Pinching pennies? Hop on a Shoreline water taxi and cruise down the river. You won't get running narration, but it's affordable (single rides range from $3 to $13, depending on route, and run) and not crowded.

For a more adventurous spin down the river, rent a canoe or a kayak. Just beware of large boats and crew shells. **Chicago Canoe and Kayak** (⊠ *3400 N. Rockwell St.* ☎ *773/704–2663* ⊕ *www.chicagoriver paddle.com*). **Chicagoland Canoe Base** (⊠ *4019 N. Narragansett Ave.* ☎ *773/777–1489* ⊕ *www.chicagolandcanoebase.com*). **Wateriders** (⊠ *900 N. Kingsbury Ave.* ☎ *312/953–9287* ⊕ *www.wateriders.com*).

Other Recommended Companies

Shoreline Sightseeing. Shoreline's been plying these waters since 1939, and has tours of both the river and Lake Michigan. ⊠ *West end of Navy Pier* ☎ *312/222–9328* ⊕ *www.shorelinesightseeing.com* ☉ *Apr.–Oct., daily; Nov., weekends only.*

Wendella Sightseeing. See the city just as the sun sets on the Chicago at Sunset tour. There's also a river architecture tour, a combined river and lake tour, and a wine tasting tour. ⊠ *400 N. Michigan Ave., at the Wrigley Building* ☎ *312/337–1446* ⊕ *www. wendellaboats.com* ☉ *Apr.–Nov., daily.*

Mercury Cruises. Mercury does quirky tours, including Canine Cruises, where dogs are welcome, and City Lights night tours that glide past Buckingham Fountain's light display. ⊠ *112 E. Wacker Dr.* ☎ *312/332–1353* ⊕ *www.mercuryskylinecruiseline.com* ☉ *May–Oct., daily.*

CITY ITINERARIES

Two Hours in Town

If you've only got a bit of time, go to a museum. Although you could spend days in any of the city's major museums, two hours will give you a quick taste of Chicago's cultural riches. Take a brisk walk around the **Art Institute** to see Grant Wood's *American Gothic,* Edward Hopper's *Nighthawks,* and one of the finest Impressionist collections in the country. Or check out the major dinosaur collection or the gorgeous Native American regalia at the **Field Museum.** Take a close look at the sharks at the **Shedd Aquarium.** If the weather's nice, stroll along the lakefront outside the **Adler Planetarium**—you'll see one of the nicest skyline views in the city. Wander down State Street, the Magnificent Mile, or around Millennium Park. If you're hungry, indulge in one of Chicago's three famous culinary treats—deep-dish pizza (head to **Pizzeria Due** to avoid the lines at **Giordano's, Gino's,** and **Pizzeria Uno**); garden-style hot dogs; or Italian beef sandwiches. After dark? Hear some music at a local club. Catch some blues at **Blue Chicago** to get a taste of authentic Chicago.

■ TIP→ Remember that many of the smaller museums are closed on Monday.

A Perfect Afternoon

Do the zoo. Spend some time at the free **Lincoln Park Zoo and Conservatory** (the tropical plants will warm you up in winter), take a ride on the exotic animal-themed carousel, and then spend a couple of hours at the nearby **Chicago History Museum** for a quirky look at the city's past. If you'd like to stay in the Lincoln Park neighborhood a bit longer, have dinner at one of many great local restaurants and then head to **The Second City,** the sketch comedy troupe that was the precursor to *Saturday Night Live.*

■ TIP→ The Second City offers free improvisation following the last performance every night but Friday.

Sightseeing in the Loop

State Street, that Great Street, is home to the old **Marshall Fields,** which has been reborn as Macy's; Louis Sullivan's ornate iron entrance to the former department store **Carson Pirie Scott;** a nascent theater district; as well as great people-watching. Start at Harold Washington Library at Van Buren Street and State Street and walk north, venturing a block east to the beautiful **Chicago Cultural Center** when you hit Randolph Street. Grab lunch at the Museum of Contemporary Art's serene Wolfgang Puck café, **Puck's at the MCA,** and then spend a couple of hours with in-your-face art. Go for steak at Morton's or the Palm before a night of Chicago theater. Broadway touring shows are on Randolph Street at the Oriental or the Cadillac Palace, or head elsewhere downtown for excellent local theater—the Goodman, Steppenwolf, Lookingglass, and Chicago Shakespeare will each give you a night to remember.

Get Outdoors

Begin with a long walk (or run) along the lakefront, or rent a bike or inline skates and watch the waves on wheels. Then catch an El train north to **Wrigley Field** for Cubs baseball; grab a dog at the seventh-inning stretch, and sing your heart out to "Take Me Out to the Ball Game." Afterward, soak up a little beer and atmosphere on the patio at one of the local sports bars. Finish up with an outdoor concert in **Grant or Millennium park.**

Family Time

Start at **Navy Pier**—or heck, spend all day there. The **Chicago Children's Museum** is a main attraction, but there's also an IMAX Theater, a Ferris wheel, a swing ride, a fun house, a stained-glass museum, and, in summer, Chicago-themed miniature golf in Pier Park. If the crowds at the Pier get to be too much, walk or take the free trolley to **Millennium Park,** where kids of all ages can ice-skate in winter and play in the fountain in summer, and where giant digital portraits of Chicagoans spit streams of water to help cool you off. Whatever the weather, make sure to get your picture taken in the mirrored center of the *Bean*—the sculpture that's formally known as *Cloud Gate.* At night in summertime, take a stroll by Buckingham Fountain, where the dancing sprays jump to music and are lit by computer-controlled colored lights, or take a turn on the dance floor during Chicago's nightly SummerDance celebration.

■ TIP→ **Fireworks explode near Navy Pier every Wednesday and Saturday night at 9** PM, **Memorial Day through Labor Day.**

Cityscapes

Start at the top. Hit the heights of the **John Hancock Center** or the **Sears Tower Skydeck** for a grand view of the city and the lake. Then take a walking tour of downtown with a well-informed docent from the **Chicago Architecture Foundation.** In the afternoon, wander north to the **Michigan Avenue Bridge,** where you can take an informative boat tour of the Chicago River. Enjoy the architecture as you float by, resting your weary feet.

Shop Chicago

Grab your bankroll and stroll the **Magnificent Mile** in search of great buys and souvenirs. Walking north from around the Michigan Avenue Bridge, window-shop your way along the many upscale stores. Hang a left on **Oak Street** for the most elite boutiques. **Accent Chicago** (875 North Michigan Ave.) or **City of Chicago Store** at the Chicago Waterworks Visitors Center are where serious souvenir hunters spent their cash. Dedicated shoppers will want to detour a little farther south to **State Street** in the Loop for a walk through the landmark Marshall Field's building, now Macy's. For a culture buzz, check out the **Museum of Contemporary Art** (closed Monday). After making a tough restaurant choice (Prime rib at Smith & Wollensky's or Lawry's? or deep-dish pizza at Giordano's?), consider a nightcap at the **Signature Room** at the 95th-floor bar on top of the John Hancock Center—the city will be spread beneath your feet.

GETTING OUTSIDE:
PARKS & ZOOS

Chicago may not be the country's biggest city, but it's arguably the prettiest. Architect Daniel Burnham designed the city to have plenty of green space so city dwellers could relax, and even the tiniest green outpost usually has some sort of public art. With winter never too far from thought, Chicagoans pour into the city's parks and zoos at the first hint of summer, or take to conservatories when the weather's less than ideal. The following are our favorite city parks and zoos.

Parks

Garfield Park Conservatory. Escape winter's cold or revel in summer sunshine inside this huge Victorian glass structure housing tropical palms, spiny cacti, and showy blooms. A children's garden delights with climbable leaf sculptures and a tube slide that winds through trees. The Sweet House now houses a permanent Sugar from the Sun exhibit focused on the elements of photosynthesis—sunlight, air, water, and sugar—in a full-sensory environment filled with spewing steam, trickling water, and chirping sounds. And don't miss the historic Jens Jensen–designed fern house with its lagoon, waterfalls, and profusion of ferns. Events include botanical-theme fashion shows, flower shows, and the annual Chocolate Fest in February, which pays homage to the conservatory's fruiting cacao trees with chef demonstrations and free samples from area chocolate shops. ⊠ *300 N. Central Park Ave., Garfield Park.*

⭐ **Fodor's Choice** **Grant Park & Buckingham Fountain.** Two of Chicago's greatest treasures reside in Grant Park—the Art Institute and Buckingham Fountain. Bordered by Lake Michigan to the east, a spectacular skyline to the west, and the Museum Campus to the south, the

ever-popular Grant Park serves as the city's front yard and unofficial gathering place. This pristine open space is decked out with walking paths, a stand of stately elm trees, and formal rose gardens, where Loop dwellers and 9-to-5-ers take refuge from the concrete and steel. The park also hosts many of the city's largest outdoor events, including the annual Taste of Chicago, a vast picnic featuring foods from more than 70 restaurants. The event precedes a fireworks show around July Fourth. The fountain is a wonderful place to people-watch.

The centerpiece of Grant Park is the gorgeous, tiered **Buckingham Fountain** (⊠ *Between Columbus and Lake Shore Drs. east of Congress Plaza*), which has intricate designs of pink-marble seashells, water-spouting fish, and bronze sculptures of sea horses. Built in 1927, it was patterned after a fountain at Versailles but is about twice the size of its model. See it in all its glory between May 1 and October 1, when it's elaborately illuminated at night and sprays colorfully lighted waters. Linger long enough to experience the spectacular water display that takes place every hour on the hour, and you'll see the center jet of water shoot 150 feet into the air. ⊠ *South Loop* ☎ *312/747–1534.*

Lincoln Park Conservatory. Green grows on green in the lush tropical main room of this refreshing city greenhouse. Stroll through permanent displays in the Palm House, Fern Room, and Orchid House, or catch one of the special shows, like the fragrant Easter Lily show in March or April and the festive Chrysanthemum Show in November. The peacefulness and abundant greenery inside the 1892 conservatory offer a refreshing respite in the heart of this bustling neighborhood.

✉ *2400 N. Stockton Dr., Lincoln Park* ☎ *312/742-7736* ⬛ *Free* �)*Daily 9–5.*

★ **Millennium Park.** The Bean, the fountains, the Disney-esque music pavilion—all the pieces of this new park quickly stole the hearts of Chicagoans and visitors alike. This is one of our favorite places to spend a sunny day.

The showstopper here is Frank Gehry's stunning **Jay Pritzker Pavilion.** Dramatic ribbons of stainless steel stretching 40 feet into the sky look like petals wrapping the music stage. The sound system, suspended by a trellis that spans the great lawn, provides concert-hall sound outside. So what can you see on this beautiful stage? Take your pick. There's the Grant Park Music Festival—a free classical-music series—as well as the city's popular free summer concerts, including the jam-packed Chicago Blues and Chicago Jazz festivals.

Hot town? Summer in the city? Cool off by letting a local resident spit on you. Okay, it's just a giant image of a Chicagoan's face—actually, dozens of Chicagoans' faces rotating through on two huge (read 50-foot-high) glass block–tower fountains. The genius behind the **Crown Fountain,** Spanish sculptor Jaume Plensa, lined up the mouths on the digital photos with an opening in the fountain. When a face purses its lips, water shoots out its "mouth." Kids love it, and we feel like kids watching it. It's at the southwest corner of the park.

You've seen the pictures. Now go, take your own. The **Cloud Gate sculpture,** otherwise known as "the Bean," awaits your delighted *ooohs* and *aaahs* as you stand beneath its gleaming seamless polished

steel. It's between Washington and Madison streets. Go on, get camera happy.

If you're feeling artsy, you can find out if there's a show playing at the indoor, underground **Harris Theater for Music and Dance,** behind the Jay Pritzker Pavilion.

In summer the carefully manicured plantings in the **Lurie Garden** bloom; in winter the **McCormick Tribune Ice Rink** is open for public skating. ✉ *Bounded by Michigan Ave., Columbus Dr., Randolph Dr., and Monroe St., Loop* ⊕ *www.millenniumpark. org* ⬛ *Free* ☉ *Daily 6 AM–11 PM.*

Zoos

★ **Brookfield Zoo.** Spend the day among nearly 3,000 animals at this gigantic zoo. The highlights? First, there's the popular **Tropic World,** a simulated tropical rain forest where monkeys, otters, birds, and other rain-forest fauna cavort in a carefully constructed setting of rocks, trees, shrubs, pools, and waterfalls. Next, test your "flying strength" in the **Be a Bird House** by flapping your "wings" on a machine that decides what kind of bird you would be, based on how you flap. We also like the **Living Coast,** where you can venture through huge glassed-in passageways to see sharks, rays, jellyfish, and turtles swimming by. Daily dolphin shows are a favorite even for adults. Walruses, seals, and sea lions inhabit a rocky seascape exhibit. Don't worry if you don't want to trek around the grounds—you can hop aboard a motorized safari tram in warm weather ($2.50) or the heated *Snowball Express* tram in the cold (free).

The two best educational exhibits are Habitat Africa and Swamp. In **Habitat Africa** you can explore two very different environments. See such tiny animals

GETTING OUTSIDE: PARKS & ZOOS

as klipspringer antelope, which are only 22 inches tall, and rock hyraxes, which resemble prairie dogs, in the savanna exhibit, which also has a water hole, rock formations characteristic of the African savanna, and termite mounds. If you look closely in the dense forest exhibit, you might be able to find animals like the okapi. The **Swamp** is about as realistic as you would want an exhibit on swamps to be, with a springy floor, push-button alligator bellows, and open habitats with low-flying birds vividly demonstrating the complex ecosystems of both southern and Illinois wetlands.

For hands-on family activities, check out the **Hamill Family Play Zoo** (🎫$3.50, *children $2.50*), where kids can learn to care for nature by playing zookeeper, gardener, or veterinarian. The **Children's Zoo** (🎫*$1.50, children $1*) includes a petting farm, excellent animal shows, and the Big Barn with its daily cow and goat milking and weekly wool-spinning demonstrations. Watch the dolphins show off and act silly at the **Seven Seas Dolphin Show** (🎫*adults $3, children $2.50*). ✉*1st Ave. and 31st St.* 🕿*708/485–0263 or 800/201–0784* ⊕*www.brookfieldzoo. org* 🎫*Zoo $11 ($7 children), free on Tues. and Thurs. Oct.–Feb.; parking $8* 🕙*Oct.–Mar., daily 10–5; Apr. and Sept., weekdays 10–5, weekends 10–6; May– Aug., daily 9:30–6; Oct.–Dec., daily 10–5.*

★ **Fodor's Choice** | **Lincoln Park Zoo.** Lions, gorillas, and bears—oh my! At this urban zoo you can face-off with lions (separated by a window, of course) outside the Lion House; watch about two-dozen gorillas go ape in the sprawling, state-of-the-art Regenstein Center for African Apes, with three separate habitats

DID YOU KNOW?

Begun in 1868 with a pair of swans donated by New York's Central Park, the Lincoln Park Zoo grew through donations of animals from wealthy Chicago residents and the purchase of a collection from the Barnum & Bailey Circus.

featuring real bamboo stands, 5,000 feet of swinging vines, and termite mounds for chimpanzee snacking; or watch some rare and endangered species of bears, such as the spectacle bear (named for the eyeglasslike markings around its eyes).

Animals both slithery (pythons) and cuddly (koalas) reside in the glass-dome Regenstein Small Mammal and Reptile House; if you're looking for the big guys (elephants, giraffes, black rhinos), they're in the large-mammal house. Bird lovers should make a beeline for the Kovler Penguin and Seabird House, where you can watch razorbills and tufted puffins frolicking on a simulated North Atlantic coast and king penguins splashing in an 18,000-gallon pool. For youngsters, there are the children's zoo, the Farm-in-the-Zoo (farm animals and a learning center with films and demonstrations), and the Conservation Station, with hands-on activities. Be sure to leave time for a ride (or two) on the Endangered Species Carousel, featuring a menagerie of 48 rare and endangered animals.

✉*2200 N. Cannon Dr., Lincoln Park* 🕿*312/742–2000* ⊕*www.lpzoo.com* 🎫*Free* 🕙*Grounds 9–6, buildings and farm 10–5 daily.*

AUTHENTIC CHICAGO

So you've done the Art Institute and the Sears Tower—now it's time to put away your tourist hat and make like a local. Luckily, it's not hard to figure out what Chicagoans like to do in their spare time. Here's how to follow in their footsteps.

Visit an Ethnic Neighborhood

Chicago is a city of neighborhoods, and in many of them you can see traces of each successive immigrant group. Each neighborhood in the city has its own flavor, reflected in its architecture, public art, restaurants, and businesses, and most have their own summer or holiday festivals. Here are a few stand-out 'hoods.

Little Italy. Though most Italians moved to the West Side a couple of generations ago, Little Italy's Italian restaurants and lemonade stands still draw them back.

Andersonville. The charming diversity of the Swedish/Middle Eastern/gay mecca of Andersonville means you can have lingonberry pancakes for breakfast, hummus for lunch, and drinks at a gay-friendly bar after dinner.

Chinatown. The Chinese New Year dragon parade is just one reason to visit Chinatown, which has dozens of restaurants and shops and a quiet riverfront park.

Devon Avenue. Devon Avenue turns from Indian to Pakistani to Russian Orthodox to Jewish within a few blocks. Try on a sari, buy a bagel or electronics, or just people-watch—it's an excellent place to spend the afternoon.

Pilsen/Little Village. The best Mexican restaurants are alongside Pilsen's famous murals. Be sure to stop into the National Museum of Mexican Art, which will give you an even deeper appreciation of the culture.

Bronzeville. Bronzeville's famous local historic figures include Ida B. Wells—a women's-rights and African-American civil-rights crusader—the trumpeter Louis Armstrong, and Bessie Coleman, the first African-American woman pilot. The area has nine landmark buildings and is rapidly gentrifying.

Enjoy the Lake

San Diego and L.A. may have the ocean, and New York its Central Park, but Chicago has the peaceful waters of Lake Michigan at its doorstep. Bikers, dog walkers, boaters, and runners crowd the lakefront paths on warm days; in winter the lake is equally beautiful, with icy towers formed from frozen sheets of water.

BIKE ALONG THE LAKESHORE

To bike any part of the gentle dips and swells of Chicago's 20 mi **lakefront bicycle path** is to see the city: the skyline, the people, the water. The breeze from the lake mixes with the sounds of the city at play as you zoom by, carefree, whiling away an afternoon.

The **Chicago Park District** (*312/742–7529 www.chicagoparkdistrict.com*) is a good source for bike maps.

For information on biking in the city, contact the **Chicagoland Bicycle Federation** (*9 W. Hubbard St., South Loop 312/427–3325 www.chibikefed.org*).

Bike Chicago (*600 E. Grand Ave., Near North 312/595–9600 or 773/327–2706 www.bikechicago.com*) can deliver a bike to your hotel and pick it up after your ride. Fees start at $8 per hour and $34 a day. It also offers lakefront, neighborhood, and nighttime bike tours for $20 to $45 (bike rental included), weather permitting.

You can rent a bike for the day or by the hour from **On the Route** (*3146 N. Lincoln*

Ave., Lakeview ☎773/477–5066 ⊕*www. ontheroute.com*), which stocks a large inventory of bicycles, including children's bikes. They also supply helmets and other safety equipment.

BOATING

Nothing beats the view of the Chicago skyline from the water, especially when the sun sets behind the sparkling skyscrapers. Plenty of boats are available to rent or charter, though you might want to leave the skippering to others if you're not familiar with Great Lakes navigation.

Sailboat lessons, rentals, and charters are available from **Chicago Sailing** (⊠*Belmont Harbor, Lakeview* ☎773/871–7245 ⊕*www.chicago sailing.com*). Chicago Sailing focuses on sailing instruction for all levels and includes a program on keeping your boat in tip-top shape.

Sailboats, Inc. (⊠*Monroe Harbor, Loop* ☎312/861–1757 or 800/826–7010 ⊕*www. sailboats-inc.com*), one of the oldest charter-certification schools in the country, prepares its students to charter any type of boat.

For a more placid water outing, paddle boats, including swan-shaped two-seaters, are available for rent at **Lincoln Park's South Lagoon** (⊠*2021 N. Stockton Dr., Lincoln Park* ☎312/742–2038), just north of Farm-in-the-Zoo.

BEACHES

One of the greatest surprises in the city is the miles of sandy beaches that Chicagoans flock to in summer. The water becomes warm enough to swim in toward the end of June, though the brave will take an icy dip through the end of October. Chicago has about 30 mi of shoreline, most of it sand or rock beach. Beaches are open to the public daily from 9 AM to 9:30 PM, Memorial Day

BEACHES	Block	Best For	Bathrooms	Changing	Facilities	Showers	Lifeguard
Far North Side							
Foster Beach	5200 N	Families	yes	no	no		yes
Montrose Beach	4400 N	Learning to sail	yes	no	yes		yes
Osterman Beach	5800 N	Quiet conversations	yes	no	yes		yes
Hyde Park							
South Shore Country Club	7100 S	Quieter beach	yes	yes	yes		yes
Jackson Beach Central	5700–5900 S	Beach trip after the Museum of Science and Industry	yes	no	no		yes
Lincoln Park							
North Avenue Beach	1600–2400 N	Margaritas at the upstairs concession	yes	yes	yes		yes
Near North							
Oak Street Beach	600–1600 N	Singles scene	yes	no	no		yes
South Loop							
12th Street Beach	1200 S at 900 E	Post museum-hopping break	yes	no	yes		yes

through Labor Day, and many beaches have changing facilities.

The **Chicago Park District** (☎312/742–7529 ⊕*www.chicagoparkdistrict.com*) provides lifeguard protection during daylight hours throughout the swimming season.

All references to north and south in beach listings refer to how far north or south of the Loop each beach is. In other words, 1600 to 2400 north means the beach begins 16 blocks north of the Loop (at Madison Street, which is the 100 block) and extends for eight blocks.

⚠ Along the lakefront you'll see plenty of broken-rock breakwaters with signs that warn NO SWIMMING OR DIVING. Although Chicagoans frequently ignore these signs, you shouldn't. The boulders below the water are slippery with seaweed and may hide sharp, rusty scraps of metal, and the water beyond is very deep. It can be dangerous even if you know the territory.

Brave the Cold

The city's brutal windy winters are infamous, but that doesn't keep Chicagoans from making the best out of the long cold months. Throw on lots of layers, lace up your ice skates, and show those city dwellers what you're made of.

★ The rink at **Millennium Park** (⊠55 N. Michigan Ave., Loop ☎312/742–1168 ⊕*www.millenniumpark.org*) has free skating seven days a week and a dazzling view of the Chicago skyline. Skate rentals are $9 a session.

On the snowiest days, some hardy souls **cross-country ski** and snowshoe on the lakeshore—bring your own equipment.

Loosen up by playing outdoor paddle tennis at **Midtown Tennis Club** (⊠2020 W. Fullerton Ave. ☎773/235–2300 ⊕*www.midtowntennisclub.com*). If it's snowing, they turn on the heated floors.

Holiday-walk Chicago's windows during the **Magnificent Mile Lights Festival**, in November, the Saturday before Thanksgiving. The celebration includes music, ice-carving contests, and stage shows, and ends in a parade and the illumination of more than one million lights.

FREE THINGS TO DO

It's easy to spend money in the big city: think shopping, museum-entrance fees, restaurants, theater. But if you'd like to put your wallet away for a while, here are some of our favorite options.

Free Art

■ Chicago has some of the most famous public art in the country, including a **Picasso** piece in Daley Plaza, **Alexander Calder's** *Flamingo* in Federal Plaza, and the *Cloud Gate* sculpture in Millennium Park. For a fairly comprehensive list, see ⊕*www.chipublib.org* or pick up a *Free Public Art* guide at a visitor center.

■ The **City Gallery** (⊠*806 N. Michigan Ave.* ☎*312/742–0808*) in the Historic Water Tower hosts rotating exhibits of Chicago-theme photography.

■ Five different galleries showcase contemporary visual art by local artists at the **Chicago Cultural Center** (⊠*78 E. Washington St.* ☎*312/744–6630* ⊕ *www.cityof chicago.org/tourism/culturalcenter/*).

Free Concerts

■ Grant Park and Millennium Park host regular classical and pop concerts in summer. For a schedule, pick up the *Chicago Reader* or buy a copy of *TimeOut Chicago*.

■ Chicago is a festival town, celebrating blues, jazz, country, gospel, Celtic, and world music during the warm months. For a schedule, see ⊕*www.cityofchicago. org*.

■ Free jazz and classical concerts are performed Monday through Wednesday and Friday at 12:15 in the **Chicago Cultural Center** (⊠*78 E. Washington St.* ☎*312/744–6630* ⊕ *www.cityofchicago. org/tourism/culturalcenter/*).

Free Movies

Every Tuesday night in summer Grant Park shows classic films at sundown on a giant screen. The films tend to be popular, so go early, spread out a blanket, and have a picnic a couple of hours beforehand. There's even a free bike valet. Local library branches and parks also have free movies—check the city's Web site for details.

Free Dance Lessons

Learn to swing, polka, step, waltz, and salsa to the beat of a live band in Grant Park during the summer-long Chicago SummerDance Festival. Chicagoans of all ages and abilities sashay around the dance floor during the lessons and the free dancing afterward. For more information, see ⊕*www.chicagoparkdistrict.com*.

Free Fireworks

Every Wednesday and Saturday night in summer Navy Pier puts on a showy display of colorful explosives. Watch from the pier or along the waterfront opposite Buckingham Fountain.

Free Trolley Rides

A free trolley circles downtown attractions like the museums and Navy Pier every 20 minutes until 9 PM on weekdays and 11 PM on weekends. For more information, call ☎*877/244–2444*.

Free Improv

The world-famous Second City comedy troupe has a free improv set following the last performance every night but Friday. For more information, go to ⊕*www.sec ondcity.com* or call ☎*312/337–3992*.

Free Museum Days

ALWAYS FREE

Jane Addams Hull-House Museum
Museum of Contemporary Photography

National Museum of Mexican Art
Oriental Institute
Smart Museum

SUNDAY:
DuSable Museum of African American History

MONDAY:
Adler Planetarium & Astronomy Museum (selected months only)
Chicago Children's Museum (for those 15 and younger the first Monday of each month)

TUESDAY:
Adler Planetarium & Astronomy Museum (selected months only)
Museum of Contemporary Art
Swedish American Museum Center (second Tuesday each month)

THURSDAY:
Art Institute of Chicago (after 5 PM)
Chicago Children's Museum (5–8 PM only)
Peggy Notebaert Nature Museum

Free TV-Show Tickets

Oprah Winfrey and Jerry Springer tape their shows in front of live audiences in Chicago. Though tickets are free, they are at a premium and must be reserved far in advance. Oprah's shows are filmed at **Harpo Studios** (✉ *1058 Washington St.* ☏ *312/591–9222 for tickets* ⊕ *www. oprah.com*). *The Jerry Springer Show* is filmed at **NBC Tower** (✉ *454 N. Columbus Dr.* ☏ *312/321–5365* ⊕ *www.jerry springertv.com*).

Sightseeing Walks

THAT GREAT STREET

The Loop—defined by the rectangle created by the El tracks—is the heart of downtown, and the heart of downtown is State Street. Begin at the south end of the Michigan Avenue Bridge, with your back to the Chicago Tribune's Gothic tower. Walk west along the river past Marina City's iconic corncob towers, perhaps taking the stairs down to the River-walk for a drink at one of the cafés. Once you're back at street level, make a left on State Street, cruising by the famous Chicago Theatre sign that marks the beginning of the theater district. Window-shop at the local landmark Marshall Field's, which is now Macy's, or just enjoy the facade of the old Carson Pirie Scott (now closed). Heading south toward Congress Parkway, gaze up at the dramatic facade of the neoclassical Harold Washington Library, with its gigantic gargoyle-like owls—then head inside to admire the airy, glass-roofed Winter Garden on the ninth (and top) floor.

ZOOTOPIA

In two hours on a beautiful day you can breeze through the Lincoln Park Zoo, stroll beside the park's lagoons, and discover the quaint, upscale neighborhood of Old Town. Beginning on North Avenue and Lake Shore Drive, walk north through the park alongside the lagoons. Watch the crew shells try to navigate past the fishing lines, or throw a line into the stocked lagoon yourself. Take your time exploring the zoo or continue north to the Lincoln Park Conservatory, pausing to admire North Pond with its lush greenery and the skyline reflected in its water. Then circle back south and slightly west to Wells Street, where the Second City improv troupe's theater and a host of tony shops and restaurants line brick streets.

CHICAGO WITH KIDS

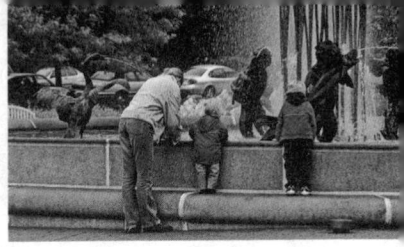

Chicago sometimes seems to have been designed with kids in mind. There are many places to play and things to do, from building sand castles at one of the lakefront's many beaches to playing 18-hole minigolf at Navy Pier in summer. Here are some suggestions for ways to show kids the sights.

Museums

Several area museums are specifically designed for kids. At the **Chicago Children's Museum** (✉ *700 E. Grand Ave., Navy Pier*), three floors of exhibits cast off with a play structure in the shape of a schooner, where kids can walk the gangplank and slide down to the lower level, and make a splash with a water playground, featuring a scaled-down river and a water wheel. Also at **Navy Pier** you'll find a Ferris wheel and Viennese swings (the kind that go around in a circle like a merry-go-round). In the summer, crowds of kids make the most of Pier Park's 18-hole minigolf course, musical carousel, and remote-control boats.

Many other Chicago museums are also kid-friendly, especially the butterfly haven and the animal habitat exhibit with its climbable treehouse at the **Peggy Notebaert Nature Museum,** the replica coal mine and hands-on Idea Factory at the **Museum of Science and Industry,** the dinosaur exhibits at the **Field Museum,** and the sharks and dolphins at the **John G. Shedd Aquarium.**

Parks, Zoos & Outside Activities

Chicago's neighborhoods are dotted with area play lots that have playground equipment as well as several ice-skating rinks for winter months. On scorching days, visit the **63rd Street Beach House,** at 63rd Street and Lake Shore Drive in Woodlawn. The interactive spiral foun-

MORE IDEAS FROM FODORS.COM FORUMS

- Holiday Lights Festival on Michigan Ave.
- Bulls, Cubs, or White Sox Game
- Day trip to Oak Park
- Gospel Brunch at House of Blues (call 312/923–2000)
- Chicago Architecture Foundation Cruise (visit www.architecture.org)

tain in the courtyard jumps and splashes, leaving kids giggling and jumping. The **North Park Village Nature Center** on the far northwest side (on Pulaski Road north of Bryn Mawr Avenue) is a wilderness oasis, serving up 46 acres of trails and a kid-oriented Nature Center with hands-on activities and fun educational programs. Deer sightings are common here. **Millennium Park** (✉ *55 N. Michigan Ave.*) has a 16,000-square-foot ice-skating rink. Skaters have an unparalleled view of downtown as they whiz around the ice.

For more structured fun, there are two zoos: the free **Lincoln Park Zoo** (✉ *2200 N. Cannon Dr. at Lake Shore Dr. and Fullerton Pkwy.*) and the large, suburban **Brookfield Zoo** (✉ *1st Ave. and 31st St., Brookfield*), which has such surprising exhibits as a wall of pulsing jellyfish. The **Buccaneer Pirate Adventure Cruise** (Wagner Charter Cruise Co. Dock, Lower Wacker Dr. between Wells St. and Franklin/Orleans St. bridges) sets sail with wannabe pirates, teaching them about the river's locks and entertaining kids with magic tricks.

FABULOUS FESTIVALS

Chicago festivals range from local neighborhood get-togethers to citywide extravaganzas. Try to catch a neighborhood street fair for some great people-watching if you're in town between June and September. On some weekends there are several festivals at once. For details, see ⊕ *www.chicagoreader.com.*

The **St. Patrick's Day parade** (☎*312/942-9188*) turns the city on its head: the Chicago River is dyed green, shamrocks decorate the street, and the center stripe of Dearborn Street is painted the color of the Irish from Wacker Drive to Van Buren Street. This is your chance to get your fill of bagpipes, green beer, and green kneesocks. It's over 4 hours, so you probably won't see the whole thing.

The **Chicago Blues Festival** (☎*312/744-3315* ⊕*www.chicagobluesfestival.org*), in Grant Park, is a popular four-day, three-stage event in June starring blues greats from Chicago and around the country. If you see only one festival in Chicago, this is the one.

The medium-size **Chicago Gospel Fest** (☎*312/744-3315*) brings its joyful sounds to Grant Park in early June.

Taste of Chicago (✉*Grant Park, Columbus Dr. between Jackson and Randolph Sts.* ☎*312/744-3315*) dishes out pizza, cheesecake, and other Chicago specialties to 3.5 million people over a 10-day period before the July Fourth holiday that includes top pop and novelty acts.

Thrill-seekers and families flock to the **Chicago Air & Water Show** (✉*Lakeshore, Fullerton Ave. to Oak St.; focal point at North Ave. Beach* ☎*312/744-3315*), a lakefront spectacle featuring aerial acrobatics and daredevil water acts. See the U.S. Navy Blue Angels perform precision flying maneuvers at the three-day event in mid-August.

The **Chicago Jazz Festival** (☎*312/744-3315*) holds sway for four days during Labor Day weekend in Grant Park.

At the **Celtic Fest,** Celtic food, art, storytelling, dance, and a bagpiper's circle celebrate everything Irish. It's held in Grant Park during the month of September.

At the weeklong **World Music Festival,** international artists play traditional and contemporary music at venues across the city in September.

Street fairs are held every week in summer, but two stand out as the best. **Halsted Market Days,** in August, is the city's largest street festival. It's held in the heart of the gay community of Lakeview and has blocks and blocks of vendors as well as some wild entertainment such as zany drag queens and radical cheerleaders. The **Taste of Randolph** is more sedate, featuring dishes from the fine restaurants lining the western end of Randolph Street in June.

The holiday season officially starts with the **Magnificent Mile Lights Festival** (⊕*www.themagnificentmile.com*), a weekend-long event at the end of every November with tons of family-friendly activities including musical performances, ice-carving contests, and stage shows. The fanfare culminates in a parade and the illumination of more than one million lights along Michigan Avenue.

GET OUT OF TOWN

You could spend a month or two just exploring the city of Chicago, but the surrounding towns are likewise rich in history, culture, and activities. The closest suburbs offer theaters and museums; the farther out you go, the more likely you are to find wooded parks and quiet places.

Brush Up on Your Ernest Hemingway

Ernest Hemingway Birthplace. Part of the literary legacy of Oak Park, this three-story, turreted Queen Anne Victorian, which stands in frilly contrast to the many streamlined Prairie-style homes elsewhere in the neighborhood, contains period-furnished rooms and many photos and artifacts pertaining to the writer's early life. Museum curators have redecorated rooms to faithfully depict the house as it looked at the turn of the 20th century; you can poke your head inside the room in which the author was born on July 21, 1899. ⊠ *339 N. Oak Park Ave.* ☎ *708/848-2222* ⊕ *www.hemingway.org* ✉ *Joint ticket with Hemingway Museum $8* ⊘ *Sun.–Fri. 1–5, Sat. 10–5.*

Ernest Hemingway Museum. How did the author's first 20 years in Oak Park impact his later work? Check out the exhibits and videos here to find out. Don't miss his first "book," a set of drawings with captions written by his mother, Grace. Holdings include reproduced manuscripts and letters. ⊠ *200 N. Oak Park Ave.* ☎ *708/848-2222* ⊕ *www.hemingway.org* ✉ *Joint ticket with Hemingway Birthplace $8* ⊘ *Sun.–Fri. 1–5, Sat. 10–5.*

Follow the Chicago Symphony Orchestra

If you enjoy music under the stars, the outdoor concerts at **Ravinia Park** are a stellar treat. The **Ravinia Festival** is the summer home of the Chicago Symphony Orchestra. Come for jazz, chamber music, pop, and dance performances. Pack a picnic and blanket and sit on the lawn for a little more than the cost of a movie ($10 to $20). Seats are also available in the pavilion for a significantly higher price ($20 to $80). Restaurants and snack bars are on park grounds. Concerts usually start at 8 PM; be at the park at 6:30 to park and get settled. ⊠ *Green Bay and Lake Cook Rds., in Highland Park, 26 mi north of downtown Chicago* ☎ *847/266-5100* ⊕ *www.ravinia.org.*

ERNEST HEMINGWAY: OAK PARK PROTÉGÉ

It seems unlikely that the rough-and-tumble adventurer and writer Ernest Hemingway was born in 1899 amid the manicured suburb of Oak Park, Illinois, a town he described as having "wide lawns and narrow minds." He excelled at writing for the high school paper—a skill that turned into his life's work. A volunteer stint as an ambulance driver introduced him to World War I and its visceral horrors—he used that experience and the lessons he learned as a reporter for the *Kansas City Star* to craft emotionally complex novels built from deceptively simple sentences, like his master work, *A Farewell to Arms.* Hemingway later lived in Toronto and Chicago. Though his return visits to Oak Park were infrequent, the residents celebrate him there to this day.

Unwind Outdoors

★ Fodor's Choice See the spectacular spring blooming season or the beautiful display of mid-June roses at the **Chicago Botanic Garden.** Among the 23 different gardens are a three-island Japanese garden, a waterfall garden, a sensory garden, and a 4-acre fruit-and-vegetable garden. Three big greenhouses showcase a desert, a rain forest, and a formal garden with flowers that bloom all winter long. ⊠ *Lake Cook Rd. and U.S. 41* ☎ *847/835–5440* ⊕ *www.chicago botanic.org* 🎟 *Free; parking $15, tram tour $5* ⊙ *Daily 8 AM–sunset; 45-min summer tours through Oct., daily 10–3, weather permitting.*

Take a quiet hike around the **Morton Arboretum,** full of woodlands, wetlands, and display gardens. Trees, shrubs, and vines flower year-round, but in spring the flowering trees are particularly spectacular. You can drive your car through some of the grounds, but we think it's much nicer to walk. There are lots of trails to take, and most take about 15 to 30 minutes. Don't miss the Daffodil Glade in early spring. Tours are scheduled most Sunday afternoons. ⊠ *4100 Illinois Rte. 53, 25 mi southwest of downtown Chicago* ☎ *630/968-0074* ⊕ *www.mortonarb.org* 🎟 *$9, Wed. $6; tram tours $5* ⊙ *Daily 7–7 (or at sunset, whichever is earlier).*

The 500-acre estate at **Cantigny Park** offers multiple attractions in one: an impressive military history museum with immersive exhibits (think touchscreen videos and re-created battle scenes), sprawling grounds with formal gardens, and its own 27-hole public golf course with separate youth links. But the centerpiece is probably the Beaux Arts–style Col. Robert R. McCormick Museum. Built for the former Chicago Tribune owner, the 35-room mansion features the Joseph Medill Library, the stately wood-paneled Freedom Hall, and an Art Deco movie theater in the basement. The hidden Prohibition-era bar alone is worth a visit—we won't ruin the surprise by revealing where it is. ⊠ *1S151 Winfield Rd., 30 mi west of downtown Chicago* ☎ *630/668–5161* ⊕ *www.cantigny.org* 🎟 *$7 per car, $8 Sat. and Sun.; grounds and museum tours free* ⊙ *In March–Dec., grounds Tues.–Sun. 9 AM–sunset, museums 10–4; in Feb., grounds Fri.–Sun. 9 AM–sunset, museums 10–4 (Feb.); closed Jan.*

Samuel Insull, partner of Thomas Edison and founder of Commonwealth Edison, built the mansion at the **Cuneo Museum and Gardens** in 1916 as a country home. After Insull lost his fortune, John Cuneo Sr., the printing-press magnate, bought the estate and fashioned it into something far more spectacular. The skylighted great hall in the main house resembles the open central courtyard of an Italian palazzo; the private family chapel has stained-glass windows; and a gilded grand piano graces the ballroom. The house is filled with antiques, porcelains, 17th-century Flemish tapestries, and Italian paintings. ⊠ *1350 N. Milwaukee Ave., 15 mi west of Lake Forest, 40 mi northwest of downtown Chicago* ☎ *847/362-3042* ⊕ *www. cuneomuseum.org* 🎟 *$7 per car; $12 per person for mansion tours* ⊙ *Tues.–Sun. 10–4; beginning in mid-May, guided mansion tours are Tues.–Sat. at 11, 1, and 3, self-guided on Sun.*

■ TIP➜ **For Frank Lloyd Wright's Oak Park, see page 141.**

CHICAGO THEN & NOW

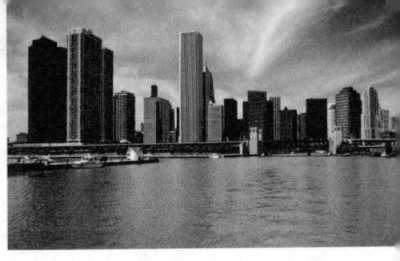

The Early Days

Before Chicago was officially "discovered" by the team of Father Jacques Marquette, a French missionary, and Louis Jolliet, a French–Canadian mapmaker and trader, in 1673, the area served as a center of trade and seasonal hunting grounds for several Native American tribes, including the Miamis, Illinois, and Pottawattomie. Villages kept close trading ties with the French, though scuffles with the Fox tribe kept the French influence at bay until 1779. That year, black French trader Jean Baptiste Point du Sable built a five-room "mansion" by the mouth of the Chicago River on the shore of Lake Michigan.

The Great Fire

The city grew until 1871, when a fire in the barn of Catherine and Patrick O'Leary spread across the city, killing hundreds. (Contrary to the legend, it was probably not started by a cow kicking over a lantern.) A recent drought coupled with crowded wooden buildings and wood-brick streets allowed the blaze to take hold quickly, destroying 18,000 structures within 36 hours.

Gangsters to the Great Migration

World War I (aka the Great War) changed the face of Chicago. Postwar—and especially during Prohibition (1920–33)—the Torrio–Capone organization expanded its gambling and liquor distribution operations, consolidating its power during the violent "beer wars" from 1924 to 1930. Hundreds of casualties include the seven victims of the infamous 1929 St. Valentine's Day Massacre. In 1934 the FBI gunned down bankrobber and "Public Enemy No. 1" John Dillinger outside the Biograph Theater on the North Side, now a theater venue and a Chicago landmark.

The Great War also led to the Great Migration, when African-Americans from the South moved to the northern cities between 1916 and 1970. World War I slowed immigration from Europe, but increased jobs in Chicago's manufacturing industry. More than 500,000 African-Americans came to the city to find work and by the mid-20th century African-Americans were a strong force in Chicago's political, economic, and cultural life.

IMPORTANT DATES IN CHICAGO HISTORY

1673	Chicago discovered by Marquette and Jolliet
1779	Jean Baptiste Point du Sable, a "free Negro," and his wife Catherine, a Pottawattamie Indian, are the first Chicago settlers.
1837	Chicago incorporated as a city
1860	First national political convention. Abraham Lincoln nominated as the Republican candidate for president
1871	Great Chicago Fire

Mayor Daley & the Notorious 1968 Democratic Convention

The Daley dynasty began when Richard J. Daley became mayor in 1955. He was reelected five times and his son, Richard M. Daley, currently runs the city.

The first Mayor Daley redrew Chicago's landscape, overseeing the construction of O'Hare International Airport, the expressway system, the University of Illinois at Chicago, and a towering skyline. He also helped John F. Kennedy get elected, thanks to his control of Chicago's Democratic party.

Despite these advances, Mayor Richard J. Daley is perhaps best known for his crackdown on student protesters during the 1968 Democratic National Convention. Americans watched on their televisions as the Chicago police beat the city's youth with sticks and blinded them with tear gas. That incident, plus his "shoot to kill" order during the riots that followed the assassination of Dr. Martin Luther King Jr., and his use of public funds to build giant, disastrous public housing projects like Cabrini–Green, eventually led to the temporary dissolution of the Democratic machine in Chicago. After Daley's death, Chicago's first black—and beloved—mayor, Harold Washington, took office in 1983.

Chicago Today

The thriving commercial and financial "City of Broad Shoulders" is spiked with gorgeous architecture and set with cultural and recreational gems, including the Art Institute, Millennium Park, 250 theater companies, and 30 mi of shoreline. Three million residents live within the city limits, and tens of thousands commute in from the surrounding (and ever-sprawling) suburbs to work downtown during the week. The current Mayor Daley gave downtown a makeover, adding wrought-iron street furniture, regular fireworks, planters of flowers, and Millennium Park. Daley's focus on eco-friendly building initiatives led to a green roof installed on City Hall, and his advocacy of bicycling has brought new bike paths and bike racks. And spectacular lights now brighten buildings along Michigan Avenue after dark. There are always controversies (recent updates to the El system have caused some delays and lots of grumbling), but most Chicagoans are proud to call the city home.

1885	First skyscraper in the country, Home Insurance Building (no longer standing), is built
1886	Haymarket Riot
1893	World's Columbian Exposition
1929	St. Valentine's Day Massacre
1968	Democratic National convention
1973	Sears Tower, tallest building in North America, completed
2005	Chicago White Sox win the World Series

FOR THE FANATICS

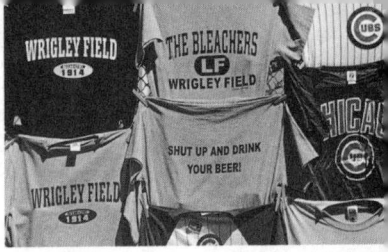

Michael Jordan, Scottie Pippin, Walter Payton, William "the Refrigerator" Perry, Ernie Banks, Sammy Sosa, Shoeless Joe Jackson. You can't mention Chicago without talking about sports. Chicagoans are fiercely devoted to their teams, whether it's baseball, basketball, or football—and whether their team's winning or losing. Come opening day for baseball season, die-hard Cubs and Sox fans take the day off work to cheer on their teams; during football season, tailgaters chow down in the parking lot before kickoff, even if it's snowy and in the single digits. One of the most fun ways to get into the Chicago spirit is to go to a game, so throw on your team's colors and join the screaming fans.

Chicago Bears

Chicago football is messy and dirty and sometimes even exciting. Don't expect to be wowed by star quarterbacks and amazing passing, but do get ready for the team's smash-mouth style that reflects the city's blue-collar persona. Legends like Walter Payton have come and gone, but after several mediocre seasons things have started to look up: they made it to the Super Bowl in 2006 but did not come away the champs.

■ **Where They Play:** *Soldier Field, 425 E. McFetridge Dr., South Loop*

■ **Season:** August–December

■ **How to Buy Tickets:** Through Ticketmaster, at ☎*312/559–1212 or* ⊕*www.chicago bears.com*

■ **Most Notable Players:** Dick Butkas, Mike Ditka, Walter Payton, William "the Refrigerator" Perry, Jim McMahon

■ **Past Highlights:** Although the Bears didn't win the 2007 Super Bowl, they won it in 1986. During that game, defensive tackle William "the Refrigerator" Perry scored a touchdown, highly rare for a defensive player.

Chicago Bulls

It's been years since Michael Jordan and Phil Jackson's "dynasty" teams played in the United Center, but the Bulls' six championships are still revered here. After Jordan's departure in 1998, the franchise became a shadow of its former self—but a new squad of fresh faces is starting to turn things around. Coach Scott Skiles and the "Baby Bulls" are back in the playoffs (2005, 2006, and 2007), and the United Center is starting to rock again.

■ **Where They Play:** *United Center, 1901 W. Madison St., Near West Side*

■ **Season:** November–April

■ **How to Buy Tickets:** From the ticket office, ☎*312/455–4000 or* ⊕*www.bulls.com*

■ **Most Notable Players:** Michael Jordan, Dennis Rodman, Scottie Pippen, Toni Kukoc

■ **Past Highlights:** The Bulls won six NBA Championship Trophies: 1991, 1992, 1993, 1996, 1997, 1998

■ **Note:** Avoid leaving the game early or wandering around this neighborhood at night

TAKE ME OUT
TO THE BALLGAME

In a city where you can get a debate going about all sorts of things—best deep-dish pizza, best blues bar, best big city (Chicago or New York?)—nothing can inspire a passionate discussion quite like Chicago baseball, an argument that's been going strong since 1901.

Your favorite team says more about you than just whether you prefer the National or American League. The rivalry plays out along geographical and class lines. South Siders, who include everyone living south of the Loop, are die-hard Sox fans. North Siders sell out afternoon Cubbies games even when the team is losing—as they do most years.

There's a legendary rivalry between Sox fans and Cubs fans. When the Sox won the World Series in 2005 for the first time in 88 years, most Cubs fans didn't even watch the games. The traitors who did were called "BiSoxual." When the Cubs made the playoffs in 2007, Sox fans actively rooted for the other team

(as the song "Ballad of the South Side Irish" goes, "When it comes to baseball there are two teams that I love, it's the go-go White Sox and whoever plays the Cubs.") One reason that the division has lasted so long is class tension. South Siders, besides the intellectual Hyde Park pocket, tend to be blue collar. North Siders tend to be professionals.

The teams have only played against each other once post-season: the 1906 World Series. The Cubs were favored, but the White Sox won. Fans on both the North and South sides agree on one thing: it would be "an El of a series" if the teams ever faced each other postseason again. As Cubs fans say, "You Gotta Believe."

CHICAGO
NATIONAL LEAGUE CHAMP
1907

SCHULTE ZIMMERMAN REULBACH LUNDGREN PEEISTER HOWARD
TINKER KLING SHECKARD McCORMICK CHANCE mgr. STEINFELDT
BROWN SLAGLE

CHICAGO CUBS

Just the Facts

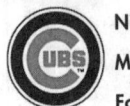

Nickname: Cubbies

Mascot: None

Founded: 1870

Last World Series appearance: 1945

World Series wins: 1907 and 1908

Most famous players: Sammy Sosa, Ron Santo, Ryne Sandberg, Ernie Banks, Billy Williams

Original name: White Stockings

Did you know?

Most hated fan: Steve Bartman, who, in the eighth inning of Game 6 in the 2003 play-offs, reached for—and caught—a foul ball at the same time as left fielder Moises Alou. Before Bartman, the Cubs were five outs away from advancing to the World Series. After Bartman's catch, the Cubs fell apart, giving up eight runs.

Lifelong Chicagoans: The Cubs are the only team to play continually in the same city since the founding of the National League in 1876.

Curse: William Sianis, the old owner of the Billy Goat Tavern, bought two tickets for one of the 1945 Cubs–Tigers World Series games: one for himself, and one for his goat. The goat was turned away, and Sianis vowed that the Cubs would never again win a World Series.

HARRY CARAY: "HOLY COW!"

Beloved for his hoarse, off-key rendition of "Take Me Out to the Ballgame," the way he mashed up players names, and his infamous "Holy Cow!", the Cubs' exuberant play-by-play broadcaster, Harry Caray (1914–1998), was as much a fixture of Wrigley Field as the bleacher bums.

Caray broadcast 8,300 games in his 53-year career. (Don't tell Cubs fans—before he came to Wrigley field, he was the voice of the St. Louis Cardinals for 25 years, the White Sox for 10.) After his death in 1998, every single player wore a caricature of Caray—with his infectious smile and goggle glasses—on their sleeves.

The curse persists, it seems, even though the current Billy Goat owner, son Sam Sianis, occasionally drags a goat back onto the field.

Best seat in the house: The bleachers. Tradition has it that the most serious fans (known as bleacher bums) sit here, on either side of the ivy covered, hand-operated scoreboard. When rival teams hit a ball into the bleachers, the fans throw it back. After the 2005 season, the Cubs' owners, the Chicago Tribune Company, expanded the bleachers for the first time since 1938.

CHICAGO WHITE SOX

Just the Facts

Mascot: Southpaw, a fuzzy, green character of indeterminate origin. He appeared in 2004.

Founded: 1893 in Sioux City, Iowa. Moved to Chicago in 1900.

Last World Series appearance: 2005

World Series wins: 1906, 1917, 2005

Notable players: "Shoeless" Joe Jackson, Roberto Hernandez, Roberto Alomar, Johnny Mostil, Frank Thomas, Germaine Dye.

Original name: White Stockings, which was also the first name of the Chicago Cubs. Charles Comiskey hoped to buy some goodwill for the new team by taking on the Cubs' former name.

Did you know?

Theme song: "Na Na Hey Hey (Kiss Him Goodbye)," is played every home game by organist Nancy Faust.

From White Sox to Black: Eight players—outfielder "Shoeless Joe" Jackson, outfielder Oscar "Happy" Felsch, pitchers Eddie Cicotte and Claude "Lefty" Williams, third baseman Buck Weaver, shortstop "Swede" Risberg, and infielders Fred McMullen and Arnold "Chick" Gandi—were accused of throwing the 1919 World Series on behalf of a group of gamblers. They were never convicted, though they were banned from baseball for life. That season's team has been known as the Black Sox ever since.

Most Famous Quote: As Shoeless Joe Jackson was leaving a Black Sox scandal hearing, a newsboy supposedly shouted out, "Say it ain't so, Joe!" This inspired headline writers after the 2005 World Series win to write: "Say it IS so!"

Strangest promotional event: Disco Demolition Night, July 12, 1979, at the old Comiskey Park. Fans were asked to bring unwanted disco records to the park for a Sox–Tigers double header; in return, the admission was lowered to a mere 98 cents. After the first game, chaos erupted—fans threw their records like Frisbees and ran onto the field where they started bonfires and mini-riots.

Fireworks: After every home run and every win, the Sox shoot fireworks into the sky from U.S. Cellular Field. They can be heard across the South Side.

WRIGLEY FIELD

Getting There

Address: 1060 West Addison St., at the corner of Addison St. and Clark St.

Phone: 773/404–CUBS

Public transportation: The Red Line's Addison stop is right outside the park. The #22 Clark bus stops at the entrance.

Driving directions: Try not to drive, but if you do, take Lake Shore Drive north to Belmont Avenue. Travel west on Belmont to North Clark Street, and north on Clark to Wrigley Field.

Parking: Parking is difficult to find around Wrigley, though business owners tend to open up their lots for exorbitant prices, as do lucky home owners with garages.

The Park: The Friendly Confines, as it's known, was built in 1914, which makes it the second-oldest ballpark in the country.

Tours: The Cubs offer 90-minute tours that provide an insider's look at 90 years of Wrigley history. Tickets are $25 per person and you must buy tickets in advance.

Box Office Hours: Mon.–Fri. 10–6. Sat.–Sun. 10–4. On game days, box office opens at 9 AM.

What to bring: Don't forget your sunscreen and umbrella/rain gear if you're in the bleachers. Bring water—the container must be one liter or less. Don't bring hard-sided coolers, large bags, thermoses, bottles, cans, or alcoholic beverages.

PLAY BALL

Tickets: Prices can range between $10 to $80. Don't expect to score tickets on short notice—games sell out early in the season.

Wrigley Field Alternatives:

- Join the crowd at Harry Caray's Restaurant in River North (⇨ see Where to Eat chapter, pg. 222).
- Check out the ticketless fans in their lawnchairs on Sheffield Avenue.
- Opt for a White Sox game (tickets are easier to come by).

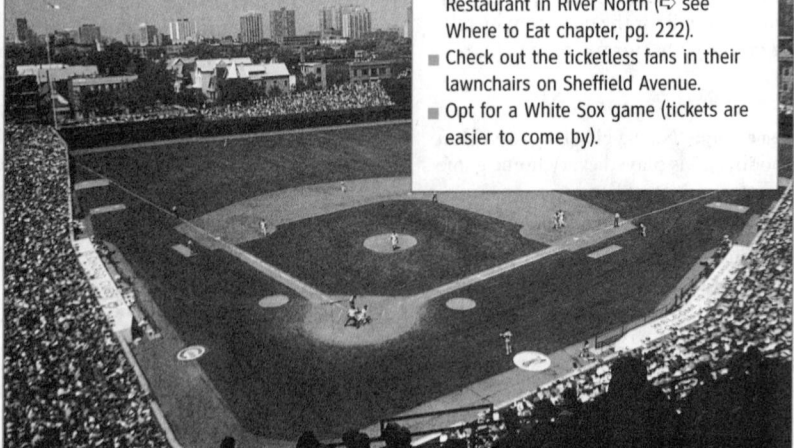

THE CELL

Getting There

Address: 333 W. 35th St.

Phone: 312/674–1000

Public transportation: Take the CTA Red Line to the 35th Street/Sox Park station of the CTA Red Line.

Driving directions: I-94 West to 35th Street; follow signs to "Sox Parking".

Parking: Parking is $20 in the lots surrounding the park. The lots open two hours prior to game time and close one hour after the game. There is no street parking.

About the name: Now it's "The Cell." But until 2003, when the White Sox made a deal to call it U.S. Cellular Field, it was Comiskey Park, named for former White Sox owner Charles A. Comiskey.

What to bring: Sunscreen and hats on hot days; jackets and small umbrellas if it looks like rain. Food in small, clear, see-through plastic bags and one sealed plastic bottle of water per person is OK–all other beverages, coolers, and large bags are not. Leave beach balls and large radios at home. The area around The Cell is sketchy—don't leave valuables in your car.

Tickets: Prices for tickets can range between $17 for a nosebleed seat to $65 for a box seat. Kids who are shorter than the turnstiles—about 36"—get in free but must sit in someone's lap. Monday home games are half price; get a second ticket free when you redeem an empty Pepsi product at ticket windows on the day of the game.

Box Office Hours:
Non-game days: Mon.–Fri., 10–6, Sat. and Sun., 10–4.
Game days: Mon.–Fri. 9–6; 9–6
Sat. 9–6 (day games); 9–8 (night games)
Sun. 9–4 (day games); 9–9 (night games).

Kids: Pontiac FUNdamentals, huge play area for kids, includes baseball and softball clinics, batting cages, and places to practice base running and pitching. It's above the left field concourse, opens 90 minutes before the game, and stays open throughout the game.

Speed pitch machine: Test your pitching speed and accuracy near section 164.

Fan Deck: Get a panoramic view of the field from a two-tiered deck. It's atop the center field concession stands. Free for all fans holding a main level ticket.

Baggage Check: Outside Gate 5 between parking lots A and B. $2 fee per bag.

ATMs: Sections 139, 531, centerfield, outside the Bullpen Sports Bar, and outside Gate 4.

Concessions: Burgers and veggie burgers, hot dogs and veggie hotdogs, and ice cream are available throughout the park. The Bullpen Sports Bar, offering more substantial food, is near ramp 2. For a small charge, you can sit in the two-tiered, open-air section. Ages 21 and over only.

FIRST GAME CERTIFICATE
The White Sox offer a certificate for guests to commemorate their first time at U.S. Cellular Field. Visit any Guest Relations Booth behind home plate to pick one up.

BEHIND THE SCENES

For a look at what (or who) makes the city tick, check out the following activities.

Black & White & Read All Over

Chicago Tribune Freedom Center. Tour the Chicago Tribune's printing plant and the *New York Times*' Midwest distribution center. ✉ *777 W. Chicago Ave., West Loop* ☎ *312/222–3040* 🎫 *Free, but there are no regular tours and you must call ahead.*

McCormick Tribune Freedom Museum. Take a peek inside the historic Tribune Tower at this two-story museum dedicated to the First Amendment. Engaging interactive exhibits examine the meaning of freedom in the U.S. and abroad. Discover democracy's ancient roots, brush up on your First Amendment rights, and listen to banned music. ✉ *445 N. Michigan Ave., inside Tribune Tower., Near North* ☎ *312/222–4860* 🌐 *www.freedommuseum.us* 🎫 *Free.*

Movers & Shakers

Graceland Cemetery. A comprehensive guide available at the entrance walks you by the graves and tombs of the people who made Chicago great, including merchandiser Marshall Field and railroad-car magnate George Pullman. ✉ *4001 N. Clark St., Far North Side* ☎ *773/525–1105* 🌐 *www.gracelandcemetery.org* 🎫 *Free.*

See Green

Federal Reserve Bank. Though they don't hand out money here, they sure do handle a lot of the green stuff. The facility processes currency and checks, scanning bills for counterfeits, destroying unfit currency, and repackaging fit currency. A visitor center in the lobby has permanent exhibits of old bills, counterfeit money, and a million dollars in $1 bills. One-hour tours explain how money travels and show a

high-speed currency-processing machine. Call in advance for tour reservations, since it's often booked in spring and fall with school groups. ✉ *230 S. LaSalle St., Loop* ☎ *312/322–2400* 🌐 *www.chicagofed.org* 🎫 *Free.*

Tour a Factory

Though Chicago isn't the industrial center it once was, you can still watch all sorts of things being made in the Chicago area, from cheesecakes to harps (Log on to 🌐 *www.factorytoursusa.com* for a complete list of tours). One of the most popular tours takes you behind the scenes at Eli's Cheesecake World, where visitors learn the company's history, tour the bakery facility, and watch cheesecake decorators at work. Of course, the tour ends with a slice of the decadent cheesecake. ✉ *6701 W. Forest Preserve Dr., at Montrose Ave.* ☎ *773/736–3417 or 773/308–7000* 🌐 *www.elicheesecake.com* ⏱ *Walk-in tours weekdays at 1* PM; *other times by reservation only .*

Neighborhoods

WORD OF MOUTH

"Lincoln Park has a great zoo and nature museum. Oak St. beach and the lakefront are the best. Hopefully you will have great weather to walk and explore."

—Lucci

"Stay in the Loop. Art Institute is a must do. Millennium Park, and a walk near the lakefront in that area is recommended."

—JJ5

2

LOOP

Sightseeing
★★★★☆

Dining
★★★☆☆

Lodging
★★★☆☆

Shopping
★★☆☆☆

Nightlife
★★★☆☆

The Loop is a living architectural museum, where shimmering modern towers stand side by side with 19th-century buildings. Striking sculptures by Picasso, Miró, and Chagall watch over plazas alive with music and farmers' markets in summer. There are noisy, mesmerizing trading centers, gigantic department stores, internationally known landmarks like the Sears Tower and the Art Institute, and the city's newest playground, Millennium Park. Rattling overhead, encircling it all, is the train system Chicagoans call the El.

Known as the Loop since the cable cars of the 1880s looped around the central business district, downtown Chicago comprises the area south of the Chicago River, west of Lake Michigan, and north of Congress Parkway/Eisenhower Expressway. The western boundary used to be the Chicago River, but the frontier continues to push westward. Handsome skyscrapers line every foot of South Wacker Drive east of the river, and new construction across the bridges is now a near constant.

WHAT'S HERE

Getting around the Loop is easy. It's laid out like a grid: State Street intersects north–south blocks, and Madison Street intersects east–west blocks. Where State and Madison converge is the zero point from where the rest of the city fans out. It's also where you find the building that once housed the department store **Carson Pirie Scott & Co.**, with its breathtaking decorative cast-iron facade—an outstanding example of Louis Sullivan's work. (The company closed the downtown location of the department store in early 2007; for the time being the building stands vacant.) Farther north on State Street—the Loop's most famous

GETTING ORIENTED

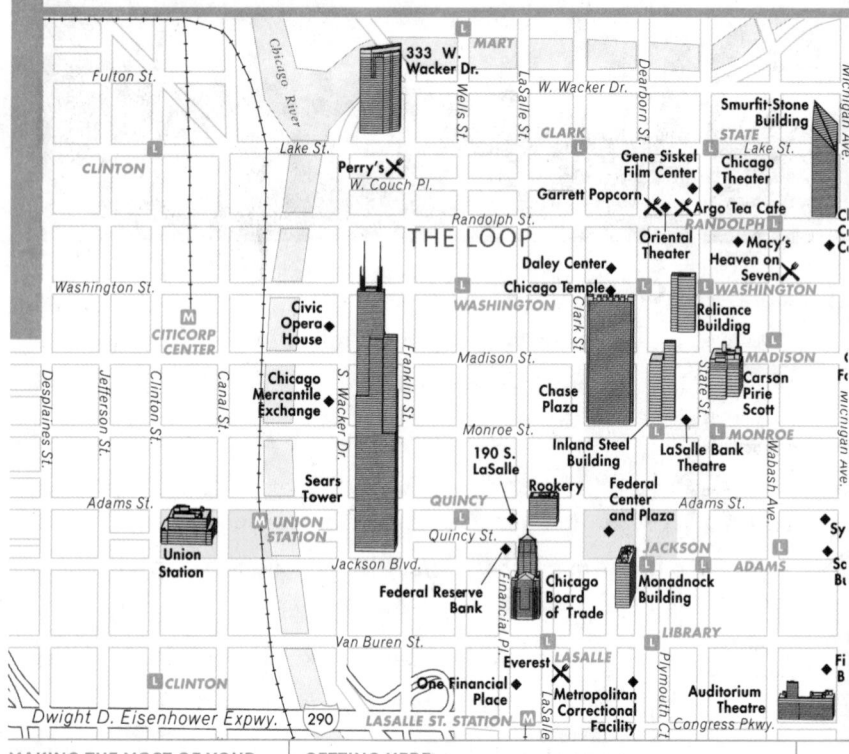

MAKING THE MOST OF YOUR TIME

If you have the time, give yourself a whole day to explore the Loop. You can easily spend half a day at the Art Institute. The rest of your day you can spend sunning yourself in Millennium Park, shopping up and down State Street, taking a trip to the top of the Sears Tower, or meandering among the architectural masterpieces and sculptures. And, of course, you'll want to allow yourself time to stand in line for Garrett Popcorn. When night falls, take in a play in the theater district.

GETTING HERE

Take a bus to Michigan Avenue and Wacker Drive. From the north, you can take Bus 3, 145, 147, or 151. Coming from the south, you can take Bus 3, 6, 145, 146, 147, or 151.

The Lake stop on the El's Red Line will put you at State and Lake streets. The Washington, Monroe, and Jackson stops are also in the Loop, just blocks from one another. The Brown, Green, Orange, Pink, and Purple lines stop at State, above ground, at Lake Street. These lines also stop at Randolph, Madison, and Adams in the Loop. If you arrive by car, you can park in the subterranean Grant Park North Garage, with an entrance on Michigan Avenue. Many side streets off Michigan Avenue also have parking garages. But be aware that parking in downtown lots can be pricey—up to $24 for five or more hours. Most streets in the Loop prohibit parking weekdays from 7 AM to 6 PM.

NEIGHBORHOOD TOP 7

1. Spend an afternoon with Georges Seurat's *A Sunday on la Grande Jatte* at the **Art Institute**.

2. Stand between the 50-foot faces screened onto the two towers of the **Crown Fountain in Millennium Park** and wait for them to spit.

3. Jump in a car and get lost in the underground world of **Lower Wacker Drive**.

4. Spend an afternoon strolling among architectural gems throughout the Loop.

5. Follow your nose and line up at one of the Loop locations of **Garret Popcorn** for a tub or two of the good stuff.

6. Explore **Grant Park** and stay for the spray at **Buckingham Fountain**.

7. Ponder the **Picasso** in Daley Plaza and decide for yourself what it resembles.

QUICK BITES

Choose from dozens of exotic varieties of tea at **Argo Tea Cafe** (⌧ *16 W. Randolph St., Loop* ☎ *312/553–1551*). Light lunch fare and sweet treats round out the menu.

The lines form early and stay long throughout the day at **Garrett Popcorn** (⌧ *26 W. Randolph St., Loop,* ☎ *312/201–0455*).

Heaven on Seven (⌧ *111 N. Wabash Ave., 7th fl., Loop* ☎ *312/263–6443*) is a Loop legend, famous for casual Cajun breakfasts and lunches that have area office workers gladly lining up to chow down.

Perry's (⌧ *180 N. Franklin St., Loop* ☎ *312/372–7557*) is a hit as much for the trivia questions Perry announces over his deli's PA system as it is for the overstuffed sandwiches.

thoroughfare—is a **Macy's** department store that until 2006 had been the flagship location for the much-mourned Marshall Field's. Despite the name change, the landmark turn-of-the-20th-century building is still beguiling.

Continuing on State, just north of Randolph Street is the old theater district. First is the ornate 1921 Beaux Arts **Chicago Theatre**, a former movie palace that now hosts live performances. Across the street is the **Gene Siskel Film Center**, which screens art, foreign, and classic movies. West on Randolph Street is the **Ford Center for the Performing Arts–Oriental Theatre**, with its long, glitzy neon sign. On Dearborn is the **Goodman Theatre**, wrapped in the 1923 Art Deco facades of the landmark Harris & Selwyn Twin Theaters. One more block west is the **Cadillac Palace Theatre**, a renovated 1926 vaudeville house that still has its original marble lobby.

Much of the impressive architecture in the Loop can be credited to the Great Chicago Fire of 1871, which leveled part of the city and cleared the way for the building of skyscrapers using steel-frame construction. One of the best things to do in the Loop is just to stroll around and take in the different types of buildings.

On Washington Street is the **Daley Center**, an outdoor plaza that has concerts and holiday and farmers' markets. Check out the unnamed Picasso sculpture, referred to simply as the *Picasso*. Opposite the Daley Center is the **Chicago Temple**, a Methodist church whose beautiful spire is so tall that it's best seen at some distance. Also on the south side of the street is Joan Miró's giant figure, *Chicago*.

DID YOU KNOW? **Controversy swirled when the Picasso was unveiled in 1967—everyone wanted to know if it was a woman's head or was inspired by one of the artist's Afghan hounds.**

To the west, following the bend of Wacker Drive, are the Art Deco **Civic Opera House**, where Chicago's Lyric Opera gives its performances, and the pale-grape-color twin towers of the **Chicago Mercantile Exchange**, where action on the trading floors is frenetic. East on Monroe Street, the sunken, bi-level **Chase Plaza** has room to rest in the shadow of the sweeping Chase Tower building that curves skyward in the shape of the letter "A." The Chagall mosaic *The Four Seasons* is at the northeast end of the plaza. Just before you get to State Street is the **LaSalle Bank Theatre** (until recently known as the Shubert Theatre). It was the tallest building in Chicago when it opened in 1906; today it's one of the top places in town to see touring Broadway shows.

Back on Michigan Avenue, just south of Wacker Drive, is the Art Deco **Carbide & Carbon Building**, a polished black granite structure with a dark green terra-cotta tower accented by gold leaf. Local lore has it the building was designed to resemble a champagne bottle with gold foil. Heading south on Michigan, between Monroe and Randolph streets, is **Millennium Park**, anchored by the immensely popular *Cloud Gate sculpture* (also known as the *Bean*) and the sweeping stainless steel Frank Gehry–designed **Jay Pritzker Pavilion**. On the west side of the

Dining in the Loop

EXPENSIVE DINING

Everest, *French*, 440 S. LaSalle St., Loop

Morton's, The Steakhouse, *Steak House*, 65 E. Wacker Pl., Loop

The Palm, *Steak House*, Swissôtel, 323 E. Wacker Dr. Loop

MODERATE DINING

Aria, *International*, Fairmont Chicago, 200 N. Columbus Dr., Loop

Atwood Cafe, *American*, Hotel Burnham, 1 W. Washington St., Loop

Nick's Fishmarket Grill, *Seafood*, 51 S. Clark St., Loop

Park Grill, *New American*, Millennium Park, 11 N. Michigan Ave., Loop

Petterino's, *Italian*, 150 N. Dearborn St., Loop

Rhapsody, *New American*, 65 E. Adams St., Loop

Russian Tea Time, *Russian*, 77 E. Adams St., Loop

Trattoria No. 10, *Italian*, 10 N. Dearborn St., Loop

Vivere, *Italian*, 71 W. Monroe St., Loop

BUDGET DINING

Exchequer Pub, *American*, 226 S. Wabash Ave., Loop

Heaven on Seven, *Cajun/Creole*, 111 N. Wabash Ave., Loop

Walnut Room, *New American*, Macy's, 7th floor, 111 N. State St., Loop

---

intersection of Randolph Street and Michigan Avenue is the **Chicago Cultural Center,** home to the **Chicago Office of Tourism Visitor Information Center.** At 200 East Randolph is the soaring **Aon Center,** the second-tallest building in Chicago after the Sears Tower. Directly west of the Aon Center is the **Prudential Building,** Chicago's tallest building until the late 1960s. Behind it rises the rocket ship–like **Two Prudential Plaza,** affectionately nicknamed Pru Two.

The southern part of the Loop balances the hub of the financial district with the fine arts. On one block are the **Art Institute of Chicago,** the grand-looking **Symphony Center** (home to the internationally acclaimed Chicago Symphony Orchestra), and the **Santa Fe Building.** Farther south on Michigan Avenue is the **Fine Arts Building.**

On Dearborn Street is the **Federal Center and Plaza,** designed by Ludwig Mies van der Rohe and anchored by Alexander Calder's red mobile *Flamingo* sculpture. Across the street from the Federal Center on Jackson Boulevard is the **Monadnock Building,** a tall masonry structure with dramatic curves. The beautiful **Rookery,** an imposing red-stone building that is one of the city's 19th-century showpieces, is on LaSalle Street; be sure to see the Frank Lloyd Wright–designed lobby. Nearby is Phillip Johnson's postmodern **190 South LaSalle,** with striking gold-leaf ceilings and a gabled roof inspired by the long-demolished Chicago landmark Masonic Temple. Across Quincy Street is the massive **Federal Reserve Bank** with its grand Corinthian colonnades; since 2001 it's been home to the Money Museum. Farther south at Jackson Boulevard the street seems to disappear in front of the commanding **Chicago Board of Trade,** which sits like a throne reigning over the financial district.

SOUTH LOOP INCLUDING PRINTER'S ROW, MUSEUM CAMPUS & BRONZEVILLE

Sightseeing
★★★★☆

Dining
★★★☆☆

Lodging
★★☆☆☆

Shopping
★☆☆☆☆

Nightlife
★★☆☆☆

The South Loop, bounded by Congress Parkway/Eisenhower Expressway on the north, Michigan Avenue on the east, Cermak Avenue on the south, and the Chicago River on the west, presents a striking contrast to the Loop, with its less-trafficked streets and more subdued—and, in some spots, grittier—vibe. Though it was one of Chicago's first residential districts, the area eventually became a symbol of urban blight. A redevelopment boom has transformed it into a residential neighborhood again, this time attracting more and more residents who like its ethnic and racial mix and growing sense of community, as well as its proximity to the Loop, great museums, and hip restaurants.

Start at the northern edge, where the Loop transitions into the South Loop, for an up-close peek at the looming **Harold Washington Library** on State Street between Van Buren and Congress. Look closely: the giant gargoyles perched atop the neoclassical building's redbrick facade are actually owls. Inside, the airy ninth-floor **Winter Garden** is well worth a visit. East on Congress at Michigan Avenue is the national landmark **Auditorium Building.** This Romanesque Revival building and opera house was designed by architects Louis Sullivan and Dankmar Adler.

Trips farther south to the Museum Campus and Printer's Row district here are musts. Perched on the lakefront, Museum Campus is a glorious spot to take in the skyline and watch the boats go by. It's home to the **Field Museum,** the **John G. Shedd Aquarium,** and the **Adler**

2

Planetarium & Astronomy Museum, all of which hold some of the most important and exciting exhibits and artifacts in the country. Printer's Row, a small enclave to the west, was once a thriving commercial area and the center of the printing trades in Chicago. Today it stands as a good example of the South Loop renaissance, with coffeehouses, shops, and restaurants inhabiting the area's beautiful buildings. Farther afield, but worth a visit if there's time, is the Bronzeville area, a historic community originally settled by waves of African-Americans fleeing the South after World War I.

WHAT'S HERE

The 57-acre Museum Campus is home to the Big Three—the **Field Museum,** the **John G. Shedd Aquarium,** and the **Adler Planetarium & Astronomy Museum,** all united in one pedestrian-friendly, parklike setting. Park your car in one of the lots just past the Field Museum on McFetridge Drive, or ride the free Museum Campus trolley (☎*877/244–2246*), which connects the three museums with other downtown tourist attractions and train stations. It operates daily from Memorial Day to Labor Day and on holidays, and runs only on weekends the rest of the year. On the west side of the campus is the Field Museum, which houses a staggering array of culture- and nature-focused exhibits. It's most famous is Sue, the largest and most complete *T. rex* skeleton in the world. No one's sure if Sue was actually a male or female. She's named for Sue Hendrickson, the fossil hunter who discovered her skeleton.

The Shedd Aquarium, on the lakefront just past the Field Museum, has bizarre and fantastically beautiful fish, plus dolphins and beluga whales. On the east side of the campus, at the far end of a peninsula that juts out into Lake Michigan is the Adler Planetarium & Astronomy Museum—the first modern planetarium in the Western Hemisphere.

FRUGAL FUN

If you're visiting all three museums, plus some of the city's other big attractions, buy a Chicago CityPass (adults $59, kids 3–11 $49). You'll avoid long lines and get access to the Field, the Shedd, and the Adler, plus the Hancock Observatory or Sears Tower Skydeck and the Museum of Science and Industry.

Just south of the Museum Campus is **Soldier Field,** the building with the massive columns reminiscent of ancient Greece and the home of the Chicago Bears. A controversial modern glass expansion was completed in 2003.

The Printer's Row district is bounded by Congress Parkway on the north, Polk Street on the south, Plymouth Court to the east, and the Chicago River to the west. It fell into disrepair in the 1960s, but a neighborhood resurgence began in the late 1970s with renovations to some of the run-down loft and office buildings. You can still see examples here of buildings by the group that represented the First Chicago School of Architecture (including Louis Sullivan), as well as **Dearborn Station,** a Romanesque Revival–style structure that was once the city's

GETTING ORIENTED

GETTING HERE

Buses 6, 12, and 146 take you to Museum Campus. If you drive, take Lake Shore Drive to the Museum Campus exit. There's some coveted meter parking as well as pricier lots adjacent to the museums. For Printer's Row, take the El's Brown, Orange, Pink, or Purple lines to the library stop, or the Red Line to Harrison. Buses 6, 22, 36, and 145 will also get you there. Drivers can take Congress Parkway to Dearborn Street. Bronzeville can be easily accessed by buses 49 and 95. To get there by car, take Lake Shore Drive to 31st Street, then travel west to Martin Luther King Jr. Drive.

MAKING THE MOST OF YOUR TIME

Plan on at least a day for a visit to the three museums (you could spend a day at the mammoth Field Museum alone). Allow extra time to enjoy the spectacular skyline and lake views from Museum Campus and to stroll along the harbor. Note that traffic can get snarled and special parking rules go into effect around Museum Campus when the Chicago Bears are playing at neighboring Soldier Field. Prairie Avenue is a quick hit, taking a couple of hours at most. A trip to Bronzeville can take from an hour or two to a half day, depending on whether you opt for one of the longer organized tours.

QUICK BITES

Bronzeville Coffee House, Inc. (⊠ *538 E. 43rd St., South Loop* ☎ *773/536–0494*) is a comfy choice for coffee and pastries.

Have a corned-beef sandwich all the other delis in town aim to beat at **Manny's Coffee Shop & Deli** (⊠ *1141 S. Jefferson St., South Loop* ☎ *312/939–2855*).

"Da Mare" himself, Richard M. Daley, has stood up for the turkey burgers at **Standing Room Only (SRO Chicago)** (⊠ *610 S. Dearborn St., South Loop* ☎ *312/360–1776*).

SAFETY

The South Loop is a changing neighborhood. Some parts can still feel sketchy, so exercise caution, particularly at night, by sticking to populated and well-lighted streets. Group tours of Bronzeville are recommended for those unfamiliar with the area.

TOURS

The **Chicago Office of Tourism** (☎ *312/742–1190*) offers a half-day bus tour of Bronzeville. Other tours are offered by the **Black Metropolis Convention and Tourism Council** (☎ *773/373–2842*), and **Tour Black Chicago** (☎ *773/684–9034*). **Black Cou-Tours** (☎ *773/233–8907*) offers a 2½-hour excursion of black culture including Bronzeville and other highlights.

NEIGHBORHOOD TOP 5

1. Spot your favorite fish at the **John G. Shedd Aquarium**, then stand next to Sue the T. rex at the **Field Museum**.

2. See the stars at the **Adler Planetarium & Astronomy Museum**.

3. Tailgate in the parking lot before a Chicago Bears game at **Soldier Field**.

4. Grab a corned-beef sandwich and potato pancake with a cross-section of Chicago at **Manny's Coffee Shop & Deli**.

5. Take a step back into Chicago's rich African-American history with a guided tour of **Bronzeville**.

Dining in the South Loop

EXPENSIVE DINING
Custom House, *Steak House*, 500 S. Dearborn St., South Loop

MODERATE DINING
Chez Joel, *Bistro*, 1119 W. Taylor St., South Loop

Chicago Firehouse, *New American*, 1401 S. Michigan Ave., South Loop

Francesca's on Taylor, *Italian*, 1400 W. Taylor St., South Loop

Gioco, *Italian*, 1312 S. Wabash Ave., South Loop

Opera, *Chinese*, 1301 S. Wabash Ave., South Loop

The Rosebud on Taylor, *Italian*, 1500 W. Taylor St., South Loop

Tuscany, *Italian*, 1014 W. Taylor St., South Loop

BUDGET DINING
Exposure Tapas, *International*, 1315 S. Wabash Ave., South Loop

Grace O'Malley's Restaurant–Pub, *Irish*, 1416 S. Michigan Ave., South Loop

Manny's Coffee Shop and Deli, *American*, 1141 S. Jefferson St., South Loop

Pompei, *Italian*, 1531 W. Taylor St., South Loop

Yolk, *Breakfast/Lunch*, 1120 S. Michigan Ave., South Loop

main passenger train hub. Today the red sandstone building houses everything from banks and law offices to a sprawling Bar Louie restaurant, and the structure's intact 12-story clock tower remains visible from several blocks in any direction. These days this section of town is best known for the annual **Printer's Row Book Fair**, a weekend-long literary celebration held each June. During the event, hundreds of book stalls line Dearborn and Harrison streets, hawking everything from small-press paperbacks to rare first editions.

DID YOU KNOW?

That futuristic round structure that seems to rise from the river west of Printer's Row on Polk Street is River City, a condominium complex and self-contained city within a city. It has its own private 1-acre park, market, clubhouse, dry cleaner, and boat slips.

The historic **Bronzeville** neighborhood, once known as Black Metropolis, roughly covers the area south of McCormick Place and north of Hyde Park between State Street and Cottage Grove Avenue. Following World War I, African-Americans moved to this neighborhood to escape race restrictions prevalent in other parts of the city. Landmarks include the symbolic entrance, a tall statue at 26th Place and Martin Luther King Jr. Drive that depicts a new arrival from the South bearing a suitcase held together with string. Walk along Martin Luther King Jr. Drive between 25th and 35th streets to follow a commemorative trail of more than 90 sidewalk plaques honoring the best and brightest of the community, including Pulitzer Prize–winner Gwendolyn Brooks, whose first book of poetry was called *A Street in Bronzeville*.

2

WEST LOOP INCLUDING GREEKTOWN

Sightseeing
★☆☆☆☆

Dining
★★★★☆

Lodging
★☆☆☆☆

Shopping
★★☆☆☆

Nightlife
★★★★☆

Most of the West Loop languished for years as a wasteland peppered with warehouses and meatpacking plants. But nowadays many of the warehouses have been converted to lofts, and a thriving art scene has emerged around Fulton Market. Eco-friendly fashion and design showrooms have transformed the area into the heart of Chicago's burgeoning green scene. Harpo Studios, the production house of Chicago's grande dame, Oprah Winfrey, is here, and there's also an ultrahip dining and nightclub scene. By day the neighborhood is a relatively quiet, concrete-heavy area where plant workers, white-collar business types, and stroller-pushing power moms share the sidewalks. When night falls, the scenesters come out of the woodwork, and a too-cool-for-school vibe reigns.

Greektown, a five-block stretch of Halsted Street within the West Loop, is a world all its own. People from all over Chicago come to the strip's restaurants, groceries, and shops for a taste of Greece that goes beyond plate breaking.

WHAT'S HERE

The West Loop is bound by Ashland Avenue on the west, the Chicago River on the east, Grand Avenue on the north, and the Eisenhower Expressway on the south. Randolph Street is the neighborhood's restaurant row and home to some of the city's most notable dining spots,

GETTING ORIENTED

By car, take the Kennedy Expressway to the Randolph Street exit. You can also get here by taking the 8 Halsted and 20 Madison buses, or the El's Green Line to Clinton. Note that the Green Line has two branches—take the Harlem/Lake branch heading west, not the Ashland/63rd branch.

For Greektown, take the Blue Line Forest Park branch (not the O'Hare branch) to UIC—Halsted. The 8 Halsted and 20 Madison buses get you here, too. If you're driving to Greektown, exit the Kennedy Expressway at Randolph or Madison streets.

Oprah fans should start their West Loop visit early with a photo op outside Harpo Studios. If you're lucky, you might catch a glimpse of a VIP guest heading into the building for a taping session. Around midday or early afternoon take a few hours to browse the galleries before heading to one of the trendy neighborhood restaurants for dinner (plan to eat early if you don't have reservations). Randolph Street offers a variety of options within easy walking distance. Then cap off the evening with a visit to a late-night club or lounge.

If your visit to Chicago happens to coincide with the last Saturday of the month (May–October), check out the Chicago Antique Market around Randolph Street and Ogden Avenue for one-of-a-kind souvenirs, including vintage dishware, clothing, handbags, and jewelry. Afterward, stroll east toward Greektown for a delicious lunch or snack—feta and olives, anyone?

2

NEIGHBORHOOD TOP 5

1. Take a picture outside **Harpo Studios,** where Oprah films her talk show.

2. Check out the funky contemporary art and design along **Fulton Market.**

3. Order the *saganaki* (flaming cheese) and shout *Opaaa!* along with waiters who set it ablaze for you tableside in **Greektown.**

4. Experience the vibrant **Randolph Street** dining and nightlife scene.

5. Bone up on Chicago history with a visit to the site of the **Haymarket Riot** at the corner of Randolph and Des Plaines streets.

SAFETY

As you reach the western part of the neighborhood around Ashland Avenue, just a stone's throw from the United Center, the gentrification comes to a halt; the streets around the Fulton Market area are deserted during off times. Exercise caution in both areas.

QUICK BITES

Artopolis Bakery, Café & Agora (⌧ *306 S. Halsted St., West Loop* ☎ *312/559–9000*) has a light menu of salads, soups, and sandwiches, and some of the best bread in the city.

For a quick and authentic taste of Greektown, or just a plain old burger and fries anytime day or night, stop in to **Greektown Gyros** (⌧ *239 S. Halsted St., West Loop* ☎ *312/236–9310*), open 24 hours a day, 7 days a week.

Smoothies and salads will fuel you up without weighing you down at the tiny **Jubilee Juice** (⌧ *140 N. Halsted St., West Loop* ☎ *312/491–8500*).

They come from all over town for the cheese grits, blue claw–crab cakes, and other examples of "Southern Reconstructionist" cooking at **Wishbone** (⌧ *1001 W. Washington Blvd., West Loop* ☎ *312/850–2663*). At breakfast and lunch, you can opt for a cafeteria line.

including French-inspired **Marché,** which many credit with jump-starting the neighborhood's turnaround in the early 1990s, and **Blackbird,** a nouveau-American hot spot lauded by critics worldwide as one of the best restaurants anywhere. Many of the restaurants offer outdoor seating in warmer months—grab a table and watch the city saunter past. Every June the **Taste of Randolph Street** festival brings entertainment and food stalls operated by dozens of nearby restaurants; many consider it the city's best culinary festival.

The corner of Randolph Street and Des Plaines Avenue was the site of the infamous Haymarket Riot, when 11 people were killed in a melee sparked by protests for an eight-hour workday in Chicago. The event led to the creation of May Day, a workers' holiday still observed the first day in May throughout much of Europe.

On Carpenter Street between Randolph Street and Washington Boulevard is **Harpo Studios** (✉ *1058 W. Washington Blvd., West Loop* ☎ *312/591–9222* ⊕ *www.oprah.com*), the taping site for Oprah Winfrey's talk show. The studio isn't open to tours, and tickets to the show can be nearly impossible to score, so a stop here isn't much more than a fun photo op. However, if you're a die-hard Oprah fan and want to attempt to get tickets, here's what you need to know: The show books audiences only for the current and following month. When you call—if you're lucky enough to get through—a staffer will give you the taping schedule and a list of available dates. You can reserve up to four seats for any one taping (all attendees must be at least 18). If you can't get tickets in advance, check the Web site for occasional last-minute tickets via e-mail.

Just to the west of Harpo on Washington is the **Museum of Holography,** where 10,000 square feet of exhibit space are dedicated to the advancement of—you guessed it—holography as an art form. The stylish **Fulton Market** district runs along Fulton Market and Lake Street between Des Plaines Street and Ashland Avenue. The trendsetting galleries, shops, and interior design showrooms that now occupy former meatpacking warehouses have transformed the area into a mecca for cutting-edge design and green living. **Pivot** boutique at 1101 W. Fulton Market showcases earth-friendly fashions made from bamboo and recycled materials. Eco-minded folks also flock to **Green Home Chicago** at 213 N. Morgan Street for sustainably made home furnishings. The art scene draws attention as well—here you'll find everything from printmaking and sculpture to photography, paintings, and glass and metalwork. One of the pioneering forces in the art community, **Mars Gallery,** has showcased contemporary pop and outsider art since 1988 at 1139 W. Fulton Market. Another contemporary art gallery worth a visit is **FLAT-FILEgalleries** at 217 N. Carpenter Street. Be aware, though, that the area remains a bustling commercial district. During the day the seafood and meatpacking plants are swarming with heavy vehicles helmed by harried drivers. Exercise caution while driving or, better yet, cab it to your destination.

Dining in the West Loop

EXPENSIVE DINING

Blackbird, *New American*, 619 W. Randolph St., West Loop

Carmichael's, *Steak House*, 1052 W. Monroe St., West Loop

Moto, *Cutting-Edge*, 945 W. Fulton Market, at N. Sangamon St., West Loop

N9NE Steakhouse, *Steak House*, 440 W. Randolph St., West Loop

one sixtyblue, *New American*, 1400 W. Randolph St., West Loop

MODERATE DINING

Avec, *New American*, 615 W. Randolph St., West Loop

Costa's, *Greek*, 340 S. Halsted St., West Loop

De Cero Taqueria, *Mexican*, 814 W. Randolph St., West Loop

Green Zebra, *Vegetarian*, 1460 W. Chicago Ave., West Loop

La Sardine, *Bistro*, 111 N. Carpenter St., West Loop

Marché, *Brasserie*, 833 W. Randolph St., West Loop

Otom, *New American*, 951 W. Fulton Market, West Loop

Red Light, *Pan Asian*, 820 W. Randolph St., West Loop

Sushi Wabi, *Japanese*, 842 W. Randolph St., West Loop

Vivo, *Italian*, 838 W. Randolph St., West Loop

West Town Tavern, *American*, 1329 W. Chicago Ave., West Loop

BUDGET DINING

Ina's, *American*, 1235 W. Randolph St., West Loop

Lou Mitchell's, *American*, 565 W. Jackson Blvd., West Loop

The Parthenon, *Greek*, 314 S. Halsted St., West Loop

Pegasus, *Greek*, 130 S. Halsted St., West Loop

The **Chicago Antique Market,** a seasonal indoor-outdoor flea market held May through October on the last Saturday of the month, has established itself as this city's answer to London's famed Portobello Road market. Centered around Randolph Street and Ogden Avenue, the market offers everything from mid-century furniture to vintage handbags. Antiques hunters with fat wallets may want to check the schedule at **Leslie Hindman Auctioneers** (⊠ *1338 W. Lake St., West Loop* ☎ *312/280–1212*), a fine-art auctioneer on Lake Street that's the fifth-largest auction house in the country. Auctions run the gamut from 20th-century decorative arts to American and European works of art to fine jewelry and timepieces.

Back on Halsted Street between Madison and Van Buren streets is **Greektown,** a small strip of the West Loop that may as well be half a world away. Greek restaurants are the main draw here. Continue west on Madison, past the slew of new condo developments and vintage conversions in progress, and you'll come to one of Chicago's latest dining and nightlife destinations. On a stretch of Madison roughly between Sangamon and Elizabeth streets you'll find up-to-the-minute boutiques, trendy bars and lounges, and popular restaurants.

NEAR NORTH INCLUDING THE GOLD COAST, MAGNIFICENT MILE & STREETERVILLE

Sightseeing
★★★★★

Dining
★★★★☆

Lodging
★★★★☆

Shopping
★★★★☆

Nightlife
★★★★☆

The city's greatest tourist magnet reads like a to-do checklist: Navy Pier, the John Hancock Building, art museums and galleries, lakefront activities, and countless shops where you could spend a few dollars or thousands. The Magnificent Mile, a stretch of Michigan Avenue between the Chicago River and Oak Street, owes its name to the swanky shops that line both sides of the street. Shoppers cram the sidewalks in summer and keep the street bustling even in winter, when the trees are twined with thousands of white lights and the buildings are aglow with colored floodlights.

East of the Magnificent Mile is upscale Streeterville, which began as a disreputable landfill that the notorious George Wellington "Cap" Streeter and his wife, Maria, claimed as their own. Along the Lake Michigan shoreline, from North Avenue on the north, Oak Street on the south, and LaSalle Street on the west, is the posh Gold Coast area. Made fashionable after the Great Chicago Fire of 1871 by the social-climbing industrialists of the day, today's Gold Coast neighborhood is still a ritzy place to live, work, shop, and mingle. Architectural styles along the East Lake Shore Drive Historic District include baroque, Renaissance, Georgian, and Beaux-Arts—though varied, they blend together beautifully.

WHAT'S HERE

The **Michigan Avenue Bridge** spans the Chicago River as a gateway to North Michigan Avenue from the south. On the east side of the river is the headquarters of the *Chicago Tribune*, in the crenellated **Tribune Tower,** behind which resides the **NBC Tower.**

2

The base of Tribune Tower is studded with pieces from more than 120 famous sites and structures around the world, including the Parthenon, the Taj Mahal, and Bunker Hill.

Across the water and due for completion in late 2008 is the much-hyped Trump International Hotel & Tower, a 92-story mixed-use behemoth on the site of the old *Chicago Sun-Times* headquarters. The construction project has been managed by the Donald's first *Apprentice,* hometown son Bill Rancic. North of the bridge on the west side of Michigan Avenue is the **Wrigley Building,** with its striking wedding-cake embellishments and clock tower. They mark the beginning of the **Magnificent Mile,** the famous stretch of shops. The tapering **John Hancock Center,** the third-tallest building in Chicago, and the elegant Fourth Presbyterian Church, with its peaceful courtyard, are near the north end of the Mile.

This stretch of Michigan Avenue was originally called the Magnificent Mile because of the architecture. Most of those elegant, small buildings are long gone, however, and the moniker now refers to the excellent shopping that attracts visitors and residents alike.

West of the Mag Mile, at Pearson and Rush streets, is **Water Tower Park,** a Chicago icon. The Water Tower and the matching Water Works Pumping Station across the street are among the few buildings to have survived the Great Chicago Fire of 1871. Since 2003 a new theater space within the historic structure has been home to the renowned Lookingglass Theatre Company. One block east is the imposing **Museum of Contemporary Art,** which concentrates on 20th-century art, principally works created after 1945.

East of the Mag Mile, on Illinois Street and Lake Michigan, is **Navy Pier,** a wonderful place to enjoy lake breezes, hop on an afternoon or evening boat cruise, catch a concert or play, or ride on the giant Ferris wheel. The **Chicago Children's Museum** is part of the Navy Pier complex, but at the time of this writing a campaign was underway to move the Chicago Children's Museum to Millennium Park. North of Navy Pier, hugging Lake Shore Drive, is the Gold Coast neighborhood. Astor Street is the grande dame of Gold Coast promenades. On the northwest corner of Astor and Burton streets, you'll find the Georgian **Patterson-McCormick Mansion** (⊠*20 E. Burton Pl.*), commissioned in 1891 by *Chicago Tribune* chief Joseph Medill. Where Astor Street jogs to meet Schiller Street stands the 1892 **Charnley–Persky House,** designed in part by Frank Lloyd Wright. On Goethe Street is the Ambassador East Hotel, home of the famous **Pump Room** restaurant. In its glory days, celebrities like Frank Sinatra, Humphrey Bogart, and Lauren Bacall

GETTING ORIENTED

Armitage Ave.

N. Lincoln Ave.

N. Clark St.

N. Mohawk St.

N. Larrabee St.

N. Sedgwick St.

LINCOLN PARK

41

North Ave.

Patterson-McCormick Mansion ◆

North Ave.

E. Burton Pl.

Astor Pl.

Wells St.

La Salle Blvd.

E. Schiller St.

Clybourn Ave.

Charnley-Persky House ◆

Astor St.

Lake Michigan

Stanton Park

GOLD COAST

Division St.

Division St.

Elm St.

Larrabee St.

RIVER NORTH

Maple St.

Oak St.

Clark St.

Dearborn St.

Parkway St.

Oak St. Beach ◆

41

Signature Room at the 95th ✕

John Hancock Center

Hudson St.

Walton St. ✕

Franklin St.

Delaware St. ✕ L'Appetito

KEY

✕ *Restaurant/Cafe*

Chestnut St.

Water Works

Bistro 110 ✕
Pearson St.

Chicago Ave.

N. Br. Chicago

Kingsbury St.

Sedgwick St.

Orleans St.

Superior St.

Huron St.

Erie St.

La Salle Blvd.

Clark St.

Dearborn St.

State St.

Wabash St.

Museum of Contemporary Art ◆

(MAGNIFICENT MILE)

Rush St.

Fairbanks Ct.

J. F. Kennedy Expwy.

Ontario St.

Ohio St.

NEAR NORTH

Garrett Popcorn Shop ✕

Grand Ave.

Illinois St.

River

Hubbard St.

Kinzie St.

Tribune Tower

NBC Tower ◆

Wrigley Building

✕ Billy Goat Tavern

Michigan Ave. Bridge ◆

0   1/4 mi

0   1/4 km

LOOP

Wacker Dr.

TO NAVY PIER & CHICAGO CHILDREN'S MUSEUM

GETTING HERE

If you're arriving from the north by car, take Lake Shore Drive south to the Michigan Avenue exit. From the south, you can start your exploring by exiting at Grand Avenue, the exit for Navy Pier. Numerous buses run along Michigan Avenue, including the 3, 4, 144, 145, 146, 167, and 151. Buses 29, 65, and 66 all service Navy Pier. If you're using the El, take the Red Line to Chicago Avenue or Clark and Division to get closest to the action.

MAKING THE MOST OF YOUR TIME

You can spend a day at a number of the attractions (or just shopping), depending on your interests. Navy Pier takes at least a couple of hours (especially if you have children); you could spend a few hours in the Chicago Children's Museum alone. Art lovers will want to set aside at least one or two hours for the Museum of Contemporary Art. A stroll through the Gold Coast can be done in an hour, but what's the hurry? Make an afternoon of it. Our favorite times are weekend afternoons in spring or fall or just before dusk any day in summer, when the neighborhood's leafy tranquillity and big-city energy converge.

NEIGHBORHOOD TOP 5

1. Have a drink or a meal at the **Signature Room** at the 95th.

2. Sunbathe with the beautiful people at **Oak Street Beach.**

3. Take one of the Chicago Architecture Foundation's amazing **boat tours** along the river.

4. Catch a glimpse of the **Tribune Tower** and find the pieces of the Taj Mahal, Parthenon, and other famous structures embedded in the base.

5. Experience the visual wit and acrobatics that characterize a **Lookingglass Theatre** performance.

QUICK BITES

For an inexpensive, hearty lunch, try **L'Appetito** (⌧ *875 N. Michigan Ave.* ☎ *312/337–0691*), a deli and grocery off the Hancock Center's lower-level plaza that has some of the best Italian sandwiches in Chicago.

Behind and one level down from the Wrigley Building is the (in)famous **Billy Goat Tavern** (⌧ *430 N. Michigan Ave.* ☎ *312/222–1525*), the inspiration for *Saturday Night Live's* classic "cheezborger, cheezborger" skit and a longtime haunt of local journalists, most notably the late columnist Mike Royko. Grab a greasy burger (and chips, of course) at this no-frills grill, or just have a beer and absorb the comic undertones.

Make a meal out of appetizers at **Bistro 110** (⌧ *110 E. Pearson St.* ☎ *312/266–3110*). The artichoke hearts are heavenly, and the gooey French onion soup is not to be missed. There are ample choices of wine by the glass. The front bar-café area is perfect for casual dining.

Garrett Popcorn Shop (⌧ *670 N. Michigan Ave.* ☎ *312/943–8464*) is a Chicago institution that has been selling popcorn on the Mag Mile for more than 50 years. Tourists and locals alike line up outside—even in the frigid months—to buy tasty warm popcorn mixed with things like macadamia nuts and caramel. (Warning: The cheese and caramel combo is a well-known diet killer.)

2

Dining in Near North

EXPENSIVE DINING

Avenues, *Cutting-Edge,* Peninsula Hotel, 108 E. Superior St., Near North

The Capital Grille, *Steak House,* 633 N. St. Clair St., Near North

David Burke's Primehouse, *Steak House,* 616 N. Rush St., Near North

Gibsons Steakhouse, *Steak House,* 1028 N. Rush St., Near North

Les Nomades, *French,* 222 E. Ontario St., Near North

NoMI, *New American,* Park Hyatt Hotel, 800 N. Michigan Ave., Near North

Pump Room, *American,* Ambassador East Hotel, 1301 N. State Pkwy, Near North

Seasons Restaurant, *New American,* Four Seasons Hotel, 120 E. Delaware Pl., Near North

Spiaggia, *Italian,* 980 N. Michigan Ave., Near North

TRU, *New American,* 676 N. Saint Clair St., Near North

MODERATE DINING

Bistro 110, *Bistro,* 110 E. Pearson St., Near North

The Caliterra Bar & Grille, *Italian,* Wyndham Chicago Hotel, 633 N. St. Clair St., Near North

Cru Café & Wine Bar, *American,* 25 E. Delaware Pl., Near North

McCormick and Schmick's, *Seafood,* 41 E. Chestnut St., Near North

Mike Ditka's Restaurant, *Steak House,* Tremont Hotel, 100 E. Chestnut St., Near North

Riva, *Seafood,* 700 E. Grand Ave., Near North

RL, *American,* 115 E. Chicago Ave., Near North

Roy's, *Pan Asian,* 720 N. State St., Near North

Shanghai Terrace, *Chinese,* Peninsula Hotel,

108 E. Superior St., Near North

Signature Room at the 95th, *American,* John Hancock Center, 875 N. Michigan Ave., Near North

Viand, *American,* 155 E. Ontario St., Near North

BUDGET DINING

Billy Goat Tavern, *Burgers,* 430 N. Michigan Ave., lower level, Near North

Fox & Obel Food Market Cafe, *Café,* 401 E. Illinois St., Near North

Heaven on Seven, *Southern,* 600 N. Michigan Ave., Near North

Joe's Be-Bop Cafe and Jazz Emporium, *Southern,* 600 E. Grand Ave., Near North

Pierrot Gourmet, *Café,* Peninsula Hotel, 108 E. Superior St., Near North

held court in the famed Booth One. Where Dearborn Street meets Oak Street is the Gold Coast's famous shopping district. Past the former **Playboy Mansion** (✉ *1340 N. State St.*), all the way to North Avenue, is a beautiful view of Lincoln Park.

GOETHE STREET

If you're ever pressed for conversation in Chicago, just solicit opinions on how Goethe Street should be pronounced. Then sit back and enjoy the fireworks.

2

RIVER NORTH

Sightseeing
★★☆☆☆
Dining
★★★★☆
Lodging
★★★★☆
Shopping
★★★★☆
Nightlife
★★★★☆

Technically a part of Near North, River North is a neighborhood that commands a strong presence all its own. Bounded on the south and west by branches of the Chicago River, River North has eastern and northern boundaries that can be hard to define. As in many other Chicago neighborhoods, the limits have expanded as the area has grown more attractive; today they extend roughly to Oak Street on the north and Rush Street on the east. Richly served by waterways and railroad tracks that ran along its western edge, the neighborhood was settled by Irish immigrants in the mid-19th century. As the 20th century approached, the area developed into a busy commercial, industrial, and warehouse district.

But as economic conditions changed and factories moved away, the neighborhood deteriorated, and River North became just another down-on-its-luck urban area. In the 1970s, artists attracted by low rents and spacious abandoned storage areas and shop floors began to move into the neighborhood, and it eventually became the go-to spot for art lovers to gallery-hop. Then developers caught the scent and began buying up properties with an eye to renovation. Today struggling artists might find it hard to afford a cup of coffee in this high-rent district dotted with tourist-pleasing restaurants and upscale retail shops.

GETTING ORIENTED

KEY
- **L** CTA lines
- ✗ Restaurant/Cafe

W. Chicago Ave.

CHICAGO **L**

N. Larrabee St.
N. Kingsbury St.
N. Hudson Ave.
N. Sedgwick St.

Brett's Kitchen ✗
W. Superior St.

W. Huron St.

RIVER NORTH

W. Erie St.

W. Erie St.

W. Ontario St.

Ed Debevic's ✗ ✗ Gino's East

John F. Kennedy Expwy.

W. Ohio St.

W. Ohio St.

N. Union Ave.
N. Des Plaines St.
N. Jefferson St.

North Branch Chicago River

N. Kingsbury St.

W. Grand Ave.

W. Illinois St.

N. Franklin St.
N. LaSalle St.

W. Hubbard St.

W. Hubbard St.

W. Kinzie St.

N. Orleans St.
N. Wells St.

W. Kinzie St.

Dan Ryan Expwy.

N. Milwaukee Ave.
N. Clinton St.
N. Canal St.

◆ Merchandise Mart

W. Wayman St.

MERCHANDISE MART **L**

GETTING HERE

The Merchandise Mart has its own stop on the El's Brown and Purple lines.

Traveling by car, there is a parking lot nearby at 350 N. Orleans Street. Or, if you are heading to the northern tip of the neighborhood, take Wells Street to Chicago Avenue.

Yours truly, can also walk west from the Mag Mile a few blocks to get to the area.

MAKING THE MOST OF YOUR TIME

You can see all there is to see in about two hours, but add another hour or more if you want to wander leisurely in and out of the shops at Tree Studios or the galleries on Superior Street and the surrounding area. Step across the State Street Bridge for a great bird's-eye view of Chicago. You'll see the Tribune Tower and Trump Tower to the east and Marina City at your back.

For a reminder of the Chicago River's ongoing importance as a working river, wait for the bridge to rise to let boats pass underneath—kids especially love seeing the bridge in action. Duck into the Bloomingdale Home store in the former Medinah Temple and admire the ornate architecture and Moorish details while shopping for bath towels. Be sure to take in a meal while you're in the area. But be forewarned: Dining without reservations at one of the touristy restaurants can entail a wait on weekends and on nice days. Most galleries are closed Sunday and Monday.

NEIGHBORHOOD TOP 7

1. Treat yourself to music during a Friday lunch at the infamous Andy's Jazz Club's **Jazz at Noon** series.

2. Spend an afternoon browsing the **art galleries.**

3. Pick up some ideas for your next home improvement project at **LuxeHome** in the Merchandise Mart.

4. Cheer on the Chicago Cubs from the comfort of a cozy barstool at **Harry Caray's Restaurant** at 33 W. Kinzie Street.

5. Admire the views north and south from the **Dearborn** or **State Street Bridge** over the Chicago River.

6. Take the kids to **Ed Debevic's** for a burger with a side of sass.

7. Catch a performance at the **House of Blues** and then head across the street to **Bin 36** for wine flights and cheese plates.

QUICK BITES

For quality over kitsch, try **Big Bowl** (✉ 60 E. Ohio St.), or fill up on both while chowing down on yummy Chicago deep-dish pizza at the graffiti-covered, tourist-happy **Ginos's East** (✉633 N. Wells St.).

Nestled under the El tracks at Superior and Franklin streets is **Brett's Kitchen** (✉233 W. Superior St., River North ☎312/664–6354), an excellent spot for a sandwich or an omelet Monday through Saturday.

Want some fries to go with that shake, honey? The purposefully sassy waitstaff at **Ed Debevic's**(✉640 N. Wells St.), a '50s-style diner, keeps the crowds entertained.

The great John-Georges Vongerichten gets casual at **Vong's Thai Kitchen** (✉6 W. Hubbard St., River North ☎312/664–8664), where sharing satays, noodle dishes, and curries is encouraged.

WHAT'S HERE

The huge **Merchandise Mart,** on the river between Orleans and Wells streets, is so commanding that it has its own zip code as well as its own stop on the El's Brown and Purple lines. Miles of corridors on its top floors are lined with trade-only furniture and home-design showrooms. LuxeHome, a collection of 30 or so upscale stores with an emphasis on home design and renovation, takes up the bottom two floors.

At Dearborn and Kinzie streets is the splendid ornamental brickwork of **33 West Kinzie Street,** the home of Harry Caray's restaurant. (The loud—and delicious—restaurant, filled with flags and giant drawings of the late Cubs broadcaster and his big glasses, is on "Harry Caray Drive," an honorary designation.) Southeast of here, just shy of the bridge that crosses the Chicago River, you can see the distinctive twin corncobs of **Marina City,** a residential complex that also includes the Hotel Sax Chicago (formerly a House of Blues hotel), the House of Blues nightclub, and a bowling alley. Fans of the old *Bob Newhart Show* may recognize Marina City from the backdrop in the show's opening credits.

A few blocks north, at the intersection of State and Ohio streets, are the **Tree Studios** shops and galleries, and the adjacent Medinah Temple, on Wabash Avenue, which houses a **Bloomingdale's Home & Furniture Store.**

THE ROOTS

The original Tree Studios were intended as living spaces for artists who were in town for the World's Columbian Exposition at the turn of the 20th century. They were used as living and working spaces by generations of creative types and were considered an artistic oasis until 2001, when a development group bought the studio buildings and the Medinah Temple.

Head west on either Ohio or Ontario Street, and as you approach LaSalle, then Wells streets, see the neighborhood transform into something of a dining Disneyland, with enormous outposts of national chains like Rainforest Café, Hooters, and the Hard Rock Café. Tourists clog the streets, eager to mob them all.

Things get a little more civilized again north on Wells Street to Superior Street, where you run into the area known as the **River North Gallery District.** Dozens of art galleries show every kind of work imaginable in the area bounded by Wells, Orleans, Chicago, and Erie streets—in fact, virtually every building on Superior Street between Wells and Orleans streets houses at least one gallery. Galleries welcome visitors, so feel free to stop into any that catch your eye. On periodic Fridays throughout the year, the galleries coordinate their exhibitions and open their doors to the public for a special night to showcase new works. Art lovers take note: though River North is still a good bet for great art, a growing number of artists have ditched the high-rent district for the cheaper, more industrial West Loop and Pilsen neighborhoods.

Dining in River North

2

EXPENSIVE DINING

Aigre Doux, *New American,* 230 W. Kinzie St., River North

Crofton on Wells, *New American,* 535 N. Wells St., River North

Fogo de Chao, *Brazilian,* 661 N. LaSalle St., River North

Joe's Seafood, *Prime Steaks & Stone Crab,* Seafood, 60 E. Grand Ave., River North

Keefer's, *Steak House,* 20 W. Kinzie St., River North

Naha, *New American,* 500 N. Clark St., River North

Ruth's Chris Steak House, *Steak House,* 431 N. Dearborn St., River North

Smith and Wollensky, *Steak House,* 318 N. State St., River North

Topolobampo, *Mexican,* 445 N. Clark St., River North

MODERATE DINING

Bin 36, *American,* 339 N. Dearborn St., River North

Blue Water Grill, *Seafood,* 520 N. Dearborn St., River North

Brasserie Jo, *Brasserie,* 59 W. Hubbard St., River North

Coco Pazzo, *Italian,* 300 W. Hubbard St., River North

DeLaCosta, *Latin,* 465 E. Illinois St., River North

Frontera Grill, *Mexican,* 445 N. Clark St., River North

Gene and Georgetti, *Steak House,* 500 N. Franklin St., River North

Harry Caray's, *Italian,* 33 W. Kinzie St., River North

Japonais, *Japanese,* 606 W. Chicago Ave., River North

Le Lan, *Asian Fusion,* 749 N. Clark St., River North

Maggiano's Little Italy, *Italian,* 516 N. Clark St., River North

mk, *New American,* 868 N. Franklin St., River North

Nacional 27, *Latin,* 325 W. Huron St., River North

Osteria via Stato, *Italian,* 620 N. State St., River North

Rockit Bar & Grill, *American,* 22 W. Hubbard St., River North

Scoozi!, *Italian,* 410 W. Huron St., River North

Shaw's Crab House and Blue Crab Lounge, *Seafood,* 21 E. Hubbard St., River North

SushiSamba Rio, *Japanese,* 504 N. Wells St., River North

BUDGET DINING

Ben Pao, *Chinese,* 52 W. Illinois St., River North

Cafe Iberico, *Spanish,* 739 N. LaSalle St., River North

Cyrano's Bistrot Wine Bar & Cabaret, *Bistro,* 546 N. Wells St., River North

Ed Debevic's, *American,* 640 N. Wells St., River North

Mr. Beef, *American,* 666 N. Orleans St., River North

Pizzeria Due, *Italian,* 619 N. Wabash Ave., River North

Pizzeria Uno, *Italian,* 29 E. Ohio St., River North

LINCOLN PARK & OLD TOWN

Sightseeing
★★★★☆

Dining
★★★★☆

Lodging
★★☆☆☆

Shopping
★★☆☆☆

Nightlife
★★★★☆

Old Town began in the 1850s as a modest neighborhood of working-class German families. Now you'll find a diverse population and some of the oldest—and most expensive—real estate in Chicago. It's bordered by Division Street to the south, Armitage Avenue to the north, Clark Street on the east, and Larrabee Street on the west, but its heart lies at the intersection of North Avenue and Wells Street. Besides its notable architecture, Old Town is home to the famous comedy clubs Zanies and the Second City.

Lincoln Park—the *park*—extends from North Avenue to Hollywood Avenue. It became the city's first public playground in 1864, named after the then recently assassinated president. The neighborhood adjacent to the original park, bordered by Armitage Avenue on the south, Diversey Parkway on the north, the lake on the east, and the Chicago River on the west, also became known as Lincoln Park. It was a sparsely settled community of truck farms and orchards that grew produce for the city of Chicago, 3 mi to the south.

In some ways, Lincoln Park today epitomizes all the things that people love to hate about yuppified urban areas: stratospheric housing prices, teeny boutiques with big-attitude salespeople, and plenty of fancy-schmancy coffee shops, wine bars, and cafés. That said, it's also got some of the prettiest residential streets in the city, that gorgeous park, a great nature museum, and a thriving arts scene.

WHAT'S HERE

There's a lot going on in Old Town and Lincoln Park. The yuck-it-up comedy clubs on Wells Street and raucous nightlife along North Lincoln Avenue and Halsted Street are a sharp contrast to the tranquillity

Dining in Lincoln Park

EXPENSIVE DINING

Alinea, *Cutting-Edge*, 1723 N. Halsted St., Lincoln Park

Charlie Trotter's, *New American*, 816 W. Armitage Ave., Lincoln Park

Geja's, *Fondue*, 340 W. Armitage Ave., Lincoln Park

North Pond, *American*, 2610 N. Cannon Dr., Lincoln Park

MODERATE DINING

Adobo Grill, *Nuevo Latino*, 1610 N. Wells St., Old Town

Bistrot Margot, *Bistro*, 1437 N. Wells St., Old Town

Black Duck Tavern and Grille, *New American*, 1800 N. Halsted St., Lincoln Park

Boka, *New American*, 1729 N. Halsted St., Lincoln Park

Landmark Grill and Lounge, *New American*, 1663 N. Halsted St., Old Town

Mon Ami Gabi, *Bistro*, 2300 N. Lincoln Park W, Lincoln Park

Sai Cafe, *Japanese*, 2010 N. Sheffield Ave., Lincoln Park

Salpicon, *Mexican*, 1252 N. Wells St., Old Town

Salvatore's, *Italian*, 525 W. Arlington Pl., Lincoln Park

Sola, *New American*, 3868 N. Lincoln Ave., Lincoln Park

Twin Anchors Restaurant & Tavern, *Barbecue*, 1655 N. Sedgwick St., Old Town

BUDGET DINING

Café Ba-Ba-Reeba!, *Spanish*, 2024 N. Halsted St., Lincoln Park

Karyn's, *Raw/Vegan*, 1901 N. Halsted St., Lincoln Park

Lalo's, *Mexican*, 1960 N. Clybourn Ave., Lincoln Park

Kamehachi, *Japanese*, 1400 N. Wells St., Old Town

Old Jerusalem, *Middle Eastern*, 1411 N. Wells St., Old Town

Raj Darbar, *Indian*, 2660 N. Halsted St., Lincoln Park

at the lagoon in Lincoln Park at Fullerton Parkway, where sometimes all the noise you hear is the flapping wings of the resident waterfowl. Between the two are plenty of historic landmarks as well as some cultural gems.

You can hear the laughs emanating from Wells Street in Old Town most any night of the week. **Zanies** has been hosting stand-up shows by some of the country's most famous comics, from Jay Leno to Dave Chappelle, for 30 years. Just up the street is **The Second City,** the legendary improv company that's served as a training ground for generations of would-be superstars.

FRUGAL FUN

Whether or not you go to a show, visit the lobby at The Second City to check out the who's who collection of photographs and caricatures of past troupe members: Alan Alda, John Belushi, Bonnie Hunt, Mike Meyers, Steve Carell, and Amy Sedaris represent just a few of the famous funny alums.

The **Chicago History Museum** (⊠*1601 N. Clark St., Lincoln Park* ☎*312/642–4600*) (formerly the Chicago Historical Society), at North Avenue and Clark Street, is housed in a Georgian structure built in

GETTING ORIENTED

Altgeld St.

Cafe Luigi

Biograph Theater

Fullerton Ave.

DePaul University

Facets Cinematheque

Belden Ave.

Webster Ave.

Nookies, too

Oz Park

Charlie Trotter's

ARMITAGE

Armitage Ave.

CLYBOURN

Cortland Ave.

Wisconsin St.

Willow St.

Steppenwolf Theatre Company

NORTH/ CLYBOURN

KEY

L CTA lines
M Metra lines
✗ Restaurant/Cafe

GETTING HERE

Take the Howard (Red Line) train or the Ravenswood (Brown Line) train to either Armitage or Fullerton avenues. Sheffield Avenue will be the nearest north–south street in both cases. Buses 11, 22, 36, and 151 take you through the area, too.

If you're driving, take Lake Shore Drive to Fullerton Avenue and drive west on Fullerton Avenue to Sheffield Avenue. Parking is scarce, especially evenings and weekends, so public transit or a cab is recommended.

MAKING THE MOST OF YOUR TIME

You could take an hour or a whole day for Lincoln Park, depending on how you prefer to spend your time. Set aside at least a couple of hours if you plan on a leisurely shopping experience along Armitage, Halsted, and Webster avenues. Tack on a couple more hours for the Peggy Notebaert Nature Museum, especially with kids. And if it's a beautiful summer day, ditch whatever else you had planned and surrender yourself to hours of frolicking in the park and on the beach. If you have kids in tow, or simply love visiting urban beasts, set aside some time for the Lincoln Park Zoo.

Come nightfall, make a beeline for The Second City or the Steppenwolf Theatre Company; do a little research ahead of time to decide what kind of performance you want to see—and how much you want to spend. Then you can plan to make a day out of enjoying Lincoln Park and Old Town. It's quintessential Chicago!

NEIGHBORHOOD TOP 7

1. Take a walk—or a run, or a bike ride—along the **lakefront path** heading south from North Avenue beach, and take in the breathtaking views of the city along Lake Michigan.

2. Catch the free improv after the show every night except Friday at **the Second City.**

3. See some of Hollywood's greats return to their roots to perform in a play at the **Steppenwolf Theatre Company.**

4. Browse the boutiques along **Armitage Avenue.**

5. Take refuge in the lush greenery of the **Lincoln Park Conservatory.**

6. Satisfy your late-night cravings after a stint at the bars with a stop at the **Wiener Circle** (at N. Clark St. and Wrightwood Ave.; walk north on Clark from Fullerton Pkwy.), where the surly service is part of the fun.

7. For a very different dining experience, splurge on a degustation at **Charlie Trotter's.**

QUICK BITES

Cafe Luigi (⊠ *2548 N. Clark St., Lincoln Park* ☎ *773/404–0200*) is a blink-and-you'll-miss-it storefront that sells New York–style pizza slices, calzones, and sausage rolls to grateful East Coast expats.

Nookies, too (⊠ *2114 N. Halsted St., Lincoln Park* ☎ *773/327–1400*) is open 24 hours on Friday and Saturday and serves heaping breakfasts anytime, making it a favorite of the neighborhood's late-night partying crowd. Cash only.

Just outside the park, **R. J. Grunt's** (⊠ *2056 N. Lincoln Park West, Lincoln Park* ☎ *773/929–5363*) has been serving killer milk shakes and burgers and stocking a salad bar for healthy types since 1971.

Twin Anchors (⊠ *1655 N. Sedgwick St., Lincoln Park* ☎ *312/266–1616* ⊙ *No lunch weekdays*), a popular Old Town restaurant and tavern for more than 60 years, is famous for its barbecued ribs.

1932. The beautiful people strut their stuff just to the east along the lake at **North Avenue Beach**, while the beasts roar nearby on Stockton Drive at **Lincoln Park Zoo**, which is free to the public. A few blocks ahead, there's a rather inconspicuous patch of grass where a garage once stood bearing the address **2122 N. Clark Street**. There's no marker, but it's the site of the infamous St. Valentine's Day Massacre, when seven men were killed on the orders of Al Capone on February 14, 1929.

DID YOU KNOW?

Another infamous Lincoln Park locale is the Biograph Theater (⊠ N. Lincoln Ave., Lincoln Park ☎ 773/871–3000), now home to the Victory Gardens Theater company, where notorious bank robber John Dillinger was shot and killed by the FBI in 1934.

One of the largest Catholic universities in the country, **DePaul University** has a 28-acre campus in Lincoln Park, bounded roughly by Webster Avenue on the south, Fullerton Avenue on the north, Halsted Street on the east, and Racine Avenue on the west. It serves more than 17,000 students, and has four other campuses in the Loop and suburbs. You might have a celebrity sighting or two on Halsted Street if you time a visit right to **Steppenwolf Theatre Company,** where ensemble members including Joan Allen, John Mahoney, Gary Sinese, and John Malkovich often perform or direct. The **Peggy Notebaert Nature Museum,** back in the park at Fullerton Parkway, is geared to kids, but outdoorsy adults will dig it, too.

On Wednesday and Saturday mornings from May to September the **Green City Market** takes over a large swath of grass at the south end of Lincoln Park. In addition to farmstands showcasing locally grown produce and sustainably produced meat, there are food booths serving up made-to-order sandwiches and savory crepes, as well as cooking demonstrations by local celebrity chefs, such as Rick Bayless of Frontera Grill.

OUR TIP

All ages get especially wide-eyed in the Notebaert's Judy Istock Butterfly Haven, where you get to commingle with 75 species of free-flying, brightly colored beauties—roughly 1,000 at any time.

Film buffs shouldn't leave Lincoln Park without a visit to **Facets Cinematheque,** which presents an eclectic selection of artistically significant films from around the world on its two screens. It also has a well-stocked video store (Facets Videotheque) that has more than 60,000 foreign, classic, and cult films.

Film fans—and younger visitors—also will relish a trip to **Oz Park**, between Webster and Dickens avenues and Burlington and Larrabee streets, for a chance to get up close with Dorothy and Toto. All the beloved movie characters are there in sculpture form. The Wizard's author, L. Frank Baum, lived in Chicago at the turn of the 20th century. The park also has a playlot for pint-size visitors.

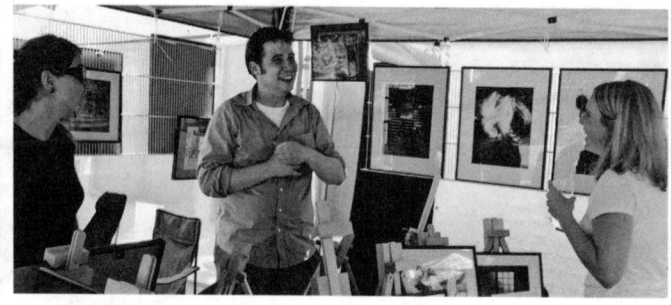

2

WICKER PARK & BUCKTOWN

Sightseeing
★★☆☆☆
Dining
★★★★☆
Lodging
★☆☆☆☆
Shopping
★★★★☆
Nightlife
★★★★☆

Creative types still cluster in Bucktown and Wicker Park, a hip, somewhat grungy enclave of side-by-side neighborhoods centered on Milwaukee, Damen, and North avenues. But they no longer lay exclusive claim to this funky part of town. These days you'll find young families, thirtysomething professionals, and university students thrown into the mix along with the immigrant communities who have lived here for generations. Within this Petri dish of gentrification, there are also cutting-edge galleries, coffeehouses, nightclubs, and a bizarre bazaar of shops. A sign of the changing times: chains like American Apparel and Urban Outfitters have opened outposts in this neighborhood, once considered a haven from corporate retail. In 2008 Marc Jacobs opened its first Chicago boutique, Marc by Marc Jacobs, in the area. Still, this area's eclectic shopping is a far cry from a suburban strip mall—or, for that matter, the Mag Mile.

Bucktown—which is said to have taken its name from the goats kept by the area's original Polish and German immigrants—encompasses the neighborhood surrounding Milwaukee Avenue north of North Avenue. The area south of North Avenue to Division Street is Wicker Park. Farther south still is Ukrainian Village, where the artsy types are now encroaching, but which still has a number of sights that are a testimony to the ethnic roots that remain strong in this neighborhood.

GETTING ORIENTED

GETTING HERE

If you're driving, take the Kennedy to North Avenue, then go west on North Avenue until you reach the triangular intersection where North meets Milwaukee and Damen avenues. Metered street parking is available but can be hard to come by, especially in the evening and on the weekend when the neighborhood is bustling. Be aware that many side streets restrict parking to residents with permits only. Most restaurants in the area offer valet service—a good alternative to driving around for an hour looking for a spot. By El train, take the Blue Line to the Damen–North Avenue stop.

QUICK BITES

bin wine cafe (✉ *1559 N. Milwaukee Ave., Wicker Park* ☎ *773/486–2233*) is a cozy little storefront where you can pair top-notch wines by the glass with global menu options.

To us, former caterer to the stars Debby Sharpe is both **The Goddess and Grocer** (✉ *1646 N. Damen Ave., Bucktown* ☎ *773/342–3200*), serving up to-die-for sandwiches and salads that please vegans and carnivores alike at her gourmet takeout shop. You can eat at the small dining room next door.

A sunny spot with a fireplace for cold winter days, **Milk & Honey Café** (✉ *1920 W. Division St., Wicker Park* ☎ *773/395–9434*) packs in neighborhood types who crave the French toast at breakfast and inventive lunchtime sandwiches served with housemade potato chips.

Fuel up with fluffy French croissants, palmiers, and cappuccinos at **Sweet Thang** (✉ *1921 W. North Ave., Bucktown* ☎ *773/772–4166*), a cute little bistro with a rich red sofa in the window and red-leather chairs with heart-shape backs. If you want to practice your French, place your order for a slice of quiche or a croque monsieur in *la belle langue*. Then settle back and imagine you're in gay Paris.

NEIGHBORHOOD TOP 5

1. Order a cup of coffee or a glass of wine and perch yourself at the window seat in a café—or at an outdoor table in warm weather—and get ready for some of the best **people-watching** in the city.

2. Catch some cutting-edge music at the **Double Door.**

3. **Shop for funky finds** at the shops along Division Street, Milwaukee Avenue, and Damen Avenue.

4. Explore the area's rich visual arts scene at the Wicker Park Bucktown Gallery Association's **Second Saturday Gallery Walk** on the second Saturday of each month.

5. Enjoy the drama at the Flatiron Arts Building's **Third Thursday Theatre Reading Series**.

MAKING THE MOST OF YOUR TIME

The best times for people-watching are in the evening when the clubs and bars draw crowds, or during Sunday brunch when the restaurants do steady business. May through October you can take your place at an outdoor patio to savor the view of hipsters and young families strolling by, soaking up the sun.

The liveliest times to visit are late August, when Bucktown hosts its annual Arts Fest, and September, during the Around the Coyote Arts Festival and the indie favorite Renegade Craft Fair.

2

AT A GLANCE

Dining in Wicker Park

EXPENSIVE DINING
Schwa, *Cutting-Edge*, 1466 N. Ashland Ave., Wicker Park

MODERATE DINING
Between Boutique Café and Lounge, *International*, 1324 N. Milwaukee Ave., Wicker Park

Café Absinthe, *New American*, 1954 W. North Ave., Bucktown

Coast, *Japanese*, 2045 N. Damen Ave., Bucktown

Crust, *Organic*, 2056 W. Division St., Wicker Park

Feast, *International*, 1616 N. Damen Ave., Bucktown

Francesca's Forno, *Italian*, 1576 N. Milwaukee Ave., Wicker Park

Hot Chocolate, *Café*, 1747 N. Damen Ave., Wicker Park

Le Bouchon, *Bistro*, 1958 N. Damen Ave., Bucktown

Mirai Sushi, *Japanese*, 2020 W. Division St., Wicker Park

Spring, *New American*, 2039 W. North Ave., Wicker Park

BUDGET DINING
Earwax, *American*, 1561 N. Milwaukee Ave., Wicker Park

Piece, *Pizza*, 1927 W. North Ave., Wicker Park

Smoke Daddy, *Southern*, 1804 W. Division St., Wicker Park

Milk & Honey Café, *Café*, 1920 W. Division St., Wicker Park

WHAT'S HERE

The anchor of the North-Milwaukee-Damen intersection is the striking triangular Art Deco–style **Northwest Tower Building**, a 12-story office building on North Avenue that's used as a reference point from miles around. Built in 1929 and nicknamed the Coyote Building for some unknown reason, it serves as the locus of the annual Around the Coyote Arts Festival. Opposite the Northwest Tower across the busy intersection is the distinctive three-story terra-cotta **Flatiron Arts Building**. Its upper floors have long served as a sort of informal arts colony, providing studio and gallery space for a number of visual artists. The beautiful facade of the **North Avenue Baths Building** (⊠ *2039 W. North Ave., Bucktown*), just west of the intersection of Milwaukee and Damen avenues, is a clue to its past life, when it was a storied meeting spot for politicians who cut deals in the hot steam rooms, where it was difficult to plant wiretaps.

Across the street is **Subterranean** (⊠ *2011 W. North Ave., Bucktown* ☎ *773/278–6600*), a bar and dance club resting atop Prohibition era escape tunnels. Also near this intersection is the **Double Door,** a late-night music venue where homegrown acts like Veruca Salt and Liz Phair and legends like the Rolling Stones have played. **Earwax Café** is a vegan- and vegetarian-friendly hangout with a video-rentals department.

FRUGAL FUN

Art spills onto the streets of Bucktown and Wicker Park every September, when the weekend-long Around the Coyote Fall Arts Festival attracts thou-

sands of collectors and browsers who scour every nook and cranny of the neighborhood.

For a reality-television fix, check out the building at the corner of Winchester and North avenues, a former *Real World* house. Back on Damen, head north for some shopping—window or otherwise—at a collection of shops selling wares you won't likely find elsewhere. Hip fashionistas from around the city head to **p.45** for the latest finds from up-and-coming designers.Homebodies *oooh* and *ahhh* over the luxurious tabletop finds at **Stitch** and antiques hunters like **Pavilion** and **Pagoda Red.**

At the southern border of Wicker Park, Division Street has become a shopping and dining destination in its own right. Bars, boutiques, and trendy restaurants line the once-gritty thoroughfare, which lent its name to journalist Studs Terkel's famous 1967 book about urban life. Heading west on the stretch of Division between Wolcott and Western avenues you'll pass by **Public I**, a popular boutique featuring clothing by independent designers; **Renegade Handmade,** an eclectic shop selling a wide variety of goods by local crafters; **Coco Rouge,** an upscale chocolatier hawking inventive spice-infused truffles; hip sushi spot **Mirai Sushi;** and **Crust,** the city's first certified organic restaurant, specializing in wood oven–fired flatbreads.

South of the North-Damen-Milwaukee intersection is the triangular **Wicker Park,** which was donated to the city in 1870 by politician Charles Wicker. Along Hoyne and Pierce streets nearby you'll find some of the biggest and best examples of Chicago's Victorian-era architecture. So many brewery owners built homes in this area that it was once dubbed **"Beer Baron Row."**

DID YOU KNOW?

■ TIP➜ Novelist Nelson Algren, whose book Chicago: City on the Make still wins praise for capturing the essence of the city, lived in the three-story home at 1958 West Evergreen Street.

For a glimpse of how the working class lived at the turn of the 20th century, head a little farther south to the **Ukrainian Village Landmark District** (on Haddon Avenue and Thomas and Cortez streets between Damen and Leavitt avenues), a well-preserved group of workers' cottages and flats. Another place to glimpse the old immigrant populations' squat leaded-glass brick homes is on Homer Street between Leavitt and Oakley streetsNearby on Chicago Avenue is the **Ukrainian Institute of Modern Art** (⊠2320 W. *Chicago Ave.* ☎773/227–5522), which has three galleries that focus on sculpture, mixed media, and paintings.

LAKEVIEW INCLUDING WRIGLEYVILLE

Sightseeing
★★☆☆☆

Dining
★★★★☆

Lodging
★☆☆☆☆

Shopping
★★★★☆

Nightlife
★★★★☆

Lakeview is a massive North Side neighborhood made up of smaller enclaves that have their own distinct personalities. There's the beer-swilling, Cubby-blue-'til-we-die sports-bar fanaticism of Wrigleyville, home of the esteemed Wrigley Field; the out-and-proud colors of the gay bars, shops, and clubs along Halsted Street in Boystown; and an air of urban chic along Southport Avenue (a street that's really a bit too far west to enjoy any lake views, but part of the neighborhood all the same), where young families stroll amid the trendy boutiques and ice-cream shops. It's a mix that means that a few blocks' walk in one direction or another will surely lead to some interesting finds.

Lakeview's first white settler was Conrad Sulzer, a grim-looking Swiss native and the son of a Protestant minister. Sulzer arrived in 1837, but the community was really established in the 1850s by James E. Rees and E. E. Hundley. Rees and Hundley built the Hotel Lake View—from which the neighborhood got its name—and then its first main road, which is now Broadway. By 1889 Chicago took the town for its own. Lakeview had, and continues to have, a large Irish population, with pubs dotting many of its streets. It's also an area that's densely populated with young urban professionals, and one of the main centers of Chicago's gay and lesbian community.

WHAT'S HERE

The venerable **Wrigley Field,** the ivy-covered home of the Chicago Cubs and the nation's second-oldest major league ballpark, is on the corner of Addison and Clark streets. Check out the **Harry Caray statue** commemorating the late Cubs announcer and sing "Take Me Out to the Ballgame" in his honor. Diagonally across the street is the **Cubby Bear Lounge** (⌧*1059 W. Addison St.* ☎*773/327–1662*), a Chicago institution since 1953. If you look up along Sheffield Avenue on the eastern side of the ballpark, you can see the rooftop patios where baseball fans pay high prices to root for the home team. Ticketless fans sit in lawn chairs on Sheffield during the games, waiting for foul balls to fly their way.

A long fly ball north of Wrigley is **Metro** (⌧*3730 N. Clark St.*), a former theater that's been converted to one of the city's best live-music venues. The Smashing Pumpkins got their start here. East on Grace Street is the 3800 north block of **Alta Vista Terrace,** a lovely residential street where 40 town houses completed as part of a single development in 1904 mirror one another diagonally across the block for a striking, harmonious effect. North again on Clark Street is **Graceland Cemetery,** which has crypts that are almost as strikingly designed as the city skyline.

DID YOU KNOW?

The names on the grave sites at Graceland read like a who's who from a Chicago history book: Marshall Field, George Pullman, Louis Sullivan, and Daniel Burnham are a few of the notables buried here. You can buy a walking-tour map at the entrance Monday through Saturday to explore on your own.

Right on Halsted Street is "Boystown," as locals often call it. Distinctive rainbow pylons line the street between Belmont and Addison avenues, marking the gay district. In June, Halsted is a sea of people, when Chicago's gay pride parade floats down the block.

On the side streets heading east and west of Boystown you'll find plenty of two- and three-story graystones and other vintage buildings on quiet tree-lined streets. Wandering Lakeview's residential streets, you might even feel transported back in time to 1920s or '30s Chicago. At least, that's what director Michael Mann must have thought. In spring 2008 a stretch of Newport Avenue between Clark and Halsted was temporarily transformed into a cobblestone thoroughfare while Mann was filming the John Dillinger flick Public Enemies (starring Johnny Depp) here. Belmont Avenue is a strip with a different character entirely. There are tattoo parlors and vintage-clothing stores, and just past the El tracks at Sheffield is the **Vic Theatre,** originally a luxurious vaudeville theater. Today it's a live-music venue that's most popular on Brew & View nights, when second- or third-run movies are screened, three bars are open, and the mood is festive.

LOCAL LIFE

Where Belmont meets up with Clark Street is a place the locals like to call "Punkin' Donuts." It's just a plain old Dunkin' Donuts, really, on a strip where lots of heavily pierced, spiky-haired types hang out.

GETTING ORIENTED

KEY

L CTA lines
✕ Restaurant/Cafe

GETTING HERE

If you're driving, take Lake Shore Drive north from the Loop to Belmont, but keep in mind that parking can be scarce. When the Cubs play, it's all but impossible—take public transit or give in and pay the exorbitant rates charged by enterprising residents with parking spots to spare.

Buses 22 and 36 will bring you here from points downtown, as will the Brown and Purple lines to Belmont or the Red Line to Addison. To get to the Southport Avenue shops, take the Brown Line to Southport.

MAKING THE MOST OF YOUR TIME

A quick walk through Wrigleyville and Lakeview will take about an hour and a half. Add another half-hour if you're wading through the post-Cubs-game crowds.

If you want to get a feel for the rest of the neighborhood, head to Graceland Cemetery—allow about an hour or two for a visit—or hit the boutiques along Southport Avenue.

You'll need a few hours more for watching an afternoon game at Wrigley Field, a pastime we consider one of the best ways to experience the *real* Chicago. To maximize the authenticity, choose a seat in the bleachers. Then follow the crowd after the game to a nearby Cubs-centric bar—such as the Cubby Bear or Murphy's Bleachers—to toast the recent win or drown your sorrows over a loss. Either method involves pitchers of beer. When night falls, catch a folk or rock show at Schubas Tavern or take in some live reggae at the Wild Hare.

2

NEIGHBORHOOD TOP 7

1. If you can score a ticket, sit in the bleachers with the locals at **Wrigley Field**—and be ready to throw the ball back onto the field if the opposing team nearly hits a homer into the stands.

2. If you can't score a ticket, hang out with the fans on **Sheffield Avenue**, who wait there to catch one of the long fly balls out of the park.

3. Catch a vintage flick at the vintage **Music Box Theatre**.

4. Indulge in a scoop of Daley (as in Mayor Richard J. Daley's) Addiction at the homegrown **Bobtail Soda Fountain**.

5. Thumb through the extensive selection of vintage vinyl and new tracks at **Reckless Records.**

6. Meet Marshall Field, George Pullman, and the other famous "residents" of **Graceland Cemetery.**

7. Experience gay Chicago in **Boystown.**

QUICK BITES

The original Swedish **Ann Sather** (✉ *909 W. Belmont Ave., Lakeview* ☎ *773/348–2378*) has legendary breakfasts: lingonberry pancakes or giant cinnamon buns.

Bobtail Soda Fountain (✉ *2951 N. Broadway, Lakeview* ☎ *773/880–7372*) serves ice cream based on an old family recipe, with specialty flavors like Lakeview Bourbon Barhopper and Daley Fudge Addiction.

The **Chicago Diner** (✉ *3411 N. Halsted St., Lakeview* ☎ *773/935–6696*) is known for its yummy vegetarian food.

Goose Island Wrigleyville (✉ *3535 N. Clark St., Wrigleyville* ☎ *773/832–9040*) has a variety of its own beers and root beers on tap, plus good burgers.

Uncommon Ground (✉ *3800 N. Clark St., Wrigleyville* ☎ *773/929–3680*) might look like a typical neighborhood coffeehouse, until you try the Jamaican jerk pork chops and Guinness French onion soup.

Dining in Lakeiew

EXPENSIVE DINING
Green Dolphin Street, *American*, 2200 N. Ashland Ave., Lakeview

MODERATE DINING
Coobah, *Latin*, 3423 N. Southport Ave., Lakeview

Erwin, New *American*, 2925 N. Halsted St., Lakeview

Mia Francesca, *Italian*, 3311 N. Clark St., Lakeview

Raw Bar, *Seafood*, 3720 N. Clark St., Lakeview

Turquoise Cafe, *Turkish*, 2147 W. Roscoe St., Lakeview

Yoshi's Cafe, *Asian Fusion*, 3257 N. Halsted St., Lakeview

BUDGET DINING
Ann Sather, *Scandinavian*, 909 W. Belmont Ave., Lakeview

Cozy Noodles and Rice, *Thai*, 3456 N. Sheffield Ave., Lakeview

Frasca Pizzeria and Wine Bar, *Pizza*, 3358 N. Paulina St., Lakeview

Harmony Grill, *American*, Schubas Tavern, 3159 N. Southport Ave., Lakeview

Heaven on Seven, *Southern*, 3478 N. Clark St., Lakeview

Hot Doug's, *Hot Dogs*, 3325 N. California Ave., Lakeview

Julius Meinl Cafe, *Café*, 3601 N. Southport Ave., Lakeview

Kitsch'n on Roscoe, *American*, 2005 W. Roscoe St., Lakeview

Orange, *American*, 3231 N. Clark St., Lakeview

Thai Classic, *Thai*, 3332 N. Clark St., Lakeview

A few blocks farther west you hit Southport Avenue, where the shopping seems to get more interesting all the time. There's not a Gap or Pottery Barn in sight—rather, the streets that travel north to Irving Park Road are lined with independent shops, many of which cater to well-dressed young women with money to burn. **Red Head Boutique** and neighboring **Krista K** are big favorites. Hipsters of both sexes, meanwhile, drool over the goods at **Jake.** Southport's main claim to fame, though, is the **Music Box Theatre,** a 1929 movie house where you can still see twinkling stars and clouds on the ceiling and hear live organ music before the independent and classic films are shown on its two screens.

Lakeview is also home to a high concentration of off-Loop theaters, many of which can be found within the small area bounded by Clark, Halsted, Belmont, and Broadway. Inside that rough square you'll find the risk-taking, experimental theater of **Red Tape Theatre Company,** the comedy-focused **Lakeshore Theater,** the historical plays of **Timeline Theater,** and **Briar Street Theatre,** the longtime Chicago performance spot for the Blue Man Group. Wander just a few blocks north on Clark Street to find **Live Bait Theater,** a veteran independent theater company that produces fresh, visually engaging works.

FAR NORTH & FAR NORTHWEST SIDES

Sightseeing
★★☆☆☆

Dining
★★★★☆

Lodging
★☆☆☆☆

Shopping
★★★★☆

Nightlife
★★★☆☆

The far north and northwest sides of Chicago are home to several of the city's most colorful, eclectic neighborhoods. History-rich Uptown was once a thriving entertainment district; there you can take in the beautiful architecture and striking old marquees. Though it's been a bit gritty for decades, new condo developments and chains like Borders and Starbucks are arriving in the area. The area centered around Broadway and Argyle Street is known alternately as Little Saigon, Little Chinatown, and North Chinatown.

Andersonville was named for the Swedish community that settled near Foster Avenue and Clark Street in the 1960s, and the area still has one of the largest concentrations of Swedes in the United States. A water tower above Clark Street is painted with the colors of the Swedish flag, and a number of businesses sell goodies like strudel and lingonberry pancakes.

Devon Avenue is a true mix of immigrant communities. In places its double street signs attest to its diversity: for a while it's Gandhi Marg, then Golda Meir Avenue. By any name, it's a sensory safari best undertaken on foot.

A straight shot south of Devon via Western Avenue is the former German enclave of Lincoln Square, now home to a buzzing dining and shopping scene.

One of the best ways to explore the ethnic diversity of these areas is by sampling the offerings at restaurants and food stores, so set out hungry. Uptown is just north of Lakeview, and Andersonville is north and west of Uptown. Devon Avenue is the farthest north and west of the three. Lincoln Square is directly south of Devon via Western Avenue.

GETTING ORIENTED

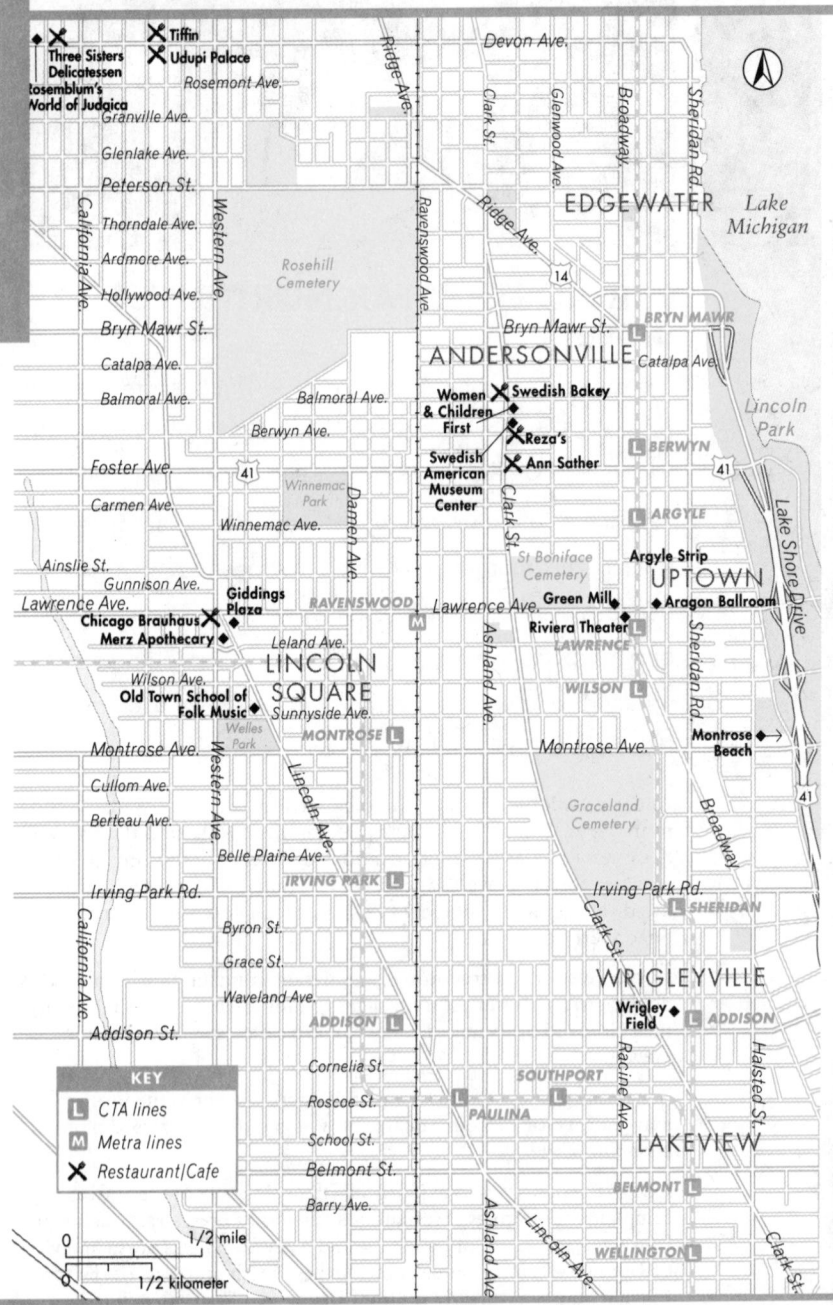

Three Sisters
Delicatessen

Tiffin

Udupi Palace

Rosemblum's
World of Judaica

Rosemont Ave.

Granville Ave.

Glenlake Ave.

Peterson St.

Thorndale Ave.

Ardmore Ave.

Hollywood Ave.

Bryn Mawr St.

Catalpa Ave.

Balmoral Ave.

Foster Ave.

Carmen Ave.

Ainslie St.

Gunnison Ave.

Lawrence Ave.

Chicago Brauhaus
Merz Apothecary

Leland Ave.

Wilson Ave.

Old Town School of
Folk Music

Sunnyside Ave.

Montrose Ave.

Cullom Ave.

Berteau Ave.

Belle Plaine Ave.

Irving Park Rd.

Byron St.

Grace St.

Waveland Ave.

Addison St.

California Ave.

Western Ave.

Ridge Ave.

Devon Ave.

Clark St.

Glenwood Ave.

Broadway

Sheridan Rd.

EDGEWATER   Lake
Michigan

Ravenswood Ave.

Ridge Ave.

14

BRYN MAWR

Bryn Mawr St.

ANDERSONVILLE   Catalpa Ave.

Balmoral Ave.

Berwyn Ave.

Rosehill
Cemetery

Women
& Children
First

Swedish Bakey

Reza's

Swedish
American
Museum
Center

Ann Sather

BERWYN

ARGYLE

Lincoln
Park

Winnemac
Park

41

Damen Ave.

Winnemac Ave.

St Boniface
Cemetery

Argyle Strip

Aragon Ballroom

UPTOWN

Giddings
Plaza

RAVENSWOOD

M

Lawrence Ave.

Green Mill

Riviera Theater

LAWRENCE

LINCOLN
SQUARE

Welles
Park

MONTROSE

Ashland Ave.

WILSON

Montrose Ave.

Graceland
Cemetery

Sheridan Rd.

Lake Shore Drive

41

Montrose
Beach

Lincoln Ave.

IRVING PARK

Irving Park Rd.

SHERIDAN

WRIGLEYVILLE

Wrigley
Field

ADDISON

Broadway

Clark St.

Racine Ave.

Halsted St.

KEY

L CTA lines

M Metra lines

✕ Restaurant/Cafe

Cornelia St.

Roscoe St.

School St.

Belmont St.

Barry Ave.

SOUTHPORT

PAULINA

Southport

LAKEVIEW

BELMONT

Ashland Ave.

Lincoln Ave.

WELLINGTON

Clark St.

0   1/2 mile

0   1/2 kilometer

GETTING HERE

Take the El's Red Line north from the Loop (toward Howard) and get off at the Lawrence stop for Uptown. In a car, take Lake Shore Drive north to Lawrence Avenue for Uptown or Foster Avenue for Andersonville. Devon Avenue is reachable via the El's Red Line (exit at the Morse Avenue station), then the 155 (Devon Avenue) bus. By car, head north up Western Avenue. For Lincoln Square, take the Brown Line El north from the Loop (toward Kimball) and exit at Western. By car, head north on Western Avenue; most of Lincoln Square's action takes place between Montrose and Lawrence.

MAKING THE MOST OF YOUR TIME

If you're planning on hitting all four neighborhoods, allow most of a day. Uptown will take about an hour; allow a couple of hours for Andersonville if you pop into the shops, and another hour to see the Swedish Museum. Devon Avenue takes about two hours—the street is crowded, especially evenings and on weekends, so walking is slow going there. Then end the day in Lincoln Square with a last peek at the boutiques followed by dinner at one of Lincoln Avenue's many restaurants.

LOCAL LIFE

Andersonville is one of the best places in Chicago to stock up on Swedish and other European foods and treats. If you have a sweet tooth, try the **Swedish Bakery** (⊠ *5348 N. Clark St., Far North Side* ☎ *773/561–8919*).

SAFETY

Be cautious in all of Uptown, especially at night. The neighborhood is slowly undergoing a resurgence, but there's still quite a bit of gang activity. Nevertheless, daytime walking, in pairs or groups, is just fine if you stick to the main drags of Broadway and Argyle.

QUICK BITES

Ann Sather (⊠ *5207 N. Clark St., Far North Side* ☎ *773/271–6677*) carries what may be the world's most addictive and enormous cinnamon rolls (buy some to carry out) and lingonberry pancakes.

At **Reza's** (⊠ *5255 N. Clark St., Far North Side* ☎ *773/561–1898*) you can dine on such outstanding Persian cuisine as kebabs, *dolmeh* (stuffed grape leaves), pomegranate juice, and charbroiled ground beef with Persian rice.

Another favorite down the street is **Tiffin** (⊠ *2536 W. Devon, Far North Side* ☎ *773/338–2143*), where the consistent crowds are a good testament to the quality of the curry.

The decor is reminiscent of a hotel lobby, and the music sounds like Indian Muzak, but the South Indian vegetarian cuisine is scrumptious at **Udupi Palace** (⊠ *2543 W. Devon, Far North Side* ☎ *773/338–2152*).

NEIGHBORHOOD TOP 5

1. Gorge yourself on cinnamon rolls at **Ann Sather.**

2. Haggle over the prices of electronics, fabric, and jewelry on **Devon Avenue.**

3. Catch a Sunday-night poetry slam at the **Green Mill,** where it all began.

4. Browse the eclectic shops along **North Lincoln Avenue.**

5. Grab a pastry to go from **Café Selmarie** and take a seat facing the fountain in **Giddings Plaza.**

WHAT'S HERE

Uptown is filled with an interesting mix of entertainment venues that attract, well, a pretty interesting mix of people to the area on any given night. Just outside the Lawrence train station is the **Aragon Ballroom** (⊠1106 W. *Lawrence Ave.* ☎773/561–9500), its large sign heralding upcoming bands—who play everything from metal to mariachi—in its dreamy, piazzalike setting. South is the marquee of the **Riviera Theatre** (⊠4746 N. *Racine Ave.* ☎773/275–6800), which draws a mosh-pit-diving crowd to see grungy bands.

DID YOU KNOW?

The Green Mill, a cramped jazz club that has drawn top names for more than a century, also sparked the national Poetry Slam movement

Nearby, Little Saigon (also known as Little Chinatown and North Chinatown) is a part of the **Argyle Strip,** which is anchored by the El's Argyle Street stop with its red pagoda. The Strip is teeming with storefront noodle shops and pan-Asian grocery stores. Roasted ducks hang in shop windows and fish peer out from large tanks.

Andersonville, just north of Uptown, still shows many signs of the Swedish settlers who founded the neighborhood. The **Swedish American Museum Center** has an interesting mix of exhibits, a separate museum complete with a Viking ship for kids, and a gift shop packed with Scandinavian items. The section of Clark Street north and just to the south of Foster Avenue is a lively mix of restaurants, bakeries, delicatessens, and boutiques. Victorian-looking street lamps and brick crosswalks complement the well-kept storefronts. An anchor of the area is the **Women & Children First** bookstore, which stocks an extensive selection of feminist and children's books.

Farther north, **Devon Avenue** is where Chicagoans go when they crave Indian food, or, as the avenue moves west, a good Jewish challah. The Indian restaurants and shops start popping up just east of Western Avenue. Besides authentic, inexpensive Indian and Pakistani food, you find the latest Bollywood flicks, electronics, jewelry, and beautifully embellished saris and fabrics. Restaurants and stores change over rapidly, however, so if the place you're looking for has closed, simply step into the next alluring spot you find. At Talman Avenue the multicultural wares transform to Jewish specialties. There are butchers and bakers and windows decorated with Russian newspapers and handmade *matrioshkas* (nesting dolls), evidence of this section's concentration of Russian Jews. At **Three Sisters Delicatessen** (⊠2854 W. *Devon Ave.* ☎773/973–1919) you can pick up an imported teapot or a doll with your Russian rye. Pick up menorahs, mezuzahs, and even stuffed matzo-ball dog toys at **Rosenblum's World of Judaica** (⊠2906 W. *Devon Ave.* ☎773/262–1700).

Bordered by Foster Avenue to the north, Montrose Avenue to the south, Damen Avenue to the east, and the Chicago River to the west, Lincoln Square has long been known for its Teutonic heritage. As proof, it's home to not one but two annual German fests—**Mayfest** in late May (held around the neighborhood's iconic 30-foot-tall maypole) and **Ger-**

man-American Fest in September. Both involve plenty of beer, brats, and German-style pretzels, as well as folks dressed in lederhosen dancing to oompah bands. In the past 10 years, however, this quiet far Northwest Side neighborhood, named for the Abraham Lincoln statue near the Lawrence-and-Western intersection, has seen its currency rise, and a spate of trendy restaurants and boutiques have moved into the area, drawing young urbanites and families.

Many credit Lincoln Square's renaissance to the relocation of the **Old Town School of Folk Music** in 1998 from its original home in Old Town to a long-vacant Art Deco building on North Lincoln Avenue. Today the area has a number of popular bars and restaurants—including **Tank Sushi, Bistro Campagne, La Bocca della Verita,** and **the Grafton**—all centered on a stretch of Lincoln Avenue between Montrose and Lawrence.

Shopping is another draw here. Trend-seekers will love browsing for threads at **the Dressing Room,** while wee fashionistas and their patient parents can browse the pint-size fashions at **City Mouse.** Head to **the Chopping Block** for cooking utensils or to attend a cooking class in the upstairs kitchen. **Eclecticity** and **Gallimaufry Gallery** are great places to snag gifts, and the **Fine Wine Brokers,** despite its highbrow-sounding name, is a low-key neighborhood wine shop hosting frequent wine tastings.

Visitors longing for a taste of Lincoln Square's ethnic roots shouldn't despair. There are still a handful of German restaurants and bars lining Lincoln Avenue—most notably, the **Chicago Brauhaus,** with its perennial Oktoberfest vibe and schnitzel dishes on the menu, and the divey German-owned **Huettenbar.** The Old World **Merz Apothecary** first opened in 1875 to cater to the area's German immigrants. Today it still retains its turn-of-the-last-century feel—walking past, you can't miss the hand-carved wooden façade with beautiful leaded glass windows—while offering an up-to-the-minute array of lovely smelling bath products. On the third Friday of each month, visit the **DANK Haus** German Cultural Center just off Lincoln on Western Avenue; the sixth-floor Skyline Lounge has German beer on tap and a patio with a fabulous view of downtown to the southeast.

Another can't-miss site is the recently rehabbed **Krause Music Store** building. Formerly the Museum of Decorative Arts and now a private office space, the 1922 landmark was the last work commissioned by architect Louis Sullivan. Passersby often stop to admire the building's ornate green terra cotta façade, with its elaborate wreathed medallion projecting above the roofline.

After shopping and dining your way through the Square, pause for a rest in **Giddings Plaza** with a view of the bronze, tiered **Giddings Square Fountain.** From May to October, the plaza comes alive with frequent outdoor concerts. It's also adjacent to the tempting bakery–restaurant **Café Selmarie,** whose tarts and chocolate croissants are impossible to resist.

PILSEN, LITTLE ITALY & UNIVERSITY VILLAGE

Sightseeing
★★☆☆☆

Dining
★★★★☆

Lodging
★☆☆☆☆

Shopping
★★☆☆☆

Nightlife
★☆☆☆☆

Stretching from the South Branch of the Chicago River to the Eisenhower Expressway (Interstate 290) this area west of the Loop on the south side of the city is a jumble of ethnic neighborhoods that has been home to immigrants of all cultures over the 20th century, most notably the Mexican community of Pilsen and the enclaves of Italian-Americans living in the shadow of the University of Illinois's Medical District and its Circle Campus.

Formerly a neighborhood of immigrants from Bohemia, Czechoslovakia, the enclave of Pilsen is now home to the largest Mexican community in the Midwest—making up roughly 85% of the neighborhood's population. Pilsen is known for its dramatic, colorful murals that show scenes from Mexican history, culture, and religion. It's also home to a thriving arts community—if you're a gallery-hopping art collector, you must visit this neighborhood. Pilsen is bordered by Halsted Street on the east and Western Avenue on the west and extends from 16th Street to the south branch of the Chicago River.

Chicago's Little Italy is to the north of Pilsen. This traditional ethnic neighborhood has been encroached upon by the expansion of the nearby university in recent years, but there are still plenty of yummy Italian restaurants, bakeries, groceries, and sandwich shops to explore. Stretching to Ashland Avenue on the west and Roosevelt on the south, Little Italy blends into University Village in its northeast corner.

The University of Illinois at Chicago anchors University Village. This booming residential area lies west of Roosevelt Road, primarily made up of a massive new mixed-use development that centers around Halsted Street and spans south to 14th Street.

WHAT'S HERE

The **National Museum of Mexican Art** (formerly the Mexican Fine Arts Center Museum), the nation's largest Latino museum, houses traditional and contemporary creations by international and local artists. In 2001 the museum tripled in size to accommodate state-of-the-art storage vaults for its 5,500-object permanent collection that spans pre-Cuauhtemoc artifacts, textiles, paintings, prints and drawings, and folk art. Its annual Day of the Dead celebration around Halloween is the largest in the city, and two annual performing arts festivals—Del Corazón Mexican Performing Arts Festival in the spring and the Sor Juana Festival honoring Mexican women in the fall—showcase Mexican performing arts from the traditional to the avant-garde.

The murals of Pilsen are one of the things that give this neighborhood its distinctive flair. You'll run into their bright colors and bold images at many turns during a walk through the neighborhood. At Ashland Avenue and 19th Street are two large murals ruminating on Latino family life and Latinos at work. More murals created by community youth groups and local artists brighten up the blocks along 18th to the east; Aztec sun-god inserts decorate the sidewalk stones.

Pilsen's main commercial strip, 18th Street, is loaded with tempting restaurants, bakeries, and Mexican grocery stores. East on 18th past the BIENVENIDOS A PILSEN sign is **Nuevo Leon**, a brightly painted family restaurant that has been an anchor in the neighborhood since the Gutiérrez family set up shop in 1962. Inhale deeply if the doors to the tortilla factory next door are open.

SWEET TOOTH

If you like sweets or have kids in tow, keep an eye out for BomBon Bakery (⊠1508 W. 18th St. ☎312/733-7788), which stocks a mind-boggling array of treats.

Halsted near 18th Street is home to an ever-growing cluster of art galleries and studios that have put Pilsen on the map as a go-to art destination. The neighborhood's low rents and low-key vibe have attracted working artists who once upon a time—as in 15 or 20 years ago—would have settled in Wicker Park. A large number of the artists live and work in the mixed-use artists' community known as the Chicago Arts District (formerly Pilsen East), centered on Halsted Street and stretching from 16th Street to Cermak Road. The community is an urban planning success story. In the early 1960s Chicago resident John Podmajersky started buying up disused commercial buildings and converting them into low-cost artists' lofts and studios. Abandoned alleyways were transformed into newly planted gardens. Today the area is a thriving arts district—a sprawling, larger-scale (and lower-cost) version of Wicker Park's Flatiron Arts Building.

Be aware that most of the area's dozen or more galleries and studio spaces are open by appointment only; a few have limited weekend hours. Notable exceptions include the combined gallery–home furnishings boutique **Grid Gallery**, the eclectic **4Art Inc.**, and the contemporary ceramics–focused **Dubhe Carreño**, all of which are open Tuesday through

GETTING ORIENTED

KEY

✗ Restaurant/Cafe

MAKING THE MOST OF YOUR TIME

Pilsen is busiest on weekends and on the first weekend of August during the Fiesta del Sol festival, as well as on Second Fridays (the second Friday of every month), when the neighborhood's art galleries stay open late for an art crawl. Little Italy is busier at night, when the restaurants and bars draw crowds. A visit to the University Village area is most rewarding on weekdays, when there's plenty of student activity on campus, or on Sunday, when you can check out the nearby Maxwell Street Market.

GETTING HERE

Take Interstate 290 west to the Damen Street exit. Go south on Damen to 19th Street. There's parking at the National Museum of Mexican Art. There's also metered parking on 18th Street and Ashland Avenue. You can also take the El's Blue Line from downtown to the 18th Street station. It's a station covered with colorful murals, and when you reach street level, take a look at the mosaic mural depicting Mexican women from pre-Columbian time to now.

To get to University Village, take the Blue Line to UIC/Halsted. The 9 Ashland bus will take you to UIC and Little Italy. If you're driving to Little Italy and University Village, take the Kennedy Expressway from either direction to the Taylor Street exit, then head west.

NEIGHBORHOOD TOP 4

1. Try the Italian lemonade—really a slushy Italian ice that comes in a rainbow of flavors—at **Mario's Lemonade Stand** on Taylor Street.

2. Gallery hop on **Second Fridays** in Pilsen, the monthly event when the art galleries stay open late.

3. Haggle over everything from TVs to tube socks at the legendary **Maxwell Street Market** on Sunday.

4. Three words: tres leches cake. Sample it at **BomBon Bakery** in Pilsen. Yum.

SAFETY

The area between Pilsen and Little Italy is railway tracks and vacant lots, and it isn't safe to walk between the two neighborhoods. If at all possible, try to drive to this area, park your car as you explore each individual neighborhood, and drive between the two. Or take the Blue Line to either UIC–Halsted or Racine to explore University Village and Little Italy, then hop back on and take it two more stops to 18th Street for Pilsen. Cabs aren't too common in this area.

QUICK BITES

Cafe Jumping Bean (✉ *1439 W. 18th St., Pilsen* ☎ *312/455-0019*), a cozy neighborhood coffee shop, displays original art by local artists on its walls. This eclectic gathering place has hot chocolate with Mexican spices, panini pizzas, and fresh sandwiches.

Picante Grill (✉ *1626 S. Halsted St., Pilsen* ☎ *312/455-8500*) is an upscale taqueria.

Pompei (✉ *1531 W. Taylor St., Little Italy* ☎ *312/421-5179*) started as a bakery selling thick, bready squares of pizza back in 1909. Today it's a part of a growing local empire of restaurants that serve salads, house-made pasta, and that same delicious pizza.

Sweet Maple Cafe (✉ *1339 W. Taylor St., Little Italy* ☎ *312/243-8908*) has a loyal following for their Southern-inspired breakfast. If you can stand the crowds on the weekend, it's worth the wait for grits, salmon cakes, and sweet-milk biscuits.

Saturday (but call first to confirm). In addition, on the second Friday evening of each month, many area artists open their studio doors to the public for the 2nd Fridays gallery walk.

In Little Italy the main thoroughfare is **Taylor Street,** which is best known for its Italian restaurants, though Thai food, tacos, and other ethnic food options are starting to fill the street as well.

The **National Italian American Sports Hall of Fame** (⌧ *1431 W. Taylor St., Little Italy* ☎ *312/226–5566*) pays tribute to athletes like Rocky Marciano, Yogi Berra, and Phil Rizzuto.

NEED A BREAK? If you visit Taylor Street from May to early September, be sure to stop at Mario's Italian Lemonade (⌧1068 W. Taylor St. ⌧No phone), where everyone from politicians like Jesse Jackson to neighborhood families lines up for old-fashioned slush-like Italian ices.

On Polk Street is **St. Basil Greek Orthodox Church** (⌧ *733 S. Ashland Ave., Little Italy* ☎ *312/243–3738*), a gorgeous Greek Revival building originally used as a Jewish synagogue. The bronze statue of Italian explorer Christopher Columbus that anchors **Arrigo Park** on Loomis Street was cast in Rome and brought to Chicago for the 1893 World's Columbian Exposition.

In University Village new luxury town homes and loft conversions mix with row houses and two-flats on a stretch of the city that not long ago was considered a wasteland. Retailers, including **Barbara's Bookstore** (⌧ *1218 S. Halsted St., University Village* ☎ *312/413–2665*), a small local chain, have been lured to the area along with the new residents. The **Jane Addams Hull-House Museum** on the UIC campus (⌧ *800 S. Halsted St., University Village* ☎ *312/413–5353*) is a city landmark as well as a memorial to Jane Addams, who launched innovative settlement-house programs. Nearby, you find the new home of the legendary **Maxwell Street Market,** which was not-so-gently nudged to the east at Canal Street and Roosevelt Road to make way for the new development. The year-round Sunday flea market is where odds and ends are sold at hundreds of stalls operated mostly by Latino immigrants. There's also live blues and food.

DID YOU KNOW? The Jane Addams Hull-House Museum is filled with exhibits about the first Hull House settlement, an innovative model for urban reform at the turn of the 20th century.

PRAIRIE AVENUE & CHINATOWN

Sightseeing
★★★☆☆

Dining
★★★★☆

Lodging
★☆☆☆☆

Shopping
★★☆☆☆

Nightlife
★☆☆☆☆

Geography is the main link between the Prairie Avenue Historic District and Chinatown. Prairie Avenue (two blocks east of Michigan Avenue, between 18th and 22nd streets) was Chicago's first Gold Coast. Many prominent merchants and manufacturers, including George Pullman and Marshall Field, built their homes here in the 1870s through the 1890s, but now only a handful of buildings recall this vanished era. New condominium construction has helped give the area more of its old vim, but it's nothing compared to the compact commotion to the west in Chinatown, a neighborhood packed with restaurants and shops. Tour the historic commercial district along Wentworth and Archer avenues and you might just forget you're in the Midwest

WHAT'S HERE

In the 19th century, many of the city's most prominent residents lived in what is now referred to as the **Prairie Avenue Historic District**. After the Chicago Fire of 1871, notable Chicagoans such as the Pullmans, the Fields, and the meatpacking family the Armours all built mansions in this neighborhood on the city's South Side.

Most of the 19th-century mansions are long gone, but you can still visit the National Historic Landmark **Glessner House Museum**(✉ *1800 S. Prairie Ave., Pilsen* ☎ *312/326–1480*) a home designed by Henry Hobson Richardson, the architect of Boston's Trinity Church. Completed in 1887, the L-shaped mansion is characteristic of "Richardson Romanesque" style, with its stone construction and short towers.

GETTING ORIENTED

GETTING HERE

To get to Chinatown by car, drive south on Michigan Avenue and take a left at 18th Street, and travel four blocks to Cermak Road/East 22nd Street. There's an inexpensive outdoor parking lot adjacent to the Chinatown Gate on Wentworth Avenue. If you dine in the area, ask the restaurant to validate your parking receipt. For the Prairie Avenue Historic District, take Michigan Avenue to East 21st Street, then travel west to Prairie Avenue. Buses 1, 3, and 4 cover both of these areas, or you can take the El's Red Line south from the Loop to the Cermak–Chinatown stop.

MAKING THE MOST OF YOUR TIME

You can easily spend a few hours browsing the shops and sampling the goodies along Wentworth Avenue or at Chinatown Square. Add an hour or two more if you're going to tour one or more of the Prairie Avenue homes. Chinatown is particularly busy on weekends throughout the year, but the big draws are Chinese New Year in January or February and the summer fair in July. Later in July, a dragon boat race draws thousands of spectators to view the ornately decorated boats on the south branch of the Chicago River.

SAFETY

Both of these areas are a little removed from the heart of the city and bordered by slowly gentrifying neighborhoods, so be cautious and aware if you are walking around the neighborhood at night. Better yet, limit your visit to well-lit and well-populated main streets after dark.

2

NEIGHBORHOOD TOP 3

1. Forgo traditional weekend brunch for dim sum with the locals at **Phoenix**.

2. Check out the digs where Chicago greats like Marshall Field and George Pullman lived in the **Prairie Avenue Historic District**.

3. Shop for tea and learn about ancient traditions at Chinatown shops like **Ten Ren Tea & Ginseng Co.** (⊠ *2247 S. Wentworth Ave.;* ☎ *312/842–1171*)

QUICK BITES

Joy Yee's Noodles (⊠ *2159 S. China Pl., in Chinatown Square Mall, Chinatown* ☎ *312/328–0001*) has a mile-long menu of Pan-Asian dishes that arrive in a flash; they claim to have introduced bubble teas to Chicagoland. Who are we to argue while we sip away?

Lao Sze Chuan (⊠ *2172 S. Archer Ave., Chinatown* ☎ *312/326–5040*) is the go-to spot for the best Szechuan in town. Try the twice-cooked pork and dry chili string beans. They're served super fast.

Phoenix (⊠ *2131 S. Archer Ave., Chinatown* ☎ *312/328–0848*) a widely popular choice, is busiest during weekend dim sum, when cart after cart of tempting dumplings and other dishes are rolled before eager diners. The food's all about comfort, but we'll warn you that the service isn't.

TOURS

Package guided tours of both the Clarke House and the Glessner House Museum are available Wednesday through Sunday, and are free on Wednesday (☎ *312/326–1480*). Wednesday tours are walk-in only and tend to fill up, so arrive early to guarantee a spot.

The Chinatown Chamber of Commerce (☎ *312/326–5320*) conducts one-hour walking tours in English and can help you arrange lunch at a neighborhood restaurant. Tours must be arranged two weeks in advance.

Nearby, the **Clarke House**(✉*1855 S. Indiana St., Pilsen* ☎*312/326–1480*), built in 1836, has the distinction of being the city's oldest surviving building. The Greek Revival–style home was built for Henry B. Clarke, a wealthy local hardware dealer. Today the home also functions as a museum, revealing what life was like for a middle-class family in the early part of the 19th century

WIDE LOAD

Clarke House has been moved three times from its original location on Michigan Avenue between 16th and 17th streets. The last time, in 1977, it had to be hoisted above the nearby elevated train tracks.

While you're in the area, don't miss the **National Vietnam Veterans Art Museum**, on the corner of 18th Street and Indiana Avenue. The museum presents a rare perspective on war through works of visual art created by combat veterans. At the intersection of Calumet and Cullerton avenues is the **Wheeler Mansion,** another of the area's great mansions that was nearly replaced by a parking lot before it was saved and painstakingly restored in the late 1990s. Today it's a contemporary boutique hotel and a fun alternative to more traditional chain lodging options nearby. ✉*2020 S. Calumet Ave., Prairie Avenue* ☎*312/945–2020.*

Three blocks farther west, on Michigan Avenue, is the handsome Gothic Revival **Second Presbyterian Church** (✉*1936 S. Michigan Ave., Prairie Avenue* ☎*312/225–4951*). Be sure to go inside this National Historic Landmark and take a look at the Tiffany stained-glass windows—one of the largest collections anywhere.

Next, walk south another block on Michigan Avenue for a tour of **Willie Dixon's Blues Heaven Foundation,** housed in the former Chess Records office and studios (✉*2120 S. Michigan Ave.*), where a cadre of music legends, from Etta James and Bo Diddley to Aretha Franklin and John Lee Hooker, have recorded.

DID YOU KNOW?

The Rolling Stones immortalized the Willie Dixon address in a blues track they recorded here in 1964 titled—you guessed it—"2120 S. Michigan Avenue."

South of the Prairie Avenue district, where Wentworth Avenue and Cermak Road/22nd Street meet, is the entrance to Chinatown. Our favorite parts are the plethora of gift shops in **Chinatown Square** (on bustling Archer Avenue) and the mouthwatering smells from the area's many restaurants and bakeries. The 11-block neighborhood is anchored by the Chinatown Gate and the enormous green-and-red pagoda towers of the Pui Tak Center, a church-based community center in the former On Leong Tong Building. Be sure to see the **Nine Dragon Wall** on Cermak Road, next to the El's Red Line Cermak-Chinatown stop, one of only four replicas worldwide of the Beijing original, and **Ping Tom Memorial Park** (✉*300 W. 19th St., Chinatown*), a multi-acre site dedicated to a neighborhood civic leader, that has views of the Chicago River.

2

HYDE PARK

Sightseeing
★★★★☆

Dining
★★☆☆☆

Lodging
★☆☆☆☆

Shopping
★☆☆☆☆

Nightlife
★★☆☆☆

Hyde Park is something of a trek from downtown Chicago, but it's worth the extra effort. Best known as the home of the University of Chicago, the neighborhood only began to see significant growth in the late 19th century, when the university opened in 1892 and the World's Columbian Exposition attracted an international influx a year later. The exposition spawned the Midway Plaisance and numerous Classical Revival buildings, including the behemoth Museum of Science and Industry. The Midway Plaisance still runs along the southern edge of the University of Chicago's original campus. Sprawling homes were soon erected for school faculty in neighboring Kenwood, and the area began to attract well-to-do types who commissioned famous architects to build them spectacular homes.

Today the neighborhood is considered a vibrant, eclectic part of the city. A number of architecturally riveting buildings are here, including two by Frank Lloyd Wright, the **Robie House** and **Heller House.** There's also a thriving theater scene and several art and history museums. Most impressive, though, is the diverse population with a strong sense of community pride and fondness for the neighborhood's pretty tree-lined streets, proximity to the lake, and slightly off-the-beaten-path vibe.

GETTING ORIENTED

KEY
- Ⓜ Metra lines
- ✕ Restaurant/Cafe

Lake Michigan

Burnham Park

HYDE PARK

E. 46th St.
E. 47th St.
E. 48th St.
E. 49th St.
E. 50th St.

S. Cottage Grove Ave.
S. Lake Shore Dr.
S. Hyde Park Blvd.

Madison Park

Heller House ◆

E. Hyde Park Ave.
E. 52nd St.
E. 53rd St.

Model Yacht Basin

S. Drexel Ave.
S. Ingleside Ave.
S. Greenwood Ave.
S. University Ave.
S. Woodlawn Ave.
S. Dorchester Ave.
S. Blackstone Ave.
S. Harper Ave.
S. Lake Park Ave.

Nichols Park

E. 53rd St.
S. Cornell Dr.
S. Hyde Park Blvd.
S. Everett Ave.

E. 54th St.
E. 54th Ave.

S. Kimbark Ave.
S. Kenwood Ave.
S. Ridgewood Ct.

E. 54th Ave.

WoodlawnTap ✕
E. 55th St.
E. 55th Pl.
E. 55th St.

David and Alfred Smart Museum of Art ◆

← DuSable Museum of African American History
E. 56th St.

Hyde Park Historical Society ◆

Windermere House and Promontory Apartments ◆
E. 56th St.

← ✕ Caffé Florian
E. 57th St.

Edwardo's Natural Pizza
Medici ✕✕

S. Ellis Ave.

Robie House ◆

Oriental Institute ◆

University Of Chicago ◆

E. 58th St.
E. 59th St.

S. Dorchester Ave.
S. Blackstone Ave.
S. Harper Ave.

Museum of Science & Industry ◆

Midway Plaisance
Midway Plaisance

Midway Plaisance

East Lagoon

E. 60th St.
E. 61st St.
E. 62nd St.

S. University Ave.
S. Dorchester Ave.
S. Stony Island Ave.
S. Cornell Ave.

Jackson Park

West Lagoon

0 ——— 600 feet
0 ——— 200 meters

GETTING HERE

By car, take Lake Shore Drive south to the 57th Street exit and turn left into the parking lot of the Museum of Science and Industry. You can also take the Metra Railroad train from Randolph Street and Michigan Avenue; get off at the 55th Street stop and walk east through the underpass two blocks, then south two blocks.

MAKING THE MOST OF YOUR TIME

If you're visiting the Museum of Science and Industry, you'll probably be spending most of your day there. Try to go during the week to avoid crowds. You could wind down the day meandering through Jackson Park or the University of Chicago campus. Then wander the Midway Plaisance, an expanse of green separating the Hyde Park neighborhood from Woodlawn to the south. The Midway was the center of activity at the World's Columbian Exposition in 1893.

QUICK BITES

Caffé Florian (⌂ *1450 E. 57th St., Hyde Park* ☎ *773/752–4100*) serves pizza and Italian entrées as well as hearty sandwiches, homemade soups and salads, decadent desserts, and lots of java.

The deep-dish pies at **Edwardo's Natural Pizza** (⌂ *1321 E. 57th St., Hyde Park* ☎ *773/241–7960*) are considered by some to be the best in the city.

You'll find several spots on 57th Street where you can get a quick bite and relax. **The Medici** (⌂ *1327 E. 57th St., Hyde Park* ☎ *773/667–7394*) has served up its specialty pizzas, burgers, and sandwiches to generations of University of Chicago students who've carved their names into the tables.

Woodlawn Tap (⌂ *1172 E. 55th St., Hyde Park* ☎ *773/643–5516* ☉ *Daily 11 AM–2 AM*) is a favored spot where locals and university students gather for a spoken-word reading or jazz concert along with pub grub.

SAFETY

Hyde Park is bordered to the west, south, and north by some less prosperous, and at times dangerous, areas. Use caution, especially in the evening, if you're uncertain about where you're heading.

TOURS

Tours of Frank Lloyd Wright's Robie House are conducted daily (☎ *708/848-1976*). Themed tours based on the children's book *The Wright 3* by Blue Balliett take place Saturday at 1:30 PM (☎ *708/848-1976* ☑ *adults $12, children 11–18 $10; 10 and under $5*).

A self-guided tour of University of Chicago architecture, *A Walking Guide to the Campus,* is available for purchase in the University of Chicago Bookstore (⌂ *Visitor Center: Reynolds Club 5706 S. University* ☎ *773/702–9739* ⊕ *www.uchicago.edu* ☉ *Weekdays 9–5*).

NEIGHBORHOOD TOP 5

1. Get lost in the massive wonder of the **Museum of Science and Industry.**

2. Do some exotic-bird-watching in **Jackson Park,** where a tropical-parrot population roosts.

3. Tour Frank Lloyd Wright's fantastic **Robie House.**

4. Pack a picnic and enjoy the views from the beautiful **Promontory Point.**

5. Get in a heated debate with a U of C Nobel Laureate over a pint at the **Woodlawn Tap.**

WHAT'S HERE

To get a good overview of the neighborhood, stop by the **Hyde Park Historical Society** (⊠*5529 S. Lake Park Ave., Hyde Park* ☎*773/493–1893* ☺ *Weekends 2–4*), which sponsors lectures and tours.

One of Hyde Park's gems is **Jackson Park** (⊠*Bounded by E. 56th and 67th Sts., S. Stony Island Ave., and the lakefront*), which was designed by Frederick Law Olmsted (who also designed Central Park in New York City) for the World's Columbian Exposition of 1893. It has lagoons, a Japanese garden with authentic Japanese statuary, and the Wooded Island, a nature retreat with wildlife and 300 species of birds.

THE BIRDS

Harold Washington Park and Jackson Park have a notable parakeet population. Rumor has it they escaped from a cage at O'Hare Airport and settled in area parks. Somehow these tropics natives were able to survive the harsh Chicago winter and have become neighborhood fixtures.

The **University of Chicago** (⊠*S. Ellis Ave.* ☎*773/702–1234*) dominates the physical and cultural landscape of Hyde Park and South Kenwood, and it's visually arresting. Much of the original campus was designed by Henry Ives Cobb. Especially of note are the International House and the Rockefeller Memorial Chapel, which has a carillon with 72 bells; a university carillonneur gives regular performances. The university's stately Gothic-style quadrangles look like something straight out of Cambridge and Oxford. Also worth a visit is the university-run Court Theatre, which stages new and classic works.

DID YOU KNOW?

"The toasters" are two U of C apartment buildings that sit on an island in the middle of the street, so named because, fittingly enough, the buildings look like two pieces of toast. They were designed by I. M. Pei, architect of the Louvre's controversial glass pyramids.

Frank Lloyd Wright's **Robie House** is a Prairie-style masterpiece and one of the most remarkable designs in modern American architecture. (It's also a place of interest for many young readers of the children's book *The Wright 3*, a fictional mystery that takes place at Robie House, which now conducts weekly tours geared to the book's fans.) **Heller House,** nearby on Harper Avenue between 52nd and 53rd streets, was designed in 1897 by Wright, 12 years prior to Robie House. Though not open to the public, the house's exterior is a good indication of his progression toward the Prairie style he achieved with Robie. The area is loaded with other architecturally significant buildings, including the **Windermere House** and **Promontory Apartments.**

Hyde Park has a bunch of smaller museums that stand in the shadow of the Museum of Science and Industry. **The DuSable Museum of African American History** has a notable permanent exhibit on slavery, and offers a cinema series and jazz and blues concerts, as well as children's programs. The **David and Alfred Smart Museum of Art** houses the fine art collection of the University of Chicago.

Museums

WORD OF MOUTH

"If you go to the Art Institute, make sure to find the Miniatures exhibit. It's wonderful, and is a collection of rooms decorated in a variety of styles and time periods."

–MP07950

"The Shedd is truly wonderful! Try to get there in time for a marine mammal show in the amazing oceanarium."

–kja

MUSEUMS PLANNER

Free Days

Always free:
Jane Addams Hull-House Museum
McCormick Tribune Freedom Museum
Museum of Contemporary Photography
National Museum of Mexican Art
Oriental Institute
Smart Museum
Ukrainian Institute of Modern Art

Sunday:
DuSable Museum of African American History

Monday:
Adler Planetarium & Astronomy Museum (selected months only)
Chicago Children's Museum (for kids 15 and younger first Mon. each month)

Tuesday:
Adler Planetarium & Astronomy Museum (selected months only)
Museum of Contemporary Art
Swedish American Museum Center (second Tues. each month)

Thursday:
Art Institute of Chicago (after 5 only)
Chicago Children's Museum (5–8 PM only)
Peggy Notebaert Nature Museum

Save Money

All the major museums are expensive; consider purchasing a Chicago CityPass instead of buying a single ticket. For about the price of admission to two museums, the pass lets you bypass the long lines and visit all of the big five—the Art Institute, Field Museum, Museum of Science and Industry, Adler Planetarium, and the Shedd Aquarium—plus the Hancock Observatory, anytime within nine days. For more information, see ⊕www.citypass.com.

Late Hours

Adler Planetarium & Astronomy Museum, first Friday of the month to 10 PM
Art Institute of Chicago, Thursday to 8 PM
Chicago Children's Museum, Thursday & Saturday to 8 PM
Museum of Contemporary Art, Tuesday to 8 PM
Museum of Contemporary Photography, Thursday to 8 PM
Oriental Institute, Wednesday to 8:30 PM
John G. Shedd Aquarium, Thursday to 10 PM (summer only)
Smart Museum, Thursday to 8 PM

Special Events

Tuesdays on the Terrace is a weekly summer event for mingling and live local jazz at the Museum of Contemporary Art. Cash bar. June–Sept., Tues. 5:30–8 PM.

DJs and local bands get things going at the Museum of Contemporary Art's First Fridays, a monthly preview of new work by Chicago artists. First Friday of every month, 6–10 PM. $15.

Feel like dinner, drinks, live jazz, and a view of the lake and the skyline? Get thee to Shedd Aquarium's Jazzin at the Shedd on the museum's terrace. June–Sept., Thurs. 5–10 PM. $10.

How Much Time?

Less than an hour:
Balzekas Museum of Lithuanian Culture
Jane Addams Hull-House Museum
Museum of Contemporary Photography
Museum of Holography
National Vietnam Veterans Art Museum
Polish Museum of America

1–2 hours:
DuSable Museum of African American History
Oriental Institute
Smart Museum of Art

2–3 hours:
Adler Planetarium & Astronomy Museum
Chicago Children's Museum
Chicago History Museum
National Museum of Mexican Art
Peggy Notebaert Nature Museum

Half day:
Museum of Contemporary Art
John G. Shedd Aquarium

Full day:
Art Institute of Chicago
Field Museum
Museum of Science and Industry

Best Gift Shops

Art Institute of Chicago. Find silk scarves, fine jewelry, glass paperweights, and other items that are reproduced from art works in the museum.

Field Museum. Everything dinosaur is sold in Field gift shops, but our guilty pleasure is the Mold-A-Rama vending machines on the lower level. These 1960s relics take heated colorful plastic and inject it into dinosaur molds.

Museum of Science and Industry. The Big Idea gift shop, on the entrance level, is packed with objects to tickle your mind, including chemistry sets, radio-controlled blimps, robot kits, and a kinetic solar-system model.

Museum of Contemporary Art. Pick up a Calder mobile or electronic chirping bird—you know, the stuff you never knew you always wanted.

Best Quirky Exhibits

Judy Istock Butterfly Haven, Peggy Notebaert Nature Museum. More than 20 local and international species of butterfly flutter through the butterfly atrium. Even more interesting are the cocoons in various stages of development. You might even catch a butterfly struggling out of its chrysalis.

Colleen Moore's Fairy Castle, Museum of Science and Industry. The MSI is full of quirky exhibits that make us wonder if we're still in a technology museum—there are live baby chicks and a moving exhibit of circus wagon miniatures—but one of the most beloved is the Fairy Castle. Built between 1928 and 1935, the final cost for this 8-foot-high palace with its 2,000 miniatures was $500,000.

Mesopotamian Gallery, Oriental Institute. The OI's largest gallery covers the entire sweep of Mesopotamian history, and includes a caveman's axe with the first trace of human blood and tablets that trace the history of writing.

Thorne Miniature Rooms, Art Institute. The 68 dollhouse-like rooms were designed by a Chicago socialite to display the miniatures she collected through her travels in Europe and America.

Updated by
Heidi Moore

Chicago's museums are the cultural heart of the city—so vital that the mayor rerouted Lake Shore Drive to create a verdant Museum Campus for the Adler Planetarium, Shedd Aquarium, and Field Museum. Treasures in Chicago's museums include Grant Wood's iconic painting *American Gothic,* at the Art Institute; "Sue," the largest T. rex ever discovered, at the Field Museum; and the only German U-boat captured during World War II, at the Museum of Science and Industry.

JUST THE HIGHLIGHTS, PLEASE

Head to the Art Institute for a quick art fix. For a tour of superlatives, see *Sky Above Clouds IV,* Georgia O'Keefe's largest painting; the largest holding of Monet's *Grainstacks* anywhere; and *A Sunday on La Grande Jatte—1884,* Georges Seurat's greatest piece.

CULTURE VULTURE

Tour the world without leaving the city. First stop? Europe. Hit the **Balzekas Museum of Lithuanian Culture,** the **Swedish American Museum Center,** the **Polish Museum of America,** and the **Ukrainian Institute of Modern Art.** Swing by the **Oriental Institute** for relics of the Near East, or brush up on Latino history at the **National Museum of Mexican Art.**

IF YOU HAVE KIDS

Besides the Chicago Children's Museum, these are our favorite kids' exhibits, sure to capture the imagination of your young ones. Don't miss the **Fairy Castle** at the Museum of Science and Industry, **"Sue,"** the T. rex, at the Field Museum, and the **dolphin show** at the Shedd Aquarium's Oceanarium. For an extra-colorful experience, **chase butterflies** at the Peggy Notebaert Nature Museum.

Chicago Museums

ANDERSONVILLE

Foster Ave.
Lawrence Ave.
Central Park Ave.
Kedzie Ave.
Western Ave.
Montrose Ave.

Swedish American Museum Center

Sheridan Rd.
Lake Shore Dr.

LAKEVIEW

Elston Ave.
Irving Park Rd.
Lincoln Ave.
Clark
Halsted

Addison
Belmont

Diversey Ave.
LINCOLN PARK & OLD TOWN
Fullerton Ave.
BUCKTOWN
Clybourn Ave.
Lincoln Park

Peggy Notebaert Nature Museum

Armitage Ave.
WICKER PARK
Armitage Ave.
Chicago History Museum

North Ave.
Milwaukee Ave.
NEAR NORTH

Lake Michigan

Division
Ukranian Institute of Modern Art
Augusta Blvd.
RIVER NORTH
McCormick Tribune Freedom Museum
Museum of Contemporary Art

Chicago Ave.
WEST LOOP
Polish Museum of America
LaSalle
State
Chicago Children's Museum

Grand Ave.
Museum of Holography
THE LOOP

Warren Blvd.
Grant Park
Michigan Ave.
John G. Shedd Aquarium

Jackson Blvd.
Eisenhower Expwy.
Museum of Contemporary Photography
Adler Planetarium & Astronomy Museum

LITTLE VILLAGE
Spertus Museum
Field Museum

Roosevelt Rd.
SOUTH LOOP

Ogden Ave.
Jane Addams Hull-House Museum
Canal
National Vietnam Veterans Art Museum

National Museum of Mexican Art
PILSEN
Cermak Rd.

25th St.
CHINATOWN
31st St.
31st St.

Archer Ave.
Ashland Ave.
Halsted
Michigan Ave.
State
Dr. Martin Luther King Jr. Dr.
Lake Shore Dr.

47th St.
51st St.
HYDE PARK
Garfield Blvd.
Washington Park
Du Sable Museum of African-American History
Museum of Science & Industry

59th St.
David & Alfred Smart Museum of Art
Oriental Institute

Balzekas Museum of Lithuanian Culture
63rd St.
65th St.
Jackson Park
Marquette Rd.
Chicago Skyway

0   2 miles
0   3 km

A GUIDE TO THE ART INSTITUTE

The Art Institute of Chicago, nestled between the contemporary public art showplace of Millennium Park and the Paris-inspired walkways of Grant Park, is both intimate and grand, a place where the rooms are human-scale and the art is transcendent.

Come for the sterling collection of Impressionists and Old Masters (an entire room is dedicated to Monet), linger over the extraordinary and comprehensive photography collection, take in a number of fine American works, and discover paintings, drawings, sculpture, design, and photography spanning the ancient to the contemporary world.

The Art Institute is more than just a museum; in fact, it was originally founded by a small group of artists in 1866 as a school with an adjoining exhibition space. Famous alumni include political cartoonist Herblock and artists Grant Wood and Ed Paschke. Walt Disney and Georgia O'Keeffe both took classes, but didn't graduate. The School of the Art Institute of Chicago, one of the finest art schools in the country, is across the street from the museum; occasionally there are lectures and discussions that are open to the public.

ORIENTATION TO THE MUSEUM

✉ 111 S. Michigan Ave., South Loop

☎ 312/443–3600

🌐 www.artic.edu/aic/

🎟 Suggested $12, Students and Seniors $7, Free Thursday 5–8

🕐 Mon.–Wed. and Fri. 10:30–5, Thu. 10:30–8, Sat.–Sun. 10–5

Take in the museum's grandeur.

Photo op: Pose with one of the two bronze lions.

The Art Institute is a complicated jumble of three difficult-to-navigate buildings—you can only change buildings on the first level of the museum, and the map the museum gives out isn't very helpful. Here are some tips to help you find your way around:

■ On the lower level are textiles, decorative arts, the Thorne Miniature Room, and the Kraft Education Center. The first level includes the non-European galleries, contemporary art, and American art to 1890. The second level holds American art from 1900 to 1950, European art from all periods, and Impressionism.

■ Pinpoint the five or six works you'd really like to see or pick two or three galleries and wander around after getting yourself there.

■ Guards expect visitors to ask for directions, so don't be shy.

■ Buy the audio tour ($6) by the coatroom as you enter—it provides descriptions for every gallery and work in the museum. All you do is key in the gallery number and the voices of curators will guide you around the room.

■ Note that a massive construction project, due to be completed in 2009, may cause the temporary closure of some exhibits (including the celebrated Chagall stained glass windows) or the relocation of some galleries.

■ Before your visit, download and listen to free podcasts from the Art Institute web site (www.artic.edu/aic)

FOR THE KIDS

Kids love the Kraft Education Center, which has rotating exhibits of child-friendly art (like paintings from picture books) and a permanent, interactive exhibit called *Faces, Places & Inner Spaces* that helps teach children how to look at different kinds of art. There's also a small stage with Kabuki costumes, actual paintings hung at kid-friendly levels, and computer-enhanced games. Nearby is the Touch Gallery, which was originally designed for the blind. You can run your fingers over several bronze works. For more suggestions, check out *Behind the Lions: A Family Guide to the Art Institute of Chicago*, available at the museum bookstore.

BEST PAINTINGS

AMERICAN GOTHIC (1930). **GALLERY 263**
Grant Wood won $300 for his iconic painting of a solemn farmer and his wife (really his sister and his dentist). Wood saw the work as a celebration of solid, work-based Midwestern values, a statement that rural America would survive the Depression and the massive migration to cities.

American Gothic (1930).

NIGHTHAWKS (1942). **GALLERY 262**
Edward Hopper's painting of four figures in a diner on the corner of a deserted New York street is a noir portrait of isolated lives and is one of the most recognized images of 20th-century art. The red-haired woman is the artist's wife, Jo.

THE CHILD'S BATH (1893). **GALLERY 273**
Mary Cassatt was the only American to become an established Impressionist and her work focused on the daily lives of women and children. In this, her most famous work, a woman gently bathes a child who is tucked up on her lap. The Bath was unconventional when it was painted because the bold patterns and cropped forms it used were more often seen in Japanese prints at the time.

Nighthawks (1942).

SKY ABOVE CLOUDS IV (1965). **GALLERY 249**
(not pictured) Georgia O'Keeffe's massive painting, the largest canvas of her career, is of clouds seen from an airplane. The rows of white rectangles stretching toward the horizon look both solid and ethereal, as if they are stepping stones for angels.

THE OLD GUITARIST (1903/04). **GALLERY 263**
(not pictured) One of the most important works of Pablo Picasso's Blue Period, this monochromatic painting is a study of the crooked figure of a blind and destitute street guitarist, singing sorrowfully. When he painted it, Picasso was feeling particularly empathetic toward the downtrodden—perhaps because of a friend's suicide—and the image of the guitarist is one of dignity amid poverty.

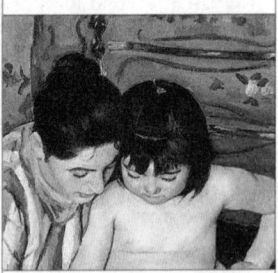
The Child's Bath (1893).

GRAINSTACK (1890/91). **GALLERY 206**
The Art Institute has the largest collection of Monet's Grainstacks in the world. The stacks rose 15 to 20 feet tall outside Monet's farmhouse in Giverny and were a symbol to the artist of sustenance and survival.

Grainstack (1890/91)

A SUNDAY ON LA GRANDE JATTE 1884 (1884-86). GALLERY 205

Georges Seurat's greatest work has inspired generations of painters and even spawned a musical—Stephen Sondheim's *Sunday in the Park with George*. A precise pattern of tiny dots creates a scene of mixed-class serenity in Paris, with rounded figures of soldiers, genteel women, children, and a monkey.

SELF-PORTRAIT (1887). GALLERY 205

Twenty-four self portraits were painted by Vincent Van Gogh, and this early example is an expressive picture made up of colorful dots and dashes. The artist's intense eyes gaze directly into yours, inviting you into his soul.

A Sunday on La Grande Jatte 1884 (1884–86).

OTHER DON'T-MISS EXHIBITS

Self-Portrait (1887).

PAPERWEIGHT COLLECTION. GALLERY 69

In the mid-nineteenth century, a newly dependable mail service made writing implements and desk accessories chic—including glass paperweights. The Art Institute's famous Arthur Rubloff Collection houses over 1,400 of these surprisingly intricate paperweights, with examples from all periods, techniques, designs, and manufacturers.

STOCK EXCHANGE TRADING ROOM.

Architects Louis Sullivan and Dankmar Adler used art glass and stenciled decorations to build a glorious trading room for the Chicago Stock Exchange. Though the Exchange was demolished in 1972, it's recreated here with pieces from the original.

TADAO ANDO. GALLERY 109

Many visitors miss this serene room of pottery and painted screens, half hidden behind a closed glass door in the Asian galleries on the first floor. The room, designed by Japanese architect and artist Tadao Ando, is notable for its rows of large wooden columns; Ando said he wanted viewers to "feel as if the wind is passing through."

THORNE MINIATURE ROOMS. GALLERY 11

Sixty-eight tiny rooms showcase interior design and decorative arts from the 13th century to 1940. Master craftsmen built them (1932–1940) for Mrs. James Ward Thorne to a scale of one inch to one foot. The rooms look like dollhouses.

Paperweight collection.

Thorne Miniature Rooms.

ADLER PLANETARIUM & ASTRONOMY MUSEUM

✉ 1300 S. Lake Shore Dr., South Loop

☎ 312/922–7827

⊕ www.adlerplanetarium.org

✉ $19 museum admission and 1 show, $23 museum admission and 2 shows. Free Mon. and Tues. Jan., Feb., Oct., and Nov. Discount weeks throughout the year

☉ 9:30 AM–4:30 PM (except 1st Fri. of month, when open until 10 PM); summer hours 9:30 AM–6 PM (except 1st Fri. of mont,h when open until 10 PM).

TIPS

 Additional charges apply for the Sky Theater planetarium shows and the Star-Rider interactive shows (*see admission prices, above*), but don't skip them—they're the reason to go.

■ Take a quick (free) ride in the Atwood Sphere, a large metal globe with punched-out stars. It provided the nation's very first planetarium experience.

■ No need to purchase the museum's audio tour. The signs in the museum are comprehensive, and the narrative doesn't add much to the experience.

■ 2–3 PM daily, the museum's Space Visualization Lab (a working laboratory where scientists, technicians, and artists drum up new ways to explore the universe) is open to the public.

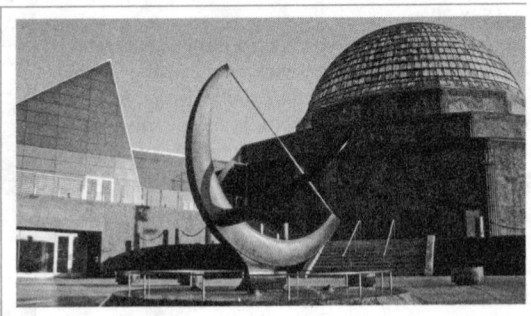

Navigate your way through the solar system with interactive and state-of-the-art exhibits that appeal to planetarium traditionalists as well as technology-savvy kids and adults. The museum uses computer games, videos, short films, and hands-on devices to teach physics and astronomy basics like the Doppler effect. Two different planetariums and a new 3-D theater unlock the mysteries of the stars.

HIGHLIGHTS

The Adler's traditional in-the-round Zeiss planetarium (called the Sky Theater) shows constellations and planets in the night sky. It's been around since the Adler opened in 1930 as the first public planetarium in the Western Hemisphere.

Peer through Chicago's largest public telescope at the Duane Observatory, located outside of and behind the main museum building. It gathers 5,000 times more light than the human eye, so filters are used to reduce the brilliant glare of the Moon.

See the restored Gemini 12, the spacecraft flown by Captain Jim Lovell and Buzz Aldrin in 1966, in the permanent exhibit "Shoot for the Moon." A collection of space artifacts once owned by Lovell is also on exhibit.

Take a digital journey into space on the interactive Star-Rider Theater, inside the high-tech Sky Pavilion. For some shows you use control buttons on your armrest to vote for what you see on screen. (Part of the technology is based on aircraft flight simulators.) Other shows wrap you in a 3-D universe of stars.

CHICAGO CHILDREN'S MUSEUM

✉ Navy Pier, 700 E. Grand Ave., Near North

☎ 312/527–1000

⊕ www.chichildrensmuseum.org

🎫 $9, free Thurs. 5–8 PM and 1st Mon. of the month for children 15 and younger

🕐 Sun.–Wed. and Fri. 10 AM–5 PM, Thurs. and Sat. 10 AM–8 PM.

3

TIPS

■ The museum issues readmission bracelets that let you leave the museum and come back on the same day—great idea for weary families that want to take a break to get a bite to eat, or simply explore other parts of Navy Pier before coming back to the museum.

■ Grab a bite at the nearby space-themed McDonald's (☎ 312/832–1640) or bring a picnic and grab a sunny seat outside (in warm weather) or gather in the Crystal Ballroom (amid tropical plants and fountains).

■ Most families spend an average of three hours visiting the museum.

■ Hour-long art workshops at Artabounds are free.

■ The museum is designed for children 2 to 12 years.

■ Adults may not enter the museum without a child.

■ Try each of the artist-created benches to figure out which one makes music when you sit on it.

"Hands-on" is the operative concept for this brightly colored Navy Pier anchor. Kids play educational video games, climb through multilevel tunnels, run their own TV stations, and, if their parents allow it, get soaking wet.

HIGHLIGHTS

Kids can don raincoats before they start splashing around in the WaterWays exhibit, which has oversize water tubs with waterwheels, pumps, brightly colored pipes, and splashing fountains. If everyone pumps hard enough, water squirts 50 feet into the air.

In the Big Backyard exhibit, children "shrink" to the size of bugs amid giant giggling flowers. Butterflies seem to flutter around their bodies and water appears to splash down on their heads, all through the magic of a tall video screen.

Parents, get ready for a workout. You and your children can scurry up a three-story-high rigging complete with crow's nest and gangplank on the Kovler Family Climbing Schooner. It's reminiscent of the boats that once sailed Lake Michigan. If you make it to the rope tunnels at the top, you can take in bird's-eye views of the museum, then slide back down to the lower level, where there are tanks of fish.

Crouch beside your child to search for fossils in Dinosaur Expedition. Brush away dirt to discover the bones of a Suchomimus, a kind of fish-eating dinosaur that's on display nearby. The exhibit re-creates a trip to the Sahara led by University of Chicago paleontologist Paul Sereno.

Collaboration is the watchword at Artabounds Gallery, where kids participate in rotating group art projects that include activities like creating a castle out of clay.

FIELD MUSEUM

✉ 1400 S. Lake Shore Dr., South Loop

☎ 312/922–9410

🌐 www.fieldmuseum.org

🎫 $14

🕓 Daily 9 AM–5 PM; last admission at 4 PM.

TIPS

■ Don't hesitate to take toddlers to the Field; the new Crown Family PlayLab, designed for kids 2–6 years old, is where they play house in a faux pueblo, sort objects by shape and color, and compare their footprints to a dinosaur's.

■ It's impossible to see the entire museum in one visit. Try to get tickets to the special exhibit of the season (go to the Web site if you'd like to order in advance) and then choose a couple of subjects you'd like to explore, like North American birds or Chinese jade.

■ The Sue Store sells a mind-boggling assortment of dinosaur-related merchandise.

■ Bring young ones to 20-minute story times, when staff and volunteers read a dinosaur-themed book and direct an art project (weekends year-round and daily July and August).

■ The lobby of the museum includes the Corner Bakery. The dining room tucked in the back has sparkling views of the lake and the Museum Campus.

★ More than 6 *acres* of exhibits fill this gigantic world-class museum, which explores cultures and environments from around the world. Interactive exhibits examine such topics as the secrets of Egyptian mummies, the people of Africa and the Pacific Northwest, and the living creatures in the soil. Originally funded by Chicago retailer Marshall Field, the museum was founded in 1893 to hold material gathered for the World's Columbian Exposition; its current classical-style home opened in 1921.

HIGHLIGHTS

Shrink to the size of a bug to burrow beneath the surface of the soil in the Underground Adventure exhibit ($8 extra). You'll come face-to-face with a giant, animatronic wolf spider twice your size, listen to the sounds of gnawing insects, and have other encounters with the life that teems under our feet.

Spend a couple hours taking in contemporary and ancient Africa. Dioramas let you feel like you're stepping inside the homes and lives of Africans from Senegal, Cameroon, and the Sahara, while the remarkable Inside Ancient Egypt complex includes a working canal, a living marsh where papyrus is grown, a shrine to the cat goddess Bastet, burial-ceremony artifacts, and 23 mummies.

The Field's dinosaur collection is one of the world's best. You can't miss 65-million-year-old "Sue," the largest and most complete *Tyrannosaurus rex* fossil ever found—it's on permanent exhibit in the lobby. Also visit the McDonald's Fossil Preparation Laboratory, where you can watch paleontologists cleaning up bones. Another favorite is the Evolving Planet, which uses video technology to explain the dawn of single-cell organisms and the advent of dinosaurs.

MUSEUM OF CONTEMPORARY ART

✉ 220 E. Chicago Ave., Near North

☎ 312/280–2660

🌐 www.mcachicago.org

🎫 $10, free Tues.

🕙 Tues. 10 AM–8 PM, Wed.–Sun. 10 AM–5 PM.

TIPS

■ The back of the MCA is one of the best spots to have lunch or Sunday brunch in the city. Run by Wolfgang Puck and called Puck's Café at the MCA, it not only has a tasty menu, but overlooks gardens, a park, and street life.

■ Try to catch one of the cutting-edge music and theater performances; one year, for example, the entire front of the museum was turned into a puppet theater. Check the Web site for more information.

■ In summer come for Tuesdays on the Terrace and be serenaded by local jazz bands. There's a cash bar from 5:30 to 8 PM and a full menu at the café.

■ On the first Friday of every month the museum hosts a party ($15) with live music and hors d'oeuvres from 6 PM to 10 PM.

■ A farmers' market sets up shop on Tuesday from mid-June through October. Pick up fresh snacks and enjoy a picnic in the museum's back-yard (free-admission) sculpture garden.

★ **Fodor's Choice** A group of art patrons who felt the great Art Institute was unresponsive to modern work founded the MCA in 1967, and it's remained a renegade art museum ever since. It doesn't have any permanent exhibits; even the works from its collection are constantly rotating. This gives it a feeling of freshness, but it also makes it impossible to predict what will be on display at any time. Special exhibits are devoted mostly to original shows you can't see anywhere else.

HIGHLIGHTS

The MCA's dramatic quarters were designed by Berlin architect Josef Paul Kleihues. From the outside, the building looks like a home for modern art—it's made of square metal plates, with round bolts in each corner.

The MCA's growing 7,000-piece collection, which includes work by René Magritte, Alexander Calder, Bruce Nauman, Sol LeWitt, Franz Kline, and June Leaf, makes up about half the museum (pieces on view continually rotate). The other half is dedicated to temporary exhibitions.

The museum showcases work in all mediums, including paintings, sculpture, works on paper, photography, video, film, and installations.

Guided "Exhibition Focus" tours dedicated to short-run exhibits happen daily; "Highlights Tours," which provide a balanced sweep of the entire museum, are offered on weekends.

The MCA Store is the place to go for well-designed jewelry and items for the home, from a porcelain eggshell from which a flower sprouts to a clock with a face that's a psychedelic swirl of color.

MUSEUM OF SCIENCE AND INDUSTRY

✉ 5700 S. Lake Shore Dr., Hyde Park

☎ 773/684-1414

🌐 www.msichicago.org

🎫 $13; museum and Omnimax admission $20; parking $14

🕐 Memorial Day–Labor Day, Mon.–Sat. 9:30–5:30, Sun. 11–5:30; Labor Day–Memorial Day, Mon.–Sat. 9:30–4, Sun. 11–4.

TIPS

■ Use the museum map to plan out your visit. Your best bet is to hit a couple of highlights (the U-boat tour alone will take at least an hour) and then see a couple of quirky exhibits.

■ If the kids get grouchy, bring them to the Idea Factory, a giant playroom where they can play with water cannons, blocks, and cranks. Limited to ages 10 and younger.

■ Relax with some ice cream in the old-fashioned ice-cream parlor, tucked away in a genteel re-creation of an Illinois main street.

■ On nice days, hordes of sunbathers and kite-flyers camp out on the giant lawn out front—it's almost as entertaining as the museum itself. Lake Michigan is across the street.

■ The museum has free-admission days, but the schedule changes often. Check the Web site for details.

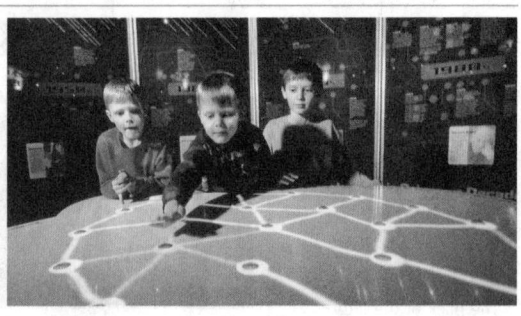

★ Fodor's Choice The beloved MSI is one of the most visited sites in Chicago, and for good reason. The sprawling open space has 2,000 exhibits on three floors, with new exhibits being added constantly. The museum's high-tech interior is hidden by the Classical Revival exterior; it was designed in 1892 by D.H. Burnham & Company as a temporary structure to house the Palace of Fine Arts for the World's Columbian Exposition. It's the fair's only surviving building. On a nice day, take a walk behind the museum to the beautifully landscaped Jackson Park and its tucked-away Osaka Garden, a Japanese-style garden with a peaceful waterfall.

HIGHLIGHTS

Descend into the depths of a simulated coal mine on a "miner"-led tour that explores the technology behind digging energy out of the ground.

Get a close-up view of a plane's flaps and wheels as a cantilevered Boeing 727 "takes off" above visitors every hour. Former United pilots explain what's going on to those sitting inside the jet as the airplane flaps raise and lower and the wheels retract.

The opulent and detailed-as-a-film-set Fairy Castle (really a giant dollhouse) has tiny chandeliers that flash with real diamonds and floors that are laid with intricate stone patterns. It's enough to make us daydream about what the world's fairy-tale characters might have lived in.

Tour the cramped quarters of the only U-505 German submarine captured during World War II (there's an additional fee). Don't feel like waiting in line? Explore just the free interactive exhibits surrounding the sub, which give stunning insight into the strategy behind the war at sea.

Learn how scientists can make frogs' eyes glow or watch baby chicks tap themselves out of their shells at the "Genetics–Decoding Life" exhibit.

JOHN G. SHEDD AQUARIUM

✉ 1200 S. Lake Shore Dr., South Loop

☎ 312/939–2438

🌐 www.sheddaquarium.org

🎟 $27.50 all-access pass

🕙 Memorial Day–Labor Day, daily 9–6, Thurs. until 10; Labor Day–Memorial Day, weekdays 9–5, weekends 9–6.

3

TIPS

■ Catch live jazz on the Shedd's north terrace on Thursday evenings from 5 to 10 PM June through August. A gorgeous view of the lake and skyline can make for a magical night. Food and a bar are available.

■ Lines for the Shedd often extend all the way down the neoclassical steps. Buy a ticket in advance to avoid the interminable wait, or spring for a CityPass.

■ Soundings restaurant is an elegant stop for lunch. The menu is pricey, but the quiet tables look over Lake Michigan—and there are very few Chicago eateries that can say that.

■ Discount admission days are offered throughout the year. Check the Web site for updates.

★ **Fodor's Choice** Take a plunge into an underwater world at the world's largest indoor aquarium. Built in 1930, the Shedd is one of the most popular aquariums in the country, housing more than 8,000 aquatic animals in realistic waterscapes.

HIGHLIGHTS

"Amazon Rising" gives you an up-close look at the animals of the Amazon River, including piranhas, snakes, and stingrays. The 8,600-square-foot exhibit, designed to resemble a flooded forest, re-creates the rise and fall of floodwaters so visitors can see how animals respond.

Sharks swim by in their 400,000-gallon tank as part of the permanent exhibit "Wild Reef," which explores the marine biodiversity and coral reefs in the Indo-Pacific. Wild Reef also has colorful corals, stingrays that slide by under your feet, and other surprising creatures, all from the waters around the Philippines.

Stare down one of the knobby-headed beluga whales (they love to people-watch), observe Pacific white-sided dolphins at play, and explore the simulated Pacific Northwest nature trail in the spectacular Oceanarium, which has pools that seem to blend into Lake Michigan. We like the daily educational dolphin presentation. Be sure to get an underwater glimpse of the dolphins and whales through the viewing windows on the lower level, where you can also find a bunch of information-packed, hands-on activities.

In the 90,000-gallon Caribbean Reef exhibit in the main building, sharks, stingrays, a sea turtle, and other denizens of the deep dart around. It's most fun to observe when divers swim within, feeding the animals and talking to the crowd gathered outside.

OTHER MUSEUMS

Sometimes the best museums are ones that you can see in an hour or less. We like Chicago's smaller museums for the unexpected, interesting, and simply fun things you can find. Some of them highlight the diverse origins that built the city; others dedicate their space to history, archaeology, or specific types of art.

FOR HIDDEN GEMS
Balzekas Museum of Lithuanian Culture. Though many of the people who come here do so for research (the museum is a large repository for genealogical information), the Balzekas has a stunning collection of Lithuanian amber. Other exhibits—armor, rare maps, stamps, and coins—chronicle Lithuanian history. ⊠ *6500 S. Pulaski Rd., Englewood* ☎ *773/582–6500* 🔖 *$5, free Mon.* 🕙 *Daily 10–4.*

WINDY CITY HISTORY
★
Chicago History Museum. The museum went through a major rehaul in late 2006 when it changed its name from the Chicago Historical Society in honor of its 150th birthday. The new permanent sights include a Costume and Textile Gallery and the exhibit entitled "Chicago: Crossroads of America," which demystifies historic tragedies like the Great Chicago Fire and Haymarket Affair. ⊠ *1601 N. Clark St., Lincoln Park* ☎ *312/642–4600* ⊕ *www.chicagohistory.org* 🔖 *$14, Mon. free* 🕙 *Mon.–Wed., Fri., and Sat. 9:30–4:30, Thurs. 9:30–8, Sun. noon–5.*

David and Alfred Smart Museum of Art. If you want to see art masterpieces but don't want to spend a long day wandering one of the major art museums, the Smart may be just your speed. The diverse, 10,000-piece permanent collection includes works by old masters; photographs by Walker Evans; furniture by Frank Lloyd Wright; sculptures by Degas, Matisse, Rodin, and Henry Moore. Temporary exhibits are a great way to see startlingly good art in a smaller, intimate space. ⊠ *5550 S. Greenwood Ave., Hyde Park* ☎ *773/702–0200* ⊕ *www.smartmuseum. uchicago.edu* 🔖 *Free* 🕙 *Tues., Wed., and Fri. 10–4, Thurs. 10–8, weekends 11–5.*

DuSable Museum of African-American History. The DuSable is a colorful—and haunting—exploration of the African-American experience, set alongside the lagoons of Washington Park. There are handwritten lyric sheets from Motown greats, letters and memorabilia of scholar W. E. B. DuBois and poet Langston Hughes, and a significant African-American art collection. The most moving exhibit is one on slavery; the poignant, disturbing artifacts include rusted shackles used on slave ships. ⊠ *740 E. 56th Pl., Hyde Park* ☎ *773/947–0600* ⊕ *www.dusablemuseum.org* 🔖 *$3, free Sun.* 🕙 *Tues.–Sat. 10–5, Sun. noon–5.*

Jane Addams Hull-House Museum. The redbrick Victorian Hull House was the birthplace of social work.. Social welfare pioneers and peace advocates Jane Addams and Ellen Gates Starr started the American settlement house movement in this house in 1889 and wrought near miracles in their surrounding community, which was then a slum for new immigrants. Pictures and letters add context to the two museum buildings, which re-create the homey setting the residents experienced.

> ## QUIET SPACES
>
> **North Terrace, Shedd Aquarium.** The entire aquarium is mesmerizing; you might find yourself staring at placidly swimming fish for hours without getting bored. But for a truly peaceful experience during mild weather, push through the doors of the North Terrace and sit at a table overlooking Lake Michigan and the city skyline. The terrace is usually deserted even on the busiest summer days.
>
> **Mammal dioramas, Field Museum.** Few visitors linger amid the long, darkened hallways of the North American mammal dioramas. Take a seat on a curved wooden bench and you won't be disturbed—unless the sight of stuffed and mounted bears and buffalo makes you queasy.
>
> **Main Street theater and Jackson Park, Museum of Science and Industry.** Olde Chicago is re-created in a corner of the MSI, complete with cobblestones and iron lamps. At the end of the street is a small theater showing silent shorts of Buster Keaton. If you'd rather be in the sunshine, take a walk around Jackson Park's lagoons and bridges behind the museum, one of the most peaceful—and overlooked—spots in all of Chicago.

✉ *800 S. Halsted St., University Village* ☎ *312/413–5353* ⊕ *www.uic. edu/jaddams/hull* ▣ *Free* ⊙ *Tues.–Fri. 10–4, Sun. noon–4.*

IF YOU ONLY HAVE TIME FOR ONE ★ **National Museum of Mexican Art.** Formerly the Mexican Fine Arts Museum Center, this sparkling site, the largest Latino museum in the country, is half art museum, half cultural exploration. After the big downtown museums, this is the one you shouldn't miss. Galleries house impressive collections of contemporary, traditional, and meso-American art from both sides of the border, as well as vivid exhibits that trace immigration woes and political fights. Every fall, the giant Day of the Dead exhibit stuns Chicagoans with its altars from artists across the country. ✉ *1852 W. 19th St., Pilsen* ☎ *312/738–1503* ⊕ *www.national museumofmexicanart.org* ▣ *Free* ⊙ *Tues.–Sun. 10–5.*

McCormick Tribune Freedom Museum. This bi-level museum dedicated to the First Amendment and the rights it describes is located, fittingly, next door to Tribune Tower, office of the Chicago Tribune (the museum is a non-profit entity of the daily paper). Inside you'll find plasma touch-screens that allow you to zoom in on electronic versions of important documents, such as the Constitution and Bill of Rights, and decipher their passages. Use headsets at the "Voices of Freedom" exhibit to hear discourses by big-time politicos like Thomas Jefferson and John Adams. The whole concept feels middle-school field trip–like, but the high-tech, interactive experiences keep things interesting. ✉ *435 N. Michigan Ave., Downtown* ☎ *312/222–4860* ⊕ *www.freedommuseum. us* ▣ *Free* ⊙ *Wed.–Mon. 10–6.*

Museum of Contemporary Photography. "Contemporary" is defined here as anything after 1936. More than 7,000 works from American-born and American-resident photographers make this an impressive collection. Don't-miss works include exhibits by Dorothea Lange, Ansel

The Local Art Scene

You don't need to be an art expert to explore the city's growing web of local neighborhood galleries. Just do as locals do and ready yourself with a free copy of *The Chicago Reader*, which has gallery and exhibition listings (available in many street dispensers, coffee shops, and record stores), or grab the *Chicago Gallery News* (or check it out on the Web at ⊕ *www.chicagogallerynews.com*)—it's the best source for maps, gallery information, and exhibition listings. Most galleries provide complimentary copies.

Here's the skinny: Chicago is divided into gallery "districts," or communities. They each have their own feel and flavor. Stop by anytime during gallery hours—no need to make an appointment—even if you're just browsing. Gallery directors and staff are always available to answer questions or provide further information on their artists.

RIVER NORTH DISTRICT
The city's first organized art neighborhood remains a vibrant community and the hub of the gallery scene.

Zolla/Lieberman (*contemporary multimedia* ⊠ *325 W. Huron St.* ☎ *312/944–1990*).

Roy Boyd (*contemporary painting and sculpture* ⊠ *739 N. Wells St.* ☎ *312/642–1606*).

Carl Hammer (*American folk and outsider art* ⊠ *740 N. Wells St.* ☎ *312/266–8512*).

Ann Nathan Gallery (*contemporary painting and sculpture* ⊠ *212 W. Superior St.* ☎ *312/664–6622*).

Stephen Daiter Gallery (*vintage black-and-white photography* ⊠ *311 W. Superior St.* ☎ *312/787–3350*).

WEST LOOP DISTRICT
Lots of galleries have opened in multilevel warehouses on Randolph Street and throughout the rest of the neighborhood.

Packer Schopf Gallery (*emerging and mid-career artists* ⊠ *942 W. Lake St.* ☎ *312/226–8984*).

Rhona Hoffman (*established and emerging contemporary artists* ⊠ *118 N. Peoria St.* ☎ *312/455–1990*).

Donald Young Gallery (*local and international contemporary art* ⊠ *933 W. Washington Blvd.* ☎ *312/455–0100*).

EAST PILSEN DISTRICT
Most artists live in their galleries in this district south and west of the Loop, and the line between reality and fantasy is often outrageously blurred.

4ArtInc. (*contemporary, artist-run* ⊠ *1932 S. Halsted St.* ☎ *312/850–1816*) and **Dubhe Carreño Gallery** (*contemporary ceramic art* ⊠ *1841 S. Halsted St.* ☎ *312/666–3150*).

WICKER PARK/BUCKTOWN
The area is home to a respectable chunk of the city's artists, but most show their work privately or in independent group shows. You can still see artists' studios if you wander around the **Flat Iron Building** (⊠ *1714 N. Damen Ave.*). Check out **Pagoda Red** (*Chinese and Tibetan art objects* ⊠ *1714 N. Damen Ave.* ☎ *773/235–1188*).

Adams, and Nicholas Nixon. Curators constantly seek out new talent and under-appreciated established photographers, which means that there are artists here you probably won't see elsewhere. Rotating exhibits have included photojournalism and scientific photography. ⊠*600 S. Michigan Ave., South Loop* ☎*312/663–5554* ⊕*www. mocp.org* ⊠*Free* ⊗*Mon.–Wed., Fri., and Sat. 10–5, Thurs. 10–8, Sun. noon–5.*

Museum of Holography. Holography seems almost quaint in our age of 3-D digital renderings. Still, it's fun to spend an hour walking from side to side in front of these glowing, three-dimensional, laser-etched portraits and pictures. ⊠*1134 W. Washington Blvd., West Loop* ☎*312/226–1007* ⊕*www.holographic center.com* ⊠*$4* ⊗*Wed.–Sun. 12:30–5.*

> ### ARTSY FESTIVALS
>
> **VISION** (☎ *312/649–0065* ⊕ *www.chicagoartdealers.org*) is a cool summertime art fest in its 13th year. Opening night is always a madhouse, with crowds spilling out of gallery doors onto the sidewalk, but things settle down in the following weeks for gallery tours and talks. Wicker Park/Bucktown throws a biannual festival called **Around the Coyote** (☎ *773/342–6777* ⊕ *www.aroundthecoyote.org*), with exhibitions and performance art taking place in and around the Flat Iron Building.

National Vietnam Veterans Art Museum. The chimelike sounds of more than 58,000 imprinted dog tags hanging from the ceiling entranceway are a melancholy memorial to the soldiers who lost their lives in the unpopular war. Take in the visual journal of the experiences of more than 122 artists who served in Vietnam through the 1,000-plus pieces of art on display here. ⊠*1801 S. Indiana Ave., South Loop* ☎*312/326–0270* ⊕*www.nvvam.org* ⊠*$10, free to service members* ⊗*Tues.–Fri. 11–6, Sat. 10–5.*

★ **Oriental Institute.** This gem began with artifacts collected by University of Chicago archaeologists in the 1930s (one is rumored to have been the model for Indiana Jones) and has expanded into an interesting, informative museum with a jaw-dropping collection from the ancient Near East, including the largest U.S. collection of Iraqi antiquities. There are amulets, mummies, limestone reliefs, gold jewelry, ivories, pottery, and bronzes from the 4th millennium BC through the 13th century AD. You won't be able to miss the 17-foot-tall statue of King Tut, excavated from the ruins of a temple in western Thebes in 1930. ⊠*1155 E. 58th St., Hyde Park* ☎*773/702–9520* ⊕*www.oi.uchicago.edu* ⊠*Free* ⊗*Tues. and Thurs.–Sat. 10–6, Wed. 10–8:30, Sun. noon–6.*

★ **Peggy Notebaert Nature Museum.** Walk among hundreds of Midwest species of butterflies and learn about the impact of rivers and lakes on daily life at this modern museum washed in natural light. Like Chicago's other science museums, it's geared to kids, with educational computer games to play and water turbines to control. But even jaded adults will be excited when bright yellow butterflies land on their shoulders. The idea is to study nature inside without forgetting graceful Lincoln

Park outside. ✉*2430 N. Cannon Dr., Lincoln Park* ☎*773/755–5100* ⊕*www.naturemuseum.org* ✆*$9, free Thurs.* ◷*Weekdays 9–4:30, weekends 10–5.*

Polish Museum of America. Chicago has the largest Polish population of any city outside Warsaw, and this museum in Ukrainian Village, just south of Wicker Park, celebrates that fact. Take a trip to the old country by strolling through exhibits of folk costumes, memorabilia from Pope John Paul II, Hussar armor, American Revolutionary War heroes Tadeusz Kosciuszko and Casimir Pulaski, pianist and composer Ignacy Paderewski, and an 8-foot-long sleigh in the shape of a dolphin that's carved from a single log. It's also a good place to catch up on your reading; the library has 60,000 volumes. ✉*984 N. Milwaukee Ave., Wicker Park* ☎*773/384–3352* ⊕*www.polishmuseumofamerica. org* ✆*$5* ◷*Fri.–Wed. 11–4.*

Spertus Museum. This museum addresses an intellectual puzzle: what does it mean to be Jewish in the modern world? Contemporary and traditional art and ritual objects illustrate daily life; a sobering Holocaust memorial with many photos and a tattered concentration camp uniform remind us to remember. The museum recently reopened in a stunning new location on the same block. ✉*618 S. Michigan Ave., South Loop* ☎*312/322–1747* ⊕*www.spertus.edu* ✆*$7* ◷*Sun.– Wed. 10–6, Thurs. 10–7, Fri. 10–3.*

★ **Swedish American Museum Center.** Though this tiny and welcoming museum does have changing exhibits that focus on the art and culture of Sweden, you don't have to be Swedish to find it interesting—much of the museum focuses on the immigrant experience. On permanent display, for example, are trunks immigrants brought with them to Chicago, and a map showing where in the city different immigrant groups settled. On the third floor, in the only children's museum in the country dedicated to immigration, kids can climb aboard a colorful Viking ship or "milk" a wooden cow, pulling rubber udders to collect streams of water in a bucket. ✉*5211 N. Clark St., Far North Side* ☎*773/728– 8111* ⊕*www.samac.org* ✆*$4, free 2nd Tues. of month* ◷*Tues.–Fri. 10–4, weekends 11–4.*

Ukrainian Institute of Modern Art. Modern and contemporary art fans head out to this small museum at the far western edge of the Ukrainian Village, near Wicker Park. Three permanent galleries feature mixed media, sculpture, painting, and even some digital art. Some of the most interesting works are abstract or playful versions of old-world themes, like Evan Prokopov's 1998 abstract bronze of a mother cradling her child. ✉*2320 W. Chicago Ave., Wicker Park* ☎*773/227–5522* ⊕*www.uima-art.org* ✆*Free* ◷*Wed.–Sun. noon–4.*

Architecture

WORD OF MOUTH

"We recently took the CAF river-only tour and loved it. Chicago architecture is amazing, and it's just fun to see it from the 'other side.'"

—dmlove

ARCHITECTURE PLANNER

In a Chicago Mood

Chicago has long been known as America's Second City, but as a visit here makes clear, this is no burg. A metropolis if there ever was one, Chicago hums with activity while its lakeside location lends a relaxed, breezy ambience. A great way to take advantage of this intermingling is to sit for a spell in Millennium Park or Grant Park and enjoy the march of buildings up Michigan Avenue. Known to some as the "Michigan Avenue Cliff," this stretch just west of the parks comprises a slew of noteworthy structures.

Good Reads

Architecture geeks won't need much introduction to the city's architectural history, but if you don't count yourself among that special breed, you might pick up *Chicago Architecture and Design*, a beautifully illustrated book with a good perspective by George A. Larson and Jay Pridmore. For a more in-depth yet highly readable study of some of the big names who worked here, check out Peter Blake's *The Master Builders*. And if you don't mind a bit of murder with your history lesson, there's Erik Larson's magnificent *The Devil in the White City*.

Walking Tours

The Chicago Architecture Foundation gives expertly guided tours. Chicago Greeter and InstaGreeter are free city services that match savvy Chicagoans with visitors for neighborhood tours. Friends of the Chicago River leads Saturday-morning tours during the warmer months.

Contacts **Chicago Architecture Foundation** (✉ *Santa Fe Bldg., 224 S. Michigan Ave.* ☎ *312/922–3432* ⊕ *www. architecture.org*). **Chicago Greeter/InstaGreeter** (✉ *Visitor Information Center at Chicago Cultural Center, 77 E. Randolph St.* ☎ *312/744–8000* ⊕ *www.chicagogreeter.com*). **Friends of the Chicago River** (✉ *40728 E. Jackson, Suite 1800* ☎ *312/939–0490* ⊕ *www.chicagoriver.org*).

Bus & Trolley Tours

A bus or trolley tour is a fun way to enjoy Chicago's architecture. Tours cost roughly $25 and last two hours or more.

Contacts **Gray Line Tours** (☎ *800/621–4153* ⊕ *www. grayline.com*). **Chicago Architecture Foundation** *(See Walking Tours)*. **Chicago Trolley and Double Decker Co.** (☎ *773/648–5000* ⊕ *www.chicagotrolley.com*).

Boat Tours

The Chicago Architecture Foundation river tour is the most authoritative ($28 weekdays; $30 on weekends and holidays). You can purchase tickets at the Chicago ArchiCenter, 224 South Michigan Avenue, or through Ticketmaster at 312/902–1500 or www.ticketmaster.com. The boat-tour season runs from the end of April to mid-November—always call ahead. Other options include:

Mercury Chicago Skyline Cruiseline (☎ *312/332–1353* ⊕ *www.mercuryskylinecruiseline.com*). **MetroDucks** (☎ *800/298–1506* ⊕ *www.metroducks.com*). **Shoreline Sightseeing** (☎ *312/222–9328* ⊕ *www.shorelinesightseeing.com*). **Wendella Sightseeing Boats** (✉ *400 N. Michigan Ave.* ☎ *312/337–1446* ⊕ *www.wendellaboats. com*). **Windy of Chicago Ltd** (☎ *312/595–5555* ⊕ *www. tallshipwindy.com*).

Updated
by Roberta
Sotonoff

Every great city has great buildings, but Chicago *is* its great
buildings. Art, culture, food, and diversion are all part of
the picture here, but everything Chicagoans do is framed
by some of the most remarkable architecture to be found
anywhere. From the sky-scraping of its tall towers to the
horizontal sweep of the Prairie School, Chicago's built environment is second to none.

DECISIONS, DECISIONS, DECISIONS

Even if you're pressed for time, you can't leave town without seeing
a few of the city's important buildings. The lovely **Reliance Building** on
State Street (home to trendy Hotel Burnham) is steps away from the
Harold Washington Library and just blocks from the Art Institute and
Millennium Park. Mies van der Rohe's **860–880 North Lake Shore Drive**
buildings are right on the lake and not too far from high-end shopping
on the Magnificent Mile.

With so many significant skyscrapers packed into the Loop, it's tough
to elevate any one above the rest. When it comes to early buildings,
the **Rookery** is hard to beat. Looking like an impenetrable terra-cotta
mass from the street, its heart is a graceful, covered court done up by
Frank Lloyd Wright. And no matter how much you may dislike modern
architecture, the **Inland Steel Building** is a beauty. Also worth a visit is
the dizzying atrium of the squat **James R. Thompson Center,** a bold inter-
pretation of a public building. Finally, for a swanky Art Deco number,
stop by the **Carbide and Carbon Building,** home to the Hard Rock Hotel
Chicago.

A TALL ORDER

If you came looking for tall buildings, Chicago certainly won't let you
down. Among the tallest are the famous **Sears Tower,** with its 103rd-
floor observatory (on clear days you can see four states); the instantly
recognizable **John Hancock Center,** with its crisscross braces and two
huge antennae (not to mention a showy bar and restaurant on the
95th floor); and the formidable **Aon Center,** which towers over Millen-

nium Park. And no building proclaims its sky-scraping ambition quite like **311 South Wacker Drive**, whose Gothic crown is ablaze with light at night.

IT'S WORTH THE TRIP

Nearby **Oak Park** is Frank Lloyd Wright's old stomping ground. The leafy community is chock-full of his work, from early examples of Prairie style to a fascinating Unitarian church. A visit to **Glessner House**— H. H. Richardson's 1887 masterpiece in the Prairie Avenue Historic District—offers the voyeuristic appeal of poking through a great home. It's enough to motivate even those who don't know an I-beam from a flying buttress.

THE LOOP

Defined by the El (the elevated train that makes a circuit around the area), the Loop is Chicago at its big-city best. A hub of retail, cultural, financial, and governmental activity, it's also home to the city's most notable skyscrapers. Ambitious walkers can cover a good part of the Loop and the surrounding areas in a day, but even a relatively short stroll will reveal some top sites.

HISTORIC BUILDINGS

★ **Auditorium Building.** Hunkered down across from Grant Park, this 110,000-ton granite-and-limestone behemoth was an instant star when it debuted in 1889, boasting a 400-room hotel, offices, and a 4,300-seat theater. It didn't hurt the careers of its designers, Dankmar Adler and Louis H. Sullivan, either. The state-of-the-art theater included electric lighting and an air-conditioning system that used 15 tons of ice per day. Adler managed the engineering—the theater's

FINDING FACTS

For more information about the city's architectural treasures, contact the Chicago Architecture Foundation at 312/922–8687 or 312/922–3432 (online at ⊕ *www. architecture.org*) or the Chicago Convention and Tourism Bureau at 312/567–8500 (online at ⊕ *www. choosechicago.com/architecture. html*).

acoustics are renowned—while Sullivan ornamented the space using mosaics, cast iron, art glass, wood, and plaster. During World War II the building was conscripted for use as a Servicemen's Center. Then Roosevelt University moved in. Thanks to Herculean restoration efforts, the theater—rechristened as the Auditorium Theatre of Roosevelt University—is once again one of the city's premiere performance venues. If you can't book a performance, call for tour details (Mon. 10 and noon). ⊠ *50 E. Congress Pkwy., Loop* ☎ *312/431–2389* ⊕ *www. auditoriumtheatre.org* 🎫 *Tour $8.*

Carson Pirie Scott & Co. Built in 1899, the old-fashioned department store's flagship location closed its doors in 2007. While shopping—window or otherwise—is no longer an option, it's worth checking out the building's facade. The work of one of Chicago's most renowned architects, it combines Louis H. Sullivan's visionary expression of modern design with intricate cast-iron ornamentation. The eye-catching rotunda and the 11 stories above it are actually an addition Sullivan made to his original building. In later years, D. H. Burnham & Co. and Holabird & Root extended Sullivan's smooth, horizontal scheme farther down State Street. ⊠ *1 S. State St., Loop.*

WORLD'S LARGEST TIFFANY DOME ★ **Chicago Cultural Center.** Built in 1897 as the city's original public library, this huge building houses the **Chicago Office of Tourism Visitor Information Center,** as well as a gift shop, café, galleries, and a concert hall. Designed by the Boston firm Shepley, Rutan & Coolidge—the team behind the Art Institute of Chicago—it's a palatial affair of Carrara marble, mosaics, gold leaf, and the world's largest Tiffany glass dome. Building tours are offered Wednesday, Friday, and Saturday at 1:15 PM. There's live music on weekdays at 12:15 PM in the café. ⊠ *78 E. Washington St., Loop* ☎ *312/346–3278 or 312/744–6630* ⊕ *www.cityofchicago.org/Tourism/CulturalCenter* ⊗ *Mon.–Thurs. 8–7, Fri. 9–6, Sat. 9–5, Sun. 10–5.*

Fine Arts Building. This creaky building was constructed in 1895 to house the showrooms of the Studebaker Company, then makers of carriages. Publishers and artists have used its spaces; today the principal tenants are professional musicians. Take a look at the handsome exterior, then step inside the marble-and-woodwork lobby. The motto engraved in the marble as you enter says, ALL PASSES—ART ALONE ENDURES. The building has an interior courtyard, across which strains of piano music and soprano voices compete with tenors as they run through exercises. Open Studios tours (4:30–9:30 on the second Friday of each month) include live music, galleries, and a peak at the studios. ⊠ *410 S. Michigan Ave., Loop* ☎ *312/566-9800* ⊕ *www.fineartsbuilding.tv.*

CHECK OUT THE CHICAGO WINDOWS ★ **Marquette Building.** Like a slipcover over a sofa, the clean, geometric facade of the Marquette Building expresses what lies beneath: in this case, a structural steel frame. Sure, the base is marked with roughly cut stone and a fancy cornice crowns the top, but the bulk of the building mirrors the cage around which it is built. Inside is another story. The intimate lobby of this 1895 Holabird & Roche building is a jewel box of a space, where a single Doric column stands surrounded by a Tiffany glass mosaic depicting the exploits of French Jesuit missionary Jacques Marquette, an early explorer of Illinois. The building is a clear example of the Chicago style, from the steel skeleton to the Chicago Windows to the terra-cotta ornamentation. ⊠ *140 S. Dearborn St., Loop.*

> ### FOR SULLIVAN FANS
>
> Bear north to Lincoln Park to see the **Louis Sullivan row houses.** The love of geometric ornamentation that Sullivan eventually brought to such projects as the Carson Pirie Scott building is already visible in these row houses built in 1885. The terra-cotta cornices and decorative window tops are especially noteworthy. ⊠ *1826–1834 N. Lincoln Park W, Lincoln Park* ⊕ *www.artic.edu/aic/libraries/rbarchives/sullivan/extant.html*

The Loop & South Loop Architecture

CARBIDE AND CARBON BUILDING/HARD ROCK HOTEL CHICAGO

SMURFIT-STONE BUILDING

S. Water St.

STATE

2 PRUDENTIAL PLAZA

AON CENTER

Wabash Ave.

ke St.

Prudential Building

RANDOLPH — Randolph St.

Randolph St. Station

WASHINGTON

Washington Blvd.

CHICAGO CULTURAL CENTER

RELIANCE BUILDING/ HOTEL BURNHAM

MADISON

Madison St.

Millennium Park

Columbus Dr.

Lake Shore Dr.

4

State St.

CARSON PIRIE SCOTT

Monroe St.

MONROE

INLAND STEEL BUILDING

Art Institute of Chicago

Adams St.

41

Grant Park

Chicago Harbor

ADAMS

SANTA FE BUILDING

Jackson Blvd.

JACKSON

Columbus Dr.

Michigan Ave.

Van Buren St.

Van Buren Station

BRARY

HAROLD WASHINGTON LIBRARY CENTER

FINE ARTS BUILDING

Congress Pkwy.

AUDITORIUM BUILDING

Congress Plaza

Buckingham Fountain

HARRISON

Hilton Chicago

I-90E

DONOHUE BUILDING

SOUTH LOOP

E 9th St

Grant Park

Plymouth Ct.

S State St.

S Wabash Ave.

S Michigan Ave.

ROOSEVELT– WABASH

0   1/4 mile

0   400 meters

WORLD'S COLUMBIAN EXPOSITION

In 1893 the city of Chicago hosted the **World's Columbian Exposition.** The fair's mix of green spaces and Beaux Arts buildings offered the vision of a more pleasantly habitable metropolis than the crammed industrial center that rose from the ashes of the Great Fire. However, a ruffled Louis Sullivan prophesied that "the damage wrought to this country by the Chicago World's Fair will last half a century." He wasn't entirely wrong in his prediction—the classicist style vied sharply over the next decades with the native creations of the Chicago and Prairie schools, all the while incorporating their technical advances. One of Hyde Park's most popular destinations—the Museum of Science and Industry—was erected as the fair's Palace of Fine Arts. It's the exposition's only building still standing.

Monadnock Building. Built in two segments a few years apart, the Monadnock captures the turning point in high-rise construction. Its northern half, designed in 1891 by Burnham & Root, was erected with traditional load-bearing masonry walls (6 feet deep at the base). In 1893, Holabird & Roche designed its southern half, which rose around the soon-to-be-common steel skeleton. The building's stone and brick exterior, shockingly unornamented for its time, led one critic to liken it to a chimney. The lobby is equally spartan: lined on either side with windowed shops, it's essentially a corridor, but one well worth traveling. Walk it from end to end and you'll feel like you're stepping back in time. ⊠ *53 W. Jackson Blvd. at S. Dearborn St., Loop* ⊕ *www. monadnockbuilding.com.*

A CHICAGO LANDMARK   **Reliance Building.** The clearly expressed, gleaming verticality that characterizes the modern skyscraper was first and most eloquently articulated in this steel-frame tower in the heart of the Loop. Completed in 1895 and now home to the stylish **Hotel Burnham,** the building was a crumbling eyesore until the late 1990s, when the city initiated a major restoration. In the early and mid-1900s it was a mixed-use office building, and Al Capone's dentist reportedly worked out of what's now Room 809. Don't

Fodor'sChoice   ★

WHAT ARE YOU LOOKIN' AT?

Terra-cotta, a baked clay that can be produced as tiles or shaped ornamentally, was commonly used by Chicago architects after the Great Fire of 1871.

Heat resistant and malleable, the material proved an effective and attractive fireproofing agent for the metal-frame buildings that otherwise would melt and collapse. The facade of the Marquette Building at 140 S. Dearborn Street is a particularly fine example.

be misled when you go looking for this masterpiece—a block away, at State and Randolph streets, a dormitory for the School of the Art Institute of Chicago shamelessly mimics this trailblazing original by Burnham, Root, and Charles Atwood. Once you've found the real thing, don't miss the mosaic floor and ironwork in the reconstructed elevator lobby. The building boasts early examples of the Chicago Window,

> **GREAT CORNERS TO LOOK UP!**
>
> ■ North Michigan Avenue and East Wacker Drive
> ■ West Adams and South LaSalle streets
> ■ North Michigan Avenue and East Chestnut Street

which define the entire building's facade by adding a shimmer and glimmer to the surrounding white terra-cotta. ⊠*1 W. Washington St., Loop* ☎*312/782–1111* ⊕*www.burnhamhotel.com.*

Fodor's Choice ★ **Rookery.** This 11-story structure, with its eclectically ornamented facade, got its name from the pigeons and politicians who roosted at the city hall that once stood on this site. Designed in 1885 by Burnham & Root, who used both masonry and the more modern steel-frame construction, the Rookery was one of the first buildings in the country to feature a central court that brought sunlight into interior office spaces. Frank Lloyd Wright, who kept an office here for a short time, renovated the two-story lobby and light court, eliminating some of the ironwork and terra-cotta and adding marble scored with geometric patterns detailed in gold leaf. The interior endured some less tasteful alterations after that, but it has since been restored to the way it looked when Wright completed his work in 1907. ⊠*209 S. LaSalle St., Loop.*

Santa Fe Building. Also known as the Railway Exchange Building, this structure was designed in 1904 by Daniel Burnham, who later moved his office here. The SANTA FE sign on its roof was put up early in the 20th century by the Santa Fe Railroad, one of several railroads that had offices here when Chicago was the rail center of the country. The fantastic **ArchiCenter of the Chicago Architecture Foundation** (☎*312/922–3432* ⊕*www.architecture.org* ☉*Daily 9:30–6:30*) occupies this historic space. ⊠*224 S. Michigan Ave., Loop.*

Symphony Center. Orchestra Hall, home to the acclaimed Chicago Symphony Orchestra (CSO), lies at the heart of this music center. The hall was built in 1904 under the supervision of Daniel Burnham. The Georgian building has a symmetrical facade of pink brick with limestone quoins, lintels, and other decorative elements. Backstage tours are available by appointment for groups of 10 or more. ⊠*220 S. Michigan Ave., Loop* ☎*312/294–3000.*

FINDING THE ART DECO

FROM BUBBLY INSPIRATION ★ **Carbide and Carbon Building.** Designed in 1929 by Daniel and Hubert Burnham, sons of the renowned architect Daniel Burnham, this is arguably the jazziest skyscraper in town. A deep-green terra-cotta tower rising from a black-granite base, its upper reaches are embellished with gold leaf. The original public spaces are a luxurious composition in marble and bronze. The story goes that the brothers Burnham got their design inspiration from a gold-foiled bottle of champagne. So perhaps it's fitting that the building now houses the **Hard Rock Hotel Chicago,** party central for those who wouldn't be caught dead at the Four Seasons. ⊠*230 N. Michigan Ave. Loop* ⊕*www.hardrockhotelchicago.com.*

★ **Chicago Board of Trade.** Rising dramatically at the end of LaSalle Street— heart of the city's financial district—Holabird & Root's building is a streamlined giant from the days when Art Deco was all the rage. The artfully lit marble lobby soars three stories; atop the roof stands Ceres, the Roman goddess of agriculture. Erected in 1930, this 45-story structure reigned as the city's tallest skyscraper until 1955, when the Prudential Center grabbed that title. ⊠*141 W. Jackson Blvd., Loop* ☎*312/435–3590.*

Civic Opera House. The handsome home of the Lyric Opera of Chicago is grand indeed, with pink-and-gray Tennessee marble floors, pillars with carved capitals, crystal chandeliers, and a sweeping staircase to the second floor. Designed by Graham, Anderson, Probst & White, it combines lavish Art Deco details with classical touches. And the show goes on, with the Lyric Opera performing regularly on the great stage within. ⊠*20 N. Wacker Dr., Loop* ☎*312/419–0033 Civic Opera House, 312/332–2244 Lyric Opera* ⊕*www.civicoperahouse.com.*

1950S & BEYOND: MEET MODERNISM

Daley Center. Named for the late mayor Richard J. Daley, this boldly plain high-rise is the headquarters of the Cook County court system, but it's best known as the site of a sculpture by Picasso. Known simply as the *Picasso,* this monumental piece provoked an outcry when it was installed in 1967; baffled Chicagoans tried to determine whether it represented a woman or an Afghan hound. In the end, they gave up guessing and simply embraced it as a unique symbol of the city. The building was constructed in 1965 of Cor-Ten steel, which weathers naturally to an attractive bronze. In summer the building's plaza is the site of concerts, political rallies, and a weekly farmers' market (Thursday); during the holidays, the city's official Christmas tree is erected here. ⊠*Bounded by Washington Blvd., Randolph, Dearborn, and Clark Sts., Loop*

MIES MEETS **Federal Center and Plaza.** Designed in 1959, but not completed until
CALDER 1974, this severe constellation of buildings around a sweeping plaza
★ was Mies van der Rohe's first mixed-use urban project. Fans of the International Style will groove on this pocket of pure modernism, while others can take comfort in the presence of the Marquette Building, which marks the north side of the site. In contrast to this dark ensemble are the great red arches of Alexander Calder's *Flamingo.* The piece was dedicated on the same day in 1974 that the artist's *The Universe* was unveiled at Sears Tower. Calder went from one event to the other, riding through the streets in a brightly colored circus wagon accompa-

nied by calliopes. The area is bound by Dearborn, Clark, and Adams streets and Jackson Boulevard. ⊠*Dirksen: 219 S. Dearborn St., Loop* ⊠*Kluczynski: 230 S. Dearborn St., Loop.*

★ **Inland Steel Building.** A runt compared to today's tall buildings, this crisp, sparkling structure from Skidmore, Owings & Merrill was a trailblazer back in the late 1950s. It was the first skyscraper built with external supports (allowing for wide-open, unobstructed floors within); the first to employ steel pilings (driven 85 feet down to bedrock); the city's first fully air-conditioned building; and the first to feature underground parking. As for looks, well, you might say it combines the friendly scale of the Reliance Building with the cool rigor of a high-rise by Mies. ⊠*30 W. Monroe St., Loop.*

4

LATE MODERNISM GIVES WAY TO POSTMODERNISM

ENJOY THE 17-
STORY ATRIUM
★

James R. Thompson Center. People either hate or love the center: former governor James Thompson, who selected the Helmut Jahn design for this state government building, hailed it in his dedication speech in 1985 as "the first building of the 21st century." For others, it's a case of postmodernism run amok. A bowl-like form topped by a truncated cylinder, the building's sky-blue and salmon color scheme scream 1980s. But the 17-story atrium, where exposed elevators zip up and down and sunlight casts dizzying patterns through the metal-and-glass skin, is one of the most animated interiors to be found anywhere in the city. The sculpture in the plaza is Jean Dubuffet's *Monument with Standing Beast.* It's nearly as controversial as the building itself. The curved shapes, in white with black traceries, have been compared to a pile of melting Chicago snow. The **Illinois Artisans Shop** (☎*312/814–5321*), on the second level of the Center, sells crafts, jewelry, and folk art by Illinois artists. ⊠*100 W. Randolph St., Loop.*

Smurfit-Stone Building. Some wags have said this building, with its diamond-shape top, looks like a giant pencil sharpener. The slanted top carves through 10 floors of this 1984 building. The painted, folded-aluminum sculpture in the plaza is Yaacov Agam's *Communication X9.* You'll see different patterns in the sculpture depending on your vantage point. ⊠*150 N. Michigan Ave., Loop.*

333 West Wacker Drive. This green-glazed beauty doesn't follow the rules. Its riverside facade echoes the curve of the Chicago River just in front of it, while the other side of the building is all business, conforming neatly to the straight lines of the street grid. This 1983 Kohn Pedersen Fox design is roughly contemporary to the James R. Thompson Center—but it has enjoyed a much more positive public reception. ⊠*333 W. Wacker Dr., between W. Lake Street and N. Orleans St., Loop.*

CHECK OUT
THE ROOF
OWLS
★
☾

Harold Washington Library Center. Gargantuan and almost goofy (the huge, gargoyle-like sculptures atop the building look like something out of Harry Potter), this granite-and-brick edifice is a uniquely postmodern homage to Chicago's great architectural past. The heavy, rusticated ground level recalls the Rookery; the stepped-back, arched

Continued on page 132

THE SKY'S THE LIMIT

Talk about baptism by fire. Although Chicago was incorporated in 1837, it wasn't until after the Great Fire of 1871 that the city really started to take shape. With four square miles gone up in flames, the town was a clean slate. The opportunity to make a mark on this metropolis drew a slew of architects, from Adler & Sullivan to H. H. Richardson and Daniel H. Burnham—names renowned in the annals of American architecture. A Windy City tradition was born: the city's continuously morphing skyline is graced with tall wonders designed by architecture's heavy hitters, including Mies van der Rohe; Skidmore, Owings & Merrill; and, if he has his way, Santiago Calatrava. In the next four pages, you'll find an eye-popping sampling of Chicago's great buildings and how they've pushed—and continue to push—the definition of even such a lofty term as "skyscraper."

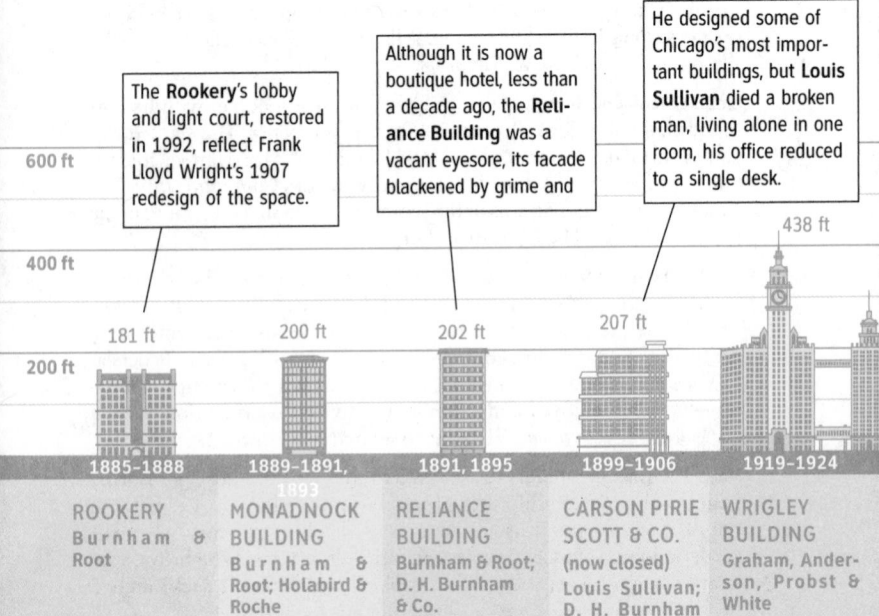

The **Rookery**'s lobby and light court, restored in 1992, reflect Frank Lloyd Wright's 1907 redesign of the space.

Although it is now a boutique hotel, less than a decade ago, the **Reliance Building** was a vacant eyesore, its facade blackened by grime and

He designed some of Chicago's most important buildings, but **Louis Sullivan** died a broken man, living alone in one room, his office reduced to a single desk.

600 ft

438 ft

400 ft

181 ft

200 ft

202 ft

207 ft

200 ft

1885–1888	1889–1891, 1893	1891, 1895	1899–1906	1919–1924
ROOKERY	MONADNOCK BUILDING	RELIANCE BUILDING	CARSON PIRIE SCOTT & CO.	WRIGLEY BUILDING
Burnham & Root	Burnham & Root; Holabird & Roche	Burnham & Root; D. H. Burnham & Co.	(now closed) Louis Sullivan; D. H. Burnham & Co.	Graham, Anderson, Probst & White

THE BIRTH OF THE SKYSCRAPER

Houses, churches, and commercial buildings of all sorts rose from the ashes after the blaze of 1871, but what truly put Chicago on the architectural map was the tall building. The earliest of these barely scrape the sky—especially when compared to what towers over us today—but in the late 19th century, structures such as William Le Baron Jenney's ten-story Home Insurance Building (1884) represented a bold push upward. Until then, the sheer weight of stone and cast-iron construction had limited how high a building could soar. But by using a lighter yet stronger steel frame and simply sheathing his building in a thin skin of masonry, Jenney blazed the way for ever taller buildings. And with only so much land available in the central business district, up was the way to go.

Although the Home Insurance Building was razed in 1931, Chicago's Loop remains a rich trove of early skyscraper design. Some of these survivors stand severe and solid as fortresses, while others manifest an almost ethereal quality. They—and their descendants along Wacker Drive, North Michigan Avenue, and Lake Shore Drive—reflect the technological, economic, and aesthetic forces that have made this city on the prairie one of the most dramatically vertical communities in the country.

Soul Train, the wildly popular dance program, first aired from WCIU–TV studios atop the **Chicago Board of Trade**.

Ludwig Mies van der Rohe was the master of the glass box, but he made his own home in a small, Italianate apartment house built

With its shops and other amenities—and initially reasonable rents—**Marina City** was designed to help stem the flood of urbanites to the suburbs.

605 ft

463 ft

270

332 ft

588 ft

1923–1925	1930	1949–1951	1954–1958	1959–1967
TRIBUNE TOWER	CHICAGO BOARD OF TRADE	860–880 N. LAKE SHORE DRIVE	INLAND STEEL BUILDING	MARINA CITY
Howells & Hood	Holabird & Root	Ludwig Mies van der Rohe	Skidmore, Owings & Merrill	Bertrand Goldberg Associates

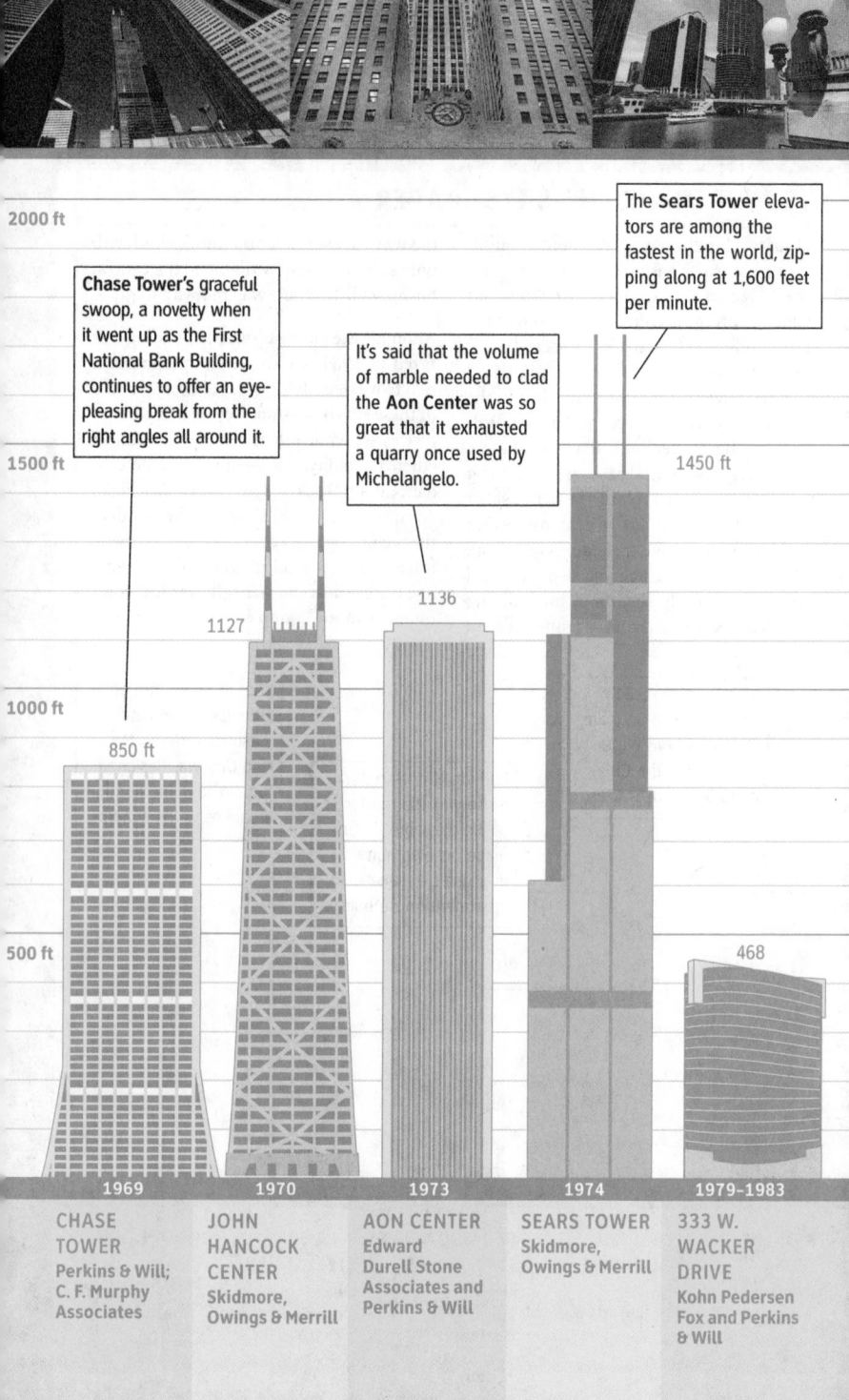

2000 ft

The **Sears Tower** elevators are among the fastest in the world, zipping along at 1,600 feet per minute.

Chase Tower's graceful swoop, a novelty when it went up as the First National Bank Building, continues to offer an eye-pleasing break from the right angles all around it.

It's said that the volume of marble needed to clad the **Aon Center** was so great that it exhausted a quarry once used by Michelangelo.

1500 ft

1450 ft

1136

1127

1000 ft

850 ft

500 ft

468

1969	1970	1973	1974	1979–1983
CHASE TOWER	JOHN HANCOCK CENTER	AON CENTER	SEARS TOWER	333 W. WACKER DRIVE
Perkins & Will; C. F. Murphy Associates	Skidmore, Owings & Merrill	Edward Durell Stone Associates and Perkins & Will	Skidmore, Owings & Merrill	Kohn Pedersen Fox and Perkins & Will

Santiago Calatrava, who designed the Turning Torso building in Malmö, Sweden, and an addition to the Milwaukee Art Museum, has grand plans for Chicago's skyline: a spiraling giant right on the lakefront.

311 S. Wacker may not be the tallest building in town, but come dark, it's one of the most visible, lit by nearly 2,000 fluorescent lights.

Although **Park Tower** hovers over nearly everything around it, this hotel/condo is considered a good neighbor, thanks to its retro styling and warmly colored facade.

2000

995 ft

961 ft

844 ft

704 ft

1990	1990	2000	2004	2006–2010
311 S. WACKER DRIVE	2 PRUDENTIAL PLAZA	PARK TOWER	HYATT CENTER	FORDHAM SPIRE
Kohn Pedersen Fox	Loebl, Schlossman & Hackl	Lucien LaGrange Architects	Pei Cobb Freed & Partners	Santiago Calatrava

windows are a reference to the great arches in the Auditorium Theatre of Roosevelt University; the swirling terra-cotta design is pinched from the Marquette Building; and the glass curtain wall on the west side is a nod to 1950s modernism. The library was named for the first African-American mayor of Chicago, and the primary architect was Thomas Beeby, of the Chicago firm Hammond, Beeby & Babka.

The excellent **Children's Library** on the second floor, an 18,000-square-foot haven, has vibrant wall-mounted figures by Chicago imagist Karl Wirsum. Works by noted Chicago artists are displayed along a second-floor walkway above the main lobby. There's also an impressive Winter Garden with skylights on the ninth floor. Free programs and performances are offered regularly at the center. ⊠*400 S. State St., Loop* ☎*312/747–4300* ⊕*www.chipublib.org* ⊗ *Mon.–Thurs. 9–9, Fri. and Sat. 9–5, Sun. 1–5.*

SKY-HIGH SANCTUARY

Chicago Temple. The Gothic-inspired headquarters of the First United Methodist Church of Chicago were built in 1923 by Holabird & Roche, complete with a first-floor sanctuary, 21 floors of office space, a sky-high chapel, and an eight-story spire (best viewed from the bridge across the Chicago River at Dearborn Street). Outside, along the building's east wall at ground level, stained-glass windows relate the history of the church in Chicago. Joan Miró's sculpture *Chicago* (1981) is in the small plaza just east of the church. ⊠*77 W. Washington St., Loop* ☎*312/236-4548* ⊕*www.chicagotemple.org.*

UP, UP, UP: THE SKYSCRAPERS

Aon Center. With the open space of Millennium Park at its doorstep, the Aon Center really stands out—even if its appearance isn't much to write home about. Originally built as the Standard Oil Building, the structure has changed names and appearances twice. Not long after it went up, its marble cladding came crashing down and the whole building was resheathed in granite. The massive building sits on a handsome (if rather sterile) plaza, where Harry Bertoia's wind-chime sculpture in the reflecting pool makes interesting sounds when a breeze blows. ⊠*200 E. Randolph Dr., Loop.*

PLAZA
BLISS: VISIT
THE MARC
CHAGALL
MOSAIC

Chase Tower. This building's graceful swoop—a novelty when it went up—continues to offer an eye-pleasing respite from all the right angles surrounding it. And its spacious plaza, with a mosaic by Marc Chagall called **The Four Seasons,** is one of the most enjoyable public spaces in the neighborhood. Designed by Perkins & Will and C. F. Murphy Associates in 1969, the building has been home to a succession of financial institutions (its most recent name was Bank One Plaza); names aside, it remains one of the more distinctive buildings around, not to mention one of the highest buildings in the Loop's true heart. ⊠*Bounded by Dearborn, Madison, Clark, and Monroe Sts., Loop.*

Hyatt Center. At 48 stories, the headquarters of this hospitality group is no giant, but it more than makes its mark on South Wacker Drive with a bold elliptical shape, a glass-faced street-level lobby rising 36 feet, and a pedestrian-friendly plaza. One of the city's newer towers, it displays a noticeable tweaking of the unrelieved curtain wall that makes many city streets forbidding canyons. Designed by Pei Cobb Freed & Partners, the building was completed in 2004. ✉ *71 S. Wacker Dr., Loop.*

CHECK OUT
THE 103RD
FLOOR
Fodor'sChoice
★
☺

Sears Tower. In Chicago, size matters. This soaring 110-story skyscraper, designed by Skidmore, Owings & Merrill in 1974, was the world's tallest building until 1996 when the Petronas Towers in Kuala Lumpur, Malaysia, claimed the title (but Petronas counts its spire as part of the building). In 2004, Taipei 101 beat out the latter. Those bragging rights aside, the **Skydeck** is really something to boast about. Enter on Jackson Boulevard to take the ear-popping ride to the 103rd-floor observatory. Video monitors turn the 70-second elevator ride into a fun-filled, thrilling trip. On a clear day a whopping four states are visible: Illinois, Michigan, Wisconsin, and Indiana. (Check the visibility ratings at the security desk before you decide to ride up and take in the view.) At the top, interactive exhibits tell about Chicago's dreamers, schemers, architects, musicians, and sports stars. Computer kiosks in six languages help international travelers key into Chicago hot spots. Knee-High Chicago, a 4-foot-high exhibit with cutouts of Chicago sports and history at a child's eye-level, will entertain the kids. The Sears Tower also has spruced up the lower level with a food court, new exhibits, and a short movie about the city. Security is very tight, so figure in a little extra time for your visit to the Skydeck. Before you leave, don't miss the spiraling Calder mobile sculpture *The Universe* in the ground-floor lobby on the Wacker Drive side. ✉ *233 S. Wacker Dr.; for Skydeck, enter on Jackson Blvd. between Wacker Dr. and Franklin St., Loop* ☎ *312/875-9696* ⊕ *www.the-skydeck.com* ✉ *$12.95* ☺ *Apr.–Sept., daily 10–10; Oct.–Mar., daily 10–8.*

NIGHT LIGHTS
SUPREME
★

311 South Wacker Drive. The first of three towers intended for the site, this pale pink building is the work of Kohn Pedersen Fox, who also designed 333 West Wacker Drive, a few blocks away. The 1990 building's most distinctive feature is its Gothic crown, blindingly lighted at

4

WHAT ARE YOU LOOKIN' AT?

The Chicago Window, a popular window design used in buildings all over America (until air-conditioning made it obsolete), consists of a large fixed central pane with smaller moveable windows on each side. The picture window offered light, while the double-hung windows let in the Lake Michigan breeze. Developed in Chicago by engineer and architect William Le Baron Jenney, who pioneered the use of metal-frame construction in the 1880s, the Chicago Window helps to define buildings across the city.

night. During migration season so many birds crashed into the illuminated tower that the building management was forced to tone down the lighting. The building has an inviting atrium, with palm trees and a splashy, romantic fountain. ⊠*311 S. Wacker Dr., at W. Jackson Blvd., Loop* ⊕*www.311southwacker.com.*

Two Prudential Plaza. Nicknamed "Two Pru," this glass-and-granite giant is the older sibling of the 1955 tower at its feet (looking very 1950s indeed). Together with their neighbors they form a block-long business-oriented minicity. Two Prudential is the tallest reinforced concrete building in the city, and its blue detailing and beveled roof are instantly recognizable from afar. ⊠*180 N. Stetson Ave., Loop* ⊕*www. pruplazachicago.com.*

SOUTH LOOP

Heading south from the heart of the Loop, you'll find Printer's Row, where lofts that once clattered with linotype machines are now luxury real-estate morsels, as well as Dearborn Park, a residential enclave reclaimed from old rail yards.

HISTORIC BUILDINGS

Dearborn Station. Chicago's oldest standing passenger train station, a South Loop landmark, now serves as a galleria. Designed in Romanesque-revival style in 1885 by the New York architect Cyrus L. W. Eidlitz, it has a wonderful clock tower and a red-sandstone and red-brick facade ornamented with terra-cotta. Striking features inside are the marble floor, wraparound brass walkway, and arching wood-frame doorways. ⊠*47 W. Polk St., South Loop* ☎*312/554–8100* ⊙*Daily 8 AM–5 PM.*

Donohue Building. The first major printing facility in Printers Row, this 1883 building's main entrance is flanked by marble columns topped by ornately carved capitals, with tile work over the entrance set into a splendid granite arch. Note the beautiful ironwork and woodwork ornamenting the first-floor retail establishments. ⊠*711 S. Dearborn St., South Loop.*

> **CURVES ON THE MARINA**
>
> **River City.** These concrete curves may look familiar; it was built in 1986 by Bertrand Goldberg, who also built the "corncobs" of Marina City. The complex features a 10-story atrium, commercial space, and 62-slip marina. It has great views of the water from the lobby. ⊠*800 S. Wells St., South Loop.*

Franklin Building. Built in 1888 and initially the home of the Franklin Company, a printing concern, this building has intricate decoration. The tile work on the facade leads up to *The First Impression*—a medieval scene illustrating the first application of the printer's craft. Above the entryway is a motto: THE EXCEL-

LENCE OF EVERY ART MUST CONSIST IN THE COMPLETE ACCOMPLISHMENT OF ITS PURPOSE. ✉ *720 S. Dearborn St., South Loop.*

OLD SCHOOL HOLABIRD & ROCHE **Pontiac Building.** An early Chicago School skyscraper—note its classic rectangular shape and flat roof—the simple, redbrick, 14-story Pontiac was designed by Holabird & Roche in 1891 and is their oldest existing building in Chicago. ✉ *542 S. Dearborn St., South Loop.*

PRAIRIE AVENUE & BEYOND

Heading even farther south parallel to the lakeshore, you'll find the Prairie Avenue Historic District; this was the neighborhood of choice for the city's movers and shakers in the mid-19th century. If you're a die-hard Mies van der Rohe fan, continue your journey south to check out his buildings on the campus of the Illinois Institute of Technology.

HISTORIC BUILDINGS

Clarke House. This Greek Revival dates from 1836, making it Chicago's oldest surviving building. It's a clapboard house in a masonry city, built for Henry and Caroline Palmer Clarke to remind them of the East Coast they left behind. The Doric columns and pilasters were an attempt to civilize Chicago's frontier image. The everyday objects and furnishings inside reveal a typical 1830s–60s middle-class home. ✉ *1827 S. Indiana Ave., Prairie Avenue District* ☎ *312/745–0040* 💲 *$10. Free Wed.; see Glessner House listing for combo-ticket information* 🕙 *Tours: Wed.–Sun. at noon and 2* PM.

Fodor'sChoice ★ **Glessner House.** This fortresslike, Romanesque Revival 1886 residence is the only surviving building in Chicago by architect H. H. Richardson, who also designed Boston's Trinity Church. It's also one of the few great mansions left on Prairie Avenue, once home to such heavy hitters as retailer Marshall Field and meat-packing magnate Philip Armour. The area has lately seen the arrival of new, high-end construction, but nothing beats a tour of Glessner House, a remarkable relic of the days when merchant princes really lived like royalty. Enjoy the lavish interiors and the many artifacts, from silver pieces and art glass to antique ceramics and Isaac Scott carvings and furnishings. ✉ *1800 S. Prairie Ave., Prairie Avenue* ☎ *312/326–1480* ⊕ *www.glessnerhouse.org* 💲 *$10. Combined admission to Glessner and nearby Clarke House $15. Free Wed.* 🕙 *Tours Wed.–Sun. at 1 and 3* PM.

NEAR NORTH & RIVER NORTH

Just a hop, skip, and a jump from the Loop's northern reaches and across the Chicago River are the Near North and River North neighborhoods. The magnet for most folks is North Michigan Avenue—aka the Magnificent Mile—a glittering stretch studded with shops and hotels. Saunter up this thoroughfare from the Michigan Avenue Bridge (or head south from Oak Street) and you'll see such sights as the Wrig-

Prairie Avenue Architecture

KEY

♦ MAJOR ARCHITECTURAL LANDMARK

♦ Minor Architectural Landmark

---

ley Building, the Tribune Tower, the Historic Water Tower, and the John Hancock Center.

HISTORIC BUILDINGS

Tribune Tower. In 1922 *Chicago Tribune* publisher Colonel Robert McCormick chose a Gothic design for the building that would house his paper, after rejecting a slew of functional modern designs by such notables as Walter Gropius, Eliel Saarinen, and Adolf Loos. Embedded in the exterior walls of the tower are chunks of material taken from famous sites around the world. Look for bits from the Parthenon, Westminster Abbey, the Alamo, St. Peter's Basilica, the Taj Mahal, and the Great Wall of China. On the ground floor are the studios of WGN radio, part of the *Chicago Tribune* empire, which also includes WGN-TV, cable-television stations, and the Chicago Cubs. (Modesty was not one of Colonel McCormick's prime traits: WGN stands for the *Tribune*'s self-bestowed nickname, World's Greatest Newspaper). ⊠ *435 N. Michigan Ave., Near North* ☎ *312/222–3232* ⊕ *www.chicago tribune.com.*

OFF THE BEATEN PATH

About 18 mi north of downtown Chicago (in Wilmette), rising near the lake, the **Baha'i House of Worship** is an intriguing, nine-sided build-

MIES VAN DER ROHE, KOOLHAAS & JAHN

Illinois Institute of Technology. "Less is more" claimed Mies van der Rohe, but for fans of the master's work, more is more at IIT. The campus holds an array of the kind of glass-and-steel structures for which he is most famous. Crown Hall is the jewel of the collection and has been designated a National Historic Landmark, but don't overlook the Robert F. Carr Memorial Chapel of St. Savior.

Additions to the campus include the McCormick Tribune Campus Center,

designed by Dutch architect Rem Koolhaas, and new student housing by Helmut Jahn. The campus is about 1 mi west of Lake Shore Drive on 31st Street. Or take the El train's Green or Red Line to the 35th Street stop, and walk east two blocks to campus. ⊠ *S. State St. between 31st and 35th Sts., Douglas, south of Chinatown* ☎ *312/567–3000* ⊕ *www. iit.edu.*

ing that incorporates architectural styles and symbols from many of the
★ world's religions. With its delicate lacelike details and massive dome, the Louis Bourgeois design emphasizes the 19th-century Persian origins of the Baha'i religion. As symmetrical and harmonious as the building are the formal gardens that surround it. The temple is the U.S. center of the Baha'i faith, which advocates spiritual unity, world peace, race unity, and equality of the sexes. The visitor center has exhibits explaining the Baha'i faith; here you can also ask for a guide to show you around. ⊠ *100 Linden Ave.* ☎ *847/853–2300* ⊕ *www.us.bahai.org* 🎫 *Free* ☉ *May–Sept., daily 10–8; Oct.–Apr., daily 10–5.*

Historic Water Tower. This famous Michigan Avenue structure, completed in 1867, was originally built to house a 137-foot standpipe that equalized the pressure of the water pumped by the similar pumping station across the street. Oscar Wilde uncharitably called it "a castellated monstrosity" studded with pepper shakers. Nonetheless, it remains a Chicago landmark and a symbol of the city's spirit of survival following the Great Chicago Fire of 1871. The small gallery inside has rotating art exhibitions of local interest. ⊠ *806 N. Michigan Ave., at Pearson St., Near North* 🎫 *Free* ☉ *Mon.–Sat. 10–6:30, Sun. 10–5.*

Water Works Pumping Station. Water is still pumped to some of the city residents at a rate of about 250 million gallons per day from this Gothic-style structure, which, along with the Water Tower across the street, survived the Great Chicago Fire of 1871. The acclaimed **Lookingglass Theatre** calls this place home. The station also houses a **Chicago Water Works Visitor Information Center** (☎ *877/244–2246* ⊕ *www.877chicago. com* ☉ *Mon.–Thurs. 8 AM–7 PM, Fri. 8 AM–6 PM, Sat. 9 AM–6 PM, Sun. 10 AM–6 PM*), which has a sandwich shop. ⊠ *163 E. Pearson St., at Michigan Ave., Near North.*

A NOD TO **Wrigley Building.** Two structures built several years apart and later
SEVILLE connected, the gleaming white Wrigley Building sports a clock tower
★ inspired by the bell tower of the grand cathedral in Seville, Spain. The

Near North & River North Architecture

KEY
- ◆ MAJOR ARCHITECTURAL LANDMARK
- ◆ Minor Architectural Landmark

Armitage Ave.

N Lincoln Ave
N Clark St.
N Larrabee St
N Mohawk St
N Sedgwick St

Baha'i House of Worship (18 miles north of downtown) ◆

LINCOLN PARK

N Clark St

GOLD COAST

North Ave.

Clybourn Ave.

Larrabee St

RIVER NORTH

Kingsbury St
Hudson St
Sedgwick St
Franklin St
Orleans St

Wells St
La Salle Blvd
Clarke St
Dearborn St
Parkway St
Astor Pl

North Ave.

Schiller St.

CHARNLEY–PERSKY HOUSE ◆

Astor St.

Division St
Elm St

Bellevue St.

Maple St
Oak St

FOURTH PRESBYTERIAN CHURCH

JOHN HANCOCK CENTER BUILDING

860 – 880 N. LAKE SHORE DRIVE

Walton St
Delaware St

Chestnut St

Quigley Seminary ◆
HISTORIC WATER TOWER

PARK TOWER →

Pearson St

Chicago Ave

Holy Name Cathedral ◆

WATER WORKS PUMPING STATION

Lake Shore Dr
Lake Michigan

Superior St
Huron St
Erie St

La Salle Blvd
Clark St
Dearborn St
State St
Wabash St.
Rush St
Michigan Ave.
Fairbanks Ct.

St. James Cathedral ◆

J. F. Kennedy Expwy

Ontario St
Ohio St

NEAR NORTH

Grand Ave
Illinois St
Hubbard St

Navy Pier ◆→

TRIBUNE TOWER

NBC Tower

WRIGLEY BUILDING

N. Branch Chicago River

Kinzie St
Carroll St

MARINA CITY

MICHIGAN AVENUE BRIDGE

Centennial Fountain and Arc

Wacker Dr.

LOOP

0 ___ 1/4 mi
0 ___ 1/4 km

landmark headquarters of the chewing-gum company—designed by Graham, Anderson, Probst & White—was instrumental in transforming Michigan Avenue from an area of warehouses to one of the most desirable spots in the city. Be sure to check it out at night, when lamps bounce light off the building's gleaming terra-cotta facade. ✉*400 and 410 N. Michigan Ave., Near North* ⊕*www.wrigley.com/wrigley/about/about_story_building.asp.*

TWO INTERPRETATIONS OF "TWINS"

Fodor'sChoice ★ **860–880 N. Lake Shore Drive.** These twin apartment towers overlooking Lake Michigan were an early and eloquent realization of Mies van der Rohe's "less is more" credo, expressed in the high-rise. I-beams running up the facade underscore the building's verticality, while, inside, mechanical systems are housed in the center so as to leave the rest of each floor free and open to the spectacular views. Completed in 1951, the buildings were built in the famed International Style, which played a key role in transforming the look of American cities. ✉*860–880 N. Lake Shore Dr., at E. Chestnut St., River North.*

SOME CALL THEM CORNCOBS **Marina City.** Likened to everything from corncobs to the towers of Antonio Gaudí's Sagrada Familia in Barcelona, Goldberg's twin towers were a bold departure from the severity of the International Style, which began to dominate high-rise architecture beginning in the 1950s. Completed in 1967, the towers house condominium apartments (all pie-shape, with curving balconies). In addition to the apartments and marina, the complex now has four restaurants, the House of Blues nightclub, the new Hotel Sax Chicago, and a huge bowling alley. ✉*329 N. Dearborn St., River North* ☎*312/923–2000.*

BRIDGE OF BRIDGES

★ **Michigan Avenue Bridge.** Chicago is a city of bridges, and this is one of its most graceful. Completed in 1920, it features impressive sculptures on its four pylons representing major Chicago events: its exploration by Marquette and Joliet, its settlement by trader Jean Baptiste Point du Sable, the Fort Dearborn Massacre of 1812, and the rebuilding of the city after the Great Chicago Fire of 1871. The site of the fort, at the southeast end of the bridge, is marked by a commemorative plaque. As you stroll Michigan Avenue, be prepared for a possible delay; the bridge rises regularly to allow boat traffic to pass underneath. ✉*Michigan Ave. at Wacker Dr., Near North.*

SKYSCRAPERS DELUXE

SKY-HIGH "BIG JOHN" Fodor'sChoice ★ **John Hancock Center.** Designed by the same team that designed the Sears Tower (Skidmore, Owings & Merrill), this multi-use skyscraper is distinguished by its tapering shape and the enormous X braces, which help stabilize its 100 stories. Soon after it went up in 1970, it earned the nickname "Big John." No wonder: at 1,127 feet (1,502 feet counting the antennae at the top), 2.8 million square feet, and 46,000 tons of

4

steel, there's nothing little about it. Packed with retail, parking, offices, a restaurant, and residences, it has been likened to a city within a city. Impressive from any angle, it offers mind-boggling views from a 94th floor observatory (as with the Sears Tower, you can see to four states on clear days). For anyone afflicted with vertigo, a sensible option is a seat in the bar of the 95th floor Signature Room. The tab will be steep, but you'll be steady on your feet—*maybe.* ⊠*875 N. Michigan Ave., Near North* ☎*312/751–3681* ⊕*www.hancock-observatory.com and www. johnhancockcenterchicago.com* ✆*Observatory $12* ⊙*Daily 9* AM– *11* PM*; last ticket sold at 10:45* PM.

Park Tower. A relative newcomer to the neighborhood (2000), this high-end hotel–condo combines retro touches (note the pitched roof) and quirky contemporary flourishes (check out the protruding bank of windows on the seventh floor). Designed by Lucien LaGrange Architects, the 67-story tower seems even taller than it really is (almost 900 feet), thanks to its unobstructed location across from the small park where the Historic Water Tower stands. ⊠*800 N. Michigan Ave., at Chicago Ave., Near North* ⊕*www.parkhyatt.com.*

CHICAGO'S ANSWER TO A GOTHIC-REVIVAL CHURCH

REST YOUR FEET IN THE GRASSY COURTYARD

Fourth Presbyterian Church. A welcome visual and physical oasis amid the high-rise hubbub of North Michigan Avenue, this Gothic Revival house of worship was designed by Ralph Adams Cram. Local architect Charles van Doren Shaw devised the cloister and companion buildings. The first big building erected on the avenue after the Chicago Fire, it counted among its congregants the city's elite. Noontime concerts are given every Friday in the sanctuary. ⊠*126 E. Chestnut St., Near North* ☎*312/787–4570* ⊕*www.fourthchurch.org.*

WHAT ARE YOU LOOKIN' AT?

"Curtain Wall" is the term for the largely glass exterior surface of many modern buildings.

Unlike masonry construction, in which stone or brick support the weight of the building, a curtain wall is not a load-bearing system; rather, it is hung on the steel or concrete frame that holds the building up.

The Reliance Building (an early example), the Sears Tower, and 333 W. Wacker Drive are all curtain-wall buildings.

FRANK LLOYD WRIGHT

1867–1959

The most famous American architect of the 20th century led a life that was as zany and scandalous as his architectural legacy was great. Behind the photo-op appearance and lordly pronouncements was a rebel visionary who left an unforgettable imprint on the world's notion of architecture. Nowhere else in the country can you experience Frank Lloyd Wright's genius as you can in Chicago and its surroundings.

Born two years after the Civil War ended, Wright did not live to see the completion of his late masterpiece, the Guggenheim Museum. His father preached and played (the Gospel and music) and dragged the family from the Midwest to New England and back before he up and left for good. Wright's Welsh-born mother, Anna Lloyd Jones, grew up in Wisconsin, and her son's roots would run deep there, too. Although his career began in Chicago and his work took him as far away as Japan, the home Wright built in Spring Green, Wisconsin—Taliesin—was his true center.

Despite all his dramas and financial instability (Wright was notoriously bad with money), the architect certainly produced. He was always ready to try something new—as long as it fit his notion of architecture as an expression of the human spirit and of human relationship with nature. By the time he died in 1959, Wright had designed over 1,000 projects, more than half of which were constructed.

Robie House, Chicago

WELCOME TO OAK PARK!

Oak Park is a leafy, quiet community just 10 miles west of downtown Chicago. When you arrive, head to the **Oak Park Visitors Center** (✉ 158 N. Forest Ave. ☎ 708/848–1500 ⊕ www.visitoakpark.com ☼ Daily 10–5, until 4 in winter) and get oriented with a free map.

Next wander to the **Frank Lloyd Wright Home and Studio** (✉ 951 Chicago Ave. ☎ 708/848–1606 🖷 708/848–1248 ⊕ www.wrightplus.org 🎟 $12; walking tour $12; combined $20 ☼ Weekday tours at 11, 1, and 3; weekend tours 11–3:30, every 20 mins. Tickets can be purchased in advance via the Web site). From the outside, the shingle-clad structure may not appear all that innovative,

but it's here that Wright developed the architectural language that still has the world talking.

Financed with a $5,000 loan from his mentor, Louis Sullivan, Wright designed the home when he was only 22. The residence manifests some of the spatial and stylistic characteristics that became hallmarks of Wright's work: there's a central fireplace from which other spaces seem to radiate and an enticing flow to the rooms. In 1974, the local Frank Lloyd Wright Home and Studio Foundation, together with the National Trust for Historic Preservation, embarked on a 13-year restoration that returned the building to its 1909 appearance.

GETTING HERE

To get to the heart of Oak Park by car, take the Eisenhower Expressway (I-290) west to Harlem Avenue. Head north on Harlem and take a right on Lake Street to get to the Oak Park Visitors Center at Forest Avenue and Lake Street (158 N. Forest Avenue), where there's ample free parking. You can also take the Green Line of the El to the last stop, the Harlem Avenue exit, or Metra's Union Pacific West Line from the Ogilvie Transportation Center in Citicorp Center downtown (500 W. Madison) to the Oak Park stop at Marion Street.

WOMEN, FIRE, SCANDAL . . . AND OVER 1,000 DESIGNS

The southeast entrance to the Frank Lloyd Wright Home & Studio in Oak Park.

1885 Wright briefly studies engineering at the University of Wisconsin.

1887 Wright strikes out for Chicago. He starts his career learning the basics with J. L. Silsbee, a residential architect. Later he joins the office of Adler & Sullivan as a drafter, just as the firm begins work on the massive Auditorium building.

1889 Wright marries Catherine Tobin; he builds her a home in suburban Oak Park, and they have six children together.

"WHILE NEW YORK HAS REPRODUCED MUCH AND PRODUCED NOTHING, CHICAGO'S ACHIEVEMENTS IN ARCHITECTURE HAVE GAINED WORLD-WIDE RECOGNITION AS A DISTINCTIVELY AMERICAN ARCHITECTURE."

Strolling Oak Park

A leisurely stroll around the neighborhood will introduce you to plenty of **Frank Lloyd Wright houses.** All are privately owned, so you'll have to be content with what you can see from the outside. Check out 1019, 1027, and 1031 Chicago Avenue. These are typical Victorians that Wright designed on the sly while working for Sullivan.

For a look at the "real" Wright, don't miss the **Moore–Dugal Home** (1895) at 333 N. Forest Avenue, which reflects Wright's evolving architectural philosophy with its huge chimney and overhanging second story. Peek also at numbers 318, 313, 238, and 210, where you can follow his emerging modernism. Around the corner at 6 Elizabeth Court is the **Laura Gale House,** a 1909 project whose cantilevered profile foreshadows the thrusting planes Wright would create at Fallingwater decades later.

Between 1889 and 1913, Wright erected over two dozen buildings in Oak Park, so unless you're making an extended visit, don't expect to see everything.

A landmark profile: the eastern facade of the architect's home and studio, Oak Park.

But don't leave town without a visit to his 1908 **Unity Temple** (✉ 875 W. Lake St. ☎ 708/383–8873), a National Historic Landmark. Take a moment to appreciate Wright's fresh take on a place of worship; his bold strokes in creating a flowing interior; his unfailing attention to what was outside (note the skylights); and his dramatic use of concrete, which helps to protect the space from traffic noise.

Interior, Unity Temple, Oak Park

1893 Wright launches his own practice in downtown Chicago.

1898 As his practice grows, Wright adds a studio to his Oak Park residence.

1905 Wright begins designing the reinforced concrete Unity Temple.

1908 Construction begins on the Robie House in Chicago's Hyde Park neighborhood.

Guided Tours

A great way to get to know Oak Park is to take advantage of the guided tours. Well-informed local guides take small groups on tours throughout the day, discussing various architectural details, pointing out artifacts from the family's life, and often telling amusing stories of the rambunctious Wright clan. Reservations are required for groups of 10 or more for the home and studio tours. Note that you need to arrive as early as possible to be assured a spot. Tours begin at the **Ginkgo Tree Bookshop**, which is part of the home and studio. The shop carries architecture-related books and gifts. You can pick up a map ($3.95) to find other examples of Wright's work that are within easy walking or driving distance, or you can join a guided tour of the neighborhood led by volunteers.

The Hemingway Connection

Frank Lloyd Wright wasn't the only creative giant to call Oak Park home. Ten years after Wright arrived, Ernest Hemingway was born here in 1899 in a proper Queen Anne, complete with turret. Wright was gone by the time Hemingway began to sow his literary oats. Good thing, too. It's doubtful the quiet village could have handled two such egos. *See* Get Out of Town: Brushing up your Ernest Hemingway pg. 26.

Frank Lloyd Wright's distinctive take on a modern dining room.

TIPS

Tickets go on sale every March 1 for the eagerly awaited annual **Wright Plus Benefit Housewalk,** your chance to see the interiors of some of Oak Park's most architecturally notable homes. Check out ⊕ www.wrightplus.org for more details.

Note that you can save time (or rest your feet) on the free **Oak Park Shuttle** (☎ 708/615–1830). Operated by PACE and the Village of Oak Park, the shuttle bus runs every 30 minutes and makes 21 stops at Oak Park sights. Regular hours are 10–5:30 daily. You can catch the shuttle outside the Frank Lloyd Wright Home and Studio.

Interior, Rookery, Chicago

1909 Wright leaves for Europe with Mamah Cheney, the wife of a former client; this puts an abrupt end to his family life, but Mrs. Wright does not consent to a divorce.

1911 Wright and Cheney settle at Taliesin, in Spring Green, Wisconsin.

1914 Mrs. Cheney, her two children, and several other people are killed by a deranged employee, who also sets fire to Taliesin. Wright rebuilds, as he does when the house burns again in 1922.

1915 With new mistress Miriam Noel in tow, the architect heads for Japan to oversee the building of the Imperial Hotel.

PRAIRIE STYLE PRIMER

Primarily a residential mode, Wright's Prairie style is characterized by ground-hugging masses; low-pitched roofs with deep eaves; and ribbon windows. Generally, Prairie houses are two-story affairs, with single story wings and terraces that project into the landscape. Brick and stone, earth tones, and unpainted wood underscore the perception of a house as an extension of the natural world. Wright designed free-flowing living spaces defined by alternating ceiling heights, natural light, and architectural screens. Although a number of other Chicago architects pursued this emerging aesthetic, Wright became its

"ALL FINE ARCHITECTURAL VALUES ARE HUMAN VALUES, ELSE NOT VALUABLE."

acknowledged master. Though Wright designed dozens of Prairie style homes, the most well-known is Robie House, in Chicago's Hyde Park neighborhood. A dynamic composition of overlapping planes, it seems both beautifully anchored to the ground and ready to sail off with the arrival of a sharp breeze.

Ribbon Windows

Eaves

SOUTH ELEVATION, ROBIE HOUSE

The architect discusses a project with his assistants in Oak Park, 1958.

1922 Wright and his wife Catherine divorce.

1924 Wright marries Miriam Noel, but Noel is emotionally unsteady and the marriage implodes three years later.

1928 Wright marries Olga (Olgivanna) Lazovich Milanoff, who remains a compelling helpmate for the remainder of his life. They have one daughter together.

1930 The Taliesin Fellowship is launched; eager apprentices arrive at Spring Green to learn from the master.

4

IN FOCUS FRANK LLOYD WRIGHT

WRIGHT BACK IN THE CITY

If you can't make it to Oak Park, there are a handful of notable—and memorable—Frank Lloyd Wright experiences to be had in the city.

★ **Fodor's Choice** Long and low, **Robie House** (1908–1910) grabs the ground and sends the eye zipping westward. Massive overhangs shoot out from the low-pitched roof and windows run along the facade in a glittering stretch. Inside, Wright's "open plan" echoes the great outdoors, as one space flows into another, while sunlight streaming through decorative leaded windows bathes the rooms in patterns. Robie House is midway through a 10-year renovation but remains open to visitors. ⊠ 5757 S. Woodlawn Ave., Hyde Park ☎ 773/834–1847 ☜ $12 ☉ Tour weekdays at 11, 1, and 3; weekends every ½ hr 11–3:30.

When he designed the **Isidore Heller House** in 1897, Frank Lloyd Wright was still moving toward the mature Prairie style achieved in the Robie House. As was common with Wright—and very uncommon then and now—the entrance to the Heller House is on the side of the structure. The house is not open to the public. ⊠ 5132 S. Woodlawn Ave., Hyde Park.

Frank Lloyd Wright designed the **Charnley–Persky House** with his mentor Louis Sullivan. This almost-austere residence represents one of Wright's first significant forays into residential design. Historians still squabble about who designed what here, but it's easy to imagine that the young go-getter had a hand in the cleanly rendered interior. Note how the geometric exterior looks unmistakably modern next to its fussy neighbors. ⊠ 1365 N. Astor St., Near North ☎ 312/915–0105 ☜ Free Wed., $10 for Sat. tour that includes Madlener House (45 min). ☉ Apr.–Nov., tours Wed. at noon, Sat. at 10 AM and 1 PM; Dec.–Mar., 10 AM only. For larger groups, make reservations well in advance.

Stand outside the **Rookery** with its dizzy-ingly detailed facade and you'll think you've taken a wrong turn in your search for Wright. This early high-rise was designed by Burnham & Root. In 1905, Wright was hired to spruce up the building's interior court, which he lightened up by replacing terra-cotta with gilded white marble; adding pendant light fixtures; and gracing the stairway with urns, one of his favorite motifs. ⊠ 209 S. LaSalle St., Loop.

1935 Fallingwater, the country home of Pittsburgh retailer Edgar J. Kaufmann, is completed at Bear Run, Pennsylvania.

1937 Wright begins construction of his winter getaway, Taliesin West, in Scottsdale, Arizona.

1956 Wright designs the Guggenheim Museum in New York. It is completed in 1959.

1957 Wright joins preservationists in saving Robie House from demolition.

1959 Wright dies at the age of 91.

Where to Eat

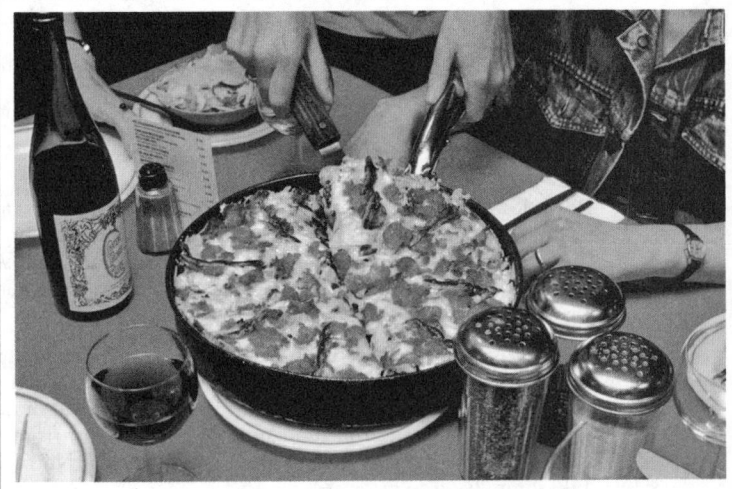

WORD OF MOUTH

"We had excellent steak dinners at Harry Caray's. The bread and salad beforehand were disappointing but my, the meat and potatoes rocked our world."

—Pisces

"Oh, I forgot about Arun's! We have lots of Thai restaurants in town, but nothing else is like Arun's. I took a friend from Seattle there who said in all his eating adventures in 62 countries he hadn't had anything like it."

—Marilynl

www.fodors.com/forums

THE SCENE

Updated by
Kate Leahy

Chicago is a city sans snobbery when it comes to food. The collective appetite champions both haute and street cuisine. Mediocrity, at any price level, just doesn't fly here, which makes Chicago a reliably tasty town to tour.

Down low, Chicago is famed for hot dogs, deep-dish pizza, and Italian beef sandwiches. On the high end, the city launched celebrity chef Charlie Trotter, cutting-edge molecular gastronomist Grant Achatz of Alinea, and Rick Bayless, who introduced the nation to authentic regional Mexican cuisine at Frontera Grill.

The city is home to more than 7,000 restaurants, the most prominent of which cluster close to downtown expense accounts. But many of the most exciting restaurants that have opened in the past several years have been in residential neighborhoods, from Alinea in Lincoln Park to Spacca Napoli and Sola on the Far North Side to Takashi in Bucktown.

Local establishments, such as barbecue-centric Smoque and hot-dog spot Hot Doug's, both on the Far North Side, find that drawing crowds from all over the city is a matter of focusing on simple food and doing it well. At the same time, downtown development hasn't slowed down, attracting big name investors (Donald Trump) and spurring local restaurant groups to open new restaurants (Bin 36's new Italian concept, A Mano, is located underneath its River North location). Meanwhile, Chicago's steak-house tradition continues to wield influence on the restaurant scene, though big-name chefs, including Christian Delouvrier and David Burke have expanded expectations, taking the experience beyond men's-club exclusive.

In coming years expect to see more outsiders in Chicago (Terrance Brennan is already on his way), eager to feed a populace that knows good food and isn't willing to accept anything less than the best.

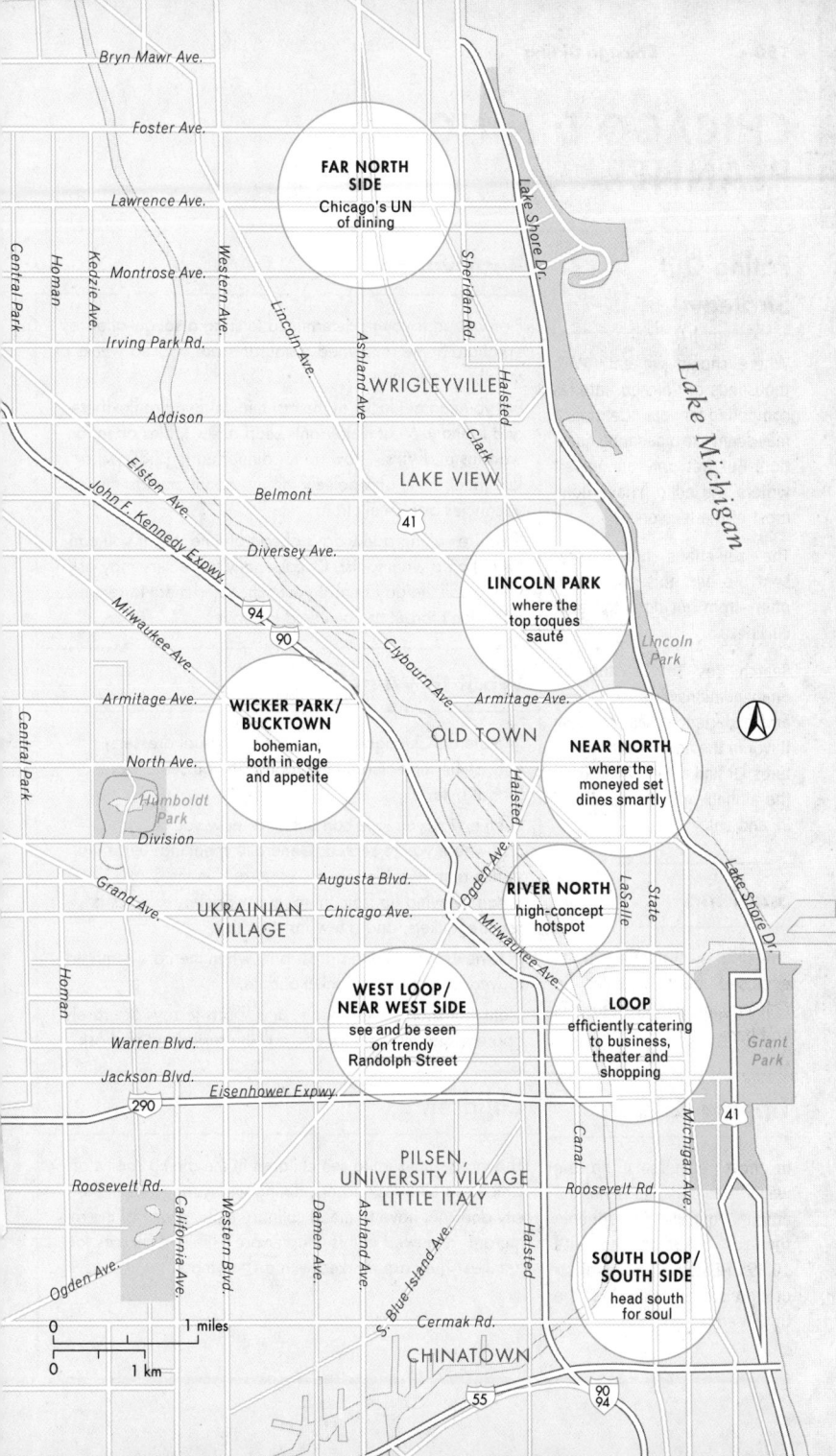

CHICAGO DINING PLANNER

Eating Out Strategy

Where should we eat? With thousands of Chicago eateries competing for your attention, it may seem like a daunting question. But fret not—our expert writers and editors have done most of the legwork.

The selections here represent the best this city has to offer—from hot dogs to haute cuisine.

Search "Best Bets" for top recommendations by price, cuisine, and experience. Sample local flavor in the neighborhood features. Or find a review quickly in the alphabetical listings. Delve in, and enjoy!

Smoking

Smoking is prohibited in all enclosed public spaces in Chicago, including restaurants and bars.

Tipping & Taxes

In most restaurants, tip the waiter 18%–20%. (To figure the amount quickly, just double the tax noted on the check—it's 10.25%.) Bills for parties of six or more sometimes include the tip already.

Reservations

Plan ahead if you're determined to snag a sought-after reservation. Some renowned restaurants are booked weeks or months in advance.

But you can get lucky at the last minute if you're flexible—and friendly. Most restaurants keep a few tables open for walk-ins and VIPs. Show up for dinner early (5:30 PM) or late (after 9 PM) and politely inquire about any last-minute vacancies or cancellations.

If you're calling a few days ahead of time, ask if you can be put on a waiting list. Occasionally, an eatery may ask you to call the day before your scheduled meal to reconfirm: don't forget or you could lose out.

What to Wear

In general, Chicagoans are neat but casual dressers; only at the top-notch dining rooms do you see a more formal style.

But the way you look can influence how you're treated—and where you're seated. Generally speaking, jeans will suffice at most table-service restaurants in the $ to $$ range. Moving up from there, many pricier restaurants require jackets, and a few insist on ties.

In reviews, we mention dress only when men are required to wear a jacket or a jacket and tie.

Note that shorts, sweatpants, and sports jerseys are rarely appropriate. When in doubt, call the restaurant and ask.

Children

Though it's unusual to see children in the dining rooms of Chicago's elite restaurants, dining with youngsters in the city does not have to mean culinary exile. Many of the restaurants reviewed in this chapter are excellent choices for families. They are marked with a ☺ symbol.

Wine

Although some of the city's top restaurants still include historic French vintages, most sommeliers are now focusing on small-production, lesser-known wineries. Some are even keeping their wine lists purposefully small, so that they can change them frequently to match the season and the menu. Half bottles are becoming more prevalent, and good wines by the glass are everywhere. Don't hesitate to ask for recommendations. Even restaurants without a sommelier on staff will appoint knowledgeable servers to lend a hand with wine selections.

Prices

If you're watching your budget, be sure to ask the price of daily specials recited by the waiter or captain. The charge for specials at some restaurants is noticeably out of line with the other prices on the menu. Beware of the $10 bottle of water; ask for tap water instead. And always review your bill.

If you eat early or late you may be able to take advantage of a prix-fixe deal not offered at peak hours. Most upscale restaurants offer great lunch deals, with special menus at cut-rate prices designed to give customers a true taste of the place.

Credit cards are widely accepted, but many restaurants (particularly smaller ones downtown) accept only cash. If you plan to use a credit card it's a good idea to double-check its acceptability when making reservations or before sitting down to eat.

WHAT IT COSTS

FOR ONE PERSON

¢	$	$$	$$$	$$$$
under $10	$10–$18	$19–$27	$28–$36	over $36

Prices are per person for a typical main course or equivalent combination of smaller dishes. Note: if a restaurant offers only prix-fixe (set-price) meals, it has been given the price category that reflects the full prix-fixe price.

In This Chapter

Spotlight On

Orientation

Throughout the chapter, you'll see mapping symbols and coordinates (✛) after property reviews. To locate the property on a map, turn to the Chicago Dining & Lodging Atlas at the end of this chapter. The first number after the (✛) symbol indicates the map number. Following that is the property's coordinate on the map grid.

5

BEST BETS FOR CHICAGO DINING

With thousands of restaurants to choose from, how will you decide where to eat? Fodor's writers and editors have selected their favorite restaurants by price, cuisine, and experience in the Best Bets lists below. In the first column, Fodor's Choice properties represent the "best of the best" in every price category. You can also search by neighborhood for excellent eats—just peruse the following pages. Or find specific details about a restaurant in the full reviews, listed alphabetically later in the chapter.

Fodor's Choice ★

Alinea, $$$$
Avec, $$
Bin 36, $$
Blackbird, $$$
Hopleaf Bar, $
Hot Doug's, ¢
North Pond, $$$
Spacca Napoli, $
Takashi, $$$

¢

Billy Goat Tavern
Hot Doug's
Milk & Honey Café
Mr. Beef
Smoque BBQ

$

Crust
Hopleaf Bar
Juicy Wine Company
Piece
Spacca Napoli

$$

A Mano
Avec
Bin 36
Frontera Grill
Hot Chocolate
West Town Tavern

$$$

Blackbird
Green Zebra
North Pond
Spring
Takashi
Table Fifty-Two

$$$$

Alinea
Charlie Trotter's
Sixteen
Spiaggia

Best by Cuisine

AMERICAN

Billy Goat Tavern, ¢
Hot Doug's, ¢
Ina's, $
Lou Mitchell's, ¢

ASIAN

Le Lan, $$
Red Light, $$
SushiSamba Rio, $$

CHINESE

Lao Sze Chuan, ¢
Phoenix, $

FRENCH

Brasserie Jo, $$
Brasserie Ruhlmann, $$$$
Everest, $$$$
Le Bouchon, $
Les Nomades, $$$$
Marché, $$

ITALIAN

A Mano, $$
Osteria via Stato, $$$
Spacca Napoli, $
Spiaggia, $$$$
Terragusto, $

JAPANESE

Japonais, $$$
Kamehachi, $
Takashi, $$$

LATIN AMERICAN

Coobah, $
DeLaCosta, $$$
Nacional 27, $$

MEXICAN

De Cero Taqueria, $
Frontera Grill, $$
Salpicón, $$
Topolobampo, $$$

PIZZA

Crust, $
Piece, $
Pizzeria Uno, $

SPANISH

Café Ba-Ba-Reeba, $
Café Iberico, $

STEAKHOUSE

Custom House, $$$
David Burke's Primehouse, $$$$
Gibsons Steakhouse, $$$$
Keefer's, $$$$

THAI

Arun's, $$$$
Thai Classic, ¢
Vong's Thai Kitchen, $$

VEGETARIAN

Charlie Trotter's, $$$$
Green Zebra, $$$$
Lula Café, $$

Best by Experience

BAR FOOD

Hopleaf Bar, $
Juicy Wine Company, $
Rockit Bar & Grill, $$
Twin Anchors Restaurant & Tavern, $$

BUSINESS DINING

NoMI, $$$$
Powerhouse Restaurant and Bar, $$$
Seasons Restaurant, $$$$
Sepia, $$$
Spiaggia, $$$$

CAFÉ EATS

Bin 36, $$
Café Selmarie, $
Julius Meinl Café, ¢
Milk & Honey, ¢
Pierrot Gourmet, $

CHICAGO CLASSICS

Billy Goat Tavern, ¢
Gene & Georgetti, $$$
Mr. Beef, ¢
Twin Anchors Restaurant & Tavern, $$
Pizzeria Uno, $

CHILD-FRIENDLY

Ann Sather, $
Café Selmarie, $
Ed Debevic's, ¢
Eleven City Diner, $
Piece, $
Scoozi!, $$
Smoque BBQ, ¢

GOOD FOR GROUPS

Fogo de Chão, $$$$
Joe's Be-Bop Cafe and Jazz Emporium, $
Park Grill, $$
The Parthenon, $

HOT SPOTS

Avec, $$
Blackbird, $$$
Brasserie Ruhlmann, $$$$
Green Zebra, $$$
Sepia, $$$
Table Fifty-Two, $$$

BEST HOTEL DINING

Avenues, $$$$
Custom House, $$$
NoMI, $$$$
Seasons Restaurant, $$$$
Sixteen, $$$$

MOST INNOVATIVE

Alinea, $$$$
Avenues, $$$$
Charlie Trotter's, $$$$
Graham Elliot, $$$
Moto, $$$$

LATE-NIGHT DINING

Avec, $$
DeLaCosta, $$$
Nacional 27, $$
Red Light, $$
Vivo, $$

PRETHEATER MEAL

Atwood Café, $$
Boka, $$–$$$
Rhapsody, $$
Riva, $$$
Sola, $$

QUIET MEAL

Arun's, $$$$
Avenues, $$$$
Charlie Trotter's, $$$$
Les Nomades, $$$$
North Pond, $$$

SPECIAL OCCASION

Charlie Trotter's, $$$$
Everest, $$$$
North Pond, $$$
Spring, $$$
TRU, $$$$

BEST VIEWS

NoMI, $$$$
North Pond, $$$
Park Grill, $$
Sixteen, $$$$
Spiaggia, $$$$

5

FAR NORTH SIDE

Some of Chicago's best ethnic food resides on the Far North Side, a vast catchall district north of Irving Park Road running all the way to suburban Evanston.

Within its borders lie several food-happy neighborhoods, none more lively than Devon Avenue, traditional home to Chicago's Indian community and lined with Indian restaurants, Bollywood video stores, and sari shops as well as Russian bakeries and Israeli eateries.

Two classic Chicago neighborhoods, the Swede-settled Andersonville and the German enclave Lincoln Square, have lured a critical mass of retailers, delis, bars, and restaurants that warrant an afternoon or evening out. Both are pedestrian-friendly; Lincoln Square lies on the Brown Line El, though Andersonville is better reached via cab. To reach the other dining destinations in this area, such as **Arun's** (✉4156 N. Kedzie Ave. ☎773/539–1909), **Hot Doug's** (✉3325 N. California Ave. ☎773/751–1500), and **Smoque BBQ** (✉3800 N. Pulaski Rd. ☎773/545–7427), you may want to consider renting a car, or expect a longish cab ride from downtown.

GASTROPUBBING

Hopleaf Bar (✉5148 N. Clark St. ☎773/334–9851) owner Michael Roper pairs food and beer, with sometimes surprising results. Here's what Roper recommends: Belgian-style mussels paired with Belgian blond ales like Leffe or Triple Karmeliet. Why: "Steamed with herbs and shallots, the mussels go great with blonds." For a snack, try a sandwich of ham, Gruyère cheese, and apple-tarragon slaw with a hoppy Lagunitas. Why: "Bigger, hoppier beers stand up to cured ham and bold cheese." On a cold night, dig into: Flemish beef stew with a pint of St. Bernardus Apt 12. Why: "Rich, malty St. Bernardus matches the caramelized beef."

NOSHING UP NORTH

German (Lincoln Square) vs. Swede (Andersonville). Germans settled Lincoln Square, and the Swedes populated Andersonville, two north-side neighborhoods not far apart. Do one, or make it a double header.

	Lincoln Square	Andersonville
Shop	Since 1875, Chicagoans have been shopping at **Merz Apothecary** (⊠ 4716 N. Lincoln Ave., at Lawrence Ave. ☎ 773/989–0900) for homeopathic remedies, health-promoting tonics and teas, and hard-to-find European lozenges and fennel digestive drops.	Stop into **City Olive** (⊠ 5408 N. Clark St., north of Foster Ave. ☎ 773/878–5408) for a carefully selected range of olive oils and non-edibles, including olive serving dishes and olive oil–based lotions.
Sip	Try a stein of Spaten or a shot of the Goldwasser, a spiced citrus liqueur with flakes of 22k gold, at the Bavarian-themed **Huettenbar** (⊠ 4721 N. Lincoln Ave., at Lawrence Ave. ☎ 773/561–2507).	Drink free coffee at the stand-up bar while noshing on pastries at **Swedish Bakery** (⊠ 5348 N. Clark St. ☎ 773/561–8919). Our favorites are the buttery spritz cookies and cinnamon streusel coffee cake.
Sup	The old-school **Chicago Brauhaus** (⊠ 4732 N. Lincoln Ave. ☎ 773/784–4444) serves up mugs of suds, platters of brats, and jovial tunes by a live oom-pah band nightly.	Herring salad, Swedish meatballs, and smorgasar (open-faced sandwiches) are on the menu at **Svea Restaurant** (⊠ 5236 N. Clark St. ☎ 773/275–7738).

RESTAURANTS IN THIS AREA

Belgian
Hopleaf Bar, $
Bistro
Bistro Campagne, $$
Café
Café Selmarie, $
German
Chicago Brauhaus, $
Hot Dogs
Hot Doug's, ¢
Italian
La Donna, $
Spacca Napoli, $
Terragusto, $
New American
Tomboy, $$
Scandinavian
Svea, ¢
Southern
Smoque BBQ, ¢
Thai
Arun's, $$$$

CHICAGO HOT DOGS

Two far-flung spots on the North Side warrant the trek for a dog. At **Superdawg Drive-In,** carhops deliver your chow (⊠ 6363 N. Milwaukee Ave., at Devon Ave. ☎ 773/763–0660). Serving haut dogs, **Hot Doug's** does the classic Chicago all-beef as well as a rotating range of exotic "encased meats," including kangaroo and rabbit (⊠ 3324 N. California, at Henderson St. ☎ 773/279–9550).

5

LINCOLN PARK & LAKEVIEW

Of Chicago's 77 official neighborhoods, the North Side's popular Lincoln Park is definitely worth exploring. From a food perspective, this neighborhood is host to several of Chicago's best restaurants, including Charlie Trotter's and Alinea.

Named for the lakefront park it borders, Lincoln Park is often a first stop for recent Chicago transplants moving to the city as well as the permanent residence of families inhabiting pricey brownstones. On commercial thoroughfares such as Clark, Halsted, and Armitage, you can spend an afternoon bouncing back and forth from great restaurants and cafés to hip shops.

For more casual fare, head north of Lincoln Park to Lakeview, which includes the sub-districts of Wrigleyville, which buffers Wrigley Field and hosts many bars serving beer and brats, and Boy's Town, which refers to the gay district along Halsted between Belmont and Addison. Here the bars are equally raucous but the food is more refined.

URBAN GARDEN

Chef Bruce Sherman has an idyllic spot in **North Pond** (✉ *2610 N. Cannon Dr.* ☎ *773/477–5845*), a restaurant lodged in a former skater's warming hut on the edge of a duck pond in the heart of Lincoln Park. To this greensward he has added a kitchen garden, growing almost all his own herbs and many of his own vegetables in the height of summer, resulting in urban-farm-to-table salads and sorbets. The only challenge is keeping the neighbors out of the garden. "Have people helped themselves? Of course, we're in a public park," Sherman says.

LINCOLN PARK—A TOP CHEF HUB

From the corner of Armitage Avenue and Halsted Street, head a half block west and you'll arrive at Charlie Trotter's, kitchen of the eponymous chef. The other way, one block south, is Alinea with its chef Grant Achatz, in many ways the next-generation Trotter.

	Charlie Trotter's (⊠*816 W. Armitage Ave.* ☎*773/248–6228*)	Alinea (⊠*1723 N. Halsted St.* ☎*312/867–0110*)
Restaurant name		
What the name means	Eponymous (Don't you know who I am?)	A typographical symbol signifying the start of a new thought
Culinary Style	Modern American; meticulous presentation; dedication to organic and free-range products	Cutting-edge American; daring presentation; flavor is as important as form
Menu	8-course degustation menus (grand and vegetable) change daily	12-course tasting menu or 22-course "tour;" menu changes often
Wow Factor	Restrained. Sources luxury ingredients (Iranian pistachios, Spanish percebes) from around the world	Unleashed. Custom service pieces reinvent fork and knife into spindles, tabletop pedestals.
Theater Analogy	Shakespearean drama	Performance art

EATING AROUND WRIGLEY FIELD

Hungry fans can find good eats in any direction, though most options run north and south of the ballpark. Go south on Sheffield Street three blocks to **Sheffield's** (*3258 N. Sheffield St., at School St.* ☎*773/281–4989*) for pulled-pork barbecue best consumed in the beer garden. Go south on Clark two blocks to **Tryst** (⊠*3485 N. Clark St., at Cornelia Ave.* ☎*773/755–3980*) for small plates such as chicken satay and beef sliders paired with strong martinis. Go north on Sheffield three blocks to **Pizza Rustica** (⊠*3913 N. Sheridan Rd., at Byron St.* ☎*773/404–8955, BYOB*) for pizza and pastas from an Italian owner.

RESTAURANTS IN THIS AREA

American
Green Dolphin Street, $
Kitsch'n on Roscoe, $
North Pond, $$$
Orange, ¢–$
Asian Fusion
Yoshi's Cafe, $$
Bistro
Mon Ami Gabi, $$
Café
Julius Meinl Cafe, ¢
Cutting-Edge
Alinea, $$$$
French
Geja's Cafe, $$$$
Italian
Mia Francesca, $
Latin American
Coobah, $
New American
Boka, $$–$$$
Charlie Trotter's, $$$$
Erwin Cafe, $$
Scandinavian
Ann Sather, $
Seafood
L20, $$$$
Spanish
Café Ba-Ba-Reeba!, $
Thai
Thai Classic, ¢
Turkish
Turquoise Restaurant and Cafe, $$

5

THE LOOP

Business, theater, and shopping converge in the Loop, the downtown district south of the Chicago River distinguished by the elevated train that circles it.

Long the city's financial center, the Loop is commuter central for inbound office workers. It is also Chicago's historic home of retail, where the flagship Marshall Field's (now Macy's) and Carson Pirie Scott (now defunct) made State Street a great shopping street. Newcomers like Old Navy and TJ Maxx update the mix, appealing to tourists as well as locals.

As a theater district, the Loop hosts the Tony-awarded Goodman Theater, which mounts its own productions, as well as the Oriental, Palace, and LaSalle theaters, which generally run Broadway tours.

In feeding these diverse audiences, Loop restaurants run the gamut from quick-service to high-volume and special-occasion. Beware noontime and pre-curtain surges (you'll need a reservation for the latter).

NEW BAGEL?

Hannah's Bretzel (✉ *180 W. Washington Ave., at Wells St.* ☎ *312/621–1111*) aims to replace the New World–popularized bagel with the Old World–ubiquitous soft pretzel. A bretzel, that is, made of organic wheat and cooked in imported German ovens by Stuttgart native and former ad exec Florian Pfahler, who quit the corporate world to train in the art of baking bretzels. Get them spread with organic butter, stuffed with Gruyère and cucumbers, or slathered in Nutella. The results are lighter and tastier than a bagel sandwich, closer to a baguette with serious holes.

TOP PICKS FOR DINING IN THE LOOP

Whether you're looking for pretheater eats, a quick bite on the go, or an intimate dining room for a special occasion, restaurants in the Loop deliver some of the city's best dining experiences.

☞ *For pre-theater dining, try*: Italian pastas and chops at **Petterino's** (⊠*150 N. Dearborn St., at Randolph St.* ☏*312/422–0150*), adjacent to the Goodman Theater; **312 Chicago** (⊠*136 N. LaSalle St., at Randolph St.* ☏*312/696–2420*) for seasonal Italian adjacent to the Palace Theater; or **Rhapsody** (⊠*65 E. Adams St., at Michigan Ave.* ☏*312/786–9911*) for contemporary American adjacent to the Chicago Symphony Center.

☞ *For a break while shopping, stop into*: **Atwood Café** (⊠*1 W. Washington Ave., at State St.* ☏*312/368–1900*) for seasonal American comfort food and picture-window views of the bustle; **Seven on State** (⊠*111 N. State St., 7th fl., at Randolph St.* ☏*312/781–1000*), within Macy's, for upscale food-court fare; or **Patty Burger** (⊠*72 E. Adams St., at Wabash Ave.* ☏*312/987–0900*) for burgers and shakes in a retro diner setting.

☞ *For a quiet dinner for two, try*: **Custom House** (⊠*500 S. Dearborn St., at Congress* ☏*312/523–0200*), a steakhouse with chef flair; **Everest** (⊠*440 S. LaSalle St., 40th fl., at Van Buren St.* ☏*312/663–8920*) serving chef Jean Joho's refined French food and city views; or **Park Grill** (⊠*11 N. Michigan Ave., at Randolph St.* ☏*312/521–7275*) in thronged Millennium Park for contemporary fare.

FAST FOOD WITH A PEDIGREE

One of Chicago's most acclaimed chefs, Rick Bayless of Frontera Grill, has opened a fast-food outlet in the Loop. Bayless call his efforts "authentic Mexican street food" at **Frontera Fresco** in the Seven on State (⊠*111 N. State St., 7th fl., at Randolph St.* ☏*312/781–1000*) food court in Macy's serving *tortas* (Mexican sandwiches), tamales, and quesadillas with Bayless's authentic regional flair.

RESTAURANTS IN THIS AREA

American
Atwood Café, $$
Tavern at the Park, $$
French
Everest, $$$$
International
Aria, $$$
Shikago, $$
Italian
312 Chicago, $$
Petterino's, $$
Trattoria No. 10, $$
New American
Park Grill, $$
Rhapsody, $$
Russian
Russian Tea Time, $$
Seafood
Catch 35, $$
Nick's Fishmarket, $$$
Southern
Heaven on Seven, $
Steakhouse
The Grillroom Chophouse & Winebar, $$
Morton's, The Steakhouse, $$$–$$$$

5

NEAR NORTH

Chicago's tony Near North district, home to shopping's Magnificent Mile and the residential Gold Coast, specializes in upscale restaurants that suit the clientele like a bespoke suit.

It's the land of posh hotels (Peninsula, Ritz-Carlton, Four Seasons, Park Hyatt) and their posh dining rooms (Avenues, The Café, Seasons Restaurant, and NoMI, respectively), as well as stand-alone stars like Tru, Spiaggia and Les Nomades. Even the Mag Mile's toniest retailers such as Polo/Ralph Lauren with the see-and-be-seen RL restaurant are in on the feed. If you're planning on dining on Michigan Avenue while you shop it, expect to spend like a platinum cardholder.

Just to the west of the Gold Coast lies the equally moneyed but more liberal Old Town district, home to Second City improv theater and a spate of restaurants that the actors can afford, at least once in a paycheck cycle.

EXPER-CHEESE

Contemporary Italian restaurant **Spiaggia** (✉ *980 N. Michigan Ave.* ☎ *312/280–2750*) works hard to get things right, down to installing a *cava di stagionatura*, or cheese cave. Why? It ages the cheese properly, says chef Tony Montuano, by controlling the temperature and humidity of between 15 and 40 cheeses the restaurant serves before or after dinner. Stocking those is Jose Flores, Spiaggia's *formaggiaio*—or cheese guy. Don't expect an atmospheric, bat-dwelling cave; this one's a 7-by-3-foot cooler visible from the dining room. Occasionally Flores will give a tour of the "cave" to help cheese aficionados choose their cheese.

CHICAGO'S CHICEST TABLES

If you want to rub elbows with Chicago's glitterati—real-estate scions, ladies who lunch, and local media figures—head to:

✘ **RL** (✉*115 E. Chicago Ave.* ☎*312/475–1100*), especially at lunch when shoppers at Ralph Lauren/Polo rest their Amex cards and order the burger made of prime beef.

✘ **NoMI** (✉*800 N. Michigan Ave.* ☎*312/239–4030*), on the 7th floor of the Park Hyatt Chicago. Be sure to specify that you want a table overlooking the landmark Water Tower under the Dale Chihuly chandeliers.

✘ **Gibsons Steakhouse** (✉*1028 N. Rush St.* ☎*312/266–8999*), a classic Chicago meat market popular with moneyed men, particularly those who play on and manage sports teams.

✘ **Bar at the Peninsula Chicago** (✉*108 E. Superior St., at Michigan Ave.* ☎*312/573–6766*), where local society types start their evenings with Champagne and end with privately blended bourbon in the leather-walled, art-filled barroom.

✘ **TRU** (✉*676 N. St. Clair St.* ☎*312/202–0001*), where there's an Andy Warhol silkscreen on the wall, a caviar course served on a table-top crystal staircase, and a multicourse dessert tasting for the truly indulgent.

BEST REFUELING STOPS FOR SHOPPERS

Around the corner from Tiffany & Co., **Pierrot Gourmet** (✉*108 E. Superior St.* ☎*312/573–6749*), run by the Peninsula Chicago hotel, serves savory soups and "tartines," open-face sandwiches. Three blocks from designer-lined Oak Street, **Big Bowl** (✉*6 E. Cedar St.* ☎*312/640–8888*) does a savory and speedy job with Asian stir-fry and noodles (and tiki-inspired tropical drinks). At Nordstrom, look no farther than the **Nordstrom Café** (✉*55 E. Grand Ave., at Michigan Ave.* ☎*312/464–1515*) on the 4th floor for paninis and salads. For post-shopping relaxation, head across the street from Nordstrom to **Eno** in the Hotel Intercontinental (✉*505 N. Michigan Ave., at Grand Ave.* ☎*312/321–8738*), and sample from flights of wine, cheese, and chocolate (in no particular order).

RESTAURANTS IN THIS AREA

American
Cru Café & Wine Bar, $
Pump Room, $$
RL, $$
Viand, $$
Barbecue
Twin Anchors Restaurant, $$
Bistro
Bistro 110, $$
Bistrot Margot, $$
Burger
Billy Goat Tavern, ¢
Café
Fox & Obel Market, ¢
Pierrot Gourmet, $
Chinese
Shanghai Terrace, $$
Cutting-Edge
Avenues, $$$$
French
Les Nomades, $$$$
Italian
Spiaggia, $$$$
Japanese
Kamehachi, $
Mexican
Salpicón, $$
New American
NoMI, $$$$
Sola, $$
TRU, $$$$
Seafood
McCormick/Schmick's, $$$
Riva, $$$
Southern
Joe's Be-Bop Cafe, $
Table Fifty-Two $$$
Steakhouse
David Burke's Primehouse, $$$$
Gibsons Steakhouse, $$$$

5

RIVER NORTH

The Chicago River bends around this 19th-century-factory district, which was refurbished and reclaimed in the 1980s by art galleries, urban-living pioneers, and chef-owned eateries to become a crown jewel in the city's dining scene.

Today the art and design trades—the mammoth Chicago Merchandise Mart anchors River North—patronize the area's trendy eateries, including Japonais, Sushi Samba Rio, and Nacional 27, as well its refined restaurants, such as mk, Naha, and Topolobampo. But while these notable restaurants have flourished, other independent eateries in the area have been forced out by soaring real-estate values and new high-rise developments. In the place of casual indie concepts, chains like Rainforest Café and ESPN Zone have taken root and gained market share.

In spite of all the change, down-home Chicago fare still thrives here, including the classic Italian beef sandwich and the famed deep-dish pizza, making River North the go-to district whether your tastes run high or low.

FOODIE DRINKS

Come cocktail hour grab a stool at the creative bar run by innovative mixologist Adam Seger at **Nacional 27** (⊠ *325 W. Huron St.* ☎ *312/664–2727*) . "I get most of my ideas from chefs and from food," says Seger, a regular farmers' market shopper who was inspired by an arugula, warm goat cheese, and mango herb-dressed salad to create his signature mango-ginger-habañero daiquiri. On Thursday evenings he pours mini drinks ($3.95 each) so you can try several. The in-demand Seger also works as beverage director at **Osteria via Stato** (⊠ *620 N. State St.* ☎ *312/642–8450*), where he creates seasonal "gastro-tails" as specials. Salut!

A STEAKHOUSE FOR ANY OCCASION

Steakhouses are a dime a dozen in River North, with its ample warehouse-sized buildings and proximity to the city center. With a meat market this robust, you can afford to be a little picky. Here are our top picks for various dining situations:

☞ A festive atmosphere that's great for groups: **Fogo de Chão** (✉ *661 N. LaSalle St.* ☎ *312/932–9330*) is an all-you-can-eat Brazilian churrascaria. The restaurant's name, which means "fire on the ground," refers to a traditional gathering around the fire with good food, family, and friends. The celebratory mood is reproduced here with interactive elements: using a two-sided red and green chip, guests indicate when they're ready to have costumed gaucho cowboys come to their table to carve the skewered and grilled meats (you can stop and start as many times as you'd like). Guests can also watch their meat being roasted in dramatic fire pit while traveling back and forth to the lavish salad bar.

☞ A Chicago classic with Italian-American flavor: **Gene & Georgetti** (✉ *500 N. Franklin St.* ☎ *312/527–3718*). Founded in 1941, this is Chicago's oldest steakhouse, and a current favorite of local politicians. On the walls you'll find autographed photos from Frank Sinatra and Lucille Ball, and on the menu you'll encounter Italian-American favorites like spaghetti and meatballs, along with classic favorites like creamed spinach. Don't miss the famed "garbage salad"—a kitchen-sink creation of greens with vegetables and meats.

☞ A stylish setting that ladies will love: **Keefer's** (✉ *20 W. Kinzie St.* ☎ *312/467–9525*) boasts a sleek, modern bistro feel, and has a broader menu than most steakhouses, with seafood, entrée salads, and roasted chicken and chops. But don't mistake this award-winning venue for steakhouse lite: its 22-ounce T-bone and 17-ounce corn-fed New York strip steak can compete with the manliest offerings in town. On the wine list you'll find more than 110 labels, with plenty of big reds.

5

SOUTH LOOP & SOUTH SIDE

The South Side of Chicago is a vast district of largely undistinguished culinary reputation that makes its foodie islands—Chinatown and South Loop—shine all the brighter.

If you're planning on exploring the South Side, especially Chicago's soul foodie Army & Lou's and other stand-alone classics, plan to drive, as distances are great and public transportation isn't, even to hubs such as the University of Chicago.

That said, you can actually spend time on foot in two rewarding South Side districts not far from the Loop. Begin at the South Loop adjacent to downtown which can easily feed Museum Campus visitors. The newly gentrifying district is home to a host of new condos and lofts, which have drawn a range of interesting diners, restaurants, and bars, primarily on Wabash Avenue. Farther south and easily accessed via the Red Line El, Chinatown is Chicago's colorful Chinese neighborhood, where traditional dim-sum specialists neighbor trendy bubble tea shops. Recently a new generation of Asian-Americans from Chicago and the suburbs have rediscovered Chinatown, energizing the scene.

CLASSIC SPOTS

Go out of your way to **Army & Lou's** (✉ *422 E. 75th St.* ☎ *773/483–3100*), a soul food favorite since 1945, for catfish, chitterlings, and smothered chicken served by bow-tied waiters on way-south 75th Street. Have the corned-beef sandwich with a side of sass from the countermen at **Manny's Coffee Shop & Deli** (✉ *1141 S. Jefferson St.* ☎ *312/939–2855*) near the Maxwell Street Market, the city's best deli. It's truly a no-frills place, but Hyde Parkers embrace the vintage cafeteria **Valois** (✉ *1518 E. 53rd St., at S. Harper Ave.* ☎ *773/667–0647*) for breakfast (pancakes), lunch (mac-'n-cheese) or dinner (barbecued ribs).

AFTERNOON IN CHINATOWN

Herbal-medicine shops, trinket sellers, candy specialists, dim-sum servers, bakeries, and noodle shops make Chinatown an entertaining day away within the city. Top stops include:

☞ Herb shop: **Yin Wall City** (✉ 2112 S. Archer Ave., at Wentworth Ave. ☎ 312/225–2888) for ginseng and Japanese mushrooms.

☞ Candy shop: **Aji Ichiban** (✉ 2117-A S. China Pl., at Cermak Rd. ☎ 312/328–9998) for dried fruit and imported candy including chocolate-covered sunflower seeds.

☞ Bakery: **Tasty Place** (✉ 2101 S. China Pl., at Cermak Rd. ☎ 312/842–2228) for coconut buns and chestnut cakes.

☞ Dim Sum: **Phoenix** (✉ 2131 S. Archer Ave. ☎ 312/328–0848) for barbecued pork buns and shrimp dumplings plucked from carts that wheel around the room on the weekend.

☞ Hot Pot: **Lao Sze Chuan** (✉ 2172 S. Archer Ave. ☎ 312/326–5040) for the all-you-can-eat Chinese fondue, where diners cook their own veggies, noodles, and meat in boiling broth at the table.

☞ Noodles: **Joy Yee's Noodle** (✉ 2159 S. China Pl., at Cermak Rd. ☎ 312/328–0001) for standout sugarcane-shrimp-pork vermicelli.

☞ Tea: **Ten Ren Tea** (✉ 2247 S. Wentworth Ave., at Cermak Rd. ☎ 312/842–1171) for bubble tea and ceramic tea sets.

BEST MUSEUM EATS

For visitors to the adjacent Museum Campus there's a South Loop dish for every interest:

☞ For visitors to the Ancient Americas exhibit at the Field Museum, the chicken in mole sauce at **Zapatista** (✉ 1307 S. Wabash Ave., at 13th St. ☎ 312/435–1307).

☞ For Shedd Aquarium goers, the albacore tuna sandwich and lox at **Eleven City Diner** (✉ 1112 S. Wabash, at 11th St. ☎ 312/212–1112).

☞ For show-goers in the Adler Planetarium's StarRider Theater, the very theatrical **Opera** (✉ 1301 S. Wabash St. ☎ 312/461–0161), with its renowned golden shrimp appetizer.

RESTAURANTS IN THIS AREA

American
Eleven City Diner, $
Manny's Coffee Shop and
Deli, ¢
Bistro
Chez Joël Bistro Français, $$
Chinese
Emperor's Choice, $
Lao Sze Chuan, ¢
Opera, $$
Phoenix, $
Italian
Gioco, $$
Pompei, ¢
Southern
Army and Lou's, ¢
Soul Queen, ¢
Steakhouse
Custom House, $$$

5

WEST LOOP & NEAR WEST SIDE

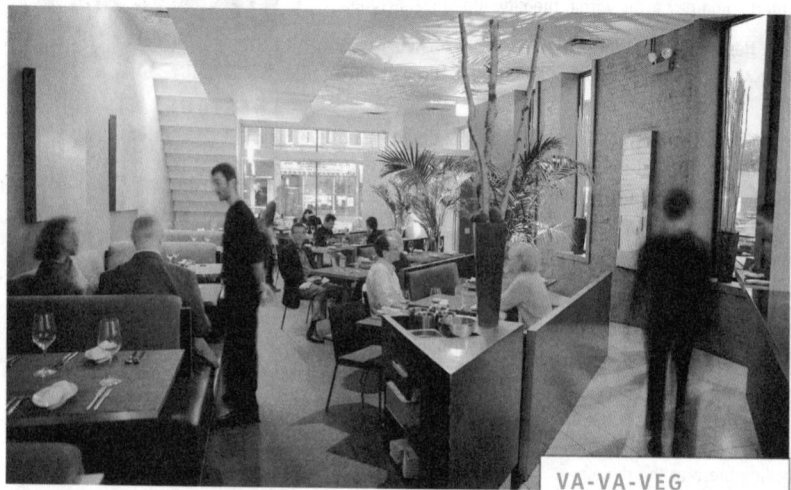

Near enough to downtown to draw a critical mass of diners, but far enough away to keep the rents down, the West Loop—and particularly Randolph Street within it—has emerged as Chicago's restaurant row, lined with upscale eateries of every ethnic persuasion.

Most restaurants here warrant a full meal, but if you haven't the time or the attention span, it's easy enough to stroll the street and feast on small bites.

The West Loop runs essentially from the south branch of the Chicago River to Ashland Avenue on the east and west, Fulton Street and Grand Avenue on the north and south, respectively. Beyond it to the north lies the unbounded but up-and-coming Near West Side. Its culinary contributions, including West Town Tavern, Juicy Wine Company, and Green Zebra, are easy to reach by cab or the El's Blue Line train.

VA-VA-VEG

Chef Shawn McClain earned raves nationwide for giving veggies the gourmet treatment at **Green Zebra** (✉ *1460 W. Chicago Ave., at Greenwood Ave.* ☎ *312/243–7100*). But don't call it vegetarian, McClain says. It's "flexitarian," mostly veggie but not strictly. "The restaurant is vegetable-focused," he says, "but we always have one fish and one chicken dish on the menu for guests who want some protein." The menu changes often, but may include dishes like a blue-cheese agnolotti with brussel sprouts, vanilla-port-swirled "ice cream," and ricotta gnocchi with eggplant caponata.

EAT YOUR WAY DOWN RANDOLPH STREET

Foodies from around the city and beyond flock to Randolph Street, aka Chicago's Restaurant Row, for excellent eats. From pizza and pasta to curry and sushi, the flavors here are sure to satisfy any culinary craving. Here are our top recommendations, dish by dish, restaurant by restaurant. Choose your own food tour from the selections below. Bon appétit!

SOUTH SIDE OF RANDOLPH STREET (the numbers refer to street addresses):

No. 615: Marinated olives and truffle-scented focaccia at **Avec** (☎ 312/377–2002).

No. 609: Bouillabaisse-like West Coast mussel soup at **Blackbird** (☎ 312/715–0708).

No. 833: Rotisserie chicken and pomme frites at **Marché** (☎ 312/226–8399).

No. 945: "Fire Breather" sausage-pepperoni-hot-pepper pizza at **Tomatohead Pizza** (✉ At Sangamon St. ☎ 312/226–1616).

No. 1235: Cheddar and black beans, fried into a disk called "scrapple" at **Ina's** (☎ 312/226–8227).

No. 1415: Global goat-cheese flight at the **Tasting Room** (✉ At Ogden Ave. ☎ 312/942–1313).

NORTH SIDE OF RANDOLPH STREET:

No. 814: Chipotle chicken tacos at **De Cero Taqueria** (☎ 312/455–8114).

No. 820: Emerald jumbo prawn curry at **Red Light** (☎ 312/733–8880).

No. 832: Dragonfly martini at **Dragonfly Mandarin** (✉ At Green St. ☎ 312/455–1400).

No. 838: Gnocchi gratinati with black truffles at **Vivo** (☎ 312/733–3379).

No. 840: Two-ounce Kobe beef burgers topped with arugula and Camembert at **Vice** (☎ 312/733–3379).

No. 842: Dragon rolls (tempura shrimp, eel, and avocado) at **Sushi Wabi** (☎ 312/563–1224).

No. 1400: Kurobuta pork tenderloin with pork belly and dates at **one sixtyblue** (☎ 312/850–0303).

RESTAURANTS IN THIS AREA

American
Ina's, $
Lou Mitchell's, ¢
West Town Tavern, $$
Asian
Red Light, $$
Bistro
La Sardine, $$
Brasserie
Marché, $$
Cutting-Edge
Moto, $$$$
Greek
Costa's, $–$$
The Parthenon, $
Italian
Vivo, $$
Japanese
Sushi Wabi, $
Mexican
De Cero Taqueria, $
New American
Avec, $$
Blackbird, $$$
Green Zebra, $$$
Juicy Wine Company, $
one sixtyblue, $$$
Otom, $$
Powerhouse Restaurant and Bar, $$$
Sepia, $$$
Steakhouse
Carmichael's Chicago Steakhouse, $$

5

WICKER PARK & BUCKTOWN

Chicago's bohemian 'hoods—neighbors Wicker Park and Bucktown—are a venturesome El stop away from downtown's deep pockets.

Artists and musicians are responsible for its 1990s rise from blighted to trendy, and although real estate prices have increased significantly, residents prize the independent spirit here, from the local record labels and hole-in-the-wall bars to one-of-a-kind boutiques and funky eateries.

Though Starbucks is, as expected, already on the scene, the food landscape here is fittingly fun and diverse, and surprisingly good at any hour, whether you want breakfast (ok, brunch, since no one gets up that early), lunch, or dinner. A handful of Bucktown and Wicker Park restaurants qualify as destinations themselves, but the best way to approach the area is to come out in the afternoon to nosh and troll the shops, stop into a bar for a drink, then head to dinner, followed by a show at Double Door, a music club.

SWEET SPOTS

A trio of sweet spots puts the cherry on the Wicker Park/Bucktown sundae. For south of the border palates, order a banana split for two served with crispy plaintains, Mexican chocolate, coconut, strawberry ice cream, and *cajeta* (caramelized condensed milk) at **Adobo Grill** (⌧ *2005 W. Division St.* ☎ *773/252–9000*). Old-school fans from infants to seniors line up for ice-cream sundaes at the family-owned **Margie's Candies** (⌧ *1960 N. Western Ave.* ☎ *773/384–1035*) dating from 1921. Progressive foodies rave about the cake and shake combo at **Hot Chocolate** (⌧ *1747 N. Damen Ave.* ☎ *773/489– 1747*), a restaurant owned by acclaimed pastry chef Mindy Segal.

WICKER PARK TWO WAYS

There are two equally satisfying ways to dine in Wicker Park & Bucktown: With money or without much.

	Save	Splurge
Foodie haunts	**Milk & Honey Café** (✉1920 W. Division St., at Damen Ave. ☎773/395–9434) distinguishes breakfast with house-made granola, and lunch with sandwiches such as crab cake with chipotle mayo.	Acclaimed chef Shawn McClain runs **Spring** (✉2039 W. North Ave., at Damen Ave. ☎773/395–7100), serving gorgeous and savory Asian-inspired seafood in a former Russian bathhouse.
Music with your meal	**Smoke Daddy** (✉1804 W. Division St., at Wood St. ☎773/772–6656) serves up finger-lickin' barbecue like pulled-pork sandwiches and rib platters along with live R&B nightly.	Put yourself in the chef's hands at the sushi bar on the lower level at **Mirai Sushi** (✉2020 W. Division St., at Damen Ave. ☎773/862–8500), then head upstairs to the lounge for music.
Unexpected flavors	Aficionados line up down the block on weekends for brunch at **Bongo Room** (✉1470 N. Milwaukee Ave., at Honore St. ☎773/427–9972), including stacks of apple-currant French toast.	Rare beverage finds at **Takashi** (✉1952 N. Damen Ave., at Cortland Ave. ☎773/772–6170) such as a sweet wine made with yuzu (a Japanese citrus), complement a globally inspired menu.

RESTAURANTS IN THIS AREA

American
Hot Chocolate, $$
Mado, Market & Eatery, $
Bistro
Le Bouchon, $
Café
Milk & Honey Café, ¢
International
Feast, $
Japanese
Takashi, $$$
New American
Spring, $$$
Pizza
Crust, $
Piece, $
Southern
Smoke Daddy, $

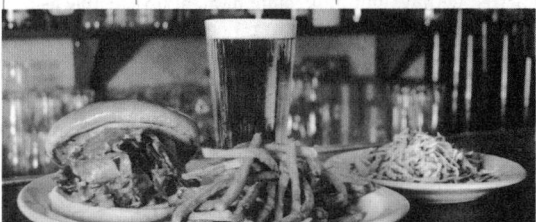

WHERE ROCKERS DINE

Come for the New Haven–style free-formed pizza and house-made brews at **Piece** (✉*1927 W. North Ave., at Damen Ave.* ☎*773/772–4422*). Stick around for the Saturday-night live-band karaoke. Co-owner Rick Nielsen is a member of Cheap Trick. Given his rep and the pies, rockers from near (Billy Corgan of Smashing Pumpkins fame, Al Jourgensen of Ministry, producer Steve Albini) and far (Todd Rundgren) frequently dine here.

$$
ITALIAN
The Loop

312 Chicago. Part handy hotel restaurant, part Loop power diner, and all Italian down to its second-generation chef, 312 Chicago earns its popularity with well-executed dishes that range from basic rigatoni with meatballs to grilled lamb chops with mascarpone and black-truffle polenta. We're tempted to carbo-load on the house-baked bread alone. Tables in the bi-level eatery are quieter aloft, though you still may see the occasional hotel guest wander through, looking for the elevator. ⊠*Hotel Allegro, 136 N. LaSalle St.* ☎*312/696–2420* ▤*AE, D, DC, MC, V* ⊗*No lunch Sat.* ✛*1:C6*

$$$
NEW AMERICAN
River North

Aigre Doux. Hidden in the shadows of its neighbor, the mammoth Merchandise Mart, this stylish spot in an unsung locale warrants searching out for the considerable talents of its husband-and-wife chef-owners. He does the savories, she the sweets. Lunch is delicious, but come back for dinner when Aigre Doux (which means "sweet and sour") is at its best, serving deftly accented dishes like heirloom squash risotto, braised rabbit pizza, and roasted lobster bucatini. Stay for desserts like sticky toffee pudding and caramelized apple bread pudding. Attentive service, a selective wine list and modern decor including exposed light bulbs create a chameleon setting conducive, like the chefs' marriage, to both business and romance. ⊠*230 W. Kinzie St.* ☎*312/329–9400* ▤*AE, D, DC, MC, V* ⊗*Closed Sun. No lunch weekends.* ✛*1:C5*

$$$$
CUTTING-EDGE
Lincoln Park
Fodor'sChoice
★

Alinea. Believe the hype and book well in advance. Chicago's most exciting restaurant—hidden on a residential block—demands an adventurous spirit and a serious commitment of time and money. If you have four hours and $225 to spare, the more than 20-course tasting menu is the best way to experience young whiz Grant Achatz's stunning cutting-edge food. The gastronomic roller coaster (there's also a less pricey 12-course version for $145) takes you on a journey through intriguing aromas, visuals, flavors, and textures. The menu changes frequently, but you might find green beans perched on a pillow that emits nutmeg-scented air, sweetbreads served with with burnt bread and toasted hay, and apple cider paired with walnut milk, cinnamon, and vegetable ash. Though some dishes—they range in size from one to four bites—may look like science projects, there's nothing gimmicky about the endless procession of bold and elegant tastes. The hours fly by in the window-less bi-level dining room, aided by the effortless service and muted decor. ⊠*1723 N. Halsted St.* ☎*312/867–0110* ⌖*Reservations essential* ▤*AE, D, DC, MC, V* ⊗*Closed Mon. and Tues. No lunch.* ✛*3:E3*

$$
ITALIAN
River North

A Mano. The proven restaurant team behind Bin 36 turned the space beneath their popular wine-centric restaurant into this Italian spot. True to its name, A Mano prides itself on making almost everything— from the pastas to the sausages—by hand. Start with burrata, a fresh, cream-filled mozzarella imported from Puglia, Italy, served with house-smoked salmon while you peruse the Italian wine list, or head to the bar to snack on $5 menu items such as thin-crust pizza, polenta fries, and cheese plates. To avoid the din (the open kitchen is in the middle of the dining room and conversation can be difficult on busy nights), dine early or on the patio next to the cypress trees. ⊠*22 N. Dearborn St.* ☎*312/629–3500* ▤ *AE, D, DC, MC, V.* ✛*3:H6*

$ Ann Sather. This Scandinavian restaurant, opened since 1945, is a Chi-
SCANDINAVIAN   cago institution, with good reason: the aroma of fresh cinnamon rolls,
Lakeview   Swedish pancakes with lingonberries, and waffles put this place on the
🕒   map, and it still draws a mob that lines up down the block for weekend breakfasts. Sure, you could try the usual eggs Benedict, but why
not sample the potato pancakes with apple sauce, or the pecan French
toast with hazelnut cream instead? Lunches offer similar Scandinavian
specialties as well as standard café sandwiches and salads. ⊠929 W.
Belmont Ave. ☎773/348–2378 ☰AE, D, DC, MC, V ⊙No dinner.
♣2:F4

$$$ Aria. Can't decide between Moroccan, Asian, or Mediterranean? Take
INTERNATIONAL   your globe-trotting taste buds to Aria, which roams the world larder
The Loop   with abandon: Asian-inspired sashimi tuna salad, free-range chicken
breast seasoned with Moroccan spices, Argentine churrasco, Malasian-
inspired soy-glazed cod, Hong Kong barbecue duck and lobster chow
mein, and the requisite American steaks. Among generous freebies,
tandoori-baked naan bread with Indian-inspired dipping sauces arrives
before the meal, and a trio of exotically spiced potatoes comes with the
entrées. In the convivial lounge, a small-plate menu and a full sushi bar
cater to abbreviated but equally adventurous appetites. ⊠*Fairmont
Chicago, 200 N. Columbus Dr.* ☎312/444–9494 ☰AE, D, DC, MC,
V. ♣1:F6

¢ Army and Lou's. First-rate home-cooked soul food banners this Far
SOUTHERN   South Side institution. The fried chicken is arguably the city's best,
South Side   but leave room for outstanding corn bread, chicken gumbo, mustard
greens, and sweet-potato pie. The setting is surprisingly genteel for such
down-home fare: waiters in bow ties, tables with starched white cloths,
and African and Haitian art on the walls. On Sunday, dress up and join
the after-church crowds. ⊠*422 E. 75th St.* ☎773/483–3100 ☰AE,
D, DC, MC, V ⊙*Closed Tues.* ♣4:F6

$$$$ Arun's. The finest Thai restaurant in Chicago—some say in the coun-
THAI   try—is also the most expensive, featuring only 12-course tasting menus
Far North Side   for a flat $85. That said, the kitchen readily adjusts its offerings to food
preferences and, of course, distastes. The kitchen artfully composes six
appetizers, four entrées, and two desserts using the freshest ingredients.
Results might include shrimp-filled golden pastry baskets, whole tama-
rind snapper, and veal medallions with ginger-lemongrass sauce. Arun's
out-of-the-way location in a residential neighborhood on the northwest
side doesn't discourage a strong following among locals and visiting
foodies. ⊠*4156 N. Kedzie Ave.* ☎773/539–1909 ⌔*Reservations
essential* ☰AE, D, DC, MC, V ⊙*Closed Mon. No lunch.* ♣2:A1

$$ Atwood Café. The Loop can be all business, even after hours, but we
AMERICAN   found an enclave of personality at this spot in the Hotel Burnham.
The Loop   Mahogany columns, cherrywood floors, gold café curtains, and curvy
banquettes provide color, and floor-to-ceiling windows provide light.
The mostly American menu includes reliables like pan-roasted chicken
breast and thick pork chops, peppered by contemporary fare such as
crispy red-lentil cakes and smoked paprika-grilled salmon fillet. ⊠*Ho-*

tel Burnham, 1 W. Washington St. ☎*312/368–1900* ▭*AE, D, DC, MC, V.* ✢*4:F1*

$$
NEW AMERICAN
West Loop
Fodor'sChoice
★

Avec. Go to this Euro-style wine bar when you're feeling gregarious; the rather stark space only has seating for 45 people, and it's all at communal tables. The results are loud and lively, though happily the shareable fare—a mix of homemade charcuterie, Mediterranean, and American dishes from a wood-burning oven—is reasonably priced. It's as popular as its next-door neighbor Blackbird (and run by the same forces), and only early birds are guaranteed tables. The doors open at—yikes!—3:30 PM. ✉*615 W. Randolph St.* ☎*312/377–2002* ▭*AE, D, DC, MC, V* ☾*No lunch.* ✢*1:A6*

$$$$
CUTTING-EDGE
Near North

Avenues. The least ostentatious of the city's cutting-edge restaurants, Avenues in the Peninsula Hotel lives a double life. The menu's most straightforward luxury items—butter-poached lobster, Kobe beef strip steak—aim to satisfy business travelers and other hotel guests, as does the contemporary black-lacquered decor. But true culinary connoisseurs come here for something else altogether. Filling the not-insignificant shoes of former chef Graham Elliot Bowles is Curtis Duffy, who has worked with some of Chicago's top toques, including Grant Achatz of Alinea and Charlie Trotter of eponymous Charlie Trotter's. Expect creative cuisine that is at once familiar and progressive as Duffy finds his stride. ✉*Peninsula Hotel, 108 E. Superior St.* ☎*312/573–6754* ▭*AE, D, DC, MC, V* ⚑*Reservations essential. Jacket required.* ☾*Closed Sun. and Mon. No lunch.* ✢*1:E3*

$
CHINESE
River North

Ben Pao. Snagging our award for the most Zen Chinese restaurant in town is this spot with minimalist black-and-gray decor and soothing water walls. The food livens up the scene, with spicy dragon noodles, Cantonese roast duck, and plenty of the tried-and-true sesame chicken and kung pao chicken. A dozen or so small-plate starters and the Asian hot pot dish—a sort of fondue that uses bubbling broth to cook meat—encourage sharing, making this a good choice for the gang. ✉*52 W. Illinois St.* ☎*312/222–1888* ▭*AE, D, DC, MC, V* ☾*No lunch weekends.* ✢*1:D4*

¢
BURGER
Near North

Billy Goat Tavern. The late comedian John Belushi immortalized the Goat's short-order cooks on *Saturday Night Live* for barking, "No Pepsi! Coke!" and "No fries! Cheeps!" at customers. They still do the shtick at this subterranean hole-in-the-wall favored by reporters posted nearby at the *Tribune* and the *Sun-Times*. Griddle-fried "cheezborgers" are the featured chow, and people-watching the favored sport. ✉*430 N. Michigan Ave., lower level* ☎*312/222–1525* ▭*No credit cards.* ✢*1:E5*

$$
AMERICAN
River North
Fodor'sChoice
★

Bin 36. This hip hybrid—fine-dining establishment, lively wine bar, and wineshop—serves wine any way you want it: by the bottle, glass, half glass, and as flights of multiple 2½ ounce tastings. The menu similarly encourages sampling, with lots of small-plate grazing choices. Contemporary entrées, such as braised lamb shank and peppercorn-crusted swordfish, are helpfully listed with wine recommendations. An all-glass west wall and 35-foot ceilings lend loft looks to the sprawling space, which can be noisy. Nonetheless, it's a good choice for group gatherings, and, since it's open all day, between-standard-mealtime nibbles. ⊠*339 N. Dearborn St.* ☎*312/755–9463* ☰*AE, D, DC, MC, V.* ✛*1:D5*

$$ **Bistro 110.** The knock against Bistro 110 is that it can be noisy and
BISTRO chaotic, but we consider that a testament to its popularity. Besides the
Near North lively bar scene and Water Tower views, the real draw is the food from the wood-burning oven. The kitchen consistently offers excellent renditions of French classics like roast chicken, and vegetarians praise the roasted-vegetable platter. The Sunday jazz brunch makes things more crowded—and louder—than usual. ⊠*110 E. Pearson St.* ☎*312/266– 3110* ☰*AE, D, DC, MC, V* ✛*1:E2.*

$$ **Bistro Campagne.** This is the place to dine on the North Side for rustic
BISTRO French fare: crispy roast chicken, steak piled with frites, goat-cheese
Far North Side salads, and ale-steamed mussels. The lovely, wood-trimmed Arts and Crafts interior provides instant attitude adjustment; in warmer weather, aim to get a table in the torch-lit garden. Prices are reasonable, including those for the French-centric wine list. ⊠*4518 N. Lincoln Ave.* ☎*773/271–6100* ☰*AE, MC, V* ⊗*No lunch.* ✛*2:B1*

$$ **Bistrot Margot.** We love this Old Town bistro for its faithfully executed
BISTRO menu, budget-friendly prices, and Parisian art nouveau interior, even
Near North if we have to sit a little too close for comfort to our neighbors. Chef-owner Joe Doppes whips up silky chicken-liver pâté, succulent *moules mariniere* (mussels in tomato sauce), escargots simmered in rich garlic butter, and soul-satisfying coq au vin. Head up to the second floor for additional seating—it has more of an intimate French country-home feel. Table spacing is tight and crowds are abundant, warranting your best behavior. ⊠*1437 N. Wells St.* ☎*312/587–3660* ☰*AE, D, DC, MC, V.* ✛*3:G3*

$$$ **Blackbird.** Being cramped next to your neighbor has never been as fun
NEW AMERICAN as it is at this hot spot run by foodie chef Paul Kahan. Celebs pepper
West Loop the sleek see-and-be-seen crowd who delve into creative dishes. While
Fodor$Choice the menu changes constantly, you'll always find items that highlight
★ seasonal ingredients, such as rack of lamb with leeks and *spigarello* (wild broccoli), in the spring, or grilled sturgeon with sauerkraut gnocchi in the winter. It all plays out against a minimalist backdrop of white walls, mohair banquettes, and aluminum chairs. Reservations aren't required, but they might as well be; the dining room is typically booked solid on Saturday night. ⊠*619 W. Randolph St.* ☎*312/715– 0708* ♙*Reservations essential* ☰*AE, D, DC, MC, V* ⊗*Closed Sun. No lunch Sat.* ✛*1:A6*

$$ **Blue Water Grill Chicago.** This isn't your standard seafood restaurant.
SEAFOOD Nightcrawlers love this spot for its sleek design, chic amenities (like
River North farewell chocolates in a small gift box), and a menu that fishes from Maine to Tokyo. The sexy L-shape interior spans a sushi bar, a cocktail lounge with low sofas, and two dining rooms with dark tables and throw pillows on the banquettes. There are the usual raw-bar oysters and steamed lobster, but the kitchen goes to work on creative maki rolls (try the spicy Baja), tempura calamari, and buttery bass. Upstairs

the jazz lounge hosts pre- and postprandial entertainment. ✉ *520 N. Dearborn St.* ☎ *312/777–1400* ⊟ *AE, D, DC, MC, V* ☉ *No lunch Sat.* ✛ *1:D4*

$$–$$$
NEW AMERICAN
Lincoln Park

Boka. If you're doing Steppenwolf pretheater dinner on North Halsted, this unpretentious, though upscale spot gets foodies' stamp of approval, particularly with Charlie Trotter alumnus Guiseppe Tentori in the kitchen. A seasonally driven menu includes standouts such as chamomile-dusted quail with caramelized fennel, and venison with Brussels sprouts, wild rice, dates, juniper berries, and a chestnut cake. The slick lounge and outdoor patio both serve food, drawing a following independent of curtain time. ✉ *1729 N. Halsted St.* ☎ *312/337–6070* ⊟ *AE, MC, V* ☉ *No lunch.* ✛ *3:E3*

$$
BRASSERIE
River North

Brasserie Jo. Come for the frites alone at Jean Joho's fun and more affordable brasserie (he of Everest fame). It's authentic down to its zinc-topped bar proffering complimentary hard-boiled eggs. Stay for the *choucroute Alsacienne* (smoked meats with Alsatian-style sauerkraut), sautéed skate wing, steamed mussels, fillet of trout, classic coq au vin, and steak tartare. It's most charming when it's bustling, though peak hours will force you to wait for a table. ✉ *59 W. Hubbard St.* ☎ *312/595–0800* ⊟ *AE, D, DC, MC, V* ☉ *No lunch.* ✛ *1:D5*

$$$$
BRASSERIE
River North

Brasserie Ruhlmann. Stroll into this cavernous space (a former Montgomery Ward building) and you're transported to a bustling French brasserie, complete with wicker bistro chairs in the bar, bold art nouveau details along the walls, and detailed tile work on the floors. Chef Christian Delouvrier (formerly of Alain Ducasse in New York City) crafts the menu around steak. But making a meal from well-executed appetizers, from the duck rillettes that arrives in a jar and the endive gratin, to the seared calamari with pesto, is far more fun (and economical). Plus, this ensures that you'll have room for classic desserts: the decadent pot de crème, also served in a jar, is not to be missed. ✉ *500 W. Superior St.* ☎ *312/494–1900* ⊟ *AE, D, DC, MC, V.* ✛ *3:F5*

$
SPANISH
Lincoln Park

Café Ba-Ba-Reeba! It has a kitschy name and is jammed with partying Lincoln Parkers, so at first you wouldn't expect much food-wise here, but expat Spaniards swear it's the best in town. Colorful Mediterranean-style interiors encourage the fiesta feel. The large assortment of cold and warm tapas ranges from garlic potato salad to beef tenderloin with blue cheese. It's worth visiting the entrée menu for paella and skewered meats. In warm weather six different flavors of sangria flow freely on the outdoor patio. ✉ *2024 N. Halsted St.* ☎ *773/935–5000* ⊟ *AE, D, DC, MC, V* ☉ *No lunch weekdays.* ✛ *3:E2*

$
SPANISH
River North

Cafe Iberico. A Spanish expat from the province of Galicia runs this tapas place hailed by a range of fans from visiting Spaniards to family clans, dating couples, and cheap chowhounds. You can easily build a meal from the many $3.95–$7 small plates on offer like baked goat cheese, Spanish ham, grilled squid, and skewered beef. When busy, it's loud and boisterous, which is only annoying on weekends when the wait can stretch to hours. Only parties of six or more may make reservations for Sunday through Thursday. ⊠*739 N. LaSalle St.* ☎*312/573–1510* ⊟*AE, D, DC, MC, V.* ✢*1:C3*

$ **Café Selmarie.** For a light meal in Lincoln Square, line up at this bak-
CAFÉ   ery-turned-café, a longstanding favorite among locals. Breakfast gets
Far North Side   you brioche French toast and corned-beef hash with eggs; lunch ranges
☺   from goat-cheese salads to turkey and Brie sandwiches; and dinner runs
to panko-crusted tilapia and roast chicken. Don't miss the sink-your-
teeth-in pastries (you can also buy them to go at the front counter).
Pass summer waits pleasantly in the neighboring plaza; during other
seasons, you're out in the cold. ⊠*4729 N. Lincoln Ave.* ☎*773/989–*
5595 ⊟*MC, V.* ✢*2:B1*

$$ **Carmichael's Chicago Steakhouse.** The look here is old-time Chicago—
STEAKHOUSE   oak and brass, black-and-white photographs, and waiters dressed in
West Loop   suspenders and shirtsleeve garters—though the true vintage is late
1990s. We forgive them the ruse for the well-priced (around $30)
Angus steaks, which make this one of the more reasonable top-tier
steakhouses in town. Planked salmon is a good nonbeef option. Live
jazz lures prowling carnivores to the lush garden in summer. ⊠*1052*
W. Monroe St. ☎*312/433–0025* ⊟*AE, D, DC, MC, V* ✆*No lunch*
weekends. ✢*4:C2*

$$ **Catch 35.** Eavesdrop on advertising types who do the after-five mix-
SEAFOOD   and-mingle at this spot in the lobby of the Leo Burnett Building. When
The Loop   it comes to the menu, have it your way: fish or shellfish comes grilled,
seared, or baked. Classic seafood appetizers are delivered with a twist,
such as coconut- and beer-battered shrimp, calamari rings with pepper
oil and fried Thai basil, and seared scallops with chive pot stickers. The
restaurant, with its marble, granite and beautifully set woodwork, is
an inviting space to relax, while the multilevel dining room provides
plenty of eye candy, plus glimpses of the Chicago River beyond. Come
Tuesday and Saturday evenings in order to catch the musical stylings
of a local jazz trio. ⊠*35 W. Wacker Dr.* ☎*312/346–3500* ⊟*AE, D,*
DC, MC, V ✆*No lunch weekends.* ✢*1:D6*

$$$$ **Charlie Trotter's.** Plan well in advance to dine at top toque Charlie Trot-
NEW AMERICAN   ter's namesake (or call the day of and hope for a cancellation). One
Lincoln Park   of the nation's most acclaimed chefs, Trotter prepares his menus daily
from the best of what's available globally. The results are daring, multi-
ingredient dishes that look like art on a dinner plate. Menus follow a
multicourse, $155 degustation format ($130 for the vegetarian ver-
sion). For a worthwhile splurge, order the wines-to-match option. This
temple of haute cuisine occupies a stately Lincoln Park town house.
⊠*816 W. Armitage Ave.* ☎*773/248–6228* ⚐*Reservations essential.*
Jacket required ⊟*AE, DC, MC, V* ✆*Closed Sun. and most Mon. No*
lunch. ✢*3:E2*

$$ **Chez Joël Bistro Français.** Breaking Taylor Street's Italian allegiance, Chez
BISTRO   Joel waves the flag for France. The sunny, cozy bistro, run by brothers
South Loop   Joël and Amed Kazouini, serves well-prepared classics like steak frites,
coq au vin, escargots, and bouillabaisse. It's a good pasta-free date
choice, and a favorite of locals thanks to its authentic bistro feel. Check

out the full bar and the reasonably priced wine list favoring French and Californian selections. On a warm Chicago day, ask for a seat outside on the patio. ✉*1119 W. Taylor St.* ☎*312/226–6479* ▱*AE, D, DC, MC, V* ⊘*Closed Mon. No lunch weekends* ✢*4:C3.*

$ **Chicago Brauhaus.** The German immigrants who settled in Lincoln
GERMAN   Square have mostly moved on, making room for a new generation of
Far North Side   urban hipsters. But they leave behind the Brauhaus, an Oktoberfest of a restaurant featuring a live band playing nightly polkas and waltzes that bring old-timers and new converts to the dance floor. Though the atmosphere is the draw over the food, you can't go wrong with the bratwurst and sauerkraut or the schnitzel. Large tables easily accommodate groups. The spacious bar and a good selection of German beers draw oompah-loving drinkers. ✉*4732 N. Lincoln Ave.* ☎*773/784–4444* ▱*AE, D, DC, MC, V* ⊘*Closed Tues.* ✢*2:B1*

$$ **Coco Pazzo.** The spread of antipasti that greets you upon entrance into
ITALIAN   this Tuscan-inspired restaurant is a sign of things to come. This restau-
River North   rant serves lusty, aggressively seasoned fare, such as homemade pasta with rabbit ragu, herb-crusted half lamb rack, and wood-grilled Florentine steaks. Stop in at lunch for pizzas fresh from the wood-fired oven. Swagged draperies and discreet but professional service work hard to soften the open loft setting of exposed brick walls and wood floors. Meanwhile, the well-rounded, exclusively Italian wine list is nothing to sniff at—Wine Spectator has lauded its selection ranging from popular to boutique producers. ✉*300 W. Hubbard St.* ☎*312/836–0900* ⌑*Reservations essential* ▱*AE, DC, MC, V* ⊘*No lunch weekends.* ✢*1:C5*

$ **Coobah.** Loud and lively Coobah loves a good party, and encourages
LATIN AMERI-   reveling to the wee hours by serving dinner until 12 AM most nights;
CAN   1 AM on Saturday. Unlike lots of lounge-restaurants, however, this
Lakeview   one doesn't rely on the mojitos and sangria to distract you from so-so food. Indeed, dishes such as tamale-baked tilapia, mussels sautéed with chili paste, and spicy pork tamales distinguish the kitchen. Weekend brunches, held 10 AM to 3 PM, lend a Latin accent to eggs and sandwiches. ✉*3423 N. Southport Ave.* ☎*773/528–2220* ▱*AE, D, DC, MC, V* ⊘*No lunch weekdays.* ✢*2:D3*

$–$$ **Costa's.** Greektown is fairly labeled monotonous, cuisine-wise. But Cos-
GREEK   ta's, a favorite among University of Illinois Chicago students, betters
West Loop   its many neighbors in both looks and taste. The multilevel Hellenic interior has terra-cotta tile work and rough-textured white walls and archways. There's a generous assortment of *mezes* (tapaslike Greek appetizers), traditional salt fish, a variety of kebabs, *dolmades* (stuffed grape leaves), fish flown in fresh daily, and roast leg of lamb. Live piano and the enthusiasm of diners tend to send the decibels soaring. ✉*340 S. Halsted St.* ☎*312/263–9700* ▱*AE, D, DC, MC, V.* ✢*4:D2*

$$$$ **Crofton on Wells.** We like this place because it's really good and still
NEW AMERICAN   manages to be rather low-key. Chef-owner Suzy Crofton breaks a few
River North   contemporary-dining rules: she doesn't pack tables too closely together in the small space, and she keeps the noise level down. Her food is

similarly short on clichés but gratifyingly long on flavor. Dig into spicy herb- and chipotle-roasted Amish chicken with Yukon Gold mashed potatoes and smoky molasses au jus, or grilled venison with baby arugula and sweet-potato spaetzle. But the menu is not meat-centric: with at least three vegetarian entrées on the menu each night, consider this a place to bring vegetarian friends. ⊠ *535 N. Wells St.* ☎ *312/755–1790* ⚱ *Reservations essential* ▤ *AE, D, DC, MC, V* ⊗ *Closed Sun. No lunch Sat.* ✛ *1:C4*

$ **Cru Café & Wine Bar.** After you've shopped Michigan Avenue and the
AMERICAN   Gold Coast and you're ready to drop, plant it at the well-located Cru
Near North   Café & Wine Bar for replenishment on a plate and in a glass. The 50-some by-the-glass pours, in addition to several hundred more bottle selections, pair well with elegant café fare such as the surf and turf lobster and beef tenderloin club sandwich, Cobb salad, and steak frites with cabernet jam. The gourmet take-out Goddess & the Grocer attached to Cru sells wine and nibbles to go if you prefer picnicking in your hotel room. ⊠ *25 E. Delaware Ave.* ☎ *312/337–4001* ▤ *AE, D, DC, MC, V.* ✛ *1:D2*

$ **Crust.** There's only a handful of restaurants around the country that are
PIZZA   certified organic, and despite the bureaucracy required for the distinc-
Wicker Park   tion (every ingredient used has to be approved by a third party certifier), this casual hipster spot is one of them. Feast on globally inspired flatbread served on wooden pizza peels; from basilico, a simple mozzarella, tomato, and basil rendition; to flammkuchen, which boasts bacon, caramelized onion, béchamel, and caraway seeds. Complement the main event with sides of roasted vegetables, local beers, or organic sodas. While Crust doesn't take reservations, call ahead to have your name added to the list; the wait can be more than an hour on Friday and Saturday nights. ⊠ *2056 W. Division St.* ☎ *773/235–5511* ⚱ *Reservations not accepted* ▤ *AE, D, MC, V.* ✛ *3:A4*

$$$ **Custom House.** Chef Shawn McClain established his renown with Asian
STEAKHOUSE   seafood at Spring and vegetables at Green Zebra before giving the stan-
South Loop   dard Chicago steak-house model a much-needed update with Custom House. The Printer's Row restaurant features sandstone block walls, cozy leather booths and picture windows, a handsome but not overly masculine setting that mirrors the food. You can get a New York strip or a flat iron steak, of course, but venturesome carnivores should try the braised veal cheeks or roast quail. Outstanding sides include gratin potatoes with sheep's-milk cheese, and desserts have a comforting quality in dishes like malted-milk chocolate mousse. ⊠ *500 S. Dearborn St.* ☎ *312/523–0200* ▤ *AE, D, DC, MC, V.* ✛ *4:F2*

$ **Cyrano's Bistrot Wine Bar & Cabaret.** Cyrano's flies under the radar in res-
BISTRO   taurant-rich River North, which works to your advantage if you want a
River North   spontaneous meal. Chef and owner Didier Durand presents the food of his birthplace, Bergerac, in this cheerful restaurant. Traditional starters such as onion tart, lobster bisque, pâtés, and rillettes lead into mains of rotisserie duck, cassoulet, and rabbit fricassee. The wine list includes many vintages from lesser-known producers in southern France. The

lower-level cabaret, Café Simone, is open on weekends and offers half-size entrées at half the price. ✉*546 N. Wells St.* ☎*312/467–0546* ▭*AE, D, DC, MC, V* ⊘*Closed Sun. and Mon. No lunch weekends.* ✛*1:C4*

$$$$
STEAKHOUSE
Near North

David Burke's Primehouse. New York celebrity chef David Burke runs Primehouse in the boutique James hotel and though local reception was initially cautious—after all, what could a New Yorker teach a Chicagoan about steak?—the restaurant has been roundly embraced for its convivial setting and sense of playfulness, including identifying 207L, the steer responsible for producing the menu's prime beef. Don't miss Burke's innovative cuts, including a 28-day-dry-aged rib eye and the bone-in filet mignon. Interactive elements including tableside tossed Caesar salads and fill-your-own doughnuts for dessert feed the considerable energy in the generally packed room. The best seats are the red-leather booths along the walls. ✉*616 N. Rush St.* ☎*312/660–6000* ▭*AE, D, MC, V.* ✛*1:E4*

$
MEXICAN
West Loop

De Cero Taqueria. Sometimes you want celebrity chef–made regional Mexican, and sometimes you just want a really good taco. For the latter, as well as zesty margaritas, a convivial setting, and lick-the-mortar-clean guacamole, grab a table at De Cero, the Mexican standout on Randolph Street's restaurant row. The highlight of the menu is the taco list. Each of 16 tacos is priced individually and made to order for a mix-and-match meal. Top choices include chipotle chicken, braised duck with corn salsa, and beef tenderloin tips braised with mushrooms. Though the spot is wood-tables-and-benches casual and very loud, beat the crowds by phoning ahead, especially on weekends. ✉*814 W. Randolph St.* ☎*312/455–8114* ▭*AE, MC, V* ⊘*Closed Sun. No lunch weekends.* ✛*3:D1*

$$$
LATIN AMERI-
CAN
River North

DeLaCosta. Hip DeLaCosta imports the Nuevo Latino food of celebrity chef Douglas Rodriguez and amps up the club vibe for a see-and-be-seen spot that manages to do a creditable job with the food. The decor is truly theatrical, down to placing menacing mannequins on the walls, renting private "cabanas" with bottle service, and swathing the public lounge area in gauzy curtains. But foodies won't be disappointed by a seat at the stylish ceviche bar (don't miss the hamachi ceviche) or orders of marlin tacos and Uruguayan beef tenderloin. The later the hour, the louder and boozier this spot becomes; reserve accordingly. ✉*465 E. Illinois St.* ☎*312/464–1700* ▭*AE, D, MC, V* ⊘*No lunch weekends.* ✛*1:H4*

¢
AMERICAN
River North
☾

Ed Debevic's. Gum-snapping waiters in garish costumes trade quips and snide remarks with customers at this tongue-in-cheek re-creation of a 1950s diner, but it's all good, clean fun (except perhaps when they dance on the counter without removing their shoes). The menu is deep and cheap with 10 different hamburgers, five chili preparations, four hot dogs, a large sandwich selection, and "deluxe plates" such as meat loaf, pot roast, and chicken-fried steak. The place is crawling with kids. Unlike a real 1950s diner, however, Ed's has a selection of cocktails and wines for their parents. ⊠*640 N. Wells St.* ☎*312/664–1707* ⌖*Reservations not accepted* ▤*AE, D, DC, MC, V.* ⊹*1:C4*

$ **Eleven City Diner.** For all its great food, Chicago is not a big deli town,
AMERICAN which endears Eleven City Diner, an old-school deli and family res-
South Loop taurant in the South Loop, to the locals. You can get breakfast all day
(bagel and lox, "hoppel poppel" scrambled eggs with salami, potatoes,
onions, and peppers), deli staples like matzoh-ball soup and pastrami
and corned-beef sandwiches, and diner options including burgers, and
soda-fountain floats and malts from the staff soda jerk. Breaking from
the deli tradition, Eleven City sells beer, wine, and cocktails. In keeping
with its theme there's an old-fashioned candy counter on your way out.
⊠*1112 S. Wabash* ☎*312/212–1112* ▤*AE, D, DC, MC, V.* ⊹*4:G3*

$ **Emperor's Choice.** This sophisticate sets out to prove that Chinese spe-
CHINESE cialties can go well beyond deep-fried prawns and kung pao chicken.
Chinatown It succeeds with strong seafood offerings, such as steamed oysters,
Peking-style lobster, and Dungeness crab, fried and served whole sea-
soned with salt. It also offers a separate menu including "delicacies"
such as shark's fin soup and pork belly. While the restaurant accom-
modates groups of 10 easily, seating is generally cramped and not for
serenity-seekers, but the decent prices, good food, and friendly service
make up for the surroundings. Discounted parking (with validation)
is available in the Cermak/Wentworth lot. ⊠*2238 S. Wentworth Ave.*
☎*312/225–8800* ▤*AE, D, MC, V.* ⊹*4:F6*

$$ **Erwin Cafe.** Striking a pose between friendly and refined, this spot has
NEW AMERICAN comforting food, a cozy setting, and polished service. Chef Erwin Dre-
Lakeview schsler often patrols the dining room of his namesake restaurant, greet-
ing regulars. The straightforward, seasonal menu may not look all that
differentiated from other upscale American menus—skate sautéed with
zucchini, cherry tomatoes, garlic, and fingerling potatoes, wood-grilled
flank steak with buttermilk-scallion mashed potatoes, and one of the
city's best burgers—but the skillful cooking and vibrant flavors give
you new respect for simplicity. The booths by the front windows are
the best for views of neighborhood comings and goings. ⊠*2925 N.
Halsted St.* ☎*773/528–7200* ▤*AE, D, DC, MC, V* ⊙*Closed Mon.
No lunch.* ⊹*2:F5*

$$$$ **Everest.** No one expects romance at the top of the Chicago Stock
FRENCH Exchange, but Everest does its best to throw you a curve wherever
The Loop and whenever. Consider the trip: two separate elevators whisk you 40
stories up, where you have sweeping views of the city's sprawl westward. Then there's the food. It's French, but with an Alsatian bent—a
nod to Chef Jean Joho's roots. He might just bring edible gold leaf to
his risotto (and you'll pay handsomely for it). And finally, there's the
redesigned space, where modern sculpture melds with art nouveau.
The whole experience, from the tuxedoed waiters to the massive wine
list, screams "special occasion!" ⊠*440 S. LaSalle St.* ☎*312/663–
8920* ⌖*Reservations essential. Jacket required* ▤*AE, D, DC, MC, V*
⊙*Closed Sun. and Mon. No lunch.* ⊹*4:F2*

$ Feast. The cozy fireplace and sofa-filled lounge create a fittingly social
INTERNATIONAL setting for the arty Bucktown locals who dine here regularly. If you
Bucktown can't find something to eat here, you're not hungry. World cuisines
from Cuba to India mingle freely on an expansive, bold menu; try the
ancho chili and maple-glazed pork chop, barbecue salmon over corn
buttermilk hot cakes, or chimichurri skirt steak. ⊠*1616 N. Damen
Ave.* ☎*773/772–7100* ⊟*AE, D, DC, MC, V.* ✛*3:B3*

$$$$ Fogo de Chão. Gaucho-clad servers parade through the dining room
BRAZILIAN brandishing carved-to-order skewered and grilled meats in this all-you-
River North can-eat Brazilian churrascaria. Diners warm up with a trip to the lavish
salad bar. Then, using a plate-side chip, signal green for "go" to bring
on lamb, pork loin, ribs, and several beef cuts, stopped only by flipping
the chip to red. You can restart as often as you like. If that's not enough,
there are starchy sides and dessert flans included in the $48.50 price as
well; only drinks are extra. Compared to traditional steakhouses, this
carnivorous all-inclusive feast is a bargain. Go on a busy night (Thursday, Friday, or Saturday) to ensure the meat's tender, and not dried out
from reheating. ⊠*661 N. LaSalle St.* ☎*312/932–9330* ⊟*AE, D, DC,
MC, V* ⊗*No lunch weekends.* ✛*1:C3*

¢ Fox & Obel Market, Café & Catering. Skip the tourist-trap funnel-cake fare
CAFÉ at Navy Pier. This riverside gourmet market a block away is a toothsome
Near North escape. The prepared fine and organic foodstuffs are treated with rev-
erence, and although service is cafeteria-style, selections are decidedly
more sophisticated. We like the Cuban sandwich with smoked Black
Forest ham, breaded pork, Swiss cheese, and the pan-seared mahimahi
topped with shrimp. But first, a word of warning: attractive chocolate
bars, exotic charcuterie, and worldly cheeses sold in the upscale grocery
can be budget busters. ⊠*401 E. Illinois St.* ☎*312/410–7301* ⊟*AE,
D, MC, V.* ✛*1:G4*

$$ Frontera Grill. Devotees of chef-owner Rick Bayless queue up for his
MEXICAN distinct fare at this casual restaurant brightly trimmed in Mexican folk
River North art. Bayless annually visits Mexico with the entire staff in tow. Servers,
consequently, are encyclopedic on the food, typified by trout in yellow
mole, red chili-marinated pork, and black-bean tamales filled with goat
cheese. The reservation policy is tricky: they're accepted for parties of
five or more, though smaller groups can phone in the same day. Oth-
erwise, do as most do and endure the two-margarita wait. ⊠*445 N.
Clark St.* ☎*312/661–1434* ⊟*AE, D, DC, MC, V* ⊗*Closed Sun. and
Mon.* ✛*1:D5*

$$$$ Geja's Cafe. For every course there's a fondue at this Lincoln Park long-
FRENCH timer. Start with the cheese fondue, then progress to the sampler plate
Lincoln Park of shellfish, chicken, beef, and vegetables cooked in a fondue pot of
hot oil (the tables are riveted to the floor to avoid disaster). Finish
by dunking fruits and sweets in liquid chocolate, if you've got room.
Candlelight, cozy dining nooks, walls filled with empty wine bottles,
and strumming guitarists mean this place is packed on Valentine's Day.
⊠*340 W. Armitage Ave.* ☎*773/281–9101* ⊟*AE, D, DC, MC, V*
⊗*No lunch.* ✛*3:G2*

Continued on page 185

CHICAGO'S HOLY TRINITY:
Pizza, Hot Dogs & Italian Beef Sandwiches

Long before Chicago's dining scene got all gussied up with boldface-named chefs and swanky hot spots, the City of Big Shoulders perfected hearty, gut-busting food for the Average Joe. Until you've pigged out on deep-dish pizza at Lou Malnati's or Gino's East, sunk your teeth into a loaded hot dog at Superdawg Drive-in, and wiped the grease off your face after devouring an Italian beef sandwich at Al's Italian Beef, you haven't done Chicago. So go on, leave your diet plans at home and get ready to sample the best of the big city.

cheese, cheese, and more mozzarella cheese to top

sausage, pepperoni, olives, onions, mushrooms, peppers, or other fillings of your choice

flaky crust on the outside, gooey on the inside

two-inch-high deep dish pan

spicy tomato sauce

TASTE 1 | DEEP-DISH PIZZA

A CALORIC HISTORY

Pizza—in one form or another—has been around since the sixth century B.C., but it only gained heft when it settled into this brash, entrepreneurial city. Pizzeria Uno founder Ike Sewell generally gets the credit for turning pizza inside out in 1943. His knife-and-fork creation started with a layer of cheese, followed by the toppings, and then the sauce, all tucked into a doughy crust that he yanked up the sides of a deep pan.

THE CRUST CONTROVERSY

The founders of Lou Malnati's pizzeria worked in Ike's kitchen at Pizzeria Uno and claim that *they* were the ones actually doing the cooking. They broke off and opened up Lou Malnati's in 1971, in Lincolnwood, a northern suburb of Chicago, and a classic Chicago rivalry was born. Today, there are more than 25 locations of Lou Malnati's in Chicago and its surrounding neighborhoods.

BEST SPOTS TO SAMPLE

Where it (supposedly) All Started: Tuck into a rich-and-gooey pie at **Pizzeria Uno** (✉ 29 E. Ohio St. ☎ 312/321–1000 ⊕ www.unos.com), where you'll be sure to encounter a wait.

Most Authentic: Aficionados of **Lou Malnati's** (✉ 439 N. Wells St. ☎ 312/828–9800 ⊕ www. loumalnatis.com) claim that their favorite pies have more flavor and like that there are fewer tourists to clog up the joint. If you're really feeling indulgent, order yours with a butter crust. Trust us.

Worth the Wait: Join the out-the-door line at **Gino's East** (✉ 633 N. Wells St. ☎ 312/943–1124 ⊕ www.-ginoseast.com) for caloric pies and a chance to add to the graffiti on the walls.

Easiest to Find: The ubiquitous **Giordano's** (✉ 730 N. Rush St. ☎ 312/951–0747) has 12 locations throughout the city besides this one.

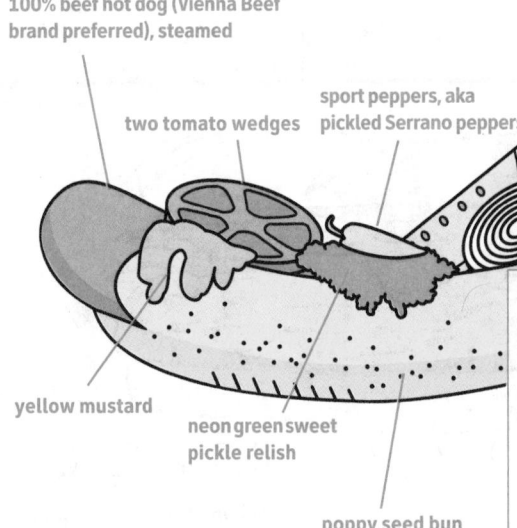

100% beef hot dog (Vienna Beef brand preferred), steamed

dill pickle spear

sport peppers, aka pickled Serrano peppers

two tomato wedges

fresh-sliced onion—bring a mint

yellow mustard

neon green sweet pickle relish

poppy seed bun

TASTE 2 | HOT DOGS

A DOG IS BORN

The iconic Chicago-style hot dog got its start at the 1893 World's Fair's Columbian Exposition. Emil Reichel and Sam Ladany, Austro-Hungarian immigrants hawked a beef frankfurter sandwich in a steamed bun piled with mustard, relish, onion, tomato, dill pickle, hot peppers, and celery salt. When the Fair moved on, the cravings persisted, launching an on-going affair with the Chicago-style hot dog.

HOW MUCH GARDEN CAN ONE BUN HOLD?

If you've walked a square block of Chicago, chances are you've passed a hot dog. Dog dealers lodge under El stops, on street corners, and at sports arenas. The one thing they all have in common? Their dogs get "dragged through the garden," or loaded with the aforementioned veggies, unless otherwise specified. Make sure to never add ketchup to your Chicago-style hot dog: a major no-no among hot dog aficionados. Don't forget to grab a fistful of napkins—these dogs are messy.

BEST SPOTS TO SAMPLE

A Chicago Institution: At Wiener's Circle (✉ 2622 N. Clark St. ☎ 773/477–7444) expect a hefty dose of attitude with your dog. This place has a cult-like following of masochistic fans who line up for insults from the sassy, crass staffers. Get the Chicago dog, and don't ask for any substitutions. You've been warned.

Get 'em Retro Style: Look for the boy dog and girl dog on the roof of **Superdawg Drive-In** (✉ 6363 N. Milwaukee Ave. ☎ 773/763–0660 ⊕ www.superdawg.com), where car-hops deliver your chow.

Poshest Pick: For a weiner on a higher plane, check out **Hot Doug's** (✉ 3324 N. California ☎ 773/279–9550 ⊕ www.hotdougs. com). In addition to the classic Chicago beef, encased meats include kangaroo or rabbit on a rotating menu.

Italian roll, split length-wise

thinly sliced, well-done beef in its juices

sautéed green bell peppers (optional)

hot giardiniera peppers

TASTE 3 | ITALIAN BEEF SANDWICHES

IT'S ALL ABOUT THE BEEF

Italian immigrants in Chicago happily adapted to the locally abundant meat supply to produce the now-classic Italian beef sandwich. Hard hats and desk jockeys crowd beef stands at lunch, joined by the occasional visiting celebrity. Don't expect much in the way of atmosphere: Here it's Formica counters, fluorescent lights, and big shoulder–to–big shoulder intimacy.

GRAB YOUR NAPKINS

The two-fister, a popular lunchtime staple, stuffs an Italian roll, split length-wise, with thin slices of medium beef. Authentic Italian beef sandwiches use sirloin rump, top round, or bottom round that's wet-roasted and dripping in a broth that's spiked with garlic, oregano, and spices. The whole thing is topped with hot giardiniera, a spicy relish of Serrano peppers, diced carrots, cauliflower, celery, and olives in oil. If you've ordered it "wet," it comes with an extra ladle of juice and a stack of napkins; if you order a cheesy beef, they melt a slice or two of mozzarella over the whole mess.

BEST SPOTS TO SAMPLE

Roll up Your Sleeves: Plant your elbows at the window counter or a picnic table in the "elegant dining room" at **Mr. Beef** (✉ 666 N. Orleans St. ☎ 312/337–8500), where famous fans get their mugs on the wall.

Join the Masses: On Little Italy's Taylor Street, standing-room-only crowds of students and local business folk pack **Al's No. 1 Italian Beef** (✉ 1079 W. Taylor St., ☎ 312/226–4017, ⊕ www.alsbeef.com).

Soak Up Nostalgia: The cavernous space at **Portillo's** (✉100 W. Ontario St. ☎ 312/587–8910) is decked out with Capone-era gangster photos and an antique car that hangs from the ceiling. Fans rave about their Italian beef sandwich, and you can buy souvenirs to commemorate the occasion.

$$$
STEAKHOUSE
River North

Gene and Georgetti. This old-school steakhouse, in business since 1941, is a Chicago institution. It thrives on the buddy network of high-powered regulars and celebrities who pop into the historic River North joint to carve up massive steaks, good chops, and the famed "garbage salad"—a kitchen-sink creation of greens with vegetables and meats. In addition, Italian-American classics such as eggplant parmigiana and veal Vesuvio are on offer along with simple seafood dishes like lobster tail, salmon, and whitefish. Service can be brusque if you're not connected, and prices can be steep, but the vibe is Chicago to the core. ⊠ *500 N. Franklin St.* ☎ *312/527–3718* ▤ *AE, DC, MC, V* ⊗ *Closed Sun.* ✛ *1:C4*

$$$$
STEAKHOUSE
Near North

Gibsons Steakhouse. Chicago movers and shakers mingle with conventioneers at Gibsons, a lively, homegrown, Gold Coast steakhouse renowned for overwhelming portions, good service, and celebrity spotting. Generous steaks and chops center the menu, but there are plenty of fish options including planked whitefish and massive Australian lobster tails. One dessert will feed a table of four. Reservations aren't required but are near essential given the hoards of fans. ⊠ *1028 N. Rush St.* ☎ *312/266–8999* ⩊ *Reservations essential* ▤ *AE, D, DC, MC, V.* ✛ *1:D1*

$$
ITALIAN
South Loop

Gioco. The name means "game" in Italian, and the restaurant fulfills the promise not with venison, but in the spirit of playing a game. The decor is distressed-urban, with plaster-spattered brick walls and well-worn hardwood floors, but the menu is comfort-Italian, with rustic fare like homemade penne pasta with prosciutto, grilled lamb chops, and sausage with beans. The Speakeasy Room, a private dining space with its own rear-alley entrance, is an homage to the building's notorious past under Prohibition. ⊠ *1312 S. Wabash Ave.* ☎ *312/939–3870* ▤ *AE, DC, MC, V.* ✛ *4:G4*

$$$
NEW AMERICAN
River North

Graham Elliot. Guests groove to the tunes of Wilco and the Police while sampling Chef Graham Elliot Bowles' inventive fare, some of which foodies may recognize from the chef's stint orchestrating elaborate tasting menus at Avenues (for reference, try the cheddar-apple risotto). Yet much of the menu, from "BLT-style" salmon (salmon served with pancetta vinaigrette) to pork prime rib will satisfy diners in far fewer courses than the old Avenues tasting menu did. Service can be unconventional: servers take dessert orders at the start of the meal, for example. Yet the boisterous space with exposed brick walls succeeds in combining a casual vibe with fine dining flourish. Bowles calls it "bistronomic;" his fans simply call it good eating. ⊠ *217 W. Huron St.* ☎ *312/624–9975* ▤ *AE, D, DC, MC, V* ⊗ *Closed Mon.* ✛ *3:G5*

$
AMERICAN
Lincoln Park

Green Dolphin Street. It's hard to pass up this one-stop dinner-and-music spot. There are globally influenced American dishes in the main dining room, a sandwiches-and-salads bar menu in the jazz club, and a seasonal outdoor patio overlooking a relatively quiet stretch of the Chicago River. Dinner in the main room gets you into the handsome club, where there are always music performances, from big band swing to Latin jazz and rhythm and blues. The venue heats up for Salsa Tuesdays, where a DJ spins salsa-worthy tracks for dancing patrons. ✉*2200 N. Ashland Ave.* ☏*773/395–0066* ▭*AE, D, DC, MC, V* ✆*Closed Sun. and Mon. No lunch.* ✛*3:C1*

$$$
NEW AMERICAN
West Loop

Green Zebra. Chef Shawn McClain of Spring fame took the vegetable side dish and ran it up the marquee. The result gives good-for-you veggies the star treatment in a sleek shop suave enough to attract the likes of Gwyneth Paltrow. All dishes are small and change seasonally. You might see roast beets with horseradish foam or sunchoke ravioli with melted goat cheese and hazelnuts. One chicken and one fish dish make do for carnivores. ✉*1460 W. Chicago Ave.* ☏*312/243–7100* ▭*AE, D, DC, MC, V* ✛*3:C5*

$$
STEAKHOUSE
The Loop

The Grillroom Chophouse & Winebar. If you're going to see a performance at the LaSalle Bank Theatre across the street, you're close enough to dash over here for a drink at intermission (we love the lengthy by-the-glass wine selections). Pre- and post-curtain, the clubby confines fill with showgoers big on beef, though there are also ample raw bar, seafood, and pasta choices. For the most relaxing experience, come after Act I commences. ✉*33 W. Monroe St.* ☏*312/960–0000* ▭*AE, D, DC, MC, V* ✆*No lunch weekends.* ✛*4:F2*

$
ITALIAN
River North

Harry Caray's Italian Steahouse. Famed Cubs announcer Harry Caray died in 1998, but his legend lives on as fans continue to pour into the namesake restaurant where Harry frequently held court. Italian-American specialties including pastas and chicken Vesuvio share menu space with top-quality prime steaks and chops. The wine list has won a number of national awards. If you're looking for a classic Chicago spot to catch a game, the generally thronged bar serves items off of the restaurant menu. Holy cow! ✉*33 W. Kinzie St.* ☏*312/828–0966* ▭*AE, D, DC, MC, V.* ✛*1:D5*

$
SOUTHERN
Multiple
Locations

Heaven on Seven. Every day is Mardi Gras at Heaven on Seven, which pursues a good time all the time—and even more so on Saturday and Sunday afternoons when a live band performs. The restaurant, with two locations in the city, has a menu centered around a daring collection of hot sauces, and the food, though it's well shy of ambrosia, is plentiful and filling. Some guests find the menu too spicy for their kids, but would go back for the well-priced Mardi Gras jambalaya, fried oyster po'boy, cheese grits, and chicory coffee. Cheddar-jalapeño biscuits and chocolate peanut-butter pie are great menu bookends. ✉ *111 N. Wabash Ave.* ☏*312/263–6443* ✉*600 N. Michigan Ave.* ☏*312/280–7774* ▭*AE, D, DC, MC, V* ✛*1:E4.*

$
BELGIAN
Far North Side
Fodor's Choice
★

Hopleaf Bar. True beer aficionados know beer is food. So when hops devotee Michael Roper added a dining room onto the back of his beloved tavern, swillers thrilled to sop their suds with delectable specialties such as Belgian-style mussels steamed in white ale with herbs, venison meat loaf with a root-vegetable gratin, and duck Reuben sandwiches on marble rye. Arrive early to avoid waiting in the bar for a table. But don't bring the kids; Roper insists that only those of legal drinking age can eat here. ✉*5148 N. Clark St.* ☏*773/334–9851* ▭*AE, D, DC, MC, V.* ✛*2:D1*

$$ **Hot Chocolate.** The city's most celebrated pastry chef, Mindy Segal,
AMERICAN strikes out solo at Hot Chocolate, a hit with, as you might expect, a
Bucktown really great dessert selection ranging from a creative soufflé tart with
salted caramel ice cream and homemade pretzels to a myriad of milk
shakes and hot chocolate flavors with homemade marshmallows. How
sweet, and how swamped, it is. The savory menu is well-crafted, with
items such as a Berkshire pork tenderloin with spaetzle and a tuna
melt made with tuna poached in olive oil, wild capers, and Wiscon-
sin cheese. ⊠*1747 N. Damen Ave.* ☎*773/489–1747* ▭*AE, MC, V*
☉*Closed Mon.* ✢*3:B3*

¢ **Hot Doug's.** Don't tell the zealots who have made Hot Doug's famous
HOT DOGS that these are *just* hot dogs—these "encased meats" go beyond your
Far North Side standard Vienna wiener. The gourmet purveyor wraps buns around
Fodor'sChoice chipotle chicken sausage, smoked crawfish and pork sausage with
★ spicy remoulade, rabbit sausage, and even rattlesnake sausage on occa-
☪ sion. Make the trek on a Friday or Saturday, when the artery-clogging
duck-fat fries are available. The clientele is a curious mix of hungry
hard-hats and serious foodies, neither of which care about the lack of
frills. ⊠*3325 N. California Ave.* ☎*773/279–9550* ▭*No credit cards*
☉*Closed Sun. No dinner.* ✢*3:A2*

$ **Ina's.** It's so cozy you almost feel like you're at a diner—there's the
AMERICAN loving presence of owner Ina Pinkney, reliable chow, and a regular fol-
West Loop lowing. But dishes like vegetable hash and "scrapple"—polenta mixed
with cheddar and black beans, fried into a disk, and served with eggs
and chorizo—at breakfast and Southern fried chicken, pork tender-
loin, and several fish entrées at dinner, there's something for everyone.
Close to Oprah's studio and loft dwellers up and down Randolph,
Ina's regularly generates a queue, especially on weekends. ⊠*1235 W.
Randolph St.* ☎*312/226–8227* ▭*AE, D, DC, MC, V* ☉*No dinner
Sun. and Mon.* ✢*4:C1*

$$$ **Japonais.** Style and substance come together at sleek and chic Japonais.
JAPANESE Don't be intimidated by the lengthy menu. Trust servers to direct you
River North to savories such as breaded oysters, sweet-vinegar-seaweed salad, and
a raft of winning maki-roll combinations including octopus with spicy
tuna. Traditional tables are supplemented by a couch-filled lounge also
serving the entire menu. Downstairs an indoor-outdoor bar provides
seasonal seating along the Chicago River—don't attempt it on weekends
unless you have sharp elbows. ⊠*606 W. Chicago Ave.* ☎*312/822–
9600* ▭*AE, D, DC, MC, V* ☉*No lunch weekends.* ✢*1:A3*

$ **Joe's Be-Bop Cafe and Jazz Emporium.** Joe's looks like a classic jazz club
SOUTHERN with a raised stage, but plays like a family restaurant on raucous Navy
Near North Pier. Hearty, hickory-smoked barbecue entrées like baby back ribs,
☪ pulled pork, and brisket as well as Creole fare such as jambalaya are
clan-pleasing, and the jazz bands—booked most nights—lift Joe's from
merely touristy to actually enjoyable. Take a seat in the colorful main
dining room or enjoy summer weather from the patio—either way,
you'll hear the slick, upbeat music during your meal. ⊠*600 E. Grand
Ave.* ☎*312/595–5299* ▭*AE, D, DC, MC, V.* ✢*1:H4*

$$-$$$
SEAFOOD
River North

Joe's Seafood, Prime Steaks & Stone Crab. You might wonder what a South Floridian like Joe's is doing so far from the ocean. Apparently, raking it in. Unlike its parent, Joe's Stone Crab in Miami Beach, this outlet doesn't close when the Florida crabs are out of season in summer, which explains the extra emphasis on other denizens of the deep and prime steaks. One thing this restaurant does share with the Miami original is its popularity—though the restaurant takes reservations, you can expect to wait when it's packed with hungry guests. ✉60 *E. Grand Ave.* ☎312/379–5637 ▭*AE, D, DC, MC, V* ✆*No lunch Sun.* ✢1:E4

$
NEW AMERICAN
Near West Side

Juicy Wine Company. Rodney Alex's smart wine bar is proof that a minimal kitchen (limited to what will fit behind the bar's counter) can still thrill foodies. Simple preparations, such as duck rillette panini seasoned with Hawaiian sea salt and aged goat cheese and slices of rare jamón ibérico, prized Spanish ham, serve to compliment the real draw: hand-picked wines from around the world poured in crystal glasses large enough to contain an entire bottle of wine. While the two-story, cork-lined space becomes a late-night chef hangout (Chef Paul Kahan from Blackbird plays DJ on occasion), head there on weekends for $5 drinks and a $5 brunch menu with offerings such as chicken and waffles. ✉ *694 N. Milwaukee Ave.* ☎312/492–6620 ▭ *AE, D, DC, MC, V* ✢3:E6

¢
CAFÉ
Lakeview

Julius Meinl Cafe. Viennese coffee roaster Julius Meinl operates this very European café in an unexpected location at the intersection of Addison and Southport, just a few blocks from Wrigley Field. Comfortable banquettes and a supply of international newspapers bid coffee sippers to stick around. Vegetable focaccia and pear and Brie sandwiches, hazelnut and blue-cheese salads, *Frittaten* (Austrian beef broth with crepe noodles), and loads of European pastries feed the peckish. We love the Austrian breakfast of poached egg, ham, and Emmentaler cheese—this is the only place in the city that serves it. Classical and jazz combos entertain Friday and Saturday, and some Tuesday evenings as well. ✉*3601 N. Southport Ave.* ☎773/868–1857 ▭*AE, D, MC, V.* ✢2:D3

$
JAPANESE
Near North

Kamehachi. It seems like there's a sushi spot on practically every corner in Chicago, but when Kamehachi opened in Old Town in 1967 it was the first. Quality fish, updated decor, and eager-to-please hospitality keep fans returning. Behind the busy sushi bar, chefs manage both restaurant orders and the many take-out calls from neighbors. We find combinations, including maki rolls, nigiri sushi, and miso soup, are often a bargain, running from $13 to $30. Belly up to the sushi bar, or take a seat in the upstairs lounge or in the flowering garden (in season). The Streeterville spin-off offers semiprivate tatami rooms ideal for groups. ✉*1400 N. Wells St.* ☎312/664–3663 ✆*No lunch Sun.* ✉*240 E. Ontario* ☎312/587–0600 ✉ *320 E. Ontario St.* ☎312/744–1900 ▭*AE, D, DC, MC, V* ✆*No lunch Sun. and Mon.* ✢1:F4

$$$$
STEAKHOUSE
River North

Keefer's. Few steakhouses advertise their broiler men, but the barrier-busting Keefer's hired acclaimed chef John Hogan to run the kitchen. Hogan's definition of a steak-house menu breaks all conventions by including his signature bistro fare, inventive daily specials (pray for the seafood-rich bouillabaisse), and plenty of fish offerings as well as New York strips and hefty porterhouses. The circular room drops the he-man pose, too. All of which explains why Keefer's pulls the most diverse and gender-balanced crowd of the meat market. ⊠*20 W. Kinzie St. ☎312/467–9525 ▤AE, D, DC, MC, V ⊗Closed Sun. No lunch Sat. ✛1:D5*

$ | **Kitsch'n on Roscoe.** If you love all things '70s, you'll love Kitsch'n as
AMERICAN | much as the regulars. It's a diner in retro garb, with lava lamps and
Lakeview | vintage toasters–turned–table lamps. Dine, with tongue firmly in cheek, on pesto-dyed "green eggs and ham" and Twinkies tiramisu. Or play it straight with hefty tuna and grilled-cheese sandwiches. Weekends are jammed; midweek is better for relaxing. ⊠*2005 W. Roscoe St. ☎773/248–7372 ▤AE, MC, V ⊗No dinner Sun. and Mon. ✛2:B4*

$$$$ | **L20.** Well before he opened this fine dining shrine to the sea, Chef Lau-
SEAFOOD | rent Gras began tempting diners by logging menu ideas onto his blog.
Lincoln Park | The results of his experiments can be found on L20's four-course prix fixe menu and 12-course tasting menu, in which hard-to-find fish varieties—such as *shimaaji*, Japanese mackerel, or *kinmedai*, fatty tuna—are smoked, cured, seared, or foamed. Guests also have the opportunity to taste delicacies such as wagyu beef imported from Miyazaki, Japan, at an additional cost. Deciphering the menu may take some assistance, but the serene, earth-toned dining room and professional staff help soothe any worries. Tradition, in the form of delicate soufflés and macaroons, return at the end of the meal for a sweet sendoff. ⊠ *2300 N. Lincoln Park W. ☎773/868–0002 ▤AE, D, DC, MC, V ⊗Closed Tues. ✛3:G1*

$ | **La Donna.** We deem this Andersonville's best Italian because of its excel-
ITALIAN | lent pastas—try the pumpkin ravioli in creamy balsamic sauce or the
Far North Side | fine penne *arrabiata* (spicy tomato sauce)—and good, cracker-crust pizzas. The generally crowded storefront dining room either makes you feel like part of a very large party or just trapped. The wine list is well chosen and fairly priced, and there's a Sunday brunch and fixed-price, three-course meal served Monday through Thursday, and both are bargains. ⊠*5146 N. Clark St. ☎773/561–9400 ▤AE, D, DC, MC, V. ✛2:D1*

$$ | **La Sardine.** We don't know if the sardine reference was meant to tele-
BISTRO | graph the seating arrangements, but, yes, it's snug here. Still, you'll find
West Loop | it easier to tolerate your neighbors with a solid menu of traditional bistro favorites including warm goat-cheese salad, bouillabaisse, and roasted chicken with mashed potatoes. Since it's across the street from Harpo Studios (where Oprah tapes her talk show), audience members and producers alike converge at La Sardine. ⊠*111 N. Carpenter St. ☎312/421–2800 ▤AE, D, DC, MC, V ⊗Closed Sun. No lunch Sat. ✛4:C1*

¢ | **Lao Sze Chuan.** If you're looking for spice, filling food, and great prices
CHINESE | in Chinatown, check out this Szechuan kitchen. Chilies, garlic, and gin-
Chinatown | ger seem to go into every dish, whether it's chicken, eggplant, or dump-

lings. The digs are nothing to write a postcard home about, but you'll feel smug for choosing it once the feast is finished. ✉2172 S. Archer Ave. ☎312/326–5040 ▤AE, D, DC, MC, V. ✣4:F6

$
BISTRO
Bucktown
Le Bouchon. The French comfort food at this charming-but-cramped bistro in Bucktown is in a league of its own. The onion tart has been a signature dish of owner Jean-Claude Poilevey for years; he also does a succulent sautéed rabbit and a definitive *salade Lyonnaise* (mixed greens topped with a

creamy vinaigrette and a poached egg). Save room for the fruit tarts. Don't attempt Le Bouchon on weekends without a reservation. ✉1958 N. Damen Ave. ☎773/862–6600 ▤AE, D, DC, MC, V ⊗Closed Sun. No lunch. ✣3:B2

$$
ASIAN
River North
Le Lan. Top toques Roland Liccioni of Le Francais and Arun Sampanthavivat of Arun's teamed up to create this elegant French-Asian boîte. We like the sophisticated-without-being-stuffy vibe—sharply dressed (yes, don your black to fit in here) foodies fill the exposed brick room that has green accents and orchids on the tables. The menu manages the same balance: the rich flavors of France are piqued by Asian notes. Look for the Asian squash dumplings and the tea-smoked duck breast ✉749 N. Clark St. ☎312/280–9100 ▤AE, D, DC, MC, V ⊗Closed Sun. No lunch. ✣1:D3

$$$$
FRENCH
Near North
Les Nomades. Intimate and elegant don't make headlines, but Les Nomades holds a torch for tender refinements. Wood-burning fireplaces and original art warm the dining rooms of the Streeterville brownstone. A carefully composed menu of contemporary French food includes the usual suspects, such as duck consommé and warm asparagus with crispy poached egg, plus earthy indulgences like roasted squab breast with crispy sweetbreads. Compose your own prix-fixe dinner from the menu; four courses cost $100; five courses cost $112. ✉222 E. Ontario St. ☎312/649–9010 ⌦Reservations essential. Jacket required ▤AE, D, DC, MC, V ⊗Closed Sun. and Mon. No lunch. ✣1:F4

¢
AMERICAN
West Loop
☾
Lou Mitchell's. Shelve your calorie and cholesterol concerns; Lou Mitchell's heeds no modern health warnings. The diner, a destination close to Union Station since 1923, specializes in high-fat breakfasts and comfort-food lunches. Start the day with double-yolk eggs and homemade hash browns by the skillet (BYO Lipitor). Later break for meat loaf and mashed potatoes. Though you have to deal with out-the-door waits, staffers dole out doughnut holes and Milk Duds to pacify hunger pangs. ✉565 W. Jackson Blvd. ☎312/939–3111 ▤AE, V ⊗No dinner. ✣4:E2

$$ Lula Café. For the kind of modern cooking made from locally sourced
AMERICAN ingredients that distinguishes downtown chefs—but at half the price
Logan Square and with zero attitude—locals throng Lula Café, a quick walk from the
Logan Square El stop. This bohemian storefront of closely set wooden
tables and chairs serves stellar cuisine such as wild bass with blood
orange and olives, and maple-scented rabbit with rosemary sweet
potatoes. Menus are seasonal, change frequently, and champion farm
sources; in fact the restaurant holds prix-fixe farm dinners each Mon-
day. Open for breakfast and lunch too, Lula is a neighborhood hang-
out for arty neighbors during the day, drawing from far and wide for
dinner, when weekend waits are common. ⊠*2537 N. Kedzie Blvd.*
☎*773/489–9554* ⊟*AE, MC, V* ⊗*Closed Tues.* ✥*3:A2*

$ Mado. Subtle, smoky aromas from a wood grill unleash appetites at
AMERICAN this modest Bucktown restaurant where the chalkboard posting the
Bucktown daily-changing menu of chef-owners Rob and Alli Levitt doubles as the
dining room's main design element. Dishes are similarly understated:
radishes with creamy salted butter, wood-grilled mushrooms, and
slow-cooked pork belly showcase locally grown or raised foodstuffs.
Small portions encourage menu exploration, and the best bet is to start
with a few antipasti—like ricotta-topped bruschetta with hazelnuts,
and arugula—to share. Although desserts change constantly, seek out
Alli Levitt's shortbread cookies when available. Mado is waiting for
its liquor license and is temporarily BYOB; call ahead to see if status
has changed. ⊠ *1647 N. Milwaukee Ave.* ☎*773/342–2340* ⊟*AE, D,
MC, V.* ⊗*Closed Mon.* ✥*3:A3*

¢ Manny's Coffee Shop and Deli. Kibitzing counter cooks provide commen-
AMERICAN tary as they sling the chow—thick pastrami sandwiches, soul-nurtur-
South Loop ing matzoh-ball soup, and piping-hot potato pancakes—at this classic
Near South Side cafeteria. Though they occasionally bark at dawdlers,
it's all in good fun; looking for seating in two teaming, fluorescent-lit
rooms is not. Don't try to pay the hash-slingers; settle up as you leave.
⊠*1141 S. Jefferson St.* ☎*312/939–2855* ⚖*Reservations not accepted*
⊟*AE, MC, V* ⊗*Closed Sun.* ✥*4:E4*

$$ Marché. If all the world's a stage, everyone from the waiters to the
BRASSERIE patrons are players at this theatrical West Loop brasserie. The set: a
West Loop lively, loftlike room trimmed in paintings from local artists and wright-
iron metal work. The program: classic French onion soup and house-
made pâté, braised lamb, and an excellent steak tartare. The finale: one
of the largest sweets list in town. Ovations at your discretion. ⊠*833 W.
Randolph St.* ☎*312/226–8399* ⊟*AE, DC, MC, V.* ✥*4:D1*

$$$ McCormick & Schmick's. If you're the indecisive type, don't even think
SEAFOOD about dining here. This link in the Oregon-based chain updates its
Near North massive menu twice daily to list the freshest fish available. Expect
six varieties of oysters, regional specialties like Louisiana crab cakes
and Wisconsin rainbow trout, and several dozen fish, like Barcelona
anchovies and Hawaiian marlin. Wood paneling, cozy booths, and high
ceilings generate a clubby setting. We love the bar, not just for the

cheap happy-hour nibbles, but because the bartenders squeeze all the juices that go into the fresh and zesty cocktails. ⊠ *41 E. Chestnut St.* ☎ *312/397–9500* ▤ *AE, D, DC, MC, V.* ✛ *1:D2*

$
ITALIAN
Multiple
Locations

Mia Francesca. Moderate prices and a smart, urbane style drive ceaseless crowds to this Lakeview storefront. Enlightened Italian dishes like classic bruschetta, *quattro formaggi* (four-cheese) pizza, sausage and wild-mushroom pasta, and roast chicken are made with fresh ingredients and avoid stereotypical heaviness. With the exception of one pricey veal dish, the limited meat options keep the prices low here. While you wait for one of the small, tightly spaced tables—and you *will* wait—you can have a drink at the bar. Or travel to other Francesca locations, such as Francesca's Forno in Wicker Park, or Francesca's on Taylor in Little Italy. ⊠ *3311 N. Clark St.* ☎ *773/281–3310* ▤ *AE, D, MC, V* ⊘ *No lunch weekdays.* ⊠ *1576 N. Milwaukee Ave.* ☎ *773/770–0184* ⊠ *1400 Taylor St.* ☎ *312/829–2828* ✛ *2:F4*

$$$
AMERICAN
Near North

Mike Ditka's. NFL Hall-of-Famer Mike Ditka was one of only two coaches to take the Bears to the Super Bowl. Sure, it was in 1985, but Bears fans have long memories, and they still love "Da Coach" as well as his clubby, sports-themed restaurant where local performer John Vincent does dead-on impressions of Frank Sinatra, Tuesdays through Saturdays. The dark-wood interior, upstairs cigar lounge, and sports memorabilia are predictable, but the menu clearly aims to please large and diverse audiences. Café staples (salads, fish) and bar food (burgers, meat loaf) join steak-house fare (steaks, chops) and a few unexpected indulgences (crab and Parmesan-crusted halibut). ⊠ *Tremont Hotel, 100 E. Chestnut St.* ☎ *312/587–8989* ▤ *AE, D, MC, V.* ✛ *1:E2*

¢
CAFÉ
Wicker Park

Milk & Honey Café. Wicker Park's Division Street has long been a prowl of night owls. But with the advent of spas and boutiques in the area, not to mention the many work-from-home locals, the boho neighborhood needed a good breakfast and lunch spot. Milk & Honey exceeds expectations with hearty (eggs) and healthful (granola) breakfasts, and creative sandwiches (avocado with smoked Gouda) at lunch. Choice seats change with the season: out on the sidewalk café in warm weather; in near the fireplace in cooler temperatures. ⊠ *1920 W. Division St.* ☎ *773/395–9434* ▤ *AE, MC, V* ⊘ *No dinner.* ✛ *3:B4*

$$$
AMERICAN
River North

mk. Foodies and fashionistas favor owner-chef Michael Kornick's ultra-hip spot for its sleek look and elegant menu. Occupying a renovated warehouse, mk weights brick walls and soaring ceilings with fine linens, expensive flatware, and designer wine stems. Menus change with the season and hew to two or three dominant flavors à la halibut with braised baby fennel and kalamata olives, and rack of pork with mustard greens. It's not cheap, but it is special. ⊠ *868 N. Franklin St.* ☎ *312/482–9179* ▤ *AE, DC, MC, V* ⊘ *No lunch.* ✛ *1:C2*

$$
BISTRO
Lincoln Park

Mon Ami Gabi. While this restaurant's corporate owner, Chicago-based Lettuce Entertain You, has opened up satellite restaurants in the suburbs and in Las Vegas, the original has not lost its charm. This little piece of Paris re-creates a classic bistro with views of Lincoln Park that could pass—with the help of a couple of glasses of *vin* from the rolling wine cart—for the Tuileries. Park-front windows let in ample natural light, warming the wood-trimmed interior. Best bites include several versions of steak frites, as well as bistro essentials such as mussels and skate with crispy garlic chips. But chef Gabino Sotelino also serves a rotating list of specials, from cassoulet served on Sunday to Dover sole on Thursday. ⊠*2300 N. Lincoln Park W* ☎*773/348–8886* ▤*AE, D, DC, MC, V* ⊙*No lunch.* ✢*3:G1*

$$$–$$$$
STEAKHOUSE
The Loop

Morton's, The Steakhouse. Morton's in the Gold Coast neighborhood can be more fun, but this is Chicago's best steakhouse, a spin-off of the Gold Coast original. Excellent service and a good wine list add to the principal attraction: beautiful, hefty steaks cooked to perfection. A kitschy tradition mandates that everything you order, from gargantuan Idahos to massive slabs of beef, is brought to the table for your approval before the chef gets started. White tablecloths and chandeliers create a classy feel. It's no place for the budget conscious, but for steak lovers it's a 16-ounce (or more) taste of heaven. ⊠*65 E. Wacker Pl.* ☎*312/201–0410* ▤*AE, D, DC, MC, V* ⊙*No lunch weekends.* ✢*1:D2*

$$$$
CUTTING-EDGE
West Loop

Moto. Mad-scientist chef Homaru Cantu has become a cult figure in the Windy City. His restaurant-cum-laboratory is sequestered in the city's still working meatpacking district. Look for the well-dressed couples handing their keys to valets (it's the only restaurant on the block). Many of the techniques perfected in the basement kitchen are later put to use in the chef's work with NASA and corporate America. Inside the minimalist dining room, patrons pay for the privilege of being literal guinea pigs. The daily changing multicourse menus—available in 5-, 10-, and 16-course options—are printed on edible paper. Flavors are seared into wine glasses by an industrial laser, rigatoni is fashioned from lychee puree, and frozen flapjacks are "cooked" tableside on a liquid-nitrogen-filled box. The spectacle is big but the portions are small. ⊠*945 W. Fulton Market* ☎*312/491–0058* ⬧*Reservations essential* ▤*AE, MC, V.* ✢*4:D1*

¢
AMERICAN
River North

Mr. Beef. A Chicago institution for two-fisted Italian beef sandwiches piled with green peppers or giardiniera and provolone cheese, Mr. Beef garners citywide fans from area hard-hats to restaurateurs and TV personalities. Service and setting—two indoor picnic tables and a dining rail—are fast-food no-nonsense. This workingman's favorite is, go figure, located near River North's art galleries. ⊠*666 N. Orleans St.* ☎*312/337–8500* ▤*No credit cards* ⊙*Closed Sun. No dinner.* ✢*1:B3*

$$
LATIN AMERI-
CAN
River North

Nacional 27. Here's a bit of trivia to spring on fellow diners: there are 27 nations south of the U.S. border, and it's the cuisine of those 27 that supposedly comprise the pan-Latin menu here. That may be an exaggeration, but the menu does offer variety. Try the tiny barbecued lamb tacos appetizer and follow with the slow-cooked pork Cubano with coconut rice, black beans, and plantains. The circular bar draws a following independent of the food. After 11 PM on weekend nights, the floor in the middle of the dining room is cleared for salsa and merengue dancing. ✉ *325 W. Huron St.* ☎ *312/664–2727* 🖃 *AE, D, DC, MC, V* 🕑 *Closed Sun. No lunch.* ✢ *1:C3*

$$$
NEW AMERICAN
River North

Naha. Cousins Carrie and Michael Nahabedian lend their name (well, the first two syllables, anyway) and considerable culinary and hospitality skills to this upscale venture. In a clean space done in shades of cream and sage, Naha presents eye-catching dishes such as wood-grilled Spanish sausage with Italian frisée, honey-lacquered duck breast, or wild bass in saffron broth. Wine is treated with reverence, from the well-chosen selection of vintages to the high-quality stemware. Solos and social-seekers can sit at the convivial bar and order from the main menu. ✉ *500 N. Clark St.* ☎ *312/321–6242* 🖃 *AE, D, DC, MC, V* 🕑 *Closed Sun. No lunch Sat.* ✢ *1:D4*

$$$
SEAFOOD
The Loop

Nick's Fishmarket. While the original owners of this Chicago institution sold it years ago, and its current owners have opened satellite locations in the suburbs, locals continue to frequent Nick's for its great down-town location, fresh seafood, and prime steaks. The bold and pricey menu matches the well-paid power lunchers who get down to business over Pacific fish, California abalone, and Maine lobster paired with wines from California or Australia. If your purse strings are tight, angle for a spot at the Grill, where the lobster comes in bisque and windows frame the Marc Chagall mosaic on the plaza outdoors. ✉ *51 S. Clark St.* ☎ *312/621–0200* 🖃 *AE, D, DC, MC, V* 🕑 *Closed Sun. No lunch Sat.* ✢ *4:F2*

$$$$
NEW AMERICAN
Near North

NoMI. The expensive linens, Limoges china, and Isamu Noguchi sculpture make NoMI completely luxurious, but the vibe here is casual, as if all this elegance were everyday and not special-occasion. This is the place to go if you're celebrating the latter or traveling on a generous expense account—you'll have one of the city's best tables, overlooking the historic Water Tower from a seven-story perch. The menu leans French, with strong Asian and Mediterranean accents. ✉ *Park Hyatt Hotel, 800 N. Michigan Ave.* ☎ *312/239–4030* 🖃 *AE, D, DC, MC, V.* ✢ *1:E3*

$$$
AMERICAN
Lincoln Park
Fodor$Choice
★

North Pond. A former Arts and Crafts–style warming house for ice-skaters at Lincoln Park's North Pond, this gem in the woods fittingly champions an uncluttered culinary style. Talented chef Bruce Sherman emphasizes organic ingredients, wild-caught fish, and artisanal farm products. Menus change seasonally, but order the Midwestern favorite walleye pike if available. Like the food, the wine list seeks out small American craft producers. The food remains top-notch at lunch but the scene, dense with strollers and high chairs, is far from serene. ✉ *2610 N. Cannon Dr.* ☎ *773/477–5845* 🖃 *AE, D, DC, MC, V* 🕑 *Closed Mon. No lunch Oct.–May.* ✢ *2:H6*

$
MEXICAN
Pilsen

Nuevo León. Fill up on the exotic (tripe soup) or the familiar (tacos) at this bustling, family-run restaurant in the heart of Pilsen, Chicago's Mexican neighborhood. Big tables accommodate big families, lending a fiesta feel to the scene. Fans love the authentic food, including *chila-quiles* (eggs scrambled with tortillas) for breakfast to dinners of shrimp fajitas, chiles rellenos, and enchiladas. Brush up your Spanglish; not all servers are fluent in English, though all are welcoming to newcomers. To wash it all down, order a tall glass of *horchata*, a milky, cinnamon-flecked rice beverage, or bring a couple of beers; Nuevo León is BYOB. ⊠*1515 W. 18th St.* ☎*312/421–1517* ⌦*Reservations not accepted* ⊟*No credit cards.* ✛*4:B5*

$$$
NEW AMERICAN
West Loop

one sixtyblue. Never mind that former Chicago Bulls superstar Michael Jordan owns a piece of this place, or that the private, cigar-friendly room has entertained its share of celebs. The real reason to travel to the tail end of West Randolph Street's restaurant row is French-trained chef Martial Noguier. Although he largely works under the radar, his food is more than just dependable. His graceful but approachable food balances challenge-me tastes, like Kurobuta pork tenderloin, with standbys like Delmonico steak with caramelized shallots (Jordan's favorite). Save room for dessert: pastry chef Suzanne Imaz's inventive desserts include milk-chocolate cream paired with cannelloni made with banana gelee and filled with mascarpone. The leather-sofa lounge makes a sexy site for nibbles and drinks. ⊠*1400 W. Randolph St.* ☎*312/850–0303* ⊟*AE, D, DC, MC, V* ⊗*Closed Sun. No lunch Sat.* ✛*4:B1*

$$
CHINESE
South Loop

Opera. Creative Chinese fare and theatrical design share the stage at Opera. Only top-flight ingredients and sparing sauces go into the cooking, distinguishing the five-spice squid, say, or lobster spring roll or roasted Scottish salmon from more familiar take-out fare. Former film-storage vaults—the building was once used by Paramount Studios—now hold a series of tables for two, providing intimacy for those who want it. Everyone else revels in the eye candy that includes Asian newspaper collages, oversize suspended lamps, and a multicolor-glass-wrapped wine cellar. ⊠*1301 S. Wabash St.* ☎*312/461–0161* ⊟*AE, DC, MC, V* ⊗*No lunch.* ✛*4:E4*

¢–$
AMERICAN
Multiple
Locations

Orange. Follow Wrigleyville's weekend crowds to the cheerful breakfast spot for inventive, and thronged, breakfasts. If you think breakfast has become too dull, try the Orange approach, which is to treat breakfast with the same innovation and focus on presentation that chefs tend to reserve for dinner. Examples include pan-seared oatmeal, fruit sushi, kebab-style skewered French toast, or jam-filled pancakes. Standard stuff is done right, too: the fruit is juiced on-site and the omelets are big enough to take you through lunch. Yet eating at this morning hot spot requires some planning. Arrive early or prepare to wait as long as an hour for tables, especially on game days, or try Orange's two other locations in Roscoe Village or in the South Loop. ⊠*3231 N. Clark St.* ☎*773/549–4400* ⊟*D, MC, V* ⊗*No dinner Mon.* ⊠ *2011 W. Roscoe St.* ☎ *773/248–0999* ⊠ *75 W. Harrison St.* ☎ *312/447–1000* ✛*2:F4*

$$$
ITALIAN
River North

Osteria via Stato. It's no-brainer Italian here, where the shtick is to feed you without asking too many questions. You pick an entrée from the $36 prix-fixe, and waiters do the rest, working the room with several rounds of communal platters of antipasti, then pasta, followed by your entrée, and dessert. There's even a "just bring me wine" program that delivers preselected Italian vino to your table throughout your meal.

The results are savory enough, but Osteria shines brightest at making you feel comfortable. If conversation is important, make a reservation here. You won't spend but a precious minute reading the menu. ⊠ *620 N. State St.* ☎ *312/642–8450* ▭ *AE, D, DC, MC, V* ⊘ *No lunch Sun.* ⊕ *1:D4*

$$ **Otom.** With its bright colors and wide-open dining room, Otom is a fine
NEW AMERICAN   addition to this industrial-chic part of town. The one-page menu offers
Near West Side   a manageable selection of simple yet delicious appetizers and entrées that fit with the restaurant's warm atmosphere. The salmon ceviche is a must, and the short-rib ravioli with goat cheese is a delight. Meat lovers should try the lamb shank, but beware the colossal portion. To top it off, Otom offers 11 martinis. The chef's sweet-potato flan is a seasonal standout. ⊠ *951 W. Fulton Market* ☎ *312/491–5804* ▭ *AE, MC, V* ⊘ *Closed Sun. No lunch.* ⊕ *4:D1*

$$ **Park Grill.** Location trumps service at Park Grill, where a seat on the
NEW AMERICAN   patio in summer, in full view of Millennium Park, is among the best in
The Loop   the city. Sadly, the waitstaff lapses—grin and bear it with another drink from the outdoor bar. The menu is divided between small, medium, and large plates, offering a something-for-everyone selection. The burgers are first-rate, as is the more ambitious seasonal fare such as blood-orange and endive salad, lamb ribs spiked with garam masala, and pineapple-glazed salmon. A grab-and-go window supplies park picnics. In winter the scene moves indoors, as indulgent calorie consumers watch ice-skating athletes through picture windows. ⊠ *Millennium Park, 11 N. Michigan Ave.* ☎ *312/521–7275* ▭ *AE, D, DC, MC, V.* ⊕ *4:G1*

$ **The Parthenon.** The claim to fame here is the *saganaki,* the Greek flam-
GREEK   ing-cheese dish, which the Parthenon says it invented in the late 1960s,
West Loop   thereby introducing "opa!" to the American vocabulary. So ordering flaming cheese here is a rite of passage for any first-time visitors, yet regulars return to this literal Greektown hot spot for lamb and chicken preparations, often skewered on sticks. In fact, the restaurant also takes credit for being the first to serve gyros stateside. True or not, indulge the legends and stick to these classics. When going, be sure to ask for pita bread and a side of *tzatziki,* a yogurt- and cucumber-based dipping sauce. The food is cheap and the atmosphere festive and family-friendly, generating happy campers. ⊠ *314 S. Halsted St.* ☎ *312/726–2407* ▭ *AE, D, DC, MC, V.* ⊕ *4:D2*

$$ **Petterino's.** Goodman, Palace, and Oriental theatergoers pack Petterino's
ITALIAN   (next door to the Goodman lobby) nightly. Not that the Italian supper
The Loop   club with framed caricatures of celebs past and present couldn't stand on its own merits. The deep, red-leather booths make a cozy stage for old-school classics like steak Diane, shrimp *de jonghe* (covered in garlicky bread crumbs then baked), tomato bisque, Bookbinder soup, plus prime steaks, seafood, and the ever-present pasta. Although the show is usually next door, for live open-mike cabaret, seek out Petterino's Monday nights and order a drink from the large, well-stocked bar.

Continued on page 201

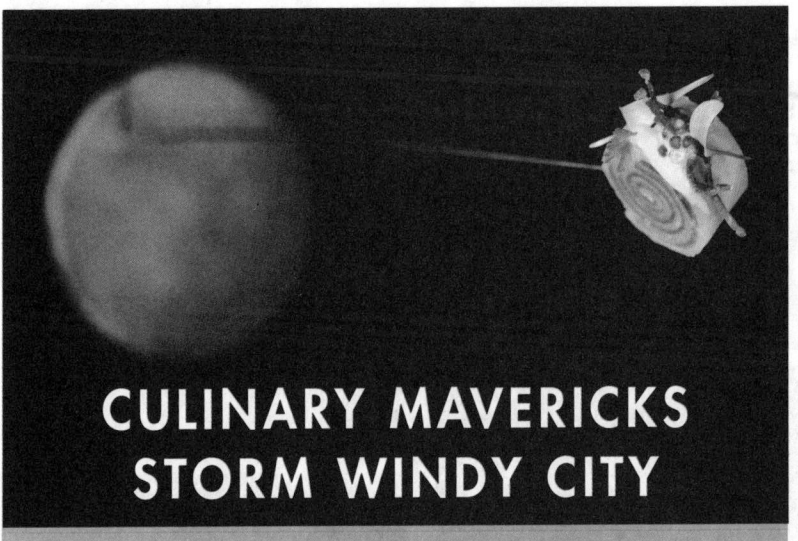

CULINARY MAVERICKS STORM WINDY CITY

Step into the kitchen, but don't forget your protective goggles. Whether "negative grilling" at minus 30 degrees Celsius or serving you an edible menu (literally—it's printed on soy paper), this trio of young chefs in Chicago is redefining haute cuisine.

Just a few years ago, three young chefs, each a veteran of local icon Charlie Trotter's kitchen, took a simultaneous gamble on the sophistication and daring of Chicago diners, unveiling cutting-edge menus the likes of which the Windy City had never seen before. Though a visit to their restaurants—Alinea, Moto, and Graham Elliot—demands an adventurous palate and serious commitment of time and money, all three places instantly thrived.

The chefs leading these restaurants—Grant Achatz, Homaru Cantu, and Graham Elliot Bowles—have brought an American touch to techniques and ideas first explored and popularized in Europe, toying with devices and chemicals more suited to a lab than a kitchen. This marriage of science and cooking is known as molecular gastronomy. Though following in the footsteps of chefs like Heston Blumenthal in Britain and Ferran Adrià in Spain, the Chicago pack prided themselves on being trailblazers, not imitators. "For Picasso to do something that looked like a Dalí would've been a sham," says Cantu. "It's the same thing in these restaurants. There's a certain amount of pride in originality."

Before long the national press began to take notice. "One chef is unique," says Bowles. "Two could be a fluke, but three guys doing this stuff in the same city, maybe something is going on." Writers from *GQ, Gourmet, The New York Times,* and *Vogue* gushed over Chicago's new "sci-fi" cuisine. The city, they wrote, had become the capital of avant-garde food in America.

by Jay Cheshes

GRANT ACHATZ

(previous page) From Alinea, a spiral of quince wrapped in prosciutto. (clockwise from top left) Grant Achatz; bacon with butterscotch, apple, and thyme; inside the Alinea kitchen; mango disc with sesame oil, soy, and bonito flakes.

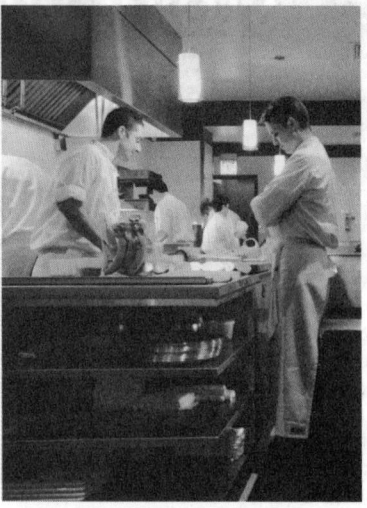

Born into a restaurant family in Michigan, Achatz, who turned 30 two years before his colleagues, is the triumvirate's senior statesman. After working at Charlie Trotter and at Thomas Keller's French Laundry in Napa, he began experimenting with molecular gastronomy at Trio in the Chicago suburbs. In 2005 he launched Alinea, his first solo project, just up the block from the Steppenwolf Theatre. The restaurant was named the best in the country by *Gourmet* barely a year after it opened.

Techniques & Trademarks

There are two dining options at Alinea—long and longer. "When we first opened we were serving 28 courses," says the chef. "People were fatiguing. When you cross over four hours you're getting into dangerous territory." Tiny one- to four-bite courses flow one into the next, with sweet dishes not just ending the meal but also interrupting it midway. "It breaks the monotony," Achatz says.

Though ingredients are as likely to be flash-frozen on a stainless steel "negative grill" (at minus 30 degrees Celsius) as seared on an old-fashioned Japanese charcoal barbecue, not much of this food (served on pedestals and prongs) will look familiar. In the kitchen you'll also find an immersion circulator (for cooking vacuum-sealed food "sous-vide") and containers of calcium lactate and sodium alginate (for encasing liquids in a yolk-like skin so they explode when you bite them).

HOMARU CANTU

Cantu, the most wildly experimental and scientifically minded of the Chicago chefs, worked in kitchens up and down the West Coast before landing at Charlie Trotter, where he eventually rose to the position of sous chef. Moto, opened in 2005 in a desolate stretch of the city's meatpacking district, is equal parts restaurant and mad-scientist workshop. The chef, who holds some two-dozen food patents, sells innovations perfected in the restaurant's basement kitchen to corporate and government clients (including NASA).

(clockwise from top left) Homaru Cantu; steamed sea bass; deconstructed mac-and-cheese; edible menu made of soybeans with food-based inks.

Techniques & Trademarks

The kitchen at Moto resembles a James Bond villain's lair. When the industrial laser is turned on, protective-goggle-clad chefs work in near darkness on orders transmitted by a computer-generated voice. The daily changing prix-fixe menus (in 5-, 10-, or 20-course options) are printed to order in edible ink on soy-based paper (one of the chef's many patents). Here theatricality and trompe l'oeil presentations rule. "When you order a tasting menu it's like going out for a night at the opera," Cantu says. "You don't get to choose Act One, Scene Five; you get the entire production as the composer intended you to see it." You might encounter chemically treated lychee puree, mimicking pasta dough, molded into translucent rigatoni. Or a new wave "nitro" sushi roll made with liquid nitrogen—treated tofu skin that emits cool smoke through your mouth and nose.

5

IN FOCUS CULINARY MAVERICKS STORM WINDY CITY

GRAHAM ELLIOT BOWLES

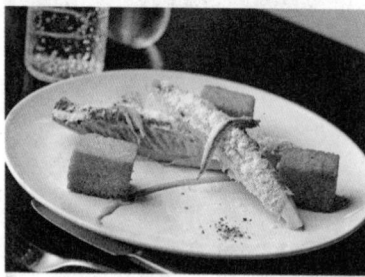

(clockwise from top left) Graham Elliot Bowles; Aged Cheddar risotto, with PBR onions, green apple, Wisconsin bacon, and Cheez-Its.; Short rib stroganoff with cremini mushrooms, egg noodles, shallot marmalade, and crème fraîche.; Caesar salad, with romaine lettuce, white anchovies, Parmesan fluff, and brioche "twinkie".

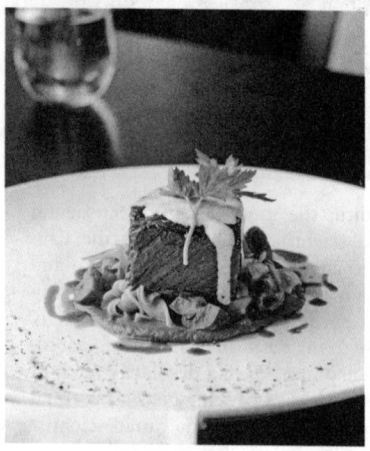

After making his professional debut at the pastoral Jackson House Inn in rural Vermont, Bowles worked alongside Cantu at Charlie Trotter. The chefs, who started two weeks apart, became good friends. Later Bowles returned to the Jackson House, where he first experimented with molecular gastronomy (and where *Food & Wine* named him one of America's best new chefs). Just as his colleagues were launching their own places, he landed the position of chef de cuisine at the flagship restaurant of Chicago's Peninsula Hotel where he won numerous awards for his inventive cooking. After his four year stint at Avenues, Chef Bowles decided to leave his highly-lauded post to open his own restaurant, Graham Elliot.

Techniques & Trademarks

Officially opening its doors in June 2008, Chef Bowles' eponymous restaurant is what he likes to call "bistronomic"—a juxtaposition of haute cuisine and a bistro-style approach. He believes his restaurant to be an extension of himself, and that too is seen in the food. An inventive take on buffalo wings is served with bleu cheese foam and Budweiser bubbles, and the cheddar risotto is served with green apple and Cheez-Its. Though his food is recognizable, it remains thought-provoking—and delicious. "It's more whimsical," says Bowles, "It's fine dining redefined."

✉ *150 N. Dearborn St.* ☎*312/422–0150* ▤*AE, D, DC, MC, V* ⊘*No lunch Sun.* ✛*1:D6*

$ **Phoenix.** This bustling dim sum house can feel overwhelming with
CHINESE the hordes of diners who flock here on weekends, and service can be
Chinatown brusque. Even so, it delivers. First Phoenix softens you up with second-floor picture-window views that frame the Loop skyline. Then,
just when you're most vulnerable, it develops the food punch—and
it's a pretty good one, too. The dim sum, dispensed from rolling carts
daily from 8 AM to 3 PM on weekends is a big draw (servers often don't
speak English; just smile and point at what you want—and don't miss
the barbecue pork buns or the shrimp dumplings). Arrive before noon
on the weekends or stew as you wait—and wait. ✉*2131 S. Archer Ave.*
☎*312/328–0848* ▤*AE, D, DC, MC, V.* ✛*4:F6*

$ **Piece.** The antithesis of Chicago-style deep-dish pizza, Piece's flat pies
PIZZA mimic those made famous in New Haven, Connecticut. The somewhat
Wicker Park free-form, eat-off-the-baking-sheet pizzas come in plain (tomato sauce,
☼ Parmesan, and garlic), white (olive oil, garlic, and mozzarella), or traditional red, with lots of topping options. Salads like the greens with Gor-
gonzola and pears are more stylish than expected, and house-brewed
beers pair perfectly with the chow. It's good enough that multipierced
Wicker Parkers are willing to risk dining alongside local families
(with kids in tow) in this former garage space. ✉*1927 W. North Ave.*
☎*773/772–4422* ▤*AE, D, DC, MC, V.* ✛*3:B3*

$ **Pierrot Gourmet.** Despite the legions of shoppers on Michigan Avenue,
CAFÉ there are few casual cafés to quell their collective hunger, making this
Near North bakery-patisserie-café a welcome neighbor. Lunches center on upscale
greens like herb salad with olives and Parmesan, along with open-face
tartine sandwiches on crusty, house-made sourdough. Break midafter-
noon for a *tarte flambé*, an Alsatian flat bread with cheese and cream,
accompanied by a glass of Riesling. Solos are accommodated at the
magazine-strewn communal table. Meals are served 7 AM to 7 PM daily.
The upscale Peninsula hotel runs Pierrot, accounting for both the high
quality and the high cost. ✉*108 E. Superior St.* ☎*312/573–6749*
▤*AE, D, DC, MC, V.* ✛*1:E3*

¢ **Pizzeria Due.** Serving up one-inch-thick pizzas in a comfortable, though
ITALIAN well-worn dining room, Pizzeria Due is where everyone goes when
River North they've found out that Uno, the original home of Chicago's deep-
☼ dish pizza up the street, has an hour-plus wait. The caveat is that Due
quickly builds its own waiting list, and it's not unusual to wait for more
than an hour here as well. The best strategy for dining out at either
spot is to arrive early or opt to come at lunch. Once here, go for the
signature dish, but feel free to customize. Due fans like the option of
ordering individual-sized pizzas rather than getting the table to agree
on fillings. ✉*619 N. Wabash Ave.* ☎*312/943–2400* ▤*AE, D, DC,
MC, V.* ✛*1:E4*

$ **Pizzeria Uno.** Chicago deep-dish pizza got its start here in 1943, and
ITALIAN both local and out-of-town fans continue to pack in for filling pies.
River North Housed in a Victorian brownstone, Uno offers a slice of old Chicago

5

in dim paneled rooms with reproduction light fixtures. Spin-off Due down the street handles the overflow. Plan on two thick, cheesy slices or less as a full meal. This is no quick-to-your-table pie, so do order salads and be prepared to entertain the kids during the inevitable wait. ⊠*29 E. Ohio St.* ☎*312/321–1000* ✚*1:E4.*

¢
ITALIAN
South Loop

Pompei. Cheap, cheerful, and fast—what's not to love about Pompei? Little Italy's only casual café with a strong kitchen specializes in square slices of pizza, each under $4, with toppings ranging from shredded onions and sausage to bread crumbs and tomato. One to two easily makes a meal. Between University of Illinois Chicago students and Rush University Medical Center workers, Pompei is jammed at lunch. If you can tolerate the self-serve system at dinner, the evening hours are more relaxing. If pizza's not your thing, salad, generous sandwiches, and homemade pastas are also on the menu. ⊠*1531 W. Taylor St.* ☎*312/421–5179* ▤*AE, D, DC, MC, V.* ✚*4:B4*

$$$
NEW AMERICAN
West Loop

Powerhouse Restaurant and Bar. Longer than a city block and punctuated by a tall smokestack, Powerhouse is an imposing sight. Yet history, not aspiration, gives the restaurant its assertive façade and name: its building once housed a coal-fired power plant. Today the kitchen turns out American dishes such as Colorado lamb, roasted chicken breast and Alaskan halibut. Professional service and a comfortable, polished dining room provide a calm and clubby atmosphere, even when trains from the nearby tracks subtly rattle your seats. ⊠ *215 N. Clinton St.* ☎*312/928–0800* ▤ *AE, D, DC, MC, V.* ✚*1:A6*

$$
AMERICAN
Near North

Pump Room. The Pump Room clings to its old-time Chicago fame, when celebrities passing through town via rail beat it to the restaurant to see and be seen. The likes of Frank Sinatra, Bette Davis, and Humphrey Bogart held court in the storied Booth One, and publicity photos taken there line the entrance to the restaurant. In keeping with tradition, the booth is off-limits to all but A-list celebs who, truthfully, don't show like they used to. Now the regulars are wealthy Gold Coasters, but new management is working hard to lure the next generation, meaning there's braised monkfish alongside the filet mignon. ⊠*1301 N. State Pkwy.* ☎*312/266–0360* ▤*AE, D, DC, MC, V.* ✚*3:H4*

$$
ASIAN
West Loop

Red Light. Sultry, all-red decor and a club sound track stoke the high-energy vibe (read: loud) at Red Light. Chinese, Thai, Vietnamese, and Indonesian dishes commingle on the pan-Asian menu, which is heavily weighted with appetizers to encourage nibbling. Standout dishes include foie gras and pork dumplings, jumbo shrimp curry, a miso-lobster seafood stew, and the signature "chocolate bag" dessert filled with white-chocolate mousse. ⊠*820 W. Randolph St.* ☎*312/733–8880* ▤*AE, D, DC, MC, V* ☉*No lunch weekends.* ✚*4:D1*

$$
NEW AMERICAN
The Loop

Rhapsody. Attached to the Symphony Center, home of the Chicago Symphony, Rhapsody is more than a handy spot for a preconcert dinner. This restaurant combines fine-dining ambitions with a pleasant urban greenhouse setting graced with potted palms and picture windows. Despite a few chef changes in recent years, the food is consistently solid. Rhapsody's handsome bar, pouring an expansive wine-by-the-glass selection, is a perfect post-performance hangout. ⊠*65 E. Adams St.* 🕾*312/786–9911* ▤*AE, D, DC, MC, V* ⊘*Closed Sun. mid-June–mid-Sept. No lunch weekends.* ✛*4:G2*

$$$ **Riva.** Riva's got the lock on upscale
SEAFOOD dining in the middle of junk-food–
Near North central Navy Pier. The restaurant relies a bit too much on the views—which, gazing southward over Lake Michigan, are admittedly fantastic—when it should concentrate on better cooking. Opt for simpler preparations, such as grilled salmon or various pastas, over the menu's more ambitious efforts. Grilled fish, shellfish, and steaks are pricey, though the hordes that crowd the place, especially in summer, don't seem to mind (good service helps). A casual grill downstairs, which spills onto the pier's promenade in summer, is kinder to your wallet. ⊠*700 E. Grand Ave.* 🕾*312/644–7482* ▤*AE, D, DC, MC, V.* ✛*1:H4*

$$ **RL.** Power brokers, moneyed locals, and Michigan Avenue shoppers
AMERICAN keep the revolving doors spinning at RL, the initials of designer Ralph
Near North Lauren who lent his name and signature soigné style to the eatery that adjoins his Polo/Ralph Lauren store. The cozy confines cluster leather banquettes under hunt-club-style art hung on wood-paneled walls. The menu of American classics, including steak tartare, Dover sole in butter, and steak Diane flamed tableside, suits the country-club-in-the-city setting. ⊠*115 E. Chicago Ave.* 🕾*312/475–1100* ▤*AE, DC, MC, V.* ✛*1:F3*

$$ **Rockit Bar & Grill.** A classic tavern for the club set, Rockit Bar & Grill
AMERICAN serves upscale bar food, pours creative cocktails, and aims to please
River North everyone from celebrity visitors (given wide berth in the barroom upstairs) to kids (served Lincoln Log-like stacks of peanut butter- and jelly-brioche French toast for brunch). The extensive menu spans salads, sandwiches, and burgers (try the Kobe version), as well as comfort-food entrées like Thanksgiving turkey and pesto-cream pasta with salmon. Oprah-famed-designer Nate Berkus did the rustic-chic interiors, including tree-stump cocktail tables and antler chandeliers. After dinner, head upstairs to shoot some pool and check out the singles scene. ⊠*22 W. Hubbard St.* 🕾*312/645–6000* ▤*AE, MC, V.* ✛*1:D5*

$$ **Russian Tea Time.** Exotica is on the menu and in the air at this spot
RUSSIAN that's favored by visitors to the nearby Art Institute and Symphony
The Loop Center. Mahogany trim, samovars, and balalaika music set the stage for dishes from Russia and neighboring republics (the owners hail from Uzbekistan), including Ukrainian borscht, *blinis* (small, savory pancakes) with salmon caviar, Moldavian meatballs, and game sausages. Chilled vodka flights (three shots) help the herring go down. ⊠*77 E. Adams St.* 🕾*312/360–0000* ⌁*Reservations essential* ▤*AE, D, DC, MC, V.* ✛*4:G2*

$$
MEXICAN
Near North

Salpicón. Anyone who does authentic Mexican in Chicago operates in the shadow of Frontera Grill's Rick Bayless, which makes it easier for those in the know to snag a table at Salpicón. Chef Priscila Satkoff grew up in Mexico City, and her renditions of Oaxacan mole pork and grilled fish with salsa fresca have unforced flair. Wash 'em down with a belt of one of 100 tequilas or 800 vintage wines. Once you try the Mexican-style Sunday brunch, with dishes like skirt steak and eggs, you'll never go back to eggs Benedict. ⊠*1252 N. Wells St.* ☎*312/988–7811* ⊟*AE, D, DC, MC, V* ⊘*No lunch.* ✛*3:G4*

> **WORD OF MOUTH**
>
> "We totally enjoyed Sepia–the atmosphere was nice, the food was great. I had a veal chop and my husband had short ribs. The presentation was cute–in cast iron pans." —drkathej

$$
ITALIAN
River North
☾

Scoozi! This ever-popular trattoria continues to attract a yuppie crowd after 5 PM and plenty of wandering suburbanites on the weekend. You'll recognize it by the gigantic tomato over the front door; inside, a sprawling, two-level dining room presents loft-chic looks of exposed-brick walls, open-truss ceiling, and steel garage doors. This place is nothing if not chameleon; groups love the shareable antipasti and pizzas, families with kids meld right into the cacophony, and couples find the energy relieves the focus on a boring date. ⊠*410 W. Huron St.* ☎*312/943–5900* ⊟*AE, D, DC, MC, V* ⊘*No lunch.* ✛*1:B3*

$$$$
NEW AMERICAN
Near North

Seasons Restaurant. How the Four Seasons's boîte manages to please business diners and traveling families is a mystery worthy of a hotel-school case study. Service is suave, the room elegant, and the seasonal food refined; altogether, it's an ideal spot for power-dining appointments. At the same time, the hotel makes a big deal about being family-friendly, which, if you read between the lines a bit, means there's a children's menu for better behaved clans (it *is* still the Four Seasons). Fixing for a good deal and a quick lunch? There's an affordable three-course daily lunch menu that's served within an hour. Dinner menus include five- and eight-course tasting options. Reservations are essential for Chicago's best (and most expensive) Sunday brunch. ⊠*Four Seasons Hotel, 120 E. Delaware Pl.* ☎*312/649–2349* ⊟*AE, D, DC, MC, V.* ✛*1:F2*

$$$
NEW AMERICAN
West Loop

Sepia. While the name evokes nostalgia for the building's gritty past as a print shop, Sepia is thoroughly forward-thinking in both its design (think glassed-in chandeliers and leather-topped tables) and its simple, seasonal dishes created by Chef Kendal Duque. Order flatbread for the table while you review the menu, which includes appetizers such as grilled octopus or pork rillettes and entrées such as rich, tender beef shortribs served with herbed noodles. Meanwhile, a well-chosen, international wine list and thoughtfully prepared classic cocktails satisfy oenophiles and mixologists alike. Though reservations can be hard to come by for dinner, seats at the communal tables are first-come, first-serve. ⊠*123 N. Jefferson St.* ☎*312/441–9447* ⊟*AE, D, DC, MC, V.* ✛*4:E1*

$$
CHINESE
Near North

Shanghai Terrace. As precious as a jewel box, and often as pricey, this red, lacquer-trimmed 80-seater hidden away in the Peninsula Hotel reveals the hotelier's Asian roots. Come for upscale dim sum, stylishly presented, and luxury-laden dishes such as steamed fish, Kobe beef rolls, roasted quail with pickled pear, and wok-fried lobster. Meanwhile, a patio seating up to 70 during warmer months lets you revel in a relaxing meal four stories above the madding crowds of Michigan Avenue. Though fans admire the attentive, professional service, some warn that diners with larger appetites might leave feeling unsatisfied. ⊠*Peninsula Hotel, 108 E. Superior St.* ☎*312/573–6744* ☰*AE, D, DC, MC, V* ☉*Closed Sun.* ✢*1:E3*

$$$
SEAFOOD
River North

Shaw's Crab House and Blue Crab Lounge. Hands down, this is one of the city's best seafood spots. Though it's held an exalted position for a long time, the restaurant doesn't rest on its laurels. The kitchen stays on track, turning out famed classics like silky crab cakes and rich halibut while updating the menu with sushi, maki, and fresh tartare selections. The seafood salad served at lunch is loaded and big enough for two. (Lunch, by the way, is a good bargain, with well-priced entrées and $1 desserts). The city's chief specialist in bivalves nurtures a split personality, spanning a clubby main dining room in nautically themed loft digs and a lively exposed-brick bar where shell shuckers work harder than the barkeeps. ⊠*21 E. Hubbard St.* ☎*312/527–2722* ☰*AE, D, DC, MC, V.* ✢*1:E5*

$$
INTERNATIONAL
The Loop

Shikago. With its ever-changing and reasonably-priced menu, Shikago lets foodies sample the work of one of Chicago's top chefs, Kevin Shikami, without skipping a car payment for the privilege. With its simple design, chunky wooden tables and soft ambient-techno music, the restaurant draws a mixed crowd; power suits by day, and hip up-and-comers by night. The Vietnamese spring rolls—a crispy blend of papaya and Korean-style short ribs—and the glazed rack of lamb are excellent. The frozen peanut mousse and flourless chocolate cake with black-currant sorbet is a must for dessert. Enter on Adams Street or you might miss it. ⊠ *190 S. LaSalle St.* ☎*312/781–7300* ☰ *AE, D, DC, MC, V.* ☉*Closed Sun. No lunch Sat.* ✢*4:D6*

$$$
AMERICAN
Near North

Signature Room at the 95th. When you've got the best view in town and a lock on the prom business, do you need to be daring with the food? Signature Room isn't; making a formal affair of dishes such as rack of lamb and grilled salmon while couples ogle the skyline views from the John Hancock's 95th floor. Avoid the clichés by calling here at lunch: the $18 buffet gets you good and stuffed, and the daytime light lets you see Lake Michigan. The appeal of the lavish and pricey Sunday brunch? The abundance of food. Brunch reservations essential. ⊠*John Hancock Center, 875 N. Michigan Ave.* ☎*312/787–9596* ☰*AE, D, DC, MC, V.* ✢*1:E2*

$$$$
NEW AMERICAN
River North

Sixteen. Uninterrupted views of the landmark Wrigley Building, Lake Michigan, and Chicago River make it easy to overlook the food at Sixteen– but you shouldn't. Located on the sixteenth floor (hence the name) of the sleek Trump International Hotel & Tower, the restaurant serves chef Frank Brunacci's unique fusion of European and Asian flavors. Dishes like Tasmanian trout or truffle lasagna are a treat for that special occasion, while coconut-lemongrass soup and upscale lobster rolls are perfect for a power lunch. The best deal might be at breakfast, when house-made crumpets, breakfast quesadillas with fried eggs, and freshly squeezed juices are an indulgent accompaniment to sunrise over the lake. ⊠ *401 N. Wabash Ave.* ☎*312/588–8001* ▤ *AE, D, DC, MC, V* ✛*3:H6*

$
SOUTHERN
Wicker Park
Smoke Daddy. A rib and blues emporium, in the gentrified though still funky Wicker Park, Smoke Daddy serves up tangy barbecued ribs with generously supplied napkins for swabbing stray sauce. Today fans pack bar stools and booths for the chow, which includes richly flavored smoked pulled pork and homemade fries, as well as for the no-cover R&B and jazz bands that play nightly after 9:30. A short walk from the Division Street El stop makes this barbecue spot an ideal point from which to explore the neighborhood's hipster scene. ⊠*1804 W. Division St.* ☎*773/772–6656* ▤*AE, D, MC, V.* ✛*3:D4*

¢
SOUTHERN
Far North Side
Smoque BBQ. The sweet smoky aroma wafting out of this casual barbecue spot always attracts a crowd. While the line to order at the counter starts out the door on weekends, it moves quickly as chowhounds catch up on neighborhood news. If you can't make up your mind between brisket or shredded pork shoulder (both tender and cooked for more than 12 hours), order the half-and-half—a sandwich with half of each. Or try a slab of ribs. A side of vinegar-spiked slaw, rich baked beans, and cornbread round out the meal, and kids love the creamy mac and cheese. Smoque is BYOB, so pick up a beer or two before arriving if desired. ⊠ *3800 N. Pulaski Rd.* ☎*773/545–7427* ♠*Reservations not accepted* ▤*AE, D, MC, V* ☾*Closed Mon.* ✛*2:A3*

$$
NEW AMERICAN
Near North
Sola. While you can dine very well in Chicago's neighborhoods, most local joints aren't as ambitious as Sola, which would be right at home downtown and probably far more expensive there. Now North Side visitors don't have to travel far for ginger-glazed salmon, bacon-wrapped pork tenderloin, and wasabi-crusted mahimahi. Chef-owner-surfer Carol Wallack's affinity for Hawaii shows in Pacific Rim fare like seaweed salad and Kauai prawns. Proving its affection for the neighborhood, the restaurant is fronted by a wall of windows and warm within, thanks to a gas fireplace. Go around the corner to Byron Street to find the front door. ⊠*3868 N. Lincoln Ave.* ☎*773/327–3868* ▤*AE, D, DC, MC, V* ☾*No lunch Mon.–Wed.* ✛*2:C2*

¢
SOUTHERN
South Side
Soul Queen Restaurant. Since 1971, family-owned and -operated Soul Queen has been sating everyone, from the famished music fans who frequent Stony Island's many jazz clubs to luminaries such as Mohhamad Ali, with one of the most generous buffets in town. For $7.75, help yourself to fried chicken, chicken and dumplings, ham hocks, turkey wings and legs, black-eyed peas, succotash, mac and cheese, peach cobbler, and more. The spread gets even more elaborate on Sunday, when the price goes up $3. ⊠*9031 S. Stony Island Ave.* ☎*773/731–3366* ♠*Reservations not accepted* ▤ MC, V. ✛*4:G6*

$ **Spacca Napoli.** Despite Chicago's renown for deep-dish pizza, locals
ITALIAN are lately swept away by Neapolitan pies bested by this bright, 68-seat
Far North Side Ravenswood gem. Finely ground Italian flour, imported buffalo moz-
Fodor$Choice zarella, hand-stretched dough, and a brick, wood-fired oven built by
★ Italian craftsmen are credited for producing bubbling, chewy crusts
that edge savory, uncut, thin pies that diners eat with a fork. Antipasti
and desserts like tiramisu round out the short menu. The proprietors
shun takeout and turn up the lights a little too high, but the food wins
out, accounting for out-the-door waits, even on weekdays. In summer,
angle for a table on the pleasant sidewalk patio, which seats more than
40. ⊠*1769 W. Sunnyside* ☏*773/878–2420* ▤*AE, MC, V* ☾*Closed
Mon. and Tues.* ♦*3:B2*

$$$$ **Spiaggia.** Refined Italian cooking dished alongside three-story picture-
ITALIAN window views of Lake Michigan make Spiaggia one of the city's top
Near North eateries. The tiered dining room guarantees good sight lines from each
table. Chef Tony Mantuano prepares elegant, seasonal dishes such as
veal-filled pasta with fennel pollen, roast guinea hen with truffle sauce,
or Mediterranean bass with saffron potato puree. Oenophiles consider
the wine list scholarly. For Spiaggia fare, minus the luxury ingredients, try lunch or dinner at the casual Café Spiaggia next door. ⊠*980
N. Michigan Ave.* ☏*312/280–2750* ⚞*Reservations essential. Jacket
required* ▤*AE, D, DC, MC, V* ☾*No lunch.* ♦*1:E2*

$$$ **Spring.** Leave pretense downtown. Chef Shawn McClain's artistic but
NEW AMERICAN unfussy fish preparations—from Kumomoto oysters with grated fresh
Wicker Park wasabi root to Atlantic skate wing, white polenta, and roasted cau-
liflower—distinguish the sophisticated Spring from the seasonal res-
taurant. Like McClain's cooking, the restaurant's interior design faces
east for inspiration, beginning with a rock garden in the foyer. Original
white glazed-tile walls hark back to the space's former life as a bath-
house. ⊠*2039 W. North Ave.* ☏*773/395–7100* ▤*AE, DC, MC, V*
☾*Closed Mon. No lunch.* ♦*3:B3*

$$ **SushiSamba Rio.** *Sex and the City* made SushiSamba a star in New York,
ASIAN and look-alike hotties make the Chicago version a scene. The trendy
River North Brazilian–Japanese hot spot combines a nightclub vibe—dramatic multilevel design, freely flowing cocktails, the co-ed bathroom—with an
inventive menu. All the usual sushi suspects are here, as well as offbeat
sashimi choices, Brazilian-style marinated fish, and fusion rolls that
don't always work. For best results sample the menu with an adventurous, party-hardy crowd on Wednesday, when there's a band and
samba dancers. An all-weather rooftop lounge, popular with the late-
night crowd, serves cocktails (try the sparkling sake) and the full menu.
⊠*504 N. Wells St.* ☏*312/595–2300* ▤*AE, DC, MC, V.* ♦*1:C4*

$ **Sushi Wabi.** This funky, West Loop sushi restaurant dances to an indus-
JAPANESE trial-pop beat—on weekend evenings, at least, when the DJ turns up
West Loop the beat (club attitude suffices on weekdays). The urban-chic brick-and-
exposed-steel interior draws a young, martini-swilling crowd. Superior
sushi and maki rolls along with straightforward entrées such as grilled
peppercorn-crusted tuna with soy and lemon, bring substance to the

style haunt. ✉ *842 W. Randolph St.* ☎ *312/563–1224* ▭ *AE, D, DC, MC, V* ⊘ *No lunch weekends.* ✛ *4:D1*

¢ **Svea.** The North Side's Andersonville neighborhood, once a haven for
SCANDINAVIAN Swedes, plays host to the humble Svea, a Swedish version of an Ameri-
Far North Side can diner. There are Swedish pancakes with lingonberries and Swedish rye *limpa* bread with eggs in the morning, and open-face Swedish
meatball sandwiches at lunch. The digs are no-frill, but the service
is friendly. ✉ *5236 N. Clark St.* ☎ *773/275–7738* ▭ *No credit cards*
⊘ *No dinner.* ✛ *2:D1*

$$$ **Table Fifty-Two.** If it feels as if everyone is a regular at chef Art Smith's
SOUTHERN Gold Coast restaurant, they very well might be. Oprah's former per-
Near North sonal chef is not short of friends and admirers. Yet newcomers lucky
enough to score a reservation feel just as welcome in its cozy, country-
home environs, particularly when the complimentary buttermilk bis-
cuits arrive. While the menu strays to Asia and Europe, at its core is a
formidable Southern lineup of dishes such as Low Country shrimp with
stone-ground grits, a fried-green-tomato Napoleon, and fried chicken
(a Sunday-only special). Save room for Smith's hummingbird cake, a
homey banana and pineapple cake topped with cream-cheese frosting.
If you're in the neighborhood without a reservation, walk in and see if
the chef's counter is available: the restaurant keeps five seats open in
front of the pizza oven. ✉ *52 W. Elm St.* ☎ *312/573–4000* ⬧ *Reser-
vations essential* ▭ *AE, MC, V* ⊘ *Closed Mon.* ✛ *3:H4*

$$$ **Takashi.** It's not often that a chef who has made a name for himself in
JAPANESE Las Vegas retreats to a neighborhood restaurant. But that's exactly
Bucktown what Takashi Yagihashi did when he left his post as executive chef of
Fodor'sChoice Okada at Wynn Las Vegas. At his intimate, dinner-only restaurant,
★ Yagihashi serves forth French- and American-inspired small and large
plates with Japanese accents, such as duck fat-fried chicken with a gin-
ger-flecked Napa cabbage slaw, and soy- and ginger-braised caramel
pork belly with pickled daikon. While the upstairs is quiet and relaxed,
request a seat downstairs to peek at the quiet action in the glassed-in
kitchen. ✉ *1952 N. Damen Ave.,* ☎ *773/772–6170* ▭ *AE, D, MC, V*
⊘ *Closed Mon.* ✛ *3:B2*

$$ **Tavern at the Park.** With its unique take on American classics and its
AMERICAN splendid view of Chicago's Millennium Park, it would be a mistake
The Loop to pass up this near-Michigan Avenue gem. Noise from the bar carries
up to the second floor, giving this spacious restaurant a lively feel. The
prime rib sliders and sticky fried shrimp are perfect starters before mov-
ing on to the blackened sea scallops and fettuccine or the slow- roasted
prime rib. Though many favor the warm blueberry-apple bread pud-
ding for dessert, the fried banana split shouldn't be missed. Don't plan
on lunch without a reservation—local businesspeople have already
made this their new hangout. ✉ *130 E. Randolph St.* ☎ *312/552–0070*
▭ *AE, D, DC, MC, V* ⊘ *Closed Sun. No lunch Sat.* ✛ *1:F6*

$ **Terragusto.** Chicago storefront dining doesn't get any better than this
ITALIAN Italian haunt in Roscoe Village. Bring your own wine and sit down in
Far North Side the exposed-brick dining room for dishes comprised mainly of organic

and sustainable ingredients and pastas made that day by your chef-cum-waiter. The house specializes in family-style service, enabling diners to choose an antipasto, salad, a couple of pastas, and entrées to split, making it a nice choice for groups who like to graze. Though it occupies an unlikely corner of Addison Street in Roscoe Village, it's only about a mile from Wrigley Field and neighbors the Brown Line El stop. ✉ *1851 Addison St.* ☎ *773/248–2777* 🖃 *AE, D, DC, MC, V* ☾ *Closed Mon. No lunch. 2:C3*

> ### WORD OF MOUTH
>
> "If you feel like getting out of downtown and up to Roscoe Village, I can recommend Terragusto on Addison and Wolcott. Excellent rustic northern Italian; organic local ingredients, pasta is hand-rolled there every morning, etc."
> —TwoFatFeet

¢ | **Thai Classic.** With apologies to Chinatown, Chicago is really a Thai
THAI town when it comes to outstanding Asian food. The assets at Thai
Lakeview | Classic include a prime location three blocks south of Wrigley Field, good service, and even better dishes. Not only are prices low, but there is no liquor license (pick up a six-pack of Singha beer from the liquor store down the street), saving you the mark-up. Bargain hunters should hit the $11.75 buffet, available Saturday afternoon and all day Sunday. Come on foot during Cubs games when parking is near impossible. ✉ *3332 N. Clark St.* ☎ *773/404–2000* 🖃 *AE, D, DC, MC, V.* ✛ *2:F4*

$$ | **Tomboy.** Here's your spot for great people-watching. A bohemian crowd
NEW AMERICAN mingles in this funky, brick-walled storefront that plates food with
Far North Side | a playful presentation. There's a fanciful "porcupine" shrimp coated with splayed-out spikes of phyllo dough and a crème brûlée served in a cookie cone inside a martini glass. With dishes that teeter between bold (ostrich cooked inside brioche) to mainstream (penne with sundried tomatoes), the menu can accommodate adventurous and timid guests alike. Meanwhile, regulars rave about the cocktails such as the electric-blue mojito. For dessert, pick from the list of sweet martinis ✉ *5402 N. Clark St.* ☎ *773/907–0636* 🖃 *AE, D, DC, MC, V* ☾ *Closed Sun.* ✛ *2:D1*

$$$ | **Topolobampo.** Chef-owner Rick Bayless wrote the book on regional
MEXICAN Mexican cuisine—several books, actually—and here he takes his faith-
River North | fully regional food upscale. Next door to the more casual Frontera Grill, Topolobampo is the higher-end room, with a more subdued mood and luxury menu, though it shares Frontera's address, phone, and dedication to quality. The ever-changing offerings showcase game, seasonal fruits and vegetables, and exotic preparations: adobo-marinated lamb and rock hen in a sauce of almonds and tomatoes are two examples. ✉ *445 N. Clark St.* ☎ *312/661–1434* 🖃 *AE, D, DC, MC, V* ☾ *Closed Sun. and Mon. No lunch Sat.* ✛ *1:D5*

$$ | **Trattoria No. 10.** It's hard to camouflage a basement location, but Tratto-
ITALIAN ria No. 10 gives it a good go with terra-cotta colors, arched entryways,
The Loop | and quarry-tile floors, all of which evoke Italy. Pretheater diners crowd

in for the house specialty ravioli filled with seasonal stuffings, classic antipasti selections like caprese salad with vine-ripened tomatoes and bufala mozzarella, and substantial *secondi piatti* like wagyu steak with roasted corn and pancetta. Cheap chowsters, meanwhile, elbow into the bar for the $12 nibbles buffet served from 5 to 7:30 PM weekdays with a $6 drink minimum. ⊠*10 N. Dearborn St.* ☏*312/984–1718* ⊟*AE, D, DC, MC, V* ⊘*Closed Sun. No lunch Sat.* ✛*4:F1*

$$$$
NEW AMERICAN
Near North

TRU. Chefs Rick Tramonto and, on pastries, Gale Gand do fine dining with a sense of humor. The quite serious food is leavened by the presentations: caviar atop a tabletop crystal staircase, between-course sorbets in cones, or dishes served over a mini fishbowl occupied by a live fighting fish. The dining room resembles a gallery, with white walls and carefully chosen art, including an Andy Warhol. The menu starts with a basic three-course prix-fixe, priced at $95, and escalates to nine courses. Several of those are dessert, so save space. ⊠*676 N. St. Clair St.* ☏*312/202–0001* ⚑*Reservations essential. Jacket required* ⊟*AE, D, DC, MC, V* ⊘*Closed Sun. No lunch.* ✛*1:F3*

$$
TURKISH
Lakeview

Turquoise Restaurant and Cafe. The bustling Turkish-owned café attempts to please every palate with a mixed menu of continental and Turkish foods, but it's the latter that star here. Can't-miss items include lamb kebabs, *sogurme* (a smoked eggplant, yogurt, and walnut dip), and homemade noodles with feta and dill. Vested waiters, a martini menu, and wood-trimmed surroundings outclass the neighborhood lot. ⊠*2147 W. Roscoe St.* ☏*773/549–3523* ⊟*AE, D, DC, MC, V.* ✛*2:B4*

$$
BARBECUE
Near North

Twin Anchors Restaurant & Tavern. For a taste of classic Chicago, stop into Twin Anchors, which has been dishing baby back ribs since 1932. The nautically-themed brick tavern was a favorite of Frank Sinatra, who still croons nightly on the jukebox. If you're not in the mood for a messy slab of mild or zesty ribs, the main draw on the menu, order the battered codfish fry or the fried chicken. In truth, dinner here is really less about cuisine and more about the scene—local and touring celebs often visit, and many locals are loyal regulars—but lovers of barrooms with personality don't mind the typically long waits during prime time. ⊠*1655 N. Sedgwick St.* ☏*312/266–1616* ⚑*Reservations not accepted* ⊟*AE, D, DC, MC, V* ⊘*No lunch weekdays.* ✛*3:G3*

$$
INTERNATIONAL
River North

Vermilion. Vermilion touts itself as a Latin–Indian fusion restaurant, but its best dishes are strictly Eastern. Skip the Latin-salute ceviche and empanadas in favor of the ribs (marinated in a special ingredient: Coca-Cola). Lots of small-plate options—led by the lamb chops and scallops—encourage sampling. Despite cool fashion photography on the walls and techno music in the air, the welcome here is warm. Late-night dining hours draw a club-going crowd. ⊠*10 W. Hubbard St.* ☏*312/527–4060* ⊟*AE, D, DC, MC, V* ⊘*No lunch Sat.* ✛*1:D5*

$$
AMERICAN
Near North

Viand. Ebullient chef-owner Steve Chiappetti's personality is written all over Viand, a lively restaurant and bar that's a breath of fresh air from the seriously designer-centric Michigan Avenue, just a half block away. "Dining should be fun," says the chef, and so it is here where

Oscar-style statuettes deliver chopsticks and the Junk Food Cart dessert option packs homemade Oreos, marshmallows, and brownies in a mini shopping cart. Don't miss the braised lamb, the four-cheese ravioli with truffle sauce, and a chat with the friendly chef. Adjacent to a Courtyard by Marriott, the restaurant serves breakfast, lunch, and dinner and has a steady bar trade. ✉*155 E. Ontario St.* ☎*312/255–8505* ▭*AE, MC, V.* ✛*1:F4*

$$ **Vivo.** Vivo was trendy on this west-of-the-Loop stretch long before Ran-
ITALIAN   dolph Street's restaurant row got hot. It still manages to be a trendset-
West Loop   ter with Vice, its new late-night lounge next door serving small plates until 1 AM on weekends. Slightly more about scene—brick walls, black ceiling, open wine racks, and lots of pretty people—than cuisine, Vivo manages reliable Italian fare. You can't go wrong with carpaccio, spaghetti vongole with littleneck clams, and free-range lamb chops. ✉*838 W. Randolph St.* ☎*312/733–3379* ▭*AE, DC, MC, V* ⊗*No lunch weekends.* ✛*4:D1*

$$ **Vong's Thai Kitchen.** This casual spin-off of chef Jean-Georges Vongeri-
THAI   chten's New York Thai–French fusion Vong, concentrates solely on
River North   Thai fare with upmarket accents and pretty presentations. Look for shrimp and crab pad Thai, and a laundry list of curries ranging from mild to "jungle" hot. Candles and palms boost the romance quotient by night, but this is also a strong candidate for a working lunch. ✉*6 W. Hubbard St.* ☎*312/644–8664* ▭*AE, D, DC, MC, V* ⊗*No lunch Sun.* ✛*1:D5*

$$ **Weber Grill Restaurant.** How cheesy is it to dine at a brand extension of a
AMERICAN   popular backyard grill? Okay, a little, but get over yourself and look for
River North   the red kettle cooker outside Weber Grill, where restaurant-sized versions of the namesake appliance demonstrate their versatility. Suburban Chicago–based Weber takes on the range of grill cookery at its River North restaurant, offering burgers, ribs, steaks, chops, veggie sides, and novelties like "beer-can chicken" on the extensive menu. Adjacent to the Hilton Garden Inn, the restaurant also serves standard breakfast fare. Spacious booths line the State Street windows and make for the best views of Chicago foot traffic. ✉*539 N. State St.* ☎*312/467–9696* ▭*AE, D, DC, MC, V.* ✛*1:E4*

$$ **West Town Tavern.** While it's a little off the beaten path, trust your cabbie
AMERICAN   to get you here. The handsome wood bar and brick walls may be tavern
West Loop   staples, but the open kitchen and oversize dining-room mirror promise more than cheeseburgers. The menu delivers with a mix of upscale comfort foods (try the beer cheese—a cheese ball made with cheddar cheese and spices—and pizza-style flat breads) and gussied-up American classics like pepper-crusted beef tenderloin in a zinfandel sauce. The focused wine list globe-trots for value. ✉*1329 W. Chicago Ave.* ☎*312/666–6175* ▭*AE, MC, V* ⊗*Closed Sun. No lunch.* ✛*3:D5*

$$ **Wildfire.** This is as close as you can get to the grill without staying home
AMERICAN   and firing up the barbie. A triple hearth of roaring fires runs along the
River North   back wall of the supper club–style joint that plays a soundtrack of vintage jazz. No culinary innovations here, just exceptional chopped salad,

roasted prime rib, and salmon roasted on a cedar plank, along with wood-fired pizzas and skillet-roasted mussels. Top taste: the horserad-ish-crusted filet mignon. ⊠*159 W. Erie St.* ☎*312/787–9000* ▭*AE, D, DC, MC, V* ☉*No lunch.* ✢*1:C4*

$$
ASIAN FUSION
Lakeview

Yoshi's Cafe. Decades ago Yoshi's launched as a pricey fine-dining res-taurant in the 'hood. We offer this history lesson to say that while the atmosphere went jeans-casual and the prices south, the cooking qual-ity remained, and remains, high. Yoshi Katsumura turns out informal French-Asian cuisine, like duck breast with baked quail egg in brioche or roasted Japanese pumpkin filled with tofu (it's good enough to con-vert a carnivore). Sunday brunch includes the expected eggs along with a Japanese-inspired breakfast (rice, tofu, and seaweed). ⊠*3257 N. Halsted St.* ☎*773/248–6160* ▭*AE, DC, MC, V* ☉*Closed Mon. Sun. brunch.* ✢*2:F4*

Chicago Dining & Lodging Atlas

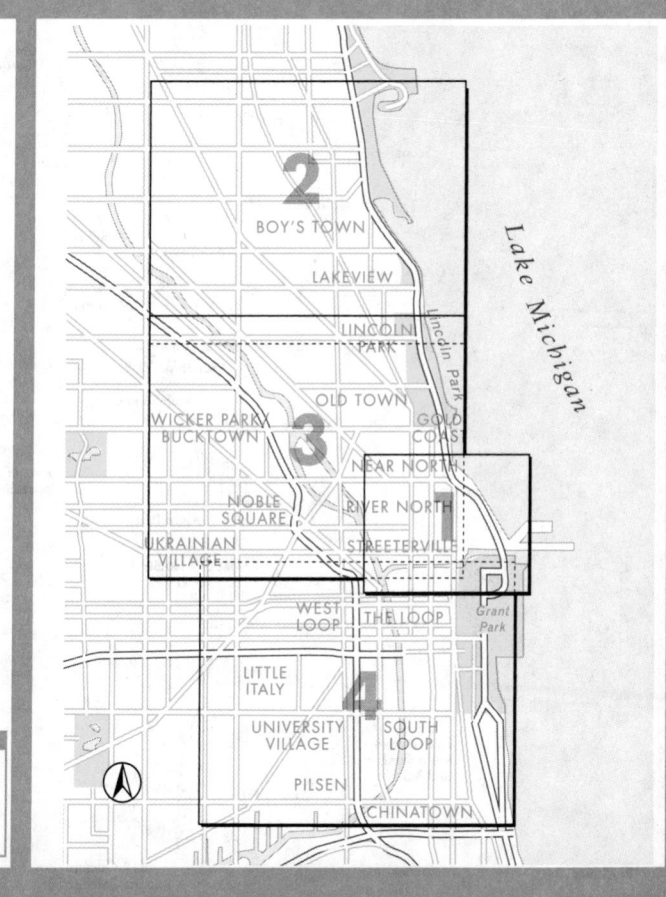

KEY

☐ Hotels
■ Restaurants
▣ Restaurant in Hotel
Ⓜ Subway Station

Map 2

- Boy's Town
- Irving Park
- Lakeview
- Lincoln Park
- Wrigleyville

UPTOWN

Montrose Harbor

Montrose Ave

Graceland Cemetery

Lincoln Park

Hazel St

Sherrida Ave

Broadway

Buena Ave

Cuyler Ave

Bittersweet Pl

Irving Park Rd

Pizza Rustica

Byron St

Grace St

Lake Michigan

WRIGLEYVILLE

Waveland Ave

Pine Grove Ave

Rec Dr.

◆ WRIGLEY FIELD

Addison St

Majestic Hotel

N Lake Shore Dr

Eddy St

Clark St

Cornelia Ave

Cornelia Ave

Halsted St

Broadway

Newport Ave

Roscoe St

Roscoe St

BOY'S TOWN

Thai Classic

Mia Francesca

Belmont Harbor

Aldine St

School St

Yoshi's Cafe

Melrose St

Orange

Belmont Ave

Ann Sather   □ **City Suites**

Fletcher St

Briar Pl

Barry St

Barry St

LAKEVIEW

Sheridan Ave

Clifton Ave

Seminary Ave

Kenmore Ave

Nelson St

Wellington Ave

Oakdale Ave

Oakdale Ave

Lincoln Park

■ **Erwin**

George St

The Willows

Surf St

Pine Grove Ave

Wolfram St

Days Inn Lincoln Park North

Diversey Pkwy

Lincoln Ave

Sheffield Ave

Wilton Ave

Mildred Ave

Dayton St

Schubert Ave

Burling St

Orchard St

Clark St

Lehmann Ct

Hampden Ct

Deming Pl

Cannon Dr

North Pond

North Pond

Wrightwood Ave

Altgeld St

LINCOLN PARK

Montana St

Arlington Pl

Larrabee St

Fullerton Ave

Fullerton Pkwy

N Lake Shore Dr

Lakewood Ave

Racine Ave

Seminary Ave

Kenmore Ave

Sheffield Ave

Lakewood Ave

Racine Ave

Wayne Ave

0 ——— 1 mi

0 ——— 1 km

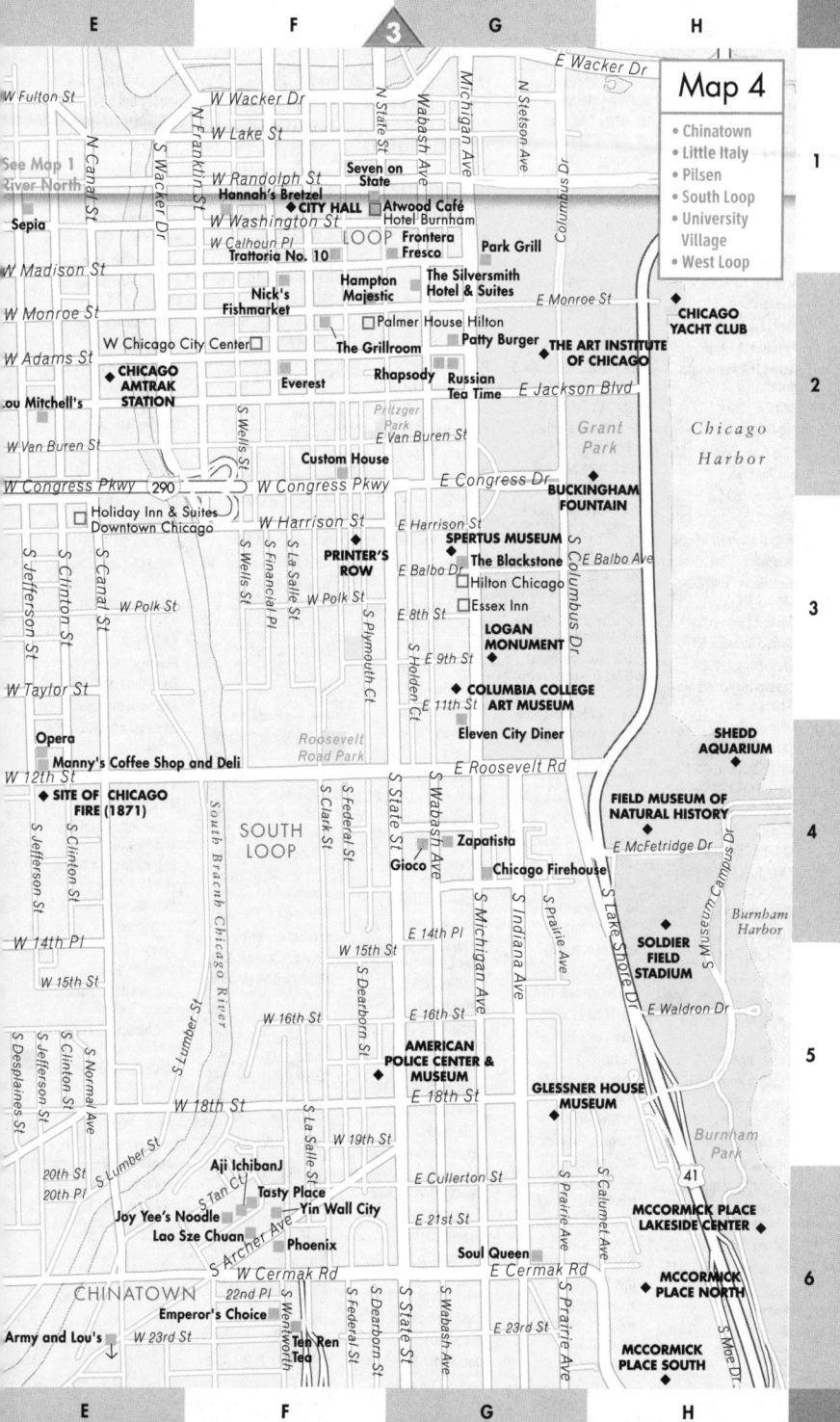

Map 4

- Chinatown
- Little Italy
- Pilsen
- South Loop
- University Village
- West Loop

E Wacker Dr

W Fulton St
W Wacker Dr
W Lake St
W Randolph St
Seven on State
Hannah's Bretzel
W Washington St
CITY HALL
Atwood Café Hotel Burnham
Sepia
W Calhoun Pl
Frontera Fresco
LOOP
Park Grill
W Madison St
Trattoria No. 10
Nick's Fishmarket
Hampton Majestic
The Silversmith Hotel & Suites
W Monroe St
E Monroe St
CHICAGO YACHT CLUB
W Adams St
W Chicago City Center
Palmer House Hilton
Patty Burger
CHICAGO AMTRAK STATION
The Grillroom
Rhapsody
Russian Tea Time
THE ART INSTITUTE OF CHICAGO
Lou Mitchell's
Everest
E Jackson Blvd
Pritzger Park
Grant Park
Chicago Harbor
W Van Buren St
E Van Buren St
Custom House
W Congress Pkwy 290
W Congress Pkwy
E Congress Dr
BUCKINGHAM FOUNTAIN
Holiday Inn & Suites Downtown Chicago
W Harrison St
E Harrison St
SPERTUS MUSEUM
PRINTER'S ROW
E Balbo Dr
The Blackstone
E Balbo Ave
W Polk St
Hilton Chicago
W Polk St
E 8th St
Essex Inn
LOGAN MONUMENT
E 9th St
COLUMBIA COLLEGE ART MUSEUM
W Taylor St
E 11th St
Roosevelt Road Park
Eleven City Diner
SHEDD AQUARIUM
Opera
Manny's Coffee Shop and Deli
E Roosevelt Rd
W 12th St
FIELD MUSEUM OF NATURAL HISTORY
SITE OF CHICAGO FIRE (1871)
SOUTH LOOP
Zapatista
E McFetridge Dr
Gioco
Chicago Firehouse
Burnham Harbor
W 14th Pl
E 14th Pl
SOLDIER FIELD STADIUM
W 15th St
W 15th St
E 16th St
E Waldron Dr
W 16th St
AMERICAN POLICE CENTER & MUSEUM
W 18th St
E 18th St
GLESSNER HOUSE MUSEUM
Burnham Park
W 19th St
41
Aji IchibanJ
E Cullerton St
Tasty Place
Yin Wall City
Joy Yee's Noodle
E 21st St
MCCORMICK PLACE LAKESIDE CENTER
Lao Sze Chuan
Phoenix
Soul Queen
W Cermak Rd
E Cermak Rd
MCCORMICK PLACE NORTH
CHINATOWN
22nd Pl
Emperor's Choice
Army and Lou's
W 23rd St
Ten Ren Tea
E 23rd St
MCCORMICK PLACE SOUTH

Where to Stay

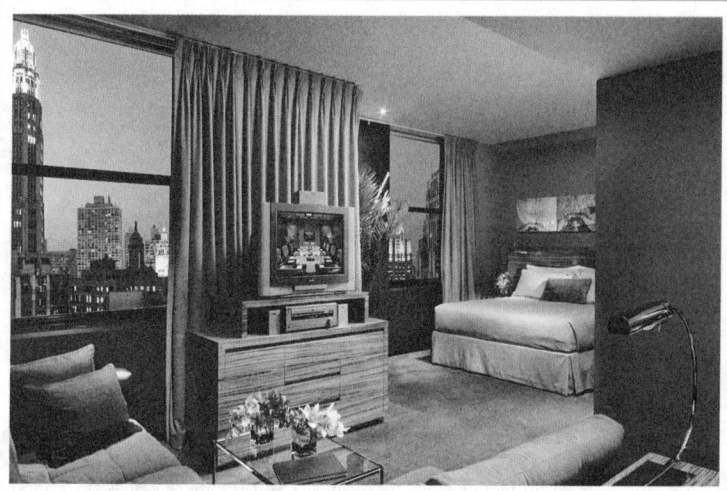

WORD OF MOUTH

"A hotel on or just off of North Michigan Avenue would provide the most options—you can walk to great shopping and restaurants. Consider The Drake (famous for afternoon tea), The Westin, The Peninsula, Park Hyatt, The Tremont, and The Ritz. Try to stay between Oak Street and the Chicago River to be centrally located."

—jen9

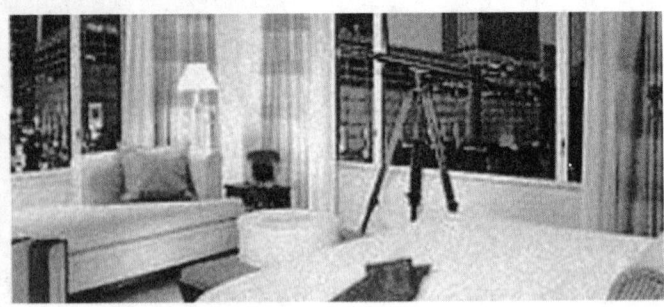

THE SCENE

Updated by Jo Napolitano

Chicago hotel rates are as temperamental as the city's climate. And just as snow in April and 70-degree weather in November are not uncommon, it is widely accepted that a hotel's room rates may drop $50 to $100 overnight—and rise again the next day. It all depends on the season (summers are most pricey, unsurprisingly) and what's happening in town (big conventions at McCormick Place, like February's annual Chicago Auto Show, throw a wrench in the system, kicking up rates citywide).

Even so, it's wise to shop around. Focus on a neighborhood of interest, such as the Michigan Avenue area, also called Near North, and you'll find budget chains like Embassy Suites, where prices start at $189, and luxury properties like the Four Seasons Hotel Chicago within a few blocks of each other.

On the lower end, expect well-maintained yet boxy and sparsely decorated rooms. The good news is that free Wi-Fi is now a feature of most budget-friendly hotels, like the Best Western and Holiday Inn chains, or local outfits like the Essex Inn.

Top-tier hotels have no problem filling their rooms: in some cases, this has little to do with amenities. Instead, their vibrant bar scenes are the draw, as is the case at the W Chicago Lakeshore, W Chicago City Center, and the James Hotel. Rooms at these hot spots usually don't go for under $300, but the "it" factor is huge, with attractive crowds queuing at the bar and lounging in the restaurants.

Looking forward, Ian Schrager, who co-founded Studio 54, announced his plans to partner with Marriott International Inc. to open a new boutique hotel called "Edition" just off the Magnificent Mile.

WHERE SHOULD I STAY?

	Neighborhood Vibe	Pros	Cons
The Loop	Mostly historic hotels of architectural interest in an area trolled by business-people on weekdays and shoppers on weekends. The scene has become increasingly hip over the years.	Accessible public transportation and abundant cabs; packed with business types during the day; the area has recently blossomed into a worthy nighttime destination.	El train noise; construction common; streets can sometimes be bare in late evening. It draws an older, more established crowd.
South Loop & West Loop	Mixed residential and business neighborhoods that are gentrifying, although empty buildings and storefronts are common. This area has seen a lot of new life in the last couple of years.	Hotels are cheaper; streets are quieter; Museum Campus and McCormick Place are within easy reach; family-friendly; appealing to hipster set with many new lounges and restaurants.	Long walks to public transportation; minimal shopping; quiet at night with many darkened streets. If you're looking for entertainment, it might require a quick drive or a long walk.
Near North	The pulse of the city, on and around North Michigan Avenue, has ritzy high-rise hotels, plenty of shopping and restaurants. The farther north you go, streets become residential.	Many lodging options, including some of the city's most luxurious hotels. Lively streets abuzz until late night; safe. The shopping couldn't be better for those with deep pockets.	Some hotels on the pricey side; crowded sidewalks; popular tourist destination. And don't expect to find many bargains here.
River North	Lots of chains, from hotels to restaurants to shops, patronized mostly by travelers. Though this is a tourist haven, the area has become home to many art galleries and antiques stores.	Affordable lodging; easy access to public transportation; attractions nearby are family-friendly, especially during the day; high concentration of nightclubs.	Area might be too touristy for some. This is Chicago's home for chain restaurants; parking is a drag.
Lincoln Park	Small, boutique hotels tucked on quiet, tree-lined streets with many independent shops and restaurants. Pedestrian-friendly area; you don't need a car to find a restaurant, bar, or bank.	Low crime; great paths for walks; lots of parkland. From hot dogs to sushi, this place has it all; eclectic collection of shops and restaurants, ranging from super-affordable to the ultrapricey.	Limited hotel selection; long walks to El train. Parking is almost impossible in some spots, and garages don't come cheap; very young and trendy crowd.
Lakeview & North of the City	Especially lively around Wrigley Field, where both Chicagoans and travelers congregate in summertime; the area's lodging is mid-sized boutique hotels and B&Bs.	Low crime; moderately priced hotels; shopping and dining options at all price ranges, including many vintage-clothing boutiques; a plethora of sports-theme bars.	Congested traffic; panhandlers common, especially around El stations and Wrigley Field. Parking is nightmarish when the Cubs are playing in town.

6

CHICAGO LODGING PLANNER

Strategy

Where should we stay? With hundreds of Chicago hotels, it may seem like a daunting question. But fret not—our expert writers and editors have done most of the legwork. The selections here represent the best this city has to offer—from the best budget motels to the sleekest designer hotels. Scan "Best Bets" on the following pages for top recommendations by price and experience. Or find a review quickly in the listings. Search by neighborhood, then alphabetically. Happy hunting!

In This Chapter

Facilities

Unless otherwise noted in the individual descriptions, all the hotels listed have private baths, central heating, air-conditioning, and private phones. Almost all hotels have Internet and phones with voice mail, as well as valet service. Many now have wireless Internet (Wi-Fi) available, although it's not always free.

Need a Reservation?

Yes. Hotel reservations are an absolute necessity when planning your trip to Chicago—hotels often fill up with convention traffic, so book your room in advance.

Orientation

Throughout the chapter, you'll see mapping symbols and coordinates (✛) after property reviews. To locate the property on a map, turn to the Chicago Dining & Lodging Atlas at the end of the Where to Eat chapter. The first number after the ✛ symbol indicates the map number. Following that is the property's coordinate on the map grid.

Prices

The prices we've printed are based on standard double rooms at high season, excluding holidays. Although we list all of the facilities that are available at a property, we don't specify what is included and what costs extra, as those policies are subject to change without notice.

WHAT IT COSTS

A STANDARD ROOM FOR TWO PEOPLE

¢	$	$$	$$$	$$$$
under $150	$151–$219	$220–$319	$320–$419	over $420

Prices exclude service charges and chicago's 15.4% room tax.

BEST BETS FOR CHICAGO LODGING

Fodor's offers a selective listing of quality lodging experiences at every price range, from the city's best budget motel to its most sophisticated luxury hotel. Here, we've compiled our top recommendations by price and experience. The best properties—those that provide a remarkable experience in their price range—are designated in the listings with the Fodor's Choice logo. Check here for our top recommendations, then read the review in the listings, which are organized alphabetically within each neighborhood.

Fodor's Choice ★

The Blackstone, p. 248

Essex Inn, p. 248

Flemish House of Chicago, p. 237

Four Seasons Hotel, p. 237

Hotel Burnham, p. 232

Hotel Sax Chicago, p. 247

The James Hotel, p. 240

Park Hyatt Chicago, p. 240

Peninsula Chicago, p. 242

Ritz-Carlton Chicago, p. 242

Sofitel Chicago Water Tower, p. 243

Trump International Hotel & Tower, p. 247

W Chicago Lakeshore, p. 244

Best by Price

¢

Margarita European Inn, p. 228

City Suites Hotel, p. 228

$

Flemish House of Chicago, p. 237

Best Western Hawthorne Terrace, p. 228

Essex Inn, p. 248

Hampton Majestic, p. 231

Millennium Knickerbocker Hotel, p. 240

$$

Hard Rock Hotel, p. 231

Hyatt Regency Chicago, p. 232

Hotel Sax Chicago, p. 247

W Chicago Lakeshore, p. 244

$$$

The Blackstone, p. 248

Four Seasons Hotel, p. 237

Hilton Chicago, p. 248

Hotel Burnham, p. 232

Trump International Hotel & Tower, p. 247

$$$$

Park Hyatt Chicago, p. 240

Peninsula Chicago, p. 242

Ritz-Carlton Chicago, p. 242

Sofitel Chicago Water Tower, p. 243

Best by Experience

BEST SPA

Four Seasons Hotel, p. 237

The James Hotel, p. 240

Trump International Hotel & Tower, p. 247

W Chicago Lakeshore, p. 244

BEST CONCIERGE

Fairmont Chicago, p. 230

Hotel Monaco, p. 232

Renaissance Chicago Hotel, p. 233

Ritz-Carlton Chicago, p. 242

GREAT POOLS

Essex Inn, p. 248

Hilton Chicago, p. 248

Hotel InterContinental Chicago, p. 238

Peninsula Chicago, p. 242

Trump International Hotel & Tower, p. 247

MOST KID-FRIENDLY

Best Western River North, p. 245

Essex Inn, p. 248

Holiday Inn & Suites Downtown, p. 249

Homewood Suites, p. 238

Hotel Allegro Chicago, p. 231

6

LISTINGS (ALPHABETICAL WITHIN NEIGHBORHOOD)

EVANSTON

¢ **Margarita European Inn.** While the tiny rooms, shared bathrooms, and narrow corridors recall a college dormitory, you won't find a more charming place to stay in Chicago's near north suburbs. The Inn was formerly an all-girls residence club built in the late 1920s, and a lot of its original features, including the iron-girded elevator shaft and antiques-laden parlor, remain intact. The staff is small but helpful. The best feature is the "borrowing" library, where guests can swap their rare and used books for those of others. If you're in no rush to go downtown, eat at the lower-level Va Pensiero restaurant, a fancy Italian spot that serves more than 10 kinds of grappa and dishes like pancetta-wrapped pork tenderloin. **Pros:** a quaint, off-the-beaten path find; close to Northwestern University and a gorgeous downtown area. **Cons:** breakfast is merely adequate; spotty service. ⊠1566 Oak Ave., Evanston ☎847/869–2273 ᗓ847/869–2353 ⊕www.margaritainn. com ➴42 rooms, 22 with bath ⌂In-hotel: restaurant, Wi-Fi, parking (fee) ⊟AE, MC, V |O|CP. ⊹ 2:D1

LAKEVIEW

Seemingly light-years away from the downtown buzz, Lakeview hotels entice with their proximity to Wrigley Field and the summertime street festivals for which the neighborhood is known. As you venture farther north, accommodations tend to be quainter and spaces more intimate.

$ **Best Western Hawthorne Terrace.** This 59-room hotel is centrally located and offers all essential amenities at a reasonable price. There's little room to relax in the American colonial–style lobby, but rooms are inviting enough; deluxe rooms come with whirlpool tubs. A stay here includes free continental breakfast, and use of business facilities and a fitness center. The hotel's front terrace becomes a place to see and be seen in the summer months, especially when street festivals roar into town. **Pros:** proximity to Wrigley Field; helpful staff; close to popular bars and restaurants. **Cons:** parking is not ideal; some guests have complained of billing problems. ⊠3434 N. Broadway, Lakeview ☎773/244–3434 or 888/675–2378 ᗓ773/244–3435 ⊕www. hawthorneterrace.com ➴46 rooms, 13 suites ⌂In-room: safe, microwave, refrigerator (some), DVD (some), Wi-Fi. In-hotel: gym, laundry facilities, laundry service, parking (fee) ⊟AE, D, DC, MC, V |O|CP. ⊹ 1:F3

¢ **City Suites Hotel.** The neighborhood is eclectic, being the stomping grounds for the city's Goth and punk kids, but it's safe and pretty appealing if you want to escape the sometimes stiff downtown scene. European travelers love the hotel for its cozy, residential feel (it's a mostly suites property, and two-thirds of the rooms have separate sitting areas and pull-out couches). Its proximity to the El train is both a blessing and a curse; you'll have easy access to downtown and the North Side, but the rumbling noise into the wee hours might not make for the most restful night. Amenities include complimentary continental breakfast, afternoon cookies, free wireless Internet access, luxury robes, and access to a nearby health club. **Pros:** located near the Briar Street Theater's Blue Man Group; close to public transportation. **Cons:** rooms are on the small side; an underwhelming breakfast. ⊠ *933 W. Belmont Ave. Lakeview* ☎ *773/404–3400 or 800/248–9108* 🖶 *773/404–3405* ⊕ *www.cityinns.com* ⇆ *16 rooms, 29 suites* ⚒ *In-room: refrigerator, Wi-Fi. In-hotel: concierge, parking (fee)* ▤ *AE, D, DC, MC, V* ⦿ *CP.* ✛ *2:F4*

$$ **Majestic Hotel.** It's no wonder lovey-dovey couples are a big part of this hotel's clientele; everything here—from the roaring fireplace in the lobby to wood-laden, cozy rooms with Prairie-style furnishings and dried flowers—says romance. Rely on the friendly concierge for just about anything, including reservations at the many restaurants in the lively Boys Town and Wrigleyville neighborhoods just outside the door. Transportation can be tricky; because the hotel is on a quiet side street, you'll have to walk a block to flag a cab, and the El train is at least five minutes away on foot. **Pros:** great ambience; friendly staff; quiet at night. **Cons:** furnishings are a bit dated; the small elevator can be a hassle for those with lots of luggage. ⊠ *528 W. Brompton Ave., Lakeview* ☎ *773/404–3499 or 800/727–5108* 🖶 *773/404–3495* ⊕ *www.cityinns.com* ⇆ *28 rooms, 23 suites* ⚒ *In-room: refrigerator (some), Wi-Fi. In-hotel: concierge, laundry service, parking (fee)* ▤ *AE, D, DC, MC, V* ⦿ *CP.* ✛ *2:G3*

$ **The Willows.** The lobby of this 1920s boutique hotel, designed in 19th-century French Provincial style, opens onto a tree-lined street in Lakeview, a lively area three blocks from the lake and central to stores, restaurants, and movie theaters. Its prime location and proximity to the El make it a top choice for visitors to Chicago. The complimentary continental breakfast and afternoon cookies make it an inviting alternative to local bed-and-breakfasts. Workout buffs don't despair: although there is no on-site fitness center, guests have access to a local Bally's Total Fitness Club. **Pro:** just steps away from bars, restaurants, and public transit. **Con:** modestly decorated rooms. ⊠ *555 W. Surf St., Lakeview* ☎ *773/528–8400 or 800/787–3108* 🖶 *773/528–8483* ⊕ *www.cityinns.com* ⇆ *51 rooms, 4 suites* ⚒ *In-room: Wi-Fi. In-hotel: concierge, laundry facilities, laundry service, parking (fee)* ▤ *AE, D, DC, MC, V* ⦿ *CP.* ✛ *2:G5*

LINCOLN PARK

Three miles of lakefront parkland draw people to this neighborhood—and most hotels here are just blocks away. Room rates are decidedly lower than those downtown, the downside being that you'll invest more in transportation to hit top sites. Parking is easier, but never a snap; plan on using the valet.

6

$$ Belden-Stratford. The 70 rooms—all with full kitchens or kitchenettes—are apartments for long-term rental, but on any given night there are plenty available for overnight stays at very reasonable rates. Don't be fooled; the feel is not that of a generic, extended-stay hotel. Its lobby, in fact, looks palatial, thanks to the polished gold chandelier, grand piano, and hand-woven tapestries. The lobby and hallways are praised for being quiet, so families should prepare to clam up their kids. The biggest treat is the on-site dining at French restaurant Mon Ami Gabi. Another highlight? The Lincoln Park Zoo is across the street and the lakefront is just a few blocks farther. **Pros:** extremely well maintained; excellent location. **Cons:** the quality of rooms is inconsistent. ⊠*2300 N. Lincoln Park W., Lincoln Park* ☎*773/281–2900 or 800/800–8301* ☎*773/880–2039* ⊕*www.beldenstratford.com* ⇨*10 rooms, 60 suites* ⌂*In-room: kitchen, Internet, Wi-Fi. In-hotel: Restaurant, gym, laundry facilities, laundry service, parking (fee)* ⊟*AE, D, DC, MC, V.* ✛ *3:G1*

$ Days Inn Chicago. This award-winning Days Inn is one of the more luxurious in the sometimes so-so chain. This boutique hotel offers an affordable stay in a prime location. The updated look of its guest rooms is one of cheery mixed patterns and light-wood furniture, white linens, and duvets. Complimentary continental breakfast and free Wi-Fi are available to all guests, as well as free use of a nearby health club. **Pros:** great location; knowledgeable staff makes it a good value for the price. **Cons:** The location—bustling even very late at night—can make it a little noisy for some guests. ⊠*644 W. Diversey Pkwy., Lincoln Park* ☎*773/525–7010 or 888/576–3297* ☎*773/525–6998* ⊕*www. daysinnchicago.net* ⇨*129 rooms, 4 suites* ⌂*In-room: safe, refrigerator (some), Wi-Fi. In-hotel: laundry facilities, laundry service, parking (fee), no-smoking rooms* ⊟*AE, D, DC, MC, V* ⎮�CP. ✛ *2:G5*

THE LOOP

Chicago's business district, laced with overhead train tracks, is a desirable—if slightly noisy—place to stay. Hotels here tend to be moderately priced; many are housed in historic buildings, giving them a charm you won't find along glitzier North Michigan Avenue. Easy access to the Art Institute and Millennium Park is a plus.

$$ Fairmont Chicago. On a quiet block near the Loop, this 45-story pink-granite tower fluctuates between the understated and the opulent, with a huge, glistening chandelier in the foyer. Good thing that it caters to the chatty; there are three telephones per room (including one hanging conspicuously on the bathroom wall). Suites offer stunning views of Lake Michigan and feature dining rooms. Coveted whirlpools are only available in grand suites, which, housed on the top floor, also boast fireplaces, libraries, and kitchenettes. Aria, an upscale restaurant within the Fairmont, attracts plenty of locals; it's a global-cuisine treasure, featuring American food with Indian, Greek, Asian, and Turkish influences. **Pros:** spacious rooms; a short walk from the heart of the city. **Cons:** rooms feel outdated. ⊠*200 N. Columbus Dr., The*

Loop ☎*312/565–8000 or 800/526–2008* 🖷*312/856–1032* ⊕*www. fairmont.com* ⮑*628 rooms, 53 suites* ☖*In-room: Internet. In-hotel: restaurant, room service, bars, spa, concierge, laundry service, public Wi-Fi, parking (fee), no-smoking rooms, some pets allowed* ▤*AE, D, DC, MC, V.* ⊹ *1:F6*

$ **Hampton Majestic, Chicago Theatre District.** The Hampton Majestic is located in one of the most high-traffic areas of town. It offers stunning and quiet guest rooms with rust-color walls, white sheets, and chocolate-brown furnishings. Online pictures, which can make the rooms look orange, don't do the place justice. The sheer curtains are a perfect touch. The downstairs lobby, nondescript and filled with luggage, is not at all a reflection of the rest of the space. The service is responsive and the common areas are large. Give this place a chance; it will truly surprise you. **Pros:** steps from the Art Institute; unique style; great complimentary breakfast. **Cons:** a hike to the Magnificent Mile; the lobby can seem too crowded with furniture. ✉*22 W. Monroe, The Loop* ☎*312/332–5052* ⊕*www.hamptonmajestic.com* ⮑*135 rooms* ☖*In-room: Wi-Fi (some). In-hotel: room service, gym, laundry service, concierge, public Internet, parking* ▤*AE, D, DC, MC, V* ❢❶ *CP.* ⊹ *4:F1*

$$ **Hard Rock Hotel.** We're not huge fans of the ubiquitous restaurant chain, but the hotel—flashy, loud, and packed with plasma TVs—has our approval. Set within the 40-story Carbide and Carbon Building, it touts modern rooms adorned with rock-and-roll paraphernalia and a brilliant dining concept called China Grill. Ask for a tower room, offering striking views of Michigan Avenue, Millennium Park, and the Chicago River. Complimentary issues of Time Out Chicago keep guests in the know about what's happening in the city. **Pros:** well-appointed rooms with great views; good location; Aveda bath products. **Cons:** the dim lighting can be bothersome to some. ✉*230 N. Michigan Ave., The Loop* ☎*312/345–1000 or 800/966–5166* 🖷*312/345–1012* ⊕*www. hardrockhotelchicago.com* ⮑*381 rooms, 20 suites* ☖*In-room: safe, DVD, Internet. In-hotel: restaurant, room service, bar, gym, concierge, executive floor, public Wi-Fi, parking (fee), some pets allowed, no-smoking rooms* ▤*AE, D, DC, MC, V.* ⊹ *1:E6*

$$$ **Hotel Allegro Chicago.** Theater lovers will relish an opportunity to stay ☾ at this recently renovated, Art Deco–theme hot spot. The new, eclectic decor—including pop art–inspired chairs and sofas—is a hit, and the lobby's black and gray wallpaper looks super sharp. The service is solid, and the rooms are a treat with their muted metallic walls and blue mohair headboards. The bathrooms are well crafted, with gleaming new gray marble and updated sinks and vanities. Rent a suite if space is your thing. The building, staying true to its original architecture, kept the rooms on the smaller side. **Pros:** Aveda products in the bathrooms; yoga equipment available upon request. **Cons:** small bathrooms and closets. ✉*171 W. Randolph St., The Loop* ☎*312/236–0123 or 800/643–1500* 🖷*312/236–0917* ⊕*www.allegrochicago.com* ⮑*451 rooms, 32 suites* ☖*In-room: DVD, Wi-Fi, refrigerator. In-hotel: 2 restaurants, room service, 2 bars, gym, children's program,* *laundry service, concierge, public Internet, parking (fee), no-smoking rooms, some pets allowed* ▭*AE, D, DC, MC, V.* ✣ *1:C6*

$$$

Hotel Burnham. Making creative use of a city landmark, this hotel is housed in the famed 13-story Reliance Building, which D.H. Burnham & Company built in 1895. The refurbished interior retains such original details as Carrara marble wainscoting and ceilings, terrazzo floors, and mahogany trim. Guest rooms, which·were once the building's offices, are compact. But we'll overlook the lack of wiggle room thanks to perks like the "pillow library," which offers everything from firm to hypoallergenic pillows. On the ground floor, the intimate Atwood Cafe has a stylish mahogany bar and serves contemporary American fare, including its popular potpies. **Pros:** property has a storied past; beautifully restored building; good location. **Cons:** small guest rooms may make it difficult to sprawl out. ⊠*1 W. Washington St., The Loop* ☎*312/782–1111 or 877/294–9712* 🖷*312/782–0899* ⊕*www.burnham hotel.com* ➩*103 rooms, 19 suites* ♿*In-room: safe, Wi-Fi, refrigerator. In-hotel: restaurant, room service, bar, gym, concierge, laundry service, public Wi-Fi, parking (fee), some pets allowed* ▭*AE, D, DC, MC, V.* ✣ *4:F1*

FodorsChoice
★

$$$

Hotel Monaco. A registration desk fashioned after a classic steamer trunk, and meeting rooms named for international destinations such as Tokyo and Paris inspire wanderlust here. Besides the bellhops dressed in safari gear, we love each room's bay windows (the Monaco is the only hotel in the city that has 'em) and the pet goldfish in a bowl provided on request. It's clear that this hotel has humor: look to the honor bars stocked with plush goldfish for the kids. Complimentary Starbucks coffee is available from 6 to 9 AM, and all guests are offered free wine each night from 5 to 6 PM. **Pros:** free coffee and wine; comfortable beds. **Cons:** small gym for a hotel of this size and splendor. ⊠*225 N. Wabash Ave., The Loop* ☎*312/960–8500 or 800/397–7661* 🖷*312/960–1883* ⊕*www.monaco-chicago.com* ➩*170 rooms, 22 suites* ♿*In-room: safe, Wi-Fi, refrigerator. In-hotel: restaurant, room service, bar, gym, concierge, laundry service, parking (fee), some pets allowed* ▭*AE, D, DC, MC, V.* ✣ *1:E6*

$$

Hyatt Regency Chicago. This 2,000-plus room hotel is one of the largest in Chicago, with illuminated signs that guide you through the labyrinth of halls. Ficus trees, palms, and gushing fountains fill the two-story greenhouse lobby. In the comfortably sized guest rooms, black-and-white photographs of Chicago landmarks give things an authentic spin. The in-house Stetson's Chop House is a convenient dining option for those who don't want to travel far for a good meal. **Pros:** great winter rates; excellent location; just steps from numerous attractions. **Cons:** thin walls can make it easy to overhear others; some guests say service didn't meet expectations for a hotel of this caliber. ⊠*151 E. Wacker Dr., The Loop* ☎*312/565–1234 or 800/233–1234* 🖷*312/239–4414* ⊕*www.chicagohyatt.com* ➩*2,019 rooms, 119 suites* ♿*In-room: safe, Internet, refrigerator (some). In-hotel: 5 restaurants, room service, gym, spa, concierge, laundry service, parking (fee), no-smoking rooms* ▭*AE, D, DC, MC, V.* ✣ *1:F5*

$$$ **Palmer House Hilton.** The *grand palais* feel of this historic property is conveyed by the huge lobby ceiling mural, which gets touched up every four years by the same Florentine gentleman who restores the art in the Sistine Chapel. Rooms—reached via a winding maze of corridors—are adequately sized. With more than 1,600 rooms, the property can seem overwhelming; luckily, one executive level, nabbed for $80 above standard rates, has its own lobby and concierge, providing a hotel-within-a-hotel feel. A 2008 renovation led to a state-of-the-art fitness center and spa, a new restaurant and bar, refurbished guest rooms, and a restored ballroom. **Pro:** recently renovated rooms with historic character left intact. **Cons:** rooms not always spotless; some rooms quite small. ✉ *17 E. Monroe St., TheLoop* ☎ *312/726–7500 or 800/445–8667* 🖷 *312/263–2556* ⊕ *www.hilton.com* ✒ *1,639 rooms, 88 suites* ♿ *In-room: Wi-Fi, kitchenette (some). In-hotel: restaurant, room service, bar, pool, gym, concierge, laundry service, public Wi-Fi, parking (fee), no-smoking rooms, some pets allowed* ▭ *AE, D, DC, MC, V.* ✛ *4:F2*

$$ **Renaissance Chicago Hotel.** The cosmopolitan Renaissance Chicago, situated on the south bank of the Chicago River, puts a premium on a good night's sleep: there's no missing the seven—yep, seven—fluffy white pillows on each bed. When you're not catching some Z's, you can enjoy views of the Chicago skyline right from your room. Stay on the hotel's slightly pricier "club levels" for a more exclusive feel and access to a private business center. **Pros:** excellent service, even when the hotel is packed to capacity; spacious rooms for a good value. **Cons:** guests complained about problems at check-in; can get pricey during high season. ✉ *1 W. Wacker Dr., The Loop* ☎ *312/372–7200 or 800/468–3571* 🖷 *312/372–0093* ⊕ *www.renaissancehotels.com* ✒ *513 rooms, 40 suites* ♿ *In-room: refrigerator, Wi-Fi. In-hotel: 2 restaurants, room service, bar, pool, gym, spa, concierge, laundry service, public Internet, public Wi-Fi, parking (fee), no-smoking rooms, some pets allowed* ▭ *AE, D, DC, MC, V.* ✛ *1:D6*

$$$ **The Silversmith Hotel and Suites.** Don't be fooled by the tiny front entrance located under the El. The guest rooms—with their 12-foot ceilings—are unusually large, each with natural light. The lobby is enormous, one of the largest in the city and covered with oak. The guest room colors—muted greens and beiges—are soft on the eyes. The furnishings are Frank Lloyd Wright–inspired, and the window seats are a treat. Steps from Millennium Park and the Art Institute, it's perfect for art and theater lovers. Popular with business folk; also great for families. **Pro:** conveniently located near public transportation. **Cons:** the entrance can be hard to find; some guests complain about outside noise. ✉ *10 S. Wabash Ave., The Loop* ☎ *312/372–7696* ⊕ *www. silversmithhotel.com* ✒ *143 rooms, 63 suites* ♿ *In-room: safe, refrigerator, Internet, Wi-Fi. In-hotel: restaurant, room service, bar, gym, laundry service, concierge, public Internet, public Wi-Fi, parking (fee), some pets allowed* ▭ *AE, D, DC, MC, V* ⦿ EP. ✛ *4:G2*

$$ **Swissôtel.** The Swissôtel's triangular Harry Weese design allows for panoramic vistas of the city, lake, or river. The comfortable, contem-

A Beautiful Stay in the Neighborhood

Chicago is, famously, a city of neighborhoods. Chicagoans like to define themselves by where they hang their hat, with attendant pride, snobbery, or aspirations to street cred (of all kinds). For visitors, setting up a temporary base in one of the neighborhoods offers many advantages. This is especially true for leisure travelers. Without an expense account to ease downtown's hotel bills and menu shock, staying right in downtown can get very costly very quickly.

When choosing accommodations, it pays to look beyond the Loop and the Magnificent Mile.

A walk up Clark Street or Lincoln Avenue in Lincoln Park opens up miles of reasonably priced dining possibilities. Along one short stretch of the former you'll pass an excellent fusion restaurant, a take-out crepes place, a grocery store, and a couple of diners where the waitress might call you "hon." Remember that the next time you're called something else in the Loop.

There's also better and cheaper parking. Downtown you'll usually pay at least $30 a day. Rates at garages in outlying neighborhoods run less. There's even a chance, albeit rather remote, of finding street parking. Some days that's like saying there's a chance of a Republican mayor, but it happens.

The best reason to stay in a neighborhood is the chance to immerse yourself in the rhythms of the city. You get a chance to live as most Chicagoans live. In the neighborhoods you'll see the sky. You'll have countless independently owned shops and restaurants to browse.

If you'd like to be somewhat near downtown, the happening Lincoln Park and Lakeview neighborhoods offer a handful of hotels. As a bonus, accommodations are relatively near the lakefront. Most also have relatively easy access to public transportation or routes well traveled by cabs. A determined walker can even get from Lincoln Park to the Magnificent Mile in a half hour.

Getting to downtown sights from farther afield may sound like too much trouble. But keep in mind that thousands upon thousands of Chicagoans make the trip every day. And, like them, you'll come home to something vital and intriguing at night. Much of the Loop, on the other hand, turns into a ghost town after rush hour. In places like Lakeview the starting gun goes off at 7 PM.

The neighborhood experience isn't for everyone. Those determined to "see it all" may find the journey in from such outposts takes too much time. Also, small hotels and B&Bs cannot offer the same pampering and facilities that are typical at the luxury digs downtown.

It's a search for small moments, for random encounters, for something indefinable—the vibe, you might say—that most appeals to visitors who stay in outer neighborhoods. Each district's rhythm is different. And it's easier to hear the city's songs away from the hustle and bustle, and tall buildings.

porary rooms have a condo feel, with two-line phones and marble bathrooms. A 42nd-floor fitness center, pool, and spa manage to draw even the most exercise-reticent, thanks to the bird's-eye views. Guests also enjoy the convenience of having The Palm restaurant located in the hotel; you don't have to travel far for a high-quality meal. **Pros:** guests love the view, the pool, and the location; modern rooms with great amenities; in-house destination restaurant. **Con:** pricey parking fees. ⊠323 E. Wacker Dr., The Loop ☎312/565–0565 or 888/737–9477 🖷312/565–0540 ⊕www.swissotelchicago.com ⇝632 rooms, 29 suites ⌂In-room: Wi-Fi. In-hotel: 2 restaurants, room service, bars, pool, gym, spa, concierge, laundry service, parking (fee), no-smoking rooms ⊟AE, D, DC, MC, V. ✛ 1:F6

$$$ W Chicago City Center. Bellhops in slick black pants and T-shirts, plus a welcome mat imprinted with "Well, Hello There," are early indicators that this hotel is hip. The couch-filled lobby (nicknamed the Living Room) is seemingly always dark (during our visit, candles were flickering at noon), and kaleidoscopic-looking film projections on walls complemented ambient music. Rooms cater to the business traveler, with desks, WebTV, and cordless phones. Whiskey Blue, the hotel bar, is frequented by celebs passing through town. **Pros:** with its sleek design and nightclub vibe, this hip and trendy hot spot is an ideal draw for a youngish visitor. **Cons:** some have complained of brusque staff; the proximity to the El can create unwanted noise. ⊠172 W. Adams St., The Loop ☎312/332–1200 or 800/621–2360 🖷312/917–5771 ⊕www.whotels.com ⇝358 rooms, 12 suites ⌂In-room: safe, DVD, Internet, Wi-Fi. In-hotel: restaurant, room service, bar, gym, spa, concierge, laundry service, public Wi-Fi, parking (fee), no-smoking rooms, some pets allowed ⊟AE, D, DC, MC, V. ✛ 4:F2

NEAR NORTH

With a cluster of accommodations around North Michigan Avenue (the "Magnificent Mile"), this area is where new hotels are springing up—or reinventing themselves, thanks to multimillion-dollar renovations. Prices hover at the high end, but there are a few deals to be found if you're willing to forgo a pool or concierge service. Consider the area's proximity to great shopping part of the bargain.

$$$ Allerton Hotel Chicago. Named a National Historic Landmark in 1998, this limestone building was a residential "club hotel" for men when it opened in 1924. A 1999 renovation restored the limestone facade and overhauled the interior. A 2008 renovation left it with a more contemporary, residential feel. The bed linens are white with navy piping, and the rooms a mix of muted blues and grays. If you want to stay in a place that is located in the middle of it all, this may be your hotel of choice. **Pros:** newly renovated rooms; delightful concierge and doormen. **Cons:** guest rooms and bathrooms are on the small-side. ⊠*701 N. Michigan Ave., Near North* ☎*312/440–1500* 🖶*312/440–1819* ⊕*www.theallertonhotel.com* ☞*359 rooms, 84 suites* ⚄*In-room: safe, Internet. In-hotel: restaurant, room service, bar, gym, concierge, laundry service, parking (fee), no-smoking rooms* ▭*AE, D, DC, MC, V.* ✛ *1:E3*

$$ **The Ambassador East.** One of the few hotels tucked in the residential Gold Coast neighborhood, this small 1920s property is a 10- to 15-minute cab ride from the Loop. The secluded setting makes it popular with celebs and literary figures, and the world-famous Pump Room still attracts a loyal following (Humphrey Bogart and Lauren Bacall celebrated their wedding in Booth One). Rooms have a certain amount of glitz, with jewel tones and cherry-wood furniture. Bookworms, take heed: the "author" suite has held book signings by the likes of John Grisham and Maya Angelou. **Pros:** the hotel is just a few minutes away from great restaurants and bars; courteous staff. **Cons:** hotel is overdue for a renovation ⊠*1301 N. State Pkwy., Near North* ☎*312/787–7200 or 800/843–6664* 🖶*312/787–4760* ⊕*www.theambassadoreasthotel. com* ☞*285 rooms, 55 suites* ⚄*In-room: refrigerator, kitchen (some), Wi-Fi. In-hotel: restaurant, room service, bar, gym, public Internet, concierge, laundry service, parking (fee), no-smoking rooms, some pets allowed* ▭*AE, D, DC, MC, V.* ✛ *3:H4*

$$$$ **Conrad Chicago.** Formerly Le Meridien hotel, this hotel's Art Deco–inspired lobby has a residential feel, with clean-lined furniture and a large mural. Rooms—featuring European duvets, oversize pillows, plush bathrobes, and slippers—aim to pamper. Don't leave without checking out the building's limestone facade, cut from the same quarries as the Empire State Building and Tribune Tower, and depicting figures from ancient mythology and the zodiac. **Pros:** large TVs; beautifully appointed lobby. **Cons:** antiquated heating and cooling systems; it takes two elevators to reach some rooms. ⊠*521 N. Rush St., Near North* ☎*312/645–1500* 🖶*312/645–1550* ⊕*www.conradhotels.com* ☞*278 rooms, 33 suites* ⚄*In-room: safe, kitchen, Internet, Wi-Fi. In-hotel: 2 restaurants, room service, bar, gym, concierge, laundry service, public Wi-Fi, parking (fee), no-smoking rooms, some pets allowed* ▭*AE, D, DC, MC, V.* ✛ *1:E4*

$$$$ **Drake Hotel.** Built in 1920, the grande dame of Chicago hotels presides over the northernmost end of Michigan Avenue. The lobby, inspired by an Italian Renaissance palace, is all deep-red walls and chandeliers dating from the 1920s. The sounds of a fountain and harpist beckon at the Palm Court, a traditional setting for afternoon tea. There's live jazz in the Coq d'Or on Thursday, Friday, and Saturday nights, and the Cape Cod Room serves to-die-for crab cakes. The downsides? No swimming pool (a bummer for the price you're paying), and some rooms are tiny. **Pros:** hotel has retained its character; beautiful lobby. **Cons:** rooms are in need of an update. ⊠*140 E. Walton Pl., Near North* ☎*312/787–2200 or 800/553–7253* 🖶*312/787–1431* ⊕*www.*

thedrakehotel.com 🗏*535 rooms, 74 suites* ⚒*In-room: safe, Wi-Fi, refrigerator. In-hotel: 4 restaurants, room service, bar, gym, concierge, laundry service, public Wi-Fi, parking (fee), no-smoking rooms* 🗏*AE, D, DC, MC, V.* ✛ *1:E2*

$ **Embassy Suites Chicago Downtown/Lakefront.** Every guest in this all-suites hotel has a view of either Lake Michigan or the Chicago skyscrapers. In addition, they also have room to roam, thanks to the spacious layout of each suite (rooms have separate bedrooms and living rooms). The sleek glass atrium is bustling in the morning due to the complimentary breakfast buffet and in the evening for complimentary manager's reception. A bonus for families on vacation is the location: within walking distance of Navy Pier and North Michigan Avenue. **Pros:** good value; free wine at night; short walk to clubs and other nightlife. **Cons:** long line for complimentary wine. ⊠*511 N. Columbus Dr., Near North* ☎*312/836–5900 or 800/362–2779* 🖷*312/836–5901* ⊕*www.chicago lakefront.embassysuites.com* 🗏*455 suites* ⚒*In-room: refrigerator, Internet. In-hotel: restaurant, room service, bar, pool, gym, concierge, laundry facilities, laundry service, parking (fee), no-smoking rooms* 🗏*AE, D, DC, MC, V* ⊠*BP.* ✛ *1:F4*

$ **Flemish House of Chicago, Apartment Bed & Breakfast.** This meticulously
Fodor'sChoice kept four-story wonder is an incredible value, considering the posh zip
★ code. Each of its seven suites has a slightly different decor, but all are roomy and well appointed, with an impressive collection of antique desks, lamps, and armoires. Built in 1892, it's classic, not old, and not a single item is amiss. The rooms are converted apartments, so each has its own kitchen, stove, dishes, cookware, and utensils. With pedestal sinks and subway tile, the bathrooms are stylish and comfortable. The owners are friendly and live on site. **Pros:** refrigerators stocked with healthy breakfast foods; complimentary use of laptops; location is ideal, in terms of restaurant choices. **Cons:** the owners don't always rent rooms for a single night, though they try to be flexible. ⊠*68 E. Cedar St., Gold Coast* ☎*312/664–9981* ⊕*www.innchicago.com* 🗏*7 rooms* ⚒ *In-room: kitchen, refrigerator, DVD, VCR, Wi-Fi. In-hotel: no elevator, laundry facilities, public Wi-Fi, no kids under 5.* 🗏*AE, D, DC, MC, V* ⊠ *CP.* ✛ *1:E1*

$$$ **Four Seasons Hotel.** At the ultrarefined Four Seasons, guest rooms begin
Fodor'sChoice on the 30th floor (the hotel sits atop the tony 900 North Michigan
★ Shops), so there's a distinct feeling of seclusion—and great views to boot. The rooms look elegant: 1940s French decor and spalike baths with honed Chinese marble. The property recently underwent a massive renovation. To get the most out of the experience, buy a package, like "Girls Just Wanna Have Fun," in which a handsome gent who makes custom martinis shows up at your room door. **Pros:** well-appointed and generously sized rooms; outstanding room service and housekeeping. **Cons:** clientele can be uptight, as can some staff. ⊠*120 E. Delaware Pl., Near North* ☎*312/280–8800 or 800/332–3442* 🖷*312/280–9184* ⊕*www.fourseasons.com* 🗏*176 rooms, 123 suites* ⚒*In-room: refrigerator, safe, Internet, Wi-Fi. In-hotel: 3 restaurants, room service, bar,*

6

pool, gym, spa, concierge, laundry service, public Wi-Fi, parking (fee), no-smoking rooms ⊟AE, D, DC, MC, V. ✤ 1:F2

$$ Gold Coast Guest House Bed & Breakfast. Set an enviable four blocks west of the Magnificent Mile, this 1873 brick town home is the ideal place to get a feel for Chicago's chi-chi side. It's located on a tree-lined street dappled with preserved town houses from which well-coiffed women wearing Prada drift in and out with their terriers in tow. Sunny but cramped, the inn's biggest draw is its backyard patio that spills into a private, statuary-splayed garden. **Pro:** Staff is warm, welcoming, and very knowledgeable about surrounding bars and restaurants. **Cons:** Spiral stairs can be troublesome for patrons with lots of luggage. *⊠113 W. Elm St., Near North ☎312/337–0361 ⊕www.bbchicago.com ➳4 rooms ⚿ In room: DVD, Wi-Fi. In hotel: no elevator, laundry facilities, parking (fee), no-smoking rooms, no children under age 10 ⊟AE, D, MC, V. ✤ 1:C1*

$$ Homewood Suites by Hilton. Suites here seem custom-designed for families, with sleeper sofas, separate bedrooms, and fully equipped kitchens. Free food isn't lacking; indulge in a complimentary breakfast buffet seven days a week, and an evening reception with drinks and a light meal Monday through Thursday. Another bonus? Work out for free at the Crunch Fitness facility in the basement. If that's not enough, the hotel is conveniently located so that guests are just a cab-ride away from Chicago's top attractions. **Pros:** great view of skyline; heated pool; free, hot breakfast. **Cons:** bathrooms feel cramped. *⊠40 E. Grand Ave., Near North ☎312/644–2222 or 800/225–5466 ⊜312/644–7777 ⊕www.homewoodsuiteschicago.com ➳233 suites ⚿In-room: kitchen, refrigerator, Wi-Fi. In-hotel: room service, pool, gym, laundry facilities, parking (fee), no-smoking rooms ⊟AE, D, DC, MC, V ⎮◎⎮BP. ✤ 1:E4*

$ Hotel Indigo. Even though this hotel caters to business travelers, there is something refreshingly non-corporate about its guest rooms and lobby dressed in plucky blues and greens and smattered with beachy Adirondack chairs. The airy guest rooms have wall-to-wall photo murals (for a real vacation feel, ask for one featuring colorful sea glass). Furthering the summer-in-Cape Cod feel are the rooms' white wooden lounge chairs and hardwood floors. It's located just on the fringe of downtown activity—expect a 10-minute cab ride to the Loop—but, on the flip side, you'll walk to Oak Street Beach, a few blocks southeast, in no time. **Pros:** chic hotel; great value; rooms are bright and uniquely designed. **Cons:** long walk to the heart of the shopping district; elevators can be a bit noisy for some guests. *⊠1244 N. Dearborn Pkwy., Near North ☎312/787–4980 ⊕www.goldcoastchicagohotel.com ➳165 rooms ⚿In room: Wi-Fi. In hotel: restaurant, room service, bar, gym, spa, laundry facilities, laundry service, concierge, public Wi-Fi, parking (fee), no-smoking rooms ⊟AE, D, DC, MC, V. ✤ 3:G4*

$$$ Hotel InterContinental Chicago. The Shriner greeting "Es Salamu Aleikum" ("Peace Be To God") etched on foyer columns and the marble lions throughout remind us of the building's past as the Medinah Men's

When Not To Go To Chicago

Here are some considerations if you're looking for headache-free travel.

■ Many leisure travelers are fazed by Chicago's frigid winters and the somewhat rough conditions they can cause (slippery roads, delayed traffic, the very thought of schlepping around in big boots). So, while museums and performances are at their max during winter, it might not be the opportune time to travel stress-free.

■ Also be aware of the more than 1,000 conventions and trade shows scheduled throughout the year. The National Restaurant Association show in May; the Manufacturing Technology show in September; the Radiological Society of America show in late November; and the National Housewares Manufacturing show in January are among the biggest. Hotel rooms may be hard to come by—and tables at popular restaurants even harder.

■ Contact the Chicago Convention and Tourism Bureau at 877/CHI-CAGO (877/244–2246) for information on conventions, trade shows, and other travel concerns before you book your trip.

■ Proximity to McCormick Place, where most of Chicago's huge trade shows hunker down, is often a conventioneer's top priority, so most wind up staying in the Loop or South Loop, where hotels are just a five-minute cab ride away from the mammoth venue. In these neighborhoods, accommodations tend to be older and somewhat less expensive—although there are certainly a few exceptions. Expect somewhat quiet nights in these parts; while the Loop boasts a revitalized theater district, come sundown there's a lot more revelry north of the Chicago River in the neighborhoods surrounding the Mag Mile. Vibrant Rush Street is the site of many bars, while River North has a high concentration of restaurants and nightclubs.

■ A meeting or convention in Rosemont or a tight flight schedule should be the only reasons to consider an airport hotel. Prices at these properties are a bit lower, but the O'Hare area is drab. Plus, trips from there to downtown may take an hour during rush hour, bad weather, or periods of heavy construction on the Kennedy Expressway.

6

Athletic Club, a private men's club. Lodging is found in two adjoining buildings. We love the contemporary air of the main building's guest rooms, featuring mahogany furniture and rich red-and-gold fabrics. The star attractions of the whole place are the junior Olympic swimming pool and a newly renovated fitness center. And be sure to check out Eno, a wine, cheese, and chocolate bar. **Pros:** you are sure to be wowed by the pool, the decor, and the view of the Magnificent Mile. **Cons:** concierge service is spotty; staff can be less than friendly. ✉*505 N. Michigan Ave., Near North* ☎*312/944–4100 or 800/628–2112* 🖷*312/944–1320* ⊕*www.chicago.intercontinental.com* ➪*720 rooms, 72 suites* ⚖*In-room: refrigerator, safe, Wi-Fi. In-hotel: 2 restaurants, room service, bar, pool, gym, spa, concierge, laundry service, public Wi-Fi, parking (fee), no-smoking rooms, some pets allowed* ▤*AE, D, DC, MC, V.* ✛ *1:E4*

Fodor'sChoice   **The James Hotel.** If you don't get the hint from the bustling bar scene
★   spilling into the lobby or the antique suitcases stacked as an art piece
$$$ near the elevator, the James further announces its hipster pedigree when
you enter your room. Preprogrammed alt-rock plays on the iPod-ready
stereo system perched on the bar beneath the ready-to-party bottles (not
minis) of vodka, whiskey, and rum. Some rooms feature not one but
two flat-screen TVs, not to mention Kiehl's bath products and design-
conscious furnishings like platform beds and full-length mirrors. The
relatively hands-off service is fitting enough—for a party hotel. **Pros:**
new and sleek with rich colors; not your typical, cookie-cutter chain.
Cons: tiny elevators; awkward room layout. ⊠ *55 E. Ontario St., at
Rush St., Near North* ☎ *312/337–1000* ⊕ *www.jameshotels.com/
chicago/* ⤳ *297 rooms* ⌂ *In-room: refrigerator, safe, Wi-Fi. In-hotel:
restaurant, room service, bar, gym, spa, concierge, laundry service,
public Wi-Fi, parking (fee), no-smoking rooms, some pets allowed*
⊟ *AE, D, DC, MC, V.* ⊹ *1:E4*

$ **Millennium Knickerbocker Hotel.** This 1927 hotel has had a number of
identities in its time—including a 1970s stint as the Playboy Hotel and
Towers under owner Hugh Hefner. Most recently, a 2008 renovation
updated guest rooms with a gold, beige, plum, and espresso color pal-
ette. This luxurious feel extends to the service: guests can hang their
kicks on the door at night and they'll be shined by morning. Your down-
time is well spent in the Lobby Bar, which offers 50 different kinds of
martinis. **Pros:** location can't be beat; generously sized rooms; friendly
front desk staff. **Cons:** service and quality of rooms are inconsistent.
⊠ *163 E. Walton Pl., Near North* ☎ *312/751–8100 or 866/866–8086*
⊟ *312/751–9205* ⊕ *www.millenniumhotels.com* ⤳ *279 rooms, 26
suites* ⌂ *In-room: Wi-Fi. In-hotel: restaurant, room service, bar, gym,
concierge, laundry service, public Wi-Fi, parking (fee), no-smoking
rooms* ⊟ *AE, D, DC, MC, V* ❖ *CP.* ⊹ *1:F2*

$$$$ **Omni Chicago Hotel.** The only all-suites hotel on Michigan Avenue has
another thing going for it: every room has a plasma TV. Large suites
with French doors separate the parlor from the bedroom, giving it a
residential atmosphere. The in-house 676 Restaurant & Bar, features
northern Italian and American cuisine with views overlooking Michi-
gan Avenue. Good choice for extended stays or those traveling with
kids—young travelers receive a backpack filled with games and books
to keep, and a goodie bag upon check-in. **Pros:** modern, comfortable
rooms with spacious sitting area, desk, and bar. **Con:** hotel can be too
noisy for some. ⊠ *676 N. Michigan Ave., Near North* ☎ *312/944–
6664 or 800/843–6664* ⊟ *312/266–3015* ⊕ *www.omnichicago.com*
⤳ *347 suites* ⌂ *In-room: safe, DVD, Internet, Wi-Fi. In-hotel: restau-
rant, room service, bar, pool, gym, concierge, laundry service, parking
(fee), no-smoking rooms, some pets allowed* ⊟ *AE, D, DC, MC, V.*
⊹ *1:E3*

$$$$ **Park Hyatt Chicago.** The 67-story Park Hyatt, which dominates the sky-
Fodor'sChoice   line high above the old Water Tower, outdoes its grand-hotel neighbors
★   by going all-out with extras. Splash out on one of their enormous suites
and you'll discover Art of Shaving amenities in the bathrooms, TVs

LODGING ALTERNATIVES

APARTMENT RENTALS

Furnished rentals can save you money, especially if you're traveling with a group. Home-exchange directories sometimes list rentals as well as exchanges.

Rental apartments are available in the Loop for temporary business lodging.

Hideaways International ✉ 767 Islington St., Portsmouth, NH 03801 ☎603/430–4433 or 800/843–4433 🖷 603/430–4444 ⊕www.hideaways.com; annual membership $145.

BED-AND-BREAKFASTS

Chicago Bed & Breakfast Association ✉ Box 14088, 6061 ☎ 773/394–2000 or 800/375–7084 🖷773/394–2002 ⊕www.chicago-bed-breakfast.com

HOME EXCHANGES

HomeLink International ✉ Box 47747, Tampa, FL 33647 ☎ 813/975–9825 or 800/638–3841 🖷 813/910–8144 ⊕www.homelink. org; $110 yearly for a listing, online access, and catalog; $70 without catalog. **Intervac U.S.** ✉ 30 Corte San Fernando Tiburon, CA 94920 ☎ 800/756–4663 🖷415/435–7440 ⊕www.intervacus.com; $125 yearly

for a listing, online access, and a catalog; $65 without catalog.

HOSTELS

No matter what your age, you can save on lodging costs by staying at hostels. In some 4,500 locations in more than 70 countries around the world, **Hostelling International (HI)**, the umbrella group for a number of national youth-hostel associations, offers single-sex, dorm-style beds and, at many hostels, rooms for couples and family accommodations. Membership in any HI national hostel association, open to travelers of all ages, allows you to stay in HI-affiliated hostels at member rates; one-year membership is about $28 for adults (C$35 for a two-year minimum membership in Canada, ✉14 in the United Kingdom, A$52 in Australia, and NZ$40 in New Zealand); hostels charge about $10–$30 per night. Members have priority if the hostel is full; they're also eligible for discounts around the world, even on rail and bus travel in some countries.

ORGANIZATIONS

Hostelling International—USA, ✉ 8401 Colesville Rd., Suite 600, Silver Spring, MD 20910 ☎301/495–1240 🖷301/495–6697 ⊕www.hiusa.org.

over the bathtubs, and motion-sensor lights in the closets. Not much here has been overlooked. For a price there are plenty more extravagances to be had, including a butler-drawn candlelit bath. The beautifully designed public spaces feature a world-class collection of sculpture and painting, including works by Gerhardt Richter and Isamu Noguchi. The sweeping views from the pool and spa look out to the horizon over Lake Michigan. **Pros:** marble bath and soaking tub; great view of the Water Tower. **Con:** hotel lobby can be noisy. ✉*800 N. Michigan Ave., Near North* ☎*312/335–1234 or 800/778–7477* 🖷*312/239–4000* ⊕*www.parkchicago.hyatt.com* ➳*198 rooms, 13 suites* ⅙*In-room: safe, refrigerator, DVD, Internet, Wi-Fi. In-hotel: restaurant,* *room service, bar, pool, gym, spa, concierge, laundry service, parking (fee), no-smoking rooms* ▭AE, D, DC, MC, V. ✤ 1:E3

$$$$ **Peninsula Chicago.** On weekend nights the Peninsula's soaring lobby
Fodor's Choice lounge becomes a chocolate fantasia, centered on an overflowing choc-
★ olate buffet. The hotel, committed to keeping its guests well fed and well rested, is also home to one of the city's most creative restaurants (Avenues), along with a lavish and popular afternoon tea. One of only three branches in the United States of the venerable Hong Kong–based Peninsula chain, its comfortable rooms feature plush pillow-top beds, Wi-Fi, and state-of-the-art bedside consoles that control both the TV and the "do not disturb" light. The rooftop lap pool is enclosed in a Zen aerie offering stunning views over the city. Make time to enjoy the property's award-winning spa. **Pros:** top-notch bath products; separate shower and bath. **Cons:** in-house dining options are not the best for families with children. ⊠*108 E. Superior St., Near North* ☎*312/337–2888 or 866/288–8889* ₰*312/751–2888* ⊕*www.chicago.peninsula. com* ↝*339 rooms, 83 suites* ☖*In-room: refrigerator, safe, Internet, Wi-Fi. In-hotel: 4 restaurants, room service, bar, pool, gym, spa, concierge, laundry service, parking (fee), no-smoking rooms, some pets allowed* ▭AE, D, DC, MC, V. ✤ 1:E3

$$ **Raffaello Hotel.** It's hard to tell what kind of crowd this hotel will attract, given its complete renovation (it was formerly the Raphael Hotel)—but the steps-from-Michigan Avenue location is working in its favor. Don't dither in the lobby; it's small and—with just a small check-in desk, a few chairs, and little else—there's not much excitement there. Guest rooms are spacious and comfortable, however. Dressed in varying shades of a neutral hay color, they have modern-looking bathrooms with rain showers, and excellent city views (ask for a room facing north for a close-up look at the John Hancock Building). **Pros:** rooms are comfortable and elegant. **Cons:** overly stringent cancellation policy (cancellations must be received at least 72 hours prior to arrival). ⊠*201 E. Delaware Pl., Near North* ☎*888/560–4977* ⊕*chicagoraffaello.com* ↝*90 rooms, 75 suites* ☖*In-room: kitchen, refrigerator, DVD, Wi-Fi. In-hotel: restaurant, room service, gym, laundry service, concierge, public Wi-Fi, airport shuttle, parking (fee), no-smoking rooms* ▭AE, D, MC, V. ✤ 1:F2

$$$$ **Ritz-Carlton Chicago.** Perched over Water Tower Place, Michigan Ave-
Fodor's Choice nue's best-known shopping mall, the Ritz-Carlton specializes in show-
★ ering guests with attention. Amenities aren't wanting: rooms are spacious, with walk-in closets and separate dressing areas. A fitness center, indoor pool, and spa services are available to guests looking for respite from their busy days. The hotel goes out of its way to cater to families with children, providing complimentary use of items such as cribs, children's DVDs, books, and toys, to name a few. The two-story, flower-filled greenhouse lobby serves afternoon tea, and the Café's chef, Mark Payne, has earned a top-notch reputation. **Pros:** guests feel pampered; great stay for families with small children. **Cons:** lobby feels worn and dated. ⊠*160 E. Pearson St., Near North* ☎*312/266–1000, 800/621–6906 outside Illinois* ₰*312/266–1194* ⊕*www.fourseasons.*

com/chicago ⇆*435 rooms, 91 suites* ⟁*In-room: refrigerator, safe, DVD (some), Wi-Fi. In-hotel: 2 restaurants, room service, bar, pool, gym, spa, concierge, laundry service, public Internet, public Wi-Fi, parking (fee), no-smoking rooms, some pets allowed* ⊟*AE, D, DC, MC, V.* ✛ *1:E2*

$$$$ **Sofitel Chicago Water Tower.** A wonder of modern architecture, this French-owned gem is a prism-shaped structure that juts over the street and widens as it rises. Design sensibility shines in guest rooms, too, with beechwood furnishings, Barcelona chairs, and marble bathrooms bedecked with bamboos (think feng shui). The sophisticated Cafe des Architectes is notable for its 30-minute executive lunch, while Le Bar is a homey den of sorts. **Pros:** modern decor; great ambience. **Cons:** the place is so sleek, some guests have a hard time finding the light switches. ✉*20 E. Chestnut St., Near North* ☎*312/324–4000 or 877/813–7700* 🖷*312/324–4026* ⊕*www.sofitel.com* ⇆*382 rooms, 33 suites* ⟁*In-room: safe, Internet, Wi-Fi. In-hotel: restaurant, room service, bars, gym, concierge, laundry service, parking (fee), no-smoking rooms, some pets allowed* ⊟*AE, D, DC, MC, V.* ✛ *1:D2*

FodorśChoice ★

$$$ **Sutton Place Hotel.** Talk about art in unexpected places: the largest single collection of original Robert Mapplethorpe floral photographs graces the walls in rooms and common spaces at this hotel. Rooms—decorated in calming sage and periwinkle tones—have sound-resistant walls, down duvets, and three phones. Splurge for a loft suite, with terraces overlooking bustling Rush Street. Rande Gerber (Cindy Crawford's husband) owns the Mexx Kitchen at the Whiskey, serving seasonal selections for breakfast, a modern Mexican lunch, and dinner. **Pros:** great location; soothing color scheme. **Cons:** some guests have complained of low water pressure and haphazard housekeeping. ✉*21 E. Bellevue Pl., Near North* ☎*312/266–2100 or 800/606–8188* 🖷*312/266–2141* ⊕*www.suttonplace.com* ⇆*206 rooms, 40 suites* ⟁*In-room: safe (some), Wi-Fi. In-hotel: restaurant, room service, bar, gym, concierge, laundry service, public Internet, parking (fee), no-smoking rooms, some pets allowed* ⊟*AE, D, DC, MC, V.* ✛ *1:D1*

6

$$$$ **Talbott.** The Talbott has a large European following, thanks to its intimacy and multilingual staff. In 2006 guest rooms were renovated with new carpets, drapes, and custom furniture, making the moderate-size lodgings even more appealing. Coffee and tea are served fireside in the lobby on winter nights—a lovely touch. Another bonus? Free Wi-Fi is available throughout the hotel, and guests get free admission to the nearby gym. **Pros:** hotel has an updated look; staff goes out of their way to please. **Cons:** rooms can be too dark and too noisy for some. ✉*20 E. Delaware Pl., Near North* ☎*312/944–4970 or 800/825–2688* 🖷*312/944–7241* ⊕*www. talbotthotel.com* ⇆*120 rooms, 29*

WORD OF MOUTH

"The Talbott is in a nice location just behind Michigan Avenue. I have had family stay there for special occasions when my own house couldn't hold all of them and everyone was impressed at the value for the money."

—laurie_ann

suites In-room: safe, Wi-Fi. In-hotel: restaurant, room service, bar, concierge, laundry service, parking (fee), no-smoking rooms, no pets allowed =AE, D, DC, MC, V. ✛ 1:D2

$$ **Tremont.** Just off North Michigan Avenue, this hotel's restaurant, Mike Ditka's, gets infinitely more attention than the rooms do. Standard guest rooms—with a cream-color theme—are on the small side, but offer all the essential amenities. Need more space? Book one of the suites, which are equipped with kitchens. Complimentary use of the fitness center is a plus for guests looking to keep up with their workout regimen even if they're on vacation. **Pros:** great location; good value. **Cons:** rooms need to be updated and cleaned; valet parking is pricey ⊠100 E. Chestnut St., Near North ☎312/751–1900 or 800/621–8133 ₪312/751–8691 ⊕www.tremontchicago.com ◔118 rooms, 12 suites In-room: refrigerators (some), safe, Wi-Fi (some). In-hotel: restaurant, bar, concierge, laundry service, public Internet, parking (fee), no-smoking rooms =AE, D, DC, MC, V. ✛ 1:E2

$$ **W Chicago Lakeshore.** Once a dreary Days Inn, this place has undergone
Fodor's Choice a complete renovation that transformed it into a sleek, high-energy
★ hotel—and the only one in Chicago directly overlooking Lake Michigan. The lobby is part lounge, part club scene, with velvety couches and DJs on weekends. The hotel's "whatever, whenever" desk—its version of a concierge service—is on call 24 hours a day. Pamper yourself at the Bliss Chicago Spa, located on the eighth floor, where hotel guests can get priority booking for their spa treatments. For those who have a hard time leaving their pets at home, the W Chicago Lakeshore allows guests to bring their furry friends. **Pros:** cool, hip vibe; guest rooms feel like swank lounges. **Cons:** service not commensurate with the price. ⊠644 N. Lake Shore Dr., Near North ☎312/943–9200 or 888/627–9034 ₪312/255–4411 ⊕www.whotels.com ◔525 rooms, 27 suites In-room: safe, DVD, Internet, Wi-Fi. In-hotel: restaurant, room service, bar, pool, gym, spa, concierge, laundry service, public Wi-Fi, airport shuttle, parking (fee), no-smoking rooms, some pets allowed =AE, D, DC, MC, V. ✛ 1:G4

$$$$ **Westin Michigan Avenue.** The lobby of the Westin reminds us of an airport hangar—long, narrow, and full of folks tapping away on laptops. Location-wise, the hotel scores big, as major malls and flagship shops are within steps of the hotel's front door. Rooms are furnished with specially designed Simmons Heavenly Beds with quilted mattresses—that guests have raved about and even purchased—as well as foam, feather, and rolled pillows. The lobby restaurant, the Grill on the Alley, is a steak house with a clubby atmosphere. **Pros:** guests love the "heavenly" beds, the proximity to area attractions, and the ever-present cabs. **Cons:** gym is a bit cramped; rooms are a bit small; elevators too slow. ⊠909 N. Michigan Ave., Near North ☎312/943–7200 or 800/937–8461 ₪312/397–5580 ⊕www.westin.com/michiganave ◔728 rooms, 23 suites In-room: safe, Internet, Wi-Fi. In-hotel: restaurant, room service, bar, gym, concierge, laundry service, public Wi-Fi, parking (fee), some pets allowed =AE, D, DC, MC, V. ✛ 1:E2

$$ Whitehall Hotel. There's a wood-land-lodge feel in this hotel's lobby, where oil paintings of hunting dogs and horses hang in gilt frames. The Old World–style rooms, many with four-poster beds, include modern luxuries such as marble bathrooms and broadband. Fornetto Mei is a Pan-Italian dining concept—with standout pizza from a wood-burning oven—that deserves more attention than it gets. The White-hall hotel also features key ameni-

ties such as a 24-hour business center and fitness facilities. Animal lovers take notice: the hotel is pet-friendly. **Pros:** hotel has a 1920s-era charm and an old-school style. **Cons:** rooms could use an update: wallpaper is faded and peeling in spots. ⊠*105 E. Delaware Pl., Near North* ☎*312/944–6300 or 800/948–4255* 🖷*312/944–8552* ⊕*www.thewhitehallhotel.com* ⬎*222 rooms, 8 suites* ⟳*In-room: safe, Internet. In-hotel: restaurant, room service, bar, gym, concierge, laundry service, public Wi-Fi, parking (fee), no-smoking rooms* ▤*AE, D, DC, MC, V* ✛ *1:E2.*

RIVER NORTH

Besides the concentration of independently owned galleries, commerce around these parts tends to be of a national-chain nature (note the Hard Rock Cafe and Red Lobster). The same can be said of the hotels. But while boutique-lodging charm is harder to find, good prices are not; you'll find plenty of competitive rates from familiar names.

$$ Amalfi Hotel Chicago. With popular magazines on the desks and well-worn books on the shelves, this well-situated hot spot is aiming for a residential feel. Check out the complimentary reception every night from 5:30 to 7 PM for free drinks, Italian beer, and antipasti, among other treats. And unlike other hotels that serve their continental breakfast in the lobby, this one offers its breakfast on every floor. The clientele is eclectic and laid-back; the reception brings everyone together. Surrounded by both upscale restaurants and famous chains—including Harry Caray's—there's no shortage of nightlife. **Pro:** Aveda products available. **Con:** some guests note that the bedding looks and feels worn. ⊠*20 W. Kinzie St., River North* ☎*312/395–9000* ⊕*amalfihotelchicago.com* ⬎*210 rooms, 5 suites* ⟳*In-room: safe, refrigerator, DVD, Wi-Fi. In-hotel: room service, bar, gym, laundry service, concierge, public Internet, public Wi-Fi, parking (fee), some pets allowed* ▤*AE, D, DC, MC, V.* ✛ *1:D5*

$ Best Western River North. Partially housed in a turn-of-the-last-century freezer building, this hotel retains a loft-like air. The somewhat forgettable lobby decor is offset by large and reasonably priced guest rooms featuring black-and-white tiled bathrooms. Parking is free, a cost-saving rarity downtown. Families convene at the on-site Pizzeria Ora for Chicago-style deep-dish pies. **Pros:** excellent service; great location; free parking—an extremely rare find in Chicago. **Cons:** creaking floors have irked some guests, especially around bedtime; rooms could use a fresher look. ⊠ *125 W. Ohio St., River North* 🕾 *312/467–0800 or 800/727–0800* 🖷 *312/467–1665* ⊕ *www.rivernorthhotel.com* 🖘 *125 rooms, 25 suites* & *In-room: safe, refrigerator (some), Wi-Fi. In-hotel: restaurant, room service, bar, pool, gym, parking (no fee), no-smoking rooms* ⊟ *AE, D, DC, MC, V.* ✛ *1:D4*

$$$ Courtyard by Marriott/Magnificent Mile. Visitors will love the location, the modern, bustling lobby, and the reasonably priced rooms. Stylish with black granite and track lighting, the hotel is modern but not cold or pretentious. The rooms are modest—with muted beige walls and white linens—but efficient. Expect lots of tourists. The double queen room sleeps five with a sofa bed, so it's great for families. Parents take notice: there is no lifeguard at the indoor pool. The restaurant, Viand, offers fine American cuisine in a dark but lively atmosphere with an attractive bar. **Pro:** great location, right in the heart of the shopping district. **Cons:** pool is on the small side; the sink is located outside the bathroom. ⊠ *165 E. Ontario, River North* 🕾 *312/573–0800* ⊕ *www.courtyardchicago.com* 🖘 *283 rooms, 23 suites* & *In-room: refrigerator (some), Internet, Wi-Fi. In-hotel: restaurant, room service, bar, pool, gym, laundry facilities, laundry service, concierge, public Internet, public Wi-Fi, parking (fee), some pets allowed* ⊟ *AE, D, DC, MC, V.* ✛ *1:F4*

$$$ Embassy Suites Downtown. The suites are arranged around an 11-story, plant-filled atrium lobby, where bubbling fountains keep noise levels relatively high. Bright rooms use space efficiently, with sensible separate living rooms with a pullout sofa, four-person dining table, and extra television. A 24-hour business center, complimentary full breakfast each morning, and cocktails each evening are especially appealing to business travelers. The indoor pool and fitness center are a plus, as is the renowned onsite restaurant, Osteria Via Stato. **Pros:** great cocktail hour; hotel is just two blocks from Navy Pier. **Cons:** paid Internet ($9.95 a day or $44.95 for 5 days). ⊠ *600 N. State St., River North* 🕾 *312/943–3800 or 800/362–2779* 🖷 *312/943–7629* ⊕ *www.embassysuiteschicago.com* 🖘 *367 suites* & *In-room: refrigerator, Wi-Fi. In-hotel: restaurant, room service, bar, pool, gym, concierge, laundry facilities, laundry service, parking (fee), no-smoking rooms* ⊟ *AE, D, DC, MC, V* ⌶◯⏐*BP.* ✛ *1:D4*

$ Hotel Cass, Holiday Inn Express. The Hotel Cass is a true boutique hotel and bears no resemblance to the chain. The crisp, white lobby is sparse and elegant, and the dramatic red hallway is offset with a touch of humor; it's lined with several austere portraits of chickens. The rooms are simple, bright, and cheerful with light-color walls and green headboards that nearly reach the ceiling. The subway-style tile in the bathroom harks back to the 1920s. The rooms are modern and warm, and the in-room artwork includes photos of 1950s fashion icons. **Pros:** stellar location; family-friendly; close to several notable art galleries.

Con: some guest rooms and bathrooms can be on the small-side. ✉ *640 N. Wabash Ave., River North* ☎*312/265–3370* ⊕*www.casshotel.com* ⇦*172 rooms, 3, suites* ⎃*In-room: safe, Internet, Wi-Fi. In-hotel: room service, laundry service, public Internet, public Wi-Fi, airport shuttle, parking (fee)* ▤*AE, D, DC, MC, V.* ✛ *3:H6*

$$ \text{Hotel Sax Chicago.}$$

$$ **Hotel Sax Chicago.** Visitors to Chicago would be hard-pressed to find a
Fodor'sChoice more chic or tech-savvy place than the Hotel Sax. Stark white walls,
★ adorned with appropriately risqué artwork, make the scented lobby feel ultra swank. In the rooms, modern furniture is chunky and ornate, and mismatched colors and patterns somehow look fabulous together. A high-tech game room leaves guests weak in the knees. Eager to please staff will download your favorite record if they don't have it already, then pipe it in while you play Guitar Hero. Another plus: free champagne in the lobby 5–8 pm on Friday and Saturday nights. **Pros:** no need to leave the hotel for nightlife, thanks to the Crimson lounge; the House of Blues is right next door. **Cons:** scented lobby is a bit much for some; rooms and hallways can be too dim. ✉ *333 N. Dearborn St., River North* ☎*312/245–0333* ⊕*www.hotelsaxchicago.com* ⇦*334 rooms, 19 suites* ⎃*In-room: safe, Internet, Wi-Fi. In-hotel: 6 restaurants, room service, 6 bars, gym, laundry service, concierge, public Internet, public Wi-Fi, parking (fee), some pets allowed* ▤*AE, D, DC, MC, V.* ✛ *1:D5*

$$$ **Trump International Hotel & Tower.** With some of the best views in Chi-
Fodor'sChoice cago, the Trump International Hotel & Tower has attracted a crowd of
★ power brokers, business travelers, and women in fur coats. The elegant guest rooms have muted gray walls, cream-colored couches, and chocolate-brown furniture; each room has its own kitchen with granite counter tops and cupboards stocked with top-of-the-line cookware, as well as a TV inside the bathroom mirror. Guests need not venture any further than Sixteen to enjoy fine dining. The full-service spa is immense. **Pros:** impeccable service; lavish amenities **Cons:** may be too decadent for some; $25 bottled water (for sale) in each room. ✉ *401 N. Wabash Ave., North Loop* ☎*312/588–8000* ⊕*www.trumpchicagohotel.com* ⇦*218 rooms, 121 suites* ⎃*In-room: safe, kitchen, refrigerator, DVD, Internet, Wi-Fi. In-hotel: restaurant, room service, 2 bars, pool, gym, spa, laundry service, concierge, public Internet, public Wi-Fi, parking (fee), some pets allowed* ▤*AE, D, DC, MC, V* ☉❘ *CP.* ✛ *3:H6*

$$$ **Westin Chicago River North.** Gym rats don't need to hoof it to the on-site fitness center, thanks to four Westin Workout Guest Rooms that come equipped with either a bicycle or a treadmill. Standard rooms—some with views of the Chicago River—have all the basics, including high-speed Internet. Nab a Deluxe Room for more square footage. This elegant hotel is centrally located near the premier shopping destination, Michigan Avenue, as well as top Chicago attractions, which makes it an ideal stay for first-time visitors. **Pros:** polite staff; the "heavenly bed" is nothing less than heavenly. **Cons:** fee for use of the fitness center; no pool. ✉ *320 N. Dearborn St., River North* ☎*312/744–1900 or 887/866–9216* ▤*312/527–2650* ⊕*www.westinchicago.com* ⇦*407 rooms, 17 suites* ⎃*In-room: Internet, Wi-Fi. In-hotel: 2 restaurants,* *room service, bar, gym, spa, concierge, laundry service, parking (fee), some pets allowed ▭AE, D, DC, MC, V. ✛ 1:D5*

SOUTH LOOP

Rapid gentrification, most apparent in the new restaurants popping up along South Michigan Avenue, has made this area increasingly popular. A hotel boom has not occurred here yet, so lodging choices are limited to a few old and reliable standards. Many hotels offer package deals with the nearby Museum Campus.

$$$ **The Blackstone.** A six-year renovation has restored this once faded build-
Fodor'sChoice ing to its original splendor. The lobby, with its gold-trimmed walls
★ and ultramodern flower arrangements, is an unusual mix of old and new. The guest rooms are simple and elegant with striking bold colors; a stunning combination of gold, red, black and white, and the ballroom–with its ornate carvings–is otherworldly. The service is exceptional; visitors are warmly greeted within seconds. Ask about the hotel's storied past; both presidents and mob bosses have stayed here. **Pro:** new owners spared no expense in this beautifully redone space. **Cons:** decor can be a bit too ornate. ✉636 S. Michigan Ave., South Loop ☎312/447–0955 ⊕www.marriott.com/hotels/travel/chirh-the-blackstone-a-renaissance-hotel ↩320 rooms, 12 suites ⚭In-room: safe, refrigerator, Internet, Wi-Fi. In-hotel: restaurant, room service, 2 bars, gym, laundry service, concierge, executive floor, public Internet, public Wi-Fi, parking (fee), some pets allowed ▭AE, D, DC, MC, V ○⦿ EP. ✛ 4:G3

$ **Essex Inn.** Don't judge this hotel on appearance alone: the nondescript,
☾ plain-brick tower containing small, boxlike guest rooms is actually
Fodor'sChoice one of the city's most accessible and family-friendly. Along with being
★ a five-minute walk from the Museum Campus, it offers package deals with popular attractions such as the Shedd Aquarium and Sears Tower. That said, you might not want to leave the hotel; its huge rooftop swimming pool is open year-round (note to anxious parents: a lifeguard is always on duty) and is surrounded by sliding-glass doors that open to views of Grant Park and Lake Michigan. **Pros:** good value; pool complete with a lifeguard. **Cons:** rooms can be drafty during winter months; staff can be slow to address complaints. ✉800 S. Michigan Ave., South Loop ☎312/939/2800 or 800/621–6909 ⊕essexinn.com ↩254 rooms ⚭In room: refrigerator (some), Wi-Fi. In hotel: restaurant, room service, pool, gym, laundry service, public Internet, parking (fee), no-smoking rooms ▭AE, D, DC, MC, V. ✛ 4:G3

$$$ **Hilton Chicago.** On a busy day the lobby of this Hilton might be mistaken for a terminal at O'Hare Airport; it's a bustling convention hotel, but one that retains its distinguished 1920s heritage in a Renaissance-inspired entrance hall and gold-and-gilt grand ballroom. We're fans of its gym, which, at 28,000 square feet, includes an indoor track and swimming pool. Tip for families: Ask for a room with two double beds and two baths (if you nab one with a view of Lake Michigan and the Museum Campus, all the better). **Pros:** spacious rooms, proximity to the museum district; well-appointed public spaces. **Cons:** a hike to the main shopping area on the Magnificent Mile; a fee for use of the fitness area. ✉*720 S. Michigan Ave., South Loop* ☎*312/922–4400 or 800/445–8667* 🖨*312/922–5240* ⊕*www.hiltonchicagosales.com* 🛏*1,544 rooms, 67 suites* ♿*In-room: Wi-Fi. In-hotel: 3 restaurants, room service, bar, pool, gym, concierge, laundry service, parking (fee), no-smoking rooms, some pets allowed* ▤*AE, D, DC, MC, V.* ✛ 3:G3

$$$ **Holiday Inn & Suites Downtown Chicago.** Thanks to its proximity to the financial district, this hotel welcomes hordes of business travelers. But leisure seekers have an added incentive to visit in the summer months: the rooftop pool. Guests appreciate the accessibility of this hotel: not only is it located near Chicago's main attractions, transportation is provided to both the Midway Airport and the O'Hare International Airport directly from the hotel (with a fee). The on-site Aurelio's, part of a popular pizza chain, serves breakfast, lunch, and dinner. **Pros:** staff goes out of their way to be helpful; convenient on-site washing machines and dryers. **Cons:** the lobby can get quite crowded; bathrooms are on the small side. ✉*506 W. Harrison St., South Loop* ☎*312/957–9100* 🖨*312/957–0474* ⊕*www.hidowntown.com* 🛏*145 rooms, 27 suites* ♿*In-room: refrigerator (some), Wi-Fi. In-hotel: restaurant, room service, bar, pool, gym, laundry facilities, laundry service, parking (fee), no-smoking rooms* ▤*AE, D, DC, MC, V.* ✛ 4:E3

WESTERN SUBURBS

$$$ **Lynfred Winery Bed & Breakfast.** Something of an anomaly amid the strip malls and big restaurant chains in nearby Schaumburg, located 45 minutes northwest of downtown Chicago, this B&B feels like a quaint country inn—one with surprising gourmet leanings. Each of its four generously sized suites has a heated bathroom floor and is decorated in the style of a different country (the French Suite has a gilded mirror and Louis IV–style chairs). The adjoining wine cellar and tasting room is where you'll try inexpensive yet tasty cabernets, aged in barrels on-site. All stays include a cellar tour and a full breakfast cooked by a Culinary Institute of America grad. **Pros:** affordable wine tastings; well-appointed rooms. **Cons:** not every wine is a hit; some guests feel that the rooms are overpriced. ✉*15 S. Roselle Rd., Western Suburbs* ☎*630/529–9463* ⊕*lynfredwinery.com* 🛏*4 rooms* ♿*In room: refrigerator, DVD, Wi-Fi. In hotel: room service, laundry facilities, laundry service, parking (no fee), no guests under 21, no-smoking rooms* ▤*AE, D, MC, V.* ✛ 4:A1

Shopping

WORD OF MOUTH

"We took our granddaughter to the American Girl store and she loved it! She wanted to have tea there (it is so cute, they have little highchairs at the tables for their dolls) but you have to have reservations and we did not."

—cd

SHOPPING PLANNER

Itineraries for the Obsessed

If art is your thing, head to River North and the West Loop, which are quick cab rides from each other and loaded with fabulous galleries.

If you're looking to head home with funky fashions, go to Bucktown and Wicker Park. Must-hits include **p. 45** (*1643 N. Damen Ave., 773/862–4523*) for women's styles; **G Boutique** for va-va-va-voom lingerie (*2131 N. Damen Ave., 773/235–1234*); and **shebang** (*1616 N. Damen Ave., 773/486–3800*) for pretty accessories.

Need to buy some things for the little ones in your life? Hit Lincoln Park's **Stinky Pants** (*844 W. Armitage Ave., 773/281–4002*) and **LMNOP** (*2574 N. Lincoln Ave., 773/975–4055*). Find treats for tiny feet at **Piggy Toes** (*2205 N. Halsted St., 773/281–5583*). For stuff for the home, best bets are **Bellini** (*2100 N. Southport Ave., 773/880–5840*) and the **Land of Nod** (*900 W. North Ave., 312/475–9903*), for stylish bedding, bath items, books, and toys.

Cold Weather Considerations

Visiting during winter or on one of Chicago's chilly days? Don't let the cold keep you from scoring some serious stash. Take a cue from weather-savvy local shoppers, who hit indoor urban malls like Water Tower Place and 900 North Michigan on the Mag Mile when the winds whip up.

If you're willing to brave the elements, dress wisely. The weather can change on a dime here, so wear layers that are easy to peel off and carry—something that'll make dressing-room acrobatics go quicker, too. We're talking warm undershirt, long-sleeved shirt, sweater or warm jacket, and windbreaker—substitute heavy winter coat for that last one if you're visiting in the dead of winter, along with the necessary accoutrements (scarf, hat, gloves). Happily, you'll find plenty of places along the way for a hot cocoa, coffee, or tea if the cold is getting the best of you.

Getting Around

Second only in size to that of New York City, the public transportation system in Chicago serves roughly 1.5 million riders a day and can get you to the city's main shopping drags with relative ease. With so many riders, it can get pretty crowded during weekday rush hours. Improvement and repair projects can cause delays on many train lines, so plan accordingly.

■ For both the bus and train (called the El, for the elevated tracks that run around the Loop) fares are $2 when using cash, $1.75 with a transit card.

■ If you plan on riding frequently, buy a transit card at any El station vending machine or at many grocery and drug stores. Bus and train rides cost $1.75 with a transit card, and transfers on both the bus and El cost an additional 25 cents; no transfers are given when paying with cash.

■ Some of the neighborhoods we mention here are easy to walk between, like the Mag Mile and River North, and parts of Lincoln Park and Lakeview, but it's best to consult a map to determine whether the distances you're planning to travel warrant wheels.

Chicago Hours

Keep these timing tips in mind as you plan out your day:

■ Most stores keep traditional retail hours, opening around 10 AM and closing at 6 or 7 PM, though different neighborhood styles and street traffic can dictate otherwise. In Bucktown and Wicker Park, for example, many shops don't open until 11 AM or noon, and may stay open later in the evening.

■ Count on mall stores to keep later hours, usually until 7 or 8 PM. Most are open (with shorter hours than other days) on Sunday.

■ If there's a particular boutique you want to visit, call ahead. Simply flip through this chapter and you'll find all the contact information you'll need.

Pamper Your Pet

Chicago is a pet-lover's city, and it's filled with fun places to shop for them. Check out the **Down Town Dog** (Macy's, 111 N. State St., 312/782–4575), a delightful boutique within Macy's that's stocked with everything for the urban pooch (and kitty).

In Bucktown, **Red Dog House** (2031 N. Damen Ave., 773/227–7341) keeps pace with the fashionable 'hood by selling spa products (such as paw balm), high-end treats (biscotti for pups), and sculptural bowls and beds. If your dog comes along for the trip, there are some retail stores that let well-behaved pups on leashes do a little browsing.

Our favorite: **Neiman Marcus** (737 N. Michigan Ave., 312/642–5900), where pedigree types can peruse Burberry carriers and other fancy items.

Word of Mouth

"I would not miss taking a walk or a bike ride along the lakefront path (my favorite is to do this on Sunday morning, maybe before breakfast?). You might also enjoy the CAF architectural river cruise, which is relaxing and informative (and Chicago architecture is, needless to see, fabulous)."

—dmlove

"Highly, highly recommend the Segway tour. My husband never wants to turn his in at the end. The route is incredibly scenic and riding the Segways is great fun."

—djkbooks

The other neighborhoods which I would recommend considering are Wicker Park/Bucktown and Lincoln Square. They each have interesting shopping options and a number of good places to eat. In addition, Lincoln Square has the Old Town School of Folk Music, which has a fine family-oriented schedule but isn't dumbed down entertainment for adults.

—exiledprincess

Updated by
Heidi Moore

A POTENT CONCENTRATION OF FAMOUS retailers around Michigan Avenue and neighborhoods bursting with one-of-a-kind shops combine to make Chicago a shopper's city. Michigan Avenue's world-class Magnificent Mile lures thousands of avid shoppers every week. How often can you find Neiman Marcus, Macy's, Nordstrom, Saks Fifth Avenue, Lord & Taylor, and Barneys New York within walking distance of one another? Neighborhood shopping areas, like fun-but-sophisticated Lincoln Park or the hipster haven of Bucktown/Wicker Park, have singular stores for specialty interests, whether Prairie-style furniture, cowboy boots, or outsider art. Those averse to paying retail won't have to venture far to unearth bargains on everything from fine jewelry to business attire. When it comes to shopping, this is one city that has it all.

Be forewarned that a gulp-inducing 10.25% sales tax is added to all purchases in the city except groceries and prescription drugs. Neighborhood shops on the North Side, especially those in Bucktown and Wicker Park, tend to open late—around 11 or noon. Most stores, particularly those on North Michigan Avenue and the North Side, are open on Sunday, although this varies by type of business; where applicable, more information is provided at the beginning of each area or category.

THE LOOP & SOUTH LOOP

This area—named for the elevated train track that encircles it—is the heart of Chicago's business and financial district. Two department stores that long defined shopping here, Marshall Field's and Carson Pirie Scott, departed from **State Street** in early 2007, a double hit for the stretch that has been striving to regain the stature it had when it was immortalized as "State Street, that great street." Carson's is empty for the time being, while Macy's has taken over the Marshall Field's building. State Street is more enticing for shoppers than it was in the 1980s and early 1990s, particularly for those interested in discount department stores, but it's still a far cry from the shopping mecca that is the Mag Mile. The blocks surrounding the intersection of Wabash Avenue and Madison Street are designated as Jewelers Row; five high-rises cater to the wholesale trade, but many showrooms sell to the public at prices 25% to 50% below retail. Despite the preponderance of working moms who spend their weekday lunch hours shopping in the area, the Loop lacks a strong presence of retail for kids, and some of the discount chains are even pulling their children's lines from Loop outposts. Not all Loop stores maintain street-level visibility: several gems are tucked away on upper floors of office buildings.

Department stores and major chains are generally open on Sunday. Smaller stores are likely to be closed on Sunday and keep limited Saturday hours. Loop workers tend to start their day early, so many stores keep pace by opening by 8:30 and closing at 5 or 6.

DEPARTMENT STORES

Filene's Basement. Patience can pay off at Filene's, where shoppers flip through racks of discounted clothing for a great find or two. Women can do well at either the State Street or Michigan Avenue location, but men will find a superior selection of designer names at State Street. Watch newspaper ads midweek for special shipments. ⊠ *1 N. State St., Loop* ☎ *312/553–1055* ⊠ *830 N. Michigan Ave., Magnificent Mile* ☎ *312/482–8918.*

★ **Macy's.** In the fall of 2006 Marshall Field's, Chicago's most famous—and perpetually struggling—department store, became a Macy's. Some of the higher-end designers Field's carried are gone from the racks, but overall the store remains the same, still standing as a glorious reminder of how grand department stores used to be. Founder Marshall Field's motto was "Give the lady what she wants!" And for many years both ladies and gentlemen had been able to find everything from furs to personalized stationery on one of the store's nine levels. The ground floor and lower level are fashioned in the model of European department stores to include leased boutiques. These stores-within-the-store include national companies like Yahoo!, selling Internet service and computer equipment, and an Yves St. Laurent accessories boutique, as well as local retailers like Merz Apothecary, a pharmacy that opened on the North Side of Chicago in 1875 and specializes in homeopathic remedies. You can still buy Field's famous Frango mints (though they're no longer made locally), and the Walnut Room restaurant on the 7th floor is still a magical place to dine at Christmas. And, the famous Tiffany Dome—designed in 1907 by Louis Comfort Tiffany—is visible from the fifth floor. ⊠ *111 N. State St., Loop* ☎ *312/781–1000* ⊠ *Water Tower Place, 835 N. Michigan Ave., Magnificent Mile* ☎ *312/335–7700.*

SPECIALTY STORES

BOOKS & MUSIC **Coulsons Music Matters.** Musicians come here to find sheet music that suits their style—whether it's jazz, classical, pop, or just about anything else. You'll also find handy accessories like piano lights and metronomes. ⊠ *75 E. Van Buren St., Loop* ☎ *312/461–1989.*

Powell's Bookstore. Marxism, the occult, and philosophy all have their own sections at Powell's, which focuses on used, rare, and discounted books and remainders with an intellectual bent. ⊠ *828 S. Wabash Ave., South Loop* ☎ *312/341–0748* ⊠ *1501 E. 57th St., Hyde Park* ☎ *773/955–7780* ⊠ *2850 N. Lincoln Ave., Lincoln Park* ☎ *773/248–1444.*

Prairie Avenue Bookshop. Massive tables amid architectural artifacts in the Prairie-style interior give browsers room to peruse nearly 20,000 new, rare, and out-of-print titles on architecture, interior design, and urban planning. ⊠ *418 S. Wabash Ave., Loop* ☎ *312/922–8311.*

Selected Works Bookstore. This charming used bookstore relocated from a warrenlike basement in Wrigleyville to a bright, sunny shop on the second floor of the Fine Arts Building. Inside you'll find an intriguing, though somewhat chaotic, selection of used books and sheet music watched over by the proprietor's friendly cat. ⊠ *410 S. Michigan Ave., Suite 210, Loop* ☎ *312/447–0068.*

The Loop & South Loop Shopping

KEY

Ⓜ Train Stations (METRA)

Ⓛ CTA Lines

CAMERAS **Central Camera.** This century-old, third-generation-owned store is
Fodor'sChoice a Loop institution, stacked to the rafters with cameras and dark-
★ room equipment at competitive prices. ⊠*230 S. Wabash Ave., Loop*
☎*312/427–5580.*

CLOTHING & **Altman's Men's Shoes and Boots.** Price tags are still written by hand at
SHOES this 75-year-old institution, which has 27 stockrooms holding 50,000
pairs of men's shoes in sizes from 5 to 19 and in widths from AAAA to
EEE. You can find anything from Timberland and Tony Lama boots to
Allen-Edmonds and Alden oxfords, all at a decent discount. ⊠*120 W.
Monroe St., Loop* ☎*312/332–0667.*

Bates Design. Barbara Bates has been designing upscale fashions with a
distinct urban edge since 1986 for a who's-who client list that includes
Oprah Winfrey, Michael Jordan, Will Smith, and Mary J. Blige. But
she's still invested in her community; her eponymous foundation
donates custom prom dresses and tuxedos to disadvantaged inner-city
teens set to graduate from high school. This new studio showcases
her couture and traditional labels. ⊠*1130 S. Wabash Ave., Suite 407,
South Loop* ☎*312/427–0284.*

Syd Jerome. Board of Trade types who like special attention and snazzy
designers come to this legendary clothier for Giorgio Armani, Ermenegildo Zegna, and on-the-spot custom alterations. Home and office con-
sultations are available. ⊠*2 N. LaSalle St., Loop* ☎*312/346–0333.*

DISCOUNT **Chicago Watch Center.** This large street-side booth in the Wabash Jew-
JEWELRY & elers Mall has one of the city's most outstanding inventories of used
WATCHES luxury watches. ⊠*Wabash Jewelers Mall, 21 N. Wabash Ave., Loop*
☎*312/609–0003.*

The Jeweler's Center at the Mallers Building. The largest concentration of
wholesale and retail jewelers in the Midwest has been housed in this
building since 1921, and is open to the general public. Roughly 190
retailers span 13 floors, offering all kinds of jewelry, watches, and related
repairs and services. ⊠*5 S. Wabash Ave., Loop* ☎*312/424–2664.*

MUSEUM **Bariff Shop for Judaica.** Come here for all your modern Jewish must-
STORES haves, like Moses action figures and Jonathan Adler yarmulkes. There's
also more traditional holiday ware, books, and music. The shop's inside
the Spertus Institute of Jewish Studies. ⊠*610 S. Michigan Ave., Loop*
☎*312/322–1740.*

Museum Shop at the Art Institute of Chicago. Museum reproductions in the
form of jewelry, posters, and Frank Lloyd Wright–inspired decorative
accessories, as well as books and toys, fill the Art Institute's gift shop.
If you're keen on one of the museum's current big exhibits, chances are
you'll find some nifty souvenirs to take away. ⊠*111 S. Michigan Ave.,
Loop* ☎*312/443–3583.*

SOUVENIRS OF **Chicago Architecture Foundation ArchiCenter Shop & Tour Center.** Daniel
CHICAGO Burnham's 1904 Santa Fe Building is a fitting home for the Chicago
Fodor'sChoice Architecture Foundation. Chock-full of architecture-related books,
★ home accessories, and everything and anything related to Frank Lloyd
Wright, the store is also the place to sign up for one of the foundation's

acclaimed tours conducted on foot or by bus, bicycle, and river cruise. ✉*224 S. Michigan Ave., Loop* ☎*312/922–3432.*

★ **Garrett Popcorn.** Bring home a tub of Chicago's famous popcorn instead of a giant pencil or T-shirt, and you'll score major points. The lines can be long, but trust us—this stuff is worth the wait. ✉*26 W. Randolph St., Loop* ☎*312/201–0511* ✉*4 E. Madison St., Loop* ☎*312/263–8087* ✉*2 W. Jackson Blvd., Loop* ☎*312/360–1108* ✉*670 N. Michigan Ave., Near North* ☎*312/944–2630.*

Illinois Artisans Shop. This store run by the Illinois State Museum culls the best jewelry, ceramics, glass, and dolls from craftspeople around the state and sells them at very reasonable prices. There are also exhibits on anything from quilting to Celtic design. ✉*James R. Thompson Center, 100 W. Randolph St., Suite 2–100, Loop* ☎*312/814–5321* ⊙*Closed weekends.*

SPECIALTY **Harlan J. Berk.** Travel back to antiquity amid this wondrous trove
STOPS of classical Greek, Roman, and Byzantine coinage and artifacts. Don't miss the gallery rooms in the back. ✉*31 N. Clark St., Loop* ☎*312/609–0016.*

★ **Iwan Ries and Co.** Iwan Ries did not just jump on the cigar bandwagon; the family-owned store has been around since 1857. Cigar smokers are welcome to light up in the smoking area, which also displays antique pipes. ■TIP➡ **Almost 100 brands of cigars are available, as are 10,000 or so pipes, deluxe Elie Bleu humidors, and all manner of smoking accessories.** ✉*19 S. Wabash Ave., 2nd fl., Loop* ☎*312/372–1306.*

WEST LOOP

Art aficionados and gallery owners are taking a new direction in Chicago. After years of doing business in River North and along Michigan Avenue, their new credo is to go west—specifically, to the West Loop, an area just west of downtown marked by Halsted Street to the east, Fulton Market (still a busy meat-packing center) to the north, Ogden Avenue to the west, and Roosevelt Avenue to the south. Large former warehouses and loft spaces coupled with more reasonable rents have led many galleries from more established neighborhoods to join what was once a sparse number of experimental artists and dealers here. Most are clustered around the northern section of the neighborhood.

ART GALLERIES

Douglas Dawson. Douglas Dawson has 8,000 square feet of space plus a sculpture garden in his West Loop space to showcase ancient and historic art from Africa, Oceania, and the Americas. ✉*400 N. Morgan St., West Loop* ☎*312/226–7975.*

G.R. N'Namdi. This gallery represents contemporary painters and sculptors, with an emphasis on African-American and Latin American artists. ✉*110 N. Peoria St., West Loop* ☎*312/563–9240.*

Gescheidle. Susan Gescheidle's focus is on challenging works in a variety of mediums by both emerging and established artists. ✉*1039 W. Lake St., 2nd fl., West Loop* ☎*312/226–3500.*

Mars Gallery. A neighborhood pioneer that showcases contemporary pop and outsider artwork, Mars Gallery shows work by Peter Mars and other well-known locals like Kevin Luthardt. ⊠*1139 W. Fulton Market, West Loop* 🕾*312/226–7808.*

Packer Schopf Gallery. Browse through an extensive collection of vintage photography and contemporary art with a special emphasis on folk and outsider pieces at this gallery run by well-known local owners Aron Packer and William Schopf. ⊠*942 W. Lake St., West Loop* 🕾*312/226–8984.*

CAMERAS & ELECTRONICS

Helix Camera & Video. Professional photographers buy and rent camera and darkroom equipment at this eight-story warehouse on Racine Avenue just west of Greektown (1½ mi west of the Loop). A good selection of used equipment is available. Underwater photography equipment is a specialty. ⊠*310 S. Racine Ave., West Loop* 🕾*312/421–6000.*

ONE-OF-KIND SOUVENIRS

Chicago Architecture Foundation ArchiCenter Shop & Tour Center (*224 S. Michigan Ave., Loop, 312/922–3432*) is chock-full of treasures to remind you of the city's glorious architecture.

Garrett Popcorn (*26 W. Randolph St., Loop, 312/2010511*) lures people off the street with its mouthwatering aromas.

City of Chicago Store (*163 E. Pearson St., Near North, 312/742—8811*) makes you forget the snow globes and lets you bring home something really authentic—like an old city parking meter.

NOTABLE MARKETS

Fodor's Choice ★ **Chicago Antique Market.** This indoor–outdoor flea market is similar to the ones you might find in London and Paris. On the last Sunday of the month in season more than 200 stalls line Randolph Street selling furniture, jewelry, books, and more. ■TIP→ **The vibe is more funky fashions and vintage treasures than tube socks and refurbished vacuums.** There's also an Indie Designer Fashion Market, showcasing one-of-a-kind wearables by up-and-coming local designers. Children under 12 get in free. ⊠*Randolph St. between Ogden Ave. and Ada St., West Loop* 🖭*$10* ☉*May–Oct., last Sun. of month.*

Maxwell Street Market. A legendary outdoor bazaar that is part of the cultural landscape of the city, the Maxwell Street Market was closed by the city of Chicago amid much controversy in the 1990s. Soon after, it reopened in its current location as the New Maxwell Street Market, where it remains a popular spot, particularly for Latino immigrants, to buy and sell wares. The finds aren't so fabulous, but the atmosphere sure is fun: live blues and stalls selling Mexican street food keep things lively. ⊠*Intersection of Canal St. and Roosevelt Rd., West Loop* 🕾*312/922–3100* 🖭*Free* ☉*Sun.* 7 AM–3 PM.

NEAR NORTH

The Near North section of Chicago encompasses the Gold Coast, which is as swanky as its name suggests. Filled with exclusive apartment buildings, luxury hotels, and top-notch restaurants, it also has some of the best shopping in the city. This is where you'll find the Magnificent Mile, Chicago's most famous shopping strip, as well as a bevy of significant shopping streets in the surrounding area. Check out the boutiques on Rush Street, which offers something for everyone—from young hipsters to ladies who lunch. Along the big avenues like Chicago and Ohio, you'll find hyper-sized versions of familiar fare.

SPECIALTY STORES

BOOKS, MUSIC & ART

Europa Books. Europa is the place for foreign-language books, newspapers, and magazines. This well-stocked bookstore carries French, Spanish, German, and Italian titles and is known for its selection of Latin American literature. ⊠*832 N. State St., Near North* ☎*312/335–9677.*

Jazz Record Mart. Billing itself as the world's largest jazz record store, this "mart" sells tens of thousands of new and used titles on CD, vinyl, and cassette. You'll also find a broad selection of world music. A vast, in-depth selection of jazz and blues and knowledgeable sales staff make the store a must for music lovers. Sometimes you can catch a live performance here on a Saturday afternoon. ⊠*27 E. Illinois St., Near North* ☎*312/222–1467.*

Museum of Contemporary Art Store and Bookstore. This outstanding museum gift shop has out-of-the-ordinary decorative accessories, tableware, and jewelry, as well as a superb collection of books on modern and contemporary art. The shop has its own street-level entrance. ⊠*220 E. Chicago Ave., Near North* ☎*312/397–4000* ☉*Closed Mon.*

FOR KIDS

American Girl Place. American Girl attracts little girls from just about everywhere with their signature dolls in tow. There's easily a day's worth of activities here—shop at the boutique, take in a live musical revue, and have lunch or afternoon tea at the café, where dolls can partake in the meal from their own "sassy seats." ⚠ **Brace yourself for long lines just to get into the store during high shopping seasons.** ⊠*111 E. Chicago Ave., Near North* ☎*877/247–5223.*

Camelot Children's Kingdom. This brightly colored boutique carries American and European clothing lines for babies and children (boys up to age 12, girls to size 14). Some of the brands you'll find are Little Mass and IKKS. Also on offer are cute Room Seven diaper bags and gifts. ⊠*1155 N. State St., Near North* ☎*312-654-1672*

Madison and Friends. Mini Mag Mile shoppers get their own high-end shopping experience at this boutique, which stocks labels like Hannah Banana and Les Tout Petits in newborn through junior sizes. They also carry top-of-the-line strollers and accessories. Adults can shop in the Denim Lounge downstairs, where the latest styles from Miss Sixty, True Religion, and other of-the-moment brands are available. ⊠*43 E. Oak St., Near North* ☎*312/642–6403.*

CLOTHING & SHOES

Adidas Originals Chicago. Old-school sneakers and hip urban fashions for a fresh generation of fans are the draw here. ⊠*923 N. Rush St., Near North* ☎*312/932–0651.*

The Daisy Shop. Gently worn new and vintage couture clothing is the draw at this high-end consignment shop. Knowledgeable staffers guide you through the collection, which features fashion's heaviest hitters as well as a well-edited selection of bags, pearls, and other accessories—all offered at a relative bargain. ⊠*67 E. Oak St., 6th fl., Near North* ☎*312/943–8880.*

Ikram. A household name in chichi Gold Coast high-rises, this 4,000-square-foot store named for owner Ikram Goldman carries an assortment of new and old fashion icons, from Alexander McQueen and Jean Paul Gaultier to Narciso Rodriguez and Zac Posen. There's also a carefully edited selection of vintage designs. ⊠*873 N. Rush St., Near North* ☎*312/587–1000.*

CLOTHING FOR MEN & WOMEN

★ **Jake.** The motto here is "fashion without victims," and the owners have taken heed to stock clothes for both sexes by up-and-coming designers you don't see elsewhere. This shop is the swanky downtown sibling of the wildly popular Southport Avenue store in Lakeview. ⊠*939 N. Rush St., Near North* ☎*312/664–5553.*

Londo Mondo. A great selection of swimwear for buff beach-ready bodies is here. You can also find workout and yoga gear and men's and women's in-line skates. ⊠*1100 N. Dearborn St., Near North* ☎*312/751–2794* ⊠*2148 N. Halsted St., Lincoln Park* ☎*773/327–2218*

FOR THE HOME

Jonathan Adler. Design guru Adler's store is chock-full of his signature fun, funky pottery and home furnishings, all arranged in a series of small living spaces. ⊠*676 Wabash Ave., Near North* ☎*312/274–9920.*

Quatrine. The washable upholstered and slipcovered furniture for dining rooms, living rooms, and bedrooms here looks decidedly chic and not at all what you'd consider child- or pet-friendly. ⊠*944 N. Rush St., Near North* ☎*312/649–1700.*

Room & Board. Straightforward yet stylish pieces with a modern sensibility blend quality craftsmanship and materials with affordable pricing. ⊠*55 E. Ohio St., Near North* ☎*312/222–0970.*

SOUVENIRS OF CHICAGO

Fodor'sChoice ★ **City of Chicago Store.** Nab unusual souvenirs of the city here—anything from a street sign to a real parking meter. It's also a good source for guidebooks, posters, and T-shirts. ⊠*Chicago Waterworks Visitor Information Center, 163 E. Pearson St., Near North* ☎*312/742–8811.*

RIVER NORTH

Contained by the Chicago River on the south and west, Clark Street on the east, and Oak Street on the north, River North is home to art galleries, high-end antiques shops, home-furnishings stores, and a few clothing boutiques. The biggest news in this neighborhood is the resurrection of Tree Studios, part of a controversial restoration project to a building originally designed as an artists' colony. On the verge of demolition a few years ago, the building is again housing retail and tenants involved in the arts, although they are no longer permitted

Near North &
River North
Shopping

Maple St.

Rush St.

Bellevue Pl.

W. Oak St.

N. Orleans St.

N. Franklin St.

Washington Square Park

N. Clark St.

N. Dearborn St.

Locust St.

W. Chestnut St.

W. Institute Pl.

Chicago Ave.

W. Superior St.

W. Huron St.

N. Wells St.

N. LaSalle St.

W. Erie St.

W. Ontario St.

N. State St.

N. Wabash Ave.

W. Ohio St.

W. Grand Ave.

W. Illinois St.

Kinzie St.

N. Water St.

Merchandise Mart

Carroll St.

7

to live here. Most of the businesses in River North have a distinctive style that fits in with this art-minded area. Strangely, it's also a wildly popular entertainment district; touristy theme restaurants such as Ed Debevic's and Rainforest Café peddle logo merchandise as aggressively as burgers.

MERCHANDISE MART

This massive marketplace between Wells and North Orleans streets just north of the Chicago River is more notable for its Art Deco design than its shopping. Much of the building is reserved for the design trade, meaning that only interior-design professionals have access to its wares. However, the first two floors have been turned into retail with the unveiling of LuxeHome, a group of 24 high-end kitchen, bath, and building showrooms that are open to the public as well as the design trade. Tenants include de Giulio kitchen design, Waterworks, and Christopher Peacock Cabinetry. The Chopping Block, a local culinary school with a loyal fan base, has a spacious location here. The Mart is usually closed on Sunday, and stores keep relatively short Saturday hours.

SPECIALTY STORES

ANTIQUES & COLLECTIBLES

Antiquarians Building. Five floors of dealers in Asian and European antiques display their wares; some examples of modernism and Art Deco are thrown in for good measure. ⊠159 W. Kinzie St., River North ☎312/527–0533.

Christa's, Ltd. Chests, cabinets, tables, and bureaus are stacked three and four high, creating narrow aisles that are precarious to negotiate but make for adventurous exploring. Look in, over, and under each and every piece to assess the gems stashed in every possible crevice. ⊠217 W. Illinois St., River North ☎312/222–2520.

Evanstonia Antique Gallery. Dealer Ziggy Osak has a rich collection of fine 19th-century English and continental antiques that are prized for being as functional as they are striking. ⊠120 W. Kinzie St., River North ☎312/907–0101.

Fly-by-Nite Gallery. Exceptional decorative and functional art objects (circa 1890–1930) are chosen with a curatorial eye. Fly-by-Nite is especially known for European art glass and pottery and antique jewelry. ⊠714 N. Wells St., River North ☎312/664–8136.

Jay Robert's Antique Warehouse. Jay Robert's has enough antique merchandise to fill a 50,000-square-foot showroom on his own. He specializes in 18th- and 19th-century European pieces, and has many large-scale armoires, dining sets, sideboards, fireplace mantels, and clocks. ⊠149 W. Kinzie St., River North ☎312/222–0167.

Continued on page 271

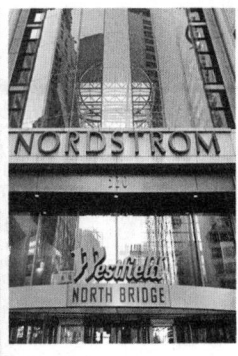

THE MAGNIFICENT MILE: A SHOPPER'S SHANGRI-LA

One mile. Nearly 500 shops. Four vertical malls.
Art galleries, haute couture, bargains, and boutiques.
Does it get any better than this?

We've got news for shopaholics who consider the Midwest nothing but flyover country: If you haven't shopped Chicago's Magnificent Mile, dare we say, you simply haven't shopped.

With four lavish malls and more than 460 stores along the stretch of Michigan Avenue that runs from the Chicago River to Oak Street, the Mag Mile is one of the best shopping strips the world over. (Swanky Oak Street is also considered part of the Mag Mile, though neighboring streets technically are not. Shops on those streets are listed in this chapter under "Near North.")

Chanel, Hermès, Gucci, and Armani are just a few of the legendary fashion houses with fabulous boutiques here. Other notables like Anne Fontaine, Kate Spade, and Prada also have Mag Mile outposts, recognizing the everybody-who's-anybody importance of the address.

Shoppers with down-to-earth budgets will find there's plenty on the Mag Mile as well, with national chains making an extra effort at their multi-level megastores here. But the Mag Mile is much more than a paradise for clothes horses, with stores for techies, furniture fiends, sports fans, art collectors, and almost anyone else with money to spend.

Following is a selective guide to stores in the area. Hours generally run from 10 AM to 7 or 8 PM Monday through Saturday, with shorter hours on Sunday.

Bellevue Pl.

Sugar Magnolia Jil Sander Palazzo
Prada Kate Spade Chasalla
Hermès
E. Oak St. Ultimo
1000 *E. Lake Shore Dr.*

Barneys Bravco Tod's Chanel
New York Beauty Colletti
Centre Gallery
Jimmy *E. Walton St.*
Choo **900 North** ● Louis Vuitton
Michigan Shops ● Anne
(with Bloomingdale's) ● Fontaine
900 *E. Delaware Pl.*

N. Wabash Ave.
John Hancock
● **Center**
Richard Gray
Gallery
E. Chestnut St.
Water Tower
● **Place (with**
N. Rush St. H&M ● **Macy's and**
Lord & Taylor)
E. Pearson St.
Water Tower ●
City of Chicago
Giorgio Armani ● Store
800 *Chicago Ave.*

Michigan Ave.
Polo/Ralph Lauren ●
Mies van der Rohe Way
Pottery Barn ● Neiman Marcus
E. Superior St. Saks Fifth Avenue
● Men's Store
Chicago Place ● The Disney Store
(with Saks Fifth Ave.) ●
● Brooks Brothers
700 *E. Huron St.*
St. Clair St.
E. Erie St.

DEPARTMENT STORES

Barneys New York. A smaller version of the Manhattan store known for austere fashions, this one's heavy on private-label merchandise, though you'll find Donna Karan and several European designers. A Vera Wang salon caters to brides. The cosmetics and Chelsea Passage gift areas have plenty of plum choices. ⊠ 25 E. Oak St. ☎ 312/587–1700.

Bloomingdale's. Chicago's Bloomie's is built in an airy style that is part Prairie School, part postmodern

(quite unlike its New York City sibling), giving you plenty of elbow room to sift through its selection of designer labels. The new Space on 5 has trendier fashions. ⊠ 900 North Michigan Shops ☎ 312/440–4460.

The Disney Store. This Mecca to the Mouse has everything little Disney disciples need for a fix: giant monitors playing Walt's classics, plus a plethora of plush toys, videos, games, and other goodies. ⊠ 717 N. Michigan Ave. ☎ 312/654–9208.

Lord & Taylor. Moderate to upscale clothing for men and women, plus shoes and accessories, form the inventory here, frequently at sale prices. ⊠ Water Tower Place, 835 N. Michigan Ave. ☎ 312/787–7400.

Neiman Marcus. Prices may be high, but they're matched by the level of taste. The selection of designer clothing and accessories is outstanding, and the gourmet top-floor food area tempts with hard-to-find delicacies and impeccable hostess gifts. ⊠ 737 N. Michigan Ave. ☎ 312/642–5900.

Nordstrom. This is a lovely department store with a killer shoe department. Note the Nordstrom Spa on the third floor. ⊠ The Shops at North Bridge, 520 N. Michigan Ave. ☎ 312/464–1515.

Saks Fifth Avenue. The smaller, less-crowded cousin of the New York flagship doesn't scrimp on its selection of designer clothes. A men's specialty store is directly across the street. ⊠ Chicago Place, 700 N. Michigan Ave. ☎ 312/944–6500 ⊠ Men's Store, 717 N. Michigan Ave. ☎ 312/944–6500.

CLOTHING FOR WOMEN

Anne Fontaine Paris. The French designer's famous takes on the classic white shirt sport hefty price tags, thanks to her attention to detail. ⊠ 909 N. Michigan Ave. ☎ 312/943–0401.

Chanel Boutique. Ensconced in the Drake Hotel, this shop carries the complete line of Chanel products, including ready-to-wear, fragrances, and cosmetics. ⊠ 935 N. Michigan Ave. ☎ 312/787–5500.

Palazzo. Chic urban brides trust Jane and Saeed Hamidi for their clean-lined bridal collection. ⊠ 49 E. Oak St. ☎ 312/337–6940.

Sugar Magnolia. Named for the Grateful Dead song, Sugar Magnolia has clothes and accessories that tap into trends with a romantic, Bohemian spin. Prices are high, but not

Bravco Beauty Centre. Need a hard-to-find shampoo, an ionic hair dryer, or simply a jar of Vaseline? Bravco is the place for all this and more. Cash or check only. ⊠ 43 E. Oak St. ☎ 312/943–4305.

over the top. ⊠ 34 E. Oak St. ☎ 312/944–0885.

Ultimo. Check out the well-edited selection of designer goods from such names as John Galliano, Michael Kors, Chloe, and Manolo Blahnik. Oprah is a customer! ⊠ 114 E. Oak St. ☎ 312/787–1171.

CLOTHING FOR MEN

Ermenegildo Zegna. The sportswear, softly tailored business attire, and dress clothes of this Italian great are gathered all under one roof. ⊠ 645 N. Michigan Ave. ☎ 312/587–9660.

Hugo BOSS. Men will find modern, well-cut suits with attention to tailoring, as well as other signature Boss clothing and accessories here. ⊠ Westfield North Bridge, 520 N. Michigan Ave. ☎ 312/660–0056.

Saks Fifth Avenue Men's Store. Spread over 30,000 square feet and three levels, Saks is the city's leading retailer for menswear. ⊠ 717 N. Michigan Ave. ☎ 312/944–6500 or 888/643–7257.

CLOTHING FOR MEN & WOMEN

Brooks Brothers. The bastion of ready-to-wear conservative fashion still sells boatloads of their classic 1837 navy blazer. But this one-stop shop for oxfords and khakis also sneaks in the occasional bold color. ⊠ 713 N. Michigan Ave. ☎ 312/915–0060.

Burberry. The label once favored by the conservatively well-dressed is now hot with young fashionistas, who can't get enough of the label's signature plaid on everything from bikinis to baby gear. ⊠ 633 N. Michigan Ave. ☎ 312/787–2500.

Chasalla. Chasalla isn't for the timid—the bold, sexy clothes and accessories of European couture houses such as Dolce & Gabbana, Gianni Versace, and Hugo Boss are the norm here. ⊠ 106 E. Oak St. ☎ 312/640–1940.

Giorgio Armani. An airy, two-floor space displays Armani's discreetly luxurious clothes and accessories, including the top-priced Black Label line. ⊠ 800 N. Michigan Ave. ☎ 312/751–2244.

Gucci. Though the prices aren't for the faint of heart, there are plenty of pieces here that will last a lifetime. ⊠ 900 North Michigan Shops ☎ 312/664–5504.

H&M. Bargain-savvy fashionistas around the world love the cheap-n-chic styles on offer; the constant crowds at the Mag Mile store prove Chicagoans are no different. ⊠ 840 N. Michigan Ave. ☎ 312/640–0060.

Hermès of Paris. The well-heeled and very well-paid shop here for suits, signature scarves, and leather accessories. ⊠ 110 E. Oak St. ☎ 312/787–8175.

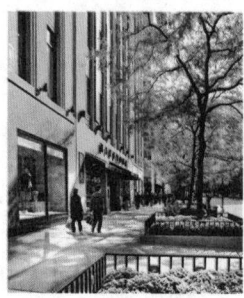

Jil Sander. This line has captured the devotion of the fashion flock for its minimalist designs and impeccable tailoring. Prices are at the upper end of the designer range. ⊠ 48 E. Oak St. ☎ 312/335–0006.

Mark Shale. Here you'll find two floors filled with stylish suits and separates from an international array of designers. ⊠ 900 North Michigan Shops ☎ 312/440–0720.

Prada. The store has a spare, cool look that matches its modern inventory of clothing, shoes, and bags. In fact, unless you're a Miuccia devotee, the three-story shop can seem almost bare. ⊠ 30 E. Oak St. ☎ 312/951–1113.

Polo/Ralph Lauren. Manor house meets mass marketing. The upper-crust chic covers men's, women's, and children's clothes and housewares. Fabrics are often enticing (suede, silk, cashmere), but expect to pay a pretty penny. ⊠ 750 N. Michigan Ave. ☎ 312/280–1655.

TECH STUFF

Apple Store. It's a multilevel fantasyland for Mac users, complete with the full range of products—from computers to iPods to digital cameras. There's an Internet café where PC fans can get a glimpse of life on the other side. ⊠ 679 N. Michigan Ave. ☎ 312/981–4104.

SHOES & ACCESSORIES

Avventura. Professional basketball players in need of European-style footwear stop here for sizes up to 16! ⊠ Water Tower Place, 835 N. Michigan Ave. ☎ 312/337–3700.

Coach. Well-designed leather goods, in the form of purses, smart shoes, briefcases, and cell phone and PDA holders, are Coach's specialty. ⊠ 625 N. Michigan Ave. ☎ 312/587–3167 ⊠ 900 North Michigan Shops ☎ 312/440–1777.

Jimmy Choo. These are the heels that have celebs and stylish women the world over drooling. Break out the plastic. ✉ 63 Oak St. ☎ 312/255–1170.

Kate Spade. The goddess of handbags has filled her two-floor boutique in the middle of Oak Street with adorable shoes, pajamas, small leather goods, men's accessories from the Jack Spade line, and, of course, her to-die-for purses. ✉ 56 E. Oak St. ☎ 312/654–8853.

Louis Vuitton. Here you have it all under one roof—the coveted purses, leather goods, and luggage bearing the beloved logo, plus men's and women's shoes and jewelry. ✉ 919 N. Michigan Ave. ☎ 312/944–2010.

Salvatore Ferragamo. The shoes have been the classic choice of the well-heeled for generations, but it's the handbags, with a fresh, contemporary sensibility, that are generating excitement of late. ✉ 645 N. Michigan Ave. ☎ 312/397–0464.

Tod's. Choose from a wide selection of the signature handbags and driving moccasins that made Tod's famous, as well as newer additions to the line, including high heels. ✉ 121 E. Oak St. ☎ 312/943–0070 or 800/457–8637.

GET SPORTY

Niketown. This is one of Chicago's top tourist attractions. Many visitors—including professional athletes—stop here to take in the sports memorabilia, road test a pair of sneakers, or watch the inspirational videos. ✉ 669 N. Michigan Ave. ☎ 312/642–6363.

ART GALLERIES

Colletti Gallery. Fine antique posters, a serious collection of

European ceramics and glass, and an eclectic selection of furniture transport you to the late 19th century. ✉ 67 E. Oak St. ☎ 312/664–6767.

Joel Oppenheimer, Inc. Established in 1969, this gallery in the Wrigley Building has an amazing collection of Audubon prints and specializes in antique natural-history pieces. ✉ 410 N. Michigan Ave. ☎ 312/642–5300.

R.-H. Love Galleries. For three decades, this gallery has specialized in museum-quality American art from the colonial period to the early 20th century. ✉ 645 N. Michigan Ave., 2nd fl. entrance on Erie St. ☎ 312/640–1300.

R.-S. Johnson Fine Art. More than 50 museums can be counted among the clients of R. S. Johnson, a Mag Mile resident for 50 years. The family-run gallery sells old masters along with art by modernists like Pablo Picasso, Edgar Degas, and Goya. ✉ 645 N. Michigan Ave., 2nd fl. entrance on Erie St. ☎ 312/943–1661.

Richard Gray Gallery. This gallery lures serious collectors with pieces by modern masters such as David Hockney and Roy Lichtenstein. ✉ John Hancock Center, 875 N. Michigan Ave., Suite 2503 ☎ 312/642–8877.

NOT LIKE THE ONE BACK HOME

On the Mag Mile, everything seems bigger and better—even chain stores, which make an extra effort in this larger-than-life atmosphere. Here are our favorites:

Banana Republic
✉ 744 N. Michigan Ave.
☎ 312/642–0020.

Crate&Barrel
✉ 646 N. Michigan Ave.
☎ 312/787–5900.

The Gap
✉ 555 N. Michigan Ave.
☎ 312/494–8580.

Pottery Barn
✉ 734 N. Michigan Ave.
☎ 312/587–9602.

Victoria's Secret
✉ 830 N. Michigan Ave.
☎ 312/664–2711.

Williams-Sonoma
✉ 900 North Michigan Shops ☎ 312/587–8080.

7

IN FOCUS THE MAGNIFICENT MILE

MIGHTY VERTICAL MALLS

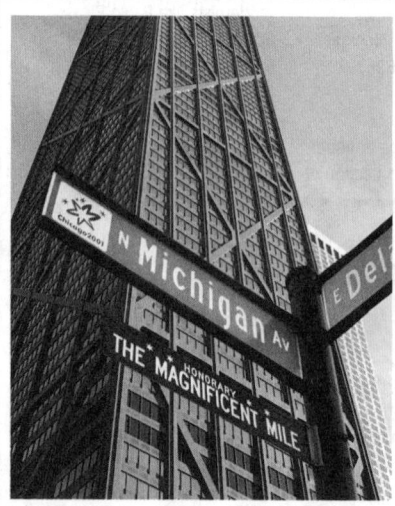

Forget all your preconceived notions about malls being suburban wastelands. Four decidedly upscale urban malls dot the Mag Mile.

The toniest of the four is 900 North Michigan, with a dazzling list of tenants, plus live weekend piano serenades. A more casual but no less entertaining shopping mecca is just blocks away at Water Tower Place. Fuel up there with a snack from **Wow Bao**, which sells steamed meat and vegetable buns that are *delish*.

Check out the beautiful views from Chicago Place's airy top-floor food court. The newest kid on the block is Westfield North Bridge, which opened in 2000.

Chicago Place. Saks Fifth Avenue is the big tenant here, and there's also a multilevel Ann Taylor. Other shops include Love from Chicago, Time-Us, Tall Girl, Russian Creations, and Kashmir Handicrafts. ⊠ 700 N. Michigan Ave. ☎ 312/642–4811.

900 North Michigan Shops. There's a ritzy feel to the mall that houses the Chicago branch of Bloomingdale's along with dozens of boutiques and specialty stores, such as Gucci, Coach, Lalique, and Fogal. ⊠ 900 N. Michigan Ave. ☎ 312/915–3916.

Water Tower Place. The Ritz-Carlton Hotel sits atop this mall, which contains branches of Macy's and Lord & Taylor, as well as seven floors of shops. The more unusual spots here include Teavana (a modern tea shop) and Jacadi (children's wear). **Foodlife**, a step above usual mall food-court fare, is a fantastic spot for a quick bite. ⊠ 835 N. Michigan Ave. ☎ 312/440–3165.

The Shops at North Bridge. The big draw here is Nordstrom. Chains like Sephora and Ann Taylor Loft share space with specialty stores like Vosges Haut-Chocolat, a local chocolatier with an international following. The third floor is for tots, with a LEGO Store, a play area, and Oilily Kids. ⊠ 520 N. Michigan Ave. ☎ 312/327–2300.

THE ANNUAL LIGHTS FESTIVAL

Chicago's holiday season officially kicks off every year at the end of November with the **Magnificent Mile Lights Festival**, a weekend-long event consisting of family-friendly activities that packs the shopping strip to the gills. Music, ice-carving contests, and stage shows kick off the celebration, which culminates in a parade and the illumination of more than one million lights along Michigan Avenue. Neighborhood stores keep late hours to accommodate the crowds. For more information, check out ⊕ www.themagnificentmile.com.

P.O.S.H. It's hard to resist the charming displays of piled-up, never-been-used, vintage hotel and restaurant china here. There's also an impressive selection of silver gravy boats, creamers, and flatware that bear the marks of ocean liners and private clubs. ✉*Tree Studios, 613 N. State St., River North* ☎*312/280–1602.*

Rita Bucheit, Ltd. Devoted to the streamlined Biedermeier aesthetic, this shop carries choice furniture and accessories from the period along with Art Deco and modern pieces that are perfect complements to the style. ✉*449 N. Wells St., River North* ☎*312/527–4080.*

ART GALLERIES The contemporary art scene continues to thrive in River North, despite losing some of its residents to a slightly lower-rent warehouse district in the nearby West Loop and a burgeoning gallery scene in Pilsen, southwest of the Loop. The neighborhood is chock-full of galleries, most open Tuesday through Saturday. ■TIP➔ **Every Saturday morning at 11, the Art Dealers Association of Chicago offers complimentary gallery tours.** Groups meet at the Starbucks at 750 North Franklin Street and are guided each week by a different gallery owner or director from the area. For more information, and to check holiday weekend schedules, call 312/649–0065 or go to www.chicagoartdealers.org.

Alan Koppel Gallery. An eclectic mix of works by modern masters and contemporary artists is balanced by a selection of French and Italian Modernist furniture from the 1920s to 1960s. ✉*210 W. Chicago Ave., River North* ☎*312/640–0730.*

Ann Nathan Gallery. The specialty here is contemporary paintings, but the gallery also showcases sculpture and singular artist-made furniture. ✉*212 W. Superior St., River North* ☎*312/664–6622.*

Byron Roche. Contemporary paintings and drawings, many by Chicago artists, are exhibited here. ✉*750 N. Franklin St., River North* ☎*312/654–0144.*

Carl Hammer Gallery. Lee Godie, Henry Darger, and Jordan Mozer are among the outsider and self-taught artists whose work is shown at this gallery. ✉*740 N. Wells St., River North* ☎*312/266–8512.*

Catherine Edelman Gallery. This gallery of contemporary photography explores the work of emerging, mixed-media, photo-based artists such as Maria Martinez-Canes and Jack Spencer. ✉*300 W. Superior St., River North* ☎*312/266–2350.*

Habatat. Collectors of fine studio art glass are drawn here by luminaries such as Dale Chihuly. ✉*222 W. Superior St., River North* ☎*312/440–0288.*

Primitive Art Works. Find ethnic and tribal art, including textiles, furniture, and jewelry, at this longtime Chicago favorite gallery. ✉*130 N. Jefferson St., River North* ☎*312/575–9600.*

Stephen Daiter Gallery. This space showcases stunning 20th-century European and American photography, particularly avant-garde photojournalism. A separate contemporary gallery highlights work by younger artists pushing the boundaries of contemporary photography. ✉*311 W. Superior St., River North* ☎*312/787–3350.*

ART SUPPLIES **Abraham Lincoln Book Shop.** The shop owner here buys, sells, and & BOOKS appraises books, paintings, documents, and other paraphernalia associated with American military and political history. It's been around since 1938. ⊠*357 W. Chicago Ave., River North* ☎*312/944–3085.*

Pearl Art & Craft Supply. Pearl is the name synonymous with the best selection of art supplies at the best prices. Paints and palettes, crafts, portfolios, tools, easels—it's all here, and it's all discounted. ⊠*225 W. Chicago Ave., River North* ☎*312/915–0200.*

CHEAP CHOCOLATE

Blommer Chocolate Outlet Store. "Why do parts of River North smell like freshly baked brownies?" is a question you hear fairly often. The oh-so-sweet reason: it's near the Blommer Chocolate Factory, which has been making wholesale chocolates here since 1939. More important, the retail outlet store is also here, so you can snap up your Blommer chocolates and candies at a discount—a handy tip to know when those smells give you a case of the munchies. ⊠*600 W. Kinzie St. at corner of N. Jefferson St., River North* ☎*312/226–7700.*

CLOTHING FOR WOMEN

Blake. A no-nonsense boutique without pomp, circumstance, or even signage, Blake displays clean-lined clothes in a pristine setting. You'll find designers like Dries van Noten, Balenciaga, and shoes and accessories of a similar subtle elegance. ⊠*212 W. Chicago Ave, River North* ☎*312/202–0047.*

Clever Alice. This women's boutique carries a well-chosen inventory of fashion from local designers like Alice in Oz and Veronica Martin Riley, plus other avant-garde labels like Kitchen Orange and Metalicus. ⊠*750 N. Franklin St., River North* ☎*312/587–8693.*

FOR THE HOME
Fodor'sChoice
★

Bloomingdale's Home & Furniture Store. The Medinah Temple once occupied this space, and Bloomie's kept the historically significant exterior intact but gutted the inside to create its first stand-alone furnishings store in Chicago. Naturally, it's stocked to the rafters with everything you need to eat, sleep, and relax in your home in high style. ⊠*600 N. Wabash Ave., Near North* ☎*312/324–7500.*

Cambium. A particularly expansive line of kitchen fittings and accoutrements is one of many temptations at this home-furnishings store. ⊠*113–119 W. Hubbard St., River North* ☎*312/832–9920.*

★ **The Chopping Block.** New and seasoned chefs appreciate an expertly edited selection of pots and pans, bakeware, gadgets, and ingredients here. The intimate cooking classes are hugely popular and taught by a fun, knowledgeable staff. (Students get 10% off store merchandise.) The Lincoln Square location has a wine shop. ⊠*Merchandise Mart Plaza, Suite 107, River North* ☎*312/644–6360* ⊠*4747 N. Lincoln Ave., Lincoln Square* ☎*773/472–6700.*

Design Within Reach. This showroom in the historic Tree Studios building is one of the home-furnishings chain's largest. Inside you'll find several floors of furnishings—from lounge designs and workspace furniture to lighting and accessories—all reflecting the store's focus on classic modern design at affordable prices. ⊠*10 E. Ohio St., River North* ☎*312/280-4677.*

Golden Triangle. This is a must-stop shop for anyone enamored of the East-meets-West aesthetic. There are 11,000 square feet of choice pieces, including antique Chinese and British colonial Raj furniture from Burma, Asian accessories, and idiosyncratic pieces from Thailand. ✉ *330 N. Clark St., River North* ☎ *312/755–1266.*

Lightology. This 20,000-square-foot showroom of modern light designs is an essential stop for designers and architects, not to mention passersby drawn to the striking designs visible from the windows. It's the brainchild of Greg Kay, who started out as a roller-disco lighting designer in the 1970s and made a name for himself in Chicago with Tech Lighting, a contemporary design gallery. ✉ *215 W. Chicago Ave., River North* ☎ *312/944–1000.*

Luminaire. The city's largest showroom of international contemporary furniture includes pieces by Philippe Starck, Antonio Citterio, Alberta Meda, and Shiro Kuromata. Sleek kitchen designs are from Italian manufacturer Bofi, and a large home accessories section has equally edgy offerings from Alessi, Zani & Zani, Rosenthal, and Mono. ✉ *301 W. Superior St., River North* ☎ *312/664–9582.*

Manifesto. In a huge, street-level space, one of the largest design ateliers in the city showcases work by furniture designer (and owner) Richard Gorman, plus contemporary furniture from Armani Casa (Giorgio Armani's furniture line and streamlined Finnish accessories). ✉ *755 N. Wells St., River North* ☎ *312/664–0733.*

Modernica. Find reissues of clean-lined and practical mid-century modernist furniture by the likes of George Nelson and Charles and Ray Eames here, plus a good selection of furniture design books. ✉ *555 N. Franklin St., River North* ☎ *312/222–1808.*

Orange Skin. The go-to resource for modern furniture, lighting, and accessories in Chicago carries pieces by Minotti, Alessi, Michael Graves, and Tisettanta. A recent move from Wicker Park to a bi-level space means a bigger inventory of goodies to choose from. ✉ *223 W. Erie St., River North* ☎ *312/335–1033.*

★ **Sawbridge Studios.** Sawbridge Studios displays custom handcrafted furniture by about 40 American artisans. The specialties include Frank Lloyd Wright reproductions, newly designed pieces with an Arts and Crafts or Shaker aesthetic, and contemporary pottery. ✉ *153 W. Ohio St., River North* ☎ *312/828–0055.*

Svenska Mobler. This store carries a hand-picked selection of Swedish antique furniture, lighting, and art, plus some mid-century pieces from Argentina. ✉ *516 N. Wells St., River North* ☎ *312/595–9320.*

GIFTS **Pops for Champagne.** Choose from well-chosen group of bubbly plus assorted accoutrements at the retail shop of this popular champagne bar. ✉ *605 N. State St., River North* ☎ *312/266–7676.*

JEWELRY & **June Blaker.** Chicago retail veteran June Blaker returns to the scene ACCESSORIES with this standout shop displaying her own jewelry line as well as an eclectic assortment of accessories, bags, clothing, and leather goods by designers such as Comme des Garçons and Brigitte Adolph. The minimalist space lets the unique merchandise take center stage. ✉ *870 N. Orleans., River North* ☎ *312/751–9220.*

PAPER **Paper Source.** Reams and reams of different types of paper are sold ★ here; much of it is eclectic and expensive. Check out the custom invitation department and good selection of rubber stamps and bookbinding supplies. Ask about the classes offered. ⊠*232 W. Chicago Ave., River North* ☎*312/337–0798* ⊠*919 W. Armitage Ave., Lincoln Park* ☎*773/525–7300.*

WICKER PARK & BUCKTOWN

Artists and musicians were the first to claim this once run-down area near the intersection of North, Damen, and Milwaukee avenues, and then, some years later, points south on and around Division Street; the trendy coffeehouses, nightclubs, and restaurants followed. Young, hip families were next, and shopping has since snowballed. Now scads of edgy clothing boutiques, art galleries, home-design ateliers, alternative-music stores, and funky kids' shops dot the area. Hipsters have been squawking about gentrification with the opening of chains like Urban Outfitters and American Apparel in the neighborhood, but this is still a one-of-a-kind-shopping destination that deserves a solid chunk of time.

Many stores don't open until at least 11 AM, some shops are closed on Monday and Tuesday, and hours can be erratic. Spend a late afternoon shopping before settling in for dinner at one of the neighborhood's popular restaurants. To get here from downtown on the El, take the Blue Line toward O'Hare and exit at Damen Avenue.

SPECIALTY STORES

ACCESSORIES & GIFTS

Paper Doll. Doll up your gift with an unusual card and handmade wrapping paper from this Wicker Park shop, where Maude, the owners' pug, holds court on the floor. Finger puppets, candles, and other gift items are also stocked here. The popular store has newer, bigger digs a few doors down from the teeny old shop. ⊠*2048 W. Division St., Wicker Park* ☎*773/227–6950.*

Red Dog House. Finally, a place in the neighborhood to shop for hipsters' four-legged friends. This boutique has everything Fido and Kitty need to sit, stay, and live pretty, from swank sweaters to made-to-order name collars, beds, and bowls. ⊠*2031 N. Damen St., Bucktown* ☎*773/227–7341.*

RR#1 Chicago. A wood-paneled 1930s pharmacy is the setting for this charming gift shop, which stocks eclectic ideas for everyone on your list, plus a tempting array of bath and beauty product lines like Barefoot Venus and Pre de Provence. ⊠*814 N. Ashland Ave., Wicker Park* ☎*312/421–9079.*

Ruby Room. This Wicker Park spa–boutique sells an eclectic mix of bath and body products from brands like Sage Spirit, Phytologie, and Surly Girl Studios. Check out the spa services, too—everything from intuitive astrology and pet healing to brow waxing and facials. ⊠*1743–45 W. Division St., 2nd fl., Wicker Park* ☎*773/635–5000.*

shebang. Accessories junkies meet up-and-coming designers at this shop chock full of handbag, jewelry, and hat finds. Super-contemporary labels include Dutchy, Hayden-Harnett, and Alexis Bittar. ⊠*1616 N. Damen Ave., Wicker Park* ☎*773/486–3800.*

Wicker Park & Bucktown Shopping

BUCKTOWN

WICKER PARK

UKRAINIAN VILLAGE

KEY

L CTA stations

M Metra Lines

0   1/4 mi

0   1/4 km

Tatine. It's hard to decide which luscious-smelling candle to choose, with such eclectic scents as sake, rose tabac, and ginger lily among the offerings. Margo Breznik hand-pours all the candles in this pretty shop herself, using soy wax, which is said to burn cleaner than traditional paraffin wax. ✉ *1742 W. Division St., Wicker Park* ☎ *773/ 342–1890.*

WORD OF MOUTH

"Definitely hit Bucktown & Wicker Park (my neighborhood) for some unique, funky boutiques and designers who aren't as well known."

–Vittrad

ANTIQUES & COLLECTIBLES

Daniels Antiques. Five blocks north of the six-way Lincoln, Belmont, and Ashland intersection, this cavernous shop shelters a huge stash of Victorian and 20th-century furnishings, especially larger pieces and complete sets. ✉ *2062 N. Damen Ave., Bucktown* ☎ *773/276-9600.*

Pagoda Red. Exceptionally well-priced Asian furnishings from owner Betsy Nathan's frequent overseas trips pack this open loft space. Among the treasures, you'll find Chinese deco chairs, Nepalese rugs, antique lanterns, and a rare collection of 20th-century Chinese advertising posters. ✉ *1714 N. Damen Ave., Bucktown* ☎ *773/235–1188.*

Pavilion. The specialty here is French, Italian, and Scandinavian antiques, but you'll be lured in by the altogether uncommon mix of industrial and decorative furnishings, accessories, and fixtures. The eclectic selection reflects the collecting acumen of its two idiosyncratic owners, who scour Europe and the Midwest for items in the perfect state of intriguing decay. ✉ *2055 N. Damen Ave., Bucktown* ☎ *773/645–0924.*

BOOKS & MUSIC

Dusty Groove America. The retail outlet of a massive online business, Dusty Groove stocks an enormous collection of older jazz, funk, soul, and blues in both LP and CD formats. They also buy used records Monday through Saturday, from noon to 5 PM. ✉ *1120 N. Ashland Ave., Wicker Park* ☎ *773/342–5800.*

★ **Myopic Books.** One of Chicago's largest used-book dealers stocks more than 80,000 titles and buys books from the public on Friday evenings and all day Saturday. ■TIP➔ **A community mainstay, Myopic also hosts regular music and poetry events, and is the meeting spot for the Wicker Park Chess Club.** ✉ *1564 N. Milwaukee Ave., Wicker Park* ☎ *773/862–4882.*

Reckless Records. Look for a varied selection of music at this sister store to the Lakeview flagship, including lots of rare stuff and rock paraphernalia. ✉ *1532 N. Milwaukee Ave., Bucktown* ☎ *773/235–3727.*

FOR KIDS

The Boring Store. Outfit your aspiring sleuth with the necessary spy paraphernalia and secret agent supplies—such as mirror glasses, fake mustaches, and voice amplifiers—at this shop run by the nonprofit group 826CHI. Proceeds help fund the group's after-school tutoring and writing programs for kids. ✉ *1331 N. Milwaukee Ave., Wicker Park* ☎ *773/772-8108.*

Grow. Kids can grow up green with this stock of organic cotton clothes, all-natural bath products and balms, and environmentally friendly nursery furniture. ✉*1943 W. Division St., Wicker Park* ☎*773/489–0009.*

Psycho Baby. The best-dressed urban tykes send their parents to this shop to spend a pretty penny on funky duds by designers like Imps & Elves, Rabbi's Daughters, and Paper Denim & Cloth. There's a great selection of shoes, plus toys and books, and a story hour every Monday and Wednesday for parents brave enough to tote their tykes along. ✉*1630 N. Damen Ave., Bucktown* ☎*773/772–2815.*

The Red Balloon Company. Known for its beautiful handmade children's furniture and stock of colorful Zutano infant wear, this charming store also carries a great selection of classic kids' books and toys, as well as blankets and art work that can be personalized. ✉*2060 N. Damen Ave., Bucktown* ☎*773/489–9800* ✉*5407 N. Clark St., Andersonville* ☎*773/989–8500 or 877/969–9800.*

CLOTHING FOR MEN

apartment number 9. Siblings Amy and Sarah Blessing offer sisterly advice to guys born without the metrosexual gene on what styles best suit them. Their store, named for the Tammy Wynette song, carries classic lines like Paul Smith, Marc Jacobs, and Michael Kors. ✉*1804 N. Damen Ave., Bucktown* ☎*773/395–2999.*

CLOTHING FOR MEN & WOMEN

Akira. Young trendsetters flock to this shop for fashion-forward threads at easy-to-swallow prices. In merely five years Akira has expanded into a mini fashion empire. The flagship women's boutique shares a stretch of North Avenue with offshoot men's clothing and women's shoe stores. ✉*1814 W. North Ave., Wicker Park* ☎*773/489–0818.* ✉*1920 W. North Ave., Wicker Park* ☎*773/276–5640* ✉*1849 W. North Ave., Wicker Park* ☎*773/342–8684 .* ✉*2357 N. Clark St., Lincoln Park* ☎*773/404–5826* ✉*122 S. State St., Loop* ☎*312/346–3034.*

Habit. Emerging independent designers are stocked by shop owner Lindsey Boland. As most pieces are only made in small quantities, this is where to go if you don't want anyone else wearing what you are. In-house alterations are available, and some lines, including Boland's Superficial, Inc., offer made-to-order designs. ✉*1951 W. Division St., Wicker Park* ☎*773/342–0093.*

Hejfina. This lifestyle boutique carries everything the mod Wicker Parker needs to get through the day stylishly: clothes by of-the-moment designers from across the globe, custom-made furniture from local designers, and books on modern art and architecture. The store also hosts art installations and speakers on design from time to time. ✉*1529 N. Milwaukee Ave., Wicker Park* ☎*773/772–0002.*

Intermix. Label hunters were thrilled when branches of this New York boutique opened in Lincoln Park and the Gold Coast. In 2008 a much-anticipated third outpost opened in Bucktown on Damen Avenue. The latest addition will offer the same mix of designer lines like Stella McCartney, M Missoni, Mint, and Diane von Furstenberg. ✉*1633 N. Damen Ave., Bucktown* ☎*773/292–0894* ✉*40 E. Delaware Pl., Gold Coast* ☎*312/640–2922* ✉*841 W. Armitage Ave., Lincoln Park* ☎*773/404–8766.*

Marc by Marc Jacobs. Neighborhood style mavens rejoiced when this store opened in Bucktown rather than on the label-conscious Mag Mile.

7

It's a fitting locale for the fashion icon, whose whimsical, slightly off-beat designs make hipsters drool. ⊠*1714 N. Damen Ave., Bucktown* ☎*773/276–2998.*

Public I. Public I prides itself on paying attention to its customers, offering plenty of helpful suggestions about which of its smart, hip, won't-find-it-down-the-street designs work best. Their inventory

> **WORD OF MOUTH**
>
> "The T-Shirt Deli (see www.tshirt deli.com for more info) was so much fun. You get to pick out your transfer and make the shirt say whatever you want. My girls had a blast here, and the shirts are very cute."   —Iacohn

includes designs by How & Wen, Isda for Men, and Emerge London. ⊠*1923 W. Division St., Wicker Park* ☎*773/772–9088.*

Riley. Put together a polished urban look at this clean, modern space. Men's lines run the gamut from Kenneth Cole to Jet Lag, and women can pick up cute wardrobe staples like QI cashmere sweaters and Michael Stars T-Shirts. ⊠*1659 N. Damen Ave., Bucktown* ☎*773/489–0101.*

Silver Moon. Vintage wedding gowns and tuxedos are a specialty here, but you can also find less formal vintage clothing and accessories. There are also new collections from Vivienne Westwood, housewares, and custom-embellished denim for babies and small kids. ⊠*1755 W. North Ave., Bucktown* ☎*773/235–5797.*

Softcore Handbuilt. Club kids go to Softcore for funky styles from Diesel, Miss Sixty, Octopussy (the store's own label), and local designer Geoffrey Mac. ⊠*1420 N. Milwaukee Ave., Wicker Park* ☎*773/227–4314.*

The T-Shirt Deli. Order up a made-to-order T-shirt with custom iron-on letters or throwback '70s decals. You'll get your T-shirt served up on the spot, wrapped in paper like a sandwich, and packed with a bag of chips for good measure. ⊠*1739 N. Damen Ave., Bucktown* ☎*773/276–6266.*

CLOTHING FOR WOMEN

Belly Dance Maternity. The hippest moms-to-be shop here for up-to-the-minute maternity fashions by Japanese Weekend, Cadeau, and Citizens of Humanity. ⊠*1647 N. Damen Ave., Bucktown* ☎*773/862–1133.*

Beta Boutique. Janice Moskoff built a following bringing occasional sample sales to young fashionistas, and now she's opened up a permanent location to hawk finds from a huge list of designers, from Cynthia Steffe to C. Ronson. The store is open Thursday to Sunday only. ⊠*2016 W. Concord Pl., Bucktown* ☎*773/276–0905* ⊗*Closed Mon.–Wed.*

G Boutique. Here's an all-in-one stop for women planning for a little romance. There's beautiful lingerie from brands like Aubade and Cosabella, plus massage oils, books, videos, and toys. There's an 18-and-over admission policy. ⊠*2131 N. Damen Ave., Bucktown* ☎*773/235–1234.*

Helen Yi. This loftlike, minimalist boutique stocks sophisticated styles from up-and-coming designers, including Shelly Steffee and local handbag maker Susan Fitch. ⊠*1645 N. Damen Ave., Bucktown* ☎*773/252–3838.*

Jade. Former stylist and fashion writer Laura Haberman's shop stands out from the crowd of women's boutiques in the neighborhood with a carefully chosen stock of must-have cocktail dresses, tops, jeans, and accessories, all displayed against a calming jade-green backdrop. ⊠1557 N. Milwaukee Ave., Wicker Park ☎773/342–5233.

Michelle Tan. Local indie design star Michelle Tan's shop also serves as a working studio where she creates clothes with an emphasis on interesting textures, most in the $200 to $300 range. You'll also find pieces by other local designers, including some students. ⊠1872 N. Damen Ave., Bucktown ☎773/252–1888.

FOR THE MOM-TO-BE

Krista K Maternity + Baby (3530 N. Southport Ave., Lakeview, 773/248–4477).

Belly Dance Maternity (1647 N. Damen Ave., Bucktown, 773/862–1133).

Shopgirl (1206 W. Webster Ave., Lincoln Park, 773/935–7467).

★ **p. 45.** This store is a must-hit for its fashion-forward collection by a cadre of hip designers like Rebecca Taylor and Ulla Johnson. Customers from all over the city and well beyond come here for adventurous to elegant styles and prices that don't get out of hand. ⊠1643 N. Damen Ave., Bucktown ☎773/862–4523.

Robin Richman. Robin Richman showcases her famous knitwear alongside designs from lesser-known European labels and local clothes designers. Chicagoland artists contribute to the shops' eclectic displays. ⊠2108 N. Damen Ave., Bucktown ☎773/278–6150.

Saffron. Merchandise as indulgent and decadent as the namesake spice lures you into this Bucktown boutique. You'll find fluid, finely finished clothes made of natural fabrics, organically inspired jewelry, and lavish bath products. ⊠2064 N. Damen Ave., Bucktown ☎773/486–7753.

Tangerine. Popular designers, such as Three Dots and Ashley, provide the fun, feminine clothes and accessories here. There's also a good denim selection, including styles by Joe's Jeans and Serfontaine. ⊠1719 N. Damen Ave., Bucktown ☎773/772–0505.

Una Mae's. This Wicker Park favorite for vintage fashions is bursting at the seams with inventory. The bulk of the bulging stock is from the 1950s through the '80s, but there are also new lines from designers like Hot Sauce and The People Have Spoken. ⊠1422 N. Milwaukee Ave., Wicker Park ☎773/276–7002.

vive la femme. The motto is "style beyond size," and the specialty is sexy, exciting clothes for women in sizes 12 to 28 from lines including Anna Scholz, Svoboda, and Z. Cavaricci. ⊠2048 N. Damen Ave., Bucktown ☎773/772–7429.

GIFTS & FOR THE HOME **Black Walnut Gallery.** The selection of beautiful handcrafted wood furniture, sculpture, and art at this gallery got even more tempting in March 2007, when it merged with neighbor "wag artworks" to add stunning and affordable ($30 to $3,000) contemporary art to the mix. ⊠2135 W. Division St., Wicker Park ☎773/772–8870.

Casa Loca. The handsome, rustic pine furniture from Mexico and South America is carved or painted, and the collection is complemented by superb vintage and antique Mexican folk art and tinware from Guanajuato. ⊠1130 N. Milwaukee Ave., Wicker Park ☎773/278–2972.

7

Jean Alan. The offerings at this design atelier, owned by a former feature-film set decorator, range from Victorian to mid-20th-century modern. There's always a healthy assortment of sofas and chairs recovered in eclectic fabrics, plus pillows made of unusual textiles and refurbished vintage lamps with marvelous shades. ⊠*2134 N. Damen Ave., Bucktown* ☎*773/278–2345.*

Kachi Bachi. What you'll find here are Claudia Ahuile's visions for home design in the way of custom throw pillows, bedding, and window treatments, even though the name (derived from a Spanish slang term for "junk") might suggest otherwise. ⊠*2041 N. Damen Ave., Bucktown* ☎*773/645–8640.*

Lille. Hidden behind a low-profile storefront in the middle of a hectic street, Lille sequesters a carefully selected mix of home furnishings and personal accessories by well-known artists (Bodo Sperlein dinnerware) and lesser-known ones (jewelry by Jeanine Payer). ⊠*1923 W. North Ave., Bucktown* ☎*773/342–0563.*

Porte Rouge. Push through the red door for housewares and pretty painted tableware. Look for copper cookware from Mauviel, Spiegelau stemware, and Mariage Fréres teas. ⊠*1911 W. Division St., Wicker Park* ☎*773/269–2800.*

Soutache. French for "braid," Soutache is all about the extras that make life so much more interesting: high-end trimmings and embellishments like tortoise shell-and-bamboo belt buckles and purse handles; exotic ostrich plumes; suede tassels; and reams and reams of ribbon. It's up to you how to get creative with all this fun stuff. ⊠*2125 N. Damen Ave., Bucktown* ☎*773/292–9110.*

Stitch. Leather goods of every ilk—purses, travel bags, desk accessories—are the main attraction here, but you also find minimalist furniture, tabletop goods, and jewelry. ⊠*1723 N. Damen Ave., Bucktown* ☎*773/782–1570.*

SHOES **City Soles/Niche.** These two shoe stores under one roof represent a version of mecca to many shoe fiends. There's a vast selection of edgy men's and women's shoes from designers like Camper and Tsubo, plus a more upscale selection of sophisticated styles from Blay, Rebecca Sanver, and others. ⊠*2001 W. North Ave., Bucktown* ☎*773/489–2001* ⊠*3432 N. Southport Ave., Lakeview* ☎*773/665–4233.*

Grace. Shoe fanatics are drawn to this shop's selection of hard-to-find footwear—mostly European lines such as London Sole, Hunter, and Jean-Michel Cazabat. The shop carries just one size per style, so it's unlikely you'll bump into someone wearing the same kicks. Also on display are handbags from designers like Alexis Hudson, Anya Hindmarch, and Cate Adair. ⊠*1917 N. Damen Ave., Bucktown* ☎*773/384–7223.*

John Fluevog. Canadian designer Fluevog's chunky platforms and bold designs have graced the famous feet of Madonna and throngs of other loyal devotees, and they can house your toes, too, if you shop here. ⊠*1539–41 N. Milwaukee Ave., Wicker Park* ☎*773/772–1983.*

Pump. High heels are in high supply here, but so are plenty of other shoe styles from well-heeled designers like Dolce Vita, Via Spiga, and Kenneth Cole. ⊠*1659 W. Division St., Wicker Park* ☎*773/384–6750.*

CLOSE UP

Ethnic Enclaves

Chicago's ethnic neighborhoods give you the chance to shop the globe without ever leaving the city. Just southwest of the Loop is **Pilsen,** the city's largest Latino neighborhood. A walk along 18th Street between Halsted Street and Western Avenue leads you to a colorful array of bakeries, religious goods shops, and a burgeoning art-gallery district. Stretching south and east from the intersection of Cermak Road and Wentworth Avenue, **Chinatown** has shops selling Far Eastern imports, including jade and ginseng root. On the north side in **Uptown,** a heavy influx of Vietnamese and other Asian trinket shops and imported food stores around the intersection of Broadway and Argyle Street have earned the area the title of "New Chinatown." In the **Lincoln Square** neighborhood on a stretch of Lincoln Avenue between Leland and Lawrence avenues on the city's North Side, you'll still find German restaurants and stores that sell European-made health and beauty products amid the swell of newer upscale clothing and gift boutiques attracting the hip singles and young families who now call this area home. Heading east to **Andersonville,** you'll find a slew of Swedish restaurants, bakeries, and gift shops along Clark Street between Foster and Balmoral avenues, plus specialty boutiques that sell everything from fine chocolates to eclectic home furnishings. Many non–U.S. visitors make the trek to a cluster of dingy but well-stocked electronics stores on **Devon Avenue** (between Western and Washtenaw avenues) in an Indian neighborhood on the city's Far North Side. The attraction is a chance to buy electronics that run on 220 volts. Because the United States has no value-added tax, it's often cheaper for international visitors to buy here than at home. ■**TIP**➔**The same stretch of Devon Avenue is also home to a cacophony of great Indian groceries, Bollywood video stores, and fabric shops where you can while away your time.**

EYEWEAR **Red Eye.** This full-service boutique stocks a wide array of specs from the likes of Anne Klein and Armani alongside stylish newcomers such as Jai Kudo, Gant, and Skago. There's even an in-house optometrist to make sure your glasses not only look good but help you look better. ✉*1869 N. Damen Ave., Wicker Park* ☎*773/782–1660.*

LINCOLN PARK & OLD TOWN

The upscale residential neighborhood of Lincoln Park entices with its mix of distinctive boutiques and well-known national chain stores. **Armitage Avenue** between Orchard Street and Racine Avenue is a great source for of-the-moment clothing, tableware, jewelry, and gifts. There are also some good finds (lingerie, French-inspired goodies) on **Webster Avenue.** On **Halsted Street,** between Armitage Avenue and Fullerton Parkway, are chains geared to the young and thin like bebe and The Blues Jean Bar. The **Clybourn Corridor** section of this neighborhood, which runs along North Avenue and Clybourn Avenue, has become akin to a giant urban strip mall, with standbys like J. Crew (*929 W. North Ave.*) and Restoration Hardware (*938 W. North Ave.*) lining the streets. The star of the show, though, is the flagship three-story

Crate&Barrel. You'll also find plenty to buy for the little ones, from children's furniture to plush and pricey clothes and gear. Just east of the Clybourn Corridor, around the intersection of **North Avenue** and **Wells Street,** you'll find the cozy, tree-lined streets of Old Town, with upscale clothiers and accessory shops. The Lincoln Park area is easily reached by taking the Ravenswood (Brown Line) El line to the Armitage stop, or the Howard (Red) El line to Clybourn. To get to Old Town, take the Ravenswood (Brown) El line to Sedgwick.

SPECIALTY STORES

ACCESSORIES **Fabrice.** The only Fabrice boutique outside of Paris stocks an abundance of French accessories: its own line of pins, necklaces, and other jewelry inspired by the gardens of Provence, plus Longchamp handbags, pretty wraps and shawls, and bath products. ✉*1714 N. Wells St., Old Town* ☎*312/280–0011.*

Isabella Fine Lingerie. Lauren Amerine, a self-confessed lingerie addict who herself has inspired many obsessions among her loyal clientele, runs this high-end jewel of a shop. Look for affordable items from Cosabella and Le Mystere mixed in with more exclusive lines like Parah and Julianne, plus bridal pieces and swimwear. ✉*840 W. Armitage Ave., Lincoln Park* ☎*773/281–2352.*

The Left Bank. An eclectic mix of antique-style French jewelry brings a touch of Paris chic to Chicago. There's also a beautiful selection of French-theme jewelry boxes, perfume bottles, and other accessories. Owner Susan Jablonski has become known for her large assortment of bridal headpieces and tiaras, and she offers wedding-planning services as well. ✉*1155 W. Webster Ave., Lincoln Park* ☎*773/929–7422.*

★ **Mint.** Mint is like a crafts fair inside a pretty storefront, selling only items—from jewelry and purses to cards and candles—from local designers. The prices are reasonable and the selection is fun and funky, not fuddy-duddy. ✉*2150 N. Seminary Ave., Lincoln Park* ☎*773/322–2944.*

Quiltology, the Urban Quilt Space. Quilting is the new knitting for funky DIY-ers, and Colette Cogley's Lincoln Park shop stocks everything they need to keep their habit going, including designs by Amy Butler and Kaffe Fassett. Classes and workshops are available in the back-room sewing lounge, too. ✉*2625 N. Halsted St., Lincoln Park* ☎*773/880–5994.*

★ **1154 Lill Studio.** Creative types design their own handbags (from chic clutches to diaper totes) from tons of fabric and shape options at this super-popular shop housed in a pretty brownstone. Some limited-edition, ready-made bags are available, too. ✉*904 W. Armitage Ave., Lincoln Park* ☎*773/477–5455.*

BEAUTY **Aroma Workshop.** Customize lotions, massage oils, and bath salts with more than 150 essential and fragrance oils in this beauty boutique. The workshop makes its own line of facial-care products, too. ✉*2050 N. Halsted St., Lincoln Park* ☎*773/871–1985.*

Endo Exo. A favorite with gotta-have-it types, this store has vintage pharmacy cabinets filled with a well-chosen stock of trendy and hard-to-find beauty lines such as Jo Wood, Bliss, and Delux Beauty. ✉*2034*

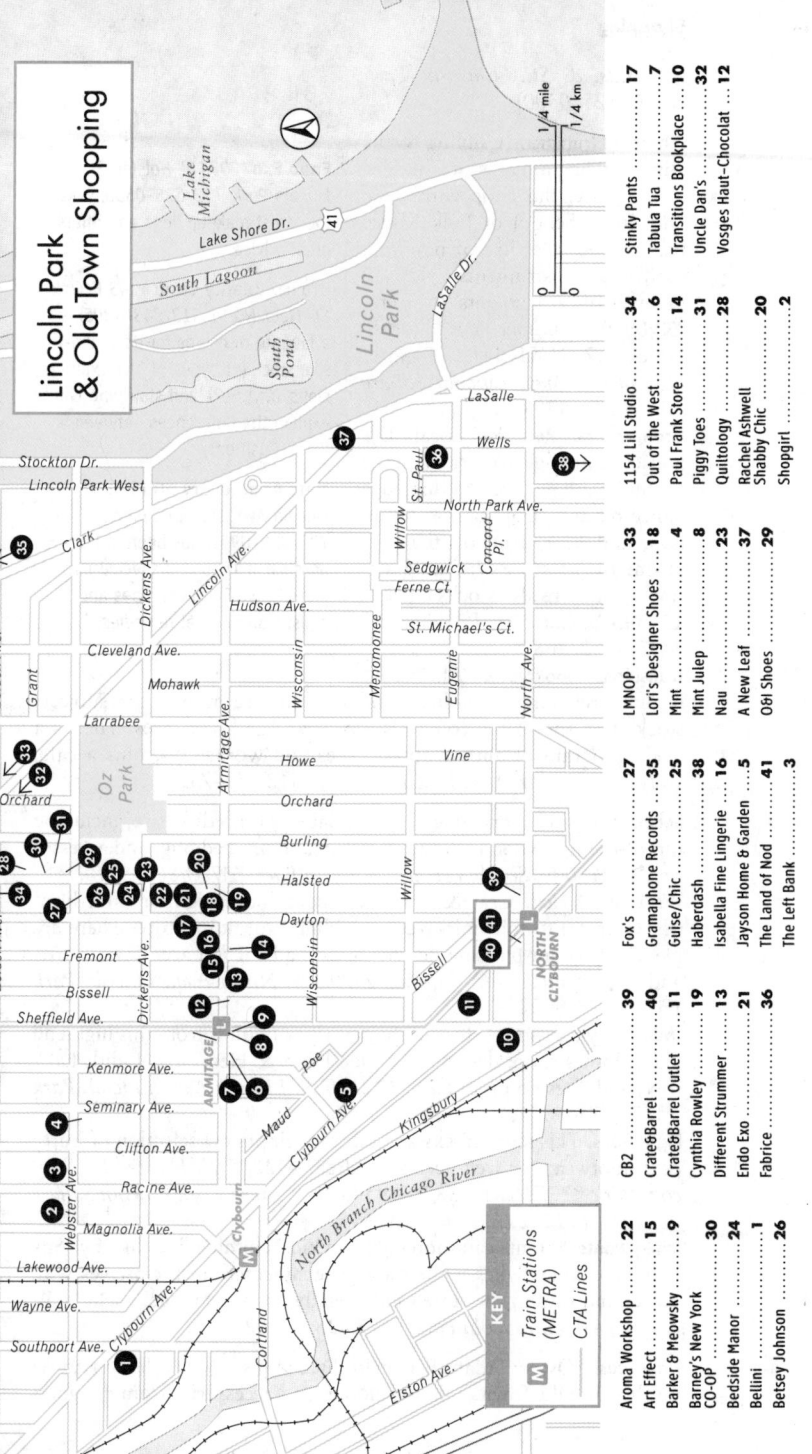

Lincoln Park & Old Town Shopping

1154 Lill Studio 34
A New Leaf 37
Aroma Workshop 22
Art Effect 15
Barker & Meowsky 9
Barney's New York CO-OP 30
Bedside Manor 24
Bellini 1
Betsey Johnson 26
CB2 39
Crate&Barrel 40
Crate&Barrel Outlet 11
Cynthia Rowley 19
Different Strummer 13
Endo Exo 21
Fabrice 36
Fox's 27
Gramaphone Records 35
Guise/Chic 25
Haberdash 38
Isabella Fine Lingerie 16
Jayson Home & Garden 5
LMNOP 33
Lori's Designer Shoes 18
Mint 4
Mint Julep 8
Nau 23
Oбi Shoes 29
Out of the West 6
Paul Frank Store 14
Piggy Toes 31
Quitology 28
Rachel Ashwell Shabby Chic 20
Shopgirl 2
Stinky Pants 17
Tabula Tua 7
Transitions Bookplace 10
Uncle Dan's 32
Vosges Haut–Chocolat 12
The Land of Nod 41
The Left Bank 3

KEY
Train Stations (METRA)
CTA Lines

1/4 mile
1/4 km

7

N. Halsted St., Lincoln Park ☎773/525–0500.

Different Strummer. A sibling to the Different Strummer store in Lincoln Square, this shop within the Old Town School of Folk Music has a good selection of new and used kids' instruments, plus all manner of instruments for rent. ✉909 W. Armitage Ave., Lincoln Park ☎773/751–3410 ✉4544 N. Lincoln Ave., Lincoln Square ☎773/751–3398.

Gramaphone Records. Local DJs and club kids go to Gramaphone to find vintage and cutting-edge dance releases, from house to hip-hop, and hear them on the spot at one of the store's listening stations. The store also stocks DJ gear. ✉2843 N. Clark St., Lincoln Park ☎773/472–3683.

Transitions Bookplace. Alternative healing, religion, mythology, and folklore are among the subjects stocked at one of the country's top New Age bookstores. There's a lively program of author appearances and workshops, plus a café. ✉1000 W. North Ave., Lincoln Park ☎312/951–7323.

Bellini. Virtually everything a stylish baby will need is here, including top-of-the-line wood bedroom furniture, luxury bedding, and accessories. ✉2100 N. Southport Ave., Lincoln Park ☎773/880–5840.

The Land of Nod. Crate&Barrel is a next-door neighbor (and business partner) to this quirky-cool children's furniture store. There are plenty of parent-pleasing designs, plus loads of fun accessories, toys, and a great music section, too. ✉900 W. North Ave., Lincoln Park ☎312/475–9903.

LMNOP. Tykes can get their posh on early with duds from this high-end kids' clothes shop; designers include Flora & Henri and Judith LaCroix, and sizes go up to an 8. ✉2570 N. Lincoln Ave., Lincoln Park ☎773/975–4055.

Piggy Toes. This store stocks a good (though pricey) selection of European footwear for well-heeled children. ✉2205 N. Halsted St., Lincoln Park ☎773/281–5583 ✉4548 N. Western Ave., Lincoln Square ☎773/878–1122.

Stinky Pants. Parents can shop high-end kids' clothing lines like Eye Spy Baby and Lucy Sykes while their progeny entertain themselves with books and toys in the store's kid-friendly "stinky lounge." ✉844 W. Armitage Ave., Lincoln Park ☎773/281–4002.

Haberdash. Owner Adam Beltzman ditched his job as a lawyer to set up shop in Old Town. Tailored clothes and accessories from designers like John Varvatos, Ted Baker, and James Perse plus leather armchairs, plasma TV, and dark-wood walls make this store decidedly masculine. ✉*1350 N. Wells St., Old Town* ☎*312/440–1300.*

CLOTHING FOR MEN & WOMEN

Barneys New York CO-OP. The CO-OP in Chicago has an urban-loft feel, an enormous inventory of designer denim, and lots of hip accessories. ✉*2209–11 N. Halsted St., Lincoln Park* ☎*773/248–0426.*

Guise/Chic. For men and women who want to look good without having to hit a dozen shops, Guise is the place. This one-stop shop stocks designer clothes from Theory, Earnest Sewn, J Brand jeans, and Filippa K. Separate salons offer shoeshines, haircuts, and barbershop-style shaves for men, and cut and color, hair extensions, and eyebrow shaping for women. Flat-screen televisions in the women's lounge are tuned to E!; in the men's, to sports channels. ✉*2128 N. Halsted St., Lincoln Park* ☎*773/929–6101.*

Out of the West. With an inventory that includes saddles, hats, and boots, there's a definite nod to urban cowboys at this Lincoln Park shop. But fashionistas won't feel left out either—especially if they're in the market for fancy-pants blue jeans from premium brands like Seven and Blue Cult. A tailor visits the store weekly to do custom alterations on jeans. ✉*1021 W. Armitage Ave., Lincoln Park* ☎*773/404–9378.*

Uncle Dan's. This is the place to go for camping, skiing, and general outdoorsy gear by brands like Marmot and The North Face. There's a good kids' selection, too. ✉*2440 N. Lincoln Ave., Lincoln Park* ☎*773/477– 1718* ✉*3551 N. Southport Ave., Lakeview* ☎*773/348–5800.*

CLOTHING FOR WOMEN

Art Effect. This modern-day general store stocks trendy clothes and accessories at approachable prices—think Michael Stars T-shirts, Weston Wear blouses, Orla Kiely babydoll dresses, and Me&Ro necklaces. There are also gifts and home furnishings ranging from candles and bath products to mortar-and-pestle sets and juicers. ✉*934 W. Armitage Ave., Lincoln Park* ☎*773/929–3600.*

Betsey Johnson. All of the bold designer's signature fun and over-the-top styles are here. ✉*2120 N. Halsted St., Lincoln Park* ☎*773/871–3961.*

Cynthia Rowley. Cynthia Rowley is a Chicago-area native, and she fills her Lincoln Park store with the exuberant, well-priced dresses, separates, and accessories that have made her so popular. ✉*808 W. Armitage Ave., Lincoln Park* ☎*773/528–6160.*

Fox's. Snap up canceled and overstocked designer clothes from the likes of Tahari and ABS at 40% to 70% discounts. New shipments come in several times a week, so there's always something new to try on. ✉*2150 N. Halsted St., Lincoln Park* ☎*773/281–0700.*

Mint Julep. Sarah Eshaghy's keen eye for style developed a loyal following at the long-popular Tribeca on the Avenue. She's outdone herself at her new Lincoln Park boutique, chock-full of fabulous fashions from the likes of Tulle, Susanna Monaco, and Shoshanna, as well as K.Amato jewelry. The best news: more than half the inventory is priced under $100, so you can stock up without breaking the bank. ✉*1013 W. Armitage Ave., Lincoln Park* ☎*773/296–2997.* ✉*3709 N. Southport Ave., Lakeview* ☎*773/472–6717.*

7

Fodor'sChoice
★ **Shopgirl.** A following of devoted customers comes here to find out what to wear next, and fall for pieces by Trina Turk, Ella Moss, and Citizens of Humanity. The owner has moved her fabulous maternity selection into this store, too. ☒*1206 W. Webster Ave., Lincoln Park* ☎*773/935–7467 or 773/935–7587.*

GIFTS **Barker & Meowsky.** This "paw firm" carries great gifts for dogs, cats, and humans. There are beautiful bowls, plush beds, picture frames, treats, and even pet massage and grooming services—just the things to get tails wagging. ☒*1003 W. Armitage Ave., Lincoln Park* ☎*773/868–0200.*

Paul Frank Store. Young fans of the designer's famous trademarked monkey, Julius, will find his likeness on stickers, slippers, and sunglasses. Scurvy, a skull and crossbones; Ellie, a pink elephant; and the designer's other kitschy characters are also well represented. ☒*851 W. Armitage Ave., Lincoln Park* ☎*773/388–3122.*

Vosges Haut-Chocolat. Local chocolatier Katrina Markoff's exotic truffles, flavored with spices like curry and ancho chili, have fans across the globe. Her ever-expanding line of goodies now includes caramels, ice cream, chocolate tortilla chips, and even yoga wear and dresses. ☒*951 W. Armitage Ave., Lincoln Park* ☎*773/296–9866* ☒*520 N. Michigan Ave., Near North* ☎*312/822–0600.*

FOR THE HOME **Bedside Manor.** Dreamland is even more inviting with these handcrafted beds and lush designer linens, many of which come in interesting jacquard weaves or are nicely trimmed and finished. ☒*2056 N. Halsted St., Lincoln Park* ☎*773/404–2020.*

Fodor'sChoice
★ **CB2.** A concept store by furniture giant Crate&Barrel, the idea is stylish, bold basics for trendy urban abodes, all sans big-ticket price tags. ☒*800 W. North Ave., Lincoln Park* ☎*312/787–8329.*

Crate&Barrel. There are plenty to "oohs" and "aahs" throughout the three floors of stylish home furnishings and kitchenware at Crate&Barrel's flagship location. There's plenty of free parking, and you can even take a break from your heavy-duty shopping at the top-floor café. ☒*850 W. North Ave., Lincoln Park* ☎*312/573–9800.*

Crate&Barrel Outlet. Around the corner from the massive outpost of the flagship store, the outlet carries odds and ends from the company's housewares and kitchen lines. Look for discounts of up to 75% on out-of-season items. ☒*1864 N. Clybourn Ave., Lincoln Park* ☎*312/787–4775.*

Jayson Home & Garden. Loaded with new and vintage European and American furnishings, this decor store carries the Mitchell Gold line. Look for oversize cupboards and armoires and decorative accessories, plus stylish garden furniture and a bevy of beautiful floral arrangements. ☒*1885 N. Clybourn Ave., Lincoln Park* ☎*773/248–8180.*

★ **A New Leaf.** You'll find one of the best selections of fresh flowers in town here. The breathtaking Wells Street space, designed by architect Cynthia Weese, is also stocked with singular antique and vintage furnishings and accessories as well as a mind-boggling selection of candles, vases, tiles, and pots. ☒*1818 N. Wells St., Old Town* ☎*312/642–*

Unpacking Crate&Barrel

Gordon and Carole Segal saw a void in the Chicago retail market in 1962, and they set out to fill it by opening the first Crate&Barrel store in an abandoned elevator factory in the then-questionable Old Town neighborhood.

"I was doing the dishes—classic Arzberg dishes we had picked up on our Caribbean honeymoon—and I said to Carole, 'How come nobody is selling this dinnerware in Chicago?'," Gordon Segal recalls. "I think we should open a store." And, as they say, the rest is history. With "more taste than money," the Segals displayed their unique housewares en masse on the crates and barrels they were shipped in, and found a niche and a name.

At a time when gas-station give-away glasses were common kitchen table fixtures, shoppers were immediately drawn to the grocery store-style displays of contemporary merchandise at reasonable prices. As the business grew, store displays became more sophisticated and the inventory more diverse.

Before the age of home-improvement cable television shows, the Segals brought accessible design into the American home. They added the Finnish fabric line Marimekko to their inventory in the late 1960s, and the bold, colorful prints became a signature style of the era.

Carole retired to raise their family, but Gordon Segal still runs the Chicago-based company they founded together 43 years ago, now a dominant home-furnishings chain with 123 stores across the United States. Always keeping his motto, "Stay humble, stay nervous," in the back of his mind, Segal has continued to fine-tune Crate&Barrel throughout its history, creating shopping environments that engage the senses. He pays close attention to the exteriors, too, focusing on building stores with architectural merit. Stores in Illinois, Pennsylvania, and Chicago have received awards for their outstanding architectural design.

The home-furnishings industry has exploded since Crate&Barrel's humble beginnings, and Segal has kept a keen eye on what interests the buying public. In 2000 Crate&Barrel launched CB2, a new concept store aimed at a young urban market with—again—a single store on Chicago's North Side. And, so that no one in the family feels left out, in 2001 Crate&Barrel formed a partnership with Land of Nod, a quirky children's furniture catalog company. They opened one store—guess where?—on Chicago's North Side to start, and have since expanded to five locations. The Segal empire just keeps growing.

–By Judy Sutton Taylor

8553 ✉1645 N. Wells St., Lincoln Park ☎312/642–1576 ✉312 S. Dearborn St., Near North ☎312/427–9097.

Rachel Ashwell Shabby Chic. Pop into this outpost (one of six nationally) of the cushy, slip-covered furniture designer. There are also pretty pastel linens and an extensive lighting collection. ✉*2146 N. Halsted St., Lincoln Park* ☎*773/327–9372.*

Tabula Tua. The colorful, contemporary, mix-and-match dishes and tabletop accessories here are worlds away from standard formal china. Other offerings include breathtaking mosaic tables handmade to order, rustic furniture crafted from old barn wood, and sleek, polished pewter pieces. ✉*1015 W. Armitage Ave., Lincoln Park* ☎*773/525–3500.*

SHOES
FodorsChoice
★

Lori's Designer Shoes. Owner Lori Andre's obsession with shoes takes her on biannual trips to Europe to scour for styles you won't likely see at department stores. The result is an inventory that many fine-footed women consider to be the best in Chicago. Shoes by designers like Gastone Lucioli, janet & janet, and better-known ones like Franco Sarto are sold at discounts of 10% to 30% in a self-serve atmosphere. Terrific handbags, jewelry, bridal shoes, and other accessories are also available. ✉*824 W. Armitage Ave., Lincoln Park* ☎*773/281–5655.*

O&I Shoes. Chic European footwear by the likes of L.A.M.B., Alexander McQueen, and Miss Sixty is sold at this shop, adjacent to swanky kids-shoe outfitter Piggy Toes. The popular store recently added men's shoes to the collection. ✉*2205 N. Halsted St., Lincoln Park* ☎*773/281–5583.*

LAKEVIEW

Lakeview, a large neighborhood just north of Lincoln Park, has spawned a number of worthwhile shopping strips, including a smattering of antiques shops around Belmont and Ashland avenues. **Clark Street** between Diversey Avenue and Addison Street has myriad clothing boutiques and specialty stores such as pet boutiques and rug dealers, as well as stores filled to the gills with Chicago Cubs paraphernalia as you approach Wrigley Field at Addison. The area farther north on **Halsted Street,** between Belmont Avenue and Addison Street, is known as Boystown; here you'll find more gift shops and boutiques, many with a gay orientation, as well as vintage-clothing and antiques stores. In West Lakeview, the latest hot spot is **Southport Avenue** between Belmont Avenue and Grace Street, where a recent onslaught of boutiques with a bent toward trendy upscale fashion has put it on the "must" list. **Broadway** between Diversey Avenue and Addison Street also claims its share of intriguing shops. The **Century Mall,** in a former movie palace at Clark Street, Broadway, and Diversey Parkway, houses some chain stores (Aveda, Victoria's Secret, Express), but has a tired feel compared with the rest of the area. To reach this neighborhood from downtown, take the 22 Clark Street bus at Dearborn Street or the 36 Broadway bus at State Street heading north. Or, take the Howard (Red Line) or Ravenswood (Brown Line) El north to the Belmont stop from downtown, which will drop you into the heart of Lakeview, near the intersection of Belmont and Sheffield avenues.

ANTIQUES DISTRICTS

BELMONT
AVENUE

Fans of Art Deco, kitchen collectibles, and bar gadgets can poke into the shops and malls lining Belmont Avenue, starting a bit west of Ashland Avenue and running to Western Avenue. You may have to scrounge around to unearth treasures in these stores, but the prices are some of the lowest in the city. The shops are usually open weekends, but may be closed on one or more weekdays. Call before making a special trip.

Blitz Tour: One-of-a-Kind Finds

Get ready for some serious spending—or at least some serious ogling. This itinerary is geared to the antiques lover in you; find exact addresses in the chapter's store listings.

Chicago tempts furniture buyers with antiques, collectibles, and architectural artifacts at prices that generally beat those on either coast. In fact, dealers from all over regularly troll these shops, which are clustered mostly in neighborhoods or malls, for stock to resell in their own shops. For a rundown on dealers, buy a copy of *Taylor's Guide to Antique Shops in Illinois & Southern Wisconsin* ($6), which is available in some bookstores and many antiques shops (to order, call ☎800/829–5677 or go to ⊕ *www. taylorsguide.com*). Many antiques districts also publish free pamphlets that list dealers in the neighborhood; look for them in the shops.

To catch the maximum number of open dealers, it's best to tackle this route after brunch on a weekend or on a Thursday or Friday. Assuming your interest runs more toward 20th-century collectibles than Biedermeier, this tour focuses mostly on the West Lakeview neighborhood (north of Lin-coln Park and west of Wrigley Field). Take the 11 Lincoln Avenue bus or a taxi to the **Chicago Antique Centre** to browse through the wares of its 35 dealers. Keep your eyes open for other antiques and vintage-clothing shops along this stretch of Lincoln Avenue. Two superb sources for adventurous, mid-20th-century, modern furnishings and collectibles are **Urban Artifacts** and **Zig Zag**. Venture farther north on Lincoln Avenue to check out the dustless vintage finds at **At Home** and the Art Deco and Art Nouveau treasures at **Smythson Yeats Antiques.**

There are three other compelling destinations for collectors that are short cab rides away. **Architectural Artifacts** is an amazing repository for statuary, garden ornaments, and the like. **Lincoln Antique Mall** stockpiles everything from kitchenware to furniture, mostly post-1920. There's also a huge selection of estate jewelry and photographs. Farthest north on the antiques trail is the **Broadway Antique Market,** with its excellent stash of mid-20th-century pieces that range from Art Deco and Arts and Crafts to modernism and beyond.

7

Antique Resources. Choice Georgian antiques are sold at fair prices. This is an excellent source for stately desks and dignified dining sets, but the true find is a huge trove—numbering more than 300—of antique crystal and gilt chandeliers from France. ⊠ *1741 W. Belmont Ave., Lakeview* ☎ *773/871–4242.*

Father Time Antiques. Father Time bills itself as the Midwest's largest restorer of vintage timepieces; it also stocks vintage Victorian and Art Deco European furniture. ⊠ *2108 W. Belmont Ave., Lakeview* ☎ *773/880–5599.*

LINCOLN AVENUE & ENVIRONS

A 1½-mi stretch of Lincoln Avenue is worth a visit for its funky antiques, collectibles, and vintage clothing. The shops start around the intersection of Lincoln Avenue and Diversey Parkway and continue until Irving Park Road. A car or the 11 Lincoln Avenue bus is the best way to navigate this area. To get the bus from downtown, take the Howard

(Red Line) or Ravenswood (Brown Line) El to the Fullerton stop; after exiting the El station, walk ½ block east to the intersection of Fullerton and Lincoln. Then catch the 11 Lincoln Avenue bus to your stop. Most of these shops are open weekends, but may be closed early in the week.

At Home. If antiques shopping can be made to feel like a modern experience, this place succeeds at it. It's clean instead of musty and is stocked with a beautiful selection of such items as armoires and vintage glassware, plus some new home accessories. ✉*3062 N. Lincoln Ave., Lakeview* ☎*773/472–0800.*

WORD OF MOUTH

"There's quite unique shopping in the Lincoln Park area with its small boutiques. Similar shopping areas radiate from Lincoln Park, such as Lakeview. Walk north along Halsted to Addison. You'll find some great vintage clothing stores. Then cross over to Broadway and head back south. Broadway has some unusual shops."

–Susie

Chicago Antique Centre. Open seven days a week, this one-stop spot houses 35 dealers on two levels, some with especially good selections of vintage dishes and jewelry. ✉*3036 N. Lincoln Ave., Lakeview* ☎*773/929–0200.*

Modlife. The emphasis here is on mid-20th-century finds from Herman Miller, Eames, Hans Olsen, and other well-known designers. You'll also find original abstract paintings and sculptures and overall affordable price points. ✉*3856 N. Lincoln Ave., Lakeview* ☎*773/868–0844.*

Smythson Yeats Antiques. An always-changing selection here includes plenty of Art Deco and Art Nouveau treasures, with an impressive selection of lamps, chandeliers, and ceramics. There are plenty of fabulous larger pieces, too—dark-wood sideboards, bookcases, and plush leather chairs. Lamp-repair service is available. ✉*3851 N. Lincoln Ave., Lakeview* ☎*773/244–6365.*

Urban Artifacts. A superb selection of furniture, lighting, and decorative accessories from the 1940s to the '70s emphasizes the industrial designs that are a popular theme in modern furnishings. ✉*2928 N. Lincoln Ave., Lakeview* ☎*773/404–1008.*

Zig Zag. Zig Zag displays a well-edited collection of pristine Art Deco and modern furnishings and jewelry. ✉*3419 N. Lincoln Ave., Lakeview* ☎*773/525–1060.*

SPECIALTY STORES

BOOKSTORES **The Bookworks.** The stock here includes more than 40,000 titles, most of them used or rare. There's an emphasis on sports (for Cubs fans strolling by from nearby Wrigley Field) and contemporary fiction. Check out the vintage-vinyl-record section. The store buys used books in good condition, too. ✉*3444 N. Clark St., Lakeview* ☎*773/871–5318.*

Powell's Bookstore. This is one of the oldest and most reliable independent bookshops around; the strength here is the section featuring art, architecture, and photography. Also check out the impressive collection of rare books. ✉*2850 N. Lincoln Ave., Lakeview* ☎*773/248–1444*

⌧*828 S. Wabash Ave., South Loop* ☎*312/341–1078* ⌧*1501 E. 57th St., Hyde Park* ☎*773/955–7780.*

Unabridged Bookstore. For more than 20 years this independent bookshop has maintained a loyal clientele who love its vast selection and dedicated staff. Known for having one of the most extensive gay and lesbian selections in the city, it also has an impressive children's section and great magazines, too. ⌧*3251 N. Broadway, Lakeview* ☎*773/883–9119.*

CLOTHING FOR MEN & WOMEN

Belmont Army Surplus. Puma, Diesel, and other funky brands get mixed in with fatigues, flak jackets, and even faux-fur coats in this neighborhood mainstay, which was forced to move to a new location by a CTA platform expansion project. Despite the name, don't expect too many bargains. ⌧*855 W. Belmont Ave., Lakeview* ☎*773/975–0626* ⌧*1318 N. Milwaukee Ave., Bucktown* ☎*773/384–8448.*

Cerulean 1. Here you'll find the latest in casual urban duds for guys and girls, including Lawd Knows, Three Dots, and Rebecca Beeson. There's a good selection of vintage T-shirts, as well as dressier options for hitting the clubs. ⌧*3657 N. Southport Ave., Lakeview* ☎*773/525–6830.*

Flirt. You'll find designs for women by Ben Sherman and Left of Center, plus the latest handbag and jewelry finds at this cute boutique. ⌧*3449 N. Southport Ave., Lakeview* ☎*773/935–4789.*

Hubba-Hubba. Flowy, feminine clothes with a retro flavor mix with vintage and modern jewelry and accessories at this packed-to-the-gills shop that feels like rummaging through your best friend's closet. ⌧*3309 N. Clark St., Lakeview* ☎*773/477–1414.*

★ **Jake.** The hip and down-to-earth owners of this ever-growing empire (it's expected to soon go national) stock men's and women's clothing by up-and-coming designers. An instant favorite from the moment it opened its doors, Jake's sister store just off the Mag Mile has the same great aesthetic, but is not as jeans-and-T-shirt heavy as the original. ⌧*3740 N. Southport Ave., Lakeview* ☎*773/929–5253* ⌧*939 N. Rush St., Near North* ☎*312/664–5533.*

Kickin'. Hip, urban women snap up their maternity wear at this new shop. There's an emphasis on workout and yoga gear. ⌧*2142 W. Roscoe St., Lakeview* ☎*773/281–6577.*

Krista K Boutique. An inventory of must-haves for women from designers like Citizens of Humanity, Theory, and Helen Wang reflects the style of the neighborhood. The shop has become the go-to spot for the latest denim trends, too. Down the street is the maternity branch, where stylish expectant moms shop a selection that includes casual non-maternity clothes with a little extra give. ⌧*3458 N. Southport Ave., Lakeview* ☎*773/248–1967* ⌧*3530 N. Southport Ave., Lakeview* ☎*773/248–4477.*

Red Head Boutique. This colorful jewel of a shop carries a limited inventory of girly clothes with a fun and funky edge, suitable for young trendoids and cool neighborhood moms alike. Look for local labels like Doris Ruth and hard-to-find ones like Beverly & Monika. ⌧*3450 N. Southport Ave., Lakeview* ☎*773/325–9898.*

Revolver Chicago. Look effortlessly rock-star cool with threads from this menswear boutique. Video games and complimentary drinks draw in even uninspired shoppers. ✉*2135 W. Belmont Ave., Lakeview* ☎*773/832–4866.*

She One. A plentiful assortment of bright T-shirts, oh-so-pretty dresses and trendy jewelry dresses the stylish young urban woman. ✉*3402 N. Southport Ave., Lakeview* ☎*773/549–9698.*

FOR THE HOME

Fodor'sChoice

★

CB2. House-proud locals with tight budgets come to this Crate&Barrel offshoot for kitchenware and accessories that look great but don't break the bank. ✉*3757 N. Lincoln Ave., Lakeview* ☎*773/755–3900.*

Equinox. Equinox literally glows from within, thanks to its Tiffany-style lamps, but the true strength here is the selection of Arts and Crafts–style art tiles and reproduction pottery. ✉*3401 N. Broadway Ave., Lakeview* ☎*773/281–9151* ✉*609 N. State St., River North* ☎*312/335–8006.*

J. Toguri Mercantile Company. This warehouse-style store carries all things Asian, including tea sets, lacquerware, kimonos, hard-to-find pots, and Japanese music. ✉*851 W. Belmont Ave., Lakeview* ☎*773/929–3500.*

FOR KIDS

Beansprout. Beansprout carries supercute kids' clothes up to size 6x for girls and 6 for boys in fabrics that won't itch, scratch, or (hopefully) become showcases for stains. ✉*3732 N. Southport Ave., Lakeview* ☎*773/472–4780.*

Little Threads. Junk Food, Oink Baby, and Zutano are just some of the funky kids' labels at this cute neighborhood shop. There's also a fun selection of children's reading material and even cool diaper bags for mom. ✉*2033 W. Roscoe St., Lakeview* ☎*773/327–9310.*

GIFTS &
GOODIES

Bourdage Pearls. Sherry Bourdage sells Chinese freshwater pearls in a staggering array of colors and styles that range from simple and inexpensive to elaborate custom designs. ✉*3530 N Southport Ave., Lakeview* ☎*773/244–1126.*

Glam to Go. The lotions and potions found here will help you stay soft and smelling good. There's also clothing by Language, Talla, Scrapbook, and others for getting glammed up. ✉*2002 W. Roscoe St., Lakeview* ☎*773/525–7004.*

Spare Parts. The selection of fine leather goods here draws on a gamut of sources, including Village Tannery, Jack Spade, and local designer Susan Fitch. Jewelry, bath and body products, and home accessories round out the selection. ✉*2947 N. Broadway, Lakeview* ☎*773/525–4242.*

Uncle Fun. The astonishing and goofy inventory of new and vintage tricks, gags, party favors, and more, delight young and old—as do the reasonable prices. ■TIP➡ **Think trendy bobble-head dolls and the Official John Travolta Picture/Postcard book.** The store is closed Monday. ✉*1338 W. Belmont Ave., Lakeview* ☎*773/477–8223.*

Waxman Candles. The candles sold here are made on the premises and come in countless shapes, colors, and scents. There's an incredible selection of holders for votives and pillars, and incense, too. ✉*3044 N. Lincoln Ave., Lakeview* ☎*773/929–3000.*

MUSIC STORE

Reckless Records. Reckless Records ranks as one of the city's leading alternative and secondhand record stores. Besides the indie offerings,

7

you can flip through jazz, classical, and soul recordings, or catch a live appearance by an up-and-comer passing through town. ✉*3161 N. Broadway, Lakeview* ☎*773/404–5080* ✉*1532 N. Milwaukee Ave., Wicker Park* ☎*773/235–3727* ✉*26 E. Madison St., Loop* ☎*312/795–0878.*

PAPER **Paper Boy.** A hip sensibility informs the cards, gift wrap, and invitations sold here by the people who bring you the quirky goods at Uncle Fun across the street. ✉*1351 W. Belmont Ave., Lakeview* ☎*773/388–8811.*

WORTH A SPECIAL TRIP

ANTIQUES & COLLECTIBLES

Architectural Artifacts. The selection matches the warehouse proportions here. The mammoth two-story space houses oversize garden ornaments (arbors, benches), statuary, iron grills, fixtures, and decorative tiles. Architectural fragments—marble, metal, wood, terra-cotta—hail from American and European historic buildings. ✉*4325 N. Ravenswood Ave., Ravenswood* ☎*773/348–0622.*

★ **Broadway Antique Market.** More than 75 hand-picked dealers, plus quality that is more carefully monitored than at most malls, make it worth the trek to the Broadway Antique Market, affectionately called BAM by its loyal fans. Mid-20th century is the primary emphasis, but items range from Arts and Crafts and Art Deco to Heywood-Wakefield. Display is the market's strong suit—the furniture, jewelry, and bibelots are wonderfully presented. The building itself is a prime example of Deco architecture; it's near the Thorndale stop on the Red Line. The Edgewater Antique Mall (6314 N. Broadway), which specializes in 20th-century goods, is a couple of blocks north. ✉*6130 N. Broadway, Edgewater* ☎*773/743–5444.*

Lincoln Antique Mall. Dozens of dealers carrying antiques and collectibles share this large space. There's a good selection of French and mid-20th-century modern furniture, plus estate jewelry, oil paintings, and photographs, but you can find virtually anything and everything here. ✉*3115 W. Irving Park Rd., Northwest Side* ☎*773/604–4700.*

★ **Salvage One.** An enormous warehouse chock-full of stained leaded glass, garden ornaments, fireplace mantels, bathtubs, bars, and other architectural artifacts draws creative home remodelers and restaurant designers from around the country. ■TIP→ **This is the place to hunt for all kinds of treasures, from vintage dental chairs to Paris street lamps.** ✉*1840 W. Hubbard St., Ukrainian Village* ☎*312/733–0098.*

APOTHECARY

★ **Merz Apothecary.** This old-fashioned druggist stocks all manner of homeopathic and herbal remedies, as well as a great selection of hard-to-find European toiletries, cosmetics, candles, and natural laundry products. It's closed Sunday. There's an outlet in the Macy's on State Street as well. ✉*4716 N. Lincoln Ave., Lincoln Square* ☎*773/989–0900.*

AUCTIONS

Susanin's Auctioneers and Appraisers. Live, usually themed, sales occur on Saturday mornings in a 35,000-square-foot location in the South Loop. Preview items are also displayed on the floor for immediate sale at a set price. Preview hours are Monday through Saturday from 10 AM to 5 PM. ⊠*900 S. Clinton St., South Loop* ☎*312/832–9800.*

BOOK & MUSIC STORES

Afrocentric Bookstore. Owner Desiree Sanders's store is dedicated entirely to African-American literature, and the store hosts many notable African-American speakers. ⊠*4655 S. King Dr., Bronzeville* ☎*773/924–3966.*

Women & Children First. This feminist bookstore 6½ mi north of the Loop stocks fiction and nonfiction, periodicals, journals, small-press publications, and a strong selection of gay and lesbian titles. The children's section has a great array of books, all politically correct. ⊠*5233 N. Clark St., Andersonville* ☎*773/769–9299.*

FACTORY OUTLETS & OFF-PRICE STORES

Mark Shale Outlet. Unsold men's and women's clothing from Mark Shale stores is available here for 30% to 70% less than the original retail price. In a strip shopping center about 2¼ mi northwest of the Loop, this outlet stocks corporate and weekend clothing from the likes of Polo and Joseph Abboud. ⊠*2593 N. Elston Ave., Logan Square* ☎*773/772–9600.*

FOR HOME & GARDEN

A Cooler Planet. Sisters Heidi Bailey and Krista White research every item they carry in their "whole lifestyle" shop. The result is a selection of attractive, practical, and guilt-free goods made from fairly traded, organic, and sustainable materials, many of which are locally made. Displays take you from morning (natural bath products, Blue Canoe yoga wear) to night (organic cotton bedding, reclaimed wood beds). ⊠*2211 W. Roscoe St., Roscoe Village* ☎*773/248–1110.*

Rotofugi. A toy store for grown-up kids, Rotofugi specializes in artist-created, limited-edition toys considered art (not playthings) by customers and owners alike. You'll find dozens of specialty lines from the United States, China, and Japan, like CiBoys Mini Destroyers and toys by H. Moto. The store also hosts a series of revolving gallery exhibitions. ⊠*1953 W. Chicago Ave., Ukrainian Village* ☎*312/491–9501.*

Sprout Home. If your tastes run toward modern furnishings, you'll drool over every nook and cranny of this store, which sells lines like Vessel, Pure, and Thomas Paul for your indoor life, plus unusual plants and gardening products for your outdoor one. ⊠*745 N. Damen Ave., Ukrainian Village* ☎*312/226–5950.*

HATS

Optimo Hat Co. One of the last stores of its kind, Optimo makes high-end custom straw and felt hats for men in an atmosphere that evokes 1930s and '40s haberdashery. The store also offers a complete line of hat services, from cleaning and blocking to repairs. ⊠*10215 S. Western Ave., Beverly* ☎*773/238–2999.*

WESTERN

Alcala's Western Wear. Alcala stocks more than 10,000 pairs of cowboy boots—many in exotic skins—for men, women, and children. About 2½ mi west of Michigan Avenue, it's a bit out of the way, but the amazing array of Stetson hats and rodeo gear makes this a must-see for cowboys, caballeros, and country-and-western dancers. ⊠ *1733 W. Chicago Ave., Ukrainian Village* ☎ *312/226–0152.*

Entertainment

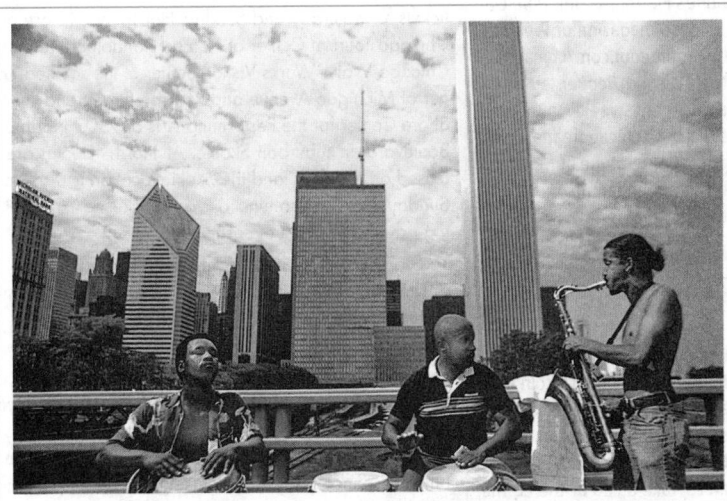

WORD OF MOUTH

"Jazz Showcase is the place to go to for serious jazz. It's a club, not a bar and they don't pack the place—nearly everyone has a seat . . . a lot of them dress up for a night out. I've been to the Showcase and been seated next to Ramsey Lewis; I think dressing well was part of the reason, since they didn't know my sparkling personality."

—patg

ENTERTAINMENT PLANNER

Find out What's Going On

To find out what's happening in the Windy City, check out the following: the *Chicago Tribune*'s Metromix.com, *Time Out Chicago* magazine or Web site (www.timeout.com/chicago), the *Chicago Reader*, an alternative newsweekly and Web site (www.chicagoreader.com), and Centerstage.net, which has a calendar of music and theater events.

Getting There

Parking in North Side neighborhoods, particularly Lincoln Park and Lakeview, is increasingly scarce, even on weeknights. If you're going out in these areas, take a cab or the El. The Red, Brown, and Blue lines will get you within a few blocks of most major entertainment destinations downtown and on the North and Near Northwest sides. If you do decide to drive, use the curbside valet service available at many restaurants and clubs for about $6 to $7. If you're headed to the South Side, be cautious about public transportation late at night. It's best to drive or cab it here.

Get Tickets

You can save money on seats at **Hot Tix** (☎ *www.hottix. org*, for listings and booth information only), where unsold tickets are available, usually at half price (plus a service charge) on the day of performance; you won't know what's available until that day. On Friday, however, you can buy tickets for Saturday and Sunday. Hot Tix booths are at the Chicago Tourism Center at 72 East Randolph Street; the Chicago Water Works Visitor Center at the southeast corner of Michigan Avenue and Pearson Street; and the North Shore Center for the Performing Arts at 9501 North Skokie Boulevard, in suburban Skokie. All Hot Tix booths are closed on Monday, and the Skokie location is also closed Sunday. Hot Tix also functions as a Ticketmaster outlet, selling advance, full-price, cash-only tickets.

You can charge full-price tickets over the phone or online at **Ticketmaster** (☎ *312/559–1212 for rock concerts and general-interest events, 312/902–1500 arts line* ⊕ *www. ticketmaster.com*).

For hot, sold-out shows, such as performances by the Chicago Symphony Orchestra or the Lyric Opera of Chicago, call a day or two before the show to see if there are any subscriber returns. Another option is to show up at the box office on concert day—a surprising number of people strike it lucky with on-the-spot tickets due to cancellations.

Small fees can have big payoffs! Many of the smaller neighborhood street festivals (there are hundreds in summer) request $5 to $10 donations upon entry, but it's often worth the expense: big-name bands are known to take the stage of even the most under-publicized festivals. For moment-to moment festival coverage, check out ⊕ *www.metromix.com*.

Don't Light Up

In January 2008, a statewide smoking ban took effect that prohibits lighting up in any public building. While most Chicagoans are breathing easier and relishing the new smoke-free scene, the throngs of smokers huddled outside nightclubs and bars may not agree, especially when temperatures drop below freezing.

Festivals

The **Chicago Humanities Festival** (☎ *312/661–1028* ⊕ *www.chfestival.org*) held the first two weeks of November, brings internationally renowned artists, authors, and cultural critics to various venues across the city for a series of lectures, films, and performances.

For the first two weeks in October, the **Chicago International Film Festival** (☎ *312/332–3456* ⊕ *www.chicagofilmfestival.org*) screens more than 100 films, including premieres of Hollywood films, international releases, documentaries, short subjects, animation, videos, and student films. Movie stars usually make appearances at the opening events.

Grant Park Music Festival (☎ *312/742–7638* ⊕ *www.grantparkmusicfestival.com*), a program of the Chicago Park District, gives free concerts June through August in the spectacular new Frank Gehry–designed Jay Pritzker Pavilion in Millennium Park. Tote along dinner and make a full night of the performance by the superb Grant Park Orchestra and Chorus. Concerts are usually Wednesday, Friday, and Saturday evenings.

The annual **Pitchfork Festival** (☎ *No phone* ⊕ *www.pitchforkmusicfestival.com*) is a three-day concert spotlighting emerging bands. It has also drawn veterans like Sonic Youth, Public Enemy, and Yoko Ono. It's held every July in Union Park on the Near West Side.

In summer you can enjoy the Chicago Symphony at the **Ravinia Festival** (☎ *847/266–5100* ⊕ *www.ravinia.org*) in Highland Park, a 25-mi train trip from Chicago. The park is lovely, and lawn seats are a fun, low-cost alternative to the pavilion. Spread a blanket and enjoy music under the stars. Ravinia also draws crowds with jazz, pop, and dance concerts.

In early June the **Chicago Blues Festival** (☎ *312/744–3370* ⊕ *www.chicagobluesfestival.org*), the largest free blues festival in the world, rocks the city. Blues legends such as B.B. King, Koko Taylor, and Buddy Guy have all headlined the festival, and blues lovers from around the world— most notably Chuck Berry and Keith Richards—have been known to attend (and sometimes take the stage).

Labor Day weekend blasts off with the unmistakable sounds of the **Chicago Jazz Festival** (☎ *312/744–3370*). Set in Grant Park, the four-day festival offers not only a prime lakefront locale, but also free performances by local, national, and international musicians and special tributes to jazz legends.

Raves & Faves

Pointe of Pride: Joffrey Ballet of Chicago

Most Wanted Tickets: Lyric Opera of Chicago

Hits Closest to Home: Steppenwolf Theatre Company

Chicest Sidewalk Café: Cru Café and Wine Bar

Sharpest Wits: The Second City

Hours

Live music starts around 9 PM at bars around town. If you want to guarantee a seat, arrive well before the band's scheduled start and stake out a spot.

Bars close at 2 AM Friday and 3 AM Saturday. A few dance clubs and late-night bars remain open until 4 AM or 5 AM.

Curtain calls for performances are usually at 7:30 or 8 PM.

8

Updated by
Heidi Moore

CHICAGO'S ARTS AND NIGHTLIFE SCENE is as vivacious and diverse as its neighborhoods. Sing along with a biographical musical at Black Ensemble Theater to the north or zip over to Lincoln Park's renowned Steppenwolf Theatre, where you just might run into longtime ensemble member John Malkovich. Head for the Loop, where renowned companies such as the Lyric Opera and the Joffrey Ballet hold court. And remember that this is the city that gave birth to the often-raucous "poetry slam" at the Green Mill jazz club.

Nighttime entertainment options before and after hours are infinite—as long as you're willing to explore. Sip an imported Belgian beer at Hopleaf, a cozy North Side tavern, or tap into your wild side at a downtown dance club such as Le Passage. And we can't forget to mention comedy: Second City has been unleashing top comedic talents, including Stephen Colbert, Mike Myers, and Tina Fey, for decades.

GREAT PERFORMANCES

If you're even mildly interested in the performing arts, Chicago has the means to put you in your seat—be it floor, mezzanine, or balcony. Just pick your preference (theater, dance, or symphony/orchestra), and let Chicago's impressive body of artists do the rest. From critically acclaimed big names to fringe groups that specialize in experimental work, there truly is a performance art for everyone.

Ticket prices vary wildly, depending on whether you're seeing a high-profile group or venturing into more obscure territory. Chicago Symphony tickets range from $15 to $200, the Lyric Opera from $30 to $180 (if you can get them). Smaller choruses and orchestras charge from $10 to $30; watch the listings for free performances. Commercial theater ranges from $15 to $75; smaller experimental ensembles might charge $5, $10, or pay-what-you-can. Movie prices range from $9 for first-run houses to as low as $1.50 at some suburban second-run houses.

■ TIP→ For free, live music in summer, head downtown to the classically oriented Grant Park Music Fest and the jam-packed Chicago Blues and Chicago Jazz festivals. Held at the visually stunning Millennium Park and Grant Park, there's no cheaper way to experience some of the best sights and sounds Chicago has to offer. See the Festivals section in the Planner for more information.

TOP 5 PERFORMANCES

Joffrey Ballet. Fine-tuned performances, such as the glittering production of *The Nutcracker,* make this Chicago's premier classical-dance company. Treat yourself to one of several annual performances at the Auditorium Theatre and help celebrate more than 50 seasons of superb ballet. ☎*312/739–0120* ⊕*www.joffrey.com.*

Lookingglass Theatre Company. Marvel at offbeat and fantastically acrobatic performances inside the belly of the historic Chicago Water Works building. The company's physically and artistically daring works incorporate theater, dance, music, and circus arts. ☎ *312/337–0665* ⊕ *www. lookingglasstheatre.org.*

Fodor'sChoice **Steppenwolf.** The alumni roster speaks for itself: John Malkovich, Gary
★ Sinise, Joan Allen, and Laurie Metcalf all honed their chops with this troupe. The company's trademark cutting-edge acting style and consistently successful productions have won national acclaim. ☎ *312/335– 1650* ⊕ *www.steppenwolf.org.*

☾ **Chicago Symphony Orchestra.** Two internationally celebrated conductors, two in-house award-winning composers, and more than 150 magnificent performances a year make the Chicago Symphony Orchestra a musical tour de force. The impressive annual roster offers regular concerts and special theme series including classical, chamber, and children's concerts. Tickets are sometimes scarce, but they do become available; call or check the Web site for status updates. If you buy your tickets online, click on the "Know Your Seats" section, where you can see photos of the views of the stage from different seats. ☎ *312/294– 3000 or 800/223–7114* ⊕ *www.cso.org* ☾ *Sept.–June.*

★ **Lyric Opera of Chicago.** The big voices of the opera world star in these top-flight productions. This is one of the top two opera companies in America today. Don't worry about understanding German or Italian; English translations are projected above the stage. All of the superb performances have sold out for more than a dozen years, and close to 90% of all Lyric tickets go to subscribers—the key to getting in is to call the Lyric in early August when individual tickets first go on sale. ☎ *312/332–2244* ⊕ *www.lyricopera.org* ☾ *Sept.–Mar.*

8

BEAUTIFUL VOICES: HIGHLY RECOMMENDED VOCAL PERFORMANCES

From a cappella to opera, the City of Big Shoulders has some of the nation's top vocal groups. Treat the kids to a sprightly concert by the Chicago Children's Choir or hear the sacred sounds of Bella Voce reverberate from the walls of a gorgeous church. The following are our picks for the most beautiful voices in the city.

CHORAL & CHAMBER GROUPS

Apollo Chorus of Chicago (☎ *312/427–5620* ⊕ *www.apollochorus.org*), formed in 1872, is one of the country's oldest oratorio societies. Don't miss the annual Handel's *Messiah* if you're here in December. Otherwise, the group performs various choral classics throughout the year at area churches.

Bella Voce (☎ *312/479–1096* ⊕ *www.bellavoce.org*). "Beautiful voices," indeed. Formerly known as His Majestie's Clerkes, the 20-person a cappella group performs a variety of sacred and secular music, including everything from early music to works by living composers. Concerts are often held in churches throughout the city, providing a powerful acoustical and visual accompaniment to the music. The season runs October through May.

☾ A performance by the **Chicago Children's Choir** (☎312/849–8300 ⊕*www. ccchoir.org*) is the closest thing we can imagine to hearing angels sing. Its members—ages 8 to 18—are culled from a broad spectrum of racial, ethnic, and economic groups. Performances, selected from an international music base, take place year during the holiday season and in May. Other concerts are scheduled periodically, sometimes in the Chicago Cultural Center's Preston Bradley Hall.

Take a step back in time with **Music of the Baroque** (☎*312/551–1414* ⊕*www.baroque.org*), one of the Midwest's leading music ensembles specializing in baroque and early classical music. See one of seven yearly programs at either Millennium Park's Harris Theater or one of several beautiful Chicago-area churches. Performances run from September to May.

The small but mighty **Oriana Singers** (☎*773/262–4558* ⊕*www.oriana. org*) are an outstanding a cappella sextet with an eclectic early, classical, and jazz repertoire. The close-knit traveling group performs from September to June, periodically in conjunction with Joffrey Ballet and other Chicago-area groups.

OPERA

Chicago Opera Theater (☎*312/704–8414* ⊕*www.chicagooperatheater. org*) shrugs off esoteric notions of opera, preferring to make productions that are accessible to aficionados and novices alike. The production of *Nixon in China,* a contemporary American opera detailing conversations between the former U.S. President and Henry Kissinger (among others), is a shining example of the company's open-mindedness toward the operatic canon. From innovative versions of traditional favorites to important lesser-known works, the emphasis is on both theatrical and musical aspects. Fear not—performances are sung in English, or in Italian with English supertitles projected above the stage. They're held at the Harris Theater for Music and Dance in Millennium Park.

Light Opera Works (☎*847/869–6300* ⊕*www.light-opera-works.org*) favors the satirical tones of the distinctly British Gilbert and Sullivan operettas, but takes on frothy Viennese, French, and other light operettas and American musicals from June to early January. Performances take place in Evanston, just north of the city and easily accessible by train or the El line.

HIGHLY RECOMMENDED DANCE & THEATER TROUPES

Chicago's reputation as a dance and theatrical powerhouse stems from its impressive roster of small, independent companies that produce every type of work you could imagine, from jazz-inflected ballets to avant-garde musicals. The groups and venues listed here are known for consistently interesting work, and a few have gained national reputations. Be open-minded when you're choosing a show; even a group you've never heard of may be harboring one or two underpaid geniuses.

The Reader carries complete dance and theater listings, plus reviews of the more avant-garde shows.

DANCE

Athenaeum Theatre (✉*2936 N. Southport Ave., Lakeview* ☎*773/935–6860* ⊕*www.athenaeumtheatre.com*) hosts innovative, small dance companies and the fall series Dance Chicago, which features innovative choreography from a wide range of Chicago dance companies.

The Dance Center of Columbia College Chicago (✉*1306 S. Michigan Ave., South Loop* ☎*312/344–8300* ⊕*www.colum.edu/dancecenter*) presents thought-provoking fare with leading national and international contemporary-dance artists.

Hubbard Street Dance Chicago (☎*312/850–9744* ⊕*www.hubbardstreetdance.com*), Chicago's most notable success story in dance, exudes a jazzy vitality that has made it extremely popular. The style mixes classical-ballet techniques, theatrical jazz, and contemporary dance.

Luna Negra Dance Theater (☎*312/337–6882* ⊕*www.lunanegra.org*) has rapidly become one of Chicago's standout dance troupes, staging highly original performances by Latino choreographers, including its Cuban-born founder and artistic director Eduardo Vilaro.

Muntu Dance Theatre of Chicago (☎*773/602–1135* ⊕*www.muntu.com*) showcases dynamic interpretations of contemporary and traditional African and African-American dance. Artistic director Amaniyea Payne travels to Africa to learn traditional dances and adapts them for the stage.

Trinity Irish Dance Co. (☎*773/529–4822* ⊕*www.trinity-dancers.com*), founded long before *Riverdance,* promotes traditional and progressive Irish dancing. In addition to the world-champion professional group, you can also catch performances by younger dancers enrolled in the Trinity Academy of Irish Dance.

THEATER

About Face Theatre (☎*773/784–8565* ⊕*www.aboutfacetheatre.com*) is the city's best-known gay, lesbian, bisexual, and transgender performing group, which in its short history has garnered awards for original works, world premieres, and adaptations presented in larger theaters like Steppenwolf and the Goodman.

Bailiwick Repertory Theatre (✉*1229 W. Belmont Ave., Lakeview* ☎*773/883–1090* ⊕*www.bailiwick.org*) stages new and classical material at its namesake Arts Center. Its Pride Performance series, held every summer, focuses on plays by gays and lesbians.

★ **Black Ensemble Theater** (✉*4520 N. Beacon St., Ravenswood* ☎*773/769–4451* ⊕*www.blackensembletheater.org*) has a penchant for long-running musicals based on popular African-American icons. Founder and executive producer Jackie Taylor has written and directed such hits as *The Jackie Wilson Story* and *The Other Cinderella.*

★ **Chicago Shakespeare Theater** (⊠*800 E. Grand Ave., Near North* ☎*312/595–5600* ⊕*www.chicagoshakes.com*) devotes its considerable talents to keeping the Bard's flame alive in the Chicago area, with at least three plays a year. The best part? The Courtyard Theater, on Navy Pier, has sparkling views of the city, and seats are never farther than 30 feet from the thrust stage.

City Lit Theatre (⊠*1020 W. Bryn Mawr Ave., Edgewater* ☎773/293–3682 ⊕*www.citylit.org*) produces notable staged readings and full productions of famous literary works—by the likes of Henry James, Alice Walker, and Raymond Carver—as well as original material with a literary bent.

Collaboraction (⊠*437 N. Wolcott Ave., Ukrainian Village* ☎312/226–9633 ⊕*www.collaboraction.org*) lets actors, artists, and musicians share the stage together in an experimental free-for-all that puts the "fun" in dysfunctional. Of its several performances a year, we recommend Sketchbook—a series of 15 to 20 seven-minute-long plays—for its color and energy.

ETA Creative Arts Foundation (⊠*7558 S. Chicago Ave., Grand Crossing* ☎773/752–3955 ⊕*www.etacreativearts.org*), a South Side performing-arts center, has established a strong presence for African-American theater. In addition to showcasing new works by black playwrights, the space is home to an art gallery and a library. The best way to get here is by taxi.

Neo-Futurists (⊠*5153 N. Ashland Ave., Uptown* ☎773/275–5255 ⊕*www.neofuturists.org*) perform their long-running, late-night hit *Too Much Light Makes the Baby Go Blind* in a space—oddly enough—above a funeral home. The piece is a series of 30 ever-changing plays performed in 60 minutes; the order of the plays is chosen by the audience. In keeping with the spirit of randomness, the admission price is set by the roll of a die, plus $7.

Fodor'sChoice **Redmoon Theater** (☎*312/850–8440* ⊕*www.redmoon.org*) tells imagi-
★ native, almost magical stories that weave together puppetry and live action. The company's annual outdoor spectacle series stages madcap theater in unlikely places, from community parks to a lagoon. The series usually takes place in the fall, but experimental theater would be nothing if not unpredictable, so be sure to call for confirmation. Other performances are held in a West Side warehouse known as Redmoon Central.

★ **Victory Gardens Theater** (⊠*2433 N. Lincoln Ave., Lincoln Park* ☎773/871–3000 ⊕*www.victorygardens.org*) is known for its workshop productions and Chicago premieres. After buying the landmark Biograph Theater (site of John Dillinger's infamous demise) in 2006, the company stages all its productions in the impressive 299-seat proscenium-thrust house. Victory Gardens' original theater, now called the Greenhouse, hosts plays by local production companies on four stages.

CINEMATHEQUE

The rowdy crowd at **Brew and View** comes for cheap flicks—both newer releases and cult faves—and beer specials. ✉ *Vic Theatre* ☎ *773/929-6713* ⊕ *www.brewview.com*.

For a change of scenery, watch current and classic films under the stars at the **Chicago Outdoor Film Festival,** which runs July through August in Grant Park on Tuesday nights. ☎ *312/742-7529*.

Facets Cinematheque shows independent and art films in its cinema and video theater. ☎ *773/281-4114* ⊕ *www.facets.org*.

Gene Siskel Film Center screens new releases from around the globe and revivals of cinematic classics; the best part is that filmmakers often make appearances at screenings. ☎ *312/846-2600* ⊕ *www.artic.edu/webspaces/siskelfilmcenter*.

If you love old theaters, old movies, and ghosts (rumor has it the theater is haunted by the spirit of its original manager), don't miss a trip to the **Music Box Theatre.** ☎ *773/871-6604* ⊕ *www.musicboxtheatre.com*.

For IMAX and OMNIMAX theaters, go to the **Museum of Science and Industry** (☎ *773/684-1414* ⊕ *www.msichicago.com*) or the **Navy Pier** (☎ *312/595-5629* ⊕ *www.navypier.com*).

AFTER DARK

Chicago's entertainment varies from loud and loose to sophisticated and sedate. You'll find classic Chicago corner bars in most neighborhoods, along with trendier alternatives like wine bars and lounges. The strains of blues and jazz provide much of the backbeat to the city's groove, and an alternative country scene is flourishing. As far as dancing is concerned, the action has switched from cavernous clubs to smaller spots with DJs spinning dance tunes; there's everything from hip-hop to swing. Wicker Park and Bucktown have the hottest nightlife, but prime spots such as Sound-Bar and Le Passage are spread throughout the city.

The Chicago Reader (distributed midweek in bookstores, record shops, and other city establishments) is your best guide to the entertainment scene. This free weekly has comprehensive, timely listings and reviews. Another reliable weekly is *Time Out Chicago* magazine. The Friday editions of the *Chicago Tribune* and *Chicago Sun-Times* are also good sources of information. Daily updates on happenings around town are listed in the *Chicago Tribune's* sister paper, *RedEye*, or on the Web at ⊕ *www.metromix.com*.

The list of blues and jazz clubs includes several South Side locations: be cautious about transportation here late at night, because some of these neighborhoods can be unsafe. Drive your own car or ask the bartender to call you a cab.

CHECK IT OUT

For complete music and theater listings, check two weeklies, *The Chicago Reader* and *TimeOut Chicago*, both published midweek; the Friday and Sunday editions of the *Chicago Tribune* and *Chicago Sun-Times*; and the monthly *Chicago* magazine.

If you're interested in Broadway-scale shows, contact the following theaters to see what's playing while you're in town.

Auditorium Theatre of Roosevelt University (☎ 312/922-2110 ⊕ www.auditoriumtheatre.org).

Chicago Theatre (☎ 312/462-6300 ⊕ www.thechicagotheatre.com).

Goodman Theatre (☎ 312/443-3800 ⊕ www.goodman-theatre.org).

Ford Center for the Performing Arts/Oriental Theatre (☎ 312/782-2004 or 312/902-1400 ⊕ www.broadwayinchicago.com).

LaSalle Bank Theatre (☎ 312/902-1400 or 312/977-1700 ⊕ www.broadwayinchicago.com).

For other performances, check out:

Athenaeum Theatre (☎ 773/935-6860 ⊕ www.athenaeumtheatre.com).

Briar Street Theatre (☎ 773/348-4000 or 800/258-3626).

Cadillac Palace Theatre (☎ 312/977-1700 ⊕ www.broadwayinchicago.com).

Drury Lane Theatre Water Tower Place (☎ 312/642-2000 ⊕ www.drurylanewatertower.com).

Joan W. and Irving B. Harris Theater for Music and Dance (☎ 312/334-7777 ⊕ www.harristheaterchicago.org).

Royal George Theatre Center (☎ 312/988-9000 ⊕ www.theroyalgeorgetheatre.com).

Storefront Theater at Gallery 37 Center for the Arts (☎ 312/742-8497 ⊕ www.dcatheater.org).

Theatre Building (☎ 773/327-5252 ⊕ www.theatrebuildingchicago.org).

Theatre on the Lake (☎ 312/742-7994 ⊕ www.chicagoparkdistrict.com).

For concerts, try the following halls:

Chicago Cultural Center (☎ 312/346-3278 or 312/744-6630 ⊕ www.cityofchicago.org).

Mandel Hall at the University of Chicago (☎ 773/702-7300 or 773/702-8068).

Newberry Library (☎ 312/943-9090 ⊕ www.newberry.org).

BARS

Chicago bars—whether they're sports bars, wine bars, neighborhood bars, or even trendy bars—are surprisingly accessible. With few exceptions, snobbishness and exclusivity are not tolerated throughout the scene, so bring your ID (many places card at the door), pocket some cash, and join the party!

■ TIP → **If you're sticking to downtown and North Side bars, it's relatively safe to patronize public transportation. But if you're planning on staying out past midnight, we suggest taking a cab home.**

LOOP, SOUTH LOOP & WEST LOOP

Sleek and sexy wine bars and lounges light up Chicago's core business district after work and on weekends. Beware: downtown bars are seldom budget-friendly (but often worth the money).

Encore (✉ *171 W. Randolph St., Loop* ☎ *312/338–3788*) is a jazzed-up hotel lounge sandwiched between the Cadillac Palace Theatre and the Hotel Allegro. Clubby seating and a classic cocktail menu make it an appealing downtown destination for post-dinner or -theater drinks, a light bite, and conversation.

Fulton Lounge (✉ *955 W. Fulton Market, West Loop* ☎ *312/942–9500*) is largely responsible for Fulton Market District's flourishing nightlife scene. The stylish lounge is all about clean-lined and understated elegance, from the slender bar right down to the low-slung swivel chairs and seasonal martinis. A sophisticated crowd mingles on the patio in summer months.

Ghost Bar (✉ *440 W. Randolph St., West Loop* ☎ *312/575–9900*) is a sexy downtown space perched above the restaurant Nine. Cool and futuristic, with cushy vinyl banquettes and designer seating, the bar is white as a, well, you know what, and the muted lighting casts the fashion-conscious crowd in silhouette.

Kitty O'Shea's (✉ *Chicago Hilton and Towers, 720 S. Michigan Ave., South Loop* ☎ *312/922–4400*), a handsome room in the Chicago Hilton and Towers, is an authentic Emerald Isle pub with all things Irish, including live music seven nights a week, beer, food, and bar staff.

The Tasting Room (✉ *1415 W. Randolph St., Loop* ☎ *312/942–1313*) makes the short list of nightspots where Chicagoans take guests they want to impress. This two-story wine bar has a casual, loft-chic look and sweeping skyline views. More than 100 wines are poured by the glass or flight, and over 300 by the bottle. Cheese, caviar, and other light bites are the perfect complement. If you love the vintage you taste here, buy a bottle to take home at the adjacent wine shop, Randolph Wine Cellars.

Whiskey Blue(✉ *172 W. Adams St., Loop* ☎ *312/782–4933*), inside the W Hotel–City Center, attracts a sophisticated crowd. The sleek, dimly lighted lounge is outfitted with leather chairs, mohair banquettes, and low-slung tables, which encourage leaning in close over an excellent martini.

NEAR NORTH & RIVER NORTH

The famous Chicago bar scene known as **Rush Street** has faded into the mists of time, although the street has found resurgent energy with the opening of a string of upscale restaurants and outdoor cafés. For the vestiges of the old Rush Street, continue north to trendy **Division Street,** between Clark and State streets. The crowd here consists mostly of suburbanites and out-of-towners on the make. The bars are crowded and noisy. Among the better-known singles' bars are **Butch McGuire's** (✉ *20 W. Division St., Near North* ☎ *312/337–9080*), the **Lodge** (✉ *21*

CLASSIC CHICAGO SPOTS

Imbibe your way through a history lesson at these Chicago institutions.

The Omni Ambassador East's glamorous **Pump Room** (✉ *1301 N. State Pkwy., Old Town* ☎ *312/266–0360*) is the spot for anyone interested in the Golden Age of Hollywood. Booth One alone has played host to more celebrities than Oprah Winfrey's couch, including Humphrey Bogart, Lauren Bacall, Irv "Kup" Kupcinet, and Judy Garland.

The **Green Mill** (✉ *4802 N. Broadway, Far North Side* ☎ *773/878–5552*), opened in 1914 in Uptown, has undergone quite a few makeovers and owners (including Al Capone). We like its current incarnation: dark-wood carvings, passionate jazz, and intimate booths

Since the 1960s, **Original Mother's** (✉ *26 W. Division St., Near North* ☎ *312/642–7251*) has been a local favorite for cutting-edge music and dance-'til-you-drop partying. The subterranean singles' destination was immortalized by Demi Moore, Jim Belushi, and Rob Lowe in the film *About Last Night.*

W. Division St., Near North ☎*312/642–4406*), and **Original Mother's** (✉*26 W. Division St., Near North* ☎*312/642–7251*).

Reprieve from the bustling Division Street scene is only a few blocks south, in the Near North and River North neighborhoods. Hunker down in a low-key lounge or sip a hearty pint of Guinness at an authentic Irish pub. Whatever your preference, plenty of conversation-friendly bars are a brief cab ride away.

Crimson Lounge(✉*333 N. Dearborn St., River North* ☎*312/923–2453*), in the Hotel Sax, delivers on its name—red leather couches, red satin perches, and plush red rugs break up the wood–dominated interior. Every detail adds to the swanky atmosphere, from the ornate furnishings to the exotic scents created for the room.

Cru Café and Wine Bar (✉*25 E. Delaware Pl., Near North* ☎*312/337–4001*) is suffused with a living-large ethos—from the oversize chandeliers to the extensive wine list to the international set that roosts here—in an appropriately sprawling space. In warmer months, a roomy Euro-style sidewalk café extends the seating options.

Fado (✉*100 W. Grand Ave., River North* ☎*312/836–0066*) uses imported wood, stone, and glass to create its Irish look. The second floor—with a bar imported from Dublin—feels more like the real thing than the first. There's expertly drawn Guinness, a fine selection of whiskeys, live music on weekends, and a menu of traditional dishes.

La Pomme Rouge (✉*108 W. Kinzie St., River North* ☎*312/245–9555*) was inspired by Belle Epoque Paris. The lavish decor, extensive champagne list, and caviar menu cater to a well-heeled crowd. One of the best places to grab a seat is a back-room lounge called Enfer (French for "Hell") decked out with fabric-covered walls and lots of plush pillows.

Lumen (✉*839 W. Fulton Market, West Town* ☎*312/733–2222*) is worth the difficulty getting here—it's in in a former meatpacking plant in the out-of-the-way warehouse district. Once inside, you'll find a clean-lined space with low-slung modular seating, sleek bamboo tables, and a stainless-steel bar. The white walls are lit by thousands of tiny lights that pulse with the music—mostly cool electronica and trip-hop beats. Best of all, there's no velvet rope or exclusionary attitude.

Motel (✉*600 W. Chicago Ave., River North* ☎*312/822–2900*) has all the comforts of a real, honest-to-goodness motel bar (TVs tuned to sports, classic cocktails, and a retro color scheme), but the atmosphere is amped-up with sexy, low-rise furniture and a "room service" menu of upscale bites.

Designer Nate Berkus assembled **Rockit's** (✉*22 W. Hubbard St., River North* ☎*312/645–6000*) hunter-lodge look: wood-plank-framed plasma TVs, antler chandeliers, and brown-leather booths. The crowd, much like the beer list, is diverse and tasteful, and despite the masculine vibe, there's a good mix of men and women. Dress to impress.

★ The **Signature Lounge** (✉*875 N. Michigan Ave., Near North* ☎*312/787–9596*) has no competition when it comes to views. Perched on the 96th floor of the John Hancock Center—above even the tower's observation deck—the bar offers stunning vistas of the skyline and lake for only the cost of a pricey drink. The ladies' room has an incredible south-facing view through floor-to-ceiling windows.

Swirl Wine Bar (✉*111 W. Hubbard St., River North* ☎*312/828–9000*) has a cozy, shabby-chic lounge and snob-free approach to wine that is enough to disarm even the most jaded oenophiles. Some 25 wines are available by the bottle, glass, quartino, and flight, and are thoughtfully arranged by flavor instead of region.

WICKER PARK & BUCKTOWN

Hip cats, artists, and yuppies converge on the famed six corners of North, Milwaukee, and Damen avenues, where the cast of Real World Chicago once resided. Previously scruffy and edgy, the area is now dotted with pricey, upscale bars, though the occasional honky-tonk still survives.

California Clipper (✉*1002 N. California Ave., Wicker Park* ☎*773/384–2547*), in Humboldt Park, just to the west of Wicker Park, has a 1940s vintage look, including a curving 60-foot-long Brunswick bar and tiny booths lining the long room back-to-back like seats on a train. Alternative country acts and soul-gospel DJs are part of the eccentric musical lineup.

The Map Room (✉ *1949 N. Hoyne Ave., Bucktown* ☎ *773/252–7636*) might help you find your way around Chicago, if not the world. Guidebooks decorate the walls of this self-described "travelers' tavern," and the beers represent much of the world. Tuesday is international buffet night; each week brings a different country's cuisine.

Northside Bar & Grill (✉ *1635 N. Damen Ave., Wicker Park* ☎ *773/384–3555*) was one of the first anchors of the now-teeming Wicker Park nightlife scene. Arty (and sometimes slightly yuppie) types come to drink, eat, shoot pool, and see and be seen. The enclosed indoor–outdoor patio lets you get the best out of the chancy Chicago weather.

The highly stylized **Rodan** (✉ *1530 N. Milwaukee Ave., Wicker Park* ☎ *773/276–7036*) is a restaurant and lounge that caters mostly to the young neighborhood hipsters who arrive at dinnertime (served until 11 PM) and stay put until closing. The narrow space often feels cramped, but if you can snag a spot at the bar or on a blue-suede banquette, an evening of major-league people-watching is in store. Snacks are served all night, so refuel with a pile of wasabi-tempura fries.

Silver Cloud Bar & Grill (✉ *1700 N. Damen Ave., Bucktown* ☎ *773/489–6212*) might be the only place in the city where you can order a champagne cocktail alongside sloppy joes and tater tots and not open yourself up to a citizen's arrest. For us, that's reason enough to go. Spacious red-leather booths, retro fringed lamps, friendly service, and an upbeat neighborhood crowd round out the good points.

★ **Sonotheque** (✉ *1444 W. Chicago Ave., Wicker Park* ☎ *312/226–7600*), with its tasteful, modern design and sparse, podlike seating, is one of the more visually interesting lounges in Chicago. A thoughtful Scotch list, high-profile DJs, and down-to-earth service bring heavy crowds to West Town, a few blocks south of Wicker Park, on weekends.

Vintage Wine Bar (✉ *1942 W. Division St., Wicker Park* ☎ *773/772–3400*) offers reasonably priced vino (many bottles clock in at around $30) in an attitude-free atmosphere. Choose a seat at the lipstick-red bar, or relax in the lounge up front, where there's a working fireplace. Hungry? A serious menu lists everything from gourmet pizzas to artisanal cheese flights.

★ **The Violet Hour** (✉ *1520 N. Damen Ave., Wicker Park* ☎ *773/252–1500*) channels a Prohibition-era speakeasy—an unmarked door in the boarded-up façade leads to a mysterious, curtained hallway. Inside, twinkling crystal chandeliers cast a glow on cornflower-blue walls, and extremely high-backed blue leather chairs encourage intimate conversations. Add to that pricey but flawlessly executed cocktails and a sign discouraging cell-phone use, and it's our idea of nightlife heaven.

LINCOLN PARK

One of the most beautiful (and bustling) neighborhoods on the north side of Chicago, Lincoln Park is largely defined by the DePaul students who inhabit the area. Irish pubs and sports bars line the streets with college students, but chic wine bars attract an older, more sophisticated set.

Clybar (⊠*2417 N. Clybourn Ave., Lincoln Park* ☏*773/388–1877*) is one of the few Lincoln Park bars not filled to the brim with frat boys. Inside, sophisticates of all ages gather to sip stiff drinks and carry on conversations. Booths and a roomy backroom couch are perfect for groups of four or more. Twinkling lights, dark-wood furniture, and a cherrywood fireplace add a touch of romance for those in the mood.

Delilah's (⊠*2771 W. Lincoln Ave., Lincoln Park* ☏*773/472–2771*) is a rare dive bar amid Lincoln Park's tonier establishments. Dark and a bit grungy, the bar has a friendly, unpretentious vibe and a standout whiskey selection (more than 300 types on offer). DJs spin punk and rockabilly.

John Barleycorn (⊠*658 W. Belden Ave., Lincoln Park* ☏*773/348–8899*), a historic pub with a long wooden bar, can get somewhat rowdy despite the classical music (played until 8 PM) and the art slides shown on video screens. It has a spacious summer beer garden, a good pub menu, and a wide selection of beers. There's another location: 3524 North Clark Street in Wrigleyville.

Krem (⊠*1750 N. Clark St., Lincoln Park* ☏*312/932–1750*) is part subterranean lounge and part South Beach–style disco, with an all-white interior awash in blue and green lights. Leather sofas and a wall-hugging lounge bed are prime seating. A champagne bar serves up bubbly, and a menu of light bites keeps patrons from going hungry.

There are two reasons to go to the newly revamped **Red Lion** (⊠*2446 N. Lincoln Ave., Lincoln Park* ☏*773/348–2695*). The first is the British kitsch: check out the London Metro maps that line the walls, duck into the hulking red phone booth, and feast on fish-and-chips and Guinness or bangers-and-mash and hard cider. The second is the legend: a bookie joint in the 1930s, it's said to be one of America's most haunted places.

Webster's Wine Bar (⊠*1480 W. Webster Ave., Lincoln Park* ☏*773/868–0608*), a romantic place for a date, stocks more than 500 bottles of wine—with at least 30 by the glass—as well as ports, sherries, single-malt Scotches, a few microbrews, and a menu of small tasting entrées at reasonable prices.

LAKEVIEW & FAR NORTH SIDE

Lakeview, Uptown, and Andersonville, all on the Far North Side, have one thing in common: affordability. Unbelievable as it sounds, there are places in the city where $20 stretches beyond the price of admission and a martini. Drink deals are frequently offered at many bars.

Enter through rowdy Jack's Bar & Grill to find the serene **404 Wine Bar** (⊠*2852 N. Southport Ave., Lakeview* ☏*773/404–5886*), a romantic spot filled with cozy nooks. The library-like back room has ornate chandeliers, shelves lined with books, and dramatic oxblood walls. You can grab a spot on the patio or near one of two fireplaces and enjoy a glass, flight, or bottle of wine accompanied by a cheese plate.

Gingerman Tavern (✉3740 N. Clark St., Lakeview ☎773/549–2050), up the street from Wrigley Field, deftly manages to avoid being pigeonholed as a sports bar. Folks here take their beer and billiards seriously, with three pool tables and—our favorite part—a list of more than 100 bottles of beer. New and vintage tunes crank out of the jukebox all night long.

Holiday Club (✉4000 N. Sheridan Rd., Far North Side ☎773/348–9600) bills itself as the "Swinger's mecca." Rat Pack aficionados will appreciate the 1950s decor and well-stocked CD jukebox, which has selections ranging from Dean Martin and Frank Sinatra to early punk. Down a pint of good beer (or even bad beer in cans) and scan the typical (but tasty) bar menu.

★ **Hopleaf** (✉5148 N. Clark St., Far North Side ☎773/334–9851), an anchor in the Andersonville corridor, continues the tradition of the classic Chicago bar hospitable to conversation (not a TV in sight). Pick one of the too-many-to-choose-from beers on the menu, with an emphasis on Belgian beers and regional microbrews. A menu of Belgian bar fare usurps typical bar food options. Don't miss the ale-steamed mussels and delectable skinny fries served with aioli.

Space is so limited at **Joie de Vine** (✉1744 W. Balmoral Ave., Far North Side ☎773/989–6846), the wine barely has room to breathe. Good design (and sidewalk tables in summer months) keeps things from feeling claustrophobic. Sit at the long wooden bar or opposing banquette and enjoy the real focal point of the room, a glass-brick wall lit up in multiple colors. All sorts of tasty delights, from wine (available in flights or by the glass) to olives and cheese, are reasonably priced. Try stopping by on a weeknight when the neighborhood regulars are least likely to crowd the slender bar.

Sheffield's (✉3258 N. Sheffield Ave., Lakeview ☎773/281–4989) spans the seasons with a shaded beer garden in summer and a roaring fireplace in winter. This laid-back neighborhood pub has billiards and more than 100 kinds of bottled beer that change seasonally, including regional microbrews, the bartender's "bad beer of the month"—a cheap can of beer (think PBR)—as well as 18 brands on tap.

CAFÉS

High-maintenance ("half-caff-double-foam-soy-latte-to-go") and low-maintenance ("cup 'o joe, black") coffee drinkers feel at home in the diverse range of cafés dotting the streets of Chicago's busiest North Side neighborhoods. Expect to spend anywhere from $2 to $6 (depending on your order) for a caffeinated beverage.

NEAR NORTH, WICKER PARK & BUCKTOWN

Café Ballou's (✉939 N. Western Ave., near Wicker Park ☎773/342–2909). European charm lies in details like a squishy couch, pressed-tin ceiling, and marble tables. The inviting atmosphere at this café nestled in the Ukrainian Village, near Wicker Park, is a far cry from Starbucks. Choose from a menu of international sippers that are served according

BARS WITH VIEWS

Vertigo is a small price to pay for these stellar views.

Castaways (✉1603 N. Lakeshore Dr., River North ☎773/281–1200) puts you so close to Lake Michigan, you might consider wearing a swimsuit. Perched atop the North Avenue Beach Boathouse, the breezy, casual bar and grill creates the perfect setup for lazy, summertime sipping.

When it comes to heights, **Signature Lounge** (✉875 N. Michigan Ave., Near North ☎312/787–9596)—set on the 96th floor of

the John Hancock Center—is in a category all its own. Drinks and appetizers are pricey but well worth it: the cityscape views are simply unmatched.

Glittering panoramic views of Lake Michigan and the city draw visitors worldwide to **Whiskey Sky** (✉644 N. Lakeshore Dr., Near North ☎312/943–9200). The W Hotel–Lakeshore's plush, low-lit lounge also offers tasty cocktails, a cool vibe, and owner Rande Gerber's seal of approval.

to tradition, like Turkish coffee brewed on a hot plate inside a mound of sand, or Russian tea drizzled with cherry compote. The friendly owner speaks fluent Polish and Ukrainian with her customers, many of whom are local neighborhood immigrants.

Caffe de Luca (✉1721 N. Damen Ave., Bucktown ☎773/342–6000) is the place to go when you crave air and light with your caffeine and calories. This sophisticated Bucktown spot hints at Tuscany with richly colored walls and a fine selection of Italian sandwiches, salads, and sorbets.

Earwax (✉1561 N. Milwaukee Ave., Wicker Park ☎773/772–4019) is a mecca for local vegans and vegetarians looking to order scrambled tofu alongside their ordinary cup of coffee. Well-worn, comfy furniture and a quirky staff go hand-in-hand with the relaxed atmosphere and kitschy decor (colorful carnival banners adorn the walls). Stop by for coffee, sweets, or a light meal.

Third Coast Café (✉1260 N. Dearborn St., Near North ☎312/649–0730), the oldest coffeehouse in the Gold Coast, pleases just about everyone with a full menu served until midnight seven nights a week. The inviting space combines warm woods, etched glass, and funky local art. A diverse clientele—from students and twentysomethings to retirees living nearby—comes for coffee, Sunday brunch, or late-night jazz sessions.

LAKEVIEW & FAR NORTH SIDE

Intelligentsia (✉3123 N. Broadway, Lakeview ☎773/348–8058) was named to invoke the pre-chain days when cafés were forums for discussion, but the long, broad farmer's tables and handsome couches are usually occupied by students and other serious types who treat the café like their office. The store does all of its own coffee roasting and sells its house blends to local restaurants.

Kopi, a Traveler's Cafe (⊠*5317 N. Clark St., Far North Side* ☎*773/989–5674*) is a study in opposites, with healthy vegetarian options as well as decadent desserts. In the Andersonville neighborhood, a 20-minute cab ride from downtown, this café has a selection of travel books, global gifts, and artfully painted tables.

The original location of **Uncommon Ground** (⊠*3800 N. Clark St., Lakeview* ☎*773/929–3680*) is roomy and inviting, with a hand-carved bar and large street-facing windows offering views of passersby. Patrons brave the wait for bowls of coffee and hot chocolate. There's also a full bar and a hearty menu. Fun perks include two fireplaces, a sidewalk café, and a steady lineup of acoustic musical acts. A hugely popular second location at 1401 West Devon Avenue on the Far Northwest Side gets bonus points for eco-friendliness, with a green roof, solar panels, and tables made from reclaimed wood.

COMEDY & IMPROV CLUBS

Improvisation has long had a successful following in Chicago; stand-up comedy hasn't fared as well. Most comedy clubs have a cover charge ($5 to $20); many have a two-drink minimum on top of that. In the stand-up circuit, keep an eye out for performances by Steve Harvey, star of his own WB television series.

Barrel of Laughs (⊠*10345 S. Central Ave., Oaklawn* ☎*708/499–2969*), in the city's southwest suburbs (a 30-minute drive from downtown), spotlights local and national comics. The dinner package includes a meal at the adjacent Senese's restaurant and reserved seats at the show.

ComedySportz (⊠*929 W. Belmont Ave., Lakeview* ☎*773/549–8080*) specializes in "competitive improv," in which two teams vie for the audience's favor. Book a family-friendly early performance or a late-night show rife with raunchy humor. The space features cabaret-style seating and a full bar.

I.O. (⊠*3541 N. Clark St., Lakeview* ☎*773/880–0199*) (formerly called ImprovOlympic) has shows with student and professional improvisation in two intimate spaces every night of the week. Team members present long-form comedic improvisations drawn on audience suggestions, including an improvised musical and a Monday-night alumni show. No drink or age minimum.

★ **Second City** (⊠*1616 N. Wells St., Near North* ☎*312/337–3992*), an institution since 1959, has served as a launching pad for some of the hottest comedians around. Alumni include Dan Aykroyd and the late John Belushi. Funny, loony skit comedy is presented on two stages, with a free improv set after the show every night but Friday.

Zanies (⊠*1548 N. Wells St., Near North* ☎*312/337–4027*) books outstanding national talent and is Chicago's best stand-up comedy spot. Jay Leno, Jerry Seinfeld, and Jackie Mason have all performed at this intimate venue.

Looking for Laughs? Try Improv

Mike Myers, Tina Fey, Bill Murray, John Belushi, Dan Aykroyd, Alan Alda, Shelley Long, Ed Asner, John Candy, Andy Dick. These are just a few of the comic actors who, were they to attempt to trace their path to stardom, might credit nights spent improvising on Chicago stages.

Chicago was the birthplace of the improvisational comedy form some 50-odd years ago, and the city remains the country's primary breeding ground for this challenging art form. Performers, usually working in an ensemble, ask the audience for a suggestion, then launch into short, long, silly, serious, or surreal scenes loosely related to that original audience input.

Second City (☎ 312/337–3992) is the anchor of Chicago improv. The revues on the company's main stage and in its smaller e.t.c. space next door are actually sketch comedy shows, but the scripts in these pre-rehearsed scenes have been developed through improvisation and there's usually a little time set aside in each show for the performers to demonstrate their quick wit. Most nights there is a free improv set after the late show, featuring cast members and invited guests (sometimes famous, sometimes not, never announced in advance). It's in **Donny's Skybox**

upstairs that you're more likely to see one of Chicago's many fledgling improv comedy troupes making their first appearance working together on freshly penned material in public.

I.O. (☎ 773/880–0199) is the city's home to long-form improvisation. The signature piece is "The Harold," in which a team of improvisers explores a single audience suggestion throughout a series of stories and characters until they all eventually weave back together to fit with the original audience idea. At **ComedySportz Chicago** (☎ 773/549–8080), teams of professional improvisers perform songs and scenes all based on your suggestions in an audience-interactive competition.

The itinerant group the **Annoyance Theatre** (☎ 773/561–4665), now settled into its new home in Uptown at 4840 North Broadway, is best known for hits like *Coed Prison Sluts* and *Splatter Theatre.*

Scope out the hordes of up-and-comers at neighborhood stages such as the **Playground Theater** (☎ 773/871–3793) at 3209 North Halsted Street. The springtime **Chicago Improv Festival** (☎ 773/935–9810), the nation's largest festival for improvisers, has stages devoted to group, pair, and single improv, sketch comedy, and more.

8

DANCE CLUBS

Most clubs don't get crowded until 11 or midnight, and they remain open into the early morning hours. Cover charges range from $5 to $20. A few dance clubs have dress codes that don't allow jeans, gym shoes, or baseball caps.

To avoid the exhausting lines and cover charges at most nightclubs, chat with your hotel concierge or even your server at dinner. Admission into the VIP lounges of Chicago's hottest clubs is often a conversation-with-the-right-person away from becoming a reality.

Great news for those who like to club-hop: most of Chicago's best dance clubs (Sound-Bar, Transit, and Le Passage, to name a few) are within the Near North and River North neighborhoods, just north of downtown. The close proximity makes it relatively easy (and cheap) to cab it from one club to another. Wicker Park and Lakeview are also good 'hoods for when you feel like dancing.

Berlin (⊠*954 W. Belmont Ave., Lakeview* ☎*773/348–4975*), a multicultural, pansexual dance club near the Belmont El station, has progressive electronic dance music and fun theme nights—Madonna and Prince are celebrated on the first and last Sunday of the month, and one Wednesday a month is devoted to disco. The crowd tends to be predominantly gay on weeknights, mixed on weekends.

Crobar—The Nightclub (⊠*1543 N. Kingsbury St., Near North* ☎*312/266–1900*) has scrapped its scruffy, Goth-like decor for a sprawling South Beach makeover complete with a glass-enclosed VIP lounge and booth-lined balcony. Top DJs spin house and techno over the enormous dance floor on Wednesday, Friday, and Saturday nights.

★ **Enclave** (⊠*220 W. Chicago Ave., River North* ☎*312/654-0234*) has a loftlike feel and three bars spread out on two floors. Sip a snazzy cocktail and groove to remixed tunes in a grown-up nightclub complete with hardwood floors, exposed brick, and a timber-beam ceiling.

Excalibur (⊠*632 N. Dearborn St., River North* ☎*312/266–1944*) won't win any prizes for breaking new ground, but this River North nightclub complex, carved out of the Romanesque fortress that was the original home of the Chicago Historical Society, has been going strong for years with its mix of dancing, dining, and posing. At the same address and phone number but with a separate entrance is the smaller, alternative-dance club called Vision. Deejays and music styles change all the time (as does the club's vibe), so call ahead for that night's selections.

Funky is the operative word for the **Funky Buddha Lounge** (⊠*728 W. Grand Ave., Wicker Park* ☎*312/666–1695*), with its diverse crowd, seductive dance music, and a big metal Buddha guarding the front door. It has an intimate bar and dark dance floor, where patrons groove as DJs spin dance hall, hip-hop, R&B, funk, and old-school house.

Le Passage (⊠*937 N. Rush St., Near North* ☎*312/255–0022*) feels like an underground Parisian nightclub, complete with low ceilings, dim lighting, and an entrance down a cobblestone alley Stop in for an early-evening cocktail and plate of French-inspired cuisine and stay for late-night dancing. DJs spin house and hip-hop Thursday through Saturday. The adjacent "culinary cocktail lounge" called the Drawing Room puts the focus on top-flight wines and small plates in a plush, intimate atmosphere.

Sound-Bar (⊠226 W. Ontario St., River North ☎312/787–4480) is a labyrinth of nine bars, each with a unique design and color scheme (some even serve matching colored cocktails). Feel like dancing? Join the pulse of Chicago's best-dressed on the huge dance floor.

Spy Bar (⊠646 N. Franklin St., River North ☎312/587–8779) pulls some smooth moves. Image is everything at this subterranean spot with a brushed stainless-steel bar and exposed brick walls. The slick, stylish crowd hits the tight dance floor for house, underground, and DJ remixes.

GAY & LESBIAN NIGHTLIFE

Chicago's gay bars appeal to mixed crowds and tastes. Most are on North Halsted Street from Belmont Avenue to Irving Park Road, an area nicknamed Boystown. Bars generally stay open until 2 AM weekends, but a few keep the lights on until 5 AM Sunday morning. The *Chicago Free Press, Windy City Times,* and *Gay Chicago* list nightspots, events, and gay and lesbian resources; all three are free and can be picked up at bookstores, bars, and some supermarkets, especially those in Boystown.

Big Chicks (⊠5024 N. Sheridan Rd., Far North Side ☎773/728–5511), in the Uptown area of the Far North Side, is a striking alternative to the Halsted strip, with a funky crowd that appreciates the owner's art collection hanging on the walls. The fun-loving staff and their self-selected eclectic music are the payoffs for the hike to get here. Special attractions include weekend dancing and free Sunday-afternoon buffets.

Charlie's (⊠3726 N. Broadway, Lakeview ☎773/871–8887), a country-and-western dance club, lets you two-step nightly to achy-breaky tunes, though dance music is played every night from about 2 AM to 4 AM. It's mostly a boots-and-denim crowd on weekends.

Circuit (⊠3641 N. Halsted St., Lakeview ☎773/325–2233), the biggest dance club in Boystown, is a stripped-down dance hall energized by flashing lights, booming sounds, and a partying crowd. Take a break in the up-front martini bar.

The **Closet** (⊠3325 N. Broadway, Lakeview ☎773/477–8533) is a basic dive bar with a gay twist. This compact bar—one of the few that caters to lesbians, though it draws gay men, too—can be especially lively after 2 AM when most other bars close. Stop by Sunday afternoons when bartenders serve up what are hailed as the best Bloody Marys in town.

Gentry (⊠440 N. State St., River North ☎312/836–0933), one of the few gay bars downtown, is a premier piano bar/cabaret, featuring local and national talent. Sophisticates linger at the upscale piano bar; the video bar downstairs attracts a younger group. A smaller Boystown branch is at 3320 North Halsted Street.

Roscoe's Tavern (⊠3356 N. Halsted St., Lakeview ☎773/281–3355), in the heart of Boystown, is a longtime favorite with a mix of amenities sure to please its peppy patrons, including a jam-packed front bar, a dance floor, a pool table, an outdoor garden, and lively music. The sidewalk café serves May through September.

The video bar **Sidetrack** (⊠ *3349 N. Halsted St., Lakeview* ☎ *773/477–9189*) is tuned into a different theme every night of the week, from show tunes on Monday to comedy on Thursday—all broadcast on TV screens that never leave your sight. The sprawling stand-and-pose bar and rooftop deck are always busy with a good-looking, professional crowd, and the vodka slushies are a house specialty.

MUSIC

COUNTRY

There are slim pickin's for country-music clubs in Chicago, even though country radio continues to draw wide audiences.

Carol's Pub (⊠ *4659 N. Clark St., Far North Side* ☎ *773/334–2402*), in the Uptown area of the Far North Side, showcased country before it was ever cool. The house band at this urban honky-tonk plays country and country-rock tunes on weekends, and the popular karaoke night on Thursday draws all walks of life, from preppie to punk.

★ **The Hideout** (⊠ *1354 W. Wabansia, Bucktown* ☎ *773/227–4433*), which is literally hidden away in a North Side industrial zone, has managed to make country music hip in Chicago. Players on the city's alternative country scene have adopted the friendly hole-in-the-wall, and bands ranging from the obscure to the semi-famous take the stage. The bluegrass band Devil in a Woodpile plays on Tuesday.

Horseshoe (⊠ *4115 N. Lincoln Ave., Far Northwest Side* ☎ *773/334–2402*) brings a slice of Texas to the Midwest, along with wicked barbecue brisket and pulled pork (and some surprisingly good vegetarian versions). Live bluegrass bands or honky-tonk jukebox tunes draw displaced Southerners, whose nostalgia is drown out by the down-home decor—think chicken-wire, scruffy floors, and horseshoe-shaped booths—and rounds of ice-cold Lone Star beer.

ECLECTIC

Clubs in this category don't limit themselves to a single type of music. Call ahead to find out what's playing.

At **Baton Show Lounge** (⊠ *436 N. Clark St., River North* ☎ *312/644–5269*), boys will be girls. The lip-synching revues with female impersonators have catered to curious out-of-towners and bachelorette parties since 1969. Some of the regular performers, such as Chili Pepper and Mimi Marks, have become Chicago cult figures. The more the audience tips, the better the show gets, so bring your bills.

North Side stalwart **Beat Kitchen** (⊠ *2100 W. Belmont Ave., Lakeview* ☎ *773/281–4444*) brings in the crowds because of its good sound system and local and touring rock, alternative-rock, country, and rockabilly acts. It also serves soups, salads, sandwiches, pizzas, and desserts.

Elbo Room (✉2871 N. Lincoln Ave., Lincoln Park ☎773/549–5549), a multilevel space in an elbow-shape corner building, has a basement rec-room feel. The bar plays host to talented live bands seven days a week, with a strong dose of nu-jazz, funk, soul, pop, and rock.

FitzGerald's (✉6615 W. Roosevelt Rd., Berwyn ☎708/788–2118), though a 30-minute schlep west of Chicago, draws crowds from all over the city and suburbs with its mix of folk, jazz, blues, zydeco, and rock. This early 1900s roadhouse has great sound and sight lines for its roots music.

★ **House of Blues** (✉329 N. Dearborn St., River North ☎312/923–2000), though its name implies otherwise, attracts big-name performers of all genres, from jazz, roots, blues, and gospel to alternative rock, hip-hop, world, and R&B. The interior is an elaborate cross between blues bar and ornate opera house. Its restaurant has live blues every night on a "second stage," as well as a satisfying Sunday gospel brunch. Part of the Marina City complex, the entrance is on State Street.

FOLK & ETHNIC

★ **Old Town School of Folk Music** (✉4544 N. Lincoln Ave., Far Northwest Side ☎773/728–6000), Chicago's first and oldest folk-music school, has served as folk central in the city since it opened in 1957. This welcoming spot in Lincoln Square hosts outstanding performances by national and local acts in an intimate-feeling 420-seat concert hall boasting excellent acoustics. If you can, book a table seat next to the stage. Each summer the school sponsors the popular Chicago Folk & Roots Festival in nearby Welles Park.

The Wild Hare (✉3530 N. Clark St., Lakeview ☎773/327–0868), with a wide-open dance floor, is the place for infectious live reggae and world-beat music seven nights a week. Take a breather at the bar and sip a rum drink or a Jamaican Red Stripe beer.

JAZZ

Jazz thrives all around town. For a recorded listing of upcoming live performances, call the **Jazz Institute Hot Line** (☎312/427–3300).

Andy's Jazz Club (✉11 E. Hubbard St., River North ☎312/642–6805), a favorite after-work watering hole with a substantial bar menu, has live music ranging from swing jazz to bebop. In addition to the evening performances, there's a jazz program at noon on weekdays—a boon for music lovers who aren't night owls.

Green Dolphin Street (✉2200 N. Ashland Ave., Lakeview ☎773/395–0066), a stylish, upscale club-restaurant with the glamour of the 1940s (in a converted auto-body shop, no less), attracts a mostly older crowd that comes to hear tight ensembles and smooth-voiced jazz divas perform big band, bebop, Latin, and world jazz.

★ **Green Mill** (✉4802 N. Broadway, Far North Side ☎773/878–5552), a Chicago institution off the beaten track in not-so-trendy Uptown, has been around since 1907. Deep leather banquettes and ornate wood paneling line the walls, and a photo of Al Capone occupies a place of honor on the piano behind the bar. The jazz entertainment is both excellent and contemporary—the club launched the careers of Kurt Elling and Patricia Barber—and the Uptown Poetry Slam, a competitive poetry reading, takes center stage on Sunday.

Pops for Champagne (✉*601 N. State St., River North* ☎*312/266–7677*) can be found in trendy River North. The bi-level space is gloriously turned out with a champagne bar, raw bar, sidewalk café, and even a retail space called Pops Shop. Grab your (champagne) flute and head downstairs to the stylish jazz lounge for live music Tuesday through Saturday.

The owner of **Velvet Lounge** (✉*67 E. Cermak Rd., Near South* ☎*312/791–9050*), saxophonist Fred Anderson, has relocated his beloved institution to a cozy Near South locale, but the heart and soul of the place remains the same. Stop in for traditional and avant-garde jazz Tuesday through Saturday. Sunday is still Jam Session day.

ROCK

Chicago has an active rock scene with many local favorites, some of which—including Smashing Pumpkins, Wilco, and Liz Phair—have won national acclaim. Bone up on Chicago's rock scene by tuning to 91.5 FM for Chicago Public Radio's Sound Opinions, a weekly radio show hosted by *Chicago Tribune* and *Chicago Sun-Times* rock critics Greg Kot and Jim DeRogatis. The program airs Friday at 8 PM and Saturday at 11 AM.

The Abbey Pub (✉*3420 W. Grace St., Far North Side* ☎*773/478–4408*), about 15 minutes northwest of downtown in the Irving Park neighborhood, showcases rock, as well as some Irish, Celtic, and country music, in a large concert hall with a separate, busy pub. By day the hall is used to show soccer and rugby games from the United Kingdom and Ireland.

Double Door (✉*1572 N. Milwaukee Ave., Wicker Park* ☎*773/489–3160*) is a hotbed for music in hip Wicker Park. The large bar books up-and-coming local and national acts from rock to acid jazz. Unannounced Rolling Stones shows have been held here. The entrance is on Damen Avenue.

Empty Bottle (✉*1035 N. Western Ave., Wicker Park* ☎*773/276–3600*), in the Ukrainian Village near Wicker Park, may have toys and knickknacks around the bar (including a case of macabre baby doll heads), but when it comes to booking rock, punk, and jazz bands from the indie scene, it's a serious place with no pretensions.

Martyrs' (✉*3855 N. Lincoln Ave., Far North Side* ☎*773/404–9869*) brings local and major-label rock bands to this small, North Side neighborhood sandwiched between Lincoln Square and Roscoe Village. Music fans can see the stage from just about any corner of the bar, while the more rhythmically inclined gyrate in the large standing-room area. A mural opposite the stage memorializes late rock greats.

Continued on page 327

CHICAGO STILL SINGS THE BLUES

The cool, electric, urban blues are the soundtrack of the Windy City. The blues traveled up the Mississippi River with the Delta sharecroppers during the Great Migration, settled down on Maxwell Street and South Side clubs, and gave birth to such big-name talent as Muddy Waters, Howlin' Wolf, Willie Dixon, and, later, Koko Taylor. Today, you can still hear the blues in a few South Side clubs where it all began, or check out the current scene on the North Side.

THE BIRTH OF THE CHICAGO BLUES

CHESS RECORDS

Founded by Philip and Leonard Chess, Polish immigrant brothers, in 1947. For the first two years, the label was called Aristocrat.

Its famous address, 2120 S. Michigan Avenue, was the nucleus of the blues scene. Up-and-comers performed on the sidewalk out front in hopes of being discovered. Even today, locals and visitors peek through the windows of the restored studio (now the Blues Heaven Foundation) looking for glimpses of past glory.

The label's first hit record was Muddy Waters' *I Can't Be Satisfied*.

The brothers were criticized for having a paternalistic relationship with their artists. They reportedly bought Muddy Waters a car off the lot when he wasn't able to finance it himself.

The label was sold in 1969 after Leonard's death.

Did you know? When the Rolling Stones recorded the track "2120 South Michigan Avenue" (off the *12 x 5* album) at the Chess Records studio in June 1964, the young Brits were reportedly so nervous about singing in front of Willie Dixon (Buddy Guy and Muddy Waters were also hanging around the studio that day) that they literally became tongue-tied. As a result, the song is purely instrumental.

WILLIE DIXON (7/1915–1/1992)

Chess Records' leading A & R (artist and repertoire) man, bass player, and composer. Founded the Blues Heaven Foundation, Chess Records' restored office and studio. *See Blues Heaven Foundation review next page.*

Famous compositions: "Hoochie Coochie Man" (recorded by Muddy Waters), "My Babe" (recorded by Little Walter), and "Wang Dang Doodle" (recorded by Koko Taylor)

MUDDY WATERS: KING OF ELECTRIC BLUES (4/1915–4/1983)

When Muddy Waters gave his guitar an electric jolt, he didn't just revolutionize the blues. His electric guitar became a magic wand: Its jive talk (and cry) turned country-blues into city-blues, and it gave birth to rock and roll. Waters' signature sound has been firmly imprinted on nearly all subsequent musical genres.

Best known for: Riveting vocals, a swooping pompadour, and, of course, plugging in the guitar

Biggest break: Leonard Chess, one of the Chess brothers of Chess Records, let Waters record two of his own songs. The record sold out in two days, and stores issued a dictum of "one per customer"

Biggest song: "Hoochie Coochie Man"

Lyrics: *Y'know I'm here / Everybody knows I'm here / And I'm the hoochie-coochie man*

Awards: 3 Grammies, Lifetime Achievement induction into the Rock and Roll Hall of Fame

Local honor: A strip of 43rd Street in Chicago is renamed Muddy Waters Drive

HOWLIN' WOLF (6/1910–1/1976)

In 1951, at the age of 41, Wolf recorded with Sun Studios in Memphis, TN. Shortly thereafter, Sun sold Wolf's only two songs, "Moanin' At Midnight" and "How Many More Years," to Chess Records, kicking off his prolific recording career with Chess.

Most popular songs: "Backdoor Man" and "Little Red Rooster"

Instruments: Electric guitar and harmonica

Dedication to his craft: Wolf was still taking guitar lessons even a year before his death, even though he was long recognized as one of the two greatest blues musicians in the world.

7

IN FOCUS CHICAGO STILL SINGS THE BLUES

THE CHICAGO BLUES TODAY

KOKO TAYLOR:
Queen of the Blues

Blessed with neither Bessie Smith's beauty nor Billie Holiday's power of seduction, Taylor offers grit; a been-there-done-that wisdom that personified urban-blues by the 1970s.

Best known for: Slam-bang stage presence and powerhouse vocals

Big break: It wasn't until Chess Records blues producer Willie Dixon saw her singing at a South Side club one night in the early 1960s that her career really took off. Dixon reportedly said, "My God, I've never heard a woman sing the blues like you," and signed her up to record

Biggest song: "Wang Dang Doodle" sold a staggering one million copies in six weeks

Lyrics: *We gonna jump and shout 'til daylight / We gonna pitch a wang dang doodle / All night long*

Most significant hardship: Gettin' paid. Though Taylor was a star, she barely saw a penny of the profits while working with Chess Records and Willie Dixon

Awards: 25 W.C. Handy Awards (more than any other recording artist, male or female); a Grammy for *Blues Explosion*, 1984; Legend of the Year by Mayor Daley in 1993

Local honor: March 3rd is Koko Taylor Day in Chicago

Catch her act: Upcoming tour information is available at www.kokotaylor.com

BEST PLACES TO HEAR THE BLUES

Checkerboard Lounge (✉ 5201 S. Harper Ct., Hyde Park ☎ 773/684–1472) has reopened in Hyde Park! It was a sad day for blues fans when the world-famous Bronzeville location, owned by Buddy Guy in the 1970s and early 1980s, closed in 2003. Though the new location's in a shopping center—a far cry from its former gritty digs—it has the same diverse selection of local and big-name blues and jazz talent. Kudos on retaining some of the old picnic tables (used inside) from the first location. Note: Call ahead for information on the cover charge, which ranges from $3 to $20 depending on who's playing.

Chicago Blues Festival (☎ 312/744–3370) There's no doubt about it; Chicago still loves to sing the blues. Each June, the city pulses with sounds from the largest free blues festival in the world, which takes place over four days and on six stages in both Grant Park and Millennium Park. The always-packed open air festival has been headlined by blues legends such as B.B. King, Koko Taylor, and Buddy Guy.

Set in an upscale part of downtown, **Blue Chicago** (✉ 536 N. Clark St., River North ☎ 312/661–0100 ✉ 736 N. Clark St., River North ☎ 312/642–6261) has none of the trademark grit or edginess of the older South Side blues clubs. It does have two bars within two blocks of each other.

BUDDY GUY

Though he recorded his first album in 1958, Guy didn't really take off until he recorded with Vanguard in 1968 and was sent on tour with blues harmonica legend Junior Wells and the Rolling Stones.

Instrument: Electric guitar

Influenced: His stinging guitar playing had strong influences on Jimi Hendrix and Eric Clapton

Catch his act: Guy is still impressing fans with his sizzling guitar and vocals both on tour and in his Chicago-based club, Buddy Guy's Legends

Honors: 2005 inductee to the Rock and Roll Hall of Fame

DON'T MISS ACTS:

If these acts are playing when you're in town, don't miss them. For contact information for the venues mentioned below, see the club reviews on this page.

Classic slide-guitar and hard-driving blues beats mixed with jazz and even rock 'n' roll influences makes **Melvin Taylor & The Slack Band** a must-see. Call Rosa's Lounge for details. **Gloria Shannon Blues Band** plays everything from Delta blues to electric blues to Chicago blues. Catch their all-ages act every Saturday "Down in the Basement" at the Blue Chicago Store. **Billy Branch and the Sons Of Blues** frequently bring their forward-thinking sounds (steeped in blues tradition) to Rosa's Lounge and Kingston Mines, though they have been known to make rousing on-stage appearances at the Chicago Blues Festival.

Both have good sound systems, regularly book female vocalists, and attract a cosmopolitan audience that's a tad more diverse than some of the baseball-capped crowds at Lincoln Park blues clubs. We like that one cover gets you into both bars.

The **Blue Chicago Store** (✉ 534 N. Clark St., River North ☎ 312/661–1003) sells a variety of Blue Chicago–related souvenirs, from CDs and T-shirts to posters and books.

★ The best part about **B.L.U.E.S.** (✉ 2519 N. Halsted St., Lincoln Park ☎ 773/528–1012) is that there isn't a bad seat in the joint. The worst part? The crowds—arrive early if you want to score

a seat. Narrow and intimate, the jam-packed North Side club has attracted the best in local talent since it opened in 1979. Big names such as Son Seals, Otis Rush, Jimmy Johnson, and Magic Slim have all played here.

Fodor's Choice **Buddy Guy's Legends** (✉ 754 S. Wabash Ave., South Loop ☎ 312/427–0333) serves up Louisiana-style barbecue along with the blues. The big club has good sound, good sight lines, and pool tables if you get restless in between sets. Look for local blues acts during the week and larger-scale touring acts on weekends. Don't miss Grammy Award winning blues performer/owner Buddy Guy in January, when he performs a

A MODERN HISTORY LESSON:

The Blues Heaven Foundation (✉ 2120 S. Michigan Ave., South Loop ☎ 312/808–1286)

Breathe the same rarefied air as blues (and rock 'n' roll) legends Muddy Waters, Howlin' Wolf, Chuck Berry, and the Rolling Stones, all of whom recorded here. Check out the Chess brothers' private offices, the recording studio, and the back stairway used only by signed musicians. Don't miss the eerie "Life Cast Portraits" wall showcasing the plaster heads of the Chess recording artists.

Note: Make a phone reservation before stopping by—the Foundation keeps irregular hours.

month-long home stand of shows (tickets go on sale one month in advance). The club has plans to move into a new spot eventually, but for now it's staying put in its storied digs.

In 1968, **Kingston Mines** (✉ 2548 N. Halsted St., Lincoln Park ☎ 773/477–4646) went down in Chicago history as the first blues club to open on the North Side. Though it's since moved to bigger digs, it still offers the same traditional sounds and late-night hours as the orig-

inal club. Swarms of blues lovers and partying singles take in the good blues and tasty barbecue.

⭐ **Fodor's Choice** **Lee's Unleaded Blues** (✉ 7401 S. South Chicago Ave., Grand Crossing ☎ 773/493–3477) has been a South Side favorite since it opened in the early 1970s. Locals come decked out in their showiest threads and University of Chicago students often pop in for a round. The cramped, triangular bar may inhibit free movement, but that doesn't seem to bother the crowd that comes for powerhouse blues and jazz. Note: the club can be difficult to find if you don't know the area, so be sure to take a cab or study a map before making the trip.

⭐ **Fodor's Choice** On a given night at **Rosa's Lounge,** (✉ 3420 W. Armitage Ave., Logan Square ☎ 773/342–0452) near Bucktown, you'll find Tony, the owner, working the crowd, and his mother, Rosa, behind the bar. What makes the club extra special is that the duo moved here from Italy out of a pure love for the blues. Stop by and partake in Rosa's winning mixture of big-name and local talent, stiff drinks, and friendly service—the same since it opened in 1984.

★ **Metro** (✉3730 N. Clark St., Lakeview ☎773/549–0203) brings in progressive, nationally known artists and the cream of the local crop. A former movie palace, it's an excellent place to see live bands, whether you're moshing on the main floor or above the fray in the balcony. In the basement is **Smart Bar,** a late-night dance club that starts hopping after midnight.

Schubas Tavern (✉3159 N. Southport Ave., Lakeview ☎773/525–2508) favors local and national power pop and indie rock bands. The wood-paneled back room has a laid-back atmosphere and good seating. The bar was built in 1900 by the Schlitz Brewing Company, and it still sells Schlitz beer—a bargain at about $2 a pop.

PIANO BARS

Coq d'Or (✉140 E. Walton St., Near North ☎312/932–4623) is a dark, wood-paneled room with red-leather booths where Chicago legend Buddy Charles held court before retiring. Fine music and cocktails served in blown-glass goblets draw hotel guests as well as neighborhood regulars.

Davenport's (✉1383 N. Milwaukee Ave., Wicker Park ☎773/278–1830), a sophisticated cabaret booking both local and touring acts, brings a grown-up presence to the Wicker Park club scene. The piano lounge is set up for casual listening, while the cabaret room is a no-chat zone that requires your full attention—as well as reservations and a two-drink minimum.

The dueling pianists at **Howl at the Moon** (✉26 W. Hubbard St., Near North ☎312/863–7427) attract a rowdy crowd that delights in belting out popular tunes. Reservations aren't accepted, but party packages are available if you're willing to shell out beaucoup bucks (around $150).

★ **Pump Room** (✉Omni Ambassador East Hotel, 1301 N. State Pkwy., Near North ☎312/266–0360) shows off its storied past with photos of celebrities covering the walls. The bar at this restaurant has live piano music and a small dance floor that calls out for dancing cheek to cheek, especially on weekends.

Zebra Lounge (✉1220 N. State St., Near North ☎312/642–5140), small and funky with zebra-stripe lamps and other kitsch, attracts an interesting crowd of dressed-up and dressed-down regulars who come to sing along to the pianist on duty.

8

OUR FAVORITE DIVE BARS

Old Town Ale House (✉ *219 W. North Ave., Near North* ☎ *312/944–7020*), just a stone's throw from Second City, has attracted a diverse cast of characters since it opened in 1958, including comedy legends John Belushi and Bill Murray. With eclectic artwork, a mural of bar denizens painted in the '70s, and a lending library on-site, it's a dingy neighborhood bar unlike any other in the city—perhaps the country.

The Matchbox (✉ *770 N. Milwaukee Ave., Wicker Park* ☎ *312/666–9292*), in West Town near Wicker Park, isn't much bigger than a you-know-what, but the hodgepodge of regulars

don't seem to mind. In fact, many claim it's the dark, cramped quarters (we're talking three feet wide at its narrowest) that keep them coming back. The crowd spills outside in summer, when iron rod tables dot the sidewalk.

Rainbo Club (✉ *1150 N. Damen Ave., Wicker Park* ☎ *773/489–5999*) is the unofficial meeting place for Chicago hipsters and indie rockers. Apart from the working photo booth wedged into a corner, the stripped-down hangout is pretty barren, but drinks are dirt-cheap and the bartenders are upbeat—and willing— conversationalists.

SPORTS BARS

Gamekeepers (✉ *345 W. Armitage Ave., Lincoln Park* ☎ *773/549–0400*) is full of former frat boys and sports fans. With more than 40 TVs, three projection screens, and complete satellite sports coverage, there's barely a game Gamekeepers doesn't get.

Hi-Tops (✉ *3551 N. Sheffield Ave., Lakeview* ☎ *773/348–0009*), within a ball's toss of Wrigley Field, may be the ultimate sports bar. Big-screen TVs, a lively crowd, and good bar food keep the Cubs fans coming. A dozen satellites and 65 TV monitors ensure that the place gets packed for a good game.

North Beach Chicago (✉ *1551 N. Sheffield Ave., Lincoln Park* ☎ *312/266–7842*) is all about channeling your inner child. Multiple large-screen TVs plus two sand-filled indoor volleyball courts, pool tables, four bowling lanes, a mechanical bull, and even Sumo wrestling all contribute to generalized regression.

Sluggers (✉ *3540 N. Clark St., Lakeview* ☎ *773/248–0055*) is packed after Cubs games in the nearby stadium, and the ballplayers make occasional appearances in summer. Check out the fast- and slow-pitch batting cages on the second floor, as well as the pool tables, air hockey tables, and electronic basketball.

UNDERSTANDING CHICAGO

Chicago Slang

Chicago at a Glance

Books & Movies

CHICAGO SLANG

Like New Yorkers and New Englanders, Chicagoans put their own *unique* twist on the English language. Here's a quick primer to help you talk like a native while you're visiting.

Beef—Short for Italian beef sandwiches, a Chicago staple made of thinly sliced roast beef served on a long crusty Italian roll. Beefs are ordered "wet" (dipped in the meat juices), "hot" (with *giardiniera*, an Italian relish containing jalapeños), and/or "sweet" (with roasted sweet peppers).

Bleacher Bums—Regulars who sit in the bleachers at the "Friendly Confines" *(see below)*.

The Blizzard of Oz—Nickname for Ozzie Guillen, the charismatic and often foulmouthed manager of the 2005 World Champion Chicago White Sox.

The Boot—Short for the Denver Boot, a contraption the city uses to lock the wheels of cars with unpaid traffic and parking tickets. Often heard around town: "My car just got booted."

Brat—Short for bratwurst, a staple at sporting events and tailgating parties (pronounced "braht").

The Cell—What White Sox fans affectionately call U.S. Cellular Field, formerly known as Comiskey Park.

Cheesehead—What the locals call people from Wisconsin.

Chicagoland—Chicago and the surrounding suburbs.

The Curse—A local legend that says that a Chicago barkeep whose pet goat was denied entry into the 1945 Chicago Cubs–Detroit Tigers World Series put a curse on the team. The Cubs lost, and have not been to a World Series since. Their last championship was in 1908.

Da Mare—"The Mayor," pronounced like a dyed-in-the-wool native.

The Edens—Commuter term referring to I-94 as it shoots north of the city, splitting from the Kennedy Expressway.

The El—The nickname for the city's public train system, short for "elevated." Even though most of the system is aboveground, the term is used even when the train goes underground.

Friendly Confines—This means Wrigley Field, home of the Chicago Cubs. A sign inside the ballpark says WELCOME TO THE FRIENDLY CONFINES OF WRIGLEY FIELD.

Gapers—Drivers who slow down traffic to look at an accident. You'll hear about "gapers blocks" or "gapers delays" on traffic reports.

The Mag Mile—A shortened term for the "Magnificent Mile," a nickname given to the retail-heavy stretch of North Michigan Avenue, between the Chicago River and Oak Street.

Pop—A soft drink, like Coca-Cola. Don't use the word "soda" here.

Reversibles—The express lanes on the Kennedy Expressway, which reverse direction depending upon the time of day.

The Riv—The hipster abbreviation for the Riviera Theater, a North Side live-music venue.

Sammitch—A sandwich, of course!

Trixies—A jabbing nickname for the young, ex-sorority types who live in and around the Lincoln Park neighborhood.

Viagra Triangle—What locals call the intersection of Clark, Dearborn, and Rush streets due to the density of bars frequented by mature gentlemen who try to pick up young ladies.

CHICAGO AT A GLANCE

FAST FACTS

Nickname: Second City, Windy City, City of the Big Shoulders, Gem of the Prairie, Hog Butcher to the World, "I Will" City, Packingtown, City in a Garden (the city's motto)

Type of government: Mayor elected every four years; 50 aldermen, one from each of the city's wards; city clerk and treasurer also elected to citywide positions

Population: 2.8 million (city); 9.6 million (metro)

Population Density: 12,750 people per square mi

Median age: 32

Crime: Violent crimes were down 2.5% in 2006

Literacy: 37% have trouble with basic reading; 35% speak a language other than English at home, usually Spanish

Ethnic groups: White 57%; Latino 19%; black 18%; Asian 5%; other 1%

Chicago seems a big city instead of merely a large place.
—A.J. Liebling

Things are so tough in Chicago that at Easter time, for bunnies the little kids use porcupines.
—Fred Allen

Chicago is not the most corrupt American city, it's the most theatrically corrupt.
—Studs Terkel

Chicago is a city of contradictions, of private visions haphazardly overlaid and linked together.
—Pat Colander

GEOGRAPHY & ENVIRONMENT

Latitude: 41° N (same as Barcelona, Spain; Istanbul, Turkey)

Longitude: 87° W (same as San Salvador, El Salvador)

Elevation: 579 feet

Land area: 228 square mi

Parkland: 7,337 acres

Terrain: Flat lakefront, extending inland to the west

Natural hazards: Extreme winter storms, tornadoes

Environmental issues: Toxic pollution, invasive species, habitat destruction, and contamination on Lake Michigan; air pollution from coal-fired power plants and diesel engines; wastewater treatment plants have exceeded pollution limits for effluents often

I miss everything about Chicago, except January and February.
—Gary Cole

ECONOMY

Per capita income: $38,439

Unemployment: 3.9%

Workforce: 4.2 million; trade, transportation, and utilities 21%; professional and business services 15%; other 14%; government 13%; manufacturing 12%; educational and health services 12%; leisure and hospitality 8%; construction 5%

Major industries: Aircraft, business services, chemicals, electronics, food processing, insurance, iron, machinery, manufacturing, meatpacking, retail, shipping, steel fabricators, trade

DID YOU KNOW?

■ The candy company MM/Mars makes 3 Musketeers and Snickers bars locally.

■ The nickname "the Windy City" doesn't come from Chicago's bitter winter conditions. Promoters of the city went to the East Coast boasting of Chicago's greatness, in hopes of securing the World's Fair of 1893. *New York Sun* editor Charles Dana tired of the bragging and bestowed the "windy" nickname.

■ Chicago's name comes from a Potawatomi Indian word meaning "wild onion" or "skunk." When Indians first arrived, the future home of America's third-largest city was a patch of rotting marshland onions.

■ The Chicago Post Office at 433 W. Van Buren is the only postal facility in the world that you can drive through.

■ Chicago's sports teams hold many distinctions, among them: the highest points-scoring average in NBA playoff games (Michael Jordan, 33.4 points), the most home runs hit in one month (Sammy Sosa, 20), and the most touchdowns in an NFL game (Ernie Nevers, 6).

■ Chicago produced the first roller skates (1884), steel-framed skyscraper (1885), elevated railway (1892), pinball game (1930), and blood bank (1937), among other things.

■ The last concert that the perennial tour band the Grateful Dead ever played was at Soldier Field in Chicago, on July 9, 1995.

■ The world's longest street is Chicago's Western Avenue.

■ In April 2000 the northwest corner of Walton Street and Michigan Avenue was named Hugh Hefner Way. The Chicago native, raised as a strict Methodist, went on to found *Playboy,* a magazine some credited with helping Americans talk about sex and others said popularized demeaning pornography.

■ Chicago counts the world's largest sewage tunnel among its many architectural and engineering distinctions. The Chicago Tunnels and Reservoir Plan (TARP) has 93 mi of machine-bored sewer tunnels 9 to 33 feet in diameter.

■ Rudolph the Red-Nosed Reindeer is a Chicago native. A copywriter for Montgomery Ward department store created the character as part of a Christmas promotion in 1939.

■ O'Hare Airport used to be a military airport named Orchard Place. That's the reason your luggage tags read ORD today.

With costs so high, restaurateurs demand formulaic, steak-and-potatoes formats. Except for Wylie Dufresne, there are no experimental chefs in New York these days. Where are they? Chicago.

–Grub Street (www.nymag.com)

BOOKS & MOVIES

Books

Native Chicagoan Saul Bellow set many novels in the city, most notably *Humboldt's Gift* and *The Adventures of Augie March*. Richard Wright's explosive *Native Son* and James T. Farrell's *Studs Lonigan* depict racial clashes in Chicago. The works of longtime resident Nelson Algren—*The Man with the Golden Arm, A Walk on the Wild Side,* and *Chicago: City on the Make*—show the city at its grittiest, as does playwright David Mamet's *American Buffalo*. Two series of detective novels use a current-day Chicago backdrop: Sara Paretsky's excellent V. I. Warshawski novels and the Monsignor Ryan mysteries of Andrew Greeley. Greeley has set other novels in Chicago as well, including *Lord of the Dance*. Local author Marcus Sakey set *The Blade Itself,* his debut novel about reunited crime partners, on Chicago's North and South sides. Sakey—with Paretsky and Chicago crime writers Sean Chercover, Barbara D'Amato, Michael Allen Dymmoch, Kevin Guilfoile, and Libby Hellman—are known collectively as "The Outfit" (check out their blog at www.theoutfitcollective.com).

Chicago was once the quintessential newspaper town; the play *The Front Page,* by Ben Hecht and Charles MacArthur, is set here. Local reporters have penned some excellent chronicles, including *Fabulous Chicago,* by Emmett Dedmon; and *Boss,* a portrait of the late mayor Richard J. Daley, by the late Mike Royko. For a selection of Royko's award-winning columns, check out *One More Time: The Best of Mike Royko.* Lois Wille's *Forever Open, Clear and Free* is a superb history of the fight to save Chicago's lakefront parks. Books by Studs Terkel, a great chronicler of Chicago, include *Division Street: America* and *Chicago.* Erik Larson traces two men, architect Daniel Burnham and serial killer Henry H. Holmes, through the Chicago World's Fair of 1893 in *The Devil in the White City. Never a City So Real* is a collection of essays by Alex Kotlowitz. Even graphic novelists have a soft spot for Chicago; one of Chicago's better known, Chris Ware, juxtaposes lovable-looking characters with disparaging dialogue in his graphic novel *Jimmy Corrigan: The Smartest Kid on Earth.*

Architecture buffs can choose from a number of excellent guidebooks. James Cornelius revised *Chicago on Foot,* by Ira J. Bach and Susan Wolfson; the book contains dozens of architecture-driven walking tours. Franz Schulze and Kevin Harrington edited the fourth edition of *Chicago's Famous Buildings,* a pocket guide to the city's most important landmarks and buildings. The *A. I. A. Guide to Chicago,* edited by Alice Sinkevitch, is an exhaustive source of information about local architecture. The pocket-size *Chicago: A Guide to Recent Architecture,* by Susanna Sirefman, covers everything from office buildings to the new airport terminal. For thought-provoking critiques of Chicago's major buildings, pick up *Why Architecture Matters: Lessons From Chicago,* a compilation of articles written by Chicago Tribune architecture critic Blair Kamin. Finally, David Garrad Lowe's *Lost Chicago* is a fascinating, heartbreaking history of vanished buildings.

Movies

Chicago has been the setting for films about everything from gangsters to restless suburbanites. Classic early gangster flicks include *Little Caesar* (1930), with Edward G. Robinson, and *Scarface* (1932), starring Paul Muni and George Raft. The theme is carried out on a lighter note in *The Sting* (1973), George Roy Hill's charming Scott Joplin–scored movie that stars Paul Newman and Robert Redford as suave con men. *Carrie* is the 1952 adaptation of Dreiser's novel about a country girl who loses her innocence in the city; Laurence Olivier and Jennifer Jones are the stars. Lorraine Hansberry's drama about a black Chicago family, *A Raisin in the Sun,* became a film with Sidney Poitier in 1961.

As Elwood and Jake, respectively, Dan Aykroyd and the late John Belushi brought wild energy and cool music to the screen in *The Blues Brothers* (1980). *Ordinary People,* the Oscar-winning 1980 film, starred Mary Tyler Moore in a drama about an affluent and agonized North Shore family. John Hughes directed 1986's *Ferris Bueller's Day Off,* in which Matthew Broderick and a couple of his high-school friends play hooky and tour Chicago for a day. In *About Last Night* (1986), which is based on the David Mamet play *Sexual Perversity in Chicago,* Demi Moore and Rob Lowe go through realistic modern dating games with the help (and hindrance) of hilarious friends played by Elizabeth Perkins and Jim Belushi. Brian De Palma's *The Untouchables* (1987) stars Kevin Costner as Eliot Ness and Robert De Niro as Al Capone in a gangster tale with a 1920s Chicago background. *Eight Men Out* (1988)—with John Cusack, John Mahoney, and Charlie Sheen—depicts baseball's infamous Black Sox scandal, when members of the Chicago White Sox took bribes to throw the 1919 World Series against the Cincinnati Reds.

Kurt Russell and William Baldwin play firefighter brothers in *Backdraft* (1991). In the action thriller *The Fugitive* (1993), Harrison Ford pulls off one narrow escape in Chicago's St. Patrick's Day parade. Steve James's *Hoop Dreams* (1994) is a powerful documentary about a couple of inner-city teens who dream that basketball will be their ticket out. In the romantic comedy *While You Were Sleeping* (1995), Sandra Bullock plays a CTA clerk who saves a man from death on the El. *My Best Friend's Wedding* (1997) is a romantic comedy starring Julia Roberts, who tries to break up the

wedding of Dermot Mulroney and Cameron Diaz. Roberts and Mulroney dance on a boat tour in the Loop.

In *High Fidelity* (2000), John Cusack is a record-store owner struggling with his past and present romantic life. In *Save the Last Dance* (2001), suburban ballerina Julia Stiles learns hip-hop from Sean Patrick Thomas on Chicago's South Side. Second City alum Nia Vardalos adapted the screenplay for the wildly popular *My Big Fat Greek Wedding* (2002) from her one-woman play. *Chicago* (2002) razzle-dazzled its way to six Oscars, helping to bring back the movie musical. *The Road to Perdition* (2002) stars Tom Hanks and Paul Newman in a 1930s gangster drama. *Barbershop* (2002) chronicles a day in the life of a South Side barbershop. Director Robert Altman and star Neve Campbell go behind the scenes with the Joffrey Ballet of Chicago in *The Company* (2003). Will Smith visits the Lake Michigan Landfill in the 2035 Chicago created in the sci-fi thriller *I, Robot* (2004). Josh Hartnett plays a young ad exec in Chicago in *Wicker Park* (2004). As a down-on-his-luck divorcé in *The Weather Man* (2004), Nicolas Cage filmed scenes in both north suburban Evanston and downtown. In *Batman Begins* (2004) Christian Bale, as Batman, is seen racing through Chicago's Lower Wacker Drive in the Batmobile. Jennifer Aniston spent some quality time in the Windy City while filming *Derailed* (2005; co-starring Clive Owen); then she was rumored to have fallen in love with Vince Vaughn while filming *The Break Up* (2006). Will Ferrell got a Golden Globe nomination for Best Actor in a Musical or Comedy for his portrayal of a regular guy whose fate is controlled by a neurotic writer in *Stranger Than Fiction* (2006), which was filmed in Chicago.

Travel Smart Chicago

WORD OF MOUTH

"You'll see almost any type of dress at the theatre. Whatever you wear, you may want to consider taking a light sweater or jacket with you. When I worked in a theatre, the matinee crowd was always thrilled to be out of the heat when they arrived, but by intermission they'd complain they were cold."

–Citylights

GETTING HERE & AROUND

Chicago is famously known as a city of neighborhoods. The Loop is Chicago's epicenter of business, finance, and government. Neighborhoods surrounding the Loop include River North (an area populated by art galleries and high-end boutiques), Streeterville (bordered by Lake Michigan and Navy Pier), and West Loop and South Loop, both up-and-coming areas with trendy residential areas and hip dining and shopping options.

Moving north, you'll encounter the Magnificent Mile (North Michigan Avenue), which gives way to the Gold Coast, so named for its luxurious mansions, stately museums, and deluxe entertainment venues. Lincoln Park, Lakeview, Wrigleyville, Lincoln Square, and Andersonville all lie north of these areas, and each has considerable charms to explore.

Neighborhoods west of the Loop include River West, West Town, Wicker Park, and Bucktown, where of-the-moment art, shopping, dining, and nightlife venues line the streets.

Beyond South Loop lies Hyde Park, home to the University of Chicago and the Museum of Science and Industry.

Traveling between neighborhoods is a relatively sane experience, thanks to the matrix of bus and train routes managed by the Chicago Transit Authority. Driving can be harried, but taxis are normally plentiful in most parts of town.

Chicago streets generally follow a grid pattern, running north–south or east–west and radiating from a center point at State and Madison streets in the Loop. East and west street numbers go up as you move away from State Street; north and south street numbers rise as you move away from Madison Street. Each block is represented by a hundred number.

■TIP→ **Ask the local tourist board about hotel and local transportation packages**

that include tickets to major museum exhibits or other special events.

▌BY AIR

To Chicago: From New York, 2 hours; from San Francisco, 4 hours; from Los Angeles, 4 hours; from Dallas, 2½ hours; from London, 7 hours; from Sydney, 17 hours.

In Chicago, the general rule is to arrive at the airport two hours before an international flight; for a domestic flight, plan to arrive 90 minutes early if you're checking luggage and 60 minutes if you're not.

There are no direct flights from Chicago to Australia or New Zealand. There are several daily direct flights to the United Kingdom by British Midland, United, and American.

Smoking policies vary from carrier to carrier. U.S. airlines prohibit smoking on all flights.

Airlines & Airports Airline and Airport Links.com (⊕ www.airlineandairportlinks.com) has links to many of the world's airlines and airports.

Airline Security Issues Transportation Security Administration (⊕ www.tsa.gov) has answers for almost every question that might come up.

AIRPORTS
The major gateway to Chicago is **O'Hare International Airport** (ORD). As one of the world's busiest airports, all major airlines pass through O'Hare. The sprawling structure is situated 19 mi from down-

town, in the far northwest corner of the city. It can take anywhere from 30 to 90 minutes to travel between downtown and O'Hare, based on time of day, weather conditions, and construction on the Kennedy Expressway (Interstate 90). The Blue Line El train offers a reliable 40-minute trip between the Loop and O'Hare.

Got some time to spend before your flight? Plenty of dining and shopping options are scattered throughout O'Hare's four terminals. Chicago favorites such as the Billy Goat Tavern, Goose Island Brewing Company, Pizzeria Uno, and Gold Coast Dogs can be found among the usual chain restaurants. Grab that last-minute souvenir or in-flight necessity at an array of shops, including the Chicago Historical Society Gift Shop, the Field Museum Gift Shop, and Landau Jewelers. Or spring for a mini-massage from the Back Rub Hub. Wi-Fi is also available throughout the building.

■TIP➜ **If you're stuck at O'Hare longer than you expected, the Hilton Chicago O'Hare (773/686-8000) is located within walking distance of all terminals.**

Midway Airport (MDW) is situated about 11 mi southwest from downtown. Midway Airport serves American, Continental, and Delta airlines along with budget carriers like Southwest, Airtran, and United Express. Driving between Midway and downtown can take 30 to 60 minutes, depending on traffic conditions on the Stevenson Expressway (Interstate 55). The Orange Line El train runs from the Loop to Midway in about 30 minutes.

Some say the recently renovated Midway has better dining options than O'Hare. With downtown standouts such as Harry Caray's, Manny's Deli, and Gold Coast Dogs all on-site, it's a good point. The Midway Boulevard area in the center of the building features cute shops such as Chicago Treasures and Kid's Corner. Wi-Fi is available throughout the airport.

An extended stay near Midway Airport can be spent at a number of nearby hotels, including Chicago Marriott Midway (800/228-9290), Hampton Inn Midway (708/496-1900), and Hilton Garden Inn Midway (708/496-2700).

Security screenings at both airports are fairly quick (it takes about 15 to 30 min-

---

SCI-FI, INDEED

If you travel frequently, look into the TSA's Registered Traveler program. The program, which is still being tested in several U.S. airports, is designed to cut down on gridlock at security checkpoints by allowing prescreened travelers to pass quickly through kiosks that scan an iris and/or a fingerprint. How sci-fi is that?

---

utes or less to get through security lines); however, during peak holiday travel, you should arrive about two hours before your flight.

■TIP➜ **Long layovers don't have to be only about sitting around or shopping. These days they can be about burning off vacation calories. Check out www.airportgyms. com for lists of health clubs that are in or near many U.S. and Canadian airports.**

Airport Information Midway Airport (☎773/838-0600 ⊕www.chicago-mdw.com or www.flychicago.com). **O'Hare International Airport** (☎773/686-2200 or 800/832-6352 ⊕www.ohare.com or www.flychicago.com).

GROUND TRANSPORTATION

If you're traveling to or from the airport by bus or car during morning or afternoon rush hours, factor in some extra time—ground transport to or from both O'Hare and Midway airports can be slow.

By Bus: Shuttle buses run between O'Hare and Midway airports and to and from either airport and various points in the city. When taking an airport shuttle bus to O'Hare or Midway to catch a departing flight, be sure to allow at least 1½ hours. When going to either airport, it's a good idea to make a reservation 24 hours in advance. Though some shuttles make regular stops at the major hotels and don't require reservations, it's best to check. Reservations are not necessary from the airports. Omega Airport Shuttle runs an hourly shuttle between the two airports for approximately $16 per person. Travel time is approximately one hour. Omega Airport Shuttle also provides an hourly service from the two airports and Hyde Park. The fare is $30 from O'Hare to Hyde Park and $17 from Midway to Hyde Park. Airport Express coaches provide service from both airports to major downtown and Near North locations and the northern suburbs. The trip downtown from O'Hare takes at least 45 minutes, depending on traffic conditions; the fare is $27, $49 round-trip. The trip downtown from Midway takes at least a half hour; the fare is $22, $37 round-trip. Call to find out times and prices for other destinations.

By Car: Depending on traffic and the time of day, driving to and from O'Hare takes about an hour, and driving to and from Midway takes at least 45 minutes. From O'Hare, follow the signs to Interstate 90 east (Kennedy Expressway), which merges with Interstate 94 (Edens Expressway). Take the eastbound exit at Ohio Street for Near North locations, the Washington or Monroe Street exit for downtown. After you exit, continue east about a mile to get to Michigan Avenue. From Midway, follow the signs to Interstate 55 east, which leads to Interstate 90.

By Taxi: Metered taxicab service is available at both O'Hare and Midway airports. Trips to and from O'Hare may incur a $1 surcharge to compensate for changing fuel costs. Expect to pay about $40 to $45 plus tip from O'Hare to Near North and downtown locations, about $30 to $35 plus tip from Midway. Some cabs, such as Checker Taxi and Yellow Cab, participate in a shared-ride program in which each cab carries up to four individual passengers going from the airport to downtown. The cost per person—a flat fee that varies according to destination— is substantially lower than the full rate, which is approximately $50.

By Train: Chicago Transit Authority (CTA) trains, called elevated or El trains (locals often refer to it simply as "the El"), are the cheapest way to and from the airports; they can also be the most convenient transfer. TRAINS TO CITY signs will guide you to the subway or elevated train line. In O'Hare Airport the Blue Line station is in the underground concourse between terminals. Travel time to the city is about 45 minutes. Get off at the station closest to your hotel, or from the first stop in the Loop (Washington and Dearborn streets) you can take a taxi to your hotel or change to other transit lines. At Midway Airport the Orange Line El runs to the Loop. The stop at Adams Street and Wabash Avenue is the closest to the hotels on South Michigan Avenue; for others, the simplest strategy is to get off anywhere in the Loop and hail a cab to your final destination. Train fare is $2, which you'll need in dollar bills (turnstiles don't give change) and/or coins. A fare card is another option. Pick up train brochures and system maps outside the entrances to the platforms; the "Downtown Transit Sightseeing Guide" is also helpful.

Transfers Between Airports O'Hare and Midway airports are located on opposite ends of the city, so moving between them can be a time-consuming and arduous task. Your best and cheapest move is hopping on the El. You will travel the Blue Line to the Orange Line, transferring at the Clark Street stop to get from O'Hare to Midway, reversing the trip to go from Midway to O'Hare. The entire journey should take you under 2 hours. If time is an issue, you may want to consider Coach USA Wisconsin, a shuttle bus that makes the trip between the two airports several times a day from 8:15 AM to

9:15 PM. The fare is $15 per person, one way; $27 round-trip. You can purchase tickets from the driver or in advance from the company's Web site. The trip should take you about 1 hour, depending on traffic conditions.

Taxis & Shuttles **American United Cab Co.** (☎773/248–7600). **Coach USA Wisconsin** (☎800/236–2028 ⊕www.coachusa.com/wisconsincoach). **Airport Express** (☎888/2THEVAN ⊕www.airportexpress.com). **Checker Taxi** (☎312/243–2537). **Flash Cab** (☎773/561–1444). **Omega Airport Shuttle** (☎773/734–6688 ⊕www.omegashuttle.com). **Yellow Cab Co.** (☎312/829–4222 ⊕www.yellowcabchicago.com).

Public Transit Information **CTA** (☎312/836–7000 ⊕www.transitchicago.com).

▌ BIKE TRAVEL

Mayor Daley's goal is to make Chicago the most bike-friendly city in the United States, and he's well on his way. One-hundred-twenty miles of designated bike routes run throughout the city, through historic areas, beautiful parks, and along city streets (look for the words BIKE LANE). Bicycling on busy city streets can be a challenge and is not for the faint of heart—cars come within inches of riders, and the doors of parked cars can swing open at any time. The best bet for a scenic ride is the lakefront, which has a traffic-free 18-mi asphalt trail affording scenic views of the skyline. When your bike is unattended, always lock it; there are bike racks throughout the city. In Millennium Park at Michigan Avenue and Randolph Street (⊕www.chicagobikestation.com), there are 300 free indoor bike spaces plus showers, lockers, and bike-rental facilities offering beach cruisers, mountain and road bikes, hybrid/comfort models, tandem styles, and add-ons for kids (wagon, baby seat, etc.). Bike rentals are also readily available at Bike Chicago, which has five locations, one at Millennium Park, one at Navy Pier, one at the Riverwalk at Wacker Drive and the Chicago River, and two along the lakefront (⊕*www.bikechicago.com*). Bike Chicago carries a good selection of mountain and cross bikes. Rates start at $8 per hour. The Chicago Department of Tourism publishes free route maps. Chicagoland Bicycle Federation maps cost $6.95. Maps are updated every few years. From April through October, Bobby's Bike Hike takes guests on cycling tours of Chicago. The three-hour tours begin at the Water Tower on the Magnificent Mile and cycle through historic neighborhoods, shopping areas, and the lakefront. A $30 to $35 fee includes bikes, helmets, and guides; book online for a 10 percent discount.

Information **Bobby's Bike Hike** (☎312/915–0995 ⊕www.bobbysbikehike.com). **Chicago Department of Tourism (CDOT)** (☎312/742–2453 ⊕egov.cityofchicago.org/Transportation) publishes free route maps. **Chicagoland Bicycle Federation** (☎312/427–3325 ⊕www.biketraffic.org).

▌ BY BOAT

Water taxis are an economical and in-the-know way to cruise parts of the Chicago River and Lake Michigan. A combination of working stiffs and tourists board these boats daily. You won't get the in-depth narrative of an architecture tour, but the views of Chicago's waterways are just as good.

Wendella Boats operates Chicago Water Taxis, which use four downtown docks (Madison Street, LaSalle Street, Michigan Avenue, and River East Plaza) along the Chicago River. The entire ride takes about a half hour, and you'll get to see a good portion of the downtown part of the Chicago River. The boats operate seven days a week, May through October. You can purchase tickets at any dock or on the company's Web site.

Shoreline Water Taxis run two routes: the River Taxi cruises between the Sears Tower and Navy Pier, and the Harbor

NAVIGATING CHICAGO

Chicago is a surprisingly well-ordered and manageable city. A few city-planning quirks do exist, however. Streets that run on a diagonal, such as Milwaukee, Elston, and Lincoln avenues, jut and hurtle drunkenly through the city. These passageways are actually old Indian trails that followed the Chicago River. Chicago also has a proliferation of double- and even triple-decker streets, Wacker Drive being the best-known example. The uppermost level is generally used for street traffic, while the lower levels serve as thoroughfares for cutting through the city rather quickly.

The most helpful landmark to help you navigate Chicago is Lake Michigan. It will always lie on the east, as it serves as the city's only eastern border. Also, look for the Sears Tower and John Hancock Center; which reach up far enough into the sky to serve as beacons. The Sears Tower is in the Loop, and the John Hancock Center is on northern Michigan Avenue.

Chicago's public transit system blankets the city well and is fairly intuitive. Major bus lines include the 151-Sheridan, which runs along the Lakefront, the 36-Broadway, which cuts through the Gold Coast, Lincoln Park, and Lakeview, and the 125-Water Tower Express, which takes a meandering route from Union Station to Water Tower. The train system (referred to as the El, short for "elevated") is an even more comprehensive network with eight train lines criss-crossing through the city and nearby suburbs. The most popular routes are the Blue Line, which runs from O'Hare Airport into the city through Bucktown and back out again through the Loop; the Red Line, which cuts a north–south swath through the city, crossing through Edgewater, Lakeview, Lincoln Park, the Gold Coast, the Loop, and the South Side; and the Brown Line, which travels from the Far Northwest Side through Lakeview and Lincoln Park, into the Loop, and back up north.

Taxi navigates Lake Michigan between Navy Pier and the Museum Campus. Water Taxis run 10 AM to 6 PM late May to early September. You can purchase tickets at any dock or in advance on the company's Web site.

Information **Shoreline Sightseeing** (⊠474 N. Lake Shore Dr., Suite 3511 ☎312/222–9328 ⊕www.shorelinesightseeing.com). **Wendella Boats** (⊠400 N. Michigan Ave. [main dock] ☎312/337–1446 ⊕www.wendellaboats.com).

▌BY BUS

Greyhound has nationwide service to its main terminal in the Loop and to neighborhood stations, at the 95th Street and Dan Ryan Expressway CTA station and at the Cumberland CTA station, near O'Hare Airport. The Harrison Street terminal is far from most hotels, so plan on another bus or a cab to your hotel.

For information on bus travel within Chicago, see By Public Transportation.

Bus Information **Chicago Transit Authority** (☎888/968–7282 ⊕www.transitchicago.com). **Greyhound Lines** (☎800/231–2222 ⊕www.greyhound.com). **Main Depot** (⊠630 W. Harrison St. ☎312/408–5800). **South Depot** (⊠14 W. 95th St. ☎312/408–5999). **Northwest Depot (O'Hare)** (⊠CTA Transit Building, 5800 N. Cumberland Ave. ☎773/693–2474).

▌BY CAR

Chicago's network of buses and rapid-transit rail is extensive, and taxis and limousines are readily available (the latter often priced competitively with metered cabs), so rent a car *only* to visit the outlying suburbs that are not accessible by public transportation. Chicago traffic is often heavy, on-street parking is nearly impossible to find, parking lots are expensive, congestion creates frustrating delays, and other drivers may be impatient with those who are unfamiliar with the city and its roads. Expect snarled traffic during rush hours. In these circumstances you may find a car to be a liability rather than an asset. The Illinois Department of Transportation gives information on expressway congestion, travel times, and lane closures and directions on state roadways.

The Illinois tollways snake around the outskirts of the city. Interstate 294 runs north and south between Wisconsin and Indiana. Interstate 90 runs northwest to western Wisconsin, including Madison and Wisconsin Dells. Interstate 88 runs east–west and goes from Eisenhower to Interstate 55. Traffic on all is sometimes just as congested as on the regular expressways. Most toll gates are unmanned, so bring lots of change if you don't have an I-Pass, which are sometimes included with rental cars. Even though tolls are double without the I-Pass, it's not cost effective to purchase one for a couple of days.

If you decide to rent a car, you'll have plenty of options, from the big rental chains to luxury options. The common rental agencies regularly stock new American-made models with standard amenities (air-conditioning, automatic transmission, AM/FM stereo).

Rates in Chicago begin around $50 a day, $130 a week or $35 a weekend for an economy car with air-conditioning, automatic transmission, and unlimited mileage. This does not include the car-rental tax of 18% plus a $2.75 surcharge per rental. If you rent from the airport, it's slightly more expensive because of airport taxes.

Gasoline Gas stations are less prevalent in downtown Chicago than in the outlying neighborhoods and suburbs. Filling up is about 50 cents higher per gallon downtown when you can find a station. Expect to pay anywhere between $3 and $4 per gallon of gas (per prices at time of writing). Major credit cards are accepted at all gas stations, and the majority of stations are completely self-serve.

Parking Most of Chicago's streets have metered parking, but during peak hours it's hard to find a spot. Most meters take quarters, buying as little as 5 minutes in high-traffic areas, up to an hour in less crowded neighborhoods. Parking lots and garages are plentiful downtown, but they're expensive. You could pay anywhere from $13 for the day in a municipal lot to $24 for three hours in a private lot. Some neighborhoods, such as the area of Lakeview known as Wrigleyville, enforce restricted parking (especially strict on game nights) and will tow cars without permits. You won't find many public parking lots in the neighborhoods. Many major thoroughfares restrict parking during peak travel hours, generally 9 to 11 AM heading toward downtown and 4 to 6 PM heading away. Read street signs carefully to determine whether a parking spot is legal. During the winter on snow days, cars parked in designated "snow route areas" will be towed. There's a $30 fine plus the cost of towing the car. In sum, Chicago isn't the most car-friendly place for visitors. Unless it's a necessity, it's best to forget renting a car and use public transportation.

Road Conditions Chicago drivers can be reckless, zipping through red lights and breaking posted speed limits. The Loop and some residential neighborhoods such as Lincoln Park, Lakeview, and Bucktown are made up of mostly one-way streets, so be sure to read signs carefully. Check both ways after a light turns green to make sure that the cross traffic has stopped.

Rush hours are 6:30 to 9:30 AM and 4 to 7 PM, but don't be surprised if the rush starts earlier or ends later, depending on weather conditions, big events, and holiday weekends. There are always bottlenecks on the expressways, particularly where the Edens and Kennedy merge, and downtown on the Dan Ryan from 22nd Street into the Loop. Sometimes anything around the airport is rough.

There are electronic signs on the expressways that post updates on the congestion. Additionally, summertime is high time for construction on highways and inner-city roads. Drive with patience.

■TIP➜ **For more information about Chicago's roadways, including up-to-the-minute road conditions, check out the Illinois Department of Transportation's Web site at www.dot.state.il.us.**

Roadside Emergencies Dial 911 in an emergency to reach police, fire, or ambulance services. AAA Chicago provides roadside assistance to members. Mr. Locks Emergency Locksmith & Security Service will unlock your vehicle 24 hours a day.

Emergency Services AAA Chicago (☎800/222–4357 [AAA–HELP)]) ⊕www.autoclubgroup.com). **Mr. Locks Emergency Locksmith & Security Service** (☎866/675–6257 ⊕www.mr-locks.com).

Rules of the Road Speed limits in Chicago vary, but on most city roads it's 35 mph. Most interstate highways, except in congested areas, have a speed limit of 55 mph. In Chicago, you may turn right at a red light after stopping if there's no oncoming traffic and no posted restrictions. When in doubt, wait for the green. Cameras have been installed at certain intersections in the city to catch drivers who run red lights. There are many one-way streets in Chicago, particularly in and around the Loop, so be alert to signs and other cars. Illinois drunk-driving laws are quite strict. Anyone caught driving with a blood-alcohol content of .08 will automatically have his or her license seized and be issued a ticket, and authorities in home states will be notified. Those with Illinois drivers' licenses can have their licenses suspended for three months on the very first offense.

Passengers are required to wear seat belts. Always strap children under age eight into approved child-safety seats.

It's illegal to use hand-held cellular phones in the city, but there aren't any restrictions in the suburbs. Headlights are compulsory if you're using windshield wipers. Radar detectors are legal in Illinois.

▌ BY PUBLIC TRANSPORTATION

Chicago's extensive public transportation network includes rapid-transit trains, buses, and a commuter-rail network. The Chicago Transit Authority, or CTA, operates the rapid-transit trains (the El), city buses, and suburban buses (PACE). Metra runs the commuter rail.

The Regional Transportation Authority (RTA) for northeastern Illinois oversees and coordinates the activities of the CTA and Metra. The RTA's Web site can be a useful first stop if you are planning to combine suburban and city public transit while in Chicago. In 2008 the state passed legislation that gives seniors a free ride—literally. Seniors age 65 and older ride free on all fixed train and bus routes operated by the CTA, Metra, and Pace. Details about where to sign up and which routes are eligible are available on the RTA's Web site.

Information RTA Travel Information Center (☎312/836–7000 ⊕www.rtachicago.com).

CTA: The El & Buses The Chicago Transit Authority (CTA) operates rapid-transit trains and buses. Chicago's rapid-transit train system is known as the El. Each of the eight lines has a color name as well as a route name: Blue (O'Hare–Congress–Douglas), Brown (Ravenswood), Green (Lake–Englewood–Jackson Park), Orange (Midway), Purple (Evanston), Red (Howard–Dan Ryan), Yellow (Skokie–Swift), and Pink (Cermak). In general, the route names indicate the first and last stop on the train. Chicagoans refer to trains both by the color and the route name. Most, but not all, rapid-transit lines operate 24 hours; some stations are closed at night. The El, though very crowded during rush hours, is the quickest way to get around (unless you're coming from the suburbs, in which case the Metra is quicker but doesn't run as often). Trains run every 15 minutes, though during rush hour they run about every 10 minutes and on weekends, every 30 minutes. Pick up the brochure "Downtown Transit Sightseeing Guide" for hours, fares, and other pertinent information. In general, late-night CTA travel is not recommended. Note that the Red and Blue lines are subways; the rest are elevated. This means if you're heading to O'Hare and looking for the Blue Line, look for a stairway down, not up.

Exact fares must be paid in cash (dollar bills or coins; no change given by turnstiles on train platforms or fare boxes on buses) or by transit card. Transit cards are flimsy plastic and credit-card size and can be purchased from machines at CTA train stations as well as at Jewel and Dominicks grocery stores and currency exchanges. These easy-to-use cards are inserted into the turnstiles at CTA train stations and into machines as you board CTA buses; directions are clearly posted. Use them to transfer between CTA vehicles. To transfer between the Loop's elevated lines and the subway or between rapid-transit trains and buses, you must either use a transit card with at least 30¢ stored on it, or, if you're not using a transit card, buy a transfer when you first board. If two CTA train lines meet, you can transfer for free. You can also obtain free train-to-train transfers from specially marked turnstiles at the Washington/State subway station or the State/Lake El station, or ask for a transfer card, good on downtown trains, at the ticket booth.

Buses generally stop on every other corner northbound and southbound (on State Street they stop at every corner). Eastbound and westbound buses generally stop on every corner. Buses from the Loop generally run north–south. Principal transfer points are on Michigan Avenue at the north side of Randolph Street for northbound buses, Adams Street and Wabash Avenue for westbound buses and the El, and State and Lake streets for southbound buses.

Buses are crowded during rush hour. Schedules vary depending on the time of day and route, and run every 8 to 15 minutes, though service is less frequent on weekends, very early in the morning, and late at night. Schedules are available online at www.transitchicago.com.

Pace runs suburban buses in a six-county region; these connect with the CTA and use CTA transit cards, transfers, and passes.

CTA Fares: The CTA fare structure is as follows: the basic fare for rapid-transit trains is $2 when paying cash or using a transit card. The basic fare for buses is $2 when paying cash and $1.75 when using a transit card. Transfers are 25¢ when using a transit card; no transfers are issued when paying cash. Transit cards can be purchased in preset denominations of $10 ($11 worth of rides) or $20 ($22 worth of rides) at many local grocery stores, currency exchanges, and stations. You can also purchase a transit card of any denomination over $2 at any CTA stop. Transfers can be used twice within a two-hour time period. Transfers between CTA train lines are free—no transfer card is needed. Transit cards may be shared.

For $5, a one-day Visitor Pass offers 24 hours of unlimited CTA riding from the time you first use it. Visitor Passes are sold at hotels, museums, and other places tourists frequent, plus all transit-card booths. A two-day pass is $9, a three-day pass is $12, and a five-day pass is $18.

Information CTA (✉ Merchandise Mart, 350 N. Wells St. ☎ 888/968–7282 ⊕ www.transitchicago.com).

Metra: Commuter Trains Metra commuter trains serve the city and surrounding suburbs. The Metra Electric railroad has a line close to Lake Michigan; its trains stop in Hyde Park. The Metra commuter rail system has 11 lines to suburbs and surrounding cities including Aurora, Elgin, Joliet, and Waukegan; one line serves the North Shore suburbs, and another has a stop at McCormick Place. Trains leave from a number of downtown terminals.

Metra trains use a fare structure based on the distance you ride. A Metra weekend pass costs $5 and is valid for rides on any of the eight operating lines all day on weekends, except for the South Shore line.

Information **Metra information line** (☎312/322-6777 ⊕www.metrarail.com).

▮ BY TAXI

You can hail a cab on just about any busy street in Chicago. Hotel doormen will hail a cab for you as well. Cabs aren't all yellow anymore, but look for standard-size sedans or, in some cases, minivans. Available taxis are sometimes indicated by an illuminated rooftop light. Chicago taxis are metered, with fares beginning at $2.25 upon entering the cab and $1.80 for each additional mile or 20¢ for every 36 seconds of wait time. A charge of $1 for the first additional passenger and 50¢ is made for each additional passenger. There's no extra baggage or credit-card charge. Taxi drivers expect a 15% tip.

Taxi Companies **American United Cab Co.** (☎773/248-7600). **Checker Taxi** (☎312/243-2537). **Flash Cab** (☎773/561-1444). **Yellow Cab Co.** (☎312/829-4222 ⊕www.yellowcabchicago.com).

▮ BY TRAIN

Amtrak offers nationwide service to Chicago's Union Station, located at 225 South Canal Street. Some trains travel overnight, and you can sleep in your seat or book a sleeper car at an additional cost. Train schedules and payment options are available by calling Amtrak directly or consulting its Web site. Amtrak trains tend to fill up, so if you don't purchase a ticket in advance at least make a reservation.

Information **Amtrak** (☎800/872-7245 ⊕www.amtrak.com).

ESSENTIALS

▮ COMMUNICATIONS

INTERNET

Chicago is more and more a wireless city, with many hotels and restaurants offering high-speed wireless access. Some hotels have a nominal fee (usually less than $10) that gets you online for 24 hours. You can also duck into places like FedEx Kinko's to check your e-mail, either on your own laptop or the available computers, but charges there can run high if you're online longer than a few minutes.

Contacts **Cybercafes** (⊕www.cybercafes.com) lists over 4,000 Internet cafés worldwide. **FedEx Kinko's** (✉444 N. Wells St. ☎312/670–4460 ⊕www.fedexkinkos.com). **Fixx Coffee Bar** (✉3053 N. Sheffield Ave. ☎773/248–0841). **Intelligentsia Coffee & Tea** (✉3123 N. Broadway St. ☎773/348–8058). **Mercury Cafe** (✉1505 W. Chicago Ave. ☎312/455–9924).**State Restaurant & Cafe** (✉935 W. Webster Ave. ☎773/975–8030). **Swim Cafe** (✉1357 W. Chicago Ave. ☎312/492–8600).

▮ DAY TOURS & GUIDES

A comprehensive collection of Chicago tours by air, water, and land can be found through **Chicago Tours** (☎888/881–3284 ⊕*www.chicagotours.us*), a travel-reservation company offering more than 75 tours, cruises, events, and activities.

BOAT TOURS

Get a fresh perspective on Chicago by taking a water tour or cruise. Boat tour schedules vary by season; be sure to call for exact times and fares. The season usually runs from May 1 through October 1. One cruise in particular stands out, though it's a bit more expensive than the rest: the Chicago Architecture Foundation river cruise aboard *Chicago's First Lady, Chicago's Little Lady,* or *Chicago's Fair Lady.* The CAF tour highlights more than 50 architecturally significant sights.

Chicago is served by two daily metro newspapers, the *Chicago Tribune* and the *Chicago Sun-Times.* Also be sure to check out the two alternative newsweeklies, *Chicago Reader,* which comes out on Thursday, and *New City,* which is available on Wednesday. For a glimpse into Chicago's social scene, pick up the free *CS* magazine from kiosks around town. The features-oriented monthly periodical *Chicago Magazine* and the entertainment-obsessed weekly *Time Out Chicago* are sold at most newsstands.

The cost is $28 on weekdays, $30 on weekends and holidays; reservations are recommended.

If you're looking for a maritime adventure, you can get a blast from the past on the *Windy,* a 148-foot ship modeled on old-time commercial vessels. Passengers may help the crew or take a turn at the wheel during sailing cruises of Lake Michigan. The cost is $30.

Boat Tours **Chicago Architecture Foundation river cruise** (☎312/922–3432 information, 312/902–1500 tickets ⊕www.architecture.org). **Mercury Chicago Skyline Cruiseline** (☎312/332–1353 recorded information ⊕www.mercuryskylinecruiseline.com). **Shoreline Marine** (☎312/222–9328 ⊕www.shorelinesightseeing.com). **Wendella Sightseeing Boats** (✉400 N. Michigan Ave. ☎312/337–1446 ⊕www.wendellaboats.com). **Windy of Chicago Ltd.** (☎312/595–5555 ⊕www.tallshipwindy.com).

BUS & TROLLEY TOURS

A narrated bus or trolley tour can be a good way to orient yourself among Chicago's main sights. Tours cost roughly $20 and normally last two hours. American Sightseeing offers two routes; combined, they cover the city quite thoroughly. The double-decker buses of Chicago Motor

Coach Company tour downtown Chicago and the lakefront.

Chicago Trolley Charters schedules stops at all the downtown attractions. You can get on and off the open-air trolleys as you like; these tours vary in price, so call for details. The Chicago Architecture Foundation's bus tours often go farther afield, exploring everything from cemeteries to movie palaces.

Bus & Trolley Tours **American Sightseeing** (☎800/621-4153 ⊕www.grayline.com). **Chicago Architecture Foundation** (Tour Center ✉Santa Fe Bldg., 224 S. Michigan Ave. ☎312/922-3432 ⊕www.architecture.org). **Chicago Trolley Charters** (☎773/648-5000 ⊕www.chicagotrolley.com).

FOREIGN-LANGUAGE TOURS

Foreign-Language Tours **Chicago Tour Guides Institute, Inc.** (☎773/276-6683 ⊕www.chicagoguide.net).

SPECIAL-INTEREST TOURS

African-American **Black Coutours** (☎773/233-8907 ⊕www.blackcoutours.com). **Tour Black Chicago** (☎773/684-9034 ⊕www.tourblackchicago.com).

Architecture ⇨ Walking Tours.

Chocolate **Accenting Chicago** (☎312/819-5363 ⊕www.accentingchicago.com). **Chicago Chocolate Tours** (☎312/863-8614 ⊕www.chicagochocolatetours.com).

Gangsters **Untouchable Tours** (☎773/881-1195 ⊕www.gangstertour.com).

Ghosts **Chicago Supernatural Ghost Tours** (☎708/499-0300 ⊕www.ghosttours.com).

Historic Neighborhoods **Black Metropolis Convention and Tourism Council** (☎773/373-2842 ⊕www.bronzevilleonline.com/bvic.htm). **Chicago Neighborhood Tours** (☎312/742-1190 ⊕www.chicagoneighborhoodtours.com).

Horse & Carriage Rides **Antique Coach and Carriage** (☎773/735-9400 ⊕www.antique-coach-carriage.com). **Chicago Horse & Carriage Ltd.** (☎312/953-9530 ⊕www.

chicagocarriage.com). **Noble Horse** (☎312/266-7878 ⊕www.noblehorsechicago.com).

WALKING TOURS

The Chicago Architecture Foundation has by far the largest selection of guided tours, with more than 50 itineraries covering everything from department stores to Frank Lloyd Wright's Oak Park buildings. Especially popular walking tours of the Loop are given daily throughout the year. Chicago Greeter and InstaGreeter (for last-minute weekend visits) are two free city services that match knowledgeable Chicagoans with visitors for tours of various sights and neighborhoods. Friends of the Chicago River has Saturday-morning walking tours along the river. The organization also has maps of the walking routes, available for a small donation.

Information **Chicago Architecture Foundation** (Tour Centers ✉Santa Fe Bldg., 224 S. Michigan Ave. ☎312/922-3432 ⊕www.architecture.org). **Chicago Greeter and InstaGreeter** (✉Chicago Office of Tourism, 78 E. Washington St. ☎312/744-2400 ⊕www.chicagogreeter.com). **Friends of the Chicago River** (✉407 S. Dearborn St., Suite 1580 ☎312/939-0490 ⊕www.chicagoriver.org).

▌HOURS OF OPERATION

Neighborhood business hours are generally 9 to 6 Friday through Wednesday, and 9 to 9 on Thursday. When holidays fall on a weekend, businesses usually close around four on the preceding Friday. On a Monday following a weekend holiday, retail businesses are rarely closed but regular businesses often are. Most stores close for Christmas, New Year's, and Easter Sunday.

Chicagoland museums are generally open daily 9 to 5, closing only on major holidays; some larger attractions keep later hours (until about 8 PM) one weeknight per week. A number of smaller museums keep limited hours; it's always advisable to phone ahead for details.

Most pharmacies are open regular business hours, starting as early as 8 AM. Some close as early as 5 PM, but many stay open later, anywhere from 6 to 10 PM.

Most businesses in Chicago are open 9 to 5 Monday through Saturday; many are open Sunday, too, but often with shorter hours (for example, noon to 4 or 5).

MONEY

Costs in Chicago are quite reasonable compared to other large cities such as San Francisco and New York. Restaurants, events, and parking costs are markedly higher in the Loop than in any other area of the city.

ATMs are plentiful. You can find them in banks, grocery stores, and hotels, as well as at some drug stores, gas stations, and convenience stores.

Prices throughout this guide are given for adults. Substantially reduced fees are almost always available for children, students, and senior citizens.

PACKING

In general, Chicago's out-and-about look is casual—jeans, a polished top, and comfortable shoes should be fine for touring around the city. The weather can change abruptly, so it's a good idea to dress in layers. Summers can be very hot and winters very cold and windy—hat, gloves, a scarf, and a warm coat are vital. Don't forget an umbrella.

For dining out, most elegant restaurants in the city require a shirt and tie for men and a dressy look for women. For mass, church, or synagogue services, people usually dress in nice slacks or skirts or dresses. Men do not always wear a suit or a sport jacket, but rarely wear jeans.

TIPS TO REMEMBER

To save money on sightseeing, buy a **Chicago CityPass** (☎ *888/330–5008* ⊕ *www.citypass.com/city/chicago*), which costs $59. The passes are good for nine days from the day of first use and include admission to the Field Museum, the Museum of Science and Industry, the Adler Planetarium, the Shedd Aquarium, and either the John Hancock Center Observatory or the Sears Tower Skydeck. You can buy the pass at any one of the participating attractions or on the Web site. The **Go Chicago Card** (☎ *800/887–9103* ⊕ *www. gochicagocard.com*) is good for more than 25 attractions and shopping, dining, and hotel discounts. The card can be purchased as a one-day or a multiday pass.

RESTROOMS

Facilities are readily available in tourist areas and throughout the downtown malls, Navy Pier, North Pier, and in many larger department stores. For the most part, restrooms are quite clean. Along the lakefront and in the park districts, public facilities close in wintertime. Most gas stations have restrooms, though sanitation standards vary.

Find a Loo **The Bathroom Diaries** (⊕ www. thebathroomdiaries.com) is flush with unsanitized info on restrooms the world over—each one located, reviewed, and rated.

SAFETY

The most common crimes in public places are pickpocketing, purse snatching, jewelry theft, and gambling scams. Men: keep your wallet in a front coat or pants pocket. Women: close your purse securely and keep it close to you. Also beware of someone jostling you and of loud arguments; these could be ploys to distract your attention while another person grabs your wallet. Leave unnecessary credit cards at home and hide valuables and jewelry from view.

Although crime on CTA buses and trains has declined, several precautions can reduce the chance of your becoming a victim: look alert and purposeful; know your route ahead of time; have your fare ready before boarding; and keep an eye on your purse or packages during the ride. Avoid taking public transit late at night.

■TIP➔ Distribute your cash, credit cards, I.D.s, and other valuables between a deep front pocket, an inside jacket or vest pocket, and a hidden money pouch. Don't reach for the money pouch once you're in public.

▌TAXES

At restaurants, you'll pay approximately 10% meal tax (thanks to special taxing initiatives, some parts of town are higher than others).

The hotel tax in Chicago is 15.4%, and slightly less in suburban hotels.

In Chicago a steep 10.25% state and county sales tax is added to all purchases except groceries, which have a 2% tax. Sales tax is already added into the initial price of prescription drugs.

▌TIME

Chicago is in the central standard time zone. It's 1 hour behind New York, 2 hours ahead of Los Angeles, 6 hours behind London, and 16 hours behind Sydney.

Time Zones **Timeanddate.com** (⊕*www. timeanddate.com/worldclock*) can help you figure out the correct time anywhere in the world.

▌TIPPING

You should tip 15% for adequate service in restaurants and up to 20% if you feel you've been treated well. At higher-end restaurants, where there are more service personnel per table who must divide the tip, up these measures by a few percentage points. An especially helpful wine steward should be acknowledged with $2 or $3. It's not necessary to tip the maître d' unless you've been done a very special favor and you intend to visit again. Tip $1 per checked coat.

Taxi drivers, bartenders, and hairdressers expect about 15%. Bellhops and porters should get about $1 per bag; valet-parking attendants $1 or $2 (but only after they bring your car to you, not when they park it), and hotel maids about $1 to $2 per room per day of your stay. On package tours, conductors and drivers usually get about $2 to $3 per day from each group member. Concierges should get tips of $5 to $10 for special service.

▌VISITOR INFORMATION

The Chicago Convention and Tourism Bureau is a great place to start planning your visit to the Windy City. The organization's Web site (⊕ www.choosechicago.com) is a veritable goldmine of information, from hotel packages, sample itineraries, event calendars, and maps. You can also call the toll-free number (☎ 877/CHICAGO) to speak with a travel consultant. The Mayor's Office of Special Events Web site will give you detailed instructions about getting around the city, neighborhood tours, and city-sponsored initiatives. The Illinois Bureau of Tourism offers much of the same Chicago information and is especially helpful if your travel plans will bring you outside of the downtown area. Once you're here, you can count on the visitor centers at the Chicago Cultural Center, Chicago Water Works, and Navy Pier. They are stocked with free maps, local publications, and knowledgeable staff to help you out.

Contacts **Chicago Convention and Tourism Bureau** (⊠2301 S. Lake Shore Dr. ☎312/567–8500 or 877/CHICAGO [877/244–2246] ⊕www.choosechicago.com). **Chicago Cultural Center** (⊠78 E. Randolph

St., ☎312/744–6630 ⊕egov.cityofchicago. org). **Chicago Water Works** (✉163 E. Pearson, ☎312/742–8811 ⊕www.choosechicago. com). **Illinois Bureau of Tourism** (✉James R. Thompson Center, 100 W. Randolph St., Suite 3-400, ☎800/2CONNECT [800/226–6632] ⊕www.enjoyillinois.com). **Mayor's Office of Special Events, General Information, and Activities** (✉121 N. LaSalle St., Room 806, ☎312/744–3315 ⊕egov.cityofchicago.org). **Navy Pier Welcome Center** (✉600 E. Grand Ave. ☎800/595–7437 or 312/595–7437 ⊕www.navypier.com).

ONLINE TRAVEL TOOLS

All About Chicago The Chicago Convention and Tourism Bureau's site, ⊕www. choosechicago.com, has plenty of general tips on the city and local events, plus helpful information on convention facilities. There's also plenty of information on the City of Chicago Web site, ⊕egov. cityofchicago.org, from festival details to neighborhood overviews and services for visitors from the Chicago Office of Tourism. For a user-friendly introduction to the city, log on to ⊕www.chicago.com.

Art For a preview of the Art Institute of Chicago, check out ⊕www.artic.edu. And to learn about gallery openings and art events, check out ⊕www.chicagoart-dealers.org.

Newspapers & Magazines The Web sites of the city's daily newspapers, the *Tribune* (⊕www.chicagotribune.com) and the *Sun-Times* (⊕www.suntimes.com/index) are great sources for reviews and events listings. The *Chicago Reader*'s site, ⊕www.chireader.com, is rich in arts, entertainment, and dining reviews. *Chicago* magazine's site, ⊕www.chicagomag.com, carries a few Web-exclusive features along with articles from the monthly. Metromix ⊕www.metromix.com thoroughly covers Chicago's entertainment scene. Another good online entertainment reference is ⊕www.timeout.com/chicago, which gives an irreverent, in-depth look at Chicago diversions.

Public Transit To sort out the public-transit system, log on to the CTA's site at ⊕www.transitchicago.com.

FOR INTERNATIONAL TRAVELERS

CURRENCY

The dollar is the basic unit of U.S. currency. It has 100 cents. Coins are the penny (1¢); the nickel (5¢), dime (10¢), quarter (25¢), half-dollar (50¢), and the very rare golden $1 coin and even rarer silver $1. Bills are denominated $1, $5, $10, $20, $50, and $100, all mostly green and identical in size; designs and background tints vary. You may come across a $2 bill, but the chances are slim.

CUSTOMS

Information **U.S. Customs and Border Protection** (⊕www.cbp.gov).

DRIVING

Driving in the United States is on the right. Speed limits are posted in miles per hour (usually between 55 mph and 70 mph). Watch for lower limits in small towns and on back roads (usually 30 mph to 40 mph). Most states require front-seat passengers to wear seat belts; many states require children to sit in the back seat and to wear seat belts. In major cities rush hour is between 7 and 10 AM; afternoon rush hour is between 4 and 7 PM. To encourage carpooling, some freeways have special lanes, ordinarily marked with a diamond, for high-occupancy vehicles (HOV)—cars carrying two people or more.

Gas stations are plentiful. Most stay open late (24 hours along major highways and in big cities) except in rural areas, where Sunday hours are limited and where you may drive for long stretches without a refueling opportunity. Along larger highways, roadside stops with restrooms, fast-food restaurants, and sundries stores are well spaced. State police and tow trucks patrol major highways. If your car breaks down on an interstate, pull onto the shoulder and wait for help.

ELECTRICITY

The U.S. standard is AC, 110 volts/60 cycles. Plugs have two flat pins set parallel to each other.

EMBASSIES

Contacts **Australia** (☎202/797–3000 ⊕www.austemb.org). **Canada** (☎202/682–1740 ⊕www.canadianembassy.org). **United Kingdom** (☎202/588–7800 ⊕www.brit-ainusa.com).

EMERGENCIES

For police, fire, or ambulance, dial 911 (0 in rural areas).

HOLIDAYS

New Year's Day (Jan. 1); Martin Luther King Day (3rd Mon. in Jan.); Presidents' Day (3rd Mon. in Feb.); Memorial Day (last Mon. in May); Independence Day (July 4); Labor Day (1st Mon. in Sept.); Columbus Day (2nd Mon. in Oct.); Thanksgiving Day (4th Thurs. in Nov.); Christmas Eve and Christmas Day (Dec. 24 and 25); and New Year's Eve (Dec. 31).

MAIL

You can buy stamps and aerograms and send letters and parcels in post offices. Stamp-dispensing machines can occasionally be found in airports, bus and train stations, office buildings, drugstores, and convenience stores. U.S. mail boxes are stout, dark blue steel bins; pickup schedules are posted inside the bin (pull down the handle to see them). Parcels weighing more than a pound must be mailed at a post office or at a private mailing center.

Within the United States a first-class letter weighing 1 ounce or less costs 41¢; each additional ounce costs 17¢. Postcards cost 26¢. Postcards or 1-ounce airmail letters to most countries costs 90¢; postcards or 1-ounce letters to Canada or Mexico cost 69¢.

To receive mail on the road, have it sent c/o General Delivery at your destination's main post office (use the correct five-digit ZIP code). You must pick up mail in person within 30 days, with a driver's license or passport for identification.

Contacts **DHL** (☎800/225–5345 ⊕www. dhl.com). **Federal Express** (☎800/463–3339 ⊕www.fedex.com). **Mail Boxes, Etc./ The UPS Store** (☎800/789–4623 ⊕www. mbe.com). **United States Postal Service** (⊕www.usps.com).

PASSPORTS & VISAS

Visitor visas aren't necessary for citizens of Australia, Canada, the United Kingdom, or most citizens of European Union countries coming for tourism and staying for fewer than 90 days. If you require a visa, the cost is $100, and waiting time can be substantial, depending on where you live. Apply for a visa at the U.S. consulate in your place of residence; also check the U.S. State Department's special Visa Web site.

Visa Information **Destination USA** (⊕www.unitedstatesvisas.gov).

PHONES

Chicago has six local area codes: 312 covers the downtown vicinity; 773 blankets the surrounding city neighborhoods. In the near west and south suburbs of Cook and Will counties, 708 fits the bill. The vast expanse of northern and northwestern suburbs in Cook, Lake, and Kane counties get the 847 area code, while the suburbs due west of the city have 630 before their phone numbers. Far outlying areas northwest and south of Chicago in McHenry, Will, and Kendall counties are outfitted with the prefix 815.

Numbers consist of a three-digit area code and a seven-digit local number. Within many local calling areas you dial only the seven digits; in others you dial "1" first and all 10 digits—just as you would for calls between area-code regions. The same is true for calls to numbers prefixed by "800," "888," "866," and "877"—all toll free. For calls to numbers prefixed by "900" you must pay—usually dearly.

For international calls, dial "011" followed by the country code and the local number. For help, dial "0" and ask for an overseas opera-

tor. Most phone books list country codes and U.S. area codes. The country code for Australia is 61, for New Zealand 64, for the United Kingdom 44. Calling Canada is the same as calling within the United States, whose country code, by the way, is 1.

For operator assistance, dial "0." For directory assistance, call 555–1212 or occasionally 411 (free at many public phones). You can reverse long-distance charges by calling "collect"; dial "0" instead of "1" before the 10-digit number.

Instructions are generally posted on pay phones. Usually you insert coins in a slot (usually 25¢ to 50¢ for local calls) and wait for a steady tone before dialing. On long-distance calls the operator tells you how much to insert; prepaid phone cards, widely available in various denominations, can be used from any phone. Follow the directions to activate the card (there's usually an access number, then an activation code), then dial your number.

Cell Phones The United States has several GSM (Global System for Mobile Communications) networks, so multiband mobiles from most countries (except for Japan) work here. Unfortunately, it's almost impossible to buy a pay-as-you-go mobile SIM card in the U.S.—which allows you to avoid roaming charges—without also buying a phone. That said, cell phones with pay-as-you-go plans are available for well under $100. The cheapest ones with decent national coverage are the GoPhone from Cingular and Virgin Mobile, which only offers pay-as-you-go service.

Contacts **Cingular** (☎888/333–6651 ⊕www.cingular.com). **Virgin Mobile** (☎888/322–1122 ⊕www.virginmobileusa. com).

INDEX

NOTES

NOTES

NOTES

NOTES

NOTES

NOTES